Baedeker's

EGYPT

CW00702509

Cover picture: Innermost gold coffin of
Tutankhamun

230 colored photographs
215 drawings and diagrams
68 maps and plans
1 fold-out map

Text:
Monika I. Baumgarten
(Geography, Vegetation, Animal life, Population,
Egyptian Pantheon, History, Glossary of Technical
Terms, Economy; Egypt from A to Z, on the basis of
Baedeker's Handbook for Travelers, "Egypt")
Professor Dr Wolfgang Hassenpflug, Kiel (Climate)

Consultant:
Professor Mohamed Abou-Zaid, Cairo

Editorial work:
Baedeker Stuttgart

English Language:
Alec Court

4th edition 1990

© Baedeker Stuttgart
Original German edition

© The Automobile Association
United Kingdom and Ireland 57260

© Jarrold and Sons Ltd
English language edition worldwide

U.S. and Canadian Edition
Prentice Hall Press

Licensed user:
Mairs Geographischer Verlag GmbH & Co.,
Ostfildern-Kemnat bei Stuttgart

Reproductions:
Gölz Repro-Service GmbH,
Ludwigsburg

The name *Baedeker* is a registered trademark

Cartography:
Ingenieurbüro für Kartographie
Huber & Oberländer, Munich
(maps, plans and diagrams in text)
Georg Schiffner, Lahr
(fold-out map)

Design and layout:
Creativ Verlagsgesellschaft mbH, Stuttgart
Ulrich Kolb, Henk Veerkamp

Conception and general direction:
Dr Peter Baumgarten, Baedeker Stuttgart

English translation:
James Hogarth

Source of illustrations: at end of book

In a time of rapid change it is difficult to ensure that all
the information given is entirely accurate and up to
date, and the possibility of error can never be entirely
eliminated. Although the publishers can accept no
responsibility for inaccuracies and omissions, they are
always grateful for corrections and suggestions for
improvement.

Printed in Italy by G. Canale & C. S.p.A. - Turin

0 7495 0046 8 UK
0-13-056358-7 U.S. and Canada

How to use this guide

The principal towns, sites and areas of tourist interest
are described in alphabetical order. The names of other
places referred to under these general headings can be
found in the Index.

Following the tradition established by Karl Baedeker
in 1844, sights of particular interest and hotels and
restaurants of particular quality are distinguished by
either one or two asterisks.

In the lists of hotels, etc., b. = beds. Only a selection of
hotels and restaurants can be given: no reflection is
implied, therefore, on establishments not included.

The symbol ⓘ at the beginning of an entry or on a
town plan indicates the local tourist office or other
organization from which further information can be
obtained. The post-horn symbol on a town plan
indicates a post office.

A brief glossary of topographical terms will be found
on p. 369, a glossary of technical terms on p. 80 and
a guide to the gods and goddesses of ancient Egypt on
p. 26.

This guidebook forms part of a completely new series of the world-famous Baedeker Guides to Europe.

The English editions are now published for the first time in this country. Each volume is the result of long and careful preparation and, true to the traditions of Baedeker, is designed in every respect to meet the needs and expectations of the modern traveler and holidaymaker.

The name of Baedeker has long been identified in the field of guidebooks with reliable, comprehensive and up-to-date information, prepared by expert writers who work from detailed, first-hand knowledge of the country concerned. Following a tradition that goes back over 150 years to the date when Karl Baedeker published the first of his handbooks for travelers, these guides have been planned to give the tourist all the essential information about the country and its inhabitants: where to go, how to get there and what to see. Baedeker's account of a country was always based on his personal observation and experience during his travels in that country. This tradition of writing a guidebook in the field rather than at an office desk has been maintained by Baedeker ever since.

Lavishly illustrated with superb color photographs and numerous specially drawn maps and street plans of the major towns, the new Baedeker Guides concentrate on making available to the modern traveler all the information he needs in a format that is both attractive and easy to follow. For every place that appears in the gazetteer, the principal features of architectural, artistic and historic interest are described, as are the main scenic beauty-spots in the locality. Selected hotels and restaurants are also included. Features of exceptional merit are indicated by either one or two asterisks.

A special section at the end of each book contains practical information to ensure a pleasant and safe journey, details of leisure activities and useful addresses. The separate road map will prove an invaluable aid to planning your route and your travel within the country.

4   Contents

Introduction to
Egypt

The transcription of Egyptian names is a perennial problem to which no agreed solution has yet been found. Since the ancient Egyptian hiero-glyphic script did not indicate vowels, place-names and personal names may appear in variant forms in different authors and in different languages, and there are also varying transliterations of some ancient Egyptian consonants. There is even more variation in the transcription of Arabic: thus the definite article, transliterated in this guide as *el-*, may appear as *al-* or *il-*, and in some cases the *l* – reflecting the normal pronunciation – may be assimilated to a following consonant; the letter transliterated in this Guide as *q* may appear as *k*, the letter trans-literated as *g* may appear as *j*; and so on.

In this Guide names are so far as pos-sible given in the forms normally used by present-day authorities writing in English; but consistency is difficult to achieve, and visitors to Egypt must be prepared to encounter a variety of alternative forms.

The Nile at Aswan

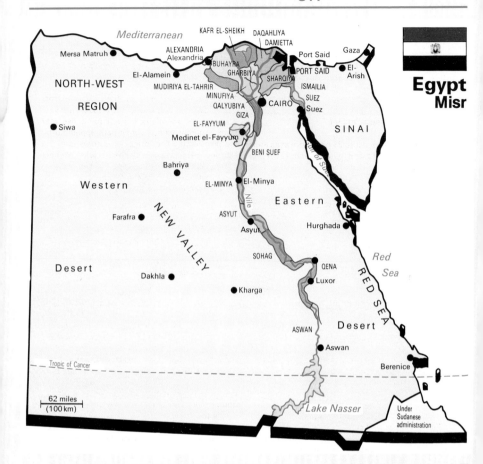

CITY GOVERNORATES	Area sq miles	sq km	Population (1986)	Administrative center
Cairo	83	214	6,052,800	Cairo
Alexandria	112	290	2,917,300	Alexandria
Port Said	153	397	399,800	Port Said
Suez	119	307	326,800	Suez
GOVERNORATES				
Lower Egypt				
Buhayra	1773	4593	3,257,200	Damanhur
Kafr el-Sheikh	1348	3492	1,800,100	Kafr el-Sheikh
Damietta	231	599	741,300	Damietta
Daqahliya	1337	3462	3,500,500	El-Mansura
Gharbiya	770	1995	2,871,000	Tanta
Sharqiya	1815	4702	3,420,100	El-Zagazig
Minufiya	585	1514	2,227,100	Shibin el-Kom
Qalyubiya	364	944	2,514,200	Benha
Ismailia	320	829	544,400	Ismailia
Central Egypt				
Giza	417	1079	3,700,100	Giza
El-Fayyum	692	1792	1,544,000	Medinet el-Fayyum
Beni Suef	507	1313	1,443,000	Beni Suef
El-Minya	878	2274	2,648,000	El-Minya
Upper Egypt				
Asyut	600	1553	2,223,000	Asyut
Sohag	595	1540	2,455,000	Sohag
Qena	699	1811	2,252,300	Qena
Aswan	341	882	801,400	Aswan
FRONTIER DISTRICTS				
North-West Region			160,600	Mersa Matruh
Sinai			200,500	
New Valley			113,800	Kharga
Red Sea			90,500	
Egypt (including Frontier Districts)	386,660	1,001,449	c. 47,000,000	Cairo

Egypt became an independent kingdom in 1922, and since 1954 has been a republic. Its official style is the **Arab Republic of Egypt** *(El-Gumhuriya Misr el-Arabiya)*. It has a total area, including the Sinai Peninsula, of 386,660 sq. miles/1,001,449 sq. km and a rapidly growing population of some 52 million.

The country is divided into **21 governorates** and **4 frontier districts**, and the governorates in turn are divided into districts and communes. The governorates and frontier districts are each headed by a *Governor,* who is assisted by a directly elected *Representative Council.* Under the Egyptian-Israeli Peace Treaty of 1979, following the Camp David Agreements, the Sinai Peninsula, which had been occupied by Israel during the Six Day War of 1967, was returned to Egypt in stages, the transfer being completed in 1982; the Gaza Strip, however, remained under Israeli control. – Egypt was united with Syria in the United Arab Republic in 1958, but this lasted only until 1961, when the union was dissolved.

Under the constitution which came into force in 1971 Egypt is a PRESIDENTIAL REPUBLIC. The original one-party system (Arab Socialist Union) has since 1976 increasingly given place to a multi-party system. The head of State and supreme commander of the armed forces is the *President,* who is appointed by the People's Assembly and confirmed in office by a National Referendum; the term of office is six years, but reappointment for a further term is possible. The President appoints the members of the *Cabinet,* which is responsible to the People's Assembly, and has wide powers of initiating and reviewing legislation. He can appoint special *National Councillors* to carry through political measures.

The People's Assembly or National Assembly (last elected 1987) consists of not less than 350 (at present 448) members elected for a five-year term, together with ten members appointed by the President. The principal *parties* are the National Democratic Party, the Socialist Workers Party and the Social Liberal Party. The National Progressive and Unionist Movement and the independent members play only a minor part.

The basis of Egyptian civil law is the *Civil Code* promulgated in 1949, which incorporates many features borrowed from French and Swiss legislation. Much of the country's personal and family law is developed from traditional religious tenets and laws, but the old ecclesiastical jurisdiction was abolished in 1956.

Egypt is a member of the United Nations, the World Health Organization and the General Agreement on Tariffs and Trade (GATT), and it has a preferential tariff agreement with the European Community. It is no longer a member of the Organization of Arab Petroleum Exporting Countries (OPAEC) or of the Arab League. It has agreements with Sudan over political, economic and military cooperation and in February 1981 the Egyptian Parliament ratified the treaty on the non-proliferation of nuclear weapons. Soon afterwards the Government signed agreements with the United States, France and West Germany for the supply and erection of several nuclear power-stations.

From time immemorial Egypt, that land of ancient civilization on the Nile, has exerted an irresistible fascination. Here the traveler finds not only the natural attractions of this Eastern country, with its mild climate and sky that is perennially clear: he encounters also the origins of Western culture, and at the same time observes the sharp contrasts between an Oriental attachment to tradition and modern technical progress. Here, too, the holiday visitor can enjoy beautiful and impressive scenery and excellent beaches.

There is a wide divergence between the area included within the frontiers of Egypt and the area actually inhabited by its population. Only about 3·5% of the total area is cultivable, and this 3·5% of the land surface is occupied by 98% of the population. The heartland of Egypt is the fertile **Nile Valley**, from the First Cataract at Aswan in the south to the wide Delta at the mouth of the river. This 930 mile/1500 km long strip of land, which above Cairo is only 6–12 miles/10–20 km wide, in places contracting to only 1100 yards/1000 m, is bounded on three sides by natural frontiers – in the north by the Mediterranean, on the east by the Eastern (Arabian) Desert, extending to the Red Sea, and on the west by the great plateau of the Western (Libyan) Desert. Only the southern frontier is without natural features to mark it, and throughout Egyptian history it was repeatedly a source of conflict.

Geography

Egypt extends for some 640 miles/
1030 km from north to south, between
latitude 31° 5′ and 22° N, and for 600
miles/960 km from west to east, between
longitude 25° 2′ and 34° 56′ E, at the
north-east corner of the African continent, bounded on the west by Libya, on
the south by Sudan, on the east by the
Red Sea – with the Sinai Peninsula
extending eastward into Asia – and on
the north by the Mediterranean.

The **Nile Valley** divides the country into
two parts, which geologically and mor-
phologically are very different from one
another: to the east the Eastern (Arabian)
Desert, to the west the Western (Libyan)
Desert. The **Delta** is a region of Quaternary limestones and calcareous
sandstones, predominantly formed from
fragments of mollusc shells, quartz, ooliths
and detritus. At many places these rocks
are overlaid by sand-dunes and other
younger geological formations. The cultivable land in the Nile Valley and the
Delta, with its north-western fringe of
limestone, consists mainly of recent
alluvial deposits, the fertile clayey mud
and the fine sand brought down by the
Nile and spread over the land by the
inundation which in the past was a regular
annual occurrence. Under this alluvium lie
coarser yellowish sands and gravels of
Pleistocene date, which outcrop here and
there in the Delta as islands of barren sand
amid the expanses of fertile agricultural
land. They are related to the late deposits
of sand and gravel in the adjacent deserts
and to the remains of Pleistocene cliffs
and shorelines which can be seen on both
sides of the Nile Valley at Cairo and
elsewhere. At Abu Sabal, NE of Nawa, a
basalt hill 65 ft/20 m high projects into the
south-eastern Delta.

The **Isthmus of Suez** consists of alluvial
deposits from the Mediterranean in the
north, Nile sediments with freshwater
molluscs in the middle section, at the El-
Gisr sill and around Lake Timsah, and
Quaternary formations along the Red Sea
in the south. Much of the shoreline of the
Gulf of Suez is fringed by fossil coral reefs
of the Quaternary era, sometimes rising to
heights of up to 985 ft/300 m – reflecting
a considerable upthrust of the mainland,
or at any rate the coastal region, which
occurred in relatively recent times and is
perhaps still continuing. There are also

The name **EGYPT** is derived from the Greek
Aigyptos ("dark") via Latin *Aegyptus*. The
ancient Egyptians called their country **Kemit**
(Kemt, Kemi), the "black land", after the dark color
of the Nile mud, contrasting it with the "red land"
of the desert. The Arabic name is **Misr** or *Masr*.

living coral reefs along large stretches of
the coast and around the islands in the
Red Sea.

To the south of the Pyramids of Giza and
at many points on the east bank of the Nile
between Cairo and el-Fashn are sandstones and marls of the Late Tertiary
(Pliocene), with well-preserved fossils. In
the small valley south of the pyramids of
Zawiyet el-Aryan is one of the richest
occurrences of Pliocene formations,
associated with the emergence during the
Pliocene of the first intimations of the Nile
Valley, originally a funnel-shaped inlet on
the Mediterranean coast.

In the Early Miocene the Nile Valley was
not yet in existence: instead there was a
mighty river flowing from the south-west
towards what is now Lower Egypt. To this
period belong the fluvio-marine deposits
at El-Maghra in the Western Desert, with
their petrified forests, and the purely
marine coarse-grained limestones on the
Libyan Plateau, to the north of the Siwa
Oasis, on the eastern edge of the Eastern
Desert (at the foot of Gebel Geneifa and
Gebel Ataqa) and around Gebel Set on
the Gulf of Suez.

The "petrified forests" near Cairo, consisting of scattered pieces of silicified
wood, and the siliceous red sandstones on
Gebel el-Ahmar and similar conical hills
along the northern edge of the Eastern
and Western Deserts were created by
siliceous hot springs which emerged
during the Oligocene among the lagoons
in these regions. These fossil tree-trunks
are still more numerous in the area north-
west of Lake Qarun, and the sandstones of
the Oligocene contain large numbers of
bones from extinct terrestrial and marine
mammals and reptiles which were carried
down by the river and buried in the alluvial
deposits at its mouth. Remains of these
animals can be seen in the Geological
Museum in Cairo.

The hills flanking the Nile Valley above
Cairo consist of fossiliferous nummulitic
limestones of the Middle and Lower
Eocene. In general the beds fall gently

away to the north-north-west, so that the strata outcropping become steadily older towards the south.

In the Edfu area we encounter sandstones of the Upper Cretaceous, which advance close to the river in Gebel Silsila and constrict it into a narrow bed. The "Nubian sandstone" covers an area of several thousand square miles extending from the oases to the Sudan. At certain points (e.g. at Aswan and, beyond the Sudanese frontier, at Wadi Halfa in the region of the Third and Fourth Cataracts) there are intrusions of crystalline rocks (granite, gneiss, diorite, etc.) which form black or reddish hills sharply contrasting with the low tabular masses of sandstone.

In the **Eastern (Arabian) Desert** a massive range up to 6560 ft/2000 m high runs close to the Red Sea coast. It consists solely of crystalline rocks (granite, gneiss, diorite, hornblende, micaceous and talc schists, andesites, etc.), which form a large group of very ancient volcanic minerals, and of porphyry (already worked in Roman times in the quarries on Gebel el-Dukhan). The sedimentary rocks on the eastern and western slopes of this chain – mostly Nubian sandstone, with some limestones and marls at the north end of the range – extend westward, forming a great plateau, of limestones in the north and sandstones in the south, in which the Nile Valley forms a narrow trough. Numerous deeply indented valleys give the Eastern Desert its characteristic aspect. Vegetation is almost wholly absent on the open plains; in the valleys it is rather more vigorous, particularly after rain; and it develops in considerable luxuriance in the gorges lying in the shelter of the mountains, where occasional springs emerge.

Totally different from the Eastern Desert is the **Western (Libyan) Desert**, a limestone plateau (about 985 ft/300 m) extending westward and looming over the lower areas of Nubian sandstone to the south. In deep indentations in these lower southern hills are the **oases** of Kharga, Dakhla and Farafra; the Bahriya Oasis occupies a depression in the higher plateau to the north. The plateau is waterless and without vegetation; and small isolated hills show how rapidly the aeolian (wind) erosion of the desert surface is proceeding. In some places long ridges of dunes 100–200 ft/30–60 m high extend from north-north-west to south-south-east, sometimes for hundreds of miles; the most striking examples are to be seen to the west of the Dakhla Oasis. The soil of the Kharga and Dakhla oases consists mainly of dark-colored sands and clays of the Upper Cretaceous, sometimes containing alum and phosphates. At many points springs emerge from clefts in the rock or from wells sunk to depths of some 400 ft/120 m, providing water which makes cultivation possible.

To the south of the oasis extends the lower plain of Nubian sandstone, the gently undulating surface of which is covered with blackened flints and deposits of iron and manganese ore. The silicified trunks of fossil trees are found in considerable numbers. Everywhere there is yellow drifting sand, only occasionally forming dunes of any great size.

Geological formations in the Western Desert

The Farafra Oasis lies farther west with the Eocene limestone plateau extending north and west to the Siwa Oasis. The Siwa area consists mainly of Miocene sedimentary rocks, with an abundance of fossils which was remarked on by Herodotus and Eratosthenes.

The **Sinai Peninsula** is also a desert region. The southern part of the peninsula is occupied by the crystalline rocks of the Mount Sinai Massif (8665 ft/2641 m), the northern half by a great limestone and sandstone plateau.

Climate

Egypt has a hot **desert climate**. Its characteristic features, heat and aridity, result from the country's situation in the great arid zone of the Old World, created by the pattern of movement of the trade winds, which extends in a wide swathe on both sides of the Tropic of Cancer from the west coast of Africa far into Asia. The Egyptians say: "The desert is a hot land which becomes very cold at night." These are regions, technically classified as arid, in which the rate of evaporation is greater than the rainfall.

The country's landscape and patterns of land use are determined by the extreme scarcity of water. There are no real rivers apart from the Nile; salt accumulates in low-lying areas; the ground forms a hard crust; the predominant features of the topography are those shaped by mechanical erosion or wind action, such as stone pavements and dunes. Vegetation on any scale, and thus any form of agricultural activity, can exist only in areas supplied with water from more humid regions. This supply is provided by the **Nile**, which carries great masses of water from the rain-rich tropics through the desert to the Mediterranean, forming an immensely long and narrow river oasis. Truly, as Herodotus said, "Egypt is the gift of the Nile."

The generally desert climate is marked by regular variations, both over the course of the year and from north to south over the great length of the country. In the north the influence of the Mediterranean is still evident, with rain falling in winter; in the central and southern regions there is practically no rainfall at all. Still farther south, in Egypt's southern neighbor the Sudan, begins the zone of increasing summer rainfall, with tropical zenithal rain.

Regional climatic characteristics are illustrated in the **climatic diagrams** on p. 13, which give monthly average temperatures and rainfall. The blue columns show the rainfall in millimeters, in accordance with the blue scale in the margin. The orange band shows the temperature in °C, the upper edge giving the average maximum day temperature (reached in the early afternoon), the lower edge the average minimum night temperature, in accordance with the red scale in the margin.

The figures given for the three weather stations selected will apply also to their immediately surrounding regions. For areas between these stations intermediate values can be interpolated. It should be borne in mind, however, that differences in altitude can produce quite considerable variations over quite short distances.

Mediterranean coast
Alexandria weather station

The climatic diagram for Alexandria applies to the narrow strip of steppe-like desert, in a zone of transition between the Mediterranean and the desert climate, which has regular though scanty winter rains. The rainfall, averaging $7\frac{1}{2}$ in./190 mm, occurs between October and April and is concentrated in a few days with abundant rain. The relative humidity of the air is high (60–70%); it is associated with onshore winds from the north (i.e. blowing off the Mediterranean) of force 3 (roughly 13 ft/4 m per second).

A feature of the spring is the *khamsin*, a hot, dry desert wind from the south which blows during this season on an average of five days in the month. It is caused by areas of low pressure moving east along the Mediterranean coast. The masses of dust which it carries with it can on occasion form dense yellow clouds.

Thanks to the proximity of the sea the daily and yearly variations in temperature are comparatively small (respectively 18° F/10 °C and 25 °F/14 °C). There are no sharp temperature changes even in winter, since even northerly winds, passing over the warm Mediterranean, are scarcely any colder than those blowing from the south.

Northern desert region
Cairo weather station

The climate here is characteristic of the deserts of northern Egypt. Rainfall over the year averages no more than 1 in./24 mm, occurring on a few days during the winter, mainly between December and February. As in other arid regions with low rainfall, however, there are considerable variations from year to year.

The relative humidity of the air is only about 50%, and in April–June falls below 40%. The duration of sunshine is correspondingly high, ranging between 236 hours per month in winter and 390 in summer. In Egypt the amount of sunshine is governed mainly by the astronomical possibilities rather than by the extent of cloud cover: the sky is cloudless, and days without sunshine are exceedingly rare. The Sahara is one of the regions in the world where solar radiation reaches its maximum.

Since with the low humidity of the air, the moderating influence of evaporation and condensation is lacking, the daily and annual temperature variations show a marked increase. In winter the average minimum night temperatures, reached shortly before sunrise, are about 50 °F/10 °C, the maximum noon temperatures

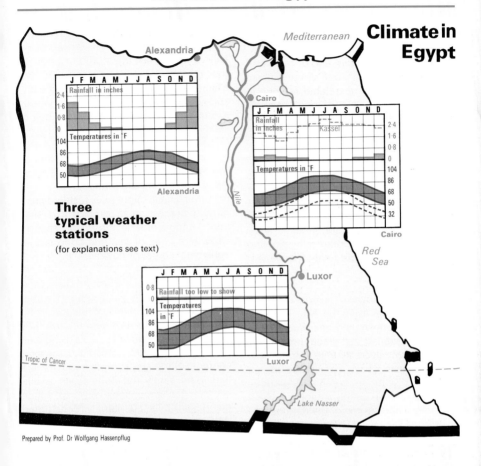

Climate in Egypt

Three typical weather stations

(for explanations see text)

Three typical weather stations shown: Alexandria, Cairo, Luxor

Prepared by Prof. Dr Wolfgang Hassenpflug

about 68 °F/20 °C; the corresponding summer figures are 72 °F/22 °C and 95 °F/35 °C. Extreme temperatures range in winter from freezing-point to 86 °F/30 °C, in summer from 59 °F/15 °C to 113 °F/45 °C.

Southern desert region
Luxor weather station

The climatic pattern of Luxor is typical of the extreme desert climate of central and southern Egypt. The average annual rainfall of ·04 of an inch/1 millimeter is too small to be shown on the diagram. This again covers wide variations from year to year: in some years 2 or 3 or even 6 millimeters have been known to fall in the form of brief showers during the winter, while in many other years hardly a single measurable drop is recorded. The average humidity of the air is always below 60%, and during the spring months falls to 30% or even lower. Temperature variations in these regions lying far from the coast are accordingly greater than in the more northerly parts of the country, as is shown by the greater width and more marked curve of the temperature band in the Luxor diagram. The variations are particularly sharp on the surface of the ground, where the midday temperature may rise above 140 °F/ 60 °C. In winter the temperature may occasionally fall below freezing-point (absolute minimum temperature for February 28 °F/−2 °C; the absolute summer maxima lie about 122 °F/50 °C (absolute maximum for June 120 °F/49 °C).

Evaporation is correspondingly high. A swimming-pool filled with water to a height of 13ft/4m would be emptied by evaporation in the course of a year (in

Cairo it would still have 12 ft/3·70 m of water after a year, in Alexandria 11½ ft/3·56 m). Lake Nasser suffers a comparable loss of water in the course of a year over its area of more than 1930 sq. miles/5000 sq. km.

Human behavior patterns – those of the local people no less than those of the unacclimatized visitor – must adapt to the conditions of this hot desert climate. The sun stands much higher in the sky than in more northerly regions, affording little possibility of shade; and the pitiless heat of the sun is reinforced by refraction from the hot ground. Provided, however, that care is taken to guard against the sun, the climate of this region, thanks to the low humidity of the air, is as a rule perfectly tolerable. Precautions should also be taken against the converse phenomenon – the correspondingly sharp fall in temperature at night, in extreme cases to below freezing-point – and some warmer clothing should always be included in the visitor's luggage.

In this desert climate it is necessary to drink plenty of water – 9 pints/5 litres per day or more. But sweating leads to a loss of minerals as well as liquid, and it is, therefore, advisable for visitors to take more salt with their food or to take special salt tablets with them.

In planning the daily program it is useful, particularly for photographers, to know the duration of daylight. The following times, given by way of illustration, relate to Cairo (latitude 30° N). Sunrise ranges between 7 a.m. in January and 5 a.m. in June, sunset between 5.10 p.m. in January and 7.05 p.m. in June, with barely half an hour of half-light in the morning and twilight in the evening.

Vegetation

Egypt lies at the eastern end of the North African belt of desert, one of the hottest, driest and most inhospitable regions in the world. In consequence more than 96% of its area has a vegetation cover of drought-resistant desert plants or no vegetation at all. The only permanent **vegetation** (i.e. consisting of plants which grow throughout the year) is found in the fertile Nile Valley, supplied with water from the Ethiopian Highlands, in the oases, which depend on artesian wells for their supply, and in some areas in the valleys of sporadically flowing rivers (wadis) which retain permanent moisture.

The Western (Libyan) Desert which extends westward from the Nile between the Mediterranean and the Sudan is a gently undulating tableland broken up by shallow depressions. Along the Mediterranean coast it is steppe-like in character, with a perennial garrigue (maquis, scrub), predominant in which are bushes and shrubs of the daphne and goosefoot families (Thymelaeaceae and Chenopodiaceae), supplemented by an ephemeral winter vegetation. Farther inland the vegetation cover becomes increasingly sparse, and eventually is reduced to sporadic clumps in which, depending on the constitution of the soil, mugworts (*Artemisia*) or capers (*Capparis*) predominate.

In salt-pans (*sebkhas*) – i.e. depressions containing brackish ground-water or terminal lakes or marshes of saline water in wadis – a salt-tolerant (halophile) vegetation is found, consisting of Chenopodiaceae, Compositae, tamarisks (Tamaricaceae), bulrushes (Typhaceae), rushes (Juncaceae) and sedges (Cyperus).

In oases fed by springs of fresh water many species common in Europe are found; but in general all the inhabited oases have been so much altered by the hand of man that their endemic vegetation survives only in remote corners or in the form of weeds. In addition to the date-palms and doum-palms, both cultivated and wild, there are tamarisks and several species of acacia. Ponds and pools are fringed by reeds (*Phragmites*) and bulrushes (*Typha*). In the wadis a sparse scrub of acacias, caper bushes, etc., may survive throughout the year.

The steppe-like strip of land along the Mediterranean coast continues east of the Nile Delta along the northern edge of the Eastern (Arabian) Desert and the Mediterranean coast of the Sinai Peninsula. To the south and south-east of this extends a barren and inhospitable belt of sandy and pebbly desert (*serir*). In the coarse sandy and gravelly soil of this region such moisture as is contributed by the very rare showers of rain rapidly seeps away, preventing the formation of a layer of humus which might have fostered plant growth. In these areas permanent vegetation is found only in the wadis, though elsewhere a fall of rain will bring out an ephemeral carpet of flowers.

In the mountains of the Eastern Desert and the Sinai Massif the water-supply is rather better than in the plains of the *serir*. Here the rain-bearing clouds, rare though they still are, come up against peaks rising well above 6500 ft/2000 m and discharge their contents. Showers are more frequent here than in the sandy and stony desert, and in addition the impervious rocks of which the desert hills are largely constituted retain the moisture in the surface soil for a relatively long period. Thus in the wadis of the mountain areas quite considerable groups of acacias, tamarisks and other drought-loving species flourish throughout the year, accompanied by a short-lived growth of smaller plants. In some of the wadis, particularly in the Sinai Peninsula, the ground-water comes to the surface, giving rise to oases in which agriculture is possible. Apart from this the

Date-palm, Memphis

rocky slopes and cliffs of the mountains are entirely without vegetation. – Along the Red Sea coast there is a narrow strip of salt- and drought-tolerant vegetation.

After millennia of cultivation the Nile Valley has almost entirely lost its endemic vegetation, and indigenous species, apart from species useful to man which are deliberately cultivated, occur only sporadically. The lotus (*Nymphaea lotus, N. cerculea* and *N. nelumbo*), once the emblem of the Egyptian kingdom, is now found only in parks. The thickets of papyrus in the marshes and along the banks of the river, once so extensive and so rich in wildlife, which appear so frequently in ancient Egyptian reliefs and paintings, disappeared during the Middle Ages, and papyrus (*Cyperus papyrus*) and giant bulrushes (*Typha elephantine*) can now be found growing wild only in the Wadi Natrun.

There were no real forests in Egypt, at any rate during the Historical period, and timber for shipbuilding and other purposes had to be imported from Lebanon, the Aegean islands and the Land of Punt (Somali coast). Natural conditions are still adverse to the development of woodland, though there are small plantations of palms and fruit trees, and trees are also planted to provide protection from wind and erosion. The villages of the fellahin are shaded by groves of date-palms, and in Nubia of doum-palms. Along promenades and country roads there are frequently acacias, tamarisks and lebbek trees (*Albizzia lebbek*). Around wells the sycamore (*Ficus sycomorus*), a tree regarded as sacred, is found. Introductions from the New World are the eucalyptus (*Eucalyptus globulus*), casuarina and prickly pear (*Opuntia*), which is common in rural areas. The olive is not common, even in Mediterranean Egypt, and except in a few oases yields fruit of poor quality.

Favorite ornamental plants are bougainvillea, jasmine, oleander, hibiscus, papyrus, poinsettia, catalpa and bamboos. – For agricultural and industrial plants see the section on Economy (agriculture), p. 86.

Animal Life

The **animal life** of Egypt is characterized by the overlapping of the Palaearctic region (animals of the northern Old World) and the Ethiopian region (animals of central and southern Africa, including Madagascar), and accordingly includes species from both of these regions.

Animal life is closely dependent on vegetation: only where plants can grow is sufficient nourishment available for animals. Thus the animals of the desert, with its limited resources of vegetable food, are confined to the smaller and less demanding species; and even these species are not found in the real desert, but on the fringes of the desert, in areas of semi-desert and steppe-like character (the latter particularly along the Mediterranean coast). In these areas and, in increasingly smaller numbers, farther south are found such mammals as the dorcas gazelle (*Gazella dorcas*), and the graceful slender-horned gazelle, the desert fox (*Fennecus cerdo*), the hyena (*Hyaena hyaena*), the jackal (*Canis aureus*), gerbils (*Meriones*) and the gundi (*Ctenodactylus gundi*). The reptiles are represented by several species of lizard, the chameleon (*Chamaeleo chamaeleo*), the desert monitor (*Varanus griseus*) and numerous snakes, many of them poisonous, including the horned viper (*Cerastes cornutus*), the spitting cobra (*Naja nigricollis*), the Egyptian cobra (*Naja haje,* the royal cobra or uraeus of the Pharaohs) and the sand-colored viper (*Psammophis schokari*). Typical endemic bird species of the arid regions are the desert sparrow (*Passer simplex*) and the Houbara bustard (*Chlamydotis undulata*); and in addition large numbers of migratory birds, including swallows, warblers, hoopoes and wagtails, pause in the oases and humid depressions during their journey south, supplied with an abundant stock of food in the myriads of insects (mosquitoes, butterflies, dragonflies).

The animal life of the Nile Valley, the Delta and the large Oasis of Fayyum is naturally more numerous and more varied, although many centuries of human encroachment on the natural setting have led to the disappearance of old-established species which feature

Dovecots, El-Minya

inaccessible mountain fastnesses of the Eastern Desert.

There are, however, large numbers of the small mammals – hares, mice, rats, etc. – which accompany human settlement and cause considerable damage to agriculture. In Lower Egypt flying foxes (Pteropodidae) are numerous. The thickets of reeds fringing river-banks are the haunt of the ichneumon or African mongoose (*Herpestes ichneumon*; "Pharaoh's rat"), which was held in high regard by the ancient Egyptians as a predator on snakes. Reptiles include geckos, agamids, Nile monitors (*Varanus niloticus*), several species of lizards, the snakes which are also found in the deserts and the Egyptian tortoise. River-banks, canals and the lakes in the Delta are populated by frogs.

prominently in ancient reliefs and paintings. Thus the hippopotamus, which at many places in ancient Egypt was venerated as divine, was ruthlessly hunted down because of the damage it caused to the fields and also for the sake of the ivory of its teeth and its hide, and was finally exterminated. A similar fate befell the crocodile, which was common in ancient times but has now completely disappeared from the lower course of the Nile, though a few survivors are said to have remained in the Abu Simbel area before the construction of the High Dam at Aswan. Other species that have disappeared from Egypt are the lion and probably also the Barbary sheep (*Ammotragus lervia*) and the oryx (*Oryx gazella*), which appears in many ancient Egyptian paintings. A few leopards are said to survive in the Sinai Peninsula; and the lynx and the wild cat have withdrawn into the

In the well-watered areas in the Delta live swarms of ducks, geese, flamingos, coots, herons, storks, rails, wagtails and other birds. Flocks of cattle egrets (*Ardeola ibis*) settle on the trees fringing the water; vultures, kites and falcons hover overhead; and everywhere there are sparrows, finches, ravens, peewits, quails, larks, snipe, guineafowl, sunbirds, sand grouse and pigeons (kept all over Egypt in dovecots which are a conspicuous feature of the landscape). The sacred ibis of the ancient Egyptians (*Threskiornis aethiopica*) is now rare, and the ostrich, which was prized for its beautiful feathers, has completely disappeared.

Cattle egrets

Dromedaries

The donkey, the mule and the dromedary are still prized by the fellahin as beasts of burden and riding animals. Cattle and water-buffalo are kept both as draft animals and for the sake of their milk and meat. Sheep and goats are the principal domestic animals of the bedouin. Pigs, held by the Muslim population to be impure, are kept only by Copts.

Insects are numerous in the hot and humid river-basins and marshy lakes of the Delta. Mosquitoes and midges spread malaria and trachoma, an eye disease common in Egypt. Locusts descend in swarms on the crops and devour everything green in a short space of time. Scorpions are feared for their painful (though rarely fatal) bite. The dung-beetle (*Scarabeus sacer*), the sacred scarab of the ancient Egyptians, can still be encountered. – A serious health problem is presented by bilharzia, a disease caused by a species of flukeworm (*Schistosoma haematobium*). The worms proliferate in an intermediate host, a species of water-snail (*Bulinus*) which lives in stagnant water, ponds and canals.

Many ancient reliefs show the abundance of fish then to be found in the Nile. Since the construction of the High Dam their numbers have been markedly reduced by the fall-off in the food-supply formerly provided by the Nile mud. – Off the Mediterranean coasts of Egypt there are large numbers of dolphins, tunny and swordfish, as well as sharks; and cuttlefish, crayfish, shellfish and sponges are also found all along the coast. – In the Red Sea sharks and rays are numerous, and the whole coast is fringed with colonies of coral.

Population

With some 52 million inhabitants, Egypt now has a population more than three times as large as in 1927, and greater by 21 million than its 1966 population; a hundred years ago, in 1882, it had only 6·8 million inhabitants. This population explosion is one of the country's most urgent problems, for all the increases in production achieved by modern technology have immediately been absorbed and overtaken by the continuing increase in population; while early marriage and religious resistance have so far frustrated all attempts to reduce the birth rate.

With an average *population density* of some 3240 inhabitants to the sq. mile (1250 to the sq. km) in the cultivated area, Egypt is one of the most densely populated countries in the world. There are particular concentrations of population around Cairo, with over 96,000 to the sq. mile (50,000 to the sq. km.), and Alexandria, with over 26,000 to the sq. mile (10,000 to the sq. km).

The *social structure* of the country is characterized by wide differences between the small but very wealthy upper stratum of the population, a middle class with a modest standard of living and the great mass of the population, impoverished and living in the most primitive conditions. Unemployment and the housing shortage have reached almost unimaginable proportions.

Some 90% of the population are descended from the ancient **Egyptians**. There are in the first place the *fellahin,* intermingled with Arab blood over many centuries, who make up four-fifths of the total population, living in very poor circumstances. Then there are the Christian *Copts* (from Greek *aigyptos* by way of Arabic *qubt*), who account for some 10% of the population and form an educated middle class living in the towns, mainly in Upper Egypt. Finally, there are the Hamitic (Negroid) *Nubians,* incomers from the south, who are largely employed in the service sector of the economy. Two small Hamitic minorities are the *Berbers* in the Oasis of Siwa and the nomadic *Bisharin* in the south-east of the country. The *bedouin* (about 100,000), who have now largely given up their nomadic way of life, are reckoned to be pure **Arabs**. Of the *Jews* who were settled in Egypt from ancient times all but a few hundred have now left following the recent wars with Israel. – In hair and skin color the Egyptians are wholly of the dark Mediterranean type.

The overwhelming majority of the population (some 93%) is *Muslim* (Sunnite). The rest are *Christians,* belonging to the Coptic Church, which broke away from

In a rural bazaar

Rome under the Patriarch of Alexandria in 451. – Polygamy has now practically died out, though it is not forbidden by Islamic law.

The official language of Egypt, and the ordinary spoken language, is *Arabic*. Many people in the upper and middle ranges of the population speak English and French, so that visitors speaking these languages should have no difficulty in making themselves understood. Coptic, which is derived from ancient Egyptian, survives only as a liturgical language. Nubian and a few Berber dialects are of only local importance.

In the field of *education* six years' school attendance has been compulsory since 1923, but there are insufficient schools, particularly in the rural areas, to cope

Village slaughterhouse

with the steadily increasing numbers of children. The country's eight universities produce more graduates than the labor market can absorb, while there are inadequate facilities for technical education.

Religion in Ancient Egypt

In spite of the great numbers of religious texts, reliefs and paintings that have come down to us from ancient Egypt we still know relatively little about Egyptian religion. We know the names of many gods and goddesses, what they looked like and where they were worshiped; but of their real nature, on the significance they had for the priests and the ordinary worshipers, on the myths associated with them we are very inadequately informed. The Egyptians themselves never evolved any clear religious system. A variety of different concepts co-existed in their religious beliefs, and they never managed to reconcile popular religion and priestly wisdom, inherited traditions and new developments.

The complex religion which finds expression in the texts of the Later Period did not exist in the early days of Egyptian history. The country was originally made up of a variety of urban and village communities, each of which had its tutelary (protective) god or goddess. Many of these *local deities* are known to us, though we cannot always be sure where they originated: Horus, who was worshiped at Behdet (Damanhur), the ancient capital of Lower Egypt; Atum, the god of Heliopolis: Thoth, the local god of

Hermopolis: Month, the god of Thebes; Khnum, patron of Herwer (Beni Hasan); Ptah of Memphis; Herishef of Heracleopolis; Sobek (Suchos), whose principal cult center was apparently in the Fayyum, etc. Among local goddesses were Neith of Sais and Hathor of Dendera. Many of these local deities had lost their original names and were worshiped under names or epithets referring to some particular quality or some feature of their myth, as in the case of the lion goddess worshiped in the Memphis area, known as Sakhmet, the "Mighty One"; the god worshiped at Asyut in the form of a wolf, known as Wepwawet, "Opener of the Ways", no doubt because his image, carried at the head of the army, opened the way into enemy territory; and the local god of This, Enhuret (Greek Onuris), known as "He who brings the Distant One", apparently reflecting an ancient legend that he brought from some distant land the lion goddess who was worshiped with him. Other local deities were merely named after the towns where they were worshiped: thus the cat goddess of the Delta town of Bast (Bubastus) was called Bastet ("She of Bastet"), the goddess of Nekhab (El-Kab) was known as Nekhbet ("She of Nekhab"), etc.

The original conceptions of these deities were extremely crude, reminiscent of the fetishism of African Negroes. Thus the people of Busiris (Djedu) and Mendes

Anubis (from Tutankhamun's Tomb)

(Djedet) venerated a curious pillar (Djed) which was later associated with Osiris and Re, and the gods Min of Coptos and Ptah of Memphis were worshiped in the form of anthropomorphic fetishes. The goddess Hathor, originally worshiped to the south of Memphis, was thought to live in a sycamore tree, the god Nefertum in a lotus flower, while the goddess Neith of Sais was venerated in the form of a shield on which two arrows were nailed crosswise. Particularly common was the belief that divinities manifested themselves in the form of animals – cows, bulls, rams, goats, crocodiles, cats, lions, ichneumons, frogs, certain species of fish, ibises, falcons, vultures, etc. Thus the god Khnum was a ram, Horus a falcon, Thoth an ibis, Sobek a crocodile, the goddess Nekhbet a vulture, the goddess of Bubastis a cat, Hathor of Dendera a cow, the local goddess of Buto a snake.

In addition to the deities worshiped in the form of animals certain *sacred animals* were worshiped in their own right. The animals, recognizable by particular signs, were kept within the precincts of the temple and when they died were buried with honor and succeeded by another of the same species. The best known of these sacred animals was the Apis bull worshiped in Memphis, which was black with white marks, a triangle on its forehead and a crescent moon on its right flank. The light-colored Mnevis bull was worshiped at Heliopolis, the Buchis bull at Hermonthis and Medamut; while a phoenix was also venerated at Heliopolis. These sacred animals were associated with the local deities: thus Apis was held to be the "servant of Ptah", Buchis the "servant of Month", the phoenix the "soul of the sun god". Later the worship of animals was carried even further, extending not only to these sacred animals but also to the animals in whose form the local deities were worshiped. These animals, too, were

kept within the temple precincts; and other animals of the same species might not be killed within the town where they were held sacred and after their death were solemnly buried in special cemeteries. From this later period date the cat tombs of Bubastis and Beni Hasan, the crocodile tombs of Kom Ombo, the ibis tombs of Ashmunein, the ram tombs of Elephantine, etc. It was no doubt this exaggerated animal cult that struck the Greeks as so extraordinary – though intimations of similar cults are found in various Oriental peoples and even in Greece and Rome (Cybele's lion, Athena's owl, Zeus's eagle).

The Egyptians moved away from their earlier fetishist beliefs when, at the beginning of the Historical period, they began to worship *deities in human form*. The god was now represented with human features and limbs, wearing the same dress as the Egyptians of that day. On his head he wore the helmet or crown of a prince and round his middle, like the kings of the Early Period, a loincloth or apron with an animal's tail to the rear; and as a symbol of his power he carried a scepter and a staff. The deities conceived as animals were now also given human form, but with the head of the animal in which they manifested themselves: thus Sobek was represented with a crocodile's head, Khnum with a ram's head, Thoth with an ibis's head, Horus with a falcon's head. The various cow goddesses were given a human head with a cow's horns; the vulture goddess Mut, who was worshiped at Thebes, was represented with a vulture over her head; and Neith of Sais, worshiped in the form of a bundle of arrows, bore the arrows on her head. Curious as all this may seem – and curious as it seemed to the Greeks – it must be recognized at least that the Egyptian artists, in both statues and reliefs, contrived the transition from a human body to an animal's head with remarkable skill.

In addition to the various local divinities, whose sphere of influence was confined to the area in which they were worshiped, there appeared at a very early stage *universal deities* worshiped throughout Egypt. Among them were the earth god Geb, the sky goddess Nut, the air god Shu, the dew goddess Tefnut, the sun god Re, the vegetation god Osiris, the Nile god Hapi and the ocean god Nun; among the star deities Orion and the goddess Sothis

(Sirius) were particularly prominent. These nature divinities were not confined to any particular place but were everywhere at home. Soon, however, these cosmic powers became associated with certain local gods and in some cases identified with them. The great sky divinities were given human form and cult centers of their own: thus the sun god Re, having become associated with Atum, was worshiped at Heliopolis, while the lionheaded divine couple, Shu and Tefnut, were venerated at Leontopolis.

At an early period the conception of many deities was extended and deepened by the increased emphasis given to particular qualities or functions. Thus the falconheaded Month, a local god worshiped at Hermonthis, became a war god; the god Min of Coptos, where the track through the hills of the Eastern Desert from the Red Sea reached the Nile Valley, became the patron of desert travelers and later also a fertility and harvest god whom the Greeks equated with Pan; Ptah of Memphis was regarded as the protective god of artists, metalworkers and smiths, the Egyptian equivalent of Hephaestus; Sakhmet, the "Mighty One" of Memphis, became a fearsome war goddess who destroyed the enemy; while Hathor of Dendera, with emphasis placed on her friendlier aspects, became a goddess of love and joy (Greek Aphrodite). Many local deities were linked with the cosmic powers, in particular the moon and the sun. Thus Thoth of Hermopolis was venerated as the moon god who had created the terrestrial order and was the "Lord of Time"; he was also credited with the invention of hieroglyphs and was accordingly the patron of scribes and scholars. Even more significantly, Horus became a sky god associated with the sun and received the name of Re-Harakhty (i.e. the Sun, Horus the Horizon-Dweller). The cow goddess Hathor ("House of Horus") became a sky goddess. Many local deities were thus worshiped throughout Egypt in virtue of particular capacities attributed to them.

There were also many *minor gods,* demons and spirits who could in certain circumstances help or injure men, and whom, therefore, men sought to propitiate. Among them were, for example, the birth goddesses who could accelerate or hinder a birth, the grotesque god Bes who was the protector of the marriage-bed and of women in childbirth, the midwife toad Heqet, various harvest

goddesses, etc. Later certain particularly notable men came to be regarded as possessing sanctity and were venerated after their death as gods, such as Imhotep of Memphis, King Djoser's architect, and the sage Amenhotep, son of Hapu.

Like men, gods frequently had wives and sons, thus forming "triads" which dwelt and were worshiped in the temple. Examples of such divine families are Ptah, his wife Sakhmet and their son Nefertum, or Osiris, Isis and Horus. The theologians of the ancient city of Heliopolis (On) went even further, establishing a group of nine gods (an "ennead") headed by Atum, the city's protective god. The other members of the group were the four cosmogonical (universal) deities Shu and his wife Tefnut, Geb and Nut, together with Osiris, his wife Isis, Seth, protective god of Upper Egypt and legendary adversary of Osiris, and his wife Nephthys. This divine ennead was imitated in many temples, with the substitution for Atum of the principal local god.

The gods were, too, equipped with human virtues and passions, and there were many accounts of their exploits and adventures. Unfortunately most of these myths and legends have been lost. Among the few that have come down to us the best known, and the most popular among the Egyptians themselves, is the tale of Osiris. According to this legend Osiris was King of Egypt, a prosperous and popular ruler. He had, however, a wicked brother named Seth, who persuaded him on the occasion of a banquet to lie down in an ingeniously contrived chest, which Seth with his 72 accomplices then locked and threw into the Nile. The river carried it down to the sea, and it was eventually cast ashore at the Phoenician town of Byblos. Meanwhile Isis, Osiris's sister and wife, had been ranging over the world in search of the chest. Finding it after a long quest, she took it back to Egypt and mourned in solitude for her dead husband; then she concealed the coffin and went to Buto, where her son Horus was brought up. During her absence Seth had found his hated brother's body while hunting wild boar, cut it up and dispersed the 14 pieces. Then Isis set out in search of the separate pieces, and when she found one buried it and set up a memorial on the spot: hence the numerous "tombs of Osiris" in Egypt. According to a later legend Isis assembled the separate parts of her husband's body, whereupon Osiris briefly returned to life in order to beget his son Horus. When Horus reached manhood he set out to wreak vengeance on his father's murderer, and eventually, after a fierce conflict, defeated and killed him. According to another account the two contestants were separated by Thoth and thereafter divided Egypt between them, Horus taking the south and Seth the north. Then, it was believed, Horus brought Osiris back to life again by magical means, and Osiris thereafter reigned in the Land of the West as King of the Dead.

Egyptian conceptions of the universe, in particular of the sky and the constellations, were also clad in the form of myth; and their picture of the world shows how narrow was the geographical horizon of the Egyptians in the Early Period. The world was conceived as an elongated oval, an island surrounded by the ocean and traversed from end to end by a broad river, the Nile, which was thought to emerge from the ocean in the south or alternatively to stem from two springs in the rocks at the Aswan cataracts. All around were high mountains, and on four of these peaks rested the sky, thought of as a level surface from which the stars hung down like lamps. Another view was that the sky was constituted like the earth, traversed by a river and dissected by numerous canals. Below the earth was another world known as Duat, the counterpart of the sky and identical to it in form, which according to a later conception was the land beyond the tomb, peopled by the dead. After the cow goddess Hathor became a sky goddess the sky was also conceived in the form of a cow with the sun set between its horns. Alternatively the sun was thought of as sailing across the cow's body during the day in a boat, as if on the celestial ocean, while at night the stars were set on its body. The air god Shu was believed to stand under the cow supporting it with his arms.

Different views were held in the various priestly schools about the two main luminaries in the sky, the sun and the moon. There was a very ancient conception that the sun and moon were the eyes of the great god who had created the world; and this great god was then identified with the sun god Re himself, giving rise to the paradoxical view that Re, the incarnation of the sun, had the sun as his eye. After Horus became the sun god the sun and the moon were also seen as his eyes. The eye of the sun featured prominently in Egyptian mythology. It was thought of in the form of the sun and became an independent goddess, an emanation of the sun god. With this eye of the sun were identified the Lower Egyptian snake goddess Uto and other goddesses such as the lion-headed Tefnut and the cow goddess Hathor. The eye of the sun was also conceived as a venomous snake, the uraeus or cobra, which reared up on the sun god's forehead and spat fire at his adversaries. Hence the cobra which was later worn by Egyptian kings as a kind of diadem on their forehead. – Another conception of the sun was that the sun god Re sailed across the sky in a boat during the day and at night continued his journey in another boat through the Underworld. Since the sun god Re-Harakhty was a falcon the sun was also seen as a falcon, flying in brilliant plumage across the sky. Alternatively, like Horus, it was a young hero engaged in constant conflict with the hostile powers of darkness. Again, it was conceived as a scarab (dung-beetle); and just as the scarab rolled in front of it a ball of dung containing its egg, so the sun god was seen in the form of a scarab pushing the round solar disc in front of it.

The world, the gods and mankind had not, it was believed, existed from the beginning of time but had been created. The view most commonly held was that the earth god Geb and the sky goddess Nut had lain in intimate union within the primal ocean, Nun, until the air god Shu separated them and raised up the sky goddess in his arms. The sun god Re was also believed to have come out of the primal ocean; or alternatively he was the child of Geb and Nut, reborn anew each day. This, of course, ran counter to the other view that Re was himself the creator of the world.

In the course of history Egyptian religion underwent many changes. Certain gods gained for a time a dominant position in the Egyptian pantheon, either through the rise to power of a dynasty or a city particularly devoted to their cult or as a result of theological speculation and myth formation. When in the Early Period two independent kingdoms came into being in Upper and Lower Egypt the local gods of the two capitals, Seth of Ombos and Horus of Behdet, became the patrons of the two States; and when the rulers of Lower Egypt established a single Egyptian kingdom, with its capital presumably at Heliopolis, Horus achieved pre-eminence and thereafter remained the protective god of the Pharaohs and of the country as a whole. In the last phase of the Prehistoric period Egypt again split into two kingdoms with capitals at Nekhab-Nekhen and Buto, whose tutelary divinities were the vulture goddess Nekhbet and the snake goddess Uto, who thus became the goddesses of Upper and Lower Egypt. Similarly, at the end of the Old Kingdom, Ptah, god of the capital city of Memphis, became the principal Egyptian god.

An important part was played in the history of Egyptian religion by the city of On (Heliopolis), which seems to have been the religious center of Egypt from a very early period. The Temple of On was the scene of the royal coronation; and here, too, according to the myth, the goddess Seshat inscribed the years of the king's reign on the leaves of the sacred tree. Here also stood the obelisk-shaped column known as Benbe, the favorite seat of the sun god. The real tutelary god of the town, however, was Atum; and the priests of On accordingly declared him equal with the sun god, maintaining that he was merely another form and another name of Re-Harakhty. This doctrine was widely diffused throughout Egypt, and other local gods began to be identified with Re and to be given his attribute, the solar disc with the royal cobra (uraeus) entwined round it. Thus, for example, the crocodile god Sobek and Amun, the god of Karnak, became sun gods. This identification of local gods with Re, beginning in the Middle Kingdom, developed on a considerable scale during the New Kingdom, throwing Egyptian religion into considerable confusion. Attempts were indeed made to distinguish the various forms of Re, for example by regarding the sun god Harakhty as the morning sun and Atum, now also a sun god, as the evening sun; but no complete systematization was ever achieved.

Similarly the female local divinities were amalgamated, particularly when they had similar characteristics. Thus the sky goddess Hathor was identified with Isis, the cat goddess Bastet with the lion goddesses Sakhmet and Pakhet, and Sakhmet with the vulture goddess Mut.

A new phase in the development of Egyptian religion began when the center of gravity of the kingdom moved south at the beginning of the New Kingdom. The god Amun of Karnak, an almost unknown deity under the Old Kingdom, who had become identified with the sun god under the name Amun-Re, was brought out of obscurity by the kings of the 12th Dynasty, some of whom were named after him (Amenemhet, "Amun is at the head"), and at the beginning of the New Kingdom, when Thebes replaced Memphis as capital, moved into the principal place in the Egyptian pantheon. The great wars waged by the Theban kings in Nubia and Asia were undertaken in his name; temples in his honor were built in the conquered territories; and the lion's share of the booty was assigned to his temples, particularly the temples in Thebes. Under the 18th Dynasty Amun became the national god of Egypt, displacing the old national god Horus (Re-Harakhty). The priests of Heliopolis, resenting this decline in their influence, took the earliest opportunity of bringing about the overthrow of Amun and restoring the sun god to his rightful place. When Amenophis IV came to the throne the sun god of Heliopolis (Re-Harakhty), in a particular form, was declared the principal god; and soon afterwards, in the sixth year of the King's reign, the sun itself (Egyptian Aten) became the sole divinity of the kingdom. One factor which undoubtedly influenced Amenophis in carrying through this revolution was his desire to put an end to the confusion in Egyptian religious doctrine and to replace the many gods long theoretically identified with the sun god by a single unique sun god. The images and names of Amun and his associated gods were everywhere destroyed. Soon after Amenophis's death, however, during the reign of Tutankhamun, the supporters of Amun gained the upper hand and the old faith was restored.

Egyptian religion thus remained in a confused state; the fusion of different divinities continued on an increasing scale, and the living faith hardened into rigidity. Men clung anxiously to the ancient traditions, and a superstitious belief in the efficacy of amulets and magic spells as man's sole protection against evil influences now gained ground. Little new religious thought is to be found in the innumerable texts which cover the walls of temples, tombs and sarcophagi. Individual Egyptian deities including Isis, Harpocrates and Sarapis (who was

Alabaster lamp from Tutankhamun's Tomb

introduced into Egypt in the Ptolemaic period) retained sufficient status to be adopted into the Greek and Roman pantheon and in Roman Imperial times to find many worshippers as far afield as Germany and Britain. Only with the coming of Christianity was Egyptian religion finally defeated.

The Egyptians never achieved any unified or systematic conception of the fate of man after death. The one generally accepted belief was that man's life did not terminate with death but that he continued to live in the same way as on earth provided that certain requirements for this continued existence were met. The main thing considered essential was to bury the dead man's body with care and to preserve it from destruction. A house was built for him in the likeness of his earthly dwelling in which he could live and which, it was believed, he could leave during the day if he wished. Statues set up in a special chamber in the tomb represented the dead man, his family and his servants. Votive offerings deposited in the tomb provided for his subsistence in the future life, and further offerings (foodstuffs, objects of everyday use, etc.) were depicted on the walls of the tomb or on the sarcophagus, in the belief that by some magical means the representations of the various objects would serve in place of the things themselves for the dead man's use. Garments, ornaments and jewelry, etc., were also placed in the tomb or represented in reliefs or paintings. The activities in which the dead man had

engaged during his life, the entertainments he had enjoyed, the honors he had gained – all these awaited him in the afterlife, and to ensure that they would be available to him were depicted on the walls of the tomb, enabling us to gain an exact picture of the life of the tomb's owner. In earlier times only the great ones of the kingdom were allowed to have tombs of their own, and lesser mortals had to be content with more modest graves; later the middle ranks of the population, provided that they could meet the considerable expense, also constructed their "houses for eternity".

The dead were under the protection of their local gods, who were responsible for watching over their burial and their security in the tomb. In addition there was a special god of the dead who was venerated in many cities – Khontamenti, "first of the inhabitants of the Western Realm" (the kingdom of the dead), who was conceived in the form of a dog. Later all these various deities were overshadowed by Osiris. Thanks to the widely diffused myth associated with him, this old vegetation god gradually became accepted throughout Egypt as the Lord of the Dead, solely responsible for their welfare, with Abydos as the principal center of his cult. The death which Osiris had suffered was the fate which awaited every man; but just as Osiris had returned to life, so every man might begin a new life, provided that the same magical formulae were pronounced for him by his son; he then joined Osiris, and indeed became one with Osiris, became himself Osiris. His entry into Osiris's kingdom depended on the recitation of magical formulae and spells, a knowledge of which had to be communicated to the dead man; but in addition it was necessary to have led a virtuous life on earth, and for this purpose the dead man had to appear in Osiris's judgment hall and declare before 42 judges that he was free of major sin. Only when this had been done, and his heart had been weighed by Thoth on the scales of justice and found not to be wanting, could he enter into the Beyond.

There were divergent views about the whereabouts of the Afterworld. It was usually thought of as being in the west, the region of hills and desert in which the sun set. Alternatively the dead were believed to live in the celestial fields of Earu, a fertile region where they plowed and harvested just as they had done on earth and where the corn grew seven cubits high – a paradise indeed for the Egyptian peasant. Since the work in the afterlife might sometimes prove too hard for the dead man, small figures known as *ushabtis* were, from the Middle Kingdom onwards, left in the tomb to help him, inscribed with a magical formula which would bring them to life and allow them to work in the fields. Another theory, designed to unify different conceptions of the afterlife, set the residence of the dead in the Underworld (Duat). This was divided into 12 sections corresponding to the 12 hours of the night, which, on one view, were separated from one another by large gates.

Alongside these conceptions there was also the popular belief that in addition to his body man also had a soul (*ba*) which lived on after his death. This was originally thought of as having the form of a bird (later a bird with a human head), which left the body after death and fluttered freely about the world, though able at any time to return to the body – always provided that the body remained intact and free from corruption. In order to enable the soul to find the right body, great pains were taken to ensure its preservation in good condition. Each man also had a *ka*, a personification of the life force and thus a kind of guardian spirit, which was born with him and accompanied him through life. Even after a man's death his *ka* lived on in order to dispense vital force to the dead man in the life beyond.

In the earliest times the dead were buried lying on their left side with their knees drawn up. During the Old Kingdom, under the influence of the Osiris myth, they began to be buried in a fully extended position – a practice perhaps first adopted in royal burials. At the same time the practice of embalming was introduced in order to preserve the bodies from dissolution. At first they were merely treated with saline solutions and asphalt and wrapped in

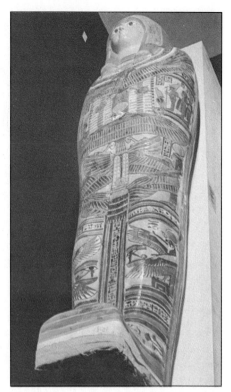

Mummy case

linen bandages and cloths. In later times the process was more elaborate. The brain was first extracted through the nostrils, using an iron hook; then the abdomen was opened with a stone knife and the entrails removed (Herodotus ii, 86). The entrails were put into four vessels (canopic jars), which in the later period had lids in the form of the four sons of Horus, who were charged with their protection. The heart was also removed from the body and replaced by a stone scarab set on the dead man's breast under the bandaging. According to Herodotus there were in the Late Period three methods of embalming, varying according to the expense to be incurred. Thanks to the great care expended on the embalming process many mummies have survived into modern times with clearly distinguishable features.

The Egyptian Pantheon

Aker

A divine couple of chthonian (Underworld) deities worshiped in Leontopolis, guardians of the entrance to the Underworld; associated with the sacred barque of the morning and evening sun. Represented as two lions back to back.

Amun (*Amon, Ammon*; the "Hidden One")

Originally a wind god venerated by the Nile boatmen. From the 11th Dynasty a creator god, the principal deity of Thebes and, as Amun-Re, elevated to the status of a sun god. From the New Kingdom worshiped as the national god of Egypt; in the reign of Amenophis IV/Akhenaten temporarily displaced by the Aten. In Hermopolis, together with his female counterpart *Amaunet*, goddess of the fresh north winds, he was worshiped as god of the air and of invisible things. Identified in Ptolemaic times with the Greek Zeus and particularly venerated, as Ammon, in the Siwa Oasis.

Represented in human form with a double feather crown, symbolizing his power over air and light; occasionally also as a ram or a goose. Occasionally, combined with Min of Coptos, ithyphallic.

Sacred animal: ram.

Anhur: see Onuris.

Antaeus

A legendary figure taken over from Greek mythology; an invincible Libyan king and giant who was identified with a curious local god. Principal place of worship: Antaeopolis (Egyptian Tukow) in Upper Egypt.

Anubis (*Anup*)

A very ancient god of the dead, local god of Kais and protective god of the 12th, 17th and 18th nomes of Upper Egypt. In later times believed to be a brother of Osiris or the son of Osiris and Nephthys, secretly conceived, exposed by his parents and brought up by Isis. His function was to show the dead the way to the Underworld. The Greeks equated him with Hermes and called him Hermanubis. Elsewhere in Egypt he was associated with Horus and Thoth. Principal place of worship: Cynopolis.

Represented as a dog or with a dog's or jackal's head. Sacred animal: dog or jackal.

Anukis (*Anqet*)

Goddess of the cataract region at Aswan; consort of Khnum. Principal place of worship: island of Sehel, Aswan.

Represented wearing a white crown with two gazelle's horns.

Anup: see Anubis.

Apis (*Hapi*)

The sacred bull of Memphis; accorded divine status as the son of Ptah (or Atum or Osiris); combined with Osiris as Osir-Hapi (Osorapis; Greek Sarapis), ruler of the Underworld. The finding of a bull with the right attributes was an occasion for great celebration throughout Egypt. When an Apis bull died it was mummified and buried with great pomp in the Serapeum at Saqqara.

Represented as a black bull with a white triangle on its forehead, a solar disc between its horns and decorative trappings.

Arsnuphis (*Harensnuphis*)

The name under which Shu was worshiped on the islands of Bigga and Philae.

Aten

The sun as the sole divinity and vital force, embracing the whole world and manifested everywhere in nature. The worship of the Aten – the first monotheistic religious doctrine – was made the State religion by Amenophis IV/Akhenaten, a fanatical opponent of the polytheism which had hitherto prevailed in Egypt. The doctrine of the Aten contains some astonishingly modern conceptions.

Represented as a solar disc with rays ending in hands.

Atum

Creator and lord of the world; the principal divinity of the Heliopolitan ennead and the local god of Pithom. Created by self-generation the divine couple Shu, the air god, and Tefnut, the dew goddess. Associated with Re and venerated as the setting sun.

Represented with the double crown, scepter and girdle; occasionally as a snake.

Bastet

Principal goddess of Bubastis, goddess of joy and love, celebrated in a lively annual festival at Bubastis. Associated from an early period with Hathor, Isis, Mut, Neith, Pakhet, Sakhmet and Tefnut.

Represented as a cat, sometimes with kittens; or cat-headed, with a pectoral bearing a lion's or cat's head, a basket on her right arm, a sistrum in her left hand. Sacred animal: cat.

Amun   **Amun-Re**   **Anubis**

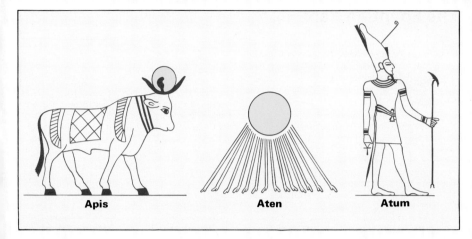

Apis   Aten   Atum

Bes
A popular god imported from the Land of Punt (Somali coast) about 1500 B.C.; protector of the marriage chamber and of women in childbirth, driver away of evil spirits and poisonous snakes. His image regularly appears in the birth-house *(mammisi)* of the larger temples.
Represented as a grotesque squatting dwarf; frequently wearing a feather crown and a cat's skin, with protruding tongue; occasionally depicted grinning grotesquely.

Buchis
The sacred bull of Hermonthis and Medamut.

Buto: see Uto.

Dedun
A Nubian god in the form of a bird of prey. Later compared with the Horus falcon.

Djehuti: see Thoth.

Duamutef
One of the four sons of Horus; protective god of the dead, guardian of the stomach.
Represented on the lid of a canopic jar with a jackal's head.

Ehi: see Ihi.

Emewet
God of the dead.

Represented with a dog's head, carrying a staff with a snake wound round it.

Enhuret *(Onuris)*
A local god of This and Sebennytus.

Epet: see Opet.

Eusos
Goddess of Heliopolis; wife of Harakhty.

Geb
Earth god and divine judge; husband of the sky goddess Nut and father of Isis, Osiris, Nephthys and Seth. He guides the first steps of the dead in the Underworld.

Hapi: see Apis.

Hapi
A Nile god and one of the manifestations of the Nile.

Hapi
One of the four sons of Horus; protective god of the dead, guardian of the lungs.
Represented on the lid of a canopic jar with a baboon's head.

Harakhty ("Horus of the Horizon")
One manifestation of the sun god Re associated with Horus, with the attributes of both gods. Associated with Re as Re-Harakhty, he was the national god

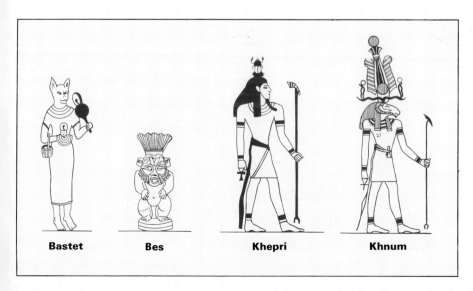

Bastet   Bes   Khepri   Khnum

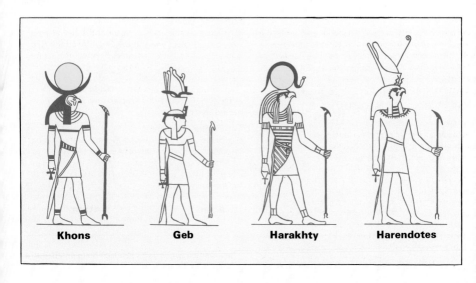

Khons   **Geb**   **Harakhty**   **Harendotes**

during the New Kingdom. Worshiped at Heliopolis and also highly venerated at many other places, sometimes in association with other gods (Re-Harakhty-Atum, Re-Harakhty-Amun, etc.).
Represented with a falcon's head, on which is the solar disc.
Sacred animal: falcon.

Harendotes (*Har-nedj-yotef*, "Horus, protector of his father Osiris")
A form of Horus. Temple at Philae.

Harkhentekhtai *(Khentekhtai)*
A crocodile (sometimes falcon) deity of Athribis (Kom el-Atrib), in the Delta.

Harmachis (*Haremakhet, Re-Harmachis*, "Horus in the Horizon")
A combination of Re and Horus, symbolizing the death-defeating powers of the sun. The name of the Sphinx of Giza.

Haroeris
The older Horus. Principal place of worship: Kom Ombo.
Represented with a falcon's head.

Harpocrates (*Hor-pa-khred*, "Horus the Child")
A form of Horus as a child, much venerated in the Late Period; to the Greeks a god of silence.
Represented with the side-lock of youth and his finger at his mouth.

Harsemtawi (*Harsomtus*, "Horus, unifier of the two lands")
Son of Horus and Hathor.

Harsiesis
Horus as a child, the son of Isis.
Represented with the side-lock of youth and his finger at his mouth.

Harsomtus: see Harsemtawi.

Hathor
Sky goddess; goddess of joy, of dancing and of love, later identified with Isis and the Greek goddess Aphrodite. At Thebes, associated with Osiris, she became the protectress of the necropolis. Venerated in Sinai as "Mistress of the Turquoises". Principal temple at Dendera; also large temples at Abu Simbel, Serabit el-Khadim (Sinai), Aphroditopolis, Aphroditespolis, etc. Represented as a cow; also in human form with a cow's horns, ears or head; later also with the solar disc between her horns. Her face appears on the capitals of pillars in her temples. Attributes: sistrum and menat (a broad collar).

Heh
God of time and of infinity.
Represented with tadpoles, each of which symbolizes 10,000 years.

Heqet
Goddess of birth.
Represented as a midwife toad.

Hathor   **Horus**   **Isis**   **Maat**

Herishef

A local god of Heracleopolis; national god during the First Intermediate Period. Closely associated with Re, Osiris and Amun; identified by the Greeks with Heracles. Cult center Hnes (later Heracleopolis Magna).
Sacred animal: ram.

Hor-pa-khred: see Harpocrates.

Horus

Worshiped everywhere as a sun god; the earliest national god of Egypt; a member of the Heliopolitan ennead. Usually regarded as son of Osiris and Isis, sometimes as son of Re and brother of Seth. The Pharaoh was believed to be an incarnation of Horus and accordingly the legitimate successor to Osiris: hence the "Horus names" of the kings which came into use at an early period. As a child Horus was known as Harsiesis or Harpocrates; the older Horus as Haroeris. His four sons Duamutef, Hapi, Imsety and Qebhsenuef – symbols of the four cardinal points – were regarded as protectors of the entrails of the dead and were frequently represented on the lids of canopic jars.
Represented in the early period as a falcon; later with a falcon's head, sometimes wearing the double crown; at Edfu as a winged solar disc.
Sacred animal: falcon.

Ihi *(Ehi)*

The young son of Hathor of Dendera; god of music and dancing; identified with the rising morning sun.
Represented with a sistrum.

Imhotep *(Imouthes)*

High Priest of Heliopolis, a great sage and adviser to King Djoser; believed to have built Djoser's Pyramid at Saqqara, and hence the patron of architects. Venerated in the Late Period as a physician and a miraculous healer, he was equated by the Greeks with Asclepius. Main cult center the Asclepieion at Saqqara; temples at Philae, Karnak, etc.
Represented with a papyrus scroll on his knees.

Imsety

One of the four sons of Horus; protective god of the dead, guardian of the liver.
Represented on the lid of a canopic jar with a human head.

Isis

A goddess much venerated in the Late Period; sister and wife of Osiris and mother of Horus; equated by the Greeks and Romans with Demeter, Ino and Hecate. The symbol of conjugal fidelity and protectress of children. Depicted on the sides of a coffin, she gave the dead man protection and vital force. Her principal temple was at Philae, where she continued to be worshiped into the Christian period; other temples at Behbeit el-Hagara (Iseum), Coptos, etc.
Represented standing erect with cow's horns and the solar disc on her head and a papyrus staff in her hand, or seated suckling the child Horus (Harsiesis or Harpocrates).

Kemuer (the "Great Black One")
Bull god of Athribis (Kom el-Atrib) in the Delta.

Khentekhtai: see Harkhentekhtai.

Khenti-Amentiu: see Khontamenti.

Khepri (the "Arising One")
The scarab (dung-beetle) as the incarnation of Re in his manifestation as the morning sun. From the Middle Kingdom scarabs of stone or pottery, with their name on the underside, were popular all over Egypt as seals or amulets.
Represented as a scarab.

Khnum

An ancient creator god, protector of the area around the First Cataract, where in the Early Period the Nile was believed to have its source. Principal temple on the island of Elephantine. As a creator god he shaped men on the potter's wheel. In the later period he was frequently identified with Osiris and Amun.
Represented with a ram's head and twisted horns.
Sacred animal: ram.

Khons (the "Wanderer")
God of the moon and of time; a member of the Theban triad, together with his parents Amun and Mut. Widely revered as a counsellor and helper in case of illness. Equated by the Greeks with Heracles. Principal temple at Karnak.
Represented with a falcon's head, often bearing the lunar crescent and lunar disc on his head; occasionally as a child with side-lock in the form of a mummy.
Sacred animal: falcon.

Khontamenti *(Khenti-Amentiu)*
A dog-headed god of the dead, particularly venerated at Abydos.

Maat

Daughter of Re (i.e. of the divine world order), goddess of truth and justice. In the judgment of the dead the dead man's heart was weighed against Maat's feather.
Represented with an ostrich feather on her head.

Mandulis

A Nubian local god, probably to be compared with Horus.

Mehit

A goddess equated with the destroying and fire-breathing cobra (uraeus), the eye of Re. In the later period associated with Hathor.
Represented in the form of a lion.

Min

Probably an ancient fertility god. Protective god of Coptos, starting-point of the caravan route across the Eastern Desert, and hence worshiped as the god of desert travelers. Later, combined with Amun, a harvest god, equated by the Greeks with Pan.
Represented as a black, ithyphallic mummiform figure with a head-dress of two feathers with a ribbon, holding a flail in his raised right hand.

Mnevis

The sacred bull of Heliopolis.

Month *(Munt)*
War god of Hermopolis, worshiped from an early period in the Thebes area (Medamut, Hermonthis, Karnak, etc.); under the 11th Dynasty protector of the royal family. Frequently associated with the Buchis bull.
Represented with a falcon's head, on which are the solar disc, a double uraeus and a double feather crown.
Sacred animal: Buchis bull.

Mut

Worshiped as a vulture goddess from an early period. A member of the Theban triad, wife of Amun and mother of Khons. Her incarnation was the queen, who accordingly sometimes wore a vulture crown. Principal temple at Karnak.
Represented with a lion's head, wearing a vulture cap or crown (either the white or the double crown).

Nefertum (the "Perfectly Beautiful")
Son of Ptah of Memphis and Sakhmet; a member of the Memphite triad. Sun child and dispenser of unguents.
Represented with a lotus-flower head-dress or two feathers; sometimes as a child seated on a lotus flower.

Min   Month   Mut   Neith

Neith
Town goddess of Sais; creator of all life and mother of the sun. Later a war goddess, closely associated with Osiris and Sobek. Watched over the bier of Osiris together with Isis, Nephthys and Selkit. Equated by the Greeks with Athena. Temples at Sais, Esna and Memphis, in the Fayyum, etc.
Represented wearing the Red Crown of Lower Egypt or two crossed arrows on her head and holding a papyrus staff and bow; occasionally with a shield as head-dress or in her hand.

Nekhbet *(Smithis)*
Goddess of Nekhab (El-Kab) and protective goddess of Upper Egypt. During the New Kingdom venerated as a birth goddess, and accordingly equated by the Greeks with Eileithyia.
Represented in the form of a vulture or with the skin of a vulture.
Sacred animal: vulture.

Nephthys
Originally a Heliopolitan goddess of the dead; sister of Osiris, Isis and Seth, wife of Seth and mother of Anubis. Together with Isis she lamented the dead Osiris on his bier. Associated with Anukis, goddess of the Aswan cataract region.
Represented in human form with the hieroglyph for "mistress of the house" on her head, holding a papyrus staff and the symbol for "life".

Nut
Sky goddess; wife of Geb and mother of Osiris, Isis,

Nephthys and Seth; alternatively mother of the sun god Re. In the cult of the dead she was closely associated with the belief in resurrection of the dead. Represented as an elongated female figure, supported by the god Shu to prevent her from falling on Geb, who swallows the sun at night to give birth to it anew in the morning.

Onnophris *(Unnefer)*
A name borne by Osiris.

Onuris: see Enhuret.

Opet (*Epet*, the "Harem")
A popular birth goddess; worshiped, particularly at Thebes, as the mother of Osiris.
Represented as a hippopotamus painted with flowers and plants.

Osiris
Son of the earth god Geb and the sky goddess Nut, brother of Isis, Nephthys and Seth. Originally a vegetation god, identified at Busiris (Nile Delta) with the local god Anedjti. Venerated from an early period as the conqueror of death and equated with the god of the dead worshiped at Abydos, the "Lord of the West". Tomb at Abydos.
Represented in mummy form wearing the White Crown of Upper Egypt with a double feather and holding a flail and crook. Attribute: *djed* pillar.

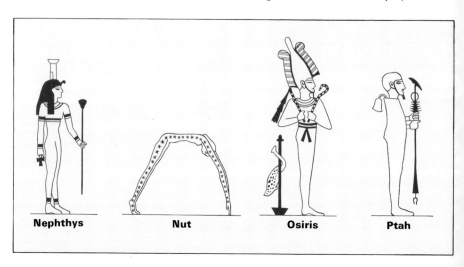

Nephthys   Nut   Osiris   Ptah

Pakhet
Goddess of the Speos Artemidos.
Represented with a cat's or lion's head.
Sacred animals: cat and lion.

Ptah
Egyptian national god; a member of the Memphite triad, together with Sakhmet and Nefertum; patron of artists and craftsmen. Originally a creator god, combined at an early period with Sokar and Osiris in the form of Ptah-Sokar-Osiris, who was associated with the Apis bull. Equated by the Greeks with Hephaestus. Temples at Thebes and Abydos, in Nubia, etc.
Represented in mummy form with a skull-cap, beard and three scepters.

Ptah-Tatjenen
A combination of Ptah with the Memphite god Tatjenen (the "High Land"), personification of the primal hill in which the primal river rose.

Qebhsenuef
One of the four sons of Horus; protective god of the dead, guardian of the entrails.
Represented on the lid of a canopic jar with a falcon's head.

Re *(Ra)*
Primal god; sun god and, as Atum, the principal figure in the Heliopolitan ennead. Combined with Harakhty at an early period to form Re-Harakhty. He was believed to sail in his boat across the heavens, appearing in the morning as a youth (Khepri), at midday as a man in the prime of life (Re) and in the evening as an old man (Atum). At night he sailed through the Underworld in the form of a ram, thus becoming a god of the dead. The solar barque of Re held for the dead the hope of a new life. Many other local gods sought and sometimes achieved upgrading by association with Re (e.g. Amun-Re, Sobek-Re, Khnum-Re). Re as the primal god may have been the origin of the monotheistic doctrine of the Aten.
The worship of Re centered on sun temples with obelisks, on the gilded tips of which (coated with electrum, an alloy of gold and silver) the rising sun could settle.
Represented in human form.

Re-Harmachis: see Harmachis.

Sakhmet
A manifestation of Bastet; a member of the Memphite triad, wife of Ptah and mother of Nefertum. War goddess and the wrathful eye of the sun god Re, whom she defends with death-bringing zeal, bringing down famine and plague on his enemies.
Represented with a lion's head.
Sacred animal: lioness.

Sarapis *(Serapis)*
A foreign god introduced into Egypt by the Ptolemies and equated with Osiris-Apis, the dead Apis bull.

Satet *(Satis)*
Protective goddess of the Aswan cataract area, worshiped at Esna, Philae and Elephantine and on the island of Sehel.
Represented with a feather crown.

Sebek: see Sobek.

Sehat-Hor
A cow goddess who fed and cared for Horus.

Selkit *(Serqet, Selkis)*
A goddess of Lower Egypt, protectress of the living and the dead, guardian of canopic jars. Together with Neith, Isis and Nephthys she watched at the bier of Osiris.
Represented in human form with a scorpion on her head; occasionally as a scorpion.
Sacred animal: scorpion.

Seshat
Goddess of writing and of scribes.
Depicted as a woman with writing materials (reeds, palette, pouches containing paint).

Seth *(Sutekh)*
God of Ombos (near Naqada) and in prehistoric times protective god of Upper Egypt, also worshiped at Tanis and Avaris. A member of the Heliopolitan ennead, as son of Geb and Nut; husband of his sister Nephthys. In the myth he was the wicked brother who slew Osiris; according to another story he was the brother and adversary of Horus. During the 22nd Dynasty he was excluded from the Egyptian pantheon and regarded as a god of the impure, of chaos, of storm and of war, equated with the Greek Typhon.
Represented with the head of an animal with a trunk-like snout, identified by the 19th c. German traveler Schweinfurth as an aardvark *(Orycteropus aethiopicus)*.

Shu
Air god, lord of the four winds. With his sister Tefnut, the dew goddess, he was equated in Leontopolis with the divine couple Aker, represented as a pair of lions.
Represented as a lion.

Sakhmet   Shu   Selkit   Seshat

Seth   **Sobek**   **Thoth**   **Thoeris**

Smithis: see Nekhbet.

Sobek *(Sebek, Suchos)*
A crocodile god, worshiped particularly in the Fayyum, at Ombos (Kom Ombo), Gebelein and Esna. From the Middle Kingdom frequently associated with Horus or Re.
Represented with a crocodile's head or as a crocodile. Sacred animal: crocodile.

Sokar *(Seker, Sokaris)*
A god of the dead worshiped in the Memphis area, guardian of the entrance to the Underworld. His festival was celebrated with processions bearing his barque. In the Late Period frequently associated with Ptah and Osiris.
Represented with a falcon's head.

Sothis
The personification of the star Sirius; goddess of water and purifier of the dead. The appearance of Sirius in the sky marked the beginning of the Nile flood.

Suchos: see Sobek.

Tatjenen: see Ptah-Tatjenen.

Taweret: see Thoeris.

Tefnut
Goddess of dew and of moisture; sister and wife of the air god Shu, and together with him equated at Leontopolis with the divine couple Aker.

Thoeris *(Taweret,* the "Great One")
A form of Opet, the hippopotamus goddess; patroness of pregnant women and women during and after childbirth.
Represented as a pregnant hippopotamus with human breasts and arms, standing erect.

Thoth *(Djehuti)*
Moon god; god of time, of measurement and later also of mathematics, learning and science; the inventor of writing. Town god of Hermopolis Parva and Hermopolis Magna, being equated by the Greeks with Hermes. He accompanied the sun god Re on his daily journey. Protector of Osiris. At the judgment of the dead he noted down all the dead man's actions.
Represented as an ibis or a baboon; also as an ibis-headed figure with the lunar crescent and disc on his head and writing materials in his hands.
Sacred animals: baboon and ibis.

Tum
God of immortality. As a primal god, in existence before the sun and moon, he was immune from death. Represented with the double crown.

Unnefer: see Onnophris.

Urthekaw: see Werthekaw.

Uto *(Buto)*
Town goddess of Buto in the Delta; protective goddess of Lower Egypt, associated with papyrus plant and cobra (uraeus). The counterpart of the Upper Egyptian goddess Nekhbet.
Represented with a lion's head, wearing the Red Crown, etc.
Sacred animals: snake, ichneumon, shrew.

Wepwawet ("Opener of the Ways")
Town god of Asyut; also worshiped as a god of the dead, corresponding to the Memphite Anubis. He accompanied Re on his journey through the Underworld.
Represented as a wolf, standing erect, or as a reclining dog.

Werthekaw *(Urthekaw)*
A lion-headed goddess, wife of Re-Harakhty.

Hieroglyphics

The term **hieroglyphics** (Greek "sacred carvings") is applied to a form of writing using picture symbols (*hieroglyphs*) devised by the ancient Egyptians, which was probably the model for the Hittite and Cretan hieroglyphic scripts; the oldest form of Babylonian cuneiform was also hieroglyphic. Hieroglyphic scripts were also used in the Indus Valley, in China (Moso script), on Easter Island and in Central America (Maya script).

After repeated attempts in modern times (e.g. by the learned Jesuit *Athanasius Kircher*, 1602–80) to decipher the Egyptian hieroglyphs and some promising preliminary work in the early 19th century by the French Orientalist *Antoine-Isaac Silvestre de Sacy* (1758–1838), the Swedish Egyptologist *Johann David Åkerblad* (1763–1819) and the English physicist *Thomas Young* (1773–1820), a French Egyptologist, *Jean-François* **Champollion** (1790–1832) finally succeeded in 1822 in identifying certain alphabetic signs and establishing the principles of the Egyptian hieroglyphic script. Thereafter he followed up his first discoveries so successfully that he is fully entitled to the credit of being the real decipherer of the hieroglyphs.

The key to the hieroglyphs was provided by the **Rosetta Stone**, an inscribed slab of basalt found by a French officer during constructional work at Fort Saint-Julien, Rosetta (some 45 miles/70 km east of Alexandria), in 1799. Coming into British hands in 1801, after the defeat of the French forces in Egypt, it was taken to London and is now in the British Museum.

The Rosetta Stone bears an inscription in three different scripts – *Egyptian hieroglyphics* at the top, *demotic* (a popular version of Egyptian which came into use in the Late Period) in the middle, and *Greek* at the bottom. The upper two are translations of the Greek text, which records a resolution by a body of Egyptian priests in honor of Ptolemy V Epiphanes dated 196 B.C. The first step in the decipherment was the realization that certain groups of signs enclosed within an oval ring represented the names of kings (the royal "cartouches") and must contain the name of Ptolemy.

After Champollion and his successors had succeeded in establishing the sound values of many hieroglyphs it became possible with the help of Coptic (the modern form of the ancient Egyptian language) not only to read the inscriptions but to understand their content. The German Egyptologist *Heinrich Karl Brugsch* (1827–94) elucidated the demotic lang-

uage and was the first to show that, like the Semitic scripts (Hebrew, Arabic), the ancient Egyptian script included only the consonants, omitting the vowels as of no significance.

The hieroglypic script consists of **ideograms**, which originally were merely pictures of particular concrete objects. Abstract conceptions and verbs could also be represented by pictures of objects associated with the concept or action concerned. Thus the verb "to rule" was expressed by the picture of a royal scepter, the name of Upper Egypt by the reed, its heraldic plant, or the verb "to write" by the representation of writing implements.

Rosetta Stone (British Museum)

A great advance was made in the development of the script when words which had no signs of their own began to be expressed by hieroglyphs which had a different meaning but the same sound value. Thus the verb "to go out", pronounced *prj*, was represented by the sign for "house", which had the same sound; the word "son" (*s´*) by the sign for "goose", which was also pronounced *s´*; "first" (*tp*) by the sign for "dagger", also *tp*. Phonetic transfers of this kind were facilitated by the fact that only the consonants, which

Hieroglyphs for concrete objects

face	moon	pigeon	eye	sun	plow

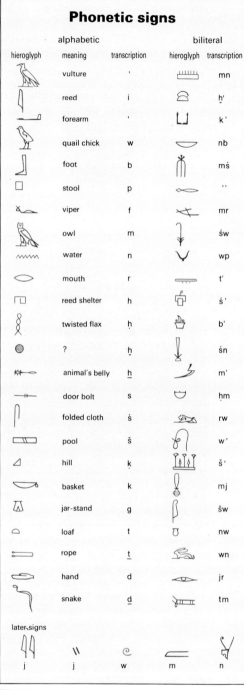

Phonetic signs

alphabetic

hieroglyph	meaning	transcription
	vulture	'
	reed	i
	forearm	'
	quail chick	w
	foot	b
	stool	p
	viper	f
	owl	m
	water	n
	mouth	r
	reed shelter	h
	twisted flax	ḥ
	?	ḫ
	animal's belly	ẖ
	door bolt	s
	folded cloth	ś
	pool	š
	hill	ḳ
	basket	k
	jar-stand	g
	loaf	t
	rope	ṯ
	hand	d
	snake	ḏ

later signs

hieroglyph	transcription
	j
	j
	w
	m
	n

biliteral

hieroglyph	transcription
	mn
	ḥ'
	k'
	nb
	mś
	''
	mr
	św
	wp
	t'
	ś'
	b'
	śn
	m'
	ḥm
	rw
	w'
	š'
	mj
	św
	nw
	wn
	jr
	tm

Determinatives

hieroglyph	meaning
	man
	woman
	tree
	house
	town
	plural
	royal cartouche

Semantic signs

original meaning

hieroglyph	meaning	transcription
	sun	r'
	front	ḥ'-t
	moon	j'ḥ
	Maat	M''t
	Re	R'
	Amun	'mn
	Horus	Ḥr
	Sobek	Śbk
	bull	k'
	be strong	nḫt
	rule (v.)	ḥw
	star	śb'

transferred meaning

hieroglyph	originally		transcription
	scepter	strong	wśr
	Osiris pillar	constant	ḏd
	hammer	majesty	ḥm
	gaming piece	strength	pḥ-t
	goose	son	s'
	animal's leg	repeat	whm
	axe	choose	śtp
	ram	soul	b'
	lake	love	mr
	column	town of	jwn
	cloth	god	nṯr
	seat	Isis	'śt
	bird	spirit	'ḫ
	basket	festival	ḥb
	sandal-strap	live	'nḫ
	bowstring	grow	rwd
	chain	gold	nb
	beetle	exist	ḫpr

Hieroglyphs were also used to represent numbers

carried the meaning of the word, needed to be taken into account.

Many signs were transferred in this way to so many words that they gradually lost their semantic value and became purely **phonetic signs** representing groups of consonants, while signs representing a single sound became alphabetic letters. Then in the Late Period some consonants were used to represent vowels. The phonetic signs thus established were put together to write whole words, together with grammatical elements such as endings and suffixes, and were also used, in the frequent cases where there was ambiguity about the sound of a particular word, to indicate its pronunciation.

In addition to the semantic signs (representing words) and the phonetic signs (representing sounds) there was a third group of hieroglyphs, the **determinatives** – signs added after a word to indicate its approximate sense. In the Late Period much use was made of these signs, which greatly simplify the reading of the inscriptions.

In the earliest Egyptian texts that have come down to us the hieroglyphic script is in fully developed form, having already completed the evolution sketched out in the preceding paragraphs, and semantic signs, phonetic signs and determinatives are all employed.

As a rule the hieroglyphic script is written from right to left, sometimes in vertical and sometimes in horizontal lines; it is quite exceptional to find it written from left to right. It goes without saying that in the course of the 3000 years or more during which the hieroglyphs were in use there were considerable changes in the form of the characters and the orthography of the words; and visitors to Egypt will soon

learn to distinguish between the large and simple hieroglyphs of the Old Kingdom, the elegant characters of the 18th Dynasty (for example in the Deir el-Bahri Temple) and the small cramped script of the Ptolemaic inscriptions.

When a text was not carved on stone but written with a reed pen on papyrus, a piece of limestone, a potsherd or a wooden tablet the hieroglyphs took on simpler and usually rounder forms. There thus developed a *literary hieroglyphic* script, found mainly in religious manuscripts. In everyday use the script was still further simplified, and in quick writing characters were frequently joined, giving rise to a cursive form which is known as the **hieratic script** used in almost all types of literary work.

Later, as a result of further abbreviation and joining up of letters, there developed out of the hieratic script a new cursive form known as the **demotic script**, used during the Graeco-Roman period in administration, in letters, contracts, accounts, etc. This script was also known to the Greeks as the *epistolographic script*.

The use of the hieroglyphic script extended over the Egyptian borders, particularly into Nubia, where it was used in the temples built by the Pharaohs; and even after the Nubian (Ethiopian) kingdom became independent of Egypt the hieroglyphics continued in use. At first they continued to be used only for writing Egyptian, but were later adapted to the native language. The hieroglyphics were considerably modified for this purpose, giving rise to a special **Meroitic script**. During the Christian era there also developed a *Meroitic cursive,* apparently based on Egyptian demotic. Although the Meroitic scripts can be read, the language cannot be understood.

Development of hieroglyphic script

Example:
"owl" (m)

hieroglyph   literary script   hieratic   demotic

History

Like other peoples of antiquity, the Egyptians had no exact system of chronology, events being usually dated according to the years of a king's reign. For this purpose the priests maintained long lists of kings, several fragments of which have survived. The *Abydos King List* gives the names of 76 kings, from Menes to Sethos I; the *Tablet of Karnak* lists 32 kings, from Menes to Tuthmosis III; the *Tablet of Saqqara* lists 47, from Merbapen (Enezib?) to Ramesses II; the *Turin Papyrus*, written in hieratic script in the 19th Dynasty and preserved in fragmentary form, gives the names of 17 kings of the Pre-Dynastic and earliest Dynastic period; and the *Palermo Stone,* probably dating from the 5th Dynasty, of which only five small fragments survive, mentions eight kings of the 1st Dynasty and nine of the 2nd.

The Abydos King List

Lists of this kind provided the basis for the "History of Egypt" written by **Manetho** of Sebennytus (now Samannud), a priest of Heliopolis in the reigns of Ptolemy I Soter and Ptolemy II Philadelphus who compiled the three volumes of his history for Ptolemy II about 300 B.C. Since Manetho, as a priest, had access to all the writings and documents preserved in the temples the information he gives is likely to be reliable. The "History" itself is unfortunately lost, but extracts from it are preserved in the writings of **Josephus** (A.D. 37/38–*c.* 100), **Julius Africanus** (*c.* A.D. 200) and **Eusebius** (*c.* A.D. 340), who, 600 years after Manetho's death, still depended on the material he assembled in writing their own works.

It was Manetho who first arranged all the rulers of Egypt from the first king, Menes, to Alexander the Great in thirty dynasties broadly corresponding to the various ruling houses which successively (or at certain periods simultaneously) held sway in Egypt. This arrangement is still generally accepted; but in addition the dynasties are now grouped together in a number of kingdoms (Old Kingdom, Middle Kingdom, New Kingdom) and periods. In view of the gaps in our sources it is usually not possible to give exact dates for the dynasties up to the time of Psammetichus I: before the 2nd millennium, therefore, the dates given are subject to a margin of error of several decades or even centuries. Nor is the identity of the early kings of the 1st Dynasty clear beyond doubt, since all the Pharaohs had several names, which sometimes makes it difficult to establish their chronological relationships.

An important contribution to exact dating is made by the so-called *Sothic dates,* obtained from events recorded as having coincided with the heliacal rising of Sirius (Sothis). Such dates are, however, available only from the beginning of the Middle Kingdom.

Much information on Egyptian history can be gleaned from the accounts by **Herodotus** (*c.* 490–420 B.C.) and **Strabo** (*c.* 63 B.C.–*c.* A.D. 25) of their visits to Egypt. They can be regarded as reliable sources, however, only so far as they record the writers' own observations.

Prehistoric period (before 60,000 to *c.* 3000 B.C.). – The Prehistoric period is still largely obscure. Later traditions held that during this period the country was ruled by gods and demigods. It can at any rate be taken as certain that there was no unified State and that Egypt was broken up into numerous tribal territories at very different stages of cultural development.

Before 60,000 B.C. **Palaeolithic period:** finds of crudely worked stone tools in gravel-beds at Luxor bear witness to human settlement in the Nile Valley almost 2 million years ago.

After 7000 B.C. **Neolithic period:** adoption of a settled way of life (villages, agriculture, stock-rearing).

Circa 5000 B.C. **Fayyum A culture:** weaving, basket-making and pottery in simple forms. **Fayyum B culture:** agriculture and pottery unknown. Traces of Neolithic village settlements on the edges of the Delta. Burials in retracted position in Upper Egypt.

After 4000 B.C. **Badarian culture** in Nubia.

Circa 3600 B.C. The **Naqada I culture** *(Amratian)* spreads: white-painted burnished pottery, stone cosmetic palettes and small amulets found as grave-goods.

Circa 3200 B.C. The **Naqada II culture** *(Gerzean)* extends to the whole of Egypt. Decorated pottery ("Egyptian faience") and finely worked stone vessels. Metalworking introduced from the Near East.

Early Period (*c.* 3000 – *c.* 2640 B.C.). – In the middle of the 4th millennium B.C. there is a rapid development of crafts, architecture and, later, writing. It is established that important cultural impulses came from Mesopotamia; but whether how far there were also influences from another advanced culture is less clear. According to the Egyptian tradition – which has found some confirmation in archaeological evidence – a foreign people which sacrificed to Horus and is now seen as a "master race" moved into the Delta and the Nile Valley, bringing with them their culture and a highly developed State structure. This people seems to have formed the aristocracy out of which grew the later Egyptian kingdom. There thus emerged within a few centuries two highly developed monarchies, Lower Egypt and Upper Egypt.

LOWER EGYPT comprised the whole of the Delta region, with Buto as its capital and the Red Crown as the symbol of royal authority. **UPPER EGYPT** extended up the Nile Valley from Memphis (Cairo) to the First Cataract at Aswan. The capital was Hieraconpolis, the symbol of royalty the White Crown. Each of these States was divided into provinces, originally no doubt independent principalities.

This division left its mark on the whole of subsequent Egyptian history. Thus when the two kingdoms were united the symbol for the new unified kingdom consisted of the two plants which had previously been the heraldic plants of Upper and Lower Egypt, the lotus and the papyrus. The king was styled "King of Upper and Lower Egypt" – a title still borne by the last

Cultures of the Ancient World

Time	Egypt	Mesopotamia	Palestine	Greece and Rome
NEOLITHIC			First temple in Jericho	
5000	Fayyum A Fayyum B	Tell Hasuna		
4000	Badarian (Nubia)		Beersheba En Gedi	
	Naqada I (Amratian)	Tell Halaf		
		Sumerians		
	Naqada II (Gerzean)	Foundation of Babylon		Sesklo Dimini
3000	1st–2nd Dynasties			
	OLD KINGDOM 3rd–6th Dyn.	1st dynasty of Ur Akkadian Empire	Amorites	Early Minoan
	1st Intermediate Period 7th–10th Dyn.			
2000	MIDDLE KINGDOM 11th–14th Dyn.	Destruction of Babylonian Empire		Middle Minoan
	Hyksos 15th–16th Dyn.	Hammurabi		
		Hittite Empire	Abraham	Late Minoan
	NEW KINGDOM 18th–24th Dyn.	Tiglath-Pileser I		Trojan War Dorian migration
1000			David Solomon	
			Hezekiah	
	LATE PERIOD 25th–31st Dyn.	Esarhaddon conquers Egypt Nebuchadnezzar II		
			Alexander the Great conquers Palestine	Persian wars Macedonian Empire
	Greek rule Ptolemies			Roman Empire
B.C.			Maccabees	
A.D.				
	Roman rule		Bar-Kochba rebellion	
				Byzantium capital of Roman Empire
	Byzantine rule			
			Abu Bekr first Caliph Omar I Spread of Islam	
1000	Arab rule			

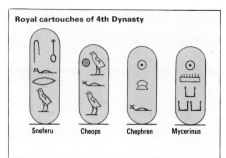

Royal cartouches of 4th Dynasty

Sneferu   Cheops   Chephren   Mycerinus

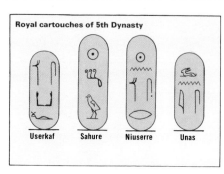

Royal cartouches of 5th Dynasty

Userkaf   Sahure   Niuserre   Unas

of the kings – or "Lord of the Two Lands", and wore the double crown, which was a combination of the White Crown of Upper Egypt and the Red Crown of Lower Egypt. At the base of the walls of the temple the nomes of the South were represented on one side, the nomes of the North on the other. And the administration of the country almost always took account of the division, which in any event was matched by the geographical diversity of the two territories.

Circa 3000–2640   The country is united and consolidated after a period of military conflict. How this unification came about is not known, but it was undoubtedly initiated from Upper Egypt; it is ascribed to the legendary king **Menes**. – The rulers of the first two dynasties had their capital at This or Thinis (Abydos) in Upper Egypt, and accordingly are known as the **Thinites**.

The *Egyptian calendar,* based on the solar year of 365 days, is in use from the Early Period. The year begins in mid July with the onset of the Nile flood.

OLD KINGDOM (*c.* 2640–*c.* 2160; 3rd–6th Dynasties). – This period sees the building of the pyramids (the symbol of supreme power, both royal and divine) and a flowering of art. Djoser (Zoser) establishes the capital at Memphis (Cairo). An official caste endowed with hereditary landed property which is exempt from taxes develops in the course of generations into a dominant feudal force which brings about the fall of the kingdom at the end of the 6th Dynasty.

3rd Dynasty
Circa 2640–2575   **Djoser** *(Zoser)* transfers the capital to Memphis and builds the Step Pyramid of Saqqara as his tomb. The earliest mastabas date from this period.

4th Dynasty
Circa 2575–2465   **Sneferu** builds the Pyramid of Meidum. **Cheops** *(Khufu),* **Chephren** *(Khafre)* and **Mycerinus** *(Menkaure)* build the three great Pyramids of Giza. *Redjedef* builds his pyramid at Abu Roash.

5th Dynasty
Circa 2465–2325   *Userkaf* founds the 5th Dynasty. Most of the kings build their pyramids at Abusir, where sun-temples are also erected in honor of the sun god Re.

Circa 2455–2443   *Sahure* carries on wars with the Libyans and Asiatics.

Circa 2416–2392   *Niuserre* builds the Sun Temple of Abu Gurab.

Circa 2355   *Unas* (Onnos), last King of the 5th Dynasty, builds his pyramid at Saqqara, the interior walls of which bear the earliest funerary reliefs and

inscriptions. After his death internal dissensions appear to have broken out, bringing a new dynasty to power.

6th Dynasty
Circa 2325–2160   The power of the kings declines as the small local principalities increasingly recover their independence. Egypt has far-reaching trading relations with the Upper Nile, the Land of Punt (Somali coast) and Syria.

Teti (Othoes), *Phiops* (Pepi) *I,* Merenre (Methusuphis) and *Phiops* (Pepi) *II* build their pyramids at Saqqara.

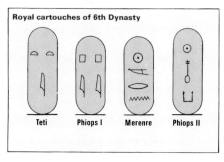

Royal cartouches of 6th Dynasty

Teti   Phiops I   Merenre   Phiops II

First Intermediate Period (*c.* 2134–*c.* 2040; 7th–10th Dynasties). – Insecurity and dynastic strife weaken the kingdom, which falls at the end of the 6th Dynasty. The descendants of that dynasty may possibly have continued to reign at Memphis as the 7th and 8th Dynasties, but a new race of kings (9th and 10th Dynasties) establish themselves at *Heracleopolis,* and may for a time have gained control of the whole of Egypt. At the Court of Heracleopolis, particularly during the reign of King *Khety* (Achthoes) there is a flowering of literature, but the art of the period is degenerate and provincial.

MIDDLE KINGDOM (*c.* 2040–*c.* 1650; 11th–14th Dynasties). – The 11th Dynasty, established by energetic Theban princes, marks the beginning of a period of prosperity and cultural flowering during which the country extends to broadly its present extent.

11th Dynasty
Circa 2040–1991   A race of Theban princes extend their power beyond their own province and gradually gain control of the whole of Egypt. Most of them bear the name of *Antef* or *Mentuhotep* (Mortuary Temple of Mentuhotep at Deir el-Bahri).

12th Dynasty
Circa 1991–1785   A prosperous period which sees much building. Remains of the structures erected by the kings of this dynasty are to be seen in almost

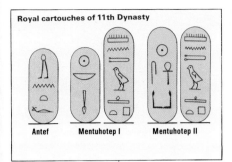

Royal cartouches of 11th Dynasty

Antef — Mentuhotep I — Mentuhotep II

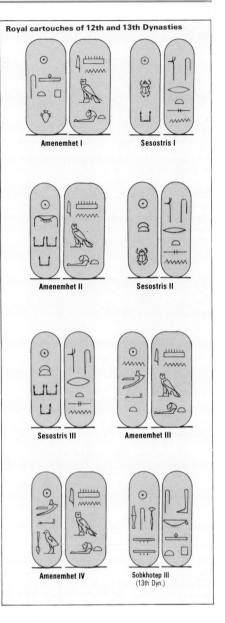

Royal cartouches of 12th and 13th Dynasties

Amenemhet I — Sesostris I

Amenemhet II — Sesostris II

Sesostris III — Amenemhet III

Amenemhet IV — Sobkhotep III (13th Dyn.)

every Egyptian town of any size. Flowering of art and literature.

1991–1962 *Amenemhet* (Ammenemes) *I* restores peace and rules over the whole of Egypt. His tomb is the Northern Pyramid at Lisht.

1971–1928 *Sesostris* (Senwosret) *I* conquers Nubia. His tomb is the Southern Pyramid at Lisht.

1929–1895 *Amenemhet* (Ammenemes) *II* builds his pyramid at Dahshur.

1897–1878 *Sesostris* (Senwosret) *II.* Pyramid at El-Lahun.

1878–1841 **Sesostris** (Senwosret) **III**, the Sesostris famed among the Greeks, consolidates his hold on Nubia. Pyramid at Dahshur.

1844–1797 *Amenemhet* (Ammenemes) *III* builds the Pyramid and the great Temple of Hawara, known as the Labyrinth.

1798–1790 *Anenemhet* (Ammenemes) *IV.*

1789–1786 Queen *Sobkneferu.*

Second Intermediate Period (*c.* 1785–*c.* 1650; 13th and 14th Dynasties). – Under the kings of this dynasty, mostly named *Sobkhotep,* the kingdom declines as a result of domestic dissensions. Many kings succeed one another, most of them reigning only for a brief period. While descendants of the old Theban kings may still have ruled in the south, a new race establishes itself in the western Delta as the 14th dynasty, with its capital at Xois. – Nubia becomes an independent State (capital Kerma).

Hyksos period (*c.* 1650–*c.* 1551; 15th and 16th Dynasties). – The *Hyksos* ("Princes of the Foreign Lands"; in the past erroneously translated "Shepherd Kings"), a people of mixed Hurrian and Semitic origin, advance into Egypt from the north-east, conquer the whole country and rule over it for a century. Few remains of this period survive, but it is evident that the Hyksos largely assimilated Egyptian culture. They introduce the horse-drawn chariot into the Nile Valley, and the scarab becomes a popular symbol of good fortune. During this period Theban princes (17th Dynasty; tombs at Dra Abu el-Naga) rule in the south, at first as vassals of the Hyksos.

Circa 1560 *Seqenenre* and his sons *Kamose* and *Ahmose* lead a rebellion against the Hyksos King *Apophis* (Apopi) *I.* (Seqenenre's mummy was found at Deir el-Bahri; his wife was Queen *Ahotep.*)

Circa 1552 *Kamose* defeats the Hyksos.

Circa 1551 *Ahmose* (Amosis) captures Avaris, the chief Hyksos stronghold in the eastern Delta, and expels the intruders. Egypt is reunited. (The Biblical story of the Exodus may possibly relate to the expulsion of the Hyksos.)

NEW KINGDOM (*c.* 1551–712; 18th–24th Dynasties). – Under the New Kingdom, with its capital at *Thebes,* Egypt becomes a Great Power. At first the culture of the New Kingdom differs little from that of the Middle Kingdom, but after the conquests of Tuthmosis III, when Egypt had close relations with western Asia, there are fundamental changes in Egyptian life and art. Enormous wealth flows into the country in the form of tribute from subject lands, especially into the capital. Splendid new buildings replace the older ones that had fallen into disrepair.

1555–1528 *Amenophis* (Amenhotep) *I.* He and his mother *Nefertari* are later regarded as guardian deities of the Theban necropolis.

1528–1510 *Tuthmosis* (Dhutmose) *I* conquers Upper Nubia. He is the first Pharaoh to have his tomb constructed in the Valley of the Kings.

1510–1490 *Tuthmosis* (Dhutmose) *II.* After his death there is conflict for the succession.

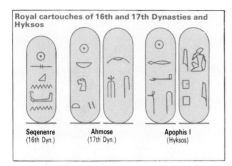

Royal cartouches of 16th and 17th Dynasties and Hyksos

| Seqenenre (16th Dyn.) | Ahmose (17th Dyn.) | Apophis I (Hyksos) |

1490–1468 **Hatshepsut**, daughter of Tuthmosis I and wife of her stepbrother Tuthmosis II, assumes the Regency on behalf of her stepson Tuthmosis III and eventually rules as Queen in her own right. Her mortuary temple is at Deir el-Bahri.

1490–1436 After Hatshepsut's death **Tuthmosis** (Dhutmose) **III** becomes sole ruler. One of the greatest of Egyptian kings, he conquers Syria and establishes Egyptian influence in western Asia. Temples at Thebes, Amada, Buhen, etc.; tomb in the Valley of the Kings.

1438–1412 *Amenophis* (Amenhotep) *II*. Temple at Karnak; tomb in the Valley of the Kings.

1412–1402 *Tuthmosis* (Dhutmose) *IV*. He has the sand cleared from the Sphinx of Giza. Tomb in the Valley of the Kings.

1402–1364 *Amenophis* (Amenhotep) *III*, known to the Greeks as *Memnon,* establishes relations with the kings of Babylon, Assyria, Mitanni (on the Upper Euphrates), etc., evidence of which is provided by the clay tablets found at Tell el-Amarna. Temples in Nubia and at Luxor, Medinet Habu, etc. His tomb and that of his wife *Tiy* are in the Valley of the Kings.

1364–1347 **Amenophis** (Amenhotep) **IV** replaces the old religion by the worship of a single deity, the Sun. The new movement is directed primarily against Amun and his fellow Theban gods, who under the New Kingdom had overshadowed all other deities, and their figures and names are erased from temples and other monuments. Since the King's name includes the name of Amun he changes it to **Akhenaten** ("the solar disc is content"). The capital is moved from Thebes to *Tell el-Amarna*, where a new art style (the "Amarna style") develops. After the King's death (tomb in the Valley of the Kings) there is a troubled period during which the new religion is abolished. Akhenaten's wife was **Nefertiti**.

1347–1338 **Tutankhamun**, Akhenaten's youthful son-in-law, moves the capital back to Memphis. The discovery in 1922 of his intact tomb in the Valley of the Kings was one of the great archaeological sensations of modern times.

1339–1335 *Ay,* perhaps Nefertiti's father, succeeds Tutankhamun after his early death.

19th Dynasty
1306–1186 Egypt recovers its strength and in the reigns of Sethos I and Ramesses II reasserts itself as a World Power.

1333–1306 *Horemheb* (Harmais), Supreme Commander of the Army and Governor of the kingdom under Amenophis IV and his successors, restores internal peace. Campaign against Nubia. Tomb in the Valley of the Kings.

1306–1304 *Ramesses I.* Tomb in the Valley of the Kings.

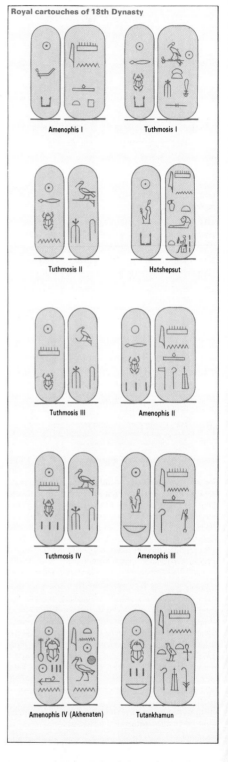

Royal cartouches of 18th Dynasty

Amenophis I   Tuthmosis I

Tuthmosis II   Hatshepsut

Tuthmosis III   Amenophis II

Tuthmosis IV   Amenophis III

Amenophis IV (Akhenaten)   Tutankhamun

1304–1290 **Sethos** (Seti) **I** wages wars against the Libyans, the Syrians and the Hittites, a powerful people who during the 18th Dynasty had advanced from Asia Minor into northern Syria and threatened Egyptian possessions in Syria and Palestine. Large temples at Karnak, Qurna and Abydos. Tomb in the Valley of the Kings.

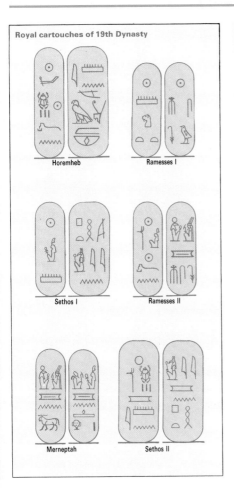

Royal cartouches of 19th Dynasty

Horemheb — Ramesses I

Sethos I — Ramesses II

Merneptah — Sethos II

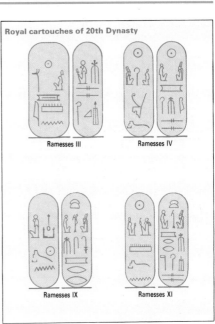

Royal cartouches of 20th Dynasty

Ramesses III — Ramesses IV

Ramesses IX — Ramesses XI

1290–1224 **Ramesses II**, the most celebrated of Egyptian kings, wages a long-drawn-out war with the Hittites (1285, Battle of Qadesh, near the present-day Syrian town of Homs). A peace treaty is signed in the 21st year of the King's reign, leaving Palestine proper in Egyptian hands, while northern Syria is required to pay tribute to the Hittites. During his 67 years' reign Ramesses develops extraordinary activity as a builder: approximately half the surviving temples date from his time, and his name is found on almost every ancient Egyptian site. Among the major temples of his reign are at Abu Simbel, Karnak, Luxor, the Ramesseum, Abydos, Memphis and Bubastis. Tomb in the Valley of the Kings. – Ramesses II has often been identified, but without any valid grounds, with the Pharaoh who oppressed the Israelites (Exodus 1: 11).

1224–1214 *Merneptah* (Menephthes), Ramesses II's only surviving son, makes war on the Libyans and the Mediterranean peoples allied with them, and on the Ethiopians. Mortuary temple in Thebes, tomb in the Valley of the Kings.

1214–1186 The reigns of *Sethos II* (1214–1208) and *Merneptah Siptah* (1208–1202) are followed by a period of anarchy and decline.

20th Dynasty

1186–1070 A brief period of relative (but deceptive) tranquility.

1186–1184 *Sethnakhte* restores peace and order. Tomb in the Valley of the Kings.

The Plagues of Egypt

The ten plagues of Egypt recorded in the Old Testament (Exodus 7: 14 to 12: 30) were ten catastrophes visited on Egypt by God which forced the Pharaohs to release the children of Israel from their captivity.

First plague:	all water turned into blood
Second plague:	frogs
Third plague:	lice
Fourth plague:	flies
Fifth plague:	murrain (cattle plague)
Sixth plague:	boils
Seventh plague:	hail
Eighth plague:	locusts
Ninth plague:	darkness
Tenth plague:	death of the first-born

1184–1153 *Ramesses III* defeats the Libyans and in two great battles repels an invasion by barbarian peoples (Philistines, etc.), on land and sea, coming from Asia Minor. The 21 years of his reign seem a time of tranquility during which great buildings such as the Temple of Medinet Habu are erected; but there are also accounts of increasing unrest and poverty. The King presents lavish gifts to the gods, particularly (like his predecessors) to Amun of Thebes. In consequence the High Priest of Amun gradually becomes the most powerful figure in the country. Tomb in the Valley of the Kings.

1153–1070 After the murder of Ramesses III his successors *Ramesses IV–XI* fall increasingly under the influence of the priests of Amun, and finally, after the death of Ramesses XI, the High Priest *Herihor* briefly occupies the throne.

21st (Tanite) Dynasty

1070–945 After the break-up of the kingdom a new dynasty arises in Tanis which contests the power of the High Priests of Thebes. By contracting marriage alliances with the Tanite Royal House *Pinudjem* (Psusennes) *VI*, priest-king of Thebes, becomes King of the whole of Egypt, while his sons obtain the

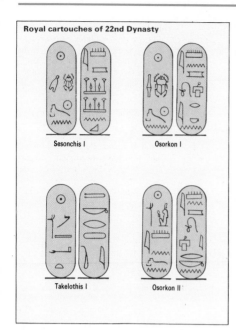

Royal cartouches of 22nd Dynasty

Sesonchis I

Osorkon I

Takelothis I

Osorkon II

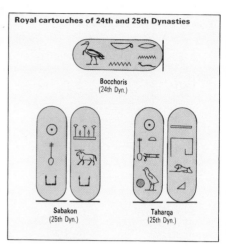

Royal cartouches of 24th and 25th Dynasties

Bocchoris
(24th Dyn.)

Sabakon
(25th Dyn.)

Taharqa
(25th Dyn.)

influential and lucrative dignity of High Priests of Thebes. Nubia becomes independent, and Egypt loses control of Palestine.

22nd Dynasty

945–722   Kings of Libyan origin, whose ancestors, belonging to the Meshwesh tribe, had come to Egypt as mercenary chieftains, settled in the eastern Delta and grew in power as the monarchy declined. Bubastis becomes the capital, and Thebes declines still further in importance. Princes of the Royal House become High Priests of Amun.

Circa 940   *Sesonchis* (Seshonq) *I,* the Shishak of the Old Testament, overthrows the Tanites. In the fifth year of the reign of King Rehoboam of Judah (924) he captures Jerusalem and plunders the Temple of Solomon, commemorating his victory by the erection of a temple at El-Hiba. – Under his successors *Osorkon, Takelothis* and *Sesonchis II* the kingdom declines and breaks up into small principalities.

23rd Dynasty

808–715   The capital of this dynasty is at Tanis. The kings of Ethiopia make themselves masters of Upper Egypt.

Circa 730   *Tefnakhte,* Prince of Sais and Memphis, attempts to gain control of the Lower Nile Valley but is defeated by the Ethiopian King *Piankhi,* who also conquers Memphis.

24th Dynasty

715–712   *Bocchoris* (Bekenrenef), Tafnakhte's son and successor, establishes sovereignty over Lower Egypt. Upper Egypt is in the hands of Ethiopian rulers. *Sabakon* (Shabaka) of Kush, son of *Kashta,* overthrows Bocchoris and has him burned to death. The whole of Egypt falls for a time into Ethiopian hands.

Late Period   (712–332; 25th–31st Dynasties). – In spite of continual wars and a period of subjection to Persia this is a time of cultural flowering and prosperity. Egypt loses its independence for many centuries, but its new rulers like to present themselves

as the legitimate successors to the earlier Pharaohs and are concerned to preserve the great Egyptian cultural heritage.

25th Dynasty

712–664   Ethiopian kings.

712–700   *Sabakon* (Shabaka) supports the small Syrian States against Assyria.

700–688   *Sebichos* (Shebitku).

688–663   *Taharqa,* the Tirhaka of the Old Testament, also supports the Syrian and Palestinian princes against the Assyrians, but is defeated about 670 by the Assyrian King Esarhaddon, who also captures Memphis, and is compelled to flee to Ethiopia. Both Upper and Lower Egypt become subject to the Assyrians; the petty kings of Egypt (Necho of Sais, etc.) retain possession of their cities as Assyrian vassals. Several unsuccessful attempts to expel the Assyrians.

663   *Tanutamun,* Shabaka's son, attempts to recover Egypt. At first successful, he is later defeated by the Assyrians and driven back into Upper Egypt. Prince Psammetichus of Sais, Necho's son, takes advantage of the absence of the main Assyrian forces, which are tied down in Babylon and Elam, to shake off the Assyrian yoke, with the help of King Gyges of Lydia. The occupying forces are expelled, the power of the small independent principalities is curbed and Egypt is again united. Ethiopia is now finally separated from Egypt.

26th Dynasty

663–525   Egypt enjoys another period of prosperity. Trade begins to flourish as a result of the relations now established with Greece, and there is a fresh flowering of the arts. Even under the Ethiopian kings there had been a return to the models of the classical period of Egyptian art, the Old and Middle Kingdoms, and occasionally also the 18th Dynasty; and the Old Kingdom was now also imitated in other fields – in literature, the orthography of inscriptions and even the titles of officials.

663–609   *Psammetichus I.*

609–593   *Necho.* While the Assyrian Empire is fighting for its existence with Babylonia and Media he conquers Syria (Battle of Megiddo, in which King Josiah of Judah is killed), but is defeated by Nebuchadnezzar of Babylon at Carchemish and loses his possessions in Syria and Palestine. – The

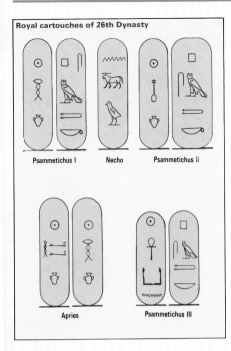

Royal cartouches of 26th Dynasty

Psammetichus I   Necho   Psammetichus II

Apries   Psammetichus III

construction of a canal from the Nile to the Red Sea is begun, but is abandoned in obedience to an oracle.

593–588 *Psammetichus II.* War with Ethiopia.

588–569 *Apries* (Wahibre), the Hophrah of the Old Testament, seeks to recover Syria, but cannot prevent the capture of Jerusalem by Nebuchadnezzar (587). Military rising in Libya: Apries's general Amasis is declared King and he himself is deposed.

569–525 *Amasis* (Ahmose) consolidates his position by marrying a daughter of Psammetichus II. After a campaign by Nebuchadnezzar against Egypt he abandons Egyptian claims to territory in Syria. Naucratis is ceded to the Greeks, and soon becomes the country's principal trading town. Friendship with Polycrates of Samos.

525 *Psammetichus III* is defeated by the Persian King Cambyses at Pelusium. Egypt becomes a Persian province.

27th (Persian) Dynasty
525–338 The Persian kings present themselves as successors to the native rulers; there is no interference with the ancient religion.

525–521 *Cambyses.* Unsuccessful expedition to the oases in the Libyan Desert; campaign against Ethiopia.

521–486 **Darius I** seeks to promote the strength and prosperity of Egypt. He completes the canal from the Nile to the Red Sea, sends a strong garrison to the Kharga Oasis and builds a Temple of Amun (Ammon) there. After the Battle of *Marathon* (490) the Egyptians temporarily expel the Persians.

486–465 **Xerxes I** recovers Egypt and appoints his brother Achaemenes satrap (provincial governor),

465–425 **Artaxerxes I.**

463 Egypt again rebels against Persian rule. *Inarus,* Prince of Marea (on Lake Mareotis), defeats Achaemenes with Athenian help, but is himself defeated and crucified by the Persian General Megabyzus at the island of Prosopitis in the Delta.

After 449 *Herodotus* visits Egypt.

424–404 *Darius II.* Decline of Persian power.

404–338 In the reigns of *Artaxerxes II* (404–362) and *Artaxerxes III* (362–338) Egypt briefly recovers independence under native rulers (Manetho's 28th–30th Dynasties).

28th Dynasty
404–399 *Amyrtaeus* of Sais maintains his authority only for a brief period. Various dynasts contend for power in Lower Egypt.

29th Dynasty
399–379 A dynasty from Mendes, which relies mainly on Greek mercenaries for support.

398–393 *Nepherites* (Nefaurud) *I.*

392–380 *Achoris* (Hagor) beats off a Persian attack in a three years' war.

379 *Psammuthis* (Pshenmut). – *Nepherites II* reigns only for a few months.

30th Dynasty
378–341 Last native dynasty.

378–361 *Nectanebo* (Nekhtnebef) *I* of Sebennytus, a powerful ruler in whose reign large temples are again built (Philae, Medinet Habu; gateway at Karnak).

360–359 *Tachos* (Djeho) advances into Syria against the Syrians, but is deposed and dies at the Persian Court.

358–341 *Nectanebo* (Nekhtharehbe) *II* rebuilds some of the old temples (Temple of Isis at Behbeit el-Hagara; Karnak).

31st Dynasty
341–332 Egypt is ruled by foreign dynasts. – Artaxerxes III again conquers Egypt for Persia. Nectanebo flees to Ethiopia; the temples are plundered.

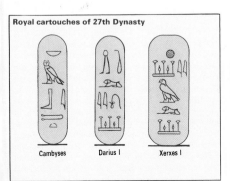

Royal cartouches of 27th Dynasty

Cambyses   Darius I   Xerxes I

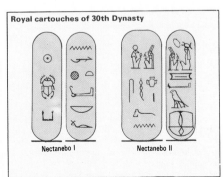

Royal cartouches of 30th Dynasty

Nectanebo I   Nectanebo II

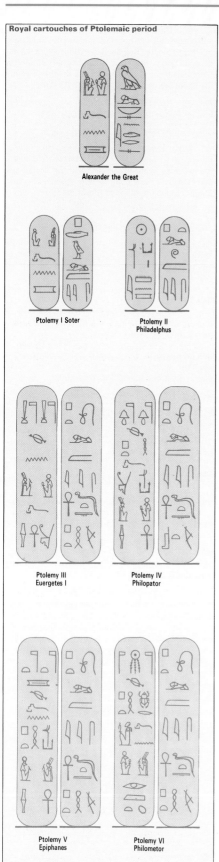

Royal cartouches of Ptolemaic period

Alexander the Great

Ptolemy I Soter

Ptolemy II Philadelphus

Ptolemy III Euergetes I

Ptolemy IV Philopator

Ptolemy V Epiphanes

Ptolemy VI Philometor

341 King *Khabash,* perhaps belonging to an Ethiopian dynasty, briefly recovers the whole of Egypt.

332 **Alexander the Great** occupies the whole of Egypt.

Greek rule (332–30 B.C.). – Under the **Ptolemies** the Lower Nile Valley is once again, for three centuries, the seat of a flourishing kingdom. At first governed by gifted rulers, it is later reduced by internal dissension and struggles for power to political impotence, and finally becomes a dependency of Rome. The Ptolemies, like the Persians, present themselves as legitimate heirs to the Pharaohs and respect Egyptian religion and customs.

332–323 **Alexander the Great** fosters the ancient religion, and in 331 travels to the Temple of Zeus Ammon in the Siwa Oasis, where he is greeted by the priests as the son of Ammon and confirmed as King of Egypt. He founds Alexandria, which soon becomes a great center of commerce and Greek culture. After Alexander's death the Macedonian Empire falls apart.

322–285 Egypt becomes the satrapy of *Ptolemy I Soter* ("Saviour"), son of Lagus. At first he acts as Regent for *Philip Arrhidaeus,* Alexander the Great's feeble-minded half-brother, and *Alexander II,* his son, and later for Alexander alone. After Alexander's death (311) he assumes the royal title (305). Foundation of the Alexandrian Museum and of the town of Ptolemais Hermiou in Upper Egypt.

285–247 *Ptolemy II Philadelphus* ("Sister-Lover"). Married first to *Arsinoe I,* daughter of Lysimachus, and then to his sister *Arsinoe II.* Arsinoe II (d. 270) becomes the protective goddess of the Fayyum, which is named the Arsinoite nome in her honor. In the reigns of Philadelphus and his successors great elephant-hunts are held on the Somali coast, and the elephants captured are taken back to Egypt to be trained for military use.

247–222 *Ptolemy III Euergetes* ("Benefactor") *I,* whose wife is *Berenice* of Cyrene, makes a short-lived conquest of the Seleucid kingdom in Asia Minor. The external power of Egypt is now at its peak. – An unsuccessful attempt is made by the priests to reform the calendar by intercalating an extra day every four years.

222–204 *Ptolemy IV Philopator* ("Father-Lover"). – He and his successors start the kingdom on the road to ruin by their mismanagement. He defeats Antiochus III (the Great) of Syria, who had threatened the Egyptian frontier, in the Battle of Raphia (217), but then concludes a dishonorable peace. His wife is *Arsinoe III,* his sister. – Two native Pharaohs, Harmachis and Anchmachis, rule at Thebes (205–184).

204–182 *Ptolemy IV Epiphanes* ("Famous") comes to the throne at the age of five under the guardianship of Agathocles and Agathocles' mother Oenanthe. A rebellion in Alexandria compels Agathocles and Oenanthe to resign their office; and Antiochus the Great of Syria and Philip V of Macedon take advantage of Egypt's domestic troubles to invade its outlying provinces. Egypt offers the guardianship of Epiphanes to the Roman Senate, which cedes Coelesyria and Palestine to Antiochus, while Egypt remains independent. Epiphanes marries Cleopatra, daughter of Antiochus. The affairs of the country fall into increasing confusion; one rebellion succeeds another, and anarchy prevails.

181   Epiphanes is poisoned.

181–146   *Ptolemy VI Philometor* ("Mother-Lover"), at first under the guardianship of his mother Cleopatra. He allows Onias to build a Jewish temple in Leontopolis (Tell el-Yahudiya).

171   *Battle of Pelusium.* Philometor is taken prisoner by Antiochus IV of Syria and Memphis is captured. His younger brother *Ptolemy VIII Physcon* ("Pot-Belly"), who at first also bears the name of Philometor, is proclaimed King by the people of Alexandria.

170–163   Philometor and Physcon, now reconciled, rule jointly, together with their sister *Cleopatra*, Philometor's wife.

163   The brothers again quarrel. Philometor, exiled by his younger brother, flees to Rome. He is brought back under Roman protection and thereafter rules alone, while Physcon becomes King of Cyrene.

146   Philometor dies and is succeeded by his son *Ptolemy VII Neos Philopator*, who reigns only a few months.

146–117   *Ptolemy VIII Euergetes II Physcon* becomes sole ruler. He marries his brother's widow and later his niece *Cleopatra III*.

130   Euergetes II is expelled in a revolution and flees to Cyprus. He is replaced by Cleopatra, with the names of *Philometor Soteira*. He murders his son *Memphis*, who had put forward a rival claim to the throne.

127–117   Euergetes II recovers the throne.

From 117   Joint rule by Euergetes' widow *Cleopatra Cocce* and her son *Ptolemy IX Soter II Lathyrus*.

106   Soter II is expelled and replaced as co-ruler by his brother *Ptolemy X Alexander I*.

88   Alexander is deposed by a rebellion and is killed in a naval battle. Soter II is recalled to the throne. – Rising in Thebes, which is taken after a long siege.

81   After Soter II's death *Ptolemy XI Alexander II* marries *Cleopatra Berenice III* and rules jointly with her.

80   Alexander has Cleopatra murdered and is then killed by the people of Alexandria.

Queens' cartouches of Ptolemaic period

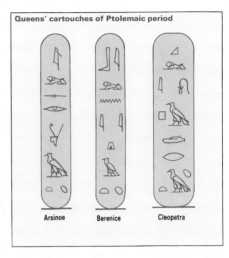

Arsinoe   Berenice   Cleopatra

81–51   *Ptolemy XI Neos Dionysos*, popularly known as Auletes (the "Flute-player"), ascends the throne and is formally recognized by Rome. In 59 he is temporarily expelled by his daughter *Berenice* (who marries *Archelaus*, putative son of King Mithridates VI of Pontus) but is restored by the Romans in 55. The Temple of Edfu is completed and the Temple of Dendera begun.

51–47   **Cleopatra VII** and *Ptolemy XIII Philopator Philadelphus*, daughter and son of Neos Dionysos, rule jointly under the protection of the Roman Senate. *Pompey* is appointed guardian.

48   Ptolemy banishes his sister Cleopatra. After his defeat in the Battle of Pharsalus (47) Pompey seeks refuge in Egypt, but, on the instigation of Ptolemy, is killed when he lands at Pelusium. – **Caesar** comes to Alexandria, takes the part of the banished Cleopatra and defeats Ptolemy, who is drowned in the Nile.

47   Caesar, now Dictator, appoints Cleopatra's 11-year-old brother *Ptolemy XIV Philopator* co-ruler.

45   Ptolemy XIV is murdered on Cleopatra's instigation and *Ptolemy XV Caesar* (Caesarion), her son by Caesar, is appointed co-ruler.

44   Caesar is murdered.

41   **Antony**, intending to call Cleopatra to account for the help given by her general Allienus, contrary to her wishes, to Brutus and Cassius in the Battle of Philippi, is captivated by her beauty and intelligence and spends years with her living a life of pleasure and indulgence. He is finally declared by the Senate an enemy of the Roman people.

31   Octavian marches against Antony, defeats him in the Battle of *Actium* and takes Alexandria. Antony commits suicide in 30 B.C. and Cleopatra also takes her own life (traditionally by the bite of an asp).

30   Egypt is now a *Roman province* directly subject to the Emperor and governed by a Prefect appointed by him.

Roman rule (30 B.C.–A.D. 395). – Like the Ptolemies, the Roman emperors present themselves to the Egyptian people as successors to the Pharaohs and maintain the appearance of an Egyptian national State. – Christianity reached Egypt at an early stage and spreads rapidly.

30/29   The first Roman Governor, *Cornelius Gallus*, represses a rebellion in Upper Egypt and fights the

Royal cartouches of Ptolemaic period

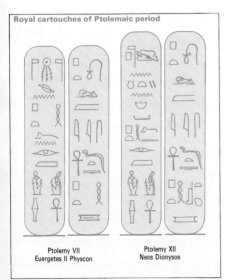

Ptolemy VII   Ptolemy XII
Euergetes II Physcon   Neos Dionysos

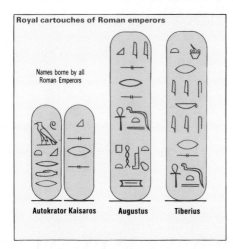

Royal cartouches of Roman emperors

Names borne by all Roman Emperors

Autokrator Kaisaros   Augustus   Tiberius

69–79 Vespasian is proclaimed Emperor in Alexandria.

79 *Titus* (Vespasian's son). He sets out from Alexandria on his expedition against Palestine, which ends in the destruction of Jerusalem in A.D. 70.

81–96 Domitian promotes the cult of Isis and Sarapis in Rome.

96–98 *Nerva.*

98–117 Trajan. Reopening of the canal between the Nile and the Red Sea, now called the Amnis Traianus (Trajan's River).

117–138 Hadrian. He visits Egypt in 130. His friend Antinous is drowned in the Nile and he founds the town of Antinoupolis in his honor.

138–161 Antoninus Pius.

Circa **150** The astronomer and mathematician Ptolemy is active in Alexandria.

161–180 Marcus Aurelius (ruling jointly with *Lucius Verus* until 169).

172/173 Rebellion by the Bucoli, cowherds living in the marshes east of Alexandria, quelled by *Avidius Cassius.*

175 Avidius Cassius is proclaimed Emperor by the legions in Egypt but is murdered in Syria.

Ethiopians. Having fallen into disfavor with the Emperor, he is recalled in 27/26 and commits suicide. – Reformed calendar introduced by Augustus.

27 B.C. Octavian becomes Emperor under the name of **Augustus.**

24 B.C. Ethiopian invasion of Egypt under Queen *Candace.* – *Strabo* visits Egypt.

A.D. **14–37 Tiberius.** He builds the Sebasteum in Alexandria.

A.D. **19** *Germanicus,* the Emperor's heir, visits Egypt.

30 The **Crucifixion.**

37–41 *Caligula.* Violent disturbances in Alexandria caused by strife between Greeks and Jews.

41–54 Claudius. The building of the vestibule of the temple at Esna and a temple at Philae is begun during his reign.

54–68 Nero. Egypt is now a center of the trade between India and Rome.

64 The Apostle *Paul* is martyred in Rome.

68–69 *Galba, Otho* and *Vitellius.*

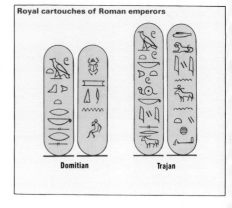

Royal cartouches of Roman emperors

Domitian   Trajan

Mediterranean

Alexandria

Mahalla
Sakha
Minyet
Ganab
Wadi Natrun

Sebennytus
(Samannūd)
Bubastis
(Tell Basta)
El-Mahammah
Bilbeis

Pelusium
(Farama)

from Bethlehem

Western
(Libyan)
Desert

El-Mariya
CAIRO
Babylon
(Old Cairo)
El-Maadi

Fayyum

Sinai
Peninsula

Nile

Beni Mazar

Gebel el-Teir

Gulf of Suez

Eastern
(Arabian)
Desert

Hermopolis Magna
(Ashmunein)
Deirut
Deir el-Maharraq
Asyut

The Holy Family in Egypt

 Halting-places

The flight of the Holy Family (Mary and Joseph with the infant Jesus) into Egypt to escape Herod's slaughter of the innocents is mentioned in the New Testament (Matthew 2: 13–15) without any further details. This map shows the main halting-places on their route, as given in various legends, which are still venerated today. – Between El-Maadi and Beni Mazar and between Gebel el-Teir and Ashmunein they would no doubt travel in sailing-boats on the Nile.

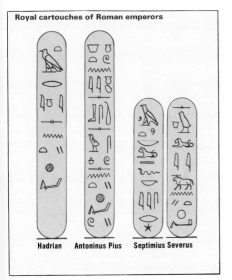

Royal cartouches of Roman emperors

Hadrian   Antoninus Pius   Septimius Severus

176   Marcus Aurelius visits Alexandria.

180–192   *Commodus.*

Circa 190   *Pantaenus,* first known head of the theological school in Alexandria; succeeded by *Clement* (*c.* 200) and *Origen* (from 203).

193–211   **Septimius Severus.**

204   Edict prohibiting Roman citizens from becoming Christians. Many Christian communities in the Delta.

211–217   **Caracalla** visits Egypt. Massacre in Alexandria.

212   *Constitutio Antonina:* Roman citizenship granted to inhabitants of Roman provinces.

217–218   *Macrinus* murders Caracalla and is recognized as Emperor by the Egyptians. After his death there are contests for the succession in Alexandria.

249–251   *Decius.* Persecution of Christians in 250 in the time of Bishop Dionysius of Alexandria.

253–260   *Valerian.* Persecution of Christians.

260–268   *Gallienus.* Christians are granted a measure of toleration. Plague in Egypt.

260   *Macrianus,* recognized as Emperor by the Egyptians, is killed in Illyria in a battle with Gallienus's general Domitian.

265   *Aemilianus (Alexander)* is proclaimed Emperor by troops in Alexandria and recognized by the people, but is defeated and put to death by the Roman legions.

268   Lower Egypt is occupied by the army of Queen *Zenobia* of Palmyra and part of Upper Egypt by the Blemmyes.

268–270   *Claudius II.*

270–275   *Aurelian.*

270   Egypt is reunited with the Empire by the Roman general Probus.

Circa 271   *Antony* (*c.* 251–356), a Copt from Coma in Middle Egypt, becomes a hermit in the desert.

276–282   *Probus* is proclaimed Emperor in Alexandria.

278   Successful campaign against the Blemmyes.

284–305   **Diocletian.**

292   Rebellion in Upper Egypt.

294   Rising in Alexandria. Diocletian captures the city (295).

303   Persecution of Christians.

305–313   *Maximinus.* Beginning of the Arian controversy.

Circa 320   *Pachomius* founds the first monastery at Tabennese.

324–337   **Constantine the Great,** the first Emperor favorable to the Christians. Reorganization of Egyptian administration: the country becomes a "diocese" and is divided into six provinces – Egypt, Augustamnica, Heptanomis (later called Arcadia), the Thebaid, Upper Egypt and Lower Egypt.

325   **Council of Nicaea.** The doctrine of *Arius* of Alexandria, who held that Christ was created by God before the world was and was thus of like nature with God *(homoiousios)* but not very God, is condemned, and the contrary doctrine of Athanasius, that the Son is of the same nature *(homoousios)* as the Father, is declared alone valid.

328   *Athanasius* Archbishop of Alexandria.

330   Byzantium (Nova Roma, Constantinopolis) becomes capital of the Empire and a new center of Greek culture and learning. – Communities of ascetics are established in the Scetic and Nitrian desert.

337–361   *Constantius* favors Arianism. Athanasius is several times banished from Alexandria.

346   Death of St Pachomius.

Circa 350   Earliest Coptic translations of the Bible.

361–363   *Julian the Apostate.*

373   Athanasius dies, having seen the triumph of his cause in the closing years of his life.

379–395   **Theodosius I, the Great.** Christianity becomes the State religion of the Empire. Persecution of Arians and pagans. Destruction of the Serapeum.

395   Division of the Roman Empire: *Arcadius* Emperor in the East, *Honorius* in the West.

Byzantine rule (395–638). – Christianity brings fundamental changes in art and intellectual life.

395–408   *Arcadius.* Patriarch *Theophilus* of Alexandria, a fierce advocate of the doctrine that God must be conceived in human form, vigorously pursues the opponents of this doctrine. – *Shenute* (d. 400), founder of the Egyptian Coptic Church, is Abbot of the White Monastery, Sohag, from about 383. – *Augustine* (354–430) Bishop of Hippo in North Africa from 395.

408–450   *Theodosius II.*

412   Theophilus dies and is succeeded as Patriarch by *Cyril.*

415   The pagan philosopher *Hypatia* is stoned to death in Alexandria.

431   At the Third Ecumenical Council, held at Ephesus, Patriarch Cyril defends the view – which is opposed by *Nestorius,* Patriarch of Constantinople since 428 – that the Virgin is the Mother of God (Theotokos).

444   Death of Cyril; he is succeeded by *Dioscurus* (until 451).

449 At the "Robber Council" of Ephesus Patriarch Dioscurus secures a declaration in favor of the doctrine of Monophysitism, which holds that before his incarnation Christ possessed two natures, human and divine, but that his human nature was afterwards absorbed into his divine nature.

450–457 *Marcian.* Wars with Nubians and Blemmyes.

451 At the Fourth Ecumenical Council, held at Chalcedon, the Monophysite doctrine is condemned and the doctrine that Christ's two natures remain unmixed and unchanged, but also indistinguishable and inseparable, is formally promulgated. The Egyptians stand by the Monophysite doctrine.

474–491 *Zeno.*

491–518 *Anastasius.*

502 Famine in Egypt.

527–565 *Justinian.* New administrative measures.

610–641 *Heraclius.*

619 The Persians under *Chosroes II* invade Egypt. Alexandria is captured. Chosroes rules with mildness and toleration.

622 **Mohammed** flees from Mecca to Medina: the *Hegira,* the starting-point of Muslim chronology.

626 The Persians are expelled by Heraclius.

632 Death of Mohammed. He is succeeded by *Abu Bekr* as first Caliph.

634 Beginning of the Arab conquest of Syria. Abu Bekr dies; Omar becomes second Caliph.

636 Decisive Arab victory over the Byzantines at the River Yarmuk; fall of Damascus.

637 Arab victory over the Persians at El-Qadisiya; fall of Ctesiphon. End of the Sassanid Empire.

638 Fall of Jerusalem. Omar in Syria.

Egypt as a province of the Caliphate (640–968). – Arab rule brings with it the conversion of the country to **Islam**. The Copts at first enjoy freedom of worship, but towards the end of the 8th century are subject to increased cultural and religious oppression.

640 *Amr ibn el-As,* Caliph Omar's general, takes Pelusium and defeats Byzantine forces at Heliopolis.

641 The fortified town of Babylon is given up to the Arabs after the intervention of Patriarch Cyrus (Muqauqis).

642 Fustat founded as a military base and seat of government. Alexandria is captured.

644–656 *Othman.* He is overthrown by a rebellion originating in Egypt.

645/646 Alexandria is occupied by a Byzantine fleet but is recovered by Amr. Egypt is now firmly in Arab hands, providing a base for naval campaigns against Byzantium and the conquest of North Africa.

656–661 Civil war fought between Caliph *Ali,* Mohammed's son-in-law, and *Muawia,* founder of the Omayyad dynasty. Egypt is at first held by Ali but in 658 falls to the Omayyads.

Omayyads

658–750 A brilliant Arab dynasty with Damascus as capital. Arab tribes settle in the Nile Valley, and the system of government is based on Arab models. Many Copts embrace Islam. Egypt is ruled by governors, many of them Omayyad princes.

744–750 *Merwan II,* last of the Omayyads, flees to Egypt and is murdered there (buried at Abusir el-Melek). The Omayyads are exterminated, with the exception of *Abd el-Rahman,* who flees to Spain and founds an independent Caliphate in Córdoba (756).

Abbasids

750–868 This new dynasty, which had risen to power on Iranian soil and with Persian assistance, transfers the capital and seat of Government of the Caliphate from Syria to Iraq. Foundation of Baghdad. The Caliphate is now at its peak. Egypt is ruled by frequently changing governors. The Copts are oppressed; frequent revolts.

813–833 *Mamun,* son of Harun el-Rashid, comes to Egypt and breaks the resistance of the Copts and rebellious bedouin tribes. The fusion of Arabs and Copts begins, and Arabic becomes the language of the fellahin.
Under Mamun's successors the Caliphate begins to decline; the Government becomes dependent on a guard of Turkish slaves, while the provinces make themselves independent.

Tulunids

868–905 Egypt enjoys a brief period of independence.

868–883 *Ahmed ibn Tulun,* Governor of Egypt, sets up as an independent Sultan and extends his authority by successful wars beyond Syria into Mesopotamia. There is great building activity during his reign and that of his son Khumaraweih.

883–895 *Khumaraweih* and his successors are unable to maintain Egyptian independence.

Abbasids

905–935 Egypt is once again governed from Baghdad.

925 An attack by the Fatimid (Shiite) caliphs of Kairouan is repelled.

Ikhshidids

935–969 The Turkish Governor of Egypt, *Mohammed el-Ikhshid* (935–946), seizes the throne and founds a short-lived dynasty.

966–968 Mohammed el-Ikhshid's successors are dependent on an Abyssinian eunuch named *Kafur,* who later usurps the throne and recognizes the suzerainty of the Abbasids. Syria and Palestine are dependencies of Egypt, and there is a brilliant Court in Old Cairo. On Kafur's death Mohammed el-Ikhshid's grandson Ahmed, a minor, succeeds to the throne, and the Fatimids take advantage of this moment of weakness to conquer Egypt.

Egypt under independent rulers (969–1517). – Having gained possession of Egypt, the *Fatimids* set up their capital at Cairo. They are followed by the *Ayyubids,* who have to contend with the armies of the Crusades. Thereafter Egypt is ruled for two and a half centuries by the *Mamelukes,* with two dynasties and a long succession of sultans.

Fatimids

969–1171 The Fatimids, rulers of a kingdom in the western part of North Africa founded in 909 on the basis of a Shiite religious movement, trace their descent from Mohammed's daughter Fatima.

969 *Gohar* conquers Egypt for the Fatimid ruler *El-Muizz* and founds the new capital of Cairo.

970 Foundation of the El-Azhar Mosque.

973 El-Muizz comes to Cairo and resides there until his death in 975. He also conquers Syria.

975–996 *El-Aziz,* El-Muizz's son, notable for his tolerance and love of learning. Egypt flourishes under his rule.

996–1021 *El-Hakim,* El-Aziz's son by a Christian mother, is a religious fanatic, a man of capricious despotic impulses and capable of great cruelty. He later declares himself to be reincarnate of Ali and claims divine veneration. He disappears during one of his nightly rides in the Moqattam Hills – probably assassinated at the instigation of his sister Sitt el-Mulk. The Druses, a sect founded by El-Darazi, believe that he withdrew from the world because of its sinfulness and will one day reappear as Messiah.

1021–36 *El-Zahir,* El-Hakim's cruel and effeminate son, comes to the throne at the age of 16. Until 1024 his aunt Sitt el-Mulk acts as Regent.

1036–94 *El-Mustansir,* a weak and indolent ruler.

1047–77 *Christodulus,* Coptic Patriarch. The seat of the Patriarchate is moved from Alexandria to Cairo.

1065 The country is ravaged for seven years by plague and famine as a result of the failure of the Nile flood. Palestine and Syria are overrun by the Seljuks, pressing forward from the east. Rebellions of Turkish and Berber mercenaries. The palace and library are plundered.

1074–94 *Badr el-Gamali,* Mustansir's Armenian Vizier, restores order in the capital and rules the country well, with almost absolute power. Building of the stone walls and gates of Cairo and the Giyushi Mosque.

1094 *El-Afdal,* Gamali's son, becomes Vizier to the young Caliph.

1094–1101 *El-Mustali,* Mustansir's son, captures Jerusalem and the Syrian coastal towns (1096–98), but loses them to the armies of the First Crusade.

1099 King *Baldwin* of Jerusalem makes an unsuccessful attack on Egypt.

1101–59 Under a succession of incapable caliphs the Fatimid kingdom declines. The viziers, El-Afdal (murdered 1121) and his successors, are the real rulers of the country.

1160–71 *El-Adid,* last of the Fatimids. The office of vizier is contested by *Shawar* and *Dirgham.* Shawar is exiled and seeks refuge with *Nur el-Din,* ruler of northern Syria (with his capital at Damascus from 1154), who restores him to his Vizierate with the help of Kurdish mercenaries commanded by *Shirkuh* and *Saladin.*

1164 Shawar falls out with the Kurds and appeals for help to *Amalric I,* King of Jerusalem, who comes to Egypt and expels the Kurds. He drives back another Kurdish army which attacks Egypt in 1167.

1168 Amalric himself seeks to obtain possession of Egypt, whereupon Shawar appeals to Nur el-Din for help and sets fire to Fustat (November 1168).

1169 On a third campaign in Egypt Shirkuh and Saladin compel Amalric to withdraw and gain control of the country. Shawar is killed and replaced as Vizier by Shirkuh.

1169–93 After Shirkuh's death he is succeeded by **Saladin** *(Salah el-Din Yusuf ibn Ayyub),* who at first rules in the name of the incapable Caliph and after his death becomes absolute ruler.

Ayyubids

1171–1250 The reign of Saladin, founder of the Ayyubid dynasty, is the most brilliant period in the medieval history of Cairo, although the Sultan lives for only eight years in the city and spends the rest of his time campaigning in Palestine, Syria and Mesopotamia. He begins the building of the Citadel and the town walls. The Shiite doctrines introduced into Egypt by the Fatimids are extirpated. Syria is conquered.

1200–18 *Malik el-Adil,* Saladin's brother, briefly preserves the unity of the Empire (which was split up on Saladin's death).

1211 Adil's wife, *El-Shemsa,* builds the Imam el-Shafii Mosque in Cairo. After Adil's death the Empire falls apart: Egypt passes to his son.

1218–38 *Malik el-Kamil,* his son, is a shrewd and capable ruler.

1218 Damietta is taken by the army of the Fifth Crusade but is given up in 1221.

1229 The Emperor *Frederick II* arrives in Palestine with a Crusading army. Kamil concludes a treaty with him under which he is granted possession of Jerusalem and the coastal towns for a period of ten years.

1238–40 El-Kamil is succeeded by his son *El-Adil II.*

1240–50 *El-Salih Ayyub,* brother of El-Adil II, who builds a castle on the island of Roda.

1249 *Louis IX* (St Louis) of France, on the Sixth Crusade, takes Damietta, but a year later is defeated and taken prisoner at El-Mansura by *Turanshah* (who had succeeded his father El-Salih). During the negotiations for Louis's release Turanshah is murdered by his bodyguard, the Mamelukes. One of the Mameluke leaders, *Aibek,* succeeds to the throne after a brief interregnum of rule by a woman, and founds a new Mameluke dynasty.

Bahrite Mamelukes

1250–1382 The Mamelukes were slaves *(mamluk,* "white slave") purchased by the sultans and trained to serve as their bodyguard or élite troops in their army. They are known as the Bahrite Mamelukes because their barracks were on the island of Roda in the Nile *(bahr,* "river"). In only 132 years of rule there are no fewer than 25 Bahrite sultans, some of whom reign several times.

1260–77 **Baibars I,** one of the ablest members of this dynasty, destroys the last remnants of the kingdom of Jerusalem in four campaigns. He brings to Cairo a scion of the Abbasid dynasty of caliphs, who had been driven into exile by the capture of Baghdad and the execution of the last Caliph, El-Mustasim, by Hulagu's Mongols, and installs him and his successors as nominal rulers (1261–1517). Building of the El-Zahir Mosque (1269).

1279–90 **Qalaun** *(El-Mansur Qalaun)* succeeds to the throne, displacing Baibars's son, who is a minor. He holds off the Mongols and establishes relations with the Emperor Rudolf of Habsburg and other rulers. Much building in Cairo: emergence of a distinctively Egyptian style of Islamic architecture.

1290–93 *El-Ashraf Khalil* captures Acre, the last Christian stronghold in Palestine (1291).

1293–1340 *Mohammed el-Nasir* (Mohammed ibn Qalaun) succeeds his elder brother Khalil at the age of nine, but is compelled by internal dissensions to flee to Syria. From 1296 Egypt is ruled by El-Mansur Lagin. With the aid of the Syrian emirs El-Nasir regains his throne in 1298, but in 1309 flees to the Castle of Kerak (to the east of the Dead Sea) in order to escape from the influence of the two emirs who hold the real power, Baibars and Sallar. *Baibars II* is chosen as Sultan, but when El-Nasir returns in 1310 he makes his submission and is killed. Thereafter El-Nasir occupies the throne until his death. Mistrustful, vindictive and greedy, he behaves with the utmost capriciousness, lavishing gifts on his emirs or having them beheaded. The only one who retains his favor was *Ismail Abulfida*, an Ayyubid, also noted as a historian, who died as Prince of Hama (Syria) in 1331. El-Nasir shows himself liberal to the mass of the people and indulgent to the priesthood. In order to provide the enormous sums required to maintain his Court and finance his building program he appoints Christians – who have a reputation for competence and astuteness – to his departments of finance and customs.

1302   Cairo destroyed by an earthquake.

1347–61   El-Nasir is succeeded by his sixth son *Hasan,* who is still under age. The emirs and Mamelukes are free to rule the country at their pleasure, and take advantage of a plague in 1348–49 which carries off whole families to confiscate property thus left ownerless. Hasan is deposed in 1351 by *Salih,* recovers his throne in 1354, but is assassinated in 1361. The Sultan Hasan Mosque in Cairo is one of the great masterpieces of Islamic architecture in Egypt. – Later sultans are increasingly dependent on the emirs.

Circassian Mamelukes
1382–1517   A Circassian slave named Barquq sets aside the six-year-old *Haggi*, El-Nasir's great-grandson, seizes the throne and founds a new dynasty.

1382–99   **Barquq's** reign is briefly interrupted in 1389/90, when he is displaced by the emirs. He wages successful wars against the Mongols of *Tamerlane* and the Ottomans under *Bayezid*.

1399–1412   *Farag,* Barquq's son, has barely ascended the throne at the age of 13 when Egypt is again threatened by the Ottomans and soon afterwards by the Mongols. He advances victoriously as far as Damascus, but is obliged to return to Cairo by dissensions among his emirs. After the Mongol victory over the Turks at Angora in 1402 Farag enters into negotiations with Tamerlane. The emirs rebel against his rule, led by Sheikh *El-Mahmudi,* later Sultan El-Muayyad. Farag is finally besieged by the rebels in Damascus, taken prisoner and executed.

1412–21   Sheikh *El-Muayyad* conducts victorious campaigns in Syria, aided by the military skill of his son *Ibrahim.* He re-enacts and rigorously enforces the laws promulgated by Omar el-Mutawakkil (847–861), El-Hakim and El-Nasir prescribing the clothes to be worn by Christians and Jews. He not only lays down the colors (for Christians dark blue clothing, a black turban and a wooden cross weighing 5 pounds hung from the neck; for Jews yellow clothing, a black turban and a black ball round the neck) but also regulates the length of the sleeves and the turban, in order to ensure that the cut as well as the colors of their garments are different from the clothes worn by Muslims.

1422–38   *El-Ashraf Bars Bey* ascends the throne, after governing for some time on behalf of an under-age Sultan. Successful campaigns against Cyprus and the Mongols.

1468–96   **Qait Bey,** one of the last independent Mameluke sultans. Both as a general and a diplomat

he maintains his position against the Turks (Sultans Mohammed II and Bayezid II), and inflicts considerable losses on them; but the refractory Mamelukes hamper his efforts and finally compel him to abdicate in favor of his 14-year-old son Mohammed.

1501–16   **El-Ghuri** (Qansuh el-Ghuri), a former slave of Qait Bey's, becomes Sultan at the age of over 60, but still possesses sufficient energy to keep the unruly emirs in check. By imposing high taxes and debasing the coinage he does further damage to Egyptian trade with India at a time when it is already endangered by the Portuguese discovery of the route round the Cape of Good Hope. Instigated by the Venetians, he sends a fleet against the Portuguese in India and wins a naval victory over Francisco d'Almeida, son of the Viceroy, at Chaul (south of Bombay); but his ships are compelled in 1509 to withdraw to Arabia. He is killed in a battle with the army of the Ottoman Sultan Selim I at Dabiq (north of Aleppo) in Syria.

1517   *Tuman Bey* is deposed by Sultan Selim I and Cairo is taken by storm. Egypt becomes a *Turkish pashalik.* Selim has *Mutawakkil (III),* last scion of the Abbasid dynasty, to be brought to Constantinople, from which he returns to Cairo after the Sultan's death. According to a tradition of somewhat doubtful authenticity, Selim compels Mutawakkil to convey to him his status as Caliph, the temporal head of all Muslim believers – an act on which the Ottoman sultans' claim to the Caliphate is based.

Turkish rule (1517–1882). – The authority of the Ottoman sultans soon declines, and with it that of their governors. The Egyptian pashas (governors) are required, before introducing any measure, to obtain the consent of 24 Mameluke leaders, the beys ("princes") who govern the provinces. The beys collect the taxes, command the militia and merely pay tribute to the pasha.

1768–73   *Ali Bey,* originally a slave, rises to the dignity of Sultan. He conquers Syria, but during his absence his son-in-law *Mohammed Bey Abu Dahab* seizes power in Egypt.

1798   **Napoleon Bonaparte** appears off Alexandria, hoping to destroy British trade in the Mediterranean and British power in India. He takes Alexandria by storm and defeats the Mameluke army in the *Battle of the Pyramids*; but soon afterwards his fleet is destroyed by Nelson in the *Battle of the Nile,* fought in Abuqir Bay.

1799   Napoleon conquers Middle and Upper Egypt and inflicts an annihilating defeat on the Turks at Abuqir. He then returns from Alexandria to France.

1800   General Kléber defeats the Turks at Matariya, but is assassinated in Cairo.

1801   The French are compelled by British forces to surrender in Cairo and Alexandria, and evacuate Egypt.

Mohammed (Mehemet) Ali and his successors
1805–82   The period of the French withdrawal saw the rise to prominence of **Mohammed (Mehemet) Ali,** the ablest ruler that the East had produced for a long time. Born at Kavala in Macedonia in 1769 (the same year as Napoleon), he was the son of Albanian parents. At first he made his living as a coffee-dealer; then, during the fighting between Turks and Mamelukes, the new Governor, Kusruf Pasha, put him in command of an Albanian Corps. In this position Mohammed Ali, under the appearance of

Napoleon's Egyptian Expedition

The French campaign in Egypt between 1798 and 1801 is known to history as the **Expédition d'Egypte**, the Egyptian Expedition.

The ostensible occasion for the expedition was an appeal for help in 1795 from the French Consul in Cairo, alarmed by the excesses of the local Bey; but its real object was to destroy British commercial predominance in the Mediterranean. The French began by seizing the island of Malta, held by the Knights of St John (June 12–13, 1798); then followed the storming of Alexandria (July 2), the defeat of the Mameluke army in the Battle of the Pyramids and the occupation of Cairo. After Nelson's destruction of the French fleet in the Battle of the Nile (August 1) the French forces in Egypt were cut off from France, but they nevertheless pressed on into Upper Egypt and routed the Turkish army at Abuqir (July 25, 1799). After Napoleon's return to France (landing at Fréjus on October 9, 1799) General Jean-Baptiste Kléber won a number of further victories over the Turks, but was murdered in Cairo on June 14, 1800. Finally the French were defeated by a British army in September 1801, surrendered in Cairo and Alexandria and left Egypt.

The French expedition was accompanied by many scholars and scientists (Orientalists, archaeologists, etc.), whose work gave a powerful boost to the study of Egypt and its antiquities (e.g. to Champollion's decipherment of the Egyptian hieroglyphics).

impartiality, maneuvered with great adroitness for the destruction of both sides and for his own establishment as ruler of Egypt.

1805 After the expulsion of the Turkish Governor Mohammed Ali proclaims himself Pasha and takes possession of the Citadel of Cairo.

1807 With the support of the Mamelukes he defeats the British forces which had occupied Alexandria and Rosetta and compels them to withdraw.

1811 On the occasion of a banquet to which 480 Mameluke leaders had been invited Mohammed Ali has them treacherously massacred by his Albanian troops. The way is now clear for him to rule with almost absolute power. – A campaign against the Wahhabis who had seized control of Arabia, undertaken on behalf of the Turkish Government, is successfully carried through by Mohammed Ali's son *Tusun* and, from 1816 by his son (or adoptive son?) **Ibrahim Pasha**, a military commander of outstanding quality.

1819 After fierce fighting the resistance of the Wahhabis collapses. Mohammed Ali turns his attention to military reforms. He employs his lawless Albanians in Nubia and the Sudan and raises an army of fellahin, which fights in Greece, under Ibrahim's command, during the Greek War of Independence (1824–27).

1827 In the Battle of *Navarino* the whole Turkish and Egyptian fleet is annihilated. – Mohammed Ali seeks to increase the strength and resources of Egypt by encouraging agricultural improvement and promoting the development of industry.

1832 After the Russian victories over Turkey in 1828–29 Mohammed Ali decides that the time has

come to shake off Turkish suzerainty. Ibrahim advances into Syria and within a year is master of Asia Minor. Following intervention by the European Powers, however, the Treaty of Kütahya is concluded, in terms favorable to the Turkish Government.

1839 The Turkish Government makes another attempt to enforce its authority on Mohammed Ali, who has now gained control of south-western Arabia. Ibrahim inflicts an annihilating defeat on the Turkish Army at *Nisibin*, to the west of the Euphrates. After the death of Sultan *Mahmud II* the entire Turkish fleet, under Ahmed Pasha, the Turkish High Admiral, goes over to Mohammed Ali. Again, however, the European Powers intervene, and Ibrahim is defeated in Lebanon by a British and Austrian expeditionary force. A fleet appears off Alexandria and compels Mohammed Ali to submit.

1841 A "firman of investiture" issued by the Sultan grants hereditary sovereignty over Egypt to Mohammed Ali's family in accordance with the Turkish law of succession. Egypt is required in future to pay tribute to the Sultan, but the Pasha is granted the right to conclude non-political treaties and to appoint all Egyptian officials and officers up to the rank of colonel.

1848 Ibrahim Pasha governs on behalf of Mohammed Ali, who has fallen into a state of imbecility, but dies in the course of the year.

1849–54 After Mohammed Ali's death he is succeeded by his grandson *Abbas I,* who is opposed to all European innovations but maintains strict discipline among his officials.

1854–63 *Said,* Mohammed Ali's fourth son, takes over the Government. He introduces a more equitable system of taxation, abolishes monopolies, builds railways and enthusiastically supports the construction of the Suez Canal.

1863–79 *Ismail,* Ibrahim Pasha's French-educated son, carries through many innovations, including factories, canals, locks, bridges, railways, the telegraph and a postal system. The **Suez Canal** is opened in 1869.

1873 Ismail, who since 1867 has had the status of Khedive or Viceroy, gains political independence for Egypt, although the tribute remains in force, and indeed is increased. His military successes extend the frontier of Egypt to the borders of Abyssinia, and his nominal authority reaches as far south as the 2nd parallel of northern latitude. Huge public works and other enterprises result in an astronomical increase in the National Debt.

1879 Ismail is compelled to abdicate. He dies in Istanbul in 1895.

1881 Under Ismail's son *Taufiq* the national finances and administration are brought under control. A nationalist revolt against increasing European influence is led by the Minister of War, *Arabi Bey*, with the slogan "Egypt for the Egyptians".

1882 British and French forces land at Alexandria in order to protect Europeans and occupy the city. Arabi is exiled to Ceylon. Thereafter British influence is predominant in Egypt.

Egypt under British administration (1882–1922). – The conflict between nationalist and Islamic aspirations on the one hand and British commercial interests on the other leads to political tensions which are reflected in repeated unrest, bloodshed and military action.

1883   *Sir Evelyn Baring* (later *Lord Cromer*), British Diplomatic Agent and Consul-General, reorganizes the country. – The Sudanese, led by *Mohammed Ahmed,* the so-called "Mahdi", shake off Egyptian control of their country, defeating two Egyptian forces under British officers, Hicks Pasha and Baker Pasha.

1884   General *Gordon* (who had been Governor of the Sudan in 1877–79) advances to Khartoum with inadequate forces and is besieged there by the Mahdi's troops. The town is taken and Gordon is killed; the relieving force led by General *Wolseley* arrives too late.

1885   The British authorities now devote their attention to developing and improving the administration of Egypt proper. Negotiations undertaken by Turkey to end the British occupation produce no result. – Agreement with France on the unconditional neutrality of the Suez Canal.

1892   *Abbas II Hilmi,* Taufiq's son, becomes Khedive. His independence of action is limited by the British presence.

1896   General *Kitchener* (from 1902 Viscount Kitchener of Khartoum) sets out from Wadi Halfa with a British and Egyptian army to recover the Sudan, annihilates a Mahdist army and takes Omdurman.

1899   Establishment of an Anglo-Egyptian Condominium in the Sudan, under a British Governor whose appointment must be confirmed by the Khedive. – In Egypt itself many reforms are carried through by the British authorities. The development of agriculture is promoted by the building of light railways and the extension of the irrigation system.

1902   The **Aswan Dam** is completed.

1904   Anglo-French agreement on the maintenance of the status quo in Egypt. – There is an upsurge of anti-European feeling.

1907   Lord Cromer is succeeded by Sir Eldon Gorst.

1911   Field-Marshal Lord Kitchener (from 1914 Earl Kitchener of Khartoum) succeeds Sir Eldon Gorst as Governor, with increased powers, and serves until the outbreak of the First World War in 1914.

1914   **First World War**: Egypt declares war on the Central Powers, and Alexandria becomes a British naval base. Egypt is declared a British Protectorate; Abbas II Hilmi, who is pro-Turkish, is deposed, and his uncle *Husein Kamil* is appointed Sultan of Egypt. Britain appoints a High Commissioner to Egypt.

1915–17   Attacks by the Senussi, under the leadership of Sheikh *Sidi Ahmed Sherif,* on the western frontiers of Egypt; Sollum and the Bahriya, Farafra and Dakhla oases are temporarily occupied. Turkish attacks on the Suez Canal in 1915 and 1916 are repelled.

1917   British advance into Palestine, supported by the new railway line from El-Qantara to El-Arish and its continuation, the Palestine Railway. – Husein Kamil dies and is succeeded as Sultan by his brother *Ahmed Fuad.*

1918   Armistice with Turkey. – In Europe, armistice between the Allies and Germany.

1919   Egyptian nationalists, led by *Saad Zaghlul Pasha,* son of a peasant in the Delta, demand full independence. The arrest and deportation to Malta of Zaghlul Pasha and three of his supporters in March is followed by serious disturbances. General *Allenby* is appointed Special High Commissioner and restores order. Zaghlul Pasha returns to Egypt.

1922   The British Protectorate comes to an end and Egypt is declared independent. Britain retains responsibility for the maintenance of communications with the British Empire, the defence of Egypt against foreign attack, the protection of European interests and the settlement of the problem of the Sudan. Sultan Ahmed Fuad becomes King under the title of *Fuad I.*

Kingdom of Egypt (1922–52). – After more than 400 years of foreign rule Egypt is now free to manage its own internal and external affairs as a largely autonomous State, no longer subject to alien tutelage or tribute.

1922 (April 19)   Promulgation of Constitution: the kingdom of Egypt a hereditary constitutional monarchy.

1923   The first General Election under the new constitution produces a strong nationalist majority. Zaghlul Pasha becomes Prime Minister. New national flag (green, with a white crescent and three stars).

1924   Opening of first Egyptian Parliament.

1927   Death of Zaghlul Pasha.

1936   Anglo-Egyptian Treaty ending the British military presence in Egypt, except in the Canal Zone. – Accession of King **Farouk**, at first under a Regency.

1937   Egypt becomes a member of the League of Nations. Under the Convention of Montreux the privileges of foreigners in Egypt are abolished.

1939   Under its defence agreement with Britain Egypt enters the **Second World War** on the side of the Allies and becomes a theater of war (El-Alamein).

1942   Britain compels King Farouk, who is of pro-German leanings, to appoint a pro-British Government. Nationalist feeling grows.

1948   Egypt intervenes in the war in Palestine and suffers considerable losses.

1949   **Nasser** *(Gamal Abd el-Nasir),* organizes resistance to the monarchy in the officer corps.

1951–52   Increasing economic difficulties enhance the prestige of the army.

Egypt as a republic (since 1952). – Economic and social reforms are carried through in an attempt to solve the country's domestic problems, but the old authoritarian style of government is still retained.

1952   General *Mohammed Neguib* seizes power. King Farouk, whose extravagant life-style has been bitterly criticized, abdicates and goes into exile in Italy. The country is governed by a Revolutionary Council consisting of members of the "League of Free Officers", which introduces a *land reform* designed to destroy the power of the nobility and the large landowners.

1954   Proclamation of a republic. Colonel Nasser becomes Prime Minister and excludes the radical Communist and clerical forces from power.

1955   As a non-aligned country Egypt distances itself from the Western Powers and seeks to improve relations with the Soviet Union and the People's Republic of China.

1956   Colonel Nasser is elected President of Egypt. – When the Western Powers withdraw their offer of assistance towards the construction of the Aswan High Dam Nasser responds by nationalizing the Suez Canal Company.

1956 October 19–November 6 **Suez crisis:** Britain and France intervene in the conflict between Egypt and Israel. Cease-fire agreed, providing for a United Nations peace-keeping force and a guarantee of free passage through the Suez Canal.

1958 Syria and Egypt combine to form the *United Arab Republic* (UAR), which is later joined by the Yemen.

1960–65 First Five Year Plan on the Soviet model: nationalization of banking and industry. Nasser's "Arab Socialism" claims to offer a model for the whole Islamic World. – The Soviet Union undertakes to provide financial and technical help for the construction of the High Dam (on which work begins in January 1960).

1961 Syria secedes from the United Arab Republic.

1964 Under a tempory constitution Egypt becomes a "Democratic Socialist State", with Islam as the national religion. The single Government party is the Arab Socialist Union.'

1965–67 Nasser seeks to distract attention from the country's increasing economic difficulties by Muslim/nationalist and anti-Israeli policies.

1967 The **Six Day War** (June 5–10) ends in a devastating military defeat, the loss of the Sinai Peninsula and the closing of the Suez Canal. The loss of revenue from the canal dues and the Sinai oilfields is an almost overwhelming blow to the Egyptian economy.

1970 Nasser dies suddenly and is succeeded by his deputy, *Mohammed Anwar el-***Sadat**. – Completion of the **Aswan High Dam**.

1971 Sadat seeks to overcome Egypt's economic difficulties by a *rapprochement* with the West. He excludes Soviet influence from every field in the country's life but concludes a Treaty of Friendship with the Soviet Union. – A new construction is approved by National Referendum: Egypt is now the *arab Republic of Egypt*, a socialist and Democratic State.

1972 Expulsion of 17,000 Soviet military advisers.

1973 The military advantages gained by Egypt in the **Yom Kippur War**, which begins with a surprise attack on Israel, strengthens Sadat's position and provide a basis for peace negotiations with Israel.

1974 A National Referendum approves the new policy of *rapprochement* with the West and a gradual liberalization of the economy.

1976 Egypt terminates the Treaty of Friendship with the Soviet Union.

1977 The ban on political parties is lifted. – Increases in the price of basic foodstuffs and everyday necessities lead to violent disturbances, demonstrations and strikes are prohibited.

November 19–20, 1977 President Sadat's historic journey to Jerusalem as the first sign of a desire for reconciliation.

1978 A National Referendum approves President Sadat's style of leadership and shows that the overwhelming majority of the population agree with the idea (bitterly opposed in the rest of the Arab World) of making peace with Israel.

1979 (March 19–20) Peace treaty with Israel on the basis of the agreements reached at Camp David (Maryland, USA). The treaty, negotiated through the mediation of US President Carter, provides for the phased return to Egypt of Israeli-occupied territory (with the exception of the Gaza Strip), the process to be completed by 1982.

1980 Foundation of the Council of the League of Arab and Islamic Peoples – a response to the expulsion of Egypt from the Arab League because of its policy of reconciliation with Israel. An amendment to the Constitution making it possible for President Sadat to be elected President for life (in place of the previous provision allowing two six-year terms) is approved in a Referendum. Some nationalized undertakings are returned to the private sector. Resumption of diplomatic relations and normalization of trade with Israel.

The ex-Shah of Iran, dying in exile in Egypt, is given a State funeral – a decision by President Sadat, which is approved by the majority of the population but arouses opposition from radical Muslim groups in sympathy with the Iranian Revolution.

1981 Tensions between Muslim fundamentalists and Copts increase still further, leading to violent riots in the working-class districts of Cairo. Sadat takes severe measures against radical groups on both the Muslim and the Coptic sides. There are mass arrests, and the head of the Coptic Church, *Shenuda III*, is banished to a monastery in the Wadi Natrun. The Government's action is approved in a National Referendum. On October 6, during a military parade on the anniversary of Egypt's victory over Israel in the Yom Kippur War, President Sadat is assassinated. He is succeeded by Air Marshal *Hosni* **Mubarak**, Vice-President since 1974, who promises to follow the political course set by President Sadat. A state of emergency is declared, to last for a year.

Many people are killed in clashes between radical Muslims and the police in Asyut (October 3–9).

1982 At the beginning of the year President Mubarak appoints his deputy *Fuad Mohieddin* as Prime Minister. Mubarak meets President Numeiri of the Sudan at Aswan (January).

The last strip of land (a strip up to 600 m wide near Taba on the Red Sea) is returned to Egypt by Israel (25 April). Extension of the state of emergency until October 1983. Huge trial of 300 members of the El-Dshihad (Holy War) movement on suspicion of implication in the murder of Sadat and of an attempted coup (December).

1983 Renewal of trade relations with Jordan which have been broken off in 1979 (April).

First meeting of the Parliament of the Nile under the chairmanship of Mubarak and Numeiri (May).

1984 Following the upsurge in the Islamic faith Christmas is removed from the official list of public holidays (January). Egypt again takes part in the conference of the Islamic Organisation (ICO; January). Extension of the emergency laws until summer 1985. Resumption of diplomatic relations with Jordan (September).

1985 The Coptic patriarch Shenuda III is restored to his spiritual office and celebrates his first mass in Cairo (January).

The hijacking of the Italian cruise liner "Achille Lauro" to Alexandria by Palestinian terrorists leads to political tension between Italy and the USA.

1986 Rebellion by the riot police (January) and numerous strikes and unrest because of continuing economic difficulties are the impetus for the Islamic fundamentalists openly to demand the introduction of Sharia (Islamic law).

1987 Early Parliamentary elections (April). On September 27 the first section of the Cairo underground railway (subway) comes into operation. In the presidential elections of October 5 Hosni Mubarak receives 95% of votes cast.

1988 The Egyptian novelist Nagib Mahfus (Naguib Mahfouz; born December 11, 1911 in Cairo) receives the Nobel Prize for Literature.

1989 Egypt accepted back into the Arab League. October 16 Mubarak meets the Libyan Muammar Al Gaddafi in Mersa Matruh.

The Art and Architecture of Ancient Egypt

Architecture

Little survives of the architecture of the Prehistoric period and Early Dynastic Period compared with the large numbers of remains ranging over the long period from the Old Kingdom to Graeco-Roman times. The remains of these early periods consist mainly of tombs, constructed of clay or sun-dried bricks of Nile mud – the materials which were also used in building houses or temples. Round palm-trunks were used to support the roof and frequently to form the roof itself; barrel-vaulted roofs were also common. – Stone began to be used in tombs and temples only at the beginning of the Old Kingdom; but brick never ceased to be the characteristic Egyptian building material. Such typical features of ancient Egyptian architecture as the cavetto cornice and torus had their origin in the primitive huts of an early period and were imitated in brick-built and later in stone structures; and the form of the round Egyptian column was modeled on the timber supports of earlier brick buildings. The square pillar, on the other hand, originated in stone architecture. Other features characteristic of stone architecture which appear at the beginning of the 3rd Dynasty in the temple buildings attached to the Step Pyramid of Saqqara are the fluted pilaster, the engaged column with papyrus capital and a semi-engaged column imitating a bundle of reeds – though these very soon go out of use as decorative elements.

The square **pillar** first appears in the tombs of the Old Kingdom. The lateral surfaces are frequently decorated with reliefs or inscriptions, the front with other forms of ornament. Thus projecting papyrus or lily stems are found on pillars of the time of Tuthmosis III at Karnak, a sistrum (a kind of rattle used by women) and the head of Hathor at Abu Simbel. The pillar was made octagonal or 16-sided by beveling off the corners, and the flat surfaces were then grooved or fluted to produce a play of light and shade. The top of the pillar, however, was left square to form a transition to the roof; and the foot rested on a round cushion-like base. Fluted 16-sided pillars, also known as

Proto-Doric columns, are found in tombs of the Middle Kingdom (Beni Hasan, Aswan) and in temples of the time of Tuthmosis III (Karnak, Deir el-Bahri). The name was suggested by certain points of resemblance to the Doric columns of the Greeks, in particular the fluting and the tapering of the shaft; but they differ from the true Doric column in lacking the echinus (rounded moulding) which is an essential constituent of a Doric capital and in resting on a base, while the Doric column springs directly from the ground. The fronts of Egyptian Proto-Doric columns are frequently not fluted but left flat for the reception of inscriptions.

From the beginning of the 5th Dynasty the square pillar and Proto-Doric column are joined by the round **column**. Its simplest form is the *tree-trunk column,* which imitates in stone the palm-trunks used as supports in an earlier period and is first found in the Mortuary Temple of Sahure at Abusir. This consists of two elements, a low circular base and a cylindrical shaft, decorated in front with a band of inscriptions.

Usually, however, the column has a third element, in the form of a capital surmounted by a square stone slab (abacus) which in turn supports the architrave bearing the stone slabs of the roof. Reflecting the Egyptians' delight in plant forms, the columns from the Old Kingdom onwards frequently have the form of plants. Two types of plant are particularly favored, a species of lotus *(Nymphaea lotus)* and papyrus *(Cyperus papyrus).* Sometimes the column represents a single plant stem, sometimes a bundle or cluster of stems held together by bands, while the capital takes the form either of a closed bud or an open flower. There are thus a variety of types – the simple plant column with either a closed (bud) capital or an open (floral or calyx) capital and cluster-columns with either closed or open capitals.

Of the various types of *lotus column* – which, to judge from the many representations of them in reliefs and paintings, were widely used – relatively few have been preserved. Lotus cluster-columns with bud capitals are found in the Old Kingdom (Mastaba of Ptah-shepses at Abusir) and Middle Kingdom (tomb at Beni Hasan), but seem to have disappeared in the New Kingdom. The

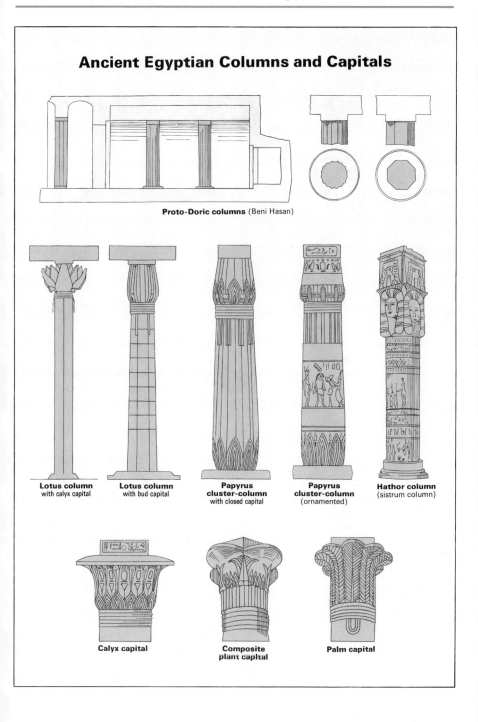

Ancient Egyptian Columns and Capitals

Proto-Doric columns (Beni Hasan)

Lotus column
with calyx capital

Lotus column
with bud capital

**Papyrus
cluster-column**
with closed capital

**Papyrus
cluster-column**
(ornamented)

Hathor column
(sistrum column)

Calyx capital

**Composite
plant capital**

Palm capital

column at Beni Hasan consists of four round stems rising from a circular base held together at the top by bands. The capital is formed of buds, the green sepals of which reach up to the top of the white petals of the corolla. Between the bands which hold the stems together at the top are smaller stems. Examples of lotus cluster-columns with calyx capitals are frequently depicted in reliefs in Old and Middle Kingdom tombs, and they are particularly common in buildings of the Late Period.

Much more common are the *papyrus columns,* which are very different from the lotus columns. In the lotus column the stems are circular in section, while in the papyrus column they are triangular, and moreover taper at the base, which is surrounded by lance-shaped leaves, a feature absent from the lotus columns.

Papyrus column, Karnak

ing foot of the papyrus column, and the capital consists of a cluster of palm branches, turned out at the top and held together by bands. The earliest and finest palm columns are those in the Mortuary Temple of Sahure at Abusir. In later periods the column is frequently found without a base. – In the Ptolemaic period the comparatively simple plant capitals of earlier times were elaborately developed into vividly colored clusters of different plants (papyrus, sedge, lilies).

In addition to these plant columns there are other different types of column. The *Hathor column* or *sistrum column* has a round shaft, at the top of which, on four sides, is a head of Hathor (with cow's ears), topped by a sistrum in the form of a temple. This representation of a sistrum (a type of rattle used by women) is found only in temples dedicated to female deities, and is particularly common in the Ptolemaic period (e.g. at Dendera). – Another curious type is the *tent-pole column,* imitating a primitive form of tent-pole. This is found, for example in the Festival Temple of Tuthmosis III at Karnak, where the capitals have the unusual form of an inverted calyx.

The capitals are also different: while in the lotus column the sepals reach up to the upper edge of the flower the leaves surrounding the umbel of the papyrus are considerably shorter. The simple papyrus column with a closed capital is known only in reliefs and paintings, but the papyrus cluster-column is very commonly found. It usually consists of eight stems held together at the top by bands, while between the stems and under the bands are smaller clusters of three stems, also fastened by bands. These smaller clusters, however, lost their independent treatment at an early period. – Towards the end of the 18th Dynasty the papyrus cluster-columns underwent a major change. In order to provide room for reliefs and inscriptions all the irregularities were abandoned and the shaft was made perfectly smooth, while the capital was rounded off and became a truncated cone, its cluster form now represented only by the ornament. – Papyrus columns with open capitals – in which it is difficult to distinguish between simple columns and cluster-columns – are found in most of the temples of the New Kingdom, usually in the higher central aisles. They invariably have a plain shaft, no longer articulated into separate stems, which is adorned with inscriptions and reliefs.

Among other, less common, types of plant column is the *palm column*. In this the shaft is round, though without the taper-

Comparatively few of the **secular buildings** of ancient Egypt, even those of the later periods, have survived. There are quite a number of remains of ancient towns; but the houses of earlier periods are almost invariably concealed under later structures and thus very difficult to examine and investigate. The remains of such earlier houses are found undisturbed by later building only in exceptional cases – beside the Valley Temple of the Pyramid of Mycerinus, at El-Lahun and most notably at Tell el-Amarna. These remains, together with the representations of houses in reliefs and paintings and the offering-tables in the form of houses, give us some idea of the structure and interior arrangements of private houses, which in many respects resembled the Arab houses of more recent times in Egypt.

The house of the simple peasant or workman was as simple then as it is today: an open courtyard in which the family lived during the day (and in summer also during the night); a few dimly lighted sleeping-rooms and stalls for livestock; and a staircase in the courtyard leading up to the flat roof, on which there might be a few smaller rooms. The houses of the more prosperous citizens of the Middle Kingdom also centered on the courtyard. On the rear side of this, on a terrace, was a portico of light columns, usually facing north, which offered protection from the sun. From here a door led into a wide hall, the roof of which was borne on columns, and beyond this a deep hall, also with columns, which was probably the dining-room. Beyond this again were bedrooms for the master of the house and his grown-up sons. Adjoining these central apartments were the women's rooms or harem, also centered on an open courtyard, and various offices (store-rooms, kitchen, stalls for livestock) and rooms for slaves. – This arrangement seems to have remained basically the same in all periods, and even in *royal palaces* (e.g. at Tell el-Amarna and Medinet Habu) the principal rooms are found in the same sequence. The 18th Dynasty houses which have been excavated at Tell el-Amarna show a rather different layout.

The walls of the private houses and palaces were built of sun-dried bricks of Nile mud; the roofs were made of wooden beams covered with straw or reeds and daubed internally and externally with Nile mud; and the columns were either of timber or stone, and in the palaces inlaid with colored stones or glass paste. Color was also used extensively in the interior: the walls were whitewashed and hung with brightly colored mats or decorated with paintings, and even the floors were often given a colored coating.

Many *fortified structures* have been preserved, including the Fort of El-Kab and the fortified town of El-Lahun (Kahun), probably dating from the Middle Kingdom. There are also the Nubian forts of Kuban, Qasr Ibrim and Aniba, now under the waters of Lake Nasser but thoroughly investigated before they disappeared, and the very many forts on Sudanese territory, to the south of Wadi Halfa (Buhen, Kor, etc.), which protected the land route between the cataracts. – Mention should also be made in this connection to the "simulated fortresses" (royal palaces built in the manner of forts) which have been found at Abydos, Kom el-Ahmar and Medinet Habu.

Since taxes were levied and salaries paid in kind, large *storehouses* were required both by the State and by temples for the reception and storage of tribute. Remains of such magazines can be seen, for example, in the Ramesseum at Thebes (West).

Surely in no other country have such large numbers of *temples* survived from ancient times within a relatively small area as in Egypt. Most of them date from the New Kingdom and the Ptolemaic period, so that we have a clear picture only of the temples of these periods; few complete temples, or none at all, have survived from the Old and Middle Kingdoms and the Late Period.

Of the *temples of the Old Kingdom*, apart from the mortuary temples associated with the pyramids, only one example of a particular kind has been preserved: the Sun Temple of King Niuserre at Abu Gurab. It consisted of a large court surrounded by covered passages and containing only a few buildings, with a large obelisk at the rear of the court. The walls of the passages and some of the chambers were decorated with reliefs depicting festivities, hunting scenes and country life.

The *temples of the Middle Kingdom* are scarcely better represented. There are only scanty remains of the great temples of Luxor and Karnak, Coptos, Abydos, Medinet el-Fayyum, Heliopolis, Bubastis and Tanis, some of which exceeded in size

Pylon and obelisk, Luxor

the temples of later periods. All probably fell into decay during the troubled period of Hyksos rule and were replaced under the 18th Dynasty by new buildings, which as far as possible incorporated masonry from the earlier temples. They appear to have been very similar in form to later temples, many of which were no doubt built on the same plan as their predecessors. The decoration was also the same as in later temples. The reliefs on the interior walls depicted the king in communion with the gods; the roofs of the halls were supported on columns of the various types; and in front of the entrance stood colossal statues of the Pharaohs and great obelisks.

Although at first sight the *temples of the New Kingdom* appear very different from one another, they can be reduced without difficulty to two basic types. One of these types – reminiscent of the Greek peripteral temple (i.e. a temple surrounded by colonnades), though the resemblance is no doubt purely accidental – was much favored during the 18th Dynasty, in the reigns of Tuthmosis III and his successors. The rectangular cella (sanctuary) which contained the sacred barque with the image of the god stands on a masonry base topped by a cavetto cornice and approached by a flight of steps. It has doorways at each end and is surrounded on all four sides by a colonnade of square pillars (or frequently Proto-Doric columns) linked by stone screens. Occasionally there may be a number of smaller subsidiary chambers to the rear of the main structure, also serving some cult function. Examples of this peripteral type of temple are the small temples of Tuthmosis III at Karnak and Medinet Habu, the southern temple from Buhen (now re-erected at Khartoum) and a Temple of Amenophis III on the island of Elephantine of which no trace now remains. Later this type went out of fashion but,

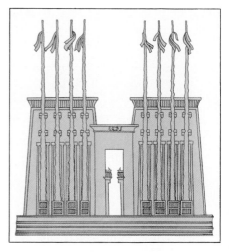

Second Pylon, Karnak (from an Egyptian relief)

curiously enough, was revived in the Ptolemaic period, with modifications, in the form of the *birth-houses (mammisi)* dedicated to the maternal goddess (Isis, Hathor) and her child which stood beside the main temple at Dendera, Edfu, Philae and other sites. In these the sanctuaries were also surrounded by colonnades, though now the roofs were supported on the curious sistrum columns topped by Hathor heads or figures of the god Bes.

The second basic type of Egyptian temple is best illustrated by the small temples built by Ramesses III at Karnak in honor of Khons and Mut. The entrance is formed by a pylon, two massive masonry towers flanking the gateway. Their walls, slightly inclined and framed by torus mouldings, afford ample space for reliefs. The imposing effect of the towers was still further enhanced by the obelisks and colossal statues which stood in front of them (features introduced in the Middle Kingdom) and the tall flagstaffs set in grooves on the façade and secured by huge clamps. The gateway leads into a spacious open court, flanked on right and left by colonnades. In the center of this court stood the great altar, round which the people assembled on festival occasions. To the rear of the court is the temple proper, standing on a terrace of moderate height topped by a cavetto cornice and approached by one or more flights of steps. The temple is entered through a vestibule or pronaos, the roof of which is borne on columns. The columns in the front row are linked by stone screens, shutting off the temple from the court. Beyond the vestibule is a hypostyle hall occupying the whole breadth of the

Mammisi (birth-house), Dendera

building. In the larger temples of the 19th and later dynasties (e.g. the Ramesseum and the Temple of Khons at Karnak) this is in the form of a multi-aisled basilica, the three central aisles being considerably higher than the lateral aisles. The roof of the central aisles is borne on four rows of columns – tall papyrus columns with open capitals in the two inner rows, lower columns with closed capitals in the outer rows. The difference in height between the inner and outer columns is made up by square pillars resting on the lower columns, with windows in the walls between the pillars. Beyond the hypostyle hall is a relatively narrow and deep chamber, the sanctuary containing the statue of the god, usually in a sacred barque, which was carried in procession by the priests. Only the king or his representative, the high priest, might enter the sanctuary and "look upon the god". If the temple was dedicated to a triad of deities (like Ramesses III's Temple at Karnak) the sanctuary of the principal god (Amun) was flanked by the chapels of the other two (Mut and Khons). Around the sanctuary were various other chambers of different sizes, serving some ritual purpose or for the storage of liturgical vessels and utensils; and staircases led up to the roof and a variety of other rooms used either for the accommodation of temple guards and attendants or for the performance of particular ceremonies.

This type of temple, which is found in most of the larger temples of the New Kingdom and continued into the Ptolemaic period, closely corresponds to the layout of the early Egyptian house or palace as described above. The open courtyard of the house, accessible to every visitor, is represented by the great temple court; the portico of the house by the pronaos of the temple; the broad hall of the house by the hypostyle hall of the temple; and the deep hall beyond this in which the master of the house spent his time by the sanctuary which was the residence of the god. And just as the main apartments of the house were surrounded by other rooms serving a variety of purposes, so the temple sanctuary had around it a range of subsidiary chambers, store-rooms, etc. Thus the temple was literally, as the Egyptians called it, the "house of the god".

In many temples the hypostyle hall is separated from the sanctuary by one or more smaller chambers (with or without columns) which steadily diminish in height. Beyond the sanctuary there are often other chambers; and not infrequently the hypostyle hall is preceded by two colonnaded courts instead of one. It is usually difficult to establish the purpose of the various additional rooms.

If some temples, such as the Temple of Luxor and the Great Temple of Amun at Karnak, show a more complex form, this is because they were not built to a unified plan but were the work of a number of different builders.

Other deviations from the normal plan might result from the nature of the site. In Lower Nubia the sandstone cliffs come so close to the Nile that the temples had to be partly or wholly hewn from the rock. Thus in the Gerf Husein Temple, now unfortunately engulfed by Lake Nasser, the court was constructed of masonry and the hypostyle hall and sanctuary hewn from the rock, while the larger temple at Abu Simbel, including the pylon and the colossal figures, was entirely rock-cut. At Abydos the part of the temple containing the slaughter-court and various subsidiary chambers was set at right angles to the main structure, giving the temple as a whole an L-shaped plan.

Although there are remains of many small *temples of the Libyan and Late Periods,* practically nothing has survived of the large temples of these periods, apart from the Temple of Hibis (Kharga Oasis), built during the period of Persian rule. Almost all the kings resided in the Delta (Bubastis, Sais) and accordingly built most of their temples in the north, where the material used was limestone. In medieval and modern times the masonry of the temples found its way into limekilns or, since building stone was scarce in the Delta, was reused in later structures, usually leaving behind only the more refractory blocks of granite. It was only in Ptolemaic times that attention was again turned to the south and many large temples were built, usually on the site of ruined temples of earlier periods. All these temples are built on a standard plan, little different from that of earlier temples (cf. the Ramesseum and the Temple of Edfu). Only two significant changes appear in most of the temples: the hypostyle hall is no longer basilician in form, with higher central aisles, but is a large hall of uniform

Colossal figures of Ramesses II, Abu Simbel

theory was the only mortal who might have commerce with the gods, appears again and again, offering gifts and homage to the deities and receiving earthly blessings from them. In the later period, particularly under the Ptolemies, the secular scenes on the outer walls and on the walls of the court give place to religious scenes: the battle scenes and triumphal processions are superseded by offering scenes and sacred ceremonies, depicted at tedious length. Only the pylons still present the traditional figures of the king smiting his enemies in the presence of the god.

Moreover to the Egyptians the temple, like any architectural structure (a house, a tomb), was a small-scale image of the world. The roof corresponded to the sky, and was accordingly adorned with stars painted on a blue ground, while over the central aisle hovered vultures, protecting the king as he passed along below. Not infrequently, particularly in the temples of the Ptolemaic period, the ceiling is covered with astronomical representations – the gods and spirits of the months and the days, the planets, various constellations and the sky goddess herself, with the solar barque sailing over her body. The floor of the temple corresponded to the earth, and here (i.e. along the base of the walls) were depicted flowers blooming and long processions of representatives of the nomes and provinces, the river and the canals, bringing their produce as offerings to the deities of the temple. And since Egypt was traditionally regarded as consisting of two parts, the South and the North, the world as represented in the temple was similarly divided into a southern and a northern half. On one side are seen the representatives of the South, on the other the representatives of the North; and this division is frequently carried into the representations of religious ceremonies. The whole temple was surrounded by a massive brick wall, the gateway in which (usually the pylon) was approached by an avenue of sphinxes or, as at Thebes, of reclining rams. Within the walls were dwellings for the priests, store-rooms, stalls for animals, etc., so that the temple itself, like a mosque of the present day, stood in the midst of a large complex of buildings.

height, and the sanctuary is surrounded on three sides by corridors with smaller chambers opening off them. This latter innovation, first attested in the Temple of Khons at Karnak, gives the temple a central chapel enclosed on all sides. Earlier temples were frequently altered to conform with this new plan and provided with a special chamber for the sacred barque (as in the temples of Luxor and Karnak). Among the smaller chambers which were also common in this period mention may be made of the small sacrificial court or offering-court and the elegant kiosk adjoining it to be seen at Edfu – features which also occur, however, in some earlier temples.

From the earliest times all flat surfaces in temples – on pylons, interior walls, column shafts and ceilings – were adorned with reliefs and inscriptions. The reliefs on the outer walls, the pylons and the walls of the courts – i.e. those parts of the temple that were exposed to public view – were mostly devoted to glorifying the king's exploits and the great events of his reign, such as military campaigns, great festivals, etc., with the object of constantly keeping the power and splendor of the Pharaoh before the eyes of his people. Elsewhere in the temple the reliefs depict the various rituals and sacred ceremonies that took place there. The king, who according to Egyptian religious

In view of the high value of cultivable land in Egypt the **tombs** of the ancient

Egyptians were from the earliest times constructed not in the alluvial soil of the valley but on the higher ground on the edge of the desert, which had the additional advantage of being out of reach of the Nile inundation and, therefore, better adapted for the preservation of the dead. The tomb always had a double function: it was a safe resting-place for the dead, and it was a place where the living might assemble on certain days and bring their gifts to the dead. It thus consisted of two parts, an underground burial chamber and a cult chamber above ground.

The earliest tombs were mere pits in which the bodies were laid, often walled with bricks and covered with wooden beams. Larger graves were divided into separate chambers by partition walls. The grave was covered with a pile of stones or a mound built up from bricks of Nile mud, on the east side of which a stela or gravestone was set up; and in front of the stela was a small court in which the mourners could assemble and deposit their offerings. From this early form of tomb developed the *mastabas* in which the dignitaries of the Old Kingdom were buried. These consist of a rectangular superstructure of bricks or limestone blocks with sloping sides, with a perpendicular shaft (10–100 ft/3–30 m in depth) or a staircase leading down to the burial chamber containing the body, often in a wooden or stone coffin. On the east side of the superstructure was a small court (now usually destroyed) with a shallow recess, the "false door", which was thought of as the entrance to the tomb and to the realm of the dead. Here the relatives of the dead man laid their offerings of food and drink and other gifts on the flat offering-table or recited their prayers for his welfare. From the end of the 3rd Dynasty a chapel was often built in front of the false door, or a cult chamber was constructed within the mastaba and the false door set on its west wall. The 5th Dynasty enlarged the inner chamber and added further rooms.

The dimensions which might be reached by these tombs can best be seen in the Mastaba of Mereruka at Saqqara, which, like any large house of the period, has a series of apartments for the dead man, another suite (the harem) for his wife and a third, to the rear, for his son, together with various store-rooms. The interior walls were adorned with inscriptions and reliefs representing the dead man enjoy-

ing his favorite recreations (hunting, fishing), the various activities on his estates, his craftsmen at work, and so on. The object of these scenes was to ensure that all the various activities and objects depicted would be available to him in the afterlife. The dead man and the members of his family were represented by statues set up in one or more special chambers, the *serdabs* ("cellars"), generally built in the thickness of the walls but occasionally separate structures, with a small aperture to admit light and air. Most of the statues now to be seen in the Egyptian Museum in Cairo came from serdabs.

Just as the streets of a town were laid out around the royal palace, so the mastabas of high dignitaries were set in rows around the king's tomb. In the earliest period this was also a large mastaba containing within the structure or underneath it chambers for the king's body, those of his relatives and the various grave-goods. Later the royal mastaba was enlarged by increasing its height and surrounding it with a series of outer casings, each lower than the one before, to produce a *stepped mastaba* or *step pyramid*, like the Step Pyramid of Saqqara or the Pyramid of Meidum. The true pyramid with a plane surface evolved from the stepped mastaba at the beginning of the 4th Dynasty and thereafter remained in use for royal tombs until the beginning of the 18th Dynasty.

The earliest true **pyramid** was the Pyramid of Sneferu at Dahshur. Under the great stone mass of the pyramid there was only a sloping shaft leading down to a corridor, closed by portcullis slabs, which gave access to the tomb chamber. Where a pyramid contains several passages and several chambers, as in the Pyramids of Giza or the Step Pyramid of Saqqara, these are the result of modifications of the original plan or of later alterations. In the early period the chambers in the interior, which after the burial were inaccessible, were almost without decoration; it was not until the end of the 5th Dynasty that the practice began of inscribing religious texts (the so-called Pyramid Texts) on the walls. – The recess or the cult chamber in which votive offerings were made to the dead in the mastabas was now replaced by a special *mortuary temple* on the east side of the pyramid, consisting of two parts, one public and the other private. The central feature of the public part was a large open court surrounded by colon-nades, off which opened five chambers for statues of the dead king, while the principal chamber in the private part was the sanctuary with the false door. The mortuary temple on the edge of the desert plateau had its counterpart in a *valley temple,* a monumental gateway on a riverside quay which was connected with the upper temple by a long covered causeway.

While the walls of the pyramid temples of the 3rd and 4th Dynasties were left bare, those of the Abusir temples frequently have reliefs, many of them of the same types as are found in the temples of the gods (the king as a griffin triumphing over foreign foes, booty captured from the enemy, military campaigns, etc.). The best-preserved mortuary temples of the Old Kingdom are Djoser's Temple beside the Step Pyramid of Saqqara, the temples of Chephren and Mycerinus at Giza and those of Sahure, Neferirkare and Niuserre at Abusir. The Middle Kingdom is represented by the mortuary temples associated with the pyramids of Lisht, Dahshur, El-Lahun and Hawara. Most

of them are badly ruined, such as Amenemhet III's Temple (the Labyrinth), while others have not been adequately excavated; the best preserved is the Mortuary Temple of Mentuhotep II (11th Dynasty) at Deir el-Bahri, though this, with its unusual terraced layout, can hardly be regarded as typical. In a much later period the pyramid as a form of royal tomb was revived by the kings of Napata and Meroe. – A type of structure which has so far remained unique is the Festival Temple within the precinct of Djoser's Step Pyramid at Saqqara, probably built on the occasion of the King's 30th Jubilee. The hypostyle hall of this temple is the earliest known example of a basilican hall with a higher central aisle.

From the end of the Old Kingdom many high dignitaries and officials preferred to be buried in their home area rather than at the foot of the king's pyramid. These provincial tombs, like the tombs within the royal funerary precinct, were built on the edge of the desert and took the form of small mastabas or small brick pyramids on a square or rectangular base. The burial chamber was either within the masonry or

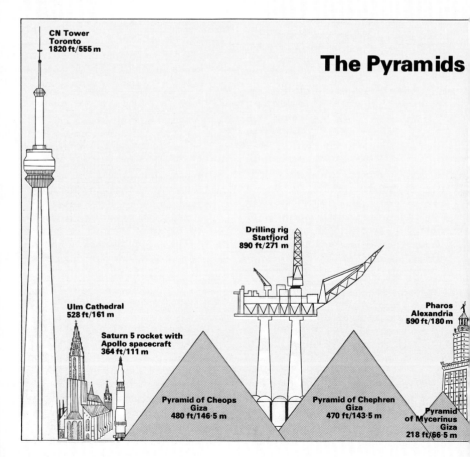

The Pyramids

CN Tower
Toronto
1820 ft/555 m

Drilling rig
Statfjord
890 ft/271 m

Ulm Cathedral
528 ft/161 m

Pharos
Alexandria
590 ft/180 m

Saturn 5 rocket with
Apollo spacecraft
364 ft/111 m

Pyramid of Cheops
Giza
480 ft/146·5 m

Pyramid of Chephren
Giza
470 ft/143·5 m

Pyramid
of Mycerinus
Giza
218 ft/66·5 m

in the underlying rock. Outside the tomb was set a gravestone in the form of a false door or a round-topped stela, in front of which the dead man's relatives recited their prayers or made their offerings. Frequently, too, the tombs were hewn from the rock on the slopes of the desert hills. The simpler tombs consisted of a single chamber with a "false door" recess, but in larger tombs chambers were cut in the rock in imitation of those in a mastaba. Usually, however, the layout was based on the conception of the tomb as the dead man's house, with the four principal elements of an ancient Egyptian dwelling-house – the open courtyard, the portico or vestibule, the broad hypostyle hall and the deep and narrow dining-room. The tombs thus consisted of an open forecourt, usually surrounded by a brick wall, a small rock-cut vestibule with two columns or pillars, a larger chamber with columns or pillars and beyond this a small chamber or recess which contained a statue of the dead man and frequently of his wife as well, also carved from the living rock, and corresponded to the serdab of the earlier mastabas. – The best examples of this type are the rock tombs of Beni Hasan and Aswan. The walls of the chambers are covered with inscriptions and reliefs, more varied in subject than those in earlier tombs but, like them, designed to enable the dead man to enjoy the activities and objects depicted. From the first chamber a shaft runs down through the rock to the undecorated tomb chamber.

The tombs of the New Kingdom are similar in form to those of the Old and Middle Kingdoms, and during this period, too, there are both free-standing tombs (mastabas and pyramids) and rock tombs, depending on the nature of the terrain. Of the free-standing tombs, however, few remains survive. From the beginning of the 18th Dynasty the kings ceased to build pyramids as their last resting-place and had their tombs hewn from the rock in a secluded valley on the west bank of the Nile opposite Thebes. These *royal tombs of the New Kingdom* consisted of long corridors and chambers adorned with religious scenes and inscriptions. Like the chambers and corridors of the pyramids, they were designed to house the sarcophagus and the grave-furnishings, with the living rock here replacing the

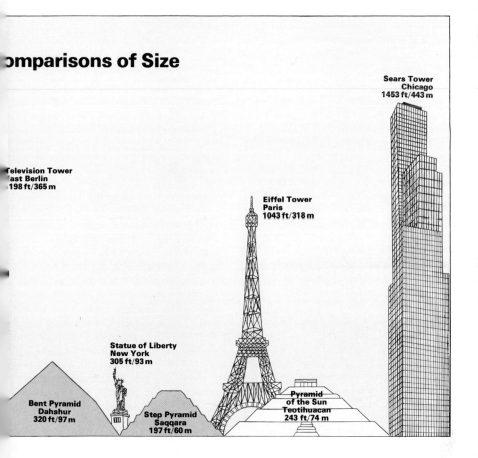

Comparisons of Size

Sears Tower
Chicago
1453 ft/443 m

Television Tower
East Berlin
1198 ft/365 m

Eiffel Tower
Paris
1043 ft/318 m

Statue of Liberty
New York
305 ft/93 m

Bent Pyramid
Dahshur
320 ft/97 m

Step Pyramid
Saqqara
197 ft/60 m

Pyramid
of the Sun
Teotihuacan
243 ft/74 m

huge masonry superstructure of the pyramid; but since there was no room for mortuary temples in the rugged desert valley these were built, usually on a large scale, in the plain below, where their remains can still be seen.

Just as the dignitaries of the Middle Kingdom frequently imitated the pyramids of their kings in constructing their own tombs, so the grandees of the Late Period, at least in Thebes, took as their model the rock-hewn tombs of the Pharaohs. The tombs, which can be seen in the Theban cemetery of El-Asasif, show a complex pattern of passages and chambers exclusively adorned with religious scenes and texts. – Of the royal tombs of the last native dynasties, constructed around the great capitals in the Delta, only those of Tanis (near the village of San el-Hagar) have so far been located and properly investigated. They imitate the form of the earlier rock tombs in the looser soil of the Delta and have a massive stone casing, the material for which had to be brought from a considerable distance away.

The tombs of the humbler classes of the population must have been much more numerous than those of the dignitaries and officials, but apart from the pits which contained the bodies and a few gravestones they have left no traces. We know from reliefs and paintings that they were frequently in the form of small brick pyramids, but few have survived the ravages of time. The poorer members of the population were frequently buried in mass graves constructed by speculative contractors within the precincts of ruined temples or in long galleries excavated under the ground. In these tombs the bodies were deposited in simple coffins, or sometimes merely on planks or on mats of palm fiber, and accompanied by modest grave-goods for their use in the life beyond. These common graves, however, have mostly been covered by drift sand, and all trace of them is lost.

Sculpture and Painting

In considering Egyptian art it must be borne in mind that it is based on a very different approach from the Classical art of Greece. The Egyptians, the Babylonians and Assyrians, the Hittites and the Cretans had all created their own styles of art before the Greeks; and one characteristic

Relief in the Mastaba of Ti, Saqqara

they shared with primitive peoples and with children was that they did not reproduce the external world merely as the eyes saw it but as the human mind conceived it. In one notable respect they departed from the visual impression of a subject: neither in painting nor in sculpture did they go in for oblique views, with the foreshortenings and distortions of angles to which they give rise. It was left to the Greeks to make the enormously important transition, about 500 B.C., from "conceptual" art to "perspectivist" art based on the visual impression

Relief sculpture and painting. – Since the pre-Greek artist is completely unaware of the foreshortening effect of perspective he depicts the human body and its various parts as if he were looking straight at them, not from a particular oblique viewpoint. Nothing is represented as if it were seen from a single point: instead the picture is built up from its separate parts without foreshortening. Objects, human figures and animals which to the observer appear behind one another tend to be represented in rows beside one another or over and under one another, and objects lying on a table are depicted as if standing on it. Figures are usually shown side by side without overlapping, though Egyptian artists realized at an early stage that when two objects lie one behind the other they cannot both be fully visible. The principal figure in any scene is depicted on a larger scale than the other figures: thus in a battle scene the king, shown dashing against the enemy in his chariot, will be considerably larger than the other persons involved in the scene.

The central element in Egyptian representational art is the human figure, which is built up from its separate parts as seen from various different viewpoints. The head is shown in profile, while the eye is depicted frontally. The shoulders are represented in their full breadth as seen from the front, without foreshortening, but the breast, abdomen, legs and feet are seen from the side. Alongside this basic form, of which the Relief of Hesire is a striking example, there gradually developed a type of representation in profile, which occasionally appears during the 5th Dynasty but is practiced with complete confidence in the second half of the 18th Dynasty. Egyptian draftsmanship then reached its peak of achievement, never thereafter surpassed. The finest examples of the work of this period are to be seen at Sheikh Abd el-Qurna and Tell el-Amarna. – Since animals were depicted almost wholly in profile, the different Egyptian approach to the representation of nature can usually be observed only in small subsidiary details.

Egyptian art had at its disposal from an early period a range of subjects which were treated again and again, though some modifications were gradually introduced. In the course of the centuries, however, new themes were introduced. Thus the art of the Old Kingdom depicts many scenes of life on large landed estates, often showing an astonishing freshness and a delicate observation of nature. Under the 5th Dynasty the repertoire is increased by the military scenes depicted in the mortuary temples, while in the Middle Kingdom there are scenes depicting life at the courts of the provincial princes and some new funerary scenes. The great increase in the range of subject-matter, however, comes under the 18th Dynasty, when Egypt had become a World Power as a result of its political relationships with western Asia and the artists' horizons had become increasingly wider. During the reign of Amenophis IV/Akhenaten even the intimate life of the royal family and the Court, which no one would previously have ventured to represent, came for a time within the field

of art. Under the 19th Dynasty and during the reign of Ramesses III artists were called on to celebrate the military exploits of the kings and depict great battle scenes. The beginnings of this trend can already be observed under the 18th Dynasty (reliefs on Tuthmosis IV's chariot in the Egyptian Museum in Cairo). At the end of the New Kingdom the range of subject-matter shrank again until it was more restricted than under the Old Kingdom. In scenes of the kind just referred to the artists had scope for invention, but in depicting ceremonial scenes – the king's commerce with the gods (praying, making offerings), the celebration of festivals, the slaughter of animals for sacrifice, etc. – they had to adhere more or less rigidly to established models.

The Egyptian artists practiced both *low relief (bas-relief)* and *sunk relief* (relief *en creux*). Low relief, the earliest and at all periods the commonest type of relief carving, was carried to a high pitch of refinement. Sunk relief, a form peculiar to Egypt in which the design is sunk below the surface of the stone, first appeared in the 4th Dynasty and always served as a cheaper substitute for bas-relief work; but the artists of the New Kingdom were able to achieve very attractive effects by skillful use of its particular characteristics. The heyday of the Egyptian relief was during the 5th Dynasty, and the technical and artistic achievement of this period is seen at its best in the mastabas of Ti and Ptah-hotep at Saqqara and the mortuary temples of the 5th Dynasty kings. Under the 6th Dynasty and the Middle Kingdom the quality of execution declined, and the earlier standard was not approached again until the 18th Dynasty (e.g. in the temples of Luxor and Deir el-Bahri and some tombs at Sheikh Abd el-Qurna). Thereafter the decline continued, though a few graceful and attractive reliefs were produced in the reign of Sethos I (e.g. in the temples of Qurna and at Abydos). In the reign of Ramesses II the excessive demands on artistic resource for the decoration of the many temples of the period led to the production of much coarse and skimped work, and the quality fell still further in the reign of Merneptah.

The artists of the Saite period also took the reliefs of the Old Kingdom as their models, though their imitative work could not achieve the standard of the earlier masters. Nevertheless the reliefs of this period offer considerable attraction with their exact and delicate execution, their elegance and their pleasing smoothness of form. – The art of the Ptolemaic period at first followed the manner of the Saite artists, but then gradually declined in standard. The subtle feeling for the right proportion between decorated and undecorated surfaces was now lost, and the temple walls were covered indiscriminately with row after row of reliefs. The figures of both men and gods became heavy and shapeless, so that their features and limbs have a swollen appearance. It is unfortunately the reliefs of this Late Period that occur most frequently and most prominently in Upper Egypt and have thus contributed to giving Egyptian relief art a much lower reputation than it deserves.

All the reliefs were originally painted, but many of them have lost their coloring. Where relief decoration is replaced by painting on a flat surface, either because of the lesser cost or on account of the poor quality of the stone (e.g. in the 18th Dynasty tombs at Abd el-Qurna) the paintings follow the same stylistic principles as the reliefs.

Sculpture in the round. – The pre-Greek approach – very different from our own – to the reproduction of nature is reflected also in Egyptian sculpture in the round, particularly the statues of men and animals, and produces a marked departure from the visual impression. In contrast to Greek sculpture with its freedom and variety of viewpoint, Egyptian statues are presented frontally. The trunk faces squarely forward, with both shoulders in the same plane, and if the head is turned at all it is turned at a right angle, while the limbs lie in a plane at right angles to the trunk. Departures from this strict frontality are very occasionally found, just as occasional examples of foreshortening occur in Egyptian reliefs. – Persons invested with particular dignity are represented

standing or seated in a chair in an attitude of repose, or sometimes seated on the ground with their legs folded under them, and are frequently shown in family groups. There is greater freedom in the statues of servants and attendants, depicted engaging in their workaday activities, which were deposited in the tomb with the dead man.

Even in the earliest period of Egyptian history we find primitive figures of men and animals, usually carved from bone or ivory. The animal figures in particular display a high degree of technical skill. The statues of the late 2nd Dynasty and *Early Old Kingdom* already show all the qualities of Egyptian sculpture, having lost their earlier primitive character, though they still have a certain stiffness, frequently attributable to the refractory nature of the material (granite, metamorphic schist, occasionally limestone). They are mostly seated figures of medium size and squat build, with the right hand resting on the breast, the left hand on the thigh. Where they bear inscriptions these are usually in relief. Even these early works of sculpture, however (among the best of which are the statues of Kings Khasekhem and Djoser), already show an attempt to depict the features in as accurate a likeness as possible.

The art of statuary reached a high point under the 4th and 5th Dynasties. The works of this period, to be seen in the Egyptian Museum in Cairo, are mostly in limestone or wood. The main stress is laid on a faithful representation of the face, while the rest of the body, in particular the hands and feet, is conventionally represented. The effect is frequently enhanced by the insertion of eyes of black and white quartz, with wooden or copper studs to represent the pupil.

After a period of decline the sculpture of the *Middle Kingdom* rose to a fresh peak of achievement. Among the masterpieces of this period are the fine figure of Amenemhet III in the Egyptian Museum in Cairo and the statues and sphinxes which were formerly attributed to the Hyksos but probably represent Amenemhet III and other rulers of the late 12th Dynasty. They are notable for their profoundly spiritual expression and deep seriousness. This period also produced work of much inferior quality, such as the conventional

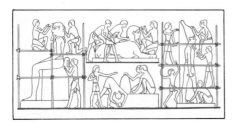
Sculptors at work (from an Egyptian relief)

Ramesses II in front of his rock temple ▶ at Abu Simbel

statues of Sesostris I from Lisht, with their vacant faces.

The statues of the *New Kingdom* (mostly designed to serve decorative purposes), which have come down to us in relatively large numbers, are very different from those of the Middle Kingdom. The rather melancholy seriousness of the earlier period now gives place to a tranquil and attractive serenity. Among the magnificent likenesses produced in this period, comparable with the finest achievements of the past, are the statue of Tuthmosis III, the portrait heads of Queen Nefertiti, the busts of a married couple, the head of King Horemheb (?), the statue of the god Khons and the head of the goddess Mut in the Egyptian Museum in Cairo and a number of works to be seen in European museums. In many cases the sculptors have abandoned portrait-like accuracy in favor of an ideal beauty, devoting much attention to the treatment of the flowing garments then fashionable, the coiffure and the ornaments and jewelry. A number of new types were created during this period, such as the figure of a man squatting on the ground clad in a voluminous cloak.

Gilded statue from Tutankhamun's Tomb

From the 20th Dynasty onwards the standard of sculpture showed a steady decline until the period of Ethiopian rule, when it enjoyed a revival based on models of the Old and Middle Kingdoms and occasionally also of the New Kingdom. This late flowering has been called the "Egyptian Renaissance". Much of the work of this period is so close to its models that it is sometimes difficult, even for a practiced eye, to distinguish between the earlier and the later work. During the Ethiopian period (*c.* 675 B.C.) there also developed a school of sculpture which went beyond mere imitation and sought to pour new wine into old bottles by striving for an exact likeness, producing such masterpieces as the head of an elderly man of Negroid type and the statue of Mentemhet, Governor of Upper Egypt under the Ethiopian ruler Taharqa. The same school produced – perhaps several centuries later – a number of fine portraits of bald-headed priests, in which subsidiary details are ignored and characteristic features (e.g. the form of the skull) reproduced with masterly skill.

These works, striving for truth to nature and then again strictly stylized, show no trace of Greek influence, but from the Ptolemaic period onwards Egyptian sculpture became increasingly subject to the influence of Greek art. Side by side with purely Greek works (chiefly in Alexandria) and with purely Egyptian works clinging mechanically to the older style we find a curious *hybrid Graeco-Egyptian style* in which a Greek figure is depicted with Egyptian garments, hairstyle and ornaments, or conversely (e.g. in the Tomb of Petosiris) the figure is of Egyptian type but the clothing is Greek. These figures are valuable for the light they throw on Egyptian culture in the Late Period, but artistically they are unsatisfying.

Much work of notable quality was produced in the field of the **applied arts**, particularly cabinet-making, glass-blowing and the production of colored faience. The finest achievements, however, were produced by the goldsmiths and metalworkers, who had attained complete mastery of their materials, practicing the techniques of enameling, damascening, etc., with consummate skill, and giving their products (especially with the aid of colored gemstones and faience inlays) a charm and brilliance which reflects the high cultural level achieved by Egyptian society.

Given the different Egyptian approach to the representation of nature, it is not always easy for people of the present day to understand and appreciate Egyptian art. The best method of getting to know it is to study the statues and reliefs in the Egyptian Museum in Cairo and the reliefs on the walls of the mastabas, rock tombs and temples, particularly the temples of Deir el-Bahri and Luxor and the Temple of Sethos I at Abydos. Genuine works of art are, it is true, relatively thin on the ground in Egypt, and amid the great mass of work that has been preserved it may sometimes be difficult for the non-expert to distinguish between work of real quality and mere journeyman work. To the latter category belong some of the most striking and prominent colossal statues, sphinxes and temple reliefs, which with few exceptions served a purely decorative function.

The Egyptian imagination, more than that of any other people, was closely tied to natural things, only occasionally evolving original concepts. It does, however, display a genuine understanding of nature and a delight in its details. At the same time it shows a trend, which may at first sight tend to put the outside observer off, towards geometrical forms and an urge towards the monumental, not only in works of gigantic size but also in its smallest products. But even those who find it difficult to appreciate the real beauty of Egyptian art cannot fail to be impressed by the supreme craftsmanship and technical mastery which still commands our admiration.

Islamic Architecture

Islamic art in Egypt begins in the 8th–9th centuries with the Nilometer and the Ibn Tulun Mosque in Cairo; but in order to understand these two monuments it is necessary to know something of the early history of Islam.

In the time of Mohammed the Arabs had nothing that could properly be called architecture. The house which he built in Medina after his flight from Mecca consisted of a large courtyard 180 ft/55 m square enclosed by 10 ft/3 m high walls, the lower part of which was built of undressed stone without mortar, the upper part of mud bricks. This court, which later became a place of prayer, was at first quite open, but later it was covered with a roof of palm leaves and daub supported on palm-trunks to give protection from the burning sun. At the south-east corner of the courtyard, outside the wall, were the huts occupied by Mohammed's wives

Sauda and Aisha, also constructed of palm leaves and daub. As Mohammed acquired other wives additional huts were built, all opening into the courtyard. There were no lamps: the evening prayers took place by the light of a fire of palm leaves.

At first the community turned when praying towards Jerusalem, under the influence of the Jews who then enjoyed great influence in Medina and had provided Mohammed with many of his religious and political conceptions. But after failing, in 18 months of discussion, to reach an understanding with them he finally broke with the Jews. The first external sign of the break was the change in the direction of prayer (the qibla): from January 10, 624 the faithful were required when praying to face not towards Jerusalem but towards the Kaaba in Mecca.

After Mohammed's death in 632 a period of great military campaigns began. The Arab armies fighting for the new faith fanned out from their peninsula, advancing north-west into Syria, where they came into contact with Syro-Byzantine civilization, and north-east towards Mesopotamia and Persia, where they encountered the civilization of the Sassanid Empire. The Arab advances in these directions had great influence on the development of Islamic architecture, as was to be demonstrated in the second half of the 7th century. – The bedouin from the interior of eastern Arabia who formed the bulk of the Islamic armies knew Mohammed and the Koran only by name and saw the campaigns as a means of winning booty rather than propagating the faith. They were not interested in art or architecture and, as nomads, disliked living in towns. When, after two generations or so, they began to adopt a settled way of life and felt a need for permanent houses they turned in Mesopotamia to Sassanid and in Syria to Byzantine architects. The semicircular prayer-niche, the pulpit and the screened-off area in a mosque for the Caliph or the provincial governor (maqsura), which first appeared at the turn of the 7th and 8th centuries, were all of non-Islamic origin.

In Syria the earliest mosques were mostly converted churches: the west doorways were built up, new entrances were constructed on the north side and the south wall gave the direction of prayer, towards

Mecca. Hence the marked preference in Syria for a sanctuary with two rows of columns (the old three-aisled basilica). – In Mesopotamia, where the principal Arab settlements were the new foundations of Kufa and Basra, a different type of mosque developed. At Basra the arrangement was very simple: an area was marked out, and within this the faithful prayed in the open. At Kufa a site for the mosque was selected, and from this spot a man fired four arrows – one to the south in the direction of the *qibla* and others to the north, east and west. The area to be occupied by the mosque was thus marked out at a square measuring two bowshots each way. Within this area, which was surrounded by a ditch, the only structure was a hypo-style hall open on all sides *(zulla)* on the south side of the enclosure, constructed with columns from the ruins of Hira. Adjoining the precinct on the south was the residence of the military commander. The type of mosque thus created in 638 remained in use for several centuries.

A far-reaching influence on the development of Islam was the fall of the Omayyads, the only genuinely Arab dynasty, in 750 and the rise of the Abbasids, who moved the seat of government to El-Mansur's new foundation of Baghdad. This change had a similar effect on Islam to the effect on the Roman Empire of the transfer of the capital from Rome to Constantinople: in both cases the center of gravity was moved eastward. The Syrian and Byzantine influence on Islamic art and architecture was now reduced and the influence of Sassanid Persia and Central Asia greatly increased. The first large mosque built in Baghdad appears to have occupied an area 395 ft/120 m square, with a court *(sahn)* in the middle and a flat-roofed sanctuary which had a hall with five rows of columns on the *qibla* side and halls with two rows of columns on the other sides. From 836 to 889 the seat of the Caliphate was in the great city of Samarra, some 60 miles/100 km farther up the Tigris, where excavation of the extensive remains has brought to light fragments of stucco ornament and (in the Caliph's palace) pointed arches.

The architecture of Egypt remained backward, since as a conquered province it was exploited over a period of two centuries by a succession of rapacious governors, few of whom remained longer than three years in office. The architecture of the Omayyad period is, therefore, not represented in Egypt. The situation changed, however, when Ahmed ibn Tulun made himself independent ruler of Egypt. A native of Samarra, he brought with him its architectural traditions. His mosque in Cairo, with a ground-plan similar to the Baghdad mosque and ornament in the style of Samarra, is an alien Mesopotamian creation on Egyptian soil. The story that it was designed by a Christian architect was no doubt invented to explain the use of pillars in place of the columns which had previously been normal. All the basic types of ornament found in Samarra reappear here, together with the earliest examples of geometric ornament in Islamic art (the lower parts of the arches on the south-west side of the court). The whole structure is built in brick, with slightly stilted pointed arches.

The *Fatimid period* (969–1171) began with the conquest of Egypt by Gohar, General of the Fatimid Caliph El-Muizz, in 969. That year saw the foundation of Cairo (El-Qahira), to the north of the earlier settlement of Fustat and Ibn Tulun's foundation of El-Qatai. The new town originally consisted of a fortified area some 1200 yds/1100 m square, with two palaces for the Caliph (a larger one to the east and a smaller one in the west), Government buildings, barracks for the garrison, a treasury, a mint, a library, a mausoleum, an arsenal, etc. Until the fall of the Fatimids (1171) no one might enter the town except members of the garrison and high officials: in this respect Cairo was reminiscent of Peking as laid out by Kublai Khan from 1267 onwards, with its Chinese town, its Tartar town and its Forbidden City. Nothing now remains of the walls or the buildings of the original foundation, though there are a few carved wooden friezes from the smaller Fatimid palace in the Museum of Islamic Art in Cairo.

In 970–971 Gohar built the El-Azhar Mosque, in which columns rather than pillars were used. In spite of the considerable changes made in later periods it is still possible to make out that the original sanctuary had five aisles and the lateral halls three; the number in the hall on the north side is uncertain. A striking feature is a kind of nave or central aisle which runs from the court *(sahn)* to the prayer-niche *(mihrab)*, interrupting the rows of arches. This is the first example of the kind in

Egypt, though it is found in the earlier Great Mosque in Damascus, built by El-Walid in 705–715. This curious feature seems to have been carried west by the last of the Omayyads, Abd el-Rahman (Great Mosque, Córdoba), and it is also found in the Great Mosque of Kairouan (Tunisia), the Fatimid capital, from which it apparently traveled east to Cairo. The two corners at the rear of the sanctuary of the El-Azhar Mosque were probably covered by domes, as in the El-Hakim Mosque built in Cairo between 990 and 1012. The El-Hakim Mosque shows very clearly the foreign influences at work in its design. Its almost square plan, its many doorways, the five aisles (each with 17 arches) of the sanctuary, the pillars and the small relieving arches above them are all Mesopotamian features; the transept and the doorways (now walled up) on the north-east and south-east sides come from Syria. The fortress-like impression created by the two large projections with the minarets is again typically Mesopotamian, found in the mosques of Baghdad and Samarra and in the Great Mosque of Bostam in northern Iran, which according to the account by the Arab geographer El-Muqaddasi (985) stood like a fortress in the center of the market-place.

Within a century Cairo had outgrown Gohar's original circuit of walls, and in 1087–92 it was surrounded with new walls by Badr el-Gamali. Of this circuit there still survive three well-preserved gates – Bab el-Nasr, Bab el-Futuh and Bab Zuwaila – and a 350 yd/300 m stretch of wall reinforced by square towers. Each of these gates is different from the others, since they were the work of different builders, three Armenian refugees from Edessa (Urfa), which a year earlier (1086) had fallen into the hands of the Seljuk Turks. The wall, gates and towers are of particular interest, since they are among the few surviving examples of Islamic military engineering of the period before the Crusades. The Bab el-Nasr has two machicolations (parapets with openings), such as are not found in Europe until the end of the 12th century. The gateways of the Bab el-Futuh and Bab Zuwaila are roofed with shallow domes of freestone borne on pendentives – the earliest example of this form in Egypt. Every feature in the structure of these fortifications, which were influenced by Byzantine practice, can be paralleled in northern Syria.

A characteristic feature of Fatimid architecture is its use of ornament remarkable for the boldness and variety of its design. It consists solely of decorative Arabic script and arabesques of consummate artistry, sometimes within a geometric framework. During this period purely geometric ornament plays an entirely subordinate part, and even the famous interlaced star pattern, which in later periods had ten, twelve or even more points, is found only in its simplest form, the eight-pointed star. In contrast to the Tulunid period, in which Mesopotamian influences had predominated, the art of the Fatimid period shows Syrian influences, which were to become increasingly prominent in the Ayyubid and Early Mameluke periods. The decorative script, on the other hand, shows Persian and northern Mesopotamian influences. A number of characteristic forms, including the intertwining of the stems of letters, is found in these areas a century earlier than in Egypt. It is not possible to reach a firm judgment on this question in view of the scarcity of contemporary examples outside Egypt; and this fact alone enhances the importance of the fine Fatimid buildings which have been preserved in Cairo.

The *Ayyubid period* (1171–1250) began with the erection by Saladin of the Citadel which still dominates Cairo and of much of the present town walls. Unfortunately none of the religious buildings which he erected in Egypt have survived. The towers on Saladin's walls were not square, like those of the Fatimids, but semicircular, measuring some 21 ft/6·5 m across; each has three loopholes for archers, one facing outwards and one on either side. The Citadel walls have a 3 ft/90 cm wide wall-walk running round the inside, but this is lacking on the town walls except on the east side, where there is a short covered passage adjoining each tower.

The most notable innovation in Saladin's fortifications is the right-angled entrance passageway of the gates, so contrived as to hold up any enemy attack. A device of this kind was known in ancient Egypt but was apparently quite unknown in Babylon, Rome, Byzantium and the Early Islamic period. The Bab el-Mudarrag in the Citadel, behind the much later Bab el-Gedid built by Mohammed Ali, is the earliest dated example in the Middle East

(1184). Another example dating from the same period is the Bab el-Qarafa on the opposite side of the Citadel, which was excavated by Creswell in 1923.

Saladin's brother El-Adil strengthened the Citadel at some points by the erection of large square towers and at other points by making the semicircular towers round and tripling their diameter; examples of this are the two large towers on the Abbasiya side. – Saladin also introduced the *medrese* (theological college) into Egypt, although its characteristic cruciform ground-plan did not appear until almost a century later.

In addition to these works of military and religious architecture the Ayyubid period was notable also for the increased use of freestone, the introduction of marble cladding for prayer-niches (e.g. in the Mosque of Sultan El-Salih Ayyub), a liking for stucco ornament of almost exaggerated elegance, the first use of glass in association with stucco lattices (Tomb of the Abbasid Caliphs) and the first beginnings of the stalactitic pendentive.

The period of the *Bahrite Mamelukes* (1250–1382) saw an important advance in the structure of mosques. The small dome over the space in front of the prayer-niche (found, for example, in the El-Hakim Mosque) now gave place to a large timber dome spanning nine bays (3×3) and dominating the sanctuary: examples can be seen in the mosques of Baibars I

(Abbasiya quarter; 1269), Mohammed el-Nasir (Citadel; 1318–35) and El-Mardani (1340). The practice of having three doorways and the form of the doorways were taken over from Syria during this period; and Baibars I also introduced from Syria the stalactitic doorway which now became a characteristic feature of Egyptian architecture. The largest building of this period was the Sultan Hasan Mosque (1356–63), which is 490 ft/150 m long and 225 ft/68 m across at its widest point and has a total area of almost 86,000 sq. ft/8000 sq. m. Anyone standing at the entrance to its great forecourt and contemplating its imposing dimensions, its rich but restrained decoration, the nobility and simplicity of its lines, the height and breadth of its dome and the richly decorated minarets at its south-west corner must surely agree that the Sultan Hasan Mosque is one of the great architectural achievements of Egypt. Under the following dynasty richer and more elegant buildings were erected, but as an expression of power and majesty this mosque can hardly be equalled.

Among the major innovations of this period was the cruciform ground-plan of the medrese. The façade was embellished by the use of banded stonework *(ablaq)*, and the stucco ornament reached its fullest development and then gradually disappeared, while the lower parts of the walls now began to be faced with many-colored marble.

Cairo – view from the Citadel of the Sultan Hasan Mosque (on left)

The architecture of the *Circassian Mamelukes* (1391–1517) followed without any break in development. The rich stucco decoration which had fallen out of favor towards the end of the preceding period was not immediately replaced by any other form of ornament. At first the stone was left bare, with marble cladding as the principal decorative feature; then about 1440, when greater skill had been achieved in the working of stone, the decoration of the wall surfaces with elaborate incised or chiseled patterns became a regular feature. This period also carried the stalactitic pendentive to its highest peak of development: the niches were set within a triangular frame, after the Syrian fashion; but, in contrast to the Syrian pendentives, each row was offset from the adjoining rows instead of cutting off the corner in a straight line. The number of rows increased considerably: seven, eight or nine commonly occur, and there may be as many as thirteen. The dome now also reached its finest form: always constructed of stone during this period, they are of incomparable lightness, beauty of line and richness of decoration. A superb example is provided by the Barquq Mosque in the cemetery of the so-called Tombs of the Caliphs. – Towards the end of the period the ground-plan of the mosque underwent a change, giving place to the type of structure previously used only for medreses.

The *Turkish Conquest* (1517) at first brought a sharp fall in building activity. Many craftsmen were sent to Constantinople, and some trades are said to have died out altogether. The architecture of the Turkish period has sometimes been dismissed as of little account; but this is not entirely fair, since it suffered not so much from a decline in artistic achievement as from a reduction in the resources devoted to large building projects. The little mosques of Sidi Sariya in the Citadel, Sinan Pasha in Bulaq and Malika Safiya can be cited in support of this view. The final blow to a distinctively Islamic architecture came later, with the steady increase in European influence, and fortunately this came much later in Egypt than elsewhere. The disastrous effects of this influence, which can be observed in Istanbul in the Nuruosmaniye Mosque, completed about 1753, and in a Baroque fountain of 1798 in Damascus, appear to have reached Egypt only about 1820.

As we have seen, the most important works of Islamic architecture are the **mosques**. These are of two types, the *gami*, the mosque for the communal Friday prayer, and the *masgid*, a place for prayer; to which may be added the *zawiya*, a small chapel. The earliest form of the communal mosque is of Mesopotamian origin (cf. the Ibn Tulun). Around an almost square court *(sahn)* lie four flat-roofed arcaded halls *(riwak)*. The main *riwak*, in the direction of Mecca, usually has five (Ibn Tulun, El-Azhar, El-Hakim) or six aisles (Baibars I), the others only two (Ibn Tulun) or three (El-Azhar, El-Hakim and Baibars I).

The religious, dogmatic, ritual, social and moral prescriptions of Islam developed in four main schools, founded by the Imams Abu Hanifa, Malik ibn Anas, El-Shafii and Ahmed ibn Hanbal. To provide instruction in these rites, and also to train the large numbers of officials required for the administration of the Seljuk Empire, the Sultans introduced in the 9th century the institution of the **medrese**, a kind of theological college. There was no hostility between the four schools of Islamic thought, and more than one rite might sometimes be housed in the same building. The first medreses were established by Nur el-Din in Syria, and after the fall of the Fatimid dynasty Saladin introduced them into Egypt in order to combat the Shiite heresy of the Fatimids and ensure the victory of the Sunnite reaction by the establishment of orthodox teaching institutions.

The medreses built in Egypt after the middle of the 13th century took the form of a square central court surrounded by four open halls *(liwan)* forming the arms of a cross. The whole structure occupied a rectangle, at the corners of which were various subsidiary structures including the main doorway, a staircase leading to the roof, teaching halls, cells for the professors, etc. In the earliest examples the liwans had barrel-vaulted roofs; later they had flat timber roofs with a single arcade on the side facing the court. The predominance of this basic form gave rise to the view that the Egyptian medreses were always built to serve all four rites; and the fact that the institution of the medrese had been taken over from Syria was seen as implying that the cruciform plan also came from Syria. Both views are erroneous. Syria has no fewer than eight medreses built before 1270, none of them with a cruciform ground-plan or four large liwans; but in Egypt Sultan Baibars I built a cruciform medrese as early as 1263. It thus seems certain that the cruciform plan was first used for a medrese in Egypt.

The cruciform plan of the medrese also influenced the development of the mosque. The disadvantage of the type of mosque with its arcaded halls bordering the inner court was the poor visibility between the preacher and the congregation – as can be seen by mounting the pulpit of the Ibn Tulun Mosque and observing how the pillars interfere with the view. In the medrese, on the other hand, there is an unobstructed view of the assembled faithful. It is not surprising, therefore, that the cruciform plan of the medrese gradually displaced the older ground-plan of the mosques, being employed occasionally in the 14th century (Emir el-Malak, 1319; Aslam el-Silahdar, 1345) and becoming common in the 15th (Gamal el-Din el-Ustadar, 1408; Gani Bek, 1427; Gohar el-Lala, 1430; Qagmas el-Ishaqi, 1481, etc.). In the final century of the Mameluke period the court became much smaller. – After the Turkish Conquest in 1517 the influence of the Byzantine/Ottoman style gave rise to a type of sanctuary roofed with a large dome, in front of which was a court surrounded by arcades covered by small domes (El-Malika Safiya, 1610).

Fountain, Alabaster Mosque, Cairo

The **exterior** of the earliest mosques was absolutely plain. The walls were crenelated, with many unpretentious doorways. Later, under Syrian influence (e.g. the Great Mosque of Damascus), the number of doorways was reduced to three (Bairbars I, 1269; El-Nasir Mohammed, 1318–35; El-Mardani, 1340). The walls were now broken up into narrow panels containing the windows, which were usually quite small. – Particular attention was paid to the *entrances*, which usually consisted of a deep rectangular recess with stalactitic vaulting. The doorway at the inner end was surmounted by an architrave and a corbeled relieving arch. The door itself was frequently covered with bronze panels in intricate geometric designs. The sill sometimes consisted of a block of granite from some ancient Egyptian monument, often with hieroglyphs still showing.

The **court** *(sahn)* usually contained a *fountain (fisuya)*, under a timber canopy supported on columns. This was not, however, used for the ritual ablutions, which after the Turkish Conquest were performed in an adjoining court. The practice which then came into favor of having a small structure surrounded by taps *(hanafiya)* in the center of the court would in earlier times have been regarded as a desecration of the mosque.

In the **sanctuary** are –
(1) the *prayer-niche (mihrab*; not *qibla*, which means merely "the direction of Mecca");
(2) the *pulpit (minbar)*, often elaborately decorated;
(3) the *dikka*, a platform supported on columns on which the *muballighin*, the assistants of the imam who leads the prayers, repeat the genuflections, etc., so that they can be seen and imitated by the whole body of worshipers;
(4) the *lamps* and lanterns *(tannur*, a large chandelier) which hang from the ceiling. Most of the old bronze chandeliers and the enamel-decorated glass lamps from the mosques of Cairo are now in the Museum of Islamic Art.

The earliest mosques had no **minarets**, the call to prayer being given from the roof of the mosque. The first minaret of the Ibn Tulun Mosque appears to have been spiral in form, following the model of the Great Mosque in Samarra. In the 11th century we find a slender square shaft topped by a small domed kiosk (El-Giyushi, 1085). In the course of time the kiosk was steadily developed and elaborated; the roof was fluted, and the lower part increased in height to such an extent that the minaret finally came to have three storeys, the bottom one square, the middle one octagonal and the top one round (Sangar el-Gauli Mosque, 1303). This development is so clear, and took place so gradually, that the old theory which asserted that the minaret was derived from the Pharos, the ancient lighthouse of Alexandria, is no longer tenable. From about 1340 the predominant form was an octagonal shaft topped by a small domed kiosk (El-Mardani Mosque, 1340; Sheikhu Mosque, 1355).

The **mausoleums** of sultans and emirs were usually incorporated in the mosques or medreses they had founded. The actual burial chamber, under ground, was undecorated. The body was wrapped in white linen, with the head in the direction of Mecca. Over the burial vault was a chamber, almost invariably square, containing a cenotaph (*tarkiba* if of stone, *tibut* if of wood); and the transition from this square plan to the circular dome presented the architects with an interesting problem. The earliest Islamic domes in Egypt (El-Hakim Mosque, El-Giyushi Mosque) rest on spherical niches at the four corners of the square, which is thus converted into an octagon providing a convenient base for the dome. Later the single niche at each corner gave place to a more elaborate structure with a lower row of three niches surmounted by a fourth (Mausoleum of Gafari and Sayyida Atika, *c.* 1125). The next step was to fill the space on either side of the upper niche with two further niches, thus producing a pendentive with two rows of three niches each (Tomb of the Abbasid Caliphs, 1242–43). A further development is seen in the Mausoleum of Sultan El-Salih Ayyub (1250), which has a comparatively large dome. Here it seems to have been felt that a gradual transition was required, and a pendentive modelled on the form used in the Tomb of the Abbasid Caliphs was surmounted by a row of four niches. Then came a pendentive with four rows of niches (Mausoleum of Baibars el-Gashenkir, 1306–09), and later with five (Mausoleum of Emir Sarghatmish, 1356). This development must have taken place in Egypt, since the Syrian type was quite different. There the rows of niches did not form an arched shape but cut across the corners, being merely blind niches carved out of projecting courses of stone. Moreover in Egypt the number of niches in each row is usually more or less the same, while in Syria there is only one niche in the bottom row, two in the second, three in the third, and so on.

Coming now to secular buildings, the fortifications of Cairo have already been discussed and the particular importance of the Fatimid walls and gates has been noted. – A number of old **palaces** have been preserved, none of them earlier than the mid 14th century. The ground floor is built of good solid masonry and has a vaulted roof, while the ceilings on the upper floor are almost always of painted and gilded wood, as in the Palace of Emir Beshtak (1341). Projecting oriel windows were a characteristic feature.

Dwelling-houses had rarely more than two storeys. On the ground floor were the men's apartments, the salamlik, on the upper floor those of the women and children, the harim. The main decorative features on the façade were the beautiful mushrabiyas (lattice-enclosed balconies or oriels). Unfortunately almost all the houses of this type have disappeared since the end of the 19th century, so that the streets of Cairo have largely lost their old-world aspect.

In general the principal rooms of a house are on the north side (the direction of the prevailing wind), facing into the courtyard. On the street side there are only a few windows, high up on the wall. The entrance passage from the street into the court turns through a right angle in order to prevent passers-by from looking in. The entrance to the harim is in a second courtyard or on the far side of the first one. The reception rooms, servants' quarters, kitchen, etc., are located around the first courtyard.

The principal apartments, which are usually the only rooms with any decoration, are the mandara, the reception-room for male visitors, with the khazna (private apartment), the takhtabosh, a square recess one or two steps above the level of the court, and the maqad, on a kind of entresol. These rooms, together with a marble-paved courtyard, form the **salamlik**. – On the upper floor is the **kaa**, the family living-room, which is similar to the mandara. Occasionally the kaa is on the ground floor (e.g. the Hall of Osman Katkhuda in the Palace of Mohammed Muhibb el-Din, Sharia Beit el-Qadi). The kaa is a long narrow room consisting of three parts with ceilings of different heights and forms. The floor of the square central section, the durqaa, is one step below the liwans on either side. The liwans are sometimes of different widths; in that event the wider one is regarded as the place of honor. The durqaa usually has a wooden cupola or lantern with windows of colored glass known as kamariyas, set in plaster frames and decorated with vases of flowers, geometric patterns, etc. The floor of the durqaa is usually paved with marble, and there is often a fountain in the middle. On one side is the suffa, a marble shelf for coffee-cups, etc., supported by graceful arches. The walls of the liwans are faced with marble to a height of 6–10 ft/ 2–3 m, and above this there is sometimes a ledge for porcelain, metal vessels and vases of various kinds. The upper part of the walls usually has a plain plaster surface. The painted and gilded wooden ceilings of the liwans are borne on a deep concave cornice, also painted and gilded. Light and air are admitted by mushrabiyas on the lower part and kamariyas on the upper part of one of the end walls.

The **public baths** have usually a quite unpretentious exterior. The Baths of Emir Beshtak in Sharia Suq el-Silah in Cairo has a beautiful little doorway.

The **caravanserais** (wikala) are often very large buildings of several storeys built round a central courtyard. On the ground floor, facing on to the street, are shops, and above these are rooms for traveling merchants or permanent residents. A monumental gateway in the center of the façade leads into the courtyard, round which are store-rooms for the merchants' goods; and above these, too, are rooms, entered from the external galleries or balconies running round the courtyard. These buildings, a combination of warehouses and dwelling-houses, were frequently used as a form of investment. Wealthy citizens desiring to make a benefaction to a mosque or medrese would often build a caravanserai, the income from which was managed by curators. A foundation of this kind was known as a waqf.

The beauty of Islamic architecture in Egypt, with its magnificent 14th- and 15th-century façades, its innumerable graceful domes and minarets and its delicate ornament, tends to be over-shadowed by the overwhelming splendors of ancient Egypt; but the better Islamic art is known, the more strongly will its particular charm and fascination be felt.

Coptic Art and Architecture

The history of Christian art in Egypt can be divided into two parts with very different characteristics, the first extending from the early 4th century to the Arab Conquest (640–642), the second from the conquest to the early modern period.

During the first period Egypt was, culturally as well as politically, a province of the Byzantine Empire, and there is clear evidence of the close relationships between the Nile Valley and the capital and between Egypt and other provinces of the Empire, particularly Syria. During this period Alexandria had developed into one of the greatest cities in the Eastern Mediterranean, a flourishing center of cultural and commercial life, with a port which handled goods from all over the East and was the meeting-place of merchants from all over the known world. The upper classes of the population were Hellenized, and although the mass of the population clung to ancient traditions the art of the period shows the dominance of the educated class. This interaction between native and imported styles led to the emergence of a local art of considerable quality.

The earliest known monuments of Christian art are **tombs**, such as the catacombs of Alexandria (near Pompey's Pillar) and the mausoleums of the Kharga necropolis. The tombs in the cemetery of Oxyrhynchus (El-Bahnasa) show the small funerary basilica in its perfected form; and the Emperor Arcadius (345–408) built a large basilica with a transept over the Tomb of St Menas in the Lake Mareotis area which is the first securely datable example of Christian architecture in Egypt. About 430 a Byzantine Prince named Caesarius built the large basilica of the Deir el-Abyad Monastery, to which the Coptic saint Shenute belonged. The characteristic feature of this basilica is the chancel with its cruciform plan of three apses, a pattern

Dancing-girl (textile, 5th c A.D. Louvre, Paris)

imitated at Deir el-Akhmar and in the basilica adjoining the Temple of Dendera. These large **arcaded basilicas**, with their many decorated niches and their frescos, originally covering the whole surface of the walls, are the finest achievements of the first period of Christian architecture in Egypt.

The churches of the Monastery of St Jeremias at Saqqara and the Monastery of St Apollonius (Apa Apollo) at Bawit are smaller, and were built at a rather later date. They were rich in decorative sculpture, the best fragments of which are now in the Egyptian Museum in Cairo. This type of church shows closer affinity to the basilicas of Syria. The Church of Deir Abu Hennis is another important church of this period, but it was much altered and rebuilt during the medieval period.

At Armant in Upper Egypt the scholars who accompanied Napoleon's Egyptian Expedition found a large basilica with an apse at each end. This has now disappeared, but the Northern Basilica at Abu Mena and a ruined church at Mersa Matruh are of the same type.

The hermits who lived in the Egyptian desert in the early days frequently chose tombs of the Pharaonic period as a suitably remote dwelling-place and converted other tombs into churches by adding long niches to serve as apses; the most interesting examples of such conversions can be seen in a number of tombs at Beni Hasan, Meir and El-Sheikh Said, in the Tomb of Penehse at Tell el-Amarna and in the tombs at Sheikh Abd el-Qurna (Nos 84, 95 and 97) in western Thebes. Several of these tombs have very interesting Christian inscriptions and frescos. Around the hermitages there gradually came into being numbers of small monasteries which used the rock tombs as churches. In the space in front of the entrance were cells, store-rooms and a tower to provide a place of refuge in case of danger. One of the best examples of an arrangement of this kind is the Monastery of the Epiphany at Sheikh Abd el-Qurna.

When the tombs of the Pharaonic period were no longer sufficient to meet the needs of the Christians they turned to the old temples and converted their vestibules into churches, as at Dendera, Edfu, Esna, Philae and elsewhere; almost all such Christian additions have been removed by the excavators of the temples in modern times. Elsewhere one of the inner chambers of a temple was converted to Christian use, as at Karnak, where the church occupied the whole of Tuthmosis III's large Festival Temple, and where the remains of frescos depicting Coptic saints can still be seen on the columns. A third possibility was to install the church in a temple court, as happened in the second court of the temple at Medinet Habu (remains of church demolished in the 1920s). – In Upper Egypt the Christians rarely destroyed the old temples. The reliefs were sometimes damaged, but for the most part merely covered with a thick coat of plaster, which preserved them in excellent condition into recent times.

The Christian buildings erected in the early period were constructed with great care. The walls were of accurately dressed stone (mainly limestone), the roofs were of timber and the apses had vaulted semi-domes. The finely worked columns of Aswan granite bore **reliefs** with crosses and other symbols, and sometimes also inscriptions by the founders. They were richly decorated with carved ornament – foliage, flowers and interlace patterns, and frequently also geometric designs. The sculptors of Middle Egypt, whose main center is believed to have been at Ahnas (Ahnasiya el-Medina), the ancient Heracleopolis, produced large compositions featuring human figures in a high relief of a depth and structure which achieved an almost Baroque interplay of light and shadow. Although the basic architectural elements – capitals, architraves, pilasters – came from Syria or Byzantium, the decoration was entirely individual, with a rich repertoire of forms

Relief with Christian symbols

Fresco, St Antony's Monastery

and motifs such as was attained by no other architecture in the Christian East.

Christian art in Egypt was fundamentally and almost exclusively decorative; and the walls, column shafts and capitals of the buildings were covered with **paintings** and **frescos**. Unfortunately only a small proportion of this work has survived, but even the fragments that remain are sufficient to throw light on the history of the period. Like the Alexandrian art from which it stemmed, this is a highly realistic art. The "Fayyum portraits" now in the Egyptian Museum in Cairo are magnificent examples of a tradition which was taken over into Christian art and found expression in the frescos from Saqqara and Bawit (also in the Egyptian Museum). With the Alexandrian tradition, however, there now mingled much more marked Oriental influences.

Greek traditions maintained their influence in decorative art. Along the base of the walls of churches were paintings

Panel-painting in Abu Sarga Church, Old Cairo

imitating marble inlays and friezes of circles and rhombs containing flowers, fruit, baskets, birds, portraits, genre scenes and symbolic figures. Higher up are broad friezes with figures of prophets and saints, monks, angels and the Virgin. In the conch of the apses Christ is frequently depicted in a chariot with the beasts of the Apocalypse. The same style is found in the famous miniatures of the "Christian Topography" (composed by Cosmas Indicopleustes of Alexandria about 547–549), which mingle the picturesqueness beloved of the Alexandrians with a monumentality more in line with the aesthetic sensibilities of Asia.

The conquest of Egypt by the **Arabs** had a major effect on the further development of Christian art. The fact that Christianity was no longer the State religion – though there was little persecution of Christians in Egypt – entailed the increasing impoverishment of the Church, so that large building projects were no longer possible. A further consequence of Arab rule was the victory of the Monophysites, who tended to be more nationalist and more attached to local traditions, over the Catholics, more closely identified with classical Greek culture. The influence of Asiatic Monophysitism, still predominant in Syria and Mesopotamia, was also strongly felt in Egyptian Christianity. Thus the link with the Greek World gave place to a still stronger leaning towards the culture of western Asia. Building techniques also changed: where previously freestone had been used, kiln-fired or sun-dried bricks were now employed even for load-bearing walls, and the shortage of timber for roofing led to the use of stone vaulting. All this brought with it changes in the ground-plan of churches, and the basilican plan was practically abandoned except in Old Cairo.

The most notable Christian buildings in northern Egypt are the **monasteries** in the *Wadi Natrun*. Of particular interest is the Deir el-Suryan (Monastery of the Syrians), which was rebuilt in the early 9th century. Its large church is an aisled basilica with a barrel-vaulted roof; the choir has the form of a transept, and the sanctuary consists of three square sections. The fine Mesopotamian-style stucco-work in the central section, probably done in the time of Abbot Moses of Nisibis (10th century), shows strong

Coptic monk

affinities with stucco ornament in the Third Style at Samarra (Mesopotamia). There are also two notable wooden doors with ivory inlays (913–914 and 926–927). The little Church of St Mary in the same monastery is modelled on the churches at Tur Abdin (25 miles/40 km north-east of Nisibis). The monasteries of Deir Amba Bshoi and Deir Abu Makar are older than Deir el-Suryan; Deir Amba Baramus was almost completely rebuilt in the 14th century. – Some 30 miles/50 km north-west of the Wadi Natrun is the Kelya area (from Latin *cella,* "cell"), which was discovered in 1964 during the construction of irrigation works and partly excavated. In the ruins of a 7th-century monastery some remarkable frescos have been preserved. There were at one time something like 700 hermitages in this area.

Mesopotamian influence is still more evident in another group of buildings in Upper Egypt. The church of St Simeon's Monastery at Aswan had one aisle roofed with two domes borne on cross ribs and others with barrel vaults – two features which are undoubtedly of Asiatic origin. The ground-plan of the church points in the same direction: there is a comparable building at Amida (now Diyarbakir) in

south-eastern Anatolia. The church of St Simeon's is the best-preserved example of the type in Egypt; the Monastery of Deir el-Shuhada at Esna has a church on similar lines.

The monasteries between Naqada and Qamula are also of interest. They are not by any means all of the same period: even within a particular monastery there are buildings of different periods. The finest are the churches of El-Adra and Mari Girgis in Deir el-Magma; the latter has a system of parallel vaulting on transverse arches which points to a model in Sassanid Persia.

During the 12th century a new type of church developed in Egypt and soon spread throughout the whole country, remaining in favor until the latter part of this period. Rectangular in plan, the church consisted of a series of square areas bounded by columns or pillars and roofed by domes. The number of domes might be very large: thus the Church of Amba Pakhom (St Pachomius) at Medamut had 29. A notable example of this type of church is the one in the Deir el-Maharraq, where, according to the Coptic legend, the Holy Family halted on their flight into Egypt.

The churches of *Old Cairo* stem from a different architectural tradition. They are

Virgin and Child (wood-carving)

medieval rebuildings of churches of the pre-Arab period, from which they inherited their general layout as well as various structural elements, such as the columns, with their bases and capitals, and the timber roof. The wood-carving shows the Western influence which reached Egypt as a result of the Crusades, and also through trading contacts with the Italian maritime republics.

In this second period the arts suffered a total decline. Sculpture in stone disappeared almost entirely after the 8th century; a few stone slabs with crude interlace designs and clumsily carved capitals dating from subsequent centuries have been found, but in the 11th century the art of stone-cutting died out altogether.

There are some examples of the painting of this second period in the monasteries of Deir el-Suryan and Deir Abu Makar in the Wadi Natrun, the White Monastery at Sohag and St Simeon's Monastery at Aswan; but though these frescos are interesting from the iconographical point of view they show strong foreign influences, particularly from Armenia. Decorative techniques are found only in wood-carving and intarsia work. The iconostasis of the Church of Abu Sarga in Old Cairo has six 11th-century carved panels, which rank with those from the Church of El-Moallaqa (now in the British Museum) as the finest of their kind. The Coptic craftsmen also produced fine carving in geometric and polygonal designs showing clear Arab influence.

In the 14th century Coptic art as a distinctive and independent form disappeared; thereafter the work of Coptic craftsmen had nothing to distinguish it from Arab and Islamic art.

Glossary of Technical Terms

Abacus:
The flat top of the capital of a column.

Aha:
Horus name of the second King of the 1st Dynasty, perhaps the legendary Menes.

Akh:
Part of a man's personality.

Akhet:
Time of the Nile inundation; the first season of the ancient Egyptian year.

Amenti:
The realm of the dead; in contrast to Duat (q.v.), the western part of the Underworld.

Amulet:
An object thought to protect its owner from evil or bring him good fortune and success. The most popular types of amulet in ancient Egypt were the scarab, the ankh sign, the winged sun and the lotus (qq.v.).

Ankh:
The hieroglyphic sign for "life", taken as a symbol for life beyond the tomb. It originally represented a sandal-strap. As an amulet, made in a wide variety of materials, it was thought to bring its bearer good fortune and a long life.

Ankham:
A bunch of flowers laid in a coffin to convey vital force to the dead man.

Apophis:
A snake-like demon, the adversary of Re and of the dead on their common journey into the Beyond.

Canopic chest (Luxor Museum)

Architrave:
A stone slab resting on columns or a wall and supporting the superstructure or roof structure.

Atef:
See *Crowns*.

Ba:
A spiritual entity associated with man, his "soul".

Barque, sacred:
The boat in which the statue of a deity traveled.

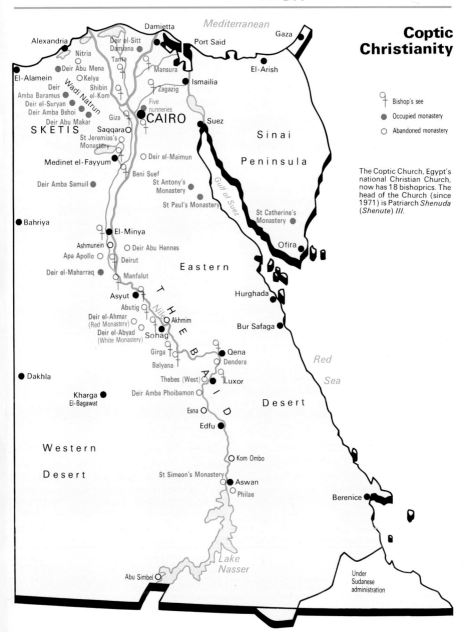

Coptic Christianity

Mediterranean
Damietta
Alexandria   Deir el-Sitt   Gaza
Damjana   Port Said
Nitria   Tanta
Deir Abu Mena   Mansura
El-Alamein   Kelya   El-Arish
Deir   Shibin   Ismailia
Amba Baramus   el-Kom   Zagazig
Deir el-Suryan
Deir Amba Bshoi   Giza   Five
Deir Abu Makar   nunneries   CAIRO
SKETIS   Saqqara   Suez
St Jeremias's
Monastery   Sinai
Medinet el-Fayyum   Deir el-Maimun   Peninsula
Deir Amba Samuel   Beni Suef
St Antony's
Monastery
St Paul's Monastery   St Catherine's
Monastery
Bahriya   El-Minya   Ofira
Ashmunein   Deir Abu Hennes
Apa Apollo   Deirut   Eastern
Deir el-Maharraq   Manfalut
Asyut   Hurghada
Abutig   Nile
Deir el-Ahmar   Akhmim   Bur Safaga
(Red Monastery)
Deir el-Abyad   Sohag
(White Monastery)   Red
Girga   Qena
Balyana   Dendera   Sea
Dakhla   Thebes (West)   Luxor
Kharga   Deir Amba Phoibamon   Desert
El-Bagawat   Esna
Edfu
Western   Kom Ombo
St Simeon's Monastery
Desert   Aswan   Berenice
Philae
THEBAID

Under
Sudanese
administration

Lake
Nasser
Abu Simbel

✝ Bishop's see
● Occupied monastery
○ Abandoned monastery

The Coptic Church, Egypt's national Christian Church, now has 18 bishoprics. The head of the Church (since 1971) is Patriarch *Shenuda* (*Shenute*) *III*.

Birth-house:
See *Mammisi*.

Blemmeyes:
A nomadic people which ranged over the southern part of the Arabian Desert in antiquity and made repeated incursions into Upper Egypt and Nubia.

"Book of the Dead":
A collection of religious and magical texts, largely derived from the older "Pyramid Texts" and "Coffin Texts". Under the New Kingdom it became the practice to deposit in tombs a selection of such texts written on papyrus.

Canopic jars:
Vessels containing the entrails of a dead man which were buried with him. They were thought to be under the protection of the four sons of Horus, represented on the lids of the jars as a man, a baboon, a dog and a falcon. The four jars might be contained in a canopic chest or shrine.

Capital:
The top of a column, usually richly ornamented, supporting the architrave. See under *Art and architecture*.

Cartouche:
An oval ring containing the name and titles of a king; originally derived from the representation of the solar disc above the horizon. For examples see under *History*.

Cataract:
The name given to the various rapids on the Nile between Khartoum (Sudan) and Aswan. Of the seven cataracts (First–Sixth and Dai Cataract) six served at different periods of Egyptian history to mark the country's southern frontier.

Cavetto cornice:
A concave moulding along the tops of walls, doorways, stelae, etc., often with relief decoration. Below it ran a torus moulding (q.v.).

Cenotaph:
An empty or simulated tomb as a place of worship or memorial.

Colonnade:
A row or rows of columns supporting a flat roof.

Column:
See chapter on *Art and architecture*.

Conch:
The semi-dome of an apse (from the Greek word for a shell).

Copts (from Greek *aiguptos,* via Arabic *qubt*):
Christian descendants of the ancient Egyptians. They now constitute about 10% of the population of Egypt, mostly belonging to the middle classes (craftsmen, shopkeepers, doctors, teachers, etc.).

Crowns:
The crowns and head-dresses worn by kings and deities in ancient Egypt derive from three main types, the **Red Crown** of Lower Egypt, the **White Crown** of Upper Egypt and the **Double Feather Crown** of the gods Amun and Min.
By the combination, alteration and elaboration of these three basic types there came into being in the course of time an extraordinary range of different crowns, the significance and symbolic value of which cannot always be satisfactorily determined. The combination of the red and white crowns produced the double crown *(pschent)* worn by the rulers of the united kingdom. The *atef* crown worn by Osiris was a combination of the red crown and the double feather crown. The *blue crown* which first appeared under the 18th Dynasty, wrongly called the "war helmet of the Pharaohs", can be seen as a modification of the double crown. The *hemhemet* is a triple *atef* crown on rams' horns with royal cobras and the solar disc.

Crypt:
An underground chamber.

Demotic (Greek "popular"):
A script developed out of hieratic (q.v.) which came into use in Lower Egypt in the 7th century B.C. and became the everyday script of the whole of Egypt in the Late and Graeco-Roman periods. It disappeared about the middle of the 5th century A.D. See the chapter on *Hieroglyphics*.

Det:
See Duat.

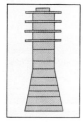

Djed:
A fetish in pillar form, the origin of which is unknown; an attribute of Osiris. Worn as an amulet, it brought stability and durability.

Duat (Det):
The Underworld, into which the sun sank in the evening and through which it traveled during the night.

Dynasty:
A family or succession of rulers. According to Manetho Egypt was ruled by 31 dynasties before Alexander the Great, normally reigning in succession to each other but occasionally concurrently.

Electrum:
An alloy of gold and silver (85% gold, 15% silver) used to gild the tips of obelisks.

Ennead (Egyptian *pesedjet,* "community of the nine")
A group of nine deities (three sub-groups of three) representing the primal forces of the universe. The best-known such group was the great Heliopolitan ennead, which was headed by the creator god *Atum* and included his son and daughter *Shu* (air) and *Tefnut* (dew), his grandson and granddaughter *Geb* (earth) and *Nut* (sky), and their children, *Isis* and *Osiris* and *Nephthys* and *Seth.* Where more than nine gods were to be venerated together a lesser ennead might be added, or the number in the group might simply be increased, though it was still referred to as an ennead.

Gods:
See the section on the *Egyptian pantheon.*

Headcloth:
See *Nemes.*

Heb-sed (Sed festival):
The king's jubilee after reigning for thirty years (thereafter celebrated every three years).

Hemhemet:
See *Crowns.*

Hieratic (from Greek *hieros,* "sacred"):
A script used throughout ancient Egyptian history but reserved in the Late Period for religious texts. See the chapter on *Hieroglyphics.*

Hieroglyphs:
See the chapter on *Hieroglyphics.*

High Priest:
The head of the local priesthood.

Hittites:
An Indo-European people settled in eastern Asia Minor (Cappadocia) from the 2nd millennium B.C.

Horbehuted:
The sun goddess, represented in the form of a winged sun, who accompanied the god Re on his journey over the sky. The winged sun was depicted on pylons and above temple doorways to protect them from collapse.

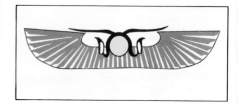

Horus name:
The first name in the king's titulature, designating him as the legitimate successor to Horus (see the section on the *Egyptian pantheon*).

Hydraeum (hydreuma):
A fortified watering-point in the desert.

Hyksos ("Princes of the Foreign Lands"):
A people of mixed Hurrian and Semitic origin who moved into Egypt from the north-east and ruled the country from 1650 to 1551 B.C. See the chapter on *History.*

Hypostyle hall:
A columned hall.

Ichneumon ("Pharaoh's rat"; *Herpestes ich-neumon*):
A small predator much esteemed as a killer of snakes and accorded divine veneration. In the Late Period large numbers of ichneumons were mummified and buried in special tombs.

Isis knot:
A sign resembling the ankh (q.v.) but with the transverse arms folded downwards.

Ithyphallic:
With erect phallus, as a symbol of fertility.

Jubilee:
The anniversary of a king's accession.

Ka:
The immortal element in man, the vital force inherent in him, which always accompanies and protects him. In the Beyond the dead man is united with his ka. Represented as an effigy or statue of the living man with his arms raised above his head, designated by the hieroglyph *ka*.

Khamsin:
A hot desert wind, blowing mainly in spring.

Kiosk:
A small open temple in which the statue of a god was set up during his festival.

Lotus:
The emblem of Pharaonic Egypt. Worn as an amulet, it was believed to give eternal youth.

Mamelukes (Arabic *mamluk*, "slave"):
Originally Turkish or Circassian slaves, who rose to become rulers of Egypt. See the chapter on *History*.

Mammisi:
The "birth-house": a term first applied by Champollion (see chapter on *Hieroglyphics*) to a small subsidiary building associated with temples of the Late Period in which the annual rebirth of the local god or the son of the local goddess was celebrated.

Mastaba (Arabic "bench"):
A private tomb of the Early Dynastic Period or Old Kingdom; a square or rectangular structure of brick or stone with slightly sloping walls and a flat roof. By the addition of further stages the mastaba developed into the step pyramid and eventually into the true pyramid.

Medrese (medersa, madrasa):
A Koranic school or Islamic theological college with the status of a university. The first medrese was founded in Baghdad in 1067. See the chapter on *Islamic architecture*.

Menat:
An attribute of Hathor; a necklace held in place by a richly ornamented counterpoise to the rear.

Mihrab:
The prayer-niche in a mosque, always on the side facing in the direction of Mecca.

Minaret (Arabic "lighthouse"):
The tower attached to a mosque from which the muezzin gives the call to prayer.

Mosque:
An Islamic place of worship. See the chapter *Islamic architecture*.

Mummy:
A body protected from decay by embalming. Herodotus gives a detailed account of the process. The brain was first extracted with the aid of a hook inserted through the nostrils, and the entrails were removed through an incision in the side and preserved in canopic jars (q.v.). The resultant cavities were then filled with natron and a variety of spices, and the body was stitched up again and immersed for 70 days in a natron bath. Now thoroughly dehydrated, it was washed in Nile water and wrapped in fine linen bandages soaked in perfumes and oils.

There were different methods of embalming, in varying degrees of thoroughness, the method selected depending on the financial resources available. This explains why royal mummies are usually better preserved than those of ordinary people.

Naos:
A small chapel or shrine for the statue of a deity.

Narthex:
A porch or vestibule leading into a church or temple.

Necropolis:
Literally, a "city of the dead". A place of burial used over a long period, usually consisting of a number of separate cemeteries.

Nemes:
The headcloth worn by a king, falling down over his shoulders and breast on both sides. The style of the royal headcloth is an important aid to the dating of statues.

Nilometer:
A device for measuring the water-level of the Nile. It consisted of a deep shaft with steps running down inside and a scale of heights marked on the wall. Communicating with the Nile by an underground channel, it filled up with water during the annual inundation, enabling the height to be measured.

Nome (Greek *nomos*; Egyptian *sepat*):
An administrative unit in ancient Egypt. The nomes developed out of the independent principalities of the Pre-Dynastic and Early Dynastic Periods, their number and size varying in the course of history. When there was a strong central power their importance was reduced, but in times of domestic dissension and weakness they grew in power and independence.

Obelisk (Greek "spit"):
A monolithic four-sided pillar, usually of pink Aswan granite, tapering towards the top and ending in a gilded apex (pyramidion); covered on all sides with hieroglyphs.
The earliest obelisks (5th and 6th Dynasties) were the central feature of the great sun-temples, the gleaming tip of the obelisk being the first resting-place of the rising sun. In later times obelisks were set up, usually in pairs, at the entrances to temples (Luxor, Karnak) to

Obelisk, Karnak

commemorate great events like victories and jubilees. During the Roman period and in the 19th century a number of obelisks were carried off to Europe (Rome, London, Paris, Munich) and to New York.

Opening of the mouth:
A ritual ceremony, performed mostly on mummies but also on statues, designed to ensure that the dead man had the use of his mouth in the Afterworld for eating, drinking and breathing.

Ostrakon:
A potsherd or small limestone tablet used as cheap writing material instead of the expensive papyrus. Large numbers of ostraka from all periods of Egyptian history have been found.

Papyrus:
A paper-like material made from the pith of the papyrus plant *(Cyperus papyrus)* by pressing it together in layers. Sheets or volumes of this material are known as papyri. It was used as a writing material in Egypt from the 3rd millennium B.C.

Papyrus staff:
The scepter of a goddess.

Pendentive:
Spherical triangle formed by intersection of dome with two adjacent arches springing from supporting columns.

Peristyle:
An open court surrounded by colonnades.

Persea:
A sacred tree of ancient Egypt *(Mimusops schimperi)*, in medieval literature identified with the lebbek tree.

Pesedjet:
See *Ennead.*

Pharaoh's rat:
See *Ichneumon.*

Pilaster:
A pillar engaged in a wall, either to strengthen the wall, articulate the interior of a building or support the roof or vaulting.

Pillar:
See the chapter on *Art and architecture.*

Portico:
The covered entrance or vestibule of a building, with its roof supported on columns and a solid rear wall.

Pronaos:
A chamber preceding the sanctuary of a temple, sometimes with columns.

Step Pyramid, Saqqara

Propylon:
A gateway set in front of a pylon.

Proto-Doric column:
A 16-sided fluted pillar on a round base, much used in Egyptian architecture. See the chapter on *Art and architecture.*

Pschent:
See *Crowns.*

Punt:
A country in East Africa, on the Somali coast, to which, from the 3rd millennium B.C., the Egyptians sent expeditions in quest of incense, resins and fine woods.

Pylon (Greek "gate"):
The monumental entrance and façade of an ancient Egyptian temple, flanked by two towers with grooves for flagstaffs. The front walls are slightly inclined, with a cavetto cornice (q.v.) along the top and torus mouldings (q.v.) down the sides. Large temples have several pylons, one behind the other. See the chapter on *Art and architecture.*

Pyramid:
A structure on a square base with four triangular sides sloping up to an apex, used for royal burials from the 3rd to the 17th Dynasty and by the Kushites (25th Dynasty). The origin of the pyramids is probably to be seen in the burial mounds of the Pre-Dynastic Period, which developed into mastabas in the Early Dynastic Period. By the addition of further stages the mastaba in turn developed into the **Step Pyramid** of Djoser (though this is not, properly speaking, a pyramid, since it still has the rectangular ground-plan of a mastaba).

The filling in of the steps of a step pyramid produced the **true pyramid**, with straight sides, which came into use in the 4th Dynasty. The major structural

Pyramid of Mycerinus and small women's pyramids, Giza

problems involved are impressively demonstrated by the Pyramid of Meidum, which collapsed under the weight of its casing, and the **Bent Pyramid** of Dahshur, in which the angle of inclination was reduced half-way up in order to lessen the weight of masonry.

The high point of pyramid-construction was reached with the three massive pyramids of Cheops, Chephren and Mycerinus at Giza, all dating from the 4th Dynasty. They are all built of sandstone blocks, originally enclosed within a casing of fine-grained Tura limestone. Later pyramids were mostly built of less durable materials and are now badly ruined or totally destroyed.

All the pyramids lay high above the Nile Valley on the edge of the desert. From the *valley temple* on the margin of the plain a *causeway* (originally open, later covered) ran straight up to the *mortuary temple* on the east side of the pyramid. Almost all the pyramids had their entrance on the north side. Until the early 4th Dynasty the *tomb chamber* was hewn from the native rock under the base of the pyramid; later it was constructed within the pyramid itself. The passages leading to the tomb chamber were barred by heavy stone portcullises and the entrance was built up. Adjoining the main pyramid were smaller *subsidiary pyramids* for female members of the royal family.

Pyramidion:

The pyramid-shaped apex of an obelisk, which was gilded with electrum (an alloy of gold and silver). The term is also applied to the apex of a pyramid, which was usually of a particularly hard stone (granite).

Qibla:

The direction in which Muslims face when praying (towards Mecca; originally towards Jerusalem).

Relief:

A work of sculpture in which the forms stand out from a flat or curved surface, with little depth. During the Old and Middle Kingdoms the favored technique was **bas-relief** or **low relief**, in which the carving might be confined to the chiseling-out of the outlines or the figures might be modeled as well. A peculiar form of low relief sometimes used was **sunk relief** (technically called *coelanaglyphic* relief), in which the surface of the stone is left as the background and the figures are incised.

Saff tomb (Arabic "row"):

A private tomb of the early 11th Dynasty preceded by a rock-cut colonnade.

Sanctuary:

The inmost shrine; in an Egyptian temple the chamber in which the god's sacred barque was kept.

Scarab:

The sacred dung-beetle *(Scarabaeus sacer)*, an anthracite-colored species of beetle common in Egypt which was seen by the ancient Egyptians as a symbol of the rising sun. A stone or pottery scarab worn as an amulet was believed to bring good fortune and a long life. A scarab with the 30th chapter of the "Book of the Dead" inscribed on its underside was placed on a mummy in the position of the heart.

Sebbakh:

The rubble from ancient sites, used as a fertilizer. Brickwork made from Nile mud yielded very fertile soil when it disintegrated.

The Sphinx of Giza

Sed festival:
See *Heb-sed.*

Sepat:
See *Nome.*

Serdab:
A walled up chamber in a tomb for the dead man's statue.

Shabti (ushabti):
Small mummiform figures placed in the tomb to act as servants to the dead man in the life beyond.

Sistrum:
A form of rattle sacred to Hathor. It had a handle with a Hathor head and a metal hoop on which were a number of metal loops.

Speos:
A cave or cave shrine.

Sphinx:
A hybrid creature with the body of a lion and the head of a king (more rarely a queen).

Talatat:
Originally a unit of measurement in Islamic architecture, the term was also applied to stones from ancient Egyptian buildings with painted or relief decoration.

Torus:
A concave moulding used on the sides of pylons, stelae, etc.

Triad:
A group of three deities (father, mother and son). The most celebrated were the Theban triad (Amun, Mut and Khons), the Memphite triad (Ptah, Sakhmet and Nefertum) and the Edfu triad (Horus, Hathor and Harsomtus). See the section on the *Egyptian pantheon.*

Udjat:
The sacred Eye of Horus. Worn as an amulet on the wrist or arm, it was believed to ward off evil, in particular snakebite, illness or a curse.

Uraeus:
The golden cobra, the sacred animal of Uto, which the

king wore on his forehead; venerated as the fiery eye of Re.

Ushabti:
See *Shabti*.

Winged sun:
See *Horbehuted*.

Economy

The main pillar of the Egyptian economy since ancient times has been **agriculture**, in particular **arable farming**. Almost half the employed population are engaged in this sector, accounting for something under a third of the national income. The main agricultural areas are the fertile Valley of the Nile, the great expanse of the Delta, the large Oasis of Fayyum and several smaller oases, some of which are being extended and linked up by irrigation schemes under the "New Valley" project.

From time immemorial the alluvial soil of the Nile Valley and the Delta, annually renewed by the inundation of the Nile, yielded one and sometimes two abundant crops. The narrow range of temperature variation over the year – a factor which influenced the choice of crops to be grown – made cultivation possible all year round had it not been for the inundation, which interrupted work in the fields for some months each year. In modern times, however, the successive steps taken to regulate the flow of the river – the Nile Dam, to the north of Cairo, built by Mohammed Ali in the first half of the 19th century, the dams constructed at Aswan, Asyut, Nag Hammadi and Esna about the turn of the century and finally the Aswan High Dam (el-Sadd el-Ali) completed in 1970 – have freed the peasants of Egypt from their dependence on the annual flood and made it possible to provide regular irrigation throughout the year.

The loss of the great quantities of fertile Nile mud which now remain in the artificial lakes above the dams, however, has made it necessary to supply the land lower down the valley with other types of fertilizer. In the past the peasants found a ready supply of fertile soil *(sebbakh)* in the mounds of rubble marking ancient sites, with their crumbling brickwork of Nile mud; but most of these mounds have

now been destroyed, and the Government is concerned, in the interests of archaeology, to preserve what still remains. Regular crop rotation, with periods of fallow, can compensate only to a limited extent for the loss of the rich Nile mud, and it is now necessary, therefore, to use artificial fertilizers to improve the soil and increase yields. The need is being met to an increasing extent from Egypt's large deposits of phosphates on the Red Sea coast and in the Dakhla and Kharga oases; but considerable quantities of artificial fertilizers still have to be imported. Government agencies are now trying out methods of dredging up Nile mud from the reservoirs and making it available for fertilizing the cultivated land.

Throughout Egyptian history **irrigation** has been vital to the cultivation of the land, and much effort was devoted from an early period to making the best use of the water-supply. Embankments were built dividing the land into basins, to which water was conducted by canals. This prevented the water from draining away too rapidly and ensured that the soil was thoroughly soaked and that the salt which threatened the fertility of the land was leached out. Various devices, still in use today in many places, were employed for raising water and feeding it into the canals. The *saqiya* is a large water-wheel (usually overshot, that is, turned by water flowing above it, but in the Fayyum

Sakiya

Tanbur (Archimedean screw)

sometimes undershot) up to 30 ft/9 m in diameter, worked by oxen, buffalo and sometimes camels and fitted with scoops or buckets *(qadus)* of wood or pottery. The *shaduf* draws water in a bucket attached to a long swiveling pole with a counterweight at the other end; a number of shadufs arranged in series can raise water through a considerable height. The *tanbur* is an Archimedean screw. These traditional methods, however, have now largely been superseded by modern pumping stations.

On small peasant holdings without modern agricultural machinery the same farming techniques and implements are used as are represented in ancient Egyptian reliefs. The plow is still of the same form as 5000 years ago. It has a shaft some 6½ ft/2 m long, to one end of which the draft animal (almost invariably an ox) is harnessed; at the lower end is a curved piece of wood shod with a triple-bladed share. A plow of this type cuts only a very shallow furrow. – Instead of a harrow a roller with iron spikes is used. Other implements employed for tilling the soil and for earth-moving are the hoe and shovel. – The corn is cut with a sickle or merely pulled out of the ground. Threshing is done with a sledge running on rollers fitted with sharp semicircular iron discs, which is drawn over the grain by oxen turning in a circle until the ears and stems are broken up. The grain is then separated from the chaff by winnowing with a large screen.

Two or even three crops are now taken off the land every year. The area under cultivation is some 7,400,000 acres, of which more than 6,900,000 acres are arable land, 346,000 acres are under permanent cultivation (pasture, fruit trees) and only 4950 acres are occupied by woodland. More than 90% of all agricultural holdings are smaller than 5 feddans (a feddan is roughly equal to an acre), and only 0·5% of all holdings are larger than 50 feddans. All these larger farms, as well as smaller holdings which have combined to form co-operatives, are equipped with modern agricultural machinery and use modern methods of cultivation.

The most important agricultural product is **cotton**, introduced into Egypt only in 1821. It is long-fibered cotton *(mako)* of excellent quality, and is for the most part processed within Egypt. More than 1,100,000 tons of raw cotton are harvested every year from an area of more than 1,500,000 acres; and cotton is the

Shaduf

country's principal export, accounting for almost two-fifths of total exports. Other crops grown include maize (3,200,000 tons), rice (2,300,000 tons), wheat (2,000,000 tons), sugar-cane (9,200,000 tons), millet (660,000 tons), barley (130,000 tons), groundnuts (25,000 tons), clover (for fodder), pulses, vegetables, onions and garlic. The Siwa and Bahriya oases produce mainly dates, citrus and tropical fruits, wine and olives. – The State-owned wine-producing estate at Abu Hummus, on the northwestern fringe of the Delta, has an annual output of some 3,300,000 gallons of *wine* from 17,300 acres of vineyards. Since Islam prohibits the consumption of alcohol, the domestic market is confined to Copts and visitors; attempts to establish an export trade have so far met with little success. A considerable proportion of the grape crop is used to produce brandy in Alexandria for export; the rest comes on to the market in the form of table grapes or raisins.

Compared with arable farming **stock-rearing** is of secondary importance. The numbers of cattle and goats are increasing, but the ancient Egyptian occupation of sheep-rearing is in decline. There are only small numbers of pigs, kept by the Christian members of the population, since to the Muslim the pig is impure. Cattle, buffalo and poultry are mainly kept by the settled fellahin, sheep and goats by the nomadic bedouin, who are able in the course of their journeying over the great expanses of steppe and semi-desert country to take advantage of seasonally available pasture. Donkeys, mules and camels are still used as beasts of burden. The rearing of poultry (chickens, ducks, pigeons, etc.) makes an important contribution to the country's meat-supply.

Egyptian agriculture is not able, however, to supply all the food required for the rapidly growing population. Although encouraging increases in agricultural yields have been achieved it is still necessary to import substantial quantities of foodstuffs.

The considerable resources of fish in Egypt's inland waters and off its coasts have not been sufficiently exploited. As a result of the difficulty of keeping fish in the hot Egyptian climate and the limited canning and preserving facilities available, the country's **fisheries** have not yet made their full contribution to the economy. The richest fishing-grounds are in the lakes and waterways of the Delta, and in recent years also in Lake Nasser, which is being artificially stocked. The numbers of fish in the Nile has fallen as a result of the reduced food-supply due to the absence of the annual inundation. Measures to develop Egyptian fisheries are planned. – *Sponge-fishing* has been practiced on Egypt's Mediterranean coasts since antiquity.

Egypt possesses a variety of **minerals**, which promote the development of **industry**. There are significant deposits of iron ore (annual output 1,100,000 tons) around Aswan and in the Bahriya Oasis, manganese in the Sinai Peninsula, chromium and tin around Mersa Alam and Bur Safaga on the Red Sea coast. Phosphates and gypsum are worked on a considerable scale (500,000 tons and 260,000 tons annually) along the Red Sea coast (between Quseir and Hurghada and around Mersa Alam), in southern Sinai (at El-Tor), in the Dakhla and Kharga oases and in the Esna area. In addition there are workable deposits of asbestos, titanium, sulphur and coal (Sinai) still awaiting exploitation. – Salt is extracted from the salt-pans in the Delta lakes.

The problem of **energy supply** is not one that ought to trouble Egypt. There are large *oilfields* in western Sinai (at Abu Rudeis), around Hurghada and to the south of El-Alamein in the Western Desert, and it is hoped to find more in the Qattara Depression. Natural gas is being worked to the south of the El-Alamein oilfields and in the Delta, near the Mediterranean coast. There are oil-refineries near Alexandria, at Tanta and Helwan, and at Port Said and Suez on the Suez Canal. The oilfields are linked by pipeline with Cairo and with the Mediterranean ports of Alexandria and El-Alamein. With an annual output of almost 30 million tons of crude oil, Egypt can not only meet its own steadily growing needs but can also earn valuable foreign currency by its increasing export of oil, its situation on the Mediterranean giving it a considerable advantage over other oil-exporting countries.

In spite of its large reserves of oil, however, Egypt still suffers from a shortage of energy, due mainly to its inadequate number of power-stations and poor distribution system. The cities of Lower Egypt obtain their electric power from thermal power-stations, while Upper Egypt is supplied with power by the hydroelectric station at the Aswan High Dam, which came into operation in 1968. Rural areas and oases which are not yet served by the national grid must rely for power on diesel generators. – In order to meet the increasing demand for power Egypt plans, with the co-operation of Western industrial States, to construct 15 nuclear power-stations by the year 2000, and agreements for this purpose have been reached with France, the United States and West Germany.

The Sphinx and the Pyramid of Cheops floodlit

The processing industries are concentrated in the main centers of population. The most important by a considerable margin is the **textile industry**, particularly cotton spinning and weaving, which accounts for 16% of the country's total exports. Other rapidly expanding industries are foodstuffs (sugar-refineries, canning factories, grain- and oil-mills), the tobacco industry, aromatics, chemicals (fertilizers), pharmaceuticals, and iron and steel (steelworks at Helwan). Foreign automobile firms are increasingly establishing assembly plants in Egypt (Volkswagen at Alexandria, Daimler-Benz utility vehicles near Cairo). The building and building materials industries are flourishing, thanks to massive State encouragement (dams, industrial plants, housing).

Egypt has a relatively well-developed **transport** system. Some 2735 miles/ 4400 km of railway lines and 16,450 miles/26,500 km of roads (including 7750 miles/12,500 km of surfaced roads and 8700 miles/14,000 km of tracks) follow the Nile Valley, spread out over the Delta and link the major oases and the Suez Canal zone with the Egyptian heartland. The number of motor vehicles in urban areas is increasing rapidly, so that the street system of central Cairo has already come up against the limits of its capacity.

Internal shipping services continue to be of great importance, handling fully half the total amount of freight carried. The largest international seaports are Alexandria, Port Said and Suez, and it is planned to develop other large ports. A major contribution to Egypt's foreign currency earnings is made by the *Suez Canal,* which still carries most of the sea traffic between Europe and the Far East. – More than 30 international airlines fly *air services* to and from Egypt. Domestic air services are provided by the national airline, EgyptAir, which also flies international services between Cairo and cities in Europe, Africa and the Middle and Far East. In addition to the major central airport of Cairo-Heliopolis there are airports at Alexandria, Luxor, Aswan, Mersa Matruh and Port Said, as well as many small airstrips.

As an important source of foreign currency, and also as a provider of employment for the increasing numbers of young people looking for jobs, **tourism** is energetically promoted by the Government. It is planned to increase and modernize the country's hotel resources and thus, in spite of its political and economic problems, to attract increasing numbers of visitors both to its antiquities and to its beaches and develop tourism into one of the major branches of the economy. Political disturbances, which sometimes expressed signs of hostility towards foreigners, have, however, inhibited further tourist development. Yet the number of foreign visitors has increased considerably (1988 over 12 million overnight stays).

Taken as a whole, however, Egypt's economic situation is unfavorable and, from the social point of view, contains potentially explosive elements. With a gross national product of 750 US dollars per head Egypt occupies a middle-ranking position among the nations of the world; but the country's very successful efforts to promote rapid industrial development have been outpaced by the enormous increase in population. The amounts of foreign currency being earned by cotton, oil, armaments, Suez Canal dues and tourism are being more than counterbalanced by steadily rising imports of foodstuffs, and further investment is possible only at the cost of ever-growing foreign debts.

Egypt
A to Z

Warning

Climbing of all Egyptian pyramids is not only dangerous but illegal.

Visitors are particularly advised not to enter the inner chambers of the pyramids, or the underground works (especially tombs) during the extremely hot summer months. The entrances are frequently alarmingly narrow and can only be negotiated by bending almost double.

Tourists suffering from heart or circulatory problems, claustrophobia or agoraphobia are strongly advised not to enter owing to the confined space, the overpowering heat and the prevailing lack of oxygen.

Pyramids of Giza▶

Abu Gurab

Middle Egypt. – Governorate: Giza.
(i) **Tourist Information Office,**
Misr Travel Tower,
Cairo – Abbasia;
tel. 82 60 16.

ACCESS. – 1½–2 hours on donkey-, camel- or horse-back or in a cross-country vehicle; or by car from Saqqara to Abusir, then 20 minutes on foot.

Some 7½ miles/12 km S of the Pyramids of Giza and ¾ mile/1 km NW of the Pyramids of Abusir, on the edge of the desert, are the imposing remains of the Sun-Temples of Abu Gurab, built by Pharaoh Niuserre (5th Dynasty) to mark the 30th anniversary of his accession.

Of the six sun-temples which are known to have been built during the 5th Dynasty (c. 2465 – c. 2325 B.C.), when the solar cult was declared the State religion and successive rulers took the name of "son of Re [the sun god]", only two have been identified – the well-preserved Temple of Abu Gurab and the nearby temple erected by Userkaf. The Temple of Abu Gurab is said to have been modelled on the Great Temple of the Sun at Heliopolis.

The temple, formerly known as the Pyramid of Righa, was excavated in 1898–1901 by the German archaeologist Ludwig Borchardt (1863–1938) on behalf of the Berlin Museum. The various finds made during the excavations, including in particular the many fine bas-reliefs with which the walls were covered, can now be seen in the museums of Cairo and Berlin.

Like earlier Egyptian temples, the sun-temples of the 5th Dynasty were built on the edge of the desert and consisted of a valley temple and the main temple, with a causeway linking the two. Unlike the earlier temples, however, they were purely temples for the worship of the divinity and not the burial-place of the Pharaoh who built them. All the sun-temples had an open courtyard enclosing the obelisk of the sun – the focal point of worship, representing the first resting-place of the rising sun. At the foot of the obelisk (the form of which can be reconstructed from hieroglyphic representations) was a massive altar on which the cult of the sun was celebrated.

Sun-temple (reconstruction drawing)

THE TEMPLE. – The **Sun-Temple of Niuserre** stands on a low, artificially levelled hill. The courtyard, 330 ft/100 m long by 245 ft/75 m wide, is surrounded by a brick-built wall with an entrance at the E end. At the W end of the enclosure stood the large obelisk of the sun. From the entrance two passages, to the left and right, originally covered, ran along the inside of the enclosure wall, with handsome relief decoration depicting festival and hunting scenes and representations of nature. The left-hand passage extended along the E and S sides of the courtyard and then turned to the right (N) to reach the obelisk. Nothing is now left of the obelisk, which reared up to a height of some 230 ft/70 m on a masonry platform (partly preserved) 65–100 ft/20–30 m high. The passage, still decorated with relief representations of nature and Egypt's three seasons, continued up though the interior of the platform to a terrace around the foot of the obelisk.

In front of the E side of the platform, in the middle of the court, stands the **Altar**, measuring 18 ft/5·5 m by 20 ft/6 m, built of five massive blocks of alabaster. – The *chapel* on the S side of the obelisk was also embellished with fine reliefs. Its entrance (on the E side) was flanked by two uninscribed granite stelae and two ablution-basins set into the ground.

At the NE corner of the court was the place where the sacrificial animals were slaughtered, with channels in the paving which carried the blood into ten *alabaster basins*, nine of which have been preserved. On the N side of the obelisk was a smaller sacrificial court. – The N side of the main court was occupied by store-rooms and treasuries, to which the covered passage to the right of the entrance gave access.

Outside the enclosure wall, some 35 yds/30 m S, is the base, built of sun-dried brick, for a solar barque, the vessel which conveyed the sun god Re on his daily journey across the sky. – Little can now be seen of the gateway in the valley below the NE side of the hill or of the covered causeway which connected it with the temple; the remains of these were excavated, but have for the most part been covered up again by the encroaching sand.

SURROUNDINGS of Abu Gurab. – To the SE of Niuserre's Temple, half-way between this and the Pyramids of Abusir, is the **Sun-Temple of Userkaf**, founder of the 5th Dynasty, the second sun-temple so far located, which was excavated by Swiss and German archaeologists in 1954–57. It is similar in layout to Niuserre's Temple but is considerably smaller (145 ft/44m by 270 ft/83 m) and is in a very poor state of preservation: much of the masonry seems to have been pulled down and reused in ancient times (in the reign of Ramesses II(?)). A black stone head, probably belonging to a statue of the goddess Neith, which was found during the excavations is now in the Egyptian Museum in Cairo.

Abu Mena

Lower Egypt. – North-West Frontier District.
(i) **Tourist Information Office,**
Midan Saad Zaghlul,
Alexandria;
tel. 80 55 71.

ACCESS. – From Bahig Station (on road and railway between Alexandria and Mersa Matruh) 9 miles/ 15 km S on a desert track.

The ruins of *Abu Mena, the City of St Menas, the greatest Christian place of pilgrimage in the East during the early medieval period and the largest Coptic town so far known, lies in the Mareotic Desert some 50 miles/80 km SW of Alexandria, half-way to the Wadi Natrun. This extensive site, known to the bedouin as Karm Abu Mina, the "Vineyard of St Menas", aroused wide international interest when it was discovered in 1905 by a German archaeologist, Carl Maria Kaufmann, and since then has been extensively excavated and studied, with long interruptions, particularly during the two world wars. Most of the finds from the site are displayed in the Coptic Museum in Cairo.

HISTORY. – The story of **St Menas,** a very popular Egyptian Saint (feast-day November 11) and the patron of merchants, is the subject of numerous legends and myths. Of Egyptian or Libyan origin, he was a Roman legionary in the time of Diocletian who was converted to the Christian faith and suffered a martyr's death in Phrygia in A.D. 296. Tradition asserts that when his comrades were carrying his body home the camels suddenly stopped on the edge of the Libyan Desert and could not be persuaded to move from the spot. Seeing this as a sign from Heaven, the soldiers buried Menas at the place indicated:

whereupon 90 springs of water gushed out of the ground and gave rise to a variety of miracles. Then pilgrims from all over the Near East began to flock to the site seeking a cure for their ailments, taking some of the water home with them in small pottery bottles made on the spot, usually decorated with a representation of St Menas between two crouching camels.

It is certain at any rate that on the site of the present burial church there was a grave of the period in question, within a cemetery bordering a settlement of some kind. In the course of time this tomb was steadily enlarged at the expense of surrounding burials, and towards the end of the 4th c. a small oratory was built over it. In the first half of the 5th c. this gave place to a basilica, which in turn was replaced at the beginning of the 6th c. by the Basilica of the Crypt, the present burial church. At about the same time the Great Basilica was built on to its eastern end, also on the site of an earlier structure. After the destruction of the holy place by fire, presumably as a result of the spread of Islam from the 7th c. onwards, the Patriarch Joseph (830–849) built, shortly before 850, a new five-aisled basilica in which much of the older church was incorporated.

Round this much-venerated shrine there grew up a magnificent city, which according to contemporary accounts was built entirely of marble and was equipped with all the attributes of an established place of pilgrimage, rather in the manner of present-day Lourdes. The heyday of the City of St Menas was in the 5th and 6th c.; but from the 7th c. onwards it was subject to repeated raids by bedouin converted to Islam, and about 900 it was plundered and devastated by the Abbasids. It was not finally abandoned by its last surviving inhabitants, however, until the 13th c. Thereafter the remains were buried under the sand of the advancing desert.

THE SITE. – Visitors are shown round the site by a monk from the nearby Monastery of St Menas. The central feature of the ancient city, the streets and houses of which can be clearly identified from the excavated remains, is the complex consisting of the Basilica of the Crypt built

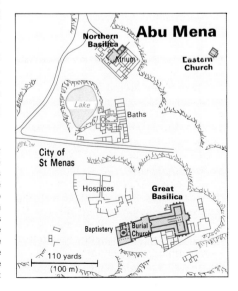

over the Saint's grave, the Great Basilica adjoining its E end and the Baptistery at its W end.

The first burial church, built at the beginning of the 6th c. over an older basilica of the early 5th c., was a tetraconch oriented from W to E, with shallow apses marked out by columns. After its destruction by fire it was replaced, shortly before the middle of the 9th c., by the **Basilica of the Crypt** now visible. This is a five-aisled basilica 125 ft/38 m long and 75 ft/22·5 m wide, built over the spacious *Crypt* which contains the Saint's tomb; lying 25 ft/8 m below the level of the church, it is approached by a staircase of 30 marble steps. – To the N of the church is an extensive complex of cisterns and baths.

Adjoining the E end of the Burial Church is the **Great Basilica** (erroneously called the *Basilica of Arcadius*), a three-aisled structure 220 ft/67 m long by 105 ft/32 m wide with aisled transepts 165 ft/50 m long by 65 ft/20 m across. Under the crossing the position of the altar is marked by four columns which once supported a baldaquin. The main entrance, with three doorways, is on the S side of the nave; there were other entrances at the NW end of the nave and in the N transept. Flanking the nave are a variety of rooms, underground burial chambers, corridors and cellars.

At the W end of the Burial Church is the octagonal **Baptistery** (5th–6th c.), enclosed within a square external structure, with a large stepped marble font in the middle. Like the Burial Church and the Great Basilica, it was several times rebuilt, but always in the original form.

In the middle of a large cemetery on the N edge of the site is the three-aisled **Northern Basilica** (7th–9th c.), with an atrium at its W end. It is surrounded by extensive residential buildings and offices. This may have been the residence of the Patriarch when visiting Abu Mena. Adjoining the right-hand aisle is an elegant *Baptistery*.

On the eastern edge of the site are the remains of the **Eastern Church**, on a centralized tetraconchal plan. The square central area probably had a timber roof; on each of the four sides is a double conch, the inner one supported on a row of columns. On the W side is an atrium. Outside the church, in the angles between the conches, are annexes, which, curiously, are built on different plans and thus disturb the strict symmetry of the plan as a whole. At the NE corner is a *Baptistery*, also containing a stepped piscina.

Among the secular buildings on the site are a number of *potters' workshops* and *kilns,* in which clay flasks for the use of pilgrims were produced in large quantities, as well as *cisterns,* Early Christian *hospices* and *bath-houses.*

Excavations by the Coptic Museum in Cairo, with the help of German archaeologists, are still in progress.

Abuqir

See under Alexandria

Abu Roash

Lower Egypt. – Governorate: Giza.
ⓘ **Tourist Information Office,**
   Misr Travel Tower,
   Cairo – Abbasia;
   tel. 82 60 16.

ACCESS. – The Pyramids of Abu Roash, NW of Giza (Mena House), can be reached by cross-country vehicle, camel, donkey or horse-drawn carriage on a track which runs along the edge of the cultivated land (canal); then a ½ hour climb on foot.

Some 5 miles/8 km NW of the Pyramids of Giza near the village of Abu Roash, commandingly situated on a steep-sided rocky plateau some 500 ft/150 m above the Nile Valley in the Western (Libyan) Desert, are the remains of the Pyramid of Djedefre (4th Dynasty), son of Cheops, and his subsidiary wife Henutsen. This is the most northerly of all the pyramids.

Djedefre ensured his succession to the throne by marrying his half-sister Hetepheres II, the legitimate heiress. During his short reign of only eight years – a period of serious internal tensions – he built his relatively small and modest pyramid well away from the burial area at Giza, opposite Heliopolis, the City of the Sun, thus demonstrating his devotion to the cult of the Sun. The cause of his death is unknown; and it is uncertain whether his pyramid was left unfinished or whether its poor state of preservation is the result of its use as a quarry of building material – a process which continued into modern times.

THE SITE. – The rocky plateau, almost inaccessible from the E, can be reached either by a steep and strenuous path on the S side or, more easily, on the ancient causeway running up from the Wadi el-Karen to the NE, which survives for a length of 1975 yds/1800 m, still carried at certain points on an embankment 40 ft/ 12 m high.

The remains of the **Pyramid of Djedefre** now stand only some 33 ft/10 m high, with a base length of 105 yds/97 m (originally 110 yds/100 m). From the top can be seen the entrance to the 140 ft/ 43 m long shaft, faced with granite blocks, leading to the *tomb chamber.* – To the E of the pyramid are the remains of the brick walling of the mortuary temple, and adjoining this a cavity in the rock which housed the solar barque. In this area were found numerous fragments of sculpture, including a fine head of Djedefre (now in the Louvre, Paris), depicted for the first time with the royal headcloth and the uraeus. – The *view from the plateau extends far into the Nile Valley and the wadis of the Western (Libyan) Desert.

Farther to the SW are the scanty remains of a smaller *stone-built pyramid.* – In the plain, N of the village of Abu Roash, was another brick-built pyramid which still stood to a height of 55 ft/17 m in the mid 19th c. but has since been entirely demolished except for the granite core containing the tomb chamber.

Some 1 mile/1·5 km E of the Abu Roash Pyramid, on a rocky spur of the plateau above the village, lies a *cemetery* of the Old Kingdom with large mastabas (excavated by French archaeologists 1922–24). Farther S, on a rocky ridge, are *tombs* of the 2nd–4th Dynasties.

SURROUNDINGS of Abu Roash. – In the nearby village of **Kerdasa** woven carpets in native traditional patterns are made and offered for sale.

Abu Simbel

Nubia. – Governorate: Aswan.

(i) **Tourist Information Office,**
Tourist Bazaar,
Aswan;
tel. 32 97.

ACCESS. – By bus or taxi from Aswan (3 hours), the bus leaving from the tourist information office each morning, or by air (several flights daily).

HOTEL. – *Nefertari* (Nov 1 to May 31 only), 60 b., SP, club.

Some 175 miles/280 km S of Aswan and 25 miles/40 km N of the Egyptian-Sudanese frontier at Wadi Halfa, near the Second Cataract (now drowned under the waters of Lake Nasser), are the****rock temples of Abu Simbel, which rank among the most stupendous monuments of ancient Egypt. Both temples were constructed during the reign of Ramesses II (1290–24 B.C.) to mark the 30th anniversary of his accession. The larger of the two temples was dedicated to Amun-Re of Thebes and Re-Harakhty of Heliopolis, the principal divinities of Upper and Lower Egypt, but Ptah of Memphis and the deified Ramesses himself were also worshiped here. The smaller temple to the N was dedicated to the goddess Hathor and Ramesses II's favorite wife Nefertari, also deified.**

HISTORY. – We can only speculate why Ramesses decided to construct such magnificent temples on this particular site. Probably there were already cave sanctuaries here at a very early period, since such sanctuaries were numerous in Nubia. With the creation of a temple dedicated to himself Ramesses became the first Pharaoh to take the final decisive step towards equating king and god; and at the same time the construction of the temples symbolized his royal and divine claim to rule the flourishing region of Nubia, the gold and copper of which were of great importance to Egypt. In addition the treasuries and store-rooms hewn deep into the rock provided a place of security for the riches acquired by war or the payment of tribute.

In the course of millennia many armies, merchants, caravans and other travelers passed this way, often leaving inscriptions and graffiti which throw light on the circumstances of the period. Traces of soot inside the temples show that they were sometimes used as dwellings. Later both temples were buried under the desert sand and sank into an oblivion which lasted until the early years of the 19th c. On March 22, 1813 the Swiss traveler Johann Ludwig Burckhardt (1784–1817) discovered the heads of the colossal figures of Ramesses emerging from the drifts of sand, but was unable to establish what they were or to penetrate into the interior of the temple. The systematic excavation of the temples was begun by an Italian,

New Abu Simbel – Ramesses II's Great Temple in its new position

Giambattista Belzoni (1778–1823), in 1817, and thereafter they ranked among the principal sights of Egypt.

New dangers threatened the Abu Simbel temples when work began on the construction of the Aswan High Dam (Sadd el-Ali) on January 9, 1960, since the site of these unique monuments would be swallowed up by the rising waters of Lake Nasser, the huge reservoir to be created by the new dam. At the joint request of Egypt and Sudan Unesco put in train a massive rescue operation which saved the two temples for posterity. After decisions had been reached on responsibility for the expenditure involved there was much discussion of possible means of saving the temples. Among the projects considered were plans (put forward by the United States) for floating both temples on pontoons, which as the lake rose would carry them up to a new site on higher ground, and a Polish proposal for enclosing the whole site within a spherical shell into which visitors would descend in lifts. Another proposal was to enclose the site in a kind of glass aquarium and take visitors down to see it in enclosed glass cabins. Most of the plans put forward were rejected on either technical or aesthetic grounds, and the only proposal which seemed acceptable was a French one. This involved cutting both temples out of the solid rock in their entirety, setting them on huge slabs of concrete and then raising them to a new site by the use of hydraulic jacks. To raise the larger temple, weighing 265,000 tons, 440 jacks would have been required; for the smaller temple, weighing 55,000 tons, 94 jacks. But this project, too – comparable in its boldness with the original construction of the temples – had to be abandoned on account of the gigantic cost.

Finally, as the level of the lake continued to rise and time grew ever shorter, the decision was taken to adopt a proposal put forward by the Egyptian sculptor Ahmad Osman for sawing the temples into manageable blocks and re-erecting them on higher ground near their original sites. The costs, estimated at 36 million US dollars, were to be shared equally by Egypt, the United States and Unesco. The contract for the execution of the project was given to a consortium of six international civil engineering firms (Grands

Travaux de Marseille, Paris; Hochtief, Essen; Impregila, Milan; Skanska, Stockholm; Sentab, Stockholm; Atlas, Cairo) under the name of "Joint Venture Abu Simbel".

Since there was no existing infrastructure at this desert site it was necessary in the first place to establish an adequate system for supplies and communications; and comfortable accommodation for 2000 people was provided, with all necessary shopping facilities and social amenities. This new settlement forms the core of a much larger town planned for the future in the center of an oasis supplied with water from Lake Nasser.

When work began on the construction of **New Abu Simbel** in the spring of 1964 the water-level of Lake Nasser was already so high that the temples had to be protected by a coffer-dam. They were then sawn up into blocks of a maximum weight of 20 tons (807 blocks for the larger temple, 235 for the smaller), the cutting lines being so arranged that the joins would be as inconspicuous as possible when the temples were re-erected. The blocks, carefully numbered, were then stored until the new site, 215 ft/65 m higher up and 200 yds/180 m farther NW, was ready to receive them. Thereafter the smaller temple had to be raised another $6\frac{1}{2}$ ft/2 m as a result in a change in the design of the High Dam, so that there is now a difference in height between the two temples of only 6 ft/1.80 m (previously $12\frac{1}{2}$ ft/3.80 m). The interior walls and ceilings of the temples were suspended from a supporting framework of reinforced concrete which provides increased stability. The loss of stone resulting from the sawing process was made good by a mortar of cement and desert sand. The re-erected temples were roofed over by massive reinforced-concrete domes with spans of 165 ft/50 m and 80 ft/24 m and internal heights of 60 ft/19 m and 25 ft/7 m respectively which provided support for the mass of rubble and rock covering the whole structure and which also accommodate the necessary tourist facilities (movie-theater, refreshment-room, etc.). By the summer of 1968 the work was completed and a cultural monument of outstanding importance had been preserved for future generations. After the re-erection of the larger temple a slight displacement of its principal axis was detected.

◀ **Abu Simbel – transport of a colossal head**

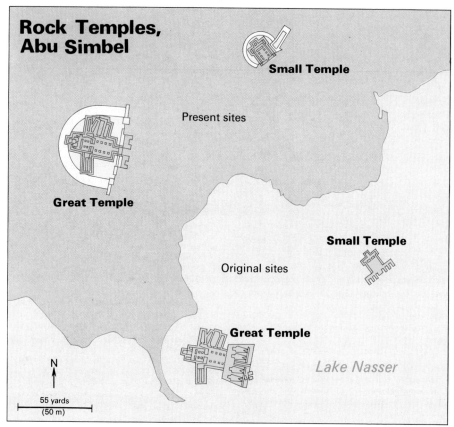

Rock Temples,
Abu Simbel

Small Temple

Present sites

Great Temple

Small Temple

Original sites

Great Temple

Lake Nasser

N

55 yards
(50 m)

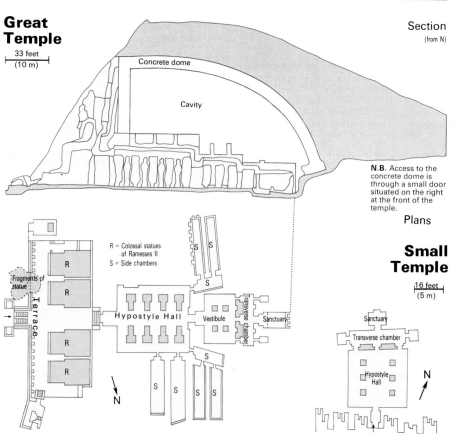

Great
Temple

Section
(from N)

33 feet
(10 m)

Concrete dome

Cavity

N.B. Access to the
concrete dome is
through a small door
situated on the right
at the front of the
temple.

Plans

R = Colossal statues
of Ramesses II
S = Side chambers

S S

S

Fragments of
statue

Terrace

R

R

Hypostyle Hall

Vestibule

Transverse chamber

Sanctuary

R

S

R

N

S   S

S   S

Small
Temple

16 feet
(5 m)

Sanctuary

Transverse chamber

Hypostyle
Hall

N

THE SITE. – The ** **Great Temple** was hewn out of the rock to a depth of 207 ft/ 63 m. The axis of the temple was aligned from W to E in such a way that twice every year, on February 20 and October 20 (now one day later, on February 21 and October 21), the rays of the rising sun reached the divine figures on the rear wall of the sanctuary.

The *forecourt* in front of the temple was enclosed on the N and S by brick walls, at the E ends of which were pylon-like towers. The E side of the court was open, looking on to the Nile, while the W side was bounded by the long temple terrace. Remains of the original brick paving have been preserved. – From the forecourt a flight of nine low steps with a ramp in the middle leads up to the *terrace* in front of the temple. To the right and left, before the ramp, are steps leading up to two recesses which probably contained basins for ritual ablutions. In the recesses are *stelae* depicting Ramesses making offerings: on the one to the right (N) he is shown burning incense to Amun-Re, Re-Harakhty and Thoth and offering them flowers, on the one to the left (S) he is making offerings to Amun-Re, Thoth and the lion-headed Sakhmet. Along the front of the terrace is a decorative frieze depicting representatives of many different peoples making obeisance to the King, and above this is a cavetto cornice. In front of the balustrade, which has a dedicatory inscription running along its

whole length, are figures of falcons alternating with small statues of the King; the figures at the S end of the balustrade were probably destroyed by the collapse of the upper part of the second of the colossal figures.

In front of the massive façade of the temple, 108 ft/33 m high, are four ** **colossal figures** hewn from the solid rock. Seated on simple thrones, they are 65 ft/ 20 m high – comparable in size with the Colossi of Memnon at Thebes (see p. 346). With their finely carved features and their stylized tranquility and harmony they dominate the mighty temple façade. All four represent the deified Ramesses II – the two on the left as Heka-tawi and Re-en-hekaw, the two on the right as Meri-Amun and Meri-Atum. The King's mild countenance and characteristic nose are best preserved in the first of the colossi (far left). The second figure lost its head and shoulders in ancient times, perhaps as a result of a rock fall or an earthquake (or a combination of both), and these now lie on the ground in front of it.

Some authorities believe that this collapse may have taken place during the reign of Ramesses II; but in that event the damage would surely have been made good, since the technical skills to do so were available in that period. It must at any rate have taken place not later than the end of the last dynasty, since in Christian times the temple was largely covered by sand. – The upper part of the third figure was repaired in the reign of Sethos II, when a support was added under the right arm.

The King wears on his head the royal headcloth, double crown and uraeus and is represented with the formal spade-like beard. His hands rest on his knees, and on his breast and upper arms and between his legs are the royal cartouches. To the right and left of each figure and between their legs are figures, on a smaller scale but still over-life-size, representing members of the royal family: flanking the first colossus the Princesses Nebt-tawi (left) and Bent-anat (right),

Colossal figures of Ramesses II on the façade of the Great Temple, Abu Simbel

with an unnamed Princess between the legs; flanking the second the King's mother, Tue (left), and his wife Queen Nefertari (right), with Prince Amen-her-khopshef between the legs. On the inner sides of the thrones of the two central colossi, flanking the entrance to the temple, are figures of the two Nile gods wreathing the floral emblems of Upper and Lower Egypt, the papyrus and the lotus, round the hieroglyphic sign meaning "unite", while below are rows of prisoners – on the left Kushites (depicted as Negroes), on the right Syrians.

On the two southern colossi are numbers of Greek, Carian and Phoenician inscriptions of great linguistic and historical interest, carved by mercenaries who had passed this way on various military expeditions. On the left leg of the second figure is a Greek inscription written by mercenaries sent by Psammetichus II (26th Dynasty; c. 595–589) from Elephantine into Nubia; after advancing as far as the Second Cataract they had left this record of their passage. The inscription reads: "When King Psammetichus had come to Elephantine this was written by those who traveled with Psammetichus, son of Theocles, and had gone beyond Kerkis so far as the river allowed. The foreigners were led by Potasimto, the Egyptians by Amasis. This was written by Archon, son of Amoibichos, and Pelekos, son of Udamos."

On the smoothed-down S wall of the terrace is a *stele* of the 34th year of Ramesses II's reign commemorating the Pharaoh's marriage with Naptera, daughter of the Hittite King Hattusilis III, who had been brought to Egypt by her father in the late summer of the year 1269 and had been given the Egyptian name of Maat-neferu-re. In the upper part of the stele is Ramesses seated between two deities under a canopy, with the Hittite Princess and her father in attitudes of veneration in front of them. – The space between the southernmost colossus and the rock face forms a small open recess entered by a doorway. On its W wall is a long poetic inscription in the name of Ramesses II. – On the W wall of the space between the northernmost colossus and the rock face is a large *memorial inscription*, also by Ramesses, representing him in the presence of Re-Harakhty. – On the N wall to the left of the entrance to the court dedicated to the worship of the sun at the northern end of the terrace is a *memorial inscription* by Merneptah Siptah (19th Dynasty; c. 1208–1202 B.C.) in which he is represented burning incense to Amun-Re, Mut, Re-Harakhty and other deities.

Behind the four colossal figures is the trapezoid *façade* of the temple, which here represents the pylon found in free-standing temples. Along the top of the façade runs a frieze of 22 praying baboons, their hands raised to greet the rising sun, and below this is a cavetto cornice with royal cartouches surrounded by uraeus serpents and representations of Amun-Re (left) and Re-Harakhty (right). Below this again is Ramesses II's dedicatory inscription to Amun-Re and Re-Harakhty. These inscriptions, together with many other representations, show that the southern part of the temple was dedicated to Amun-Re and the northern part to Re-Harakhty.

Above the *entrance doorway* in the center of the façade is a large figural relief giving the King's name in the form of a rebus. In the middle is the falcon-headed figure of the sun god, flanked by the jackal-headed staff known as *user* and by Maat, goddess of truth and justice. Taken together, these give the King's coronation name, User-Maat-Re. On either side of the relief are representations of Ramesses making offerings to

the sun god and to his own deified name. On the door-lintel he is shown laying the foundation-stone of the temple in the presence of Amun and Mut (left) and Re-Harakhty and his lion-headed spouse Wert-hekaw (right). The doorway was closed by a single door, opening on the S side.

The doorway gives access to the large **Hypostyle Hall**, 58 ft/17·7 m long by 54 ft/16·43 m across, which here replaces the pillared court of free-standing temples. It is divided into three aisles, the central one being twice the width of the other two, by two rows of four square pillars, on the inner sides of which are *Osiris figures* of the King holding the scourge and the crook, almost 33 ft/10 m high. The figures on the right-hand side were the double crown of Upper and Lower Egypt, those on the left the crown of Upper Egypt. The stylized symmetry of these massive figures is very striking. The finest is the fourth on the right, with its energetic features and well-preserved powerful nose. On the other sides of the pillars are representations of the King making offerings, his favorite wife Nefertari and his daughter (later his wife) Bent-anat. The ceiling of the central aisle has paintings of flying vultures; those of the lateral aisles are adorned with stars.

In the Hypostyle Hall of the Great Temple

The ***mural reliefs**, some of which have preserved their vivid colors, are of great historical interest. On the right-hand side of the entrance wall the King, accompanied by his *ka*, is shown smiting his enemies in the presence of Re-Harakhty, who hands him a curved sword; below this scene are the Princesses with their sistra. On the left-hand side of the entrance wall is a similar representation of the King in the presence of Amun-Re, with his sons in the lower part of the scene. – On the S wall (to the left), in the upper register, are five magnificent *reliefs, mainly of religious content, notable among them being the fourth scene, which shows the King kneeling before Re-Harakhty under the sacred persea tree; the fruits of the tree bear his name. In the lower register are three large battle scenes. To the left the King is shown storming a Syrian fortress in his war chariot under the protection of the weapon god Month and shooting the enemy on the battlements, who sue for mercy; he is followed by three Princes, while below a herdsman is shown fleeing into the town with his herd. In the middle scene the King is shown piercing a prostrate Libyan with his lance. The right-hand scene depicts his triumphal return from battle with his African prisoners.

On the N wall (to the right) are scenes from the King's campaign against the Hittites, also depicted in the temples of Abydos and Luxor and in the Ramesseum. In the lower register can be seen, at the left-hand end, the Egyptian army on the march; then, between two

New Abu Simbel – the Small Temple

doors to side chambers, the Egyptian camp, with shields set round it in a kind of stockade. The various activities in the camp are depicted in a lively way – the horses being given their fodder, the troops resting after their march, the camp-followers and servants, etc. To the right is the royal tent. The third scene shows the King and Princes holding a Council of War, while below two enemy spies are being beaten. The last scene depicts the battle between Egyptian and Hittite charioteers. – The scenes in the upper register take us into the thick of the battle. To the left the King is shown dashing against his enemies, who have surrounded him with their chariots, in the center is the enemy stronghold of Qadesh, encircled by the River Orontes, with the defenders looking down from the battlements; and to the right the King in his chariot watches while his officers count the severed hands and limbs of the enemy and bring in prisoners.

In the right-hand half of the rear wall Ramesses is shown leading two files of Hittite prisoners into the presence of Re-Harakhty, his own deified effigy and the lion-headed Wert-hekaw. In the left-hand half he presents Negro (Kushite) prisoners to Amun, the deified Ramesses and Mut. – Between the last two pillars on the left is a stela dating from the 35th year of Ramesses's reign recording in florid language the buildings and the gifts dedicated by him to Ptah of Memphis.

To the right and left of the Hypostyle Hall are eight small *side chambers*, some of which served as treasuries and store-rooms. Their decoration is of varying quality, but in general is simpler than that of the main chambers of the temple. Some of the rooms have stone tables along the walls.

Beyond the Hypostyle Hall is a second hypostyle hall or **Vestibule**, 36 ft/11 m by 25 ft/7·58 m, divided into three aisles by four square pillars. On the sides of the pillars are representations of the King being received into the company of the gods. On the S wall is the barque of Amun-Re, on the N wall that of the deified Ramesses in the form of the divine unity Ramses-meri-Imen-em-pa-per-Ramses. The barques are borne in

procession, preceded by the King and his wife Nefertari making offerings of food and incense. On the S wall the royal couple are shown wearing sandals; on the N wall they are barefoot.

From the Vestibule three doorways lead into a long and narrow **Transverse Chamber**. On the walls of this chamber the King is shown making offerings to Min, Horus and Khnum (left-hand end) and to Atum, Thoth and Ptah (right-hand end), who were also worshiped here, almost with the status of guest divinities. – From the Transverse Chamber three doors lead into three small rooms at the farthest end of the temple. In the center is the rectangular **Sanctuary**, which could be entered only by the King. On the right-hand and left-hand walls Ramesses is depicted burning incense. On the rear wall are over-life-size figures of Ptah, Amun-Re, the King himself and Re-Harakhty (from left to right) – again giving expression to the King's complete equality with the gods.

Every year on February 20 and October 20 (one of which may have been the date of Ramesses II's Coronation) the rays of the rising sun penetrated into the Sanctuary, illuminating the faces of the divine figures. This recurring phenomenon was undoubtedly an occasion for ritual celebration, and is still an impressive spectacle. – In front of the figures is the square base, hewn from the rock, of the sacred barque which was kept here.

To the N of the Great Temple, reached by way of a gate constructed by Ramesses in the brick wall enclosing the forecourt, is the *Small Temple of Abu Simbel (Temple of Hathor),* originally situated on a rocky promontory reaching out towards the Nile and separated from the Great Temple by a sand-filled valley. Also built by Ramesses II, this was dedicated to Hathor, goddess of love, and to the deified Nefertari, Ramesses's wife. It is oriented from NW to SE. During the Nile inundation it could be reached directly from the river by way of a quay of which no trace survives; it had no forecourt.

The *façade*, 92 ft/28 m long and 39 ft/12 m high, is hewn from the rock in imitation of a pylon with a cavetto cornice (now missing). It does not form an exact right angle with the main axis of the temple, so that there is a gap between the N end of the façade and the rock face. Here the Royal Steward and Scribe Iuni of Heracleopolis, who was probably in charge of the construction of the Abu Simbel temples, had himself represented in the act of demonstrating his devotion to his royal and divine master.

Along the façade are six *colossal statues, more than 33 ft/10 m high, of Ramesses and his Queen. The colossal figures on either side of the doorway represent the King in the union of the divine beings Heka-tawi with Meri-Imen (to the left) and Re-en-hekaw with Meri-Atum (to the right). On either side of these central figures are statues of Queen Nefertari, and beyond these again are two further statues of the King. Unusually, the Queen is the same size as the King. Flanking the colossal statues are smaller figures of the royal children, the Princesses (depicted with their left foot advanced in front of them) being larger than the Princes. Beside the figure of Nefertari are the Princesses Merit-Amun (right) and Hent-tawi (left); beside the figures of Ramesses at each end of the façade are the Princes Meri-Atum (right) and Meri-Re (left); and beside the central figures of the King are Amen-her-khopshef (right) and Re-her-unemef (left). Between the colossal figures are projecting sections of rock like buttresses, so that the statues appear to be set in niches. In view of the extreme friability of the stone the whole area of the façade was plastered and painted. All the buttresses are covered with hieroglyphic inscriptions.

The *doorway* is cut through the rather wider central buttress; above it is a broad frieze of royal cobras. In the center of the façade, high above the doorway,

is a block of undressed stone, which may have been reserved for a carving of the Hathor cow.

The doorway leads into an almost exactly square *Hypostyle Hall,* divided into three aisles by six pillars, on the fronts of which are sistra with the head of the cow-eared goddess Hathor. On the other sides of the pillars are figures of the royal couple and various deities.

The *mural reliefs* are simpler and less colorful than those in the Great Temple but are also of great artistic and historical value. On the entrance wall the King, accompanied by the Queen, is shown smiting a Libyan in the presence of Re-Harakhty and a Negro (Kushite) in the presence of Amun-Re. On the left-hand wall, from left to right, are: 1. Ramesses in the presence of Hathor; 2. Ramesses crowned by Seth and Horus; 3. The Queen in the presence of Anukis; 4. Ramesses presenting an image of Maat to Amun. On the right-hand wall, from right to left, are: 1. Ramesses offering food to Ptah; 2. Ramesses in the presence of the ram-headed god Herishef of Heracleopolis; 3. The Queen in the presence of Hathor; 4. Ramesses offering wine to Re-Harakhty. On the rear wall the Queen is depicted in the presence of Hathor (left) and of Mut (right).

From the Hypostyle Hall three doorways lead into a narrow *Transverse Chamber,* with reliefs of less interest. To the left and right are two unfinished side chambers, over the doors of which are fine reliefs of the Hathor cow in a papyrus marsh, worshiped respectively by the King and the Queen. Beyond the Transverse Chamber is the *Sanctuary* in the rear wall of which is a recess in the form of a chapel, its roof supported by sistra. In this recess is a figure in high relief of the goddess Hathor as a cow; under her head (and thus under her protection) is the King. On the left-hand wall the Queen offers incense to Mut and Hathor; on the right-hand wall the King offers incense and pours a libation in front of his own image and that of the Queen.

There are no official guides (or *dragomen*) to the temples but the entrance fee includes an evening visit, when the temples are floodlit inside and out, and a second visit next day at dawn when the first rays of the sun provide the most spectacular setting of all.

In **Abu Simbel village**, an exhibition demonstrates the relocation of the Abu Simbel temples, through the use of models and diagrams. Some may wish to see this before they visit the site.

Abusir

Middle Egypt. – Governorate: Giza.
(i) **Tourist Information Office,**
Misr Travel Tower,
Cairo – Abbasia;
tel. 82 60 16.

ACCESS. – By road from Giza: 7½ miles/12 km S.

The *Pyramids of Abusir stand on a low bluff above the W bank of the Nile near the village of that name, roughly half-way between the Pyramids of Giza and the Step Pyramid of Djoser near Saqqara. They were erected by three kings of the 5th Dynasty – Sahure (2455–2443), Neferirkare (2443–2423) and Niuserre (2416–2392). The first ruler of the 4th Dynasty and the kings

Relief in the Small Temple of Abu Simbel

of the 6th Dynasty built their funerary monuments farther S, around Saqqara. – The Abusir Pyramids, originally 14 in number, were first excavated in 1901–08 by the German Oriental Society under the direction of Ludwig Borchardt. Further investigations were carried out in 1955–57.

The solar cult reached its climax under the 5th Dynasty. The rulers of this dynasty no longer saw themselves merely as the sons of their deified predecessor but as sons of their divine father Re, the Sun which gave life and light to the world. The mortuary temples now became temples of the sun which were the king's home after his death. – The mortuary temples of Abusir are similar to those of earlier rulers: the only new feature is the extraordinary profusion of relief decoration. This has unfortunately been decimated by stone robbery; and most of the reliefs still surviving when the monuments were excavated were removed and are now in museums, mostly in Europe. These magnificent reliefs depict everyday events and special occasions in the life of the king: scenes of religious ritual are relatively rare. Built of soft limestone, often with no great care, the Pyramids and temples of Abusir have suffered much damage in the course of the centuries.

The northernmost monument in the group is the **Pyramid of Sahure**. As the earliest of the three kings, Sahure selected the best site for his pyramid, a low-lying area within convenient reach of the Nile Valley. The vertical height of the pyramid was originally 228 ft/69·4 m (now 115 ft/35 m), the length of the base 257 ft/78·3 m (now 216 ft/65·8 m), the angle of incline 51° 42′ 35″. It was originally faced with smooth marble slabs and probably had a cap (pyramidion) of red Aswan granite with the King's cartouche. From the N side of the pyramid a passage walled and paved with granite led down to the tomb chamber (now destroyed) containing the royal sarcophagus.

On the E side of the pyramid are the extensive remains of the **mortuary temple**, laid out on a clearly articulated axial plan, which was connected with the valley temple by a gently sloping causeway 245 yds/225 m long, once richly decorated with reliefs.

A narrow rectangular vestibule on the E side of the temple gives access to a large *colonnaded court* (80 ft/24 m by 55 ft/17 m) which is the central feature of the plan. Fragments of the 16 granite palm columns (6 along the sides and 4 along the ends) which once supported the roof of the colonnade around the walls of the court are scattered about. The columns bore the names and titles of the King and dedicatory inscriptions, while the walls were decorated with reliefs depicting important and glorious events in his reign. The basalt paving of the court is well preserved. At the rear end of the court stood the altar of light-colored alabaster, decorated with incised representations of religious themes. – Around the outside of the court ran a passage, also richly decorated with reliefs. In the southern part of this there is a well-preserved scene depicting the King hunting hoofed game; in the northern part he is shown hunting wildfowl and hippopotamuses in a papyrus marsh.

From the court a narrow passage runs W into a transverse chamber, beyond which, on a slightly higher level, is a small room with five niches in its rear wall which originally contained statues of the King in his five divine qualities. From here a side door on the left led through narrow passages to the innermost sanctuary at the foot of the pyramid, with the large false door which symbolized the entrance to the Realm of the Dead. – To N and S of the sanctuary are a series of two-storeyed *store-rooms* and *treasuries* for the provisions and equipment which the King would require in his afterlife.

At the SE corner of the temple, in a separate court but still within the precinct wall of the temple, was the small Pyramid of the Queen.

Under the New Kingdom Sahure's Mortuary Temple gained increased importance through the introduction of the cult of the goddess Sakhmet, who was probably worshiped here into Ptolemaic times. During the Roman period the temple fell into disuse and was systematically demolished by stone-robbers. In Early Christian times a modest Coptic church was built in the colonnaded court, but this, too, has now disappeared.

S of the Pyramid of Sahure is the **Pyramid of Niuserre** (2416–2392), the ruins of whose once-mighty sun-temple lie a short distance away to the NW at Abu Gurab (see that entry). The layout of the funerary complex is similar to that of Sahure, but the structures are in a much worse state of preservation. From the *valley temple,* of which practically nothing is left, a covered causeway led up to the Pyramid of Neferirkare (see below) – perhaps making use of the earlier causeway leading to that pyramid – and then, reaching the higher ground, turned towards Niuserre's Mortuary Temple. A massive precinct wall enclosed the pyramid, the mortuary temple to the E of the pyramid and a smaller subsidiary pyramid at its SE corner. The causeway led into a forecourt, on either side of which were store-rooms. Adjoining this was an open court paved with basalt slabs and originally surrounded by papyrus columns, fragments of which lie about. Little trace is left of the temple itself. To the N, outside the enclosure wall, are large *mastabas* for female members of the Royal House and high dignitaries. In the Mastaba of Userkafankh, a High Priest and Court official, which stood close to the temple, was found a statue of Userkafankh himself (now in the Liebieghaus in Frankfurt).

A few paces SE of the Pyramid of Sahure is the *Mastaba of Ptahshepses* (5th Dynasty), Niuserre's son-in-law, the largest and most richly furnished private tomb of the Old Kingdom. From the large hypostyle hall (only partly cleared) with 20 square columns a doorway leads into another room with three niches for statues. On the walls are reliefs (gold-smiths and workmen carving statues of the dead man in wood and metal). In a third room (to the right) were found the two oldest and largest known lotus cluster-columns of the Old and Middle Kingdoms (height 20 ft 5 in./6·28 m, diameter 3 ft 5 in./1·05 m) and remains of fine mural reliefs (ships, market scenes, craftsmen, etc.).

A short distance SW of the Pyramid of Niuserre stands the **Pyramid of Neferirkare**, the largest of the Abusir group. It originally had a base length of 360 ft/109 m (now 325 ft/99 m) and a height of 225 ft/69 m (now 165 ft/50 m). On the E side are remains of the *mortuary temple*, built of freestone and brick. – Farther S is the **Pyramid of Neferefre**, fifth King of the 5th Dynasty, who ruled only a few days in 2416 B.C.

Abusir (Busiris)

See under Behbeit el-Hagara

Abusir (Taposiris Magna)

See under Alexandria

Abydos

Upper Egypt. – Governorate: Sohag.
ⓘ **Tourist Information Office,**
Tourist Bazaar,
Luxor;
tel. 22 15.

ACCESS. – By car from Sohag (28 miles/45 km, going S along the Nile road) or Luxor (87 miles/140 km: NW via Qena and Nag Hammadi to El-Balyana, then 7½ miles/12 km SW). – By rail to El-Balyana, then taxi.

Some 95 miles/150 km NW of Luxor on the W bank of the Nile, between the villages of El-Khirba and El-Araba el-Madfuna (the "buried" village), are the ruins of the** Temples of Abydos (Egyptian Abodu), with one of the oldest necropolises in Egypt, associated with the nearby city of Thinis (This), the first Egyptian capital. From the time of the 1st and 2nd Dynasties (beginning of 3rd millennium B.C.) Abydos played an important role as the burial-place of kings and high Court dignitaries. Here were celebrated the rituals for the burial of the dead king and the accession of his successor, symbolizing the transitory and recurrent character of all earthly things.

HISTORY. – The city and its necropolis were both devoted to the worship of the death god Khontamenti, "first of the inhabitants of the Western Kingdom", who had the form of a dog. Even under the Old Kingdom, however, the cult of Osiris, which originated in the Delta, had gained a foothold at Abydos; and thereafter Osiris took possession of the ancient temple and was recognized as Khontamenti's equal. The nearby hill of Umm el-Gaab was believed to be Osiris's Tomb, and from the 6th Dynasty onwards the dead from all over Egypt were buried at Abydos. Several kings of the Middle Kingdom as well as wealthy private citizens erected cenotaphs or stelae here, for to the pious Egyptian there was no greater bliss than to be buried beside the Tomb of Osiris, or failing this to have his mummy brought temporarily to Abydos to receive the desired consecration, or at the very least to recommend himself to the favor of Osiris, lord of the Underworld, by the erection of a cenotaph or a memorial stone. In the mystery plays performed annually at Abydos in honour of Osiris the eternal terrestrial cycle of death and rebirth was celebrated. Osiris's sister and wife Isis, their son Horus and, under the New Kingdom, Ptah, Re-Harakhty and Amun were also worshiped at Abydos.

Strabo gives an interesting account of Abydos: "Above Ptolemais lies Abydos, the site of the Memnonium, a wonderful palace built of stone in the manner of the Labyrinth but with fewer passages and corridors. Under the Memnonium is a spring, reached by passages with low vaults consisting of a single stone and notable for their extent and mode of construction. This spring is connected with the Nile by a canal, which flows through a grove of thorn-acacias sacred to Apollo. Abydos seems once to have been a

A *sakiya* bringing up water for irrigation near Abydos

The chief feature of interest is the ****Temple of Sethos I**, Strabo's *Memnonium*. This magnificent structure, completed by Sethos's son and successor Ramesses II, was almost completely excavated in 1859 by the French Egyptologist Auguste Mariette (1821–81) at the expense of the then Viceroy, Said.

Anubis (Temple of Sethos I)

large city, second only to Thebes, but now it is only a small place." – Ammianus Marcellinus (4th c. A.D. speaks of the oracle of the god Bes which flourished here.

SIGHTS. – The most important part of ancient Abydos was its extensive **Necropolis**, situated in the desert. Four separate areas can be identified. In the most southerly part of the necropolis, near El-Araba, are the tombs of the New Kingdom, the temples of Sethos I and Ramesses II and the so-called Osireion. To the N of this is a hill containing burials of the Late Old Kingdom. Still farther N, between the Sanctuary of Osiris and the remains of walls at Shunet el-Zebib, are the tombs of the Middle Kingdom, many of them in the form of small brick pyramids; here, too, are burials of other periods, particularly the 18th–20th Dynasties (*c.* 1500–*c.* 1000 B.C.) and the Late Dynastic Period. Finally in the hill of Umm el-Gaab, to the W, are the royal tombs of the earliest dynasties and the sacred Tomb of Osiris.

The temple complex is laid out on three levels. The walls are built of fine-grained limestone, the columns, architraves and door-posts of a harder limestone. The layout differs in many respects from that of other Egyptian temples. There are not one but no fewer than seven chapels, dedicated to Osiris, Isis, Horus, Ptah, Re-Harakhty, Amun and the deified Sethos. The front part of the temple is thus divided into seven individual temples, each with its own doorway, and the chambers behind the chapels are not arranged behind one another, as in other temples, but side by side. Another unusual feature is the wing, containing various subsidiary chambers, which branches off the main

Temple of Sethos I (Memnonium)

structure at right angles. Of particular interest is the decoration of the temple, in particular the **reliefs dating from the reign of Sethos I, which rank among the finest achievements of Egyptian sculpture. A short distance to the NE is a resthouse offering simple fare.

The temple is entered from the NE. In front of it, to the left, is the façade wall of a small building, probably a festival temple, facing on to the axis of the main temple. The first pylon is in ruins; on its rear side are shallow niches which contained statues of Sethos I and Ramesses II in the form of Osiris. – The **First Court** is largely destroyed. On its SE wall (to the left) are scenes from Ramesses II's wars and victories in Asia (Battle of Qadesh against the Hittites; counting of the severed hands of the enemy dead; dedication of booty to Amun). On the SW side of the court, on a higher level, is a *Hypostyle Hall,* with representations of Ramesses II's children on the base of the walls; the scenes are continued on the rear wall of the second pylon. In front of the hall can be seen two wells.

The **Second Court** is better preserved. To the right and left are dedicatory inscriptions in the name of Ramesses II. Ramesses is also depicted making offerings to various deities and smiting his enemies in the presence of Amun. On the far side of the court a low ramp leads up to the TEMPLE proper, which stands on a platform. It comes first to a vestibule, which, like the Hypostyle Hall in the First Court, had 12 pillars constructed of blocks of sandstone and limestone. It originally had seven doors in the rear wall. On the wall to the left of the main doorway is an inscription in 95 vertical columns recording the completion of the temple by Ramesses II. The reliefs depict Ramesses in the presence of various deities; one scene (adjoining the doorway) shows him presenting an image of the goddess Maat to the triad of Osiris, Isis and Sethos I (here taking the place of Horus). – The seven doors corresponded to the temple's seven chapels. Processions in honor of the King passed through the first door, at the left-hand end, while the other doors were used by processions honoring Ptah, Re-Harakhty, Amun, Osiris, Isis and Horus. Six of these doors were walled up by Ramesses II, leaving only the one in the middle as the main entrance.

The central doorway leads into the **First Hypostyle Hall** (170 ft/52 m by 35 ft/11 m), the roof of which (partly fallen in) is supported on 24 papyrus cluster-columns with bud capitals. The columns are so arranged that the five central processional aisles leading to the chapels are flanked by two pairs of columns, while the two outermost aisles are bounded on one side by the walls of the hall. The reliefs on the shafts of the columns show the King in the presence of the god to whose chapel the aisle leads, sometimes accompanied by the other deities of his triad. The carving is of mediocre quality; the reliefs date from the time of Ramesses II, who caused Sethos I's bas-reliefs to be chiseled out and replaced by sunk reliefs. Notable among the other reliefs are those in the lower row on the end wall to the right. They show (to the right) Thoth and Horus pouring holy water, in the form of the hieroglyphs for "purity" and "life", over Ramesses II; to the left the dog-headed Wepwawet and the falcon-headed Horus, "avenger of his father", lead the King into the temple and hold the hieroglyph for "life" to his nostrils, with Hathor of Dendera to the left; farther to the left Ramesses presents to Osiris, who is accompanied by Isis and Horus, a case for papyrus rolls in the shape of a column held by a kneeling king, with a falcon's head on the top as a lid.

Seven doors, corresponding to the walled-up entrance doorways, lead into the **Second Hypostyle Hall**, with 36 columns set in three rows supporting the architraves and the roofing slabs which rest on them. The arrangement of the columns flanking the processional aisles is similar to that in the preceding hall. The 24 columns in the first two rows have closed papyrus capitals. The columns in the third row, set on a raised platform, are tree-trunk columns with cylindrical shafts and no capitals, on which rest stone slabs forming an abacus for the support of the architrave.

The inscriptions and reliefs on the walls and columns, which date from the time of Sethos I, are of excellent workmanship, but the subjects are of little interest. Particular attention should be paid, however, to the magnificent *reliefs on the right-hand end wall. To the right Sethos is shown standing before Osiris and Horus holding a censer and pouring water out of three flower-decked vases. In the next scene the King, with his censer, stands in front of a shrine in which Osiris is enthroned, with Maat and Ronpet (goddess of the year) in front of him and Isis, Amentet (goddess of the West) and Nephthys behind him and nine small gods in the background. On the pier at the far end of the wall is a richly decorated *djed* pillar, the emblem of Osiris of Busiris, flanked on the right and left by a figure of the King wearing the crown of Lower Egypt (cf. the representation on the corresponding pier at the other end of the hall). To the left of the pier Sethos is depicted presenting an image of the goddess Maat to Osiris, Isis and Horus. In all these figures of the King his profile, evidently a faithful likeness, is executed with great artistic skill.

Adjoining this hall, in a direct line with the seven entrance doorways, are seven CHAPELS. The one in the middle is dedicated to Amun, the principal god of the New Kingdom, the three on the right to Osiris, Isis and Horus and the three on the left to Re-Harakhty, Ptah and the King. In each chapel stood the sacred barque of the particular deity. The chapels, which were originally closed by double doors, are approached by ramps, with the exception of the central one, which has a flight of steps. The roofs of the chapels, which are formed by projecting courses of stone capped by roof-slabs, are decorated with stars and the names of Sethos I. The walls are covered with *reliefs* depicting the ceremonies which took place in the chapels. The colors are excellently preserved. In the piers between the entrances to the chapels are square niches, also decorated with reliefs.

The following description of the chapels and the niches goes from left to right. – KING'S CHAPEL. Left-hand wall, lower row (left to right): three falcon-headed and three dog-headed gods bear the King into the chapel, preceded by a priest (with the side-lock of youth and a panther skin) offering incense; the King seated on a throne at a banquet, with his guardian spirit behind him and the ibis-headed god Thoth in front of him; the gifts offered by the King are detailed in a long list presented to the god. Left-hand wall, upper row: the priest before nine gods (in three rows); the King between Thoth and Nekhbet (on the right) and Horus and Buto (on the left), who bestow blessings on him; Thoth and the priest making offerings to the sacred barque, which has heads of the King on the bow and stern and stands in a shrine crowned with serpents (the priest in front of the King has been effaced). Right-hand wall, lower row (left to right): the King, his guardian spirit and the priest, as on the opposite wall; the King seated between Nekhbet and Buto on a throne which is supported by the hieroglyph for "union", around which Thoth and

Horus twine papyrus and lotus, the emblems of Lower and Upper Egypt (symbolizing the unification of the two parts of the country under one king); Seshet inscribes the King's name for eternity; the priest in the presence of nine gods. Right-hand wall, upper row: the priest and Thoth in front of the (defaced) image of the King, while six dog-headed and falcon-headed gods bring him vases; Month and Atum conduct the King to the temple, followed by Isis. – As in all the other chapels except that of Osiris, the rear wall was occupied by two false doors, the rounded pediments of which (only partly preserved) were richly ornamented. Between the two doors is a plant on which a serpent lies. – Niche to the right of the chapel: Thoth holds the hieroglyph for "life" to the King's nostrils (left); the priest of the dead offering incense to the King (rear); Thoth and the King seated opposite one another (right).

Relief in the Temple of Sethos I

The CHAPEL OF PTAH is partly destroyed. On the side walls the King is shown worshiping Ptah. – Niche to the right of the chapel: Sethos before Sakhmet (left), Ptah (rear) and Re-Harakhty (right.)

CHAPEL OF RE-HARAKHTY. The reliefs depict the King before Re-Harakhty, Atum, the goddess Eusos of Heliopolis and Hathor. – Niche to the right: the King before Harakhty, to whom he presents an image of Maat (left), Amun-Re (rear) and Mut (right).

CHAPEL OF AMUN. The colors of the reliefs in this chapel are excellently preserved. Sethos is depicted offering sacrifices to Amun in his various forms and burning incense before the sacred barques of Amun (decorated with rams' heads), Khons and Mut (decorated with the heads of these deities), which stand in a shrine. On the false door are inscriptions dating from the Greek period. – Niche to the right: the King sacrifices to Mut (left), anoints Amun (rear) and offers incense to Khons (right).

CHAPEL OF OSIRIS. The King before the various forms of Osiris, who is frequently accompanied by Isis or other deities. On the right-hand wall (above) he sacrifices to the sacred barque of Isis; on the left-hand wall (above) he offers incense to the reliquary of Osiris at Abydos, which stands under a canopy with five images of deities borne on poles in front of it. To right and left of the entrance the King is depicted before the dog-headed Wepwawet. – Niche to the right: the King before Osiris, Isis and Nut.

CHAPEL OF ISIS. Sethos appears before Isis, who is frequently accompanied by her son, the falcon-headed Horus, and the goddess's barque. – Niche to the right: the King before Osiris, Horus and Isis.

CHAPEL OF HORUS. The King before the falcon-headed Horus, Isis and Horus's barque.

A door in the Chapel of Osiris leads into a series of rooms dedicated to the special cult of Osiris. The first is a hall, the roof of which was supported on ten columns without capitals. To the right of this are three chapels with fine colored reliefs, dedicated respectively (from left to right) to Isis, the King revered as Osiris and Horus. Behind the chapels is another room (not accessible). To the left of the hall is a small room with four columns, on the E wall of which are four niches containing reliefs. Adjoining are three small chapels, largely destroyed.

The SOUTH WING contains a slaughter-yard, a well, store-rooms, etc., as well as a *Chapel of Ptah-Sokar*, the death-god of Memphis, which is entered from the Second Hypostyle Hall, turning left immediately in front of the King's Chapel. The roof is supported by three tree-trunk columns. The fine reliefs show Sethos I revering Ptah-Sokar, his son Nefertum and other deities. In the E wall are four niches decorated with reliefs. – Off the main chapel open two smaller ones roofed with false (corbeled) vaults, dedicated to Sokar (right) and Nefertum (left). On the left-hand wall of the former is a relief of Horus and Isis by the bier of Osiris, on whose mummy sits a falcon (Isis); at the head and foot are two other falcons with drooping wings. On the right-hand wall are Isis and Horus at the bier of Sokar-Osiris, who holds his left hand to his brow and grasps his phallus in his right.

By far the most important feature of the S wing, however, is the **Gallery of the Kings**, a long and gradually rising corridor which is entered from the Second Hypostyle Hall (doorway between the second and third rows of columns). On the right-hand wall of the gallery is the famous ****Abydos King List** (illustration, p.36), which has yielded important information on the sequence of Egyptian rulers. It depicts Sethos I with a censer and the Crown Prince, later Ramesses II (with the side-lock of youth), who is reciting hymns from a papyrus roll. They are revering their royal ancestors, 76 of whom are listed in the two upper rows. The list begins with the first King of Egypt, Menes (Hor-aha?), and continues to Sethos, the names of unimportant or illegitimate rulers being omitted. The inscription above the list reads as follows: "The performance of the prayer for the dead ('May Ptah-Sokar-Osiris, lord of the tomb, who dwells in the temple of Sethos, increase the gifts for the kings of Upper and Lower Egypt') by King Sethos: 1000 loaves of bread, 1000 barrels of beer, 1000 head of cattle, 1000 geese, 1000 offerings of incense, etc., by King Sethos for King Menes, . . .", followed by the list. In the bottom row the phrases "by King Men-matre" and "by the son of Re, Sethos" are repeated over and over again. – On the left-hand wall of the gallery Sethos, holding a censer in his left hand, is depicted with Ramesses, wearing the panther skin of a priest, who pours a libation on the altar. The inscription gives a long list of the names and shrines of the gods to whom they are making sacrificial offerings.

A door half-way along the right-hand wall of the Gallery of the Kings leads into a passage, beyond which is a vaulted stone staircase, originally leading out of the temple but walled up in ancient times. The reliefs in the passage date from the reign of Ramesses II. On the right-hand wall the King and a Prince are shown lassoing a bull in the presence of the dog-headed god Wepwawet, to whom (farther left) they sacrifice it. On the left-hand wall Ramesses conducts four sacred oxen to Khons and King Sethos. Beyond this are other scenes: Ramesses pacing out the precincts of the temple; Ramesses and four gods catching birds in a net; Ramesses and a Prince offering the captured

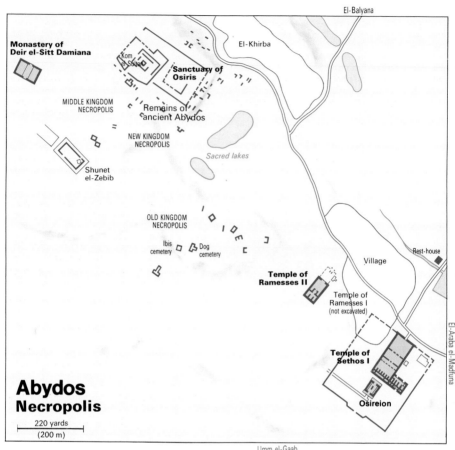

El-Balyana

El-Khirba

Monastery of
Deir el-Sitt Damiana

Kom
el-Sultan

Sanctuary of
Osiris

MIDDLE KINGDOM
NECROPOLIS

Remains of
ancient Abydos

NEW KINGDOM
NECROPOLIS

Sacred lakes

Shunet
el-Zebib

OLD KINGDOM
NECROPOLIS

Ibis
cemetery

Dog
cemetery

Rest-house

Village

Temple of
Ramesses II

Temple of
Ramesses I
(not excavated)

Temple of
Sethos I

El-Araba el-Madfuna

Abydos
Necropolis

Osireion

220 yards
(200 m)

Umm el-Gaab

geese to Amun and Mut. – On the walls of the staircase are numerous Phoenician and Aramaic inscriptions left by Semitic visitors to the temple.

Another door in the right-hand wall of the Gallery of the Kings leads into a small **Hypostyle Hall** (six columns), with paintings (designs for reliefs which were never completed) dating from the reign of Sethos I and sunk reliefs of Ramesses II's reign. Along the walls are benches, probably for offerings.

From the S end of the Gallery of the Kings, where there are Coptic inscriptions (prayers) in red paint, a doorway leads into the **slaughter-court**, with a colonnade (never completed) of seven columns. The scenes and hieroglyphics on the walls were sketched in color in the reign of Sethos I, but only a few of them were later finished as sunk reliefs. They depict Sethos sacrificing to various deities and (in the lower row) the slaughter and cutting up of sacrificial animals. The screen between the first column and the left-hand wall was intended to block the view from the Gallery of the Kings into the slaughter-court.

Adjoining this court are four unfinished rooms, two of which are closed. In three of them the scenes on the walls are merely sketched in; in the fourth they have been completed in color. From the first room (immediately on the right, close to the doorway into the slaughter-court) a staircase leads up to five other rooms (two of them closed) containing unfinished paintings dating from the reign of Merneptah. From the middle room a doorway leads into the open air and

to the Osireion. – Beyond the E corner of the S wing, outside the temple proper, is a deep circular *well.*

SW of the Temple of Sethos I, its rear wall only 26 ft/8 m away, stands the large structure known as the **Osireion**, reminiscent in its majestic simplicity of Chephren's Temple at Giza. Often taken for the Tomb of Osiris, it is in reality a cenotaph of Sethos I, closely associated with the main temple. It was discovered in 1903 by Margaret A. Murray and excavated between 1911 and 1926 by the Egypt Exploration Society under the direction of E. Naville and Dr Frankfort. The building, originally covered by an artificial mound and surrounded by trees, was erected by Sethos I, but remained unfinished. Later some rooms were decorated with religious scenes and inscriptions by Merneptah. The main structure is built of white limestone and reddish sandstone, red granite being used only for the pillars and roof of the main hall and some of the doorways.

The *entrance,* on the N side of the building, was roofed with a strong brick vault and was reached by a vertical shaft, brick-lined, running down through the mound. From the entrance a sloping corridor 120 yds/110 m long, its walls decorated with scenes and texts from the books of the Underworld dating from the reigns of Sethos I and Merneptah (on the right-hand wall from the "Book of Gates", on the left-hand wall from the "Book of what is in the Underworld"), leads into an *antechamber*, also decorated with religious scenes and texts, with another small room to the right of it. From the antechamber another corridor runs E to a large saddle-roofed *transverse chamber* (20 ft/ 6 m by 66 ft/20 m), also decorated with religious texts ("Book of the Dead") dating from the reign of Merneptah. Adjoining this is a large three-aisled *Hypostyle Hall* (98 ft/30 m by 66 ft/20 m) surrounded by 16 small chambers opening off a narrow corridor only 2 ft/60 cm wide. Between the central hall and the small chambers runs a ditch, perhaps symbolizing the primal water out of which, according to the Egyptian creation myth, the terrestrial hill (the earth) emerged along with the sun god. At the end of the central hall (representing the terrestrial hill) steps lead down to the water. Between the two rows of pillars in the hall are two cavities in the floor, a rectangular one in the middle which may have housed a sarcophagus and a square one at the E end, perhaps for a canopic chest. At the far end of the hall is another *transverse chamber*, the shape of which may represent the royal sarcophagus; on its well-preserved saddle roof are fine *reliefs* dating from the reign of Sethos I (representations of the sky; the sky goddess Nut supported by the air god Shu; Nut screening the dead King with her arms).

NW of the Temple of Sethos I, lying partly under the modern village, is a Temple of Ramesses I, and a short distance away is the (destroyed) *Temple of Ramesses II*, also dedicated to Osiris and the cult of the dead King. In front of the present entrance was a large court of which only a few traces remain. The masonry of the temple itself is preserved only to a height of 6½ ft/ 2 m, but it is still possible to trace the outlines of a court surrounded by colonnades with pillars and Osiris figures (as in the Ramesseum), two halls with chapels at their far ends and many subsidiary rooms. To judge from the surviving remains, the temple was much more sumptuous and more carefully built than any of the other buildings of Ramesses II known to us. It was constructed of fine-grained limestone, with red and black granite for the doorways, sandstone for the columns and alabaster for the innermost sanctuary. The mural decorations, the colors of which are remarkably well preserved, are in delicate low relief, reminiscent of the fine work done in the reign of Sethos I, in the rooms to the rear; the cruder sunk reliefs are found only in the court, the first hall and the rooms adjoining that hall. The reliefs in the first court depict a sacrificial procession. On the outer walls are warlike scenes, on the S wall lists of donations to the temple.

On the right-hand (N) wall peasants are shown bringing various sacrificial animals (oxen, antelopes, geese) to four priests, the first of whom records the gifts, while the second offers incense. Farther right the animals are being slaughtered. On the left-hand (E and S) walls are similar scenes. To the left of the entrance are people with sacrificial offerings, who are met by a procession of priests, soldiers, the royal war chariot, Negro and Asian prisoners, etc. The colors are surprisingly fresh. – In the rooms to the rear are badly damaged religious scenes.

The reliefs on the outside of the temple (N and W sides), worked in fine white limestone, are among the finest produced in the reign of Ramesses II. They depict scenes from the King's war against the Hittites; adjoining is an account of the campaign. On the S wall is a long inscription recording the building of the temple and its endowments.

NW of Ramesses II's temple are the ruins of **Shunet el-Zebib**, surrounded by an outer and an inner (and higher) wall of sun-dried brick. The complex, 145 yds/ 133 m long, probably dates from the 2nd Dynasty and may have been a palace. The popular view of this structure as a fortress is undoubtedly erroneous.

A few hundred yards NE of Shunet el-Zebib, near the village of El-Khirba, are the remains of the **ancient city of Abydos** and the *Sanctuary of Osiris,* which dates back to the beginnings of Egyptian history. Of the sanctuary there remain only the brick enclosure walls built during the Middle Kingdom and scanty remains of the temple. – To the W is the Coptic Monastery of *Deir el-Sitt Damiana* (or Amba Musa), which dates from year 1306 of the Coptic era (A.D. 1590); it scarcely repays a visit.

1 mile/1·5 km SW of the Temple of Ramesses II is a mound of rubble known as the **Umm el-Gaab** ("mother of pots"), in which Amelineau and Flinders Petrie found the cenotaphs of kings of the 1st and 2nd Dynasties, including those of Djer (1st Dynasty), believed during the Middle Kingdom to be the Tomb of Osiris, Usaphais (1st Dynasty; *c.* 3100 B.C.) and Miebis (1st Dynasty; *c.* 3100 B.C.). Practically nothing of these monuments is now to be seen. – S of Abydos, at *Nag el-Ghabat,* is an ancient quarry.

Agilka
See under Philae

Ain Sukhna
See under Red Sea

Akhmim

Upper Egypt. – Governorate: Sohag.
(i) **Tourist Information Office,**
Tourist Bazaar,
Luxor;
tel. 22 15.

ACCESS. – By car or taxi from Sohag, crossing to the right bank of the Nile on the 725 yd/665 m long bridge (middle section swing bridge).

The modest district capital of Akhmim lies 3 miles/5 km E of Sohag on the right bank of the Nile, just N of a wide loop in the river. It has a number of cotton-mills and a lively bazaar. Akhmim is one of the great centers of the Coptic faith, with several churches.

HISTORY. – Akhmim occupies the site of the ancient **Chemmis** or **Panopolis**, which was the chief town of a nome. The Egyptians called it *Epu*, and also *Khente-Min*, after its protective deity, the ithyphallic harvest god Min: hence the Coptic name of Shmin and the Arabic Akhmim. Herodotus (ii, 91) praises the citizens of Chemmis as the only Egyptians who favored Greek customs and relates that they erected a temple to Perseus and worshiped him with Hellenic rites. Strabo refers to the weavers and stone-cutters of Panopolis. The town continued to flourish during the Roman period, and its ancient and famous temple was enlarged in the 12th year of Trajan's reign (A.D. 109). In Christian times many religious houses were built around Panopolis. The Patriarch of Constantinople, Nestorius, who had been banished to the Kharga Oasis because he did not acknowledge the Virgin Mary to be the Mother of God, died in Panopolis. Even after the Arab Conquest Akhmim was described by Abulfida and other writers as a great city, with temples which were among the finest remains of the Pharaonic period.

Until recently only scanty remains of this once-flourishing ancient city were visible. In 1981 the *colossal statue* of an Egyptian queen, with an estimated height of 33 ft/10 m, was uncovered. During excavations in 1987 remains of *temple c.* 2392 sq. yds/2000 sq m, several **Monumental statues** of Pharoah Ramses II and one of his daughters, and a marble statue of the Greek goddess Aphrodite were brought to light.

SURROUNDINGS of Akhmim. – Extensive **necropolises** have been found in the low hills some 3 miles/5 km NE of Akhmim. They are reached by way of the village of *El-Hawawish* (2½ miles/4 km), just beyond which, in a hill, are many ancient tombs, now totally destroyed. N and W of the village extends a Christian cemetery used from the 5th to the 15th c. In the vicinity is a *Coptic monastery*. The tombs farther to the N are older, dating from the Roman, Ptolemaic and Egyptian periods. Higher up in the hills lie 6th Dynasty tombs. – S of Akhmim is a rock chapel constructed in the reign of King Ay (18th Dynasty). – **Sohag**: see separate entry.

El-Alamein

Western Mediterranean coast. – North-West Frontier District.
(i) **Tourist Information Office,**
Shari' Salah Salem 33,
Alexandria;
tel. 2 50 25.

ACCOMMODATION. – *Rest-house* at British military cemetary. – In Sidi Abdel Rahman: Hotel Alamein I, 304 b. (some in chalets).

ACCESS. – Good asphalt road from Alexandria (68 miles/110 km; bus services). – By rail from Alexandria.

The modest village of El-Alamein gained a place in history during the Second World War, when, in the late summer and autumn of 1942, the advance of Rommel's Afrika Korps was halted by British forces in a series of bloody battles in which some 80,000 men on both sides were killed or wounded. El-Alamein (rather prophetically meaning "two flags" in Arabic) now attract many visitors to its military cemetary and war memorials.

In 1966 promising reserves of oil were found in the vicinity, and extraction began in 1968, giving a considerable boost to the economy of the area.

HISTORY. – During the German-Italian offensive in North Africa, which had been ordered by Hitler and Mussolini, a German and Italian armored force commanded by General Erwin Rommel (1891–1944) advanced from Tobruk (Libya) and on June 30, 1942, in the First Battle of El-Alamein, captured Hill 26 and occupied positions at El-Alamein. Their further advance towards Cairo, however, was thwarted by the resistance of British forces, who had established a defensive line between El-Alamein and the Qattara Depression. Then on October 23, 1942 the British Eighth Army commanded by Generals Montgomery and Alexander launched a major offensive and in the Second Battle of El-Alamein compelled Rommel to retreat on November 4, in spite of Hitler's order to hold the position at any cost. British military superiority in North Africa was thus assured, and the way was clear for the advance into Italy.

At km 105 (65 miles) on the road from Alexandria, in an extensive depression below the road on the left, is the **British Military Cemetery**, containing 7500 graves. In the middle of the cemetery stands a huge stone cross. On the opposite side of the road is a *rest-house*

German Memorial, El-Alamein

(accommodation). – Some 550 yds/ 500 m from the cemetery a *Museum,* established in 1965, contains weapons, documents and displays illustrating the course of the battles. In the courtyard is a collection of armored vehicles, guns and other heavy armament. – Beyond this point in the direction of Mersa Matruh sand-filled trenches, bunkers and other evidence of the battles of 1942 can be seen on both sides of the road.

Some 6 miles/10 km farther W, at km 115 (71 miles), the **German Memorial** stands on a hill near the sea. Erected in 1959, this is an octagonal structure of light-colored stone modelled on the Castel del Monte in Apulia. Here are buried 4200 of the 4500 Germans who died in the fighting. In the central courtyard stands a basalt obelisk 38 ft/ 11·5 m high.

Some 2½ miles/4 km farther W is the **Italian Memorial**, built of white marble with a high central tower. Beyond this is *Tell el-Eissa* (Hill 33), where the fate of the Afrika Korps was decided. The German-Italian military cemetery which

was laid out on the SE side of the hill after the war had to be abandoned on account of unfavorable climatic and geological conditions, and the remains of the fallen were removed to the new memorials, were removed to the new memorials.

SURROUNDINGS of El-Alamein. – 14 miles/23 km W is the little resort of **Sidi Abd el-Rahman**, named after a holy man revered by the bedouin as a prophet; the local mosque also bears his name. Here there are an excellent *beach in a beautiful setting and a modern luxury hotel. It is planned to lay a pipeline from the El-Alamein oilfield to Sidi Abd el-Rahman, which will be developed into a modern oil terminal. – From Sidi Abd el-Rahman the road continues W via *El-Dabaa,* the ancient Zephirium, to **Mersa Matruh** (80 miles/128 km; see separate entry).

Alexandria, Qattara Depression and **Western Desert**: see separate entries.

Alexandria/ El-Iskandariya

Lower Egypt. – Governorate: Alexandria.
Altitude: sea-level. – Population: 3,000,000.
ⓘ **Tourist Information Office,**
23 El Mina El Saa-kia Saad Zaghloul Sq,
tel. 003 020;
Misr Travel, Shari' Salah Salem 33,
tel. 2 50 25;
Main Railway Station,
tel. 2 59 85;
Maritime Station,
tel. 80 01 00.
Tourist Police,
in Midan Saad Zaghlul and at Main Railway Station, Maritime Station and Montazah Palace, tel. 863 804.
Automobile et Touring Club d'Egypte,
Shari' Salah Salem 15;
tel. 96 94 94–95.
Misr Travel,
Shari' Salah Salem 33;
tel. 2 50 25.

El-Alamein War Cemetery and Memorial, Commonwealth War Graves Commission

CONSULATES. – *United Kingdom:* Shari' Mina 3, Roushy Pasha; tel. 4 71 66. – *United States:* Shari'

Gamal Abdel Nasser 110; tel. 80 19 11.

HOTELS. – *Palestine*, in Montazah Palace, L, 416 b.; *Montazah Sheraton*, Corniche el Nil, near Montazah Palace, L, 660 b., SP private beach; *Ramada Renaissance*, Sharia el-Gúeish, 544, L, 360 b.; *Phenicia*, Sharia el-Nasr 21, I, 280 b.; *San Stefano*, San Stefano Sharia Abdel-Salam Aref, I, 244 b.; *Landmark*, San Stefano, Sharia Abdel-Salam Aref 163, I, 244 b.; *Windsor*, Sharia el Shohada 17, Raml Station, I, 200 b.; *Maamoura Palace*, in El-Maamura, 193 b.; *Alexandria*, Midan el-Nasr 23, El-Mansheya, I, 189 b.; *Cecil*, Midan Saad Saglul 16, I, 171 b.; *Salamlek*, near Montazah Palace, I, 110 b.; *Al-Mehreuk*, Sharia-el Gueish 133, 176 b.; *Summer Moon*, Betash, Beach, El Agami, 140 b.; *Al Haram*, Sharia el Gueish 162, Cleopatra, II 430 b.; *Hannoville*, Hannoville Beach, El Agami, II, 300 b.; *Mecca*, Sharia el-Gueish 44, Camp Cesar, II, 290 b.; *Amoun*, Midan el-Nasr 32 Mansheya, II, 240 b.; *Delta*, Sharia Champolion 14, Mazarita, II, 126 b.; *Admiral*, Shari Amin Fikri, II, 120 b.; *Metropole*, Sharia Saad Zaghoul 52, Raml Station, II, 120 b.; *Qasr el-Agami*, Bitash Beach, El Agami, II, 106 b.; *San Giovani*, Sharia el-Gueish 205, Stanley, II, 60 b.; *Isis*, near main railway station, Sharia Isis, III, 120 b.; *Dubai*, Sharia Hehia 13, III, 110 b.; *Noble*, Cleopatra, Sharia -el-Gueish 152, III 80 b.; *New Admiral*, in Agami Hannoville, III, 80 b.; *Borg el-Thaghr*, Sharia Safija Saglul/Sharia el Hurreja, III, 69 b.; *New Capri*, near Miyami Beach, Sharia el-Mina el Sharkija, III, 64 b.; *Lolowa*, Sharia Mustafa Naguib, III, 59 b.; *Corail*, Mandara, Sharia el-Gueish 802, III, 52 b.; *Swiss Cottage*, Sharia el-Gueish 347, III, 46 b.; *Le Roy*, Sharia Talaat Harb, IV, 140 b.; *El-Andalos*, Sharia Port-Said 273, IV, 133 b.; *Minas*, El-Agami, IV, 120 b.; *Gordon*, Midan Saad Saglul 19, IV, 100 b.; *Hyde Park*, Sharia Amin Fikri 21, IV, 95 b.; others – in Sidi Krer, 134 km W of Alexandria: *Sidi Krer*, II, 60 b.; At King Mariut, 135 km SW of Alexandria: *Desert Home*, II, 28 b.; *King Mariut*, III, 40 b.; *Mont Ribo*, IV, 30 b.

YOUTH HOSTEL: Sharia Port Said 13. – Y.M.C.A./ Y.W.C.A., El-Asarita, Sharia Sultan Abd el-Asis 18; Y.M.M.A., near Shoban Moslemin railway station.

CAMPING SITES at *Abuqir*, 18 miles/29 km NE and at *Sidi Krer*, 21 miles/34 km W.

CAFÉS: *Delices*, opposite the Hotel Cecil; *Athineos*, at Babel-Ahtar.

BEACHES: *Chatby, Ibrahimiya, Sporting, Cleopatra, Sidi Gaber, Stanley, San Stefano, Sidi Bishr, Miyami, Mandara, Montazah, Maamura, Abuqir.*

LEISURE: *Watersports, golf course (18 holes), horse riding, tennis.*

The ancient and famous city of ** Alexandria (Arabic El-Iskandariya), Egypt's second largest city and principal port, lies at the western extremity of the Nile Delta on the sandy strip of land which separates Lake Mareotis (Maryut) from the Mediterranean. Alexandria remains the most European of Egyptian cities, even with the Islamic influence becoming more apparent recently. The old town preserves the atmosphere and activities of the East.

Alexandria is a great center of the Egyptian cotton trade (Cotton Exchange), and there are many spinning-mills, weaving-mills and other textile-working establishments in and around the city. Other major industrial activities include a thriving foodstuffs industry, cigarette factories, tanneries and an oil-refinery.

Thanks to its economic importance as a center of trade in the Eastern Mediterranean, Alexandria has long had a considerable foreign colony. Most of the Europeans who make up some 4% of the population are Greeks and Italians. – Alexandria is the seat of an Orthodox

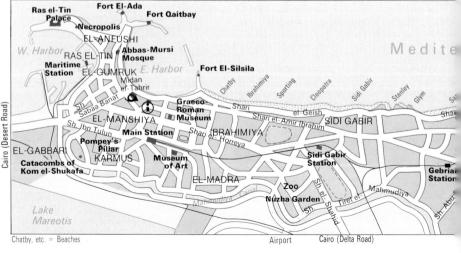

Chatby, etc. = Beaches

Patriarch. The head of the Egyptian Coptic Church, who bears the style of Patriarch of Alexandria, resides in Cairo, as does the Patriarch of the Coptic Catholic Church.

HISTORY. – Alexandria was founded in 331 B.C. by *Alexander the Great*, whose object was to link the land of the Pharaohs, both materially and culturally, with the Greek world empire which it was his great ambition to establish. The site he selected opposite the island of Pharos, near the Egyptian village of Rhakotis, between the Mediterranean and Lake Mareotis, which was connected with the Nile by several navigable channels, was well chosen, for the older harbors to the E were threatened with silting-up by the Nile mud as a result of the current which flowed along the North African coast from the Strait of Gibraltar. The planning and building of the new city was entrusted to the Greek architect Deinocrates. Under Alexander's lieutenant and successor, Ptolemy I Soter (322–285 B.C.), Alexandria became the resort of artists and scholars, among them the philosopher Demetrius of Phaleron, who suggested the foundation of the famous Library, the painters Apelles and Antiphilus, the celebrated mathematician Euclid and the physicians Erasistratus and Herophilus. Ptolemy also founded the Museum (Mouseion), a splendid complex of buildings dedicated to the pursuit of science and literature in which a whole range of scholars dwelt, studied and taught.

In spite of the continual dissensions among the Ptolemies over succession to the throne Alexandria continued to flourish as the world's greatest commercial center and the principal seat of Greek learning. In 48 B.C., when Rome intervened in the quarrel between Cleopatra and her brother and husband Ptolemy XIV, the city was at the peak of its fame. After the murder of Pompey at Pelusium Caesar entered Alexandria in triumph, but was then attacked by the citizens and Ptolemy XIV's army and had considerable difficulty in maintaining his position in the Regia or "Royal City" (see box on next page). Cleopatra was able to win over by her charms first Caesar and later Antony, who lived with her in Alexandria from 42 to 30 B.C. Augustus enlarged the city by the addition of the suburb of Nicopolis. At this prosperous period Alexandria was said to have a population of more than

half a million; the Greek element predominated, followed by the Egyptian, while there was also a separate Jewish community, originally established in the time of Ptolemy I.

In A.D. 69 Vespasian was proclaimed Emperor by the citizens of Alexandria, largely as a result of the influence of the philosophers of the Museum. In the reign of Trajan (98–117) the Jews, who then constituted a third of the population, were the cause of bloody riots. In the year 130 the Emperor Hadrian (117–138) visited Alexandria and instituted public disputations in the Museum. Marcus Aurelius (161–180) attended the lectures of the grammarians Athenaeus, Harpocration, Hephaestion, Julius Pollux and other scholars. During this period, too, the Greek satirical writer Lucian lived in Alexandria as Secretary to the Prefect of Egypt. Septimius Severus (193–211) visited the city in 199 and granted it a municipal consitution. The next Imperial visit was disastrous, for Caracalla (211–217) was derided by the citizens and revenged himself by a bloody massacre and the closure of the Academy. Alexandria suffered still more cruelly during the fighting between Palmyrene and Imperial forces in the second half of the 3rd c., when a large part of the population was carried away by the sword, famine and pestilence.

Christianity established itself in Alexandria at an early stage. According to tradition the Gospel was first preached here by St Mark (whose remains were carried off to Venice in 828). The first great persecution of the Christians in the reign of Decius (250) hit Alexandria hard. The city had been for many years the seat of a bishop, and had had since 190 a theological school, presided over by Pantaenus and, at the beginning of the 3rd c., by Clement of Alexandria, which sought to combine Christianity with the Neo-Platonism which developed about this period and was taught by Ammonius Saccas, Herennius, Plotinus, Porphyrius, Iamblichus and others. A second persecution took place in 257 during the reign of Valerian, and soon afterwards, in the reign of Gallienus, plague carried off a large part of the population. Nevertheless Alexandria still remained the principal seat of Christian learning and the orthodox faith (Athanasian Creed) until it was compelled to yield this position to the newly founded city of Constantinople. Sanguinary quarrels took place between the Athanasian party and the Arians under their unworthy bishop Georgius. During the reign of

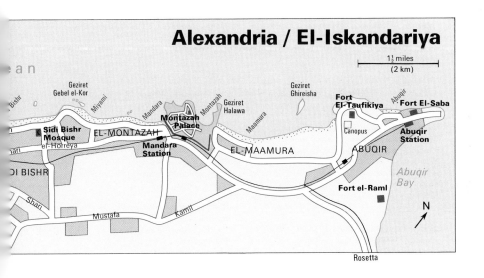

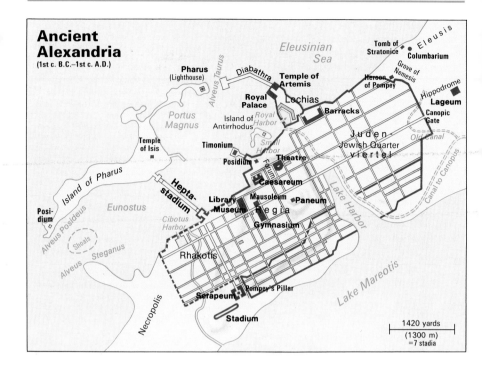

Ancient Alexandria (1st c. B.C.–1st c. A.D.)

In the 17th book of his "Geographica" the Greek scholar *Strabo* (63 B.C.–A.D. 20) describes Alexandria as it was in the third decade B.C.

On the former island of **Pharus** *(Pharos)*, then linked to the mainland by a causeway, the Heptastadium (Heptastadion), stood the famous **Lighthouse**, one of the Seven Wonders of the World. Built of white limestone by Sostratus the Cnidian in the reign of Ptolemy II Philadephus, it was completed in 280–279 B.C. Its original height is said to have been 400 cubits (590 ft/180 m: cf. p. 62); and though even in antiquity it was several times in danger of collapsing, part of the ancient tower still stood erect after the great earthquakes of 1303 and 1326. Sections of the old masonry were incorporated in Fort Qaitbay when it was built in the 15th c.

The **Heptastadion** was also constructed in the reign of Ptolemy II, or perhaps of Ptolemy I. As the name indicates, it was 7 stadia (1400 yds/ 1300 m) long. It was pierced by two passages, both bridged over, and before the time of Caesar served also as an aqueduct.

Strabo refers to a number of the principal quarters of the city: the NECROPOLIS, at the W end of the area, "where there are many gardens, tombs and establishments for embalming bodies"; RHAKOTIS, "the quarter of Alexandria situated above the naval arsenal", which was chiefly inhabited by Egyptians; the REGIA or "Royal City" (later known as Bruchium), with various public buildings, which lay between the Heptastadion and the Lochias Peninsula and was later enclosed by walls; and the JEWISH QUARTER, to the E of the Regia.

Outside the Canopic Gate at the E end of the city was the Hippodrome, and farther to the E,

30 stadia from the city, was the suburb of NICOPOLIS, which had an amphitheatre and a racecourse.

The city was laid out on a regular plan, with streets intersecting at right angles. The principal thoroughfare was the long street which ran W from the Canopic Gate.

Only a few scanty remnants of the buildings of ancient Alexandria can now be identified. – The **Caesareum** was a large temple begun by Cleopatra in honor of Antony and completed by Augustus as a center of the Imperial cult. At the entrance stood the two "Cleopatra's Needles" which are now in London and New York. – The **Paneum** was probably the hill now known as Kom el-Dik; the **Gymnasium** may have stood on the E side of the hill.

The Theater, the Sema and the Museum were in the "Royal City". The **Theater** was situated opposite the island of Antirrhodus, so that the spectators had the sea as a backdrop to the performance. The *Sema*, near the Royal Palace, was an enclosed space within which were the tombs of Alexander the Great and the Ptolemies. The **Museum** *(Mouseion, "seat of the Muses")* had "a hall for walking, another for sitting and a large building with a refectory for the scholars attached to the Museum". Associated with the Museum was the great Alexandrian **Library**, which as early as the reign of Ptolemy II Philadelphus possessed 400,000 papyrus rolls, a figure which had risen to almost 900,000 in the time of Caesar.

The **Serapeum** *(Serapeion)*, dedicated to the worship of Serapis, god of the Underworld – a cult introduced by the Ptolemies – stood on the hill now crowned by Pompey's Pillar.

Julian the Apostate (361–363) the Christians of Alexandria were again persecuted. Under Theodosius (379–395), however, paganism received its death-blow. Patriarch Theophilus of Alexandria showed the utmost zeal in destroying pagan temples and monuments, and the famous statue of Serapis was destroyed by fire. The material prosperity of the city now declined, so that it could no longer meet the cost of cleansing the Nile and keeping the canals open. Its revenues were reduced still further when the Jews were expelled from the city by Patriarch Cyril. In 415 the learned and beautiful pagan Hypatia, the principal opponent of the fanatical Cyril, was stoned to death by a mob. The pagan schools were finally closed during the reign of Justinian (527–565).

In 619 Alexandria was captured by King Chosroes II of Persia, but the Christians were not molested. In 626 the Persians were driven out by Heraclius; but soon afterwards the armies of the Caliph Omar advanced into Egypt under the banner of Islam, and in October 641 the city was taken after a prolonged siege. Omar's general, Amr ibn el-As, treated the inhabitants with moderation; but Alexandria now continued to decline, while the new capital of Cairo prospered. The discovery of America and the sea route to India finally destroyed the city's commerce.

The decay of Alexandria, which by 1800 had a population of only 5000, was finally arrested by *Mohammed (Mehemet) Ali*, who improved the harbor and constructed a number of canals. His main contribution was the construction of the Mahmudiya Canal (begun in 1819), named after the reigning Sultan Mahmud II, which irrigated the surrounding country and linked Alexandria with the rest of Egypt, whose products had hitherto been shipped from Rosetta and Damietta. During Arabi's Rising in 1882 much of the European quarter was burned down. Thereafter, however, Alexandria began to recover its prosperity, and it is now the largest and most important city in Egypt after Cairo. In 1988 Cleopatra's main palace was uncovered. There are plans to have the ancient library restored.

Sightseeing in Alexandria

The hub of the city's life is the **Midan el-Tahrir** (Freedom Square), in which are an equestrian statue of Mohammed Ali,

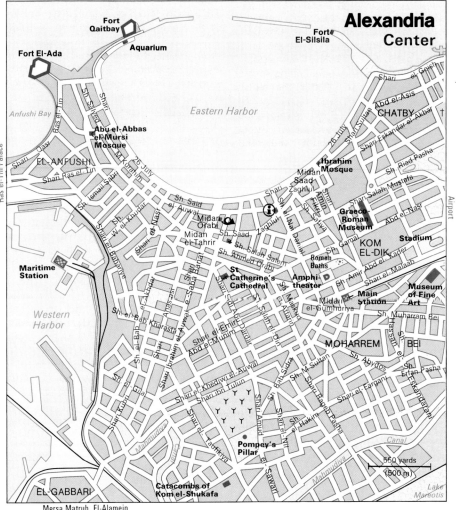

Eastern Harbor and Fort Qaitbay, Alexandria

(1872) the *Law Courts*, the Anglican *St Mark's Church*. – Immediately N is the Midan Ahmed Orabi, also laid out in gardens, which leads to the magnificent seafront promenade known as the *Corniche (Sharia July 26), running round the S side of the old EASTERN HARBOR, the principal harbor (Portus Magnus) of the ancient city, in a wide arc. Within the harbor archaeologists have recently discovered, at a depth of some 26 ft/8 m, remains of Cleopatra's palaces, of which Strabo gives a detailed account, and other ancient buildings and quays.

SW of the old harbor is the modern WESTERN HARBOR, known in antiquity as *Eunostos* ("Harbor of the Safe Return"). It consists of the small *Inner Harbor* within the Coal Pier and the *Outer Harbor*, protected by a breakwater 2 miles/ 3·25 km long, which can accommodate large vessels.

The tongue of land between the eastern and western harbors developed out of the ancient causeway known as the Heptastadion which led out to the island of **Pharos**, site of the famous Lighthouse which was one of the Seven Wonders of the World. On this are the picturesque ARAB and TURKISH QUARTERS. Two notable buildings to be seen here are the *Abu el-Abbas el-Mursi Mosque, built in 1796 over the tomb of the 13th c. holy man Abu el-Abbas, who is much revered in Alexandria, and the *Mosque of Ibrahim Terbana* (1648), which incorporates Graeco-Roman columns. – At the northern tip of Pharos, on the site of the

ancient Lighthouse (finally destroyed by two earthquakes in the 14th c.), is the 15th c. **Fort Qaitbay**, which houses a small naval Museum. A short distance SW is the *Hydrobiological Institute*, with an Aquarium containing a colorful collection from the Mediterranean, Red Sea and the Nile (open 9 a.m. to 2 p.m.). – At the NW end of the Pharos Peninsular is the sumptuous **Ras el-Tin Palace** (Ras el-Tin="Cape of Figs"), which in the time of Mohammed Ali was the royal summer residence, it now provides accommodation for visiting dignitaries and is not open to the public. – E of the palace is the Greek *Anfushi Necropolis*, which dates from the Ptolemaic period (2nd c. B.C.).

To the S of Midan el-Tahrir stands the Roman Catholic **St Catherine's Cathedral**. In the crypt is the tomb of King Victor Emmanuel III of Italy, who died in exile in Egypt in 1947; it is planned to transfer his remains to Italy.

In a side street opening off the wide tree-lined Tariq Gamal Abdel Nasser we find the important *Graeco-Roman Museum** (open, winter 9 a.m. to 4 p.m.; closed Friday from 11.30 a.m. to 1.30 p.m.). Most of its collection comes from Alexandria itself, mainly from tombs ranging in date between 300 B.C. and A.D. 300.

To the right of the *Vestibule* (prehistoric material; two sphinxes from the time of Apries) is *Room 1:* Christian antiquities, in particular tombstones, stelae and numbers of "St Menas flasks" for holding holy water and oil from the Tomb of St Menas (martyred A.D. 296: see under Abu Mena). – *Rooms 2–5:* Early Christian Coptic art and part of the large collection (some 50,000 in all) of Alexandrian coins (300 B.C.–A.D. 500). – *Room 6:* Greek and Latin documents of the

Abu el-Abbas el-Mursi Mosque, Alexandria

Graeco-Roman Museum   Alexandria

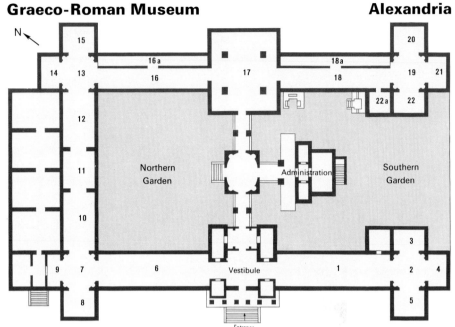

town's history. – *Rooms 7–9:* Egyptian antiquities. Particularly notable are a colossal statue of Ramesses II in reddish granite (Room 7) and a crocodile mummy from the Fayyum which yielded important papyri (Room 9). – *Room 10:* the Antoniades Collection of small Egyptian sculpture, including scarabs, amulets, statuettes, canopic jars, etc. – *Room 11:* Graeco-Egyptian and Roman-Egyptian sculpture, architectural fragments and mosaics. – *Room 12:* portrait busts and small sculpture. – *Rooms 13–15:* Sculpture and architectural fragments of the Hellenistic period; Medusa mosaic from Gabbari (Room 14); Roman fresco depicting a wheel for raising water (*sakiya:* Room 15). – *Room 16:* Greek sculpture and sculptural fragments, including a large eagle in white marble. – *Room 16a:* small sculpture. – *Room 17:* sculpture; mosaic pavement (banquet with musicians); sarcophagi. – *Room 18:* small objects, mosaics, pottery. – *Room 18a:* terracottas and Tanagra figures of the Early Ptolemaic period. – *Room 19:* glass and pottery vessels; mosaics. – *Room 20:* grave-goods and garlands from local cemeteries. – *Room 21:* pottery figures, urns and vases from tombs at Chatby and Ibrahimiya. – *Room 22:* glass of the Ptolemaic and Roman periods. – *Room 22a:* bronze sculpture. – *Room 23:* coins and jewelry from the Ptolemaic period.

Northern Garden: Egyptian sculpture. – *Southern Garden:* two reconstructed tombs (3rd c. B.C., 1st c. A.D.); sarcophagi.

A short distance W of the Graeco-Roman Museum is the excavation site of **Kom el-Dik**, formerly occupied by a fort, where a Roman *Amphitheater* and remains of baths (3rd c.) and an odeon have been brought to light. The amphitheater, the only one of the Roman era to be found in Egypt, is in almost perfect condition. Thirteen rows of marble seating compose the semi-circular structure and capitals from broken pillars indicate some of the original ornamentation. The site may be entered either from Shari Abdel Moneim,

close to the main railway station, or from Shari Safiya Zaghlul. – SE of the Graeco-Roman Museum, beyond the railway lines leading to the *Main Railway Station,* is the **Museum of Fine Art** (Egyptian and European painting of the 16th-19th c.).

In the SW of the city, near the large Arab cemetery, is a hill littered with the remains of ancient walls, architectural fragments and rubble on which stands Alexandria's largest ancient monument, ***Pompey's Pillar**, rising from the ruins of the ancient and famous Serapeion (Temple of

Pompey's Pillar, Alexandria

Serapis). This column of red Aswan granite with a Corinthian capital, standing on a badly ruined substructure and rising to a height of almost 90 ft/27 m, is traditionally believed to have been erected by the Emperor Theodosius to commemorate the victory of Christianity over paganism and the destruction of the Serapeion in 391. More probably, however, it was set up in 292 in honor of Diocletian, who supplied food for the starving population after the siege of the city.

SW of Pompey's Pillar, near the small *El-Miri Mosque*, is the entrance to the *Catacombs of Kom el-Shukafa ("Hill of Potsherds"), hewn from the rock on the southern slopes of a hill, which probably date from the 2nd c. A.D. and offer an admirable example of the characteristic Alexandrian fusion of the Egyptian and Graeco-Roman styles.

The catacombs, which may have been the burial-place of a particular religious community, were discovered in 1900. Laid out on several levels, they have been made conveniently accessible by the provision of wooden gangways and electric light. A spiral staircase with a large circular *light-shaft* runs down two storeys, the lower of which is generally under water; near the

top of the staircase is a *sarcophagus chamber* of later construction. Off the upper level opens a *rotunda* with a domed roof, to the right of which are two smaller chambers with niches, sarcophagi and loculi (shelf tombs); to the left is a large room, the *Triclinium funebre*, used for banquets in honor of the dead. From the rotunda a staircase continues down and then divides: from this point there is a view of the main burial chambers. At the foot of the stairs is the entrance to the *Sepulchral Chapel*, with three niches containing sarcophagi. In the central niche the mummy lies on a bier, surrounded by the three gods of the Underworld, Horus, Thoth and Anubis. Round the sepulchral chapel runs a gallery, entered from the vestibule to the chapel, containing 91 loculi, each large enough to accommodate at least three or four mummies. – In the vicinity of the Kom el-Shukafa catacombs are other small and less important catacombs of the Graeco-Roman period.

Stanley Beach, Alexandria

In the SE of the city the beautiful *Nuzha Gardens* incorporate a small *Zoo*. Immediately S of this are the no less attractive *Antoniadis Gardens*, once the country estate of a wealthy Greek citizen.

From the Eastern Harbor the seafront promenade, the *Corniche* (Sharia el-Geish), extends E for 10 miles/17 km, past picturesque coves and beautiful sandy beaches, to the *Park* of **Montazah Palace**, formerly a royal summer residence and now used by the government for meetings. Next to it is the luxury "Palestine" hotel (residence of well-to-do Palestinians).

SURROUNDINGS of Alexandria

7½ miles/12 km NE of the Montazah Palace, on a promontory defended on all sides by old forts, is the fishing village of **Abuqir** (Aboukir). In Abuqir Bay was fought the Battle of the Nile (August 1, 1798), in which Nelson inflicted an annihilating defeat on the French fleet. Here, too, in 1799, Napoleon defeated a numerically much superior Turkish force; and here in 1801 Sir Ralph Abercromby defeated the remnants of

Alexandria   **Catacombs of Kom el-Shukafa**

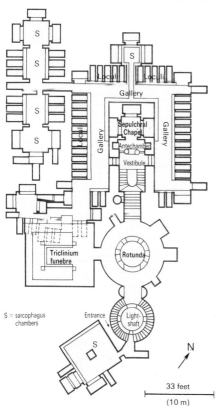

S = sarcophagus chambers

Montazah Palace, Alexandria

the French army and compelled them to evacuate Egypt. – SW of the village is the site of the important ancient port of *Canopus*, of which only scanty remains survive; the site is now in a military area and closed to the public.

Some 28 miles/45 km SW of Alexandria we come to *Abusir, with the scanty remains of the ancient city of *Taposiris Magna*, which lay in the plain. On a limestone ridge rising from the seashore, however, are the well-preserved remains of the enclosure wall of an *Egyptian temple*, which the Greek name of the city suggests may have been dedicated to Osiris. The temple, oriented from E to W, was entered by a handsome pylon, which, like the rest of the walls, was built of limestone blocks. In the interior of each of the two towers is a staircase (fine *view from top). Adjoining the pylon is the temple (interior destroyed), which was 295 ft/90 m long and surrounded by high walls. – A little way N of the temple are the remains of a Roman lighthouse. The rocks in the neighborhood contain many old quarries and Roman tombs. Near the temple a bath has been excavated, and rather farther away is an animal cemetery.

See also *Abu Mena, Damanhur, *El-Alamein, Nile Delta, Rosetta, *Wadi Natrun and Western Desert.

Amada

Upper Egypt. – Governorate: Aswan.
ⓘ **Tourist Information Office,**
Tourist Bazaar,
Aswan;
tel. 32 97.

Some 125 miles/200 km S of Aswan, in the most fertile part of Nubia, is the *Rock Temple of Amada. Constructed on its original site, on the left bank of the Nile, by Tuthmosis III

and Amenophis II (18th Dynasty), it was dedicated to Amun-Re and Re-Harakhty. Tuthmosis IV later enlarged it by the addition of a Hypostyle Hall. The figures of Amun, defaced by Amenophis IV, were restored by Sethos I. In Christian times the temple became a church and the reliefs were covered over, and as a result have preserved their original brilliant coloring.

With the construction of the Aswan High Dam the rising waters of Lake Nasser threatened to engulf this monument along with many others; and in a rescue operation carried out by a French firm the entire temple was sawn out of the solid rock and re-erected on a new site – now known as **New Amada** – 1½ miles/2·6 km farther N and 213 ft/65 m above its original level.

THE TEMPLE. – The *Temple of Amada, oriented roughly N and S, is entered through a stone *gateway,* originally flanked by brick pylon towers. On the right-hand side is Tuthmosis III and on the left Amenophis II in the presence of Re-Harakhty. On the inside of the gateway, to the left, is an inscription referring to a campaign by Merneptah against the Ethiopians, and beyond this is the praying figure of Setaw, Governor of Nubia in the reign of Ramesses II.

Beyond the pylon there was originally a court enclosed by brick walls, on the far side of which was a hall with four Proto-Doric columns. This court was later converted by Tuthmosis IV into a covered **Hypostyle Hall** (32½ ft/9·95 m long, 26–28½ ft/7·90–8·70 m wide, 14½ ft/4·40 m high), still excellently preserved, by the addition of 12 pillars and stone lateral walls. The reliefs on the pillars and the walls show Tuthmosis IV holding converse with the gods. The inscriptions on the architraves are also in his name. The columns bear dedicatory inscriptions by Tuthmosis III and Amenophis II, who are also depicted on the rear wall.

Adjoining the Hypostyle Hall is a **Transverse Chamber** (25 ft/7·50 m long, 7 ft/2·10 m deep, 12 ft/3·65 m high). On the right-hand side of the entrance wall are Tuthmosis III being embraced by Isis and Amenophis II sacrificing to Amun-Re. On the left-hand side the gods Thoth and Horus of Edfu are depicted pouring the consecrating water, in the form of the hieroglyphs for "life", over Amenophis II.

In the rear wall of the Transverse Chamber are three doors. The two side doors each lead into a chamber; the right-hand one has reliefs depicting the ceremonies associated with the foundation of a temple. The central door gives access to the **Sanctuary**, on the rear wall of which is an *inscription* of great historical importance dating from the third year of Amenophis II's reign. It records the completion of the temple and a campaign in Syria during which Amenophis captured seven Syrian princes and hanged six of them on the walls of Thebes and the seventh at Napata. Above the inscription is the solar barque with the gods Re-Harakhty and Amun, to whom the King is making a libation of wine. – At the far end of the sanctuary, to the right and left, are two small rooms, which were connected with the side chambers entered from the Transverse Chamber by doors of later construction (now walled up).

SURROUNDINGS. – Near the Amada Temple stands another temple moved from its original site to save it from being submerged, the **Rock Temple of El-Derr**. Before its removal in 1964 it was the only Nubian temple on the right bank of the river, situated some 7 miles/11 km SW of New Amada near the district capital of El-Derr (now beneath Lake Nasser). This "Temple of Ramesses in the house of Re", dedicated to the sun god Re-Harakhty, is also oriented N and S. The pylon and the court constructed in front of the rock-cut temple have disappeared.

The visitor now enters directly into the much-ruined **Hypostyle Hall**, partly hewn from the rock and partly constructed. The roof was supported by 12 square pillars in three rows, but only those in the back row, against which were statues of Ramesses, still stand to any height. Only the lower parts of the walls, the reliefs on which were of considerable historical importance, are left. On the left-hand side of the entrance wall are traces of chariots and warriors. On the right-hand (W) wall are scenes from Ramesses's Nubian campaign. In the upper row (much damaged) he is shown in his chariot, accompanied by his lion, conducting a group of prisoners to the god; in the adjoining scene he is sacrificing to Amun-Re. In the lower row he is depicted in his chariot shooting arrows at his fleeing foes; the fugitives are seen conveying their wounded

to the mountains, where a herdsman's family, surrounded by their livestock, wait anxiously; to the left Egyptian soldiers are shown bringing in Negro (Kushite) prisoners. On the left-hand (E) wall are the remains of several reliefs: (from left to right) prisoners brought before the King; the King in battle; the King on foot, smiting his enemies; the King leading two files of prisoners to Re-Harakhty to serve as slaves in his temple. Above, the King is depicted in the presence of Amun.

On the rear wall, to the left of the door, the King is shown grasping his enemies by the hair and smiting them with a club, while his lion seizes one of the enemy by the leg and the falcon-headed Re-Harakhty hands the King the sickle-shaped sword. To the right the King presents an image of Maat to the ram-headed Khnum. At the foot of the wall are the royal Princes with their fans. To the right of the door the King is depicted smiting his enemies in the presence of Amun-Re; to the left, above, he makes a libation of wine to Ptah and another god; below, he burns incense before Thoth.

The following **Ceremonial Hall** has six square pillars with reliefs depicting the King before various deities. In a scene on the W wall he is shown burning incense before the sacred barque of Re-Harakhty, which is adorned with falcons' heads and carried by priests. In another scene on the E wall he is seen offering flowers to the barque. – Beyond this hall are three chapels, the central one being the **Sanctuary**, in which the sacred barque was kept. On the rear wall are four seated figures (partly destroyed) of the gods worshiped in the temple: (from left to right) Re-Harakhty, the deified Ramesses II, Amun-Re and Ptah.

Another monument brought to Amada to save it from the rising waters is the **Rock Tomb of Pennut**, Steward of Ramesses VI (20th Dynasty) in the district of Wawat in Lower Nubia. It is of interest for its rich and well-preserved *decoration, with extensive inscriptions. This was the latest tomb in an extensive necropolis of the New Kingdom situated some 25 miles/40 km S on the right bank of the Nile, near the village (now submerged) of Aniba, which occupied the site of the ancient Mem or Miam, capital of Lower Nubia and residence of the Egyptian Viceroy.

The tomb is of the very simplest form. The entrance leads straight into a transverse chamber (21 ft/6·5 m wide by 9 ft/2·8 m deep), in the rear wall of which is a niche. The scenes on the right-hand (E) side depict life in this world, those on the left-hand side the life Beyond. There are two registers on all the walls. – To the left of the entrance are Pennut and his wife in prayer.

Right-hand side. – Entrance wall: a 20-line inscription recording donations in honor of a statue of Ramesses VI; adjoining, above, Ramesses's Governor presents two silver vessels to Pennut, and the Governor and a steward in the presence of the royal family; Pennut robed by two servants; below, Pennut and his wife praying and sacrificing to their ancestors. – Rear wall: Pennut, his wife and his six sons praying before Re-Harakhty and (below) before Osiris.

Left-hand side. – Entrance wall, above: Pennut before the doorway into the Beyond; Pennut and his wife praying in the world Beyond; Anubis weighing Pennut's heart against truth and justice, with Thoth recording the result. – Entrance wall, below: "opening of the mouth" scene; lamentation for Pennut; Harsiesis leads Pennut and his wife to the throne of Osiris; Anubis at Pennut's bier; text from the "Book of the Dead"; Pennut and his wife praying. – Rear wall, above: Pennut praying before the Hathor cow; Pennut and his wife before Re-Khepri. – Rear wall, below: Anubis and Thoth pouring the consecrating water over the dead couple; Pennut and his wife praying before Ptah, Sokar and Osiris. – Around the entrance to the niche are scenes of prayer; above, the sacred barque. In the niche are three unfinished divine statues.

Wadi el-Sebwa: see separate entry.

Amarna
See Tell el-Amarna

El-Arish

Sinai Peninsula. – Sinai Frontier District.
Population: 30,000.
(i) **Tourist Information Office,**
Misr Travel Tower,
Cairo – Abbasia;
tel. 82 60 16.

ACCESS. – Expressway from Cairo to Ismailia (75 miles/120 km), then 118 miles/190 km on the coast road along the N side of the Sinai Peninsula. – By air from Cairo (regular flights).

HOTELS. – *Oberoi El-Arish,* I, 300 b.; Sinai Beach, II, 48 b.; *Al-Ubur*; *Al-Salam*; *Moon-Light*; *Golden Beach*; *Misr*; *Al-Nasr*; *Kouieder*; etc. – CAMPSITE belonging to the Automobile Club.

El-Arish, chief town of the Sinai Frontier District, the largest town on the peninsula and seat of a faculty of the Suez Canal University, lies amid beautiful groves of date-palms and fertile oasis gardens on the Mediterranean coast at the mouth of the Wadi el-Arish, Sinai's largest river (dry for part of the year). El-Arish is a fishing port and a bedouin settlement with some recently established industries.

HISTORY. – The town is said to have been founded in Pharaonic times as a place of banishment. In the Ptolemaic period it was known as *Rhinocorura* or *Rhinocolura* ("severed nose"), perhaps because prisoners confined here had their noses cut off to distinguish them as such. – With its abundant springs and ancient groves of date-palms, the town was from an early period an important staging-point on the Via Maris, the military road and trading-route between Palestine and Egypt. – In the Byzantine period the town, then known as *Laris,* was the see of a bishop. – In the 11th c. its population consisted predominantly of Jews, who called it *Hazor.* Baldwin I, King of Jerusalem, died here in 1118. – In 1799 Napoleon took the town but was compelled to give it up again under the Convention of El-Arish (January 24, 1800).

The Arabic name El-Arish means "hut" – referring to a legend that Jacob stayed here in a hut which he constructed for himself during his journey from Canaan into Egypt. This was one factor which led Theodor Herzl to see the town and the Arish Valley as the nucleus of a new Jewish State: a project which foundered on British resistance. – In 1948 El-Arish was a base for Egyptian bombers. It was briefly occupied by Israel in 1956, and again after the Six Day War of 1967. In 1980, under the Camp David Agreements, it was returned to Egypt. The return to Egypt of further territory in Sinai in 1982 moved the Egyptian-Israeli frontier some 25 miles/40 km E of El-Arish, adjoining the Gaza Strip.

The most notable features of this popular resort are its groves of *date-palms*, which are cultivated by the bedouin in considerable numbers and represent a major source of wealth for their owners. They practice an unusual method of cultivation, found only here, digging down until they find moist soil and planting palm cuttings in the sheltered depressions thus created; the excavated soil is consolidated with stones to provide further protection. After some years – by which time the holes have been filled by drifting sand – the young palms are strong enough to stand up to the harsh desert conditions. The palms supply the bedouin not only with food but also with building material for the light palm huts which are still commonly found in this area. Bedouin life is portrayed in the *Sinai Museum*, on the outskirts of town on the road to Rafah. – The magnificent white-sand *beach* of El-Arish is crowded in summer.

Sinai: see separate entry.

Armant
See under Tod

Ashmunein
See under Mallawi

Aswan – a general view

Aswan

Upper Egypt. – Governorate: Aswan.
Population: 200,000.

ⓘ **Tourist Information Office,**
Tourist Bazaar;
tel. 332 297.

Tourist Police,
Tourist Bazaar;
tel. 323 163.

Misr Travel,
Tourist Bazaar;
tel. 23 23.

ACCOMMODATION. – *Sheraton-Amon Village,* Sahara City, L, 504 b., upper part of Lake Nasser; *New Cataract Hotel,* Sharia Abtal el-Tahrir, L, 280 b., and *Cataract Hotel,* Sharia Abtal el-Tahrir, I, 215 b., beautifully situated above the Nile; *Aswan Oberoi,* L, 274 b., on the island of Elephantine; *Kalabsha,* Sharia Abtal el-Tahrir, I, 220 b., beyond the Cataract Hotel; *Isis,* I, 160 b.; *Amoun,* I, 72 b., on the island of that name; *Cleopatra,* Sharia Saad Zaghloul, II, 200 b.; *Abu Simbel,* II, 132 b.; *Nile City,* II, 108 b.; *Gran Hotel,* III, 325 b.; *Philae,* III, 68 b.; also Club Méditerranée "Amoun". – YOUTH HOSTEL. Sharia Abtal el-Tahrir.

ACCESS. – Road from Cairo along E bank of Nile (590 miles/950 km). – By rail from Cairo, 16 hours. – By air from Cairo via Luxor, 2½ hours. – Nile cruise ships run by the Hilton and Sheraton hotel groups, offering a high standard of amenity; smaller boats run by Egyptian companies, with more modest standards of comfort.

The town *Aswan (ancient Greek Syene) in Upper Egypt, celebrated for its cleanliness, lies in latitude 24° 5 N below the First Cataract. Situated on the E bank of the Nile, partly on low ground and partly on a hill, it is a much-favored winter resort thanks to its equable dry and warm climate and its sand-baths, which are efficacious in the treatment of diseases of the joints. Aswan, the capital of Egypt's most southerly governorate and the terminus of the railway line along the Nile Valley, has a university which is still in course of development. (A Nubian museum is planned.) – As a result of the construction of the **High Dam farther up the valley Aswan is now becoming one of the country's principal industrial centers (steel, nitrogen, electric power).

At Aswan the Nile divides into several arms, separated by large granite rocks and islands, in particular the island of Elephantine. There is only a narrow strip of cultivable land, supporting almost nothing but date-palms; the dates produced here are considered the best in Egypt. – The Southern Cross constellation is visible here in January about 3 a.m., in April about 10 p.m.

HISTORY. – The area around modern Aswan, including the island of Elephantine, was known in antiquity as *Yebu* ("Elephant Land"), perhaps because the Egyptians saw elephants here for the first time or because the rocks in the river, worn smooth by the water, were thought to resemble the backs of a herd of elephants. At a later date the name was restricted to the island and town of Elephantine. From the earliest times down to the Roman period the quarries of Yebu, which became known in the Ptolemaic period as *Syene,* supplied the Egyptians with fine colored granite (containing quartz, yellow and brick-red felspar and blackish mica) for their buildings and statues. The term "syenite" applied to this rock by Pliny is now, however, used by geologists to denote a different kind of stone containing a higher proportion of hornblende.

Yebu was also of strategic importance, commanding as it did the Nile cataracts and traffic by water between Egypt and Nubia. It was also the starting-point of the great caravan route to Nubia and the Sudan, along which passed the commercial and military expeditions of the Egyptians. The ancient capital of the province, also called Yebu, lay at the S end of the island. In the 6th and 5th c. B.C. there was a Jewish military colony here, with a Temple of Yahweh, as was shown by Aramaic papyri found here in 1906–08 (now in the Egyptian Museum, West Berlin, and the Bode Museum, East Berlin).

On the E bank of the river was the town of *Swenet,* the Greek **Syene,** which rose to importance only in a later period. In the early 2nd c. A.D. the Roman garrison here was commanded by the satirical poet Juvenal, who had been posted to this remote frontier of the Empire

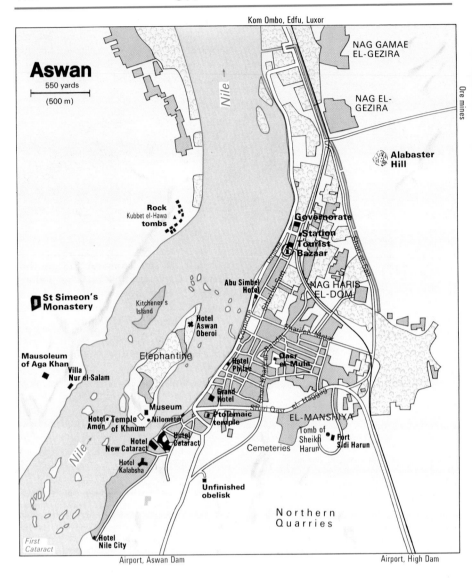

Kom Ombo, Edfu, Luxor

Aswan

550 yards

(500 m)

Nile

NAG GAMAE
EL-GEZIRA

NAG EL-
GEZIRA

Ore mines

Alabaster
Hill

Rock
Kubbet el-Hawa
tombs

Governorate
Station
Tourist
Bazaar

St Simeon's
Monastery

Kitchener's
Island

Abu Simbel
Hotel

NAG HARIS
EL-DOM

Hotel
Aswan
Oberoi

Mausoleum
of Aga Khan

Villa
Nur el-Salam

Elephantine

Qasr
el-Mula

Hotel
Philae

Grand
Hotel

Sharia el-Haggag

Museum

Nilometer

Ptolemaic
temple

EL-MANSHIYA

Hotel Temple
Amon of Khnum

Hotel
Cataract

Tomb of
Sheikh
Harun

Fort
Sidi Harun

Hotel
New Cataract

Cemeteries

Hotel
Kalabsha

Unfinished
obelisk

Northern
Quarries

First
Cataract

Hotel
Nile City

Airport, Aswan Dam

Airport, High Dam

as a punishment for his biting attacks on the Court. A celebrated curiosity of ancient Syene was a well into which the sun's rays descended perpendicularly at the summer solstice, casting no shadow; and this led the Athenian scholar Eratosthenes (276–196 B.C.), who was attached to the Museum in Alexandria, to devise his method of measuring the size of the earth. – The town suffered greatly at the hands of the Blemmyes, but became the see of a Christian bishop, and seems to have regained its prosperity under the Caliphs. Arab writers record that a plague carried off 20,000 of its inhabitants, which points to a very large total population. From the end of the 12th c. Aswan suffered severely from the incursions of plundering bedouin tribes, which were ended only when the Turkish Sultan Selim stationed a garrison in the town in 1517.

SIGHTS. – There are only scanty remains of the ancient city of **Syene** on the right bank of the Nile – mainly inscriptions on rocks and architectural fragments built into modern houses. In the S of the town

are the ruins of the *Qasr el-Mula,* situated on a hill amid beautiful gardens, and a small Ptolemaic temple (see below).

From the *railway station,* at the N end of the town, a street leads W to the *Corniche,* a riverside promenade on which are the offices of the Governorate, several hotels and the *Tourist Bazaar,* with the Tourist Information Office. On the opposite side of the river can be seen the Kubbet el-Hawa, a sheikh's tomb, crowning a hill which contains rock tombs of the Old and Middle Kingdoms. – From the station *Sharia el-Suq* runs S, parallel to the river, to the center of the town. In this street and the adjoining side streets is the **Bazaar,** a magnet for visitors with its many little shops and stalls and its colorful bustle of activity.

Street in the Bazaar, Aswan

Amenophis IV. On the right is Men, "Superintendent of Works", before an image of Amenophis III; to the left his son Bek, Chief Architect at Tell el-Amarna, before an image (defaced) of Amenophis IV, on which the sun's rays descend.

SURROUNDINGS of Aswan

From the *Tomb of Sheikh Harun*, on a hill in the desert to the SE of the town, there is a fine *view of the town.

In the desert to the S of the town are ancient **Arab cemeteries**. The graves are marked by rectangles of undressed stone and a slab bearing an inscription, those of wealthy people by small domed structures. On higher ground is a sheikh's tomb. – On the surrounding hills large mosque-like *cenotaphs* commemorate celebrated holy men and women such as Sheikh Mahmud, Sheikh Ali and the Lady (Sayyida) Zeinab, whose birthdays *(mulis)* are celebrated here.

At the S end of the town is a small **Ptolemaic temple** (unfinished and poorly preserved) built by Ptolemaios III, Euergetes I, Ptolemaios IV and Philopator and dedicated to Isis of Syene.

The main *doorway* is crowned by a cavetto cornice. On the left-hand door-post, above, Euergetes presents an image of the goddess Maat to Amun; below, Euergetes in the presence of Min-Amun and of Mut and Isis. On the lintel Euergetes (in one case accompanied by his wife Berenice) is depicted before various gods. Within the doorway the King is shown in the presence of Thoth (right) and Harsiesis (left), with an inscription above each scene. – The interior consists of a hall with two pillars in which are several bases for statues and sacred boats, and three *chapels*. On the rear wall of the middle chapel are reliefs depicting Euergetes (accompanied in one scene by Berenice) in the presence of the deities of Syene.

Cataract Hotel and New Cataract Hotel, Aswan

Beyond this, in a magnificent *situation on the banks of the Nile with a view of the island of Elephantine, stands the old **Cataract Hotel**, set in beautiful gardens reaching down to the river, with a spacious shady terrace and a swimming-pool. Adjoining it is the modern *New Cataract Hotel.* – To the E of the Cataract Hotel, on a granite rock below a stone wall of the Roman period, can be seen an *inscription* dating from the reign of

To the SE of the town are the ancient granite **quarries** from which the Egyptians obtained the fine reddish Aswan granite for their buildings and statues. In the *Northern Quarries* can be seen an *unfinished obelisk (137 ft/41·75 m long, 14 ft/4.20 m across at the broader end), no doubt abandoned because of a crack in the stone. It is estimated that the completed obelisk would have weighed 1168 tons and would

Domed tombs in an Arab cemetery

Unfinished obelisk

have been the largest ever hewn. Round the obelisk has been cut a trench 2½ ft/75 cm wide. On the surrounding rock faces, which are of moderate height, can be seen many traces of the work of ancient stone-cutters. The blocks were detached from the rock by boring holes along a prescribed line, driving wedges into these and then soaking the wedges with water to detach the block. Statues, sarcophagi, obelisks, etc., were usually roughly dressed before removal in order to reduce the weight for transport. From the hill above the obelisk there are extensive *views; to the W, in a desert valley on the far side of the Nile, can be seen St Simeon's Monastery. – From the quarries a massive causeway (still in use today) ran down to Aswan to facilitate the transport of the huge blocks to the banks of the Nile.

From the quarries the causeway continues S, first passing through the hills and then descending into a picturesque valley, after which it follows a level course and comes in some 45 minutes to the *Southern Quarries*, facing eastward towards the desert. Here, too, there are rough-hewn blocks abandoned by the ancient stone-cutters. On a rock face is carved an inscription in the name of Amenophis III, but the name and figure of the stone-cutter who carved it have been obliterated. Beside it are two trough-shaped sarcophagi of the Ptolemaic or Imperial period on which work has only been begun, and near by are a *colossal statue* of a king (of which all but the feet have been covered with sand) and a large rectangular block, perhaps intended for the shrine of a god. Some 5 minutes' walk farther on, near the top of the cliff above the wide valley through which the railway runs on to Shellal, stands a figure of Osiris (popularly called Rameses), measuring some 20 ft/6 m, with a crown and beard, the arms crossed over the breast. From here there is a fine *view over the desert to Lake Nasser, with the Temple of Philae (see that entry).

To the N of the town rises the Alabaster Hill, an ancient quarry of quartz from which the Egyptians

obtained the material required for the polishing of hard stones.

The verdant island of ***Elephantine** (1650 yds/1500 m long, 550 yds/500 m wide), with its luxuriant growth of palms, known in Arabic as **Geziret Aswan** or *El-Gesira* ("the Island") for short, can be reached by boat (preferably a felucca) in a few minutes. It is one of Aswan's principal tourist attractions, and accordingly is in danger of losing its quiet idyllic charm. On the island are two picturesque *Nubian villages,* the inhabitants of which still speak Nubian and preserve their national traditions. (A Nubian museum is planned.)

Near the primitive landing-stage on the E side of the island, facing Aswan, is a flight of steps leading to the ***Nilometer**, of which Strabo gives a precise description. After more than a thousand years of neglect it was restored to use by Mahmud Bey in 1870 during the reign of Viceroy Ismail, as is recorded in French and Arabic inscriptions; since the construction of the High Dam, however, it no longer functions. The scales date from the Late Empire, the heights (in cubits) being given in both Greek and demotic characters. The new scale is inscribed on marble tablets.

> The description of the Nilometer by the Greek geographer *Strabo* (c. 63 B.C.–A.D. 20) is still accurate:
>
> "The Nilometer is a well built of regular hewn stone on the bank of the Nile, in which is recorded the rise of the stream: not only the highest and the lowest rises but also those in between, for the water in the well rises and falls with the stream. On the side of the well are marks, measuring the height sufficient for irrigation and other water-levels. These are observed and made known to all.... This is of importance to the peasants for the management of the water, the embankments, the canals and so on, and also to the officials for the purpose of taxation; for the higher the rise of the water the higher are the taxes."

At the head of the steps leading to the Nilometer, set in beautiful gardens, is the ***Aswan Museum**, established in 1912 in a villa which belonged to Sir William Willcocks, designer of the first Aswan Dam; it contains a notable collection of antiquities from excavations in Lower Nubia which give an excellent view of the culture of the region.

In the *Colonnade* are statues, stelae and architectural fragments, including the torso of a woman and a

Coastal scenery, Elephantine

Kitchener's Island, seen from the left bank of the Nile

terracotta sarcophagus of the Roman period. – *Entrance Hall*: mummy of a sacred ram in a gilded sarcophagus; Egyptian, Greek and Coptic grave-stones; votive tablets, including one with a Meroitic inscription.

Room 1 (reached from Room 2; prehistoric material, 4000 – 3200 B.C.): burnished red vessels with a black rim, light-colored jugs with dark red painted decoration (ships, human figures, animals), hand-made stone vessels; cosmetic-palettes, combs, awls and needles made of bone; chains, amulets, cylinder-seals; flint mace-heads, knives and arrowheads. – *Room 2* (Old Kingdom, 3200–2100 B.C.): pottery; copper weapons and implements; pear-shaped mace-heads; a skull with a healed fracture; pottery doll; ostrich eggs with incised figures of animals; porphyry bowl; strings of beads and bracelets. – Now through the entrance hall to *Room 3* (Middle and New Kingdoms, 2100–1500 B.C.): pottery, notably red and black burnished ware with incised patterns lined in white; bracelets of quartz; crude figures of women and cattle; alabaster vessels; cosmetic caskets; small painted plaster masks placed over the wrappings of mummies; faience; Mycenaean stirrup-jar; board game of blue faience; mirrors, daggers and knives of copper and bronze; chains, rings, amulets; a small steatite memorial stone depicting Amun as a ram; scarabs. – *Room 4* (Late Period, after 1500 B.C.): mummies of the Ptolemaic period with cases of painted cartonnage, including those of a priest and priestess of Isis of Philae; bronze vessels and lance-heads; heavy bronze bracelets, Meroitic glass flasks with incised designs; Nubian pottery of the Late Roman period (c. A.D. 400); strings of beads; a pottery censer and a small bronze incense vessel from a Christian church at El-Madiq in Lower Nubia (now submerged by Lake Nasser).

Garden: architectural fragments of the 18th Dynasty (c. 1555–1308 B.C.), incorporated in later buildings erected by Nectanebo II in Elephantine.

A Nubian Museum designed to house material recovered during the rescue operations on the Nubian temples is under construction.

S of the Nilometer, opposite the Cataract Hotel, is a massive *ancient embankment,* many of the stones in which were taken from older buildings and bear inscriptions. There are also many inscriptions on the rocks along the water's edge, including some large inscriptions in the name of Psammetichus.

South of Aswan

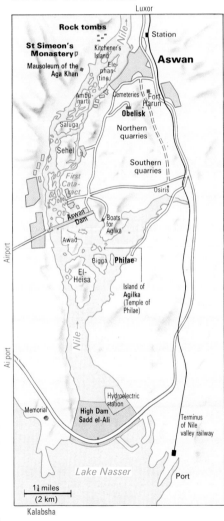

The whole of the southern part of the island, part of which is occupied by the more southerly of the two villages, was once covered by the **ancient town of Elephantine**, the remains of which were first explored in the 19th c. and since 1969 have been undergoing excavation and investigation by modern methods. A few paces W of the Nilometer, surrounded by brick walls, are the substructures of a small *Temple of Satet*, built over an earlier temple and incorporating a variety of architectural fragments (column drums, blocks bearing the name of Tuthmosis III, Ramesses III, etc.). The inscriptions on the solitary stump of column still standing refer to Trajan as the builder, but there was a temple on this site as early as *c.* 2900 B.C. The temple is being reconstructed, with financial assistance from German industrial firms, to show its successive phases.

Some 50 yards SW a granite doorway originally gave access to a **Temple of Khnum** built by Nectanebo II over an earlier temple. During the Roman period large terraces were built on the river side of both temples. The reliefs show Alexander II, son of Alexander the Great, offering sacrifices to various gods, in particular the ram-headed Khnum. On a section of wall which is still standing the Emperor, followed by Nile gods, is shown sacrificing to Khnum; the faces of both the Emperor and the god have been deliberately defaced. Close to the Temple of Khnum is the cemetery of the sacred rams, with sarcophagi still *in situ* (mummies in the Aswan Museum and the Egyptian Museum in Cairo). – To the N, between the temples of Satet and Khnum, are the remains of a small *temple,* formed out of three earlier chapels, dedicated to Hekaib, Prince of the Nome of Elephantine, whose rock tomb is on the W bank.

Various other buildings described by the French expedition in the early 19th c. were later pulled down, among them two temples built respectively by Amenophis III and Tuthmosis III. The residential area of the ancient town lay to the SW of the temple area. During the Old Kingdom the town was enclosed by a wall on the S side, and a gateway in this wall can still be identified. – SW of the site of the ancient town, at the southern tip of the island, is the so-called *Kalabsha Kiosk,* a structure in the style of a temple of the Ptolemaic period put together from fragments of the Kalabsha Temple left here during the operation for the rescue of the Nubian temples, in the course of which the stones of the Kalabsha Temple were temporarily stored on Elephantine (see under Kalabsha).

From the higher parts of the island, particularly from the Hill of *Kom,* there are fine *views of the rocks of the

First Cataract – some brown and some black, some rugged and some smooth – between which the Nile pursues a tranquil course.

A *felucca trip* round the island is full of interest. Some 550 yds/500 m S, near the right bank of the Nile, is a small islet on which can be seen a number of "pot-holes", gouged out of the rock and worn smooth by the Nile flood. – Between Elephantine and the left bank is the island of *El-Atrun* or *Kitchener's Island*, more recently known as **Botanical Island**. Once the property of Lord Kitchener, it now belongs to the State, and with its luxuriant abundance of plants and flowers is one of the great attractions of Aswan.

On the WEST BANK of the Nile, opposite the S end of Elephantine, is the *Villa Nur el-Salam,* set in carefully tended gardens, which belonged to Aga Khan III (Sultan Mohammed Shah, b. 1887 in Karachi, d. 1957 at Versoix in Switzerland), spiritual head of the Khojas, a branch of the Ismaili sect. The Khojas, who revere him as the 48th Imam, live mainly in India and East Africa. For many years the Aga Khan spent the winter months at Aswan, seeking relief from a rheumatic complaint. – Commandingly situated on a hill above the villa, with magnificent *views, is the **Mausoleum of the Aga Khan**, built here, in accordance with his wishes, by the Begum, his French-born wife and former beauty queen Yvette Labrousse (b. 1906). A stiff climb on a stepped path brings the visitor to a spacious esplanade from which a broad flight of steps leads up to the entrance. The mausoleum is built of ochre-colored calcareous sandstone in a severely restrained style; the interior (in which absolute silence must be observed) is finished in light colors, floored with red carpets and immaculately maintained. On the Begum's instructions a fresh red rose is laid on the sarcophagus (of white marble, with Koranic texts carved in relief) every day.

Farther N, on the hill crowned by the little sheikh's tomb known as *Kubbet el-Hawa*, are the *rock tombs* of the princes and grandees of Elephantine. The tombs date from the end of the Old Kingdom and the Middle Kingdom – i.e. from the same period as the tombs of Beni Hasan (see that entry), which they resemble both in construction and in decoration. There are fine *views from the hill.

Mausoleum and villa of the Aga Khan, Aswan

From the boat landing-place a sandy path (moderate gradient, but fairly strenuous) climbs up to Tomb 31. Even more testing is the ancient staircase, consisting of two parallel flights of steps separated by a ramp up which the sarcophagi were drawn, which leads up to Tombs 25 and 26.

The tour of the tombs begins at the S end with No. 25, the **tomb of Mekhu** (6th Dynasty), the construction and decoration of which are somewhat crude. In front of the entrance are two small obelisks without inscriptions. The chamber contains 18 roughly worked columns, in three rows. Opposite the entrance, between two columns, stands a three-legged stone table, presumably an altar, and in the rear wall beyond this is a niche approached by steps and closed by a stone screen, within which is a false door. On the walls are various scenes depicting the dead man receiving offerings. To the right of the entrance sacrifices are being made to him; to the left are agricultural scenes (plowing, harvesting; donkeys bringing in the harvest).

Immediately adjoining No. 25 is No. 26, the *Tomb of Sabni I*, Mekhu's son. This has an unusual type of doorway, divided into two parts by a cross-beam; in front of it are two small obelisks and a sacrificial basin. The chamber is divided into three aisles by 14 square pillars. On the rear wall the dead man is depicted with his daughters in a boat, hunting in the marshes: on the left he holds a throwing-stick in one hand and the slain birds in the others; on the right he is catching two fish with his harpoon; in the middle birds are flying over a papyrus thicket.

To the right of this double tomb the path continues up past two tombs buried in sand (Nos. 27 and 29) to *Tomb 30*, belonging to one Hekaib (Middle Kingdom). The chamber, divided into three aisles by six pillars, has a barrel-vaulted roof. In the rear wall is a niche with the figures of two men and a papyrus plant, symbolizing the life-force. – Beyond No. 30 is the *Tomb of Hekaib I* (No. 28), of modest size and decoration, with a figure of the dead man, depicted as a Nubian with a curious curled wig and dark skin.

Farther on we come to the * **Tomb of Prince Sarenput II** (No. 31), son of Satethotep and a contemporary of King Amenemhet II (12th Dynasty). This is one of the largest and best-preserved tombs in the necropolis. The narrow entrance leads into a hall with six pillars, which taper towards the top; it has no decoration, but on the right is a handsome granite offering-table. Beyond this is a corridor with three niches on either side, each containing a rock-cut statue of the dead man in the guise of the Osiris mummy. To the left of the first niche is a figure of the dead man and his son, the colors of which are excellently preserved. The corridor leads into a small chamber with four pillars, on each of which there are figures of the dead man; on some of them can be seen the grid of lines used by the artist in setting out his picture. In the rear wall of this chamber is a niche containing finely executed reliefs: the dead man at table, with his son in front of him carrying flowers (rear); the dead man standing on the right, with his mother at table on the left (right-hand wall); the dead man with his son behind him and his wife in front of him (left-hand wall).

Beyond this are the *Tomb of Aku* (No. 32), with a niche containing a representation of the dead man with his wife and son seated at a meal in an arbor; the *Tomb of Khui* (sanded up); and the *Tomb of Khunes*

(No. 34h; 6th Dynasty), an eight-pillared chamber containing fine representations of various craftsmen (bakers, potters, metalworkers beside a furnace, brewers, leather-workers, etc.). The two last-named tombs were later occupied by Coptic monks, who left a variety of inscriptions. – From the Tomb of Khunes a flight of steps leads to the *Tomb of Setka* (First Intermediate Period), with wall-paintings, badly damaged but with astonishingly vivid colors, which are among the few surviving examples of the decorative art of this period.

Then follows the *Tomb of Harhuf* (No. 34n). On the outer wall, flanking the entrance, are figures of the dead man (depicted on the left leaning on a staff, with his son holding a censer), with important inscriptions recording four successful trading expeditions in Nubia, three of them during the reign of Merenre and the fourth (on which the goods he brought back included a dwarf) in the reign of Pepi II (6th Dynasty). – Adjoining is the small *Tomb of Pepinakht* (No. 35; sanded up), with inscriptions on either side of the entrance glorifying the dead man's exploits in campaigns against the Nubians and the inhabitants of the Eastern Desert during the reign of Pepi II (6th Dynasty).

Adjoining the tomb of Pepinakht is the recently cleared *Tomb of Hekaib II* (No. 35d), whose mortuary temple has been found on the island of Elephantine. Constructed on an irregular plan, it has a large forecourt and vestibule. The tomb chamber itself is small and modestly decorated, but was notable for the quantity of grave-goods and votive tablets found in it (now in the Aswan Museum). – To the left of the forecourt are doorways leading to other tombs, including the *Tomb of Sabni II*, son of Hekaib II.

Finally we come to the* **Tomb of Prince Sarenput I** (No. 36), son of Satseni, who lived in the reign of Sesostris I (12th Dynasty). A doorway of fine limestone with figures of the dead man leads into the court, with six pillars, formerly supporting the roof of a colonnade, bearing inscriptions and representations of the dead man. Rear wall, to the left of the door: a large figure of the dead man followed by his sandal-bearer and two dogs; cattle are brought to the dead man (note particularly the enraged bulls); Sarenput in a boat spearing fish. To the right of the door: a large figure of the dead man, followed by his bow-bearer, a dog and his three sons; above, the dead man seated in a colonnade, with four women in front of him holding flowers; below, a woman and two men gaming. The paintings, on stucco, are badly damaged. A vaulted passage, now closed by a modern wall, leads into a second chamber, with four pillars, from which another passage continues into a small chamber with two pillars and a cult-niche. Here, too, there are many scenes of everyday life, much damaged, on the walls and pillars.

To the NE is the **Tomb of Kakemet** (reign of Amenophis III), with fine *ceiling-paintings (flying birds, spirals with bulls' heads). On the pillars the dead man is shown before Osiris and the Hathor cow. Excavations still in progress have brought a third row of tombs to light. – Above the necropolis are the remains of a Coptic monastery.

It is worth the effort of climbing to the top of the hill, with the small sheikh's tomb known as the *Kubbet el-Hawa*, for the sake of the fine *view. From here a 45-minute camel or donkey ride brings the visitor to St Simeon's Monastery.

St Simeon's Monastery, Aswan

The ruined *Monastery of St Simeon (*Deir Amba Samaan* or *Deir Amba Hadra*), situated on a hill in the desert on the W bank of the Nile, can be reached from the river-bank on a footpath running up a desert valley opposite the S end of Elephantine; the climb takes 20 minutes. One of the largest and best-preserved Coptic monasteries, it was founded in the 7th c. and abandoned in the 13th because of water shortage. The buildings, standing on a rock shelf on two levels, are surrounded by a wall 20–23 ft/6–7 m high, the lower part of which is constructed of undressed stone, the upper part of sun-dried bricks; on the W side the lower part is hewn from the rock.

The buildings on the LOWER LEVEL (excavated and restored 1925–26) are reached by way of a *tower* on the E side which leads into the *forecourt*. To the left is a porter's lodge, to the right a large bench *(mastaba)* on which pilgrims could sleep. On the S side of the court is the **Church**, an aisled basilica. At the E end of the wide nave, once covered by two domes, is the large *apse*, with three rectangular niches under semi-domes. In the central niche are the remains of a fresco depicting Christ enthroned between angels. To the right and left of the apse are Coptic inscriptions. Adjoining is the *Baptistery*, with a piscina. At the W end of the nave a small apse has remains of frescos. – A small door at the W end of the N aisle leads into a small *rock chapel* with fine decoration (8th c.) on the ceiling and a niche containing six medallions of saints. – To the N and W of the church are various subsidiary buildings and small grottoes. – To the SE of the church is a court, with a tomb built against its S wall. Along the E side of the court are bedrooms, each with three beds, and other barrel-vaulted rooms.

Remains of frescos in the church

To the NW of the church is a flight of stone steps leading to the UPPER LEVEL, some 16 ft/5 m higher up. On this level are the large three-storeyed **living-quarters** *(qasr)*, the two lower floors of which are well preserved. On each floor is a large vaulted corridor, flanked by the monks' cells with their brick-built

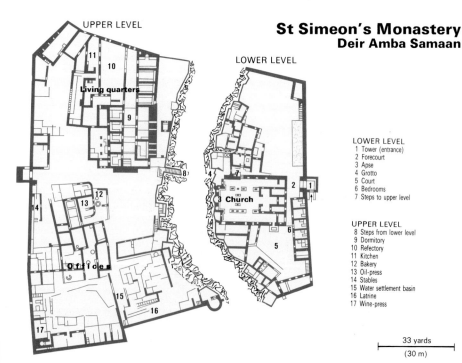

UPPER LEVEL

LOWER LEVEL

St Simeon's Monastery
Deir Amba Samaan

LOWER LEVEL
1 Tower (entrance)
2 Forecourt
3 Apse
4 Grotto
5 Court
6 Bedrooms
7 Steps to upper level

UPPER LEVEL
8 Steps from lower level
9 Dormitory
10 Refectory
11 Kitchen
12 Bakery
13 Oil-press
14 Stables
15 Water settlement basin
16 Latrine
17 Wine-press

33 yards
(30 m)

beds. On the walls are Coptic and Arabic inscriptions. To the S of this block are various *offices* (a mill, a bakery, oil- and wine-presses, store-rooms, a bath-house, etc.) and a small domed *chapel*.

Half an hour's walk S of the monastery are two conspicuous high cliffs, one of which is covered with inscriptions. – 10 minutes beyond this is a hill of dark-colored stone from which there is a superb* view of the cataract area, extending N to the island of Bahrif. – The path down to the bank of the Nile runs past a large *cemetery*. On the river-bank are many *rock tombs*.

An interesting excursion from here (2 hours by camel or donkey) is to the **sandstone quarries** which lie on the banks of the Nile to the N of St Simeon's Monastery. Here can be seen the upper part of an unfinished obelisk with carvings and an inscription in the name of Sethos I.

Some 3 miles/5 km upstream from Aswan is the *Aswan Dam* (Arabic *El-Sadd*, "the Dam", or *El-Khassan*, "the Reservoir"), constructed between 1898 and 1912. At the time of its construction it was the largest dam in the world, and until the building of the High Dam in 1971 it remained the world's longest. It was designed to put an end to the annual inundation of the Nile by pounding its water and distributing it regularly over the year, thus making it possible to irrigate the cultivated land throughout the year, extending its area and enabling two or three crops to be taken off it every year.

Designed by Sir William Willcocks, the British engineer who was also responsible for the Asyut Dam, and built by the firm of John Aird and Co., it is constructed of blocks of Aswan granite. It originally ran straight across the river for a distance of 2145 yds/ 1960 m, 130 ft/40 m high, 100 ft/30 m thick at the base and 23 ft/7 m thick at the top. After being enlarged in 1907–12 and again in 1929–34 the dam is now 2340 yds/2140 m long and 165 ft/51 m high. The water-level is regulated by 180 sluice-gates, the 140

lower sluices (each measuring 23 ft/7 m by 6½ ft/2 m) being used for the distribution of the water and the 40 upper sluices (11½ ft/3·5 m by 6½ ft/2 m) for the escape of surplus water.

To the W of the dam is a *navigation canal* 1¼ miles/ 2 km long which enables boats of some size to move up- and downstream, overcoming the difference in level (75 ft/23 m) by the use of four locks 230 ft/70 m long and 31 ft/9·5 m wide. The two uppermost lock-gates are 62 ft/19 m high, the other five 49 ft/15 m, 39 ft/12 m and 36 ft/11 m.

The increase in agricultural output resulting from the construction of the dam was soon overtaken by the rapid increase in the population: in the first half of this century it was doubled, and it has now been multiplied fivefold. Moreover, the degree of regulation achieved by the dam turned out to be insufficient. Accordingly after the Second World War, when the country's economic problems were increasingly pressing, it became a matter of urgency to consider the extension and improvement of the arrangements for the regulation of the Nile by the construction of a dam higher up the river.

President Nasser, who came to power in 1952 after a military coup, energetically promoted a project of truly Pharaonic dimensions which should both benefit the nation and redound to his own glory, in the form of a high dam for which plans were first put forward by two German firms (Hochtief of Essen and Union-Brückenbau of Dortmund) in 1955. Financial assistance was offered by Britain, the United States and the World Bank; but when the Western Powers withdrew their offer in 1956 because of Nasser's policy of neutrality, Nasser sought to obtain part of the resources required by nationalizing the Suez Canal. The gap was then filled by the Soviet Union, which contributed by the granting of credits and the provision of some 2000 engineers and technicians to the realization of the project on the basis of the German plans with some modification.

The old Aswan Dam

Overleaf: The Aswan High Dam (el-Sadd el-Ali) and Lake Nasser

Illustrative picture half-way along the High Dam

Work began on January 9, 1960 with the ceremonial laying of the foundation-stone, and on May 14, 1964 the bypass canal on the E bank of the Nile was opened. The solemn inauguration of the High Dam took place on January 15, 1971. Some 35,000 workers and engineers had been employed on its construction, and 451 men had lost their lives. The rising of the water above the dam made it necessary to rehouse almost 60,000 Nubians and Sudanese, and in addition gave rise to an unprecedented international rescue program for saving many historical monuments (temples, tombs, churches, monasteries, etc.) dating from ancient and medieval times by removing them from areas due to be flooded and re-erecting them on new sites.

Memorial at west end

The****High Dam**, or **el-Sadd el-Ali**, some 4 miles/7 km above the old Aswan Dam, is a massive accumulation of 55.9 billion cu. yds/42.7 billion cu. m (17 times the volume of the Pyramid of Cheops) of stones and sand with a clay core and a concrete facing. With a total length of $2\frac{1}{4}$ miles/3·6 km, it pounds the waters of the Nile, which was originally 550 yds/500 m wide at this point. It is no less than 1070 yds/980 m thick at the base, reducing to 44 yds/40 m at the top. The top of the dam is 364 ft/111 m above the base and 643 ft/196 m above sea-level. The average capacity of the reservoir (Lake Nasser) formed by the dam is some 177 billion cu. yds/135 billion cu. m, its maximum capacity 205 billion cu. yds/157 billion cu. m. Of this total quantity 110 billion cu. yds/84 billion cu. m – the average annual flow of the Nile – are assigned to irrigation, Egypt receiving 73 billion cu. yds/5·5 billion cu. m and Sudan 24 billion cu. yds/18·5 billion cu. m. It is estimated that over the next 500 years some 39 billion cu. yds/30 billion cu. m of capacity will be lost by the deposition of sediment; and some 8 billion cu. yds/6 billion cu. m of water are lost every year by evaporation. The remaining 48 billion cu. yds/37 billion cu. m of capacity are held in reserve against an unexpectedly high flow of water. – A four-lane road runs across the top of the dam. A *memorial*, a *triumphal arch* and an inscription commemorate the completion of this huge enterprise and the co-operation between Egypt and the Soviet Union in its realization.

Triumphal Arch at highest point

Hydroelectric station at east end

On the E bank of the river is a bypass canal 1750 yds/ 1600 m long. After passing through six tunnels with a total length of 308 yds/282 m this drives the turbines of a hydroelectric station which produces 10 billion kWh of power annually, making a major contribution to the industrial development of the Nile Valley.

The damming of the Nile by the High Dam has created an immense reservoir, *LAKE NASSER, with an area of 2025 sq. miles/5250 sq. km – the largest artificial lake in the world after the one formed by the Kariba Dam on the Zambezi. The lake is 317 miles/510 km long (a third of this length being in Sudanese territory) and 3–22 miles/5–35 km wide. The average altitude of the surface of the lake is about 600 ft/182 m above sea-level. – It is planned to build several towns and villages on the shores of the lake.

It is not yet possible to assess completely the positive and negative effects of the High Dam. One undoubted benefit has been an increase of 20–30% (1,250,000–2,000,000 acres) in cultivated land, together with increased agricultural yields as a result of even and regular irrigation. Other clear gains are the increased output of electricity, the elimination of unpredictable floods and droughts, the possibility of navigation on the Nile throughout the year and the resources of food yielded by the fish of Lake Nasser. One negative result has been the loss of the fertilizing mud formerly deposited by the Nile, which now has to be made good by expensive artificial fertilizers; and consideration is now being given to the possibility of mechanical means of swirling the water in the reservoir in order to prevent it from depositing its alluvium there. Other disadvantageous effects have been the fall in the underground water-table in consequence of the faster and more direct flow of the river and the build-up of salt in the soil, which is no longer washed out by regular flooding with fresh water. In order to obviate these side-effects it will be necessary to construct further dams between Aswan and Cairo. The coastal regions of the Nile Delta have also suffered by the loss of the fertile alluvium formerly carried down by the Nile; and the lack of natural foodstuffs in the water of the river has led to a considerable reduction in the stocks of fish in the south-eastern Mediterranean. – Another potential cause for concern is the possibility of damage to the High Dam by enemy action. The bursting of the dam would devastate the whole of Egypt and wipe out 98% of the population; and even the arrangements already provided for to bring about a rapid fall in the level of Lake Nasser cannot eliminate the danger that would result from a surprise attack.

Abu Simbel, *Amada, *Kalabsha, *Kom Ombo, *Nile, Nubia, *Philae, Silsila, *Wadi el-Sebwa and Western Desert: see separate entries.

Asyut

Upper Egypt. – Governorate: Asyut.
Population: 250,000.

ACCESS. – By the road along the Nile or by rail.

The lively provincial capital of Asyut, the largest town in Upper Egypt, is one of the centers of Coptic Christianity, and also has an excellent Islamic university associated with the El-Azhar University in Cairo, a technical college and a number of secondary schools. Situated on the left bank of the Nile, with a small older quarter and extensive modern districts, it has few features of tourist interest.

The town is noted for its craft products – pottery, marquetry-work, ivory-carvings, leather articles, woven fabrics, colored woollen blankets, tulle shawls with gold and silver embroidery. Here as elsewhere, however, locally made articles of considerable artistic quality are gradually been driven out by industrial products in European style. – Asyut has a busy river port handling soda, cotton and grain, and is a market center for the agricultural produce of the very fertile surrounding area.

HISTORY. – Asyut (ancient Egyptian *Syut*) was a place of considerable importance in antiquity thanks to its situation in a large and fertile plain extending between the Libyan and the Arabian mountains – a distance of some $12\frac{1}{2}$ miles/20 km – at the end of the "road of the forty days", an important caravan route which led to the oases in the Libyan Desert and on to the Darfur Oasis in what is now Sudan. Politically, however, it achieved prominence only occasionally, as during the First Intermediate Period, when it played a considerable part in the conflicts between Thebes and Heracleopolis. Asyut was the capital of the 13th nome of Upper Egypt, the Sycamore nome, and the principal center of the cult of the war god Wopwawot, who was represented as a desert wolf: hence the town's Greek name of **Lycopolis**, "city of the wolf". – Asyut was the birthplace of Plotinus (A.D. 205–270), the greatest of the Neo-Platonic philosophers, whose system was influenced to some degree by the priestly doctrines of his native town. – At the beginning of the 4th c. Christianity became dominant in the town, and pious believers moved into the caves of the necropolis to live a life of penitence. Among them was John of Lycopolis (end of 4th c.), who gained the reputation of a saint and a prophet: thus when the Emperor Theodosius sent an envoy to ask about the outcome of his conflict with his rival Eugenius he correctly foretold the Emperor's victory. – During the medieval period the town enjoyed considerable prosperity thanks to its extensive trading connections and to its slave market, the largest in Egypt. – Soon after the murder of President Sadat in October 1981 there were bloody conflicts in Asyut between Muslim radicals and the police.

SIGHTS. – To the E of the railway station is a shady promenade on the banks of the *Nile*. This leads N to the bridge over the sluice-gates on the *Ibrahimiya Canal* and continues to the Asyut Dam (see below). – The little OLD TOWN, with its busy bazaar, lies W of the railway.

Asyut has an interesting little **Museum** containing the collection of antiquities assembled between 1910 and 1914 by a wealthy Asyut citizen, Sayyid Pasha Khashaba, from excavations in the ancient necropolises of Asyut and Meir. The collection includes wooden sarcophagi, including some with fine colored door ornaments and a mummiform sarcophagus of granite; large quantities of grave-goods, in particular domestic and agricultural equipment; a limestone group depicting a princely couple (from Meir; 6th Dynasty); fine reliefs from a 19th Dynasty tomb (the dead man at table, the dead man and his relatives in the presence of the gods of the dead); and a famous over-life-size *statue of an official named Iuni holding a chapel with the image of Osiris.

From the square in front of the railway station Sharia el-Mahatta (Station Road) runs W past the old town and then bears SW, crosses the *Sohagiya Canal* and continues to the foot of the desert hills, on the slopes of which are the ***rock tombs** of ancient Asyut. A track zigzags steeply uphill to the large *Tomb of Hapidjefa I* (12th Dynasty), Prince of the nome in the reign of Sesostris I. The tomb is of a size previously found only in royal burials.

From a court in front of the tomb we enter a surprisingly high *longitudinal chamber,* the vaulted ceiling of which was decorated with painted stars. On the right-hand wall is a figure of the dead man, with a long and barely legible inscription. From this chamber a doorway, on each side of which is a figure of the dead man with a long staff, leads ito a *transverse chamber.* On the right-hand entrance wall is a long inscription containing the text of ten contracts concluded by the dead man with various priesthoods in his native town in order to secure the proper sacrificial offerings to himself and to provide for the performance of other ceremonies. The corresponding inscription on the left-hand entrance wall contains invocations to visitors to the tomb and a recital of the dead man's merits. The flat ceiling is decorated with a variety of colored spiral, meander and woven patterns. In the rear wall, between two niches, is a door leading into a vaulted passage and beyond this into a *second transverse hall* with three niches. In the middle niche, on the rear wall, was a figure of the dead man, with four women holding lotus flowers in front of him; the side walls show him at table, with three files of priests and servants bringing him gifts or performing sacred ceremonies. The left-hand niche leads to the *mummy-shaft.*

The *view from this tomb is very fine. To the left, lower down, is the Arab cemetery; in the fertile plain is the widely spreading town with its minarets and palms and the Ibharimiya Canal with its busy boat traffic; and in the distance can be seen the edge of the desert. – A still more extensive and more attractive *view can be enjoyed from the tombs higher up the hill. Here can be seen three adjoining tombs (the most northerly of which is ruined) dating from the Heracleopolitan period (9th and 10th Dynasties) of the Middle Kingdom.

The middle tomb is the *Tomb of Kheti,* Prince of the nome under the 10th Dynasty. On the right-hand wall of the vestibule are the dead man and his wife Tefyeb, with a long text, partly destroyed, referring to King Merikare (10th Dynasty). On the S wall of the main chamber, in which only one pillar is left standing, are depicted several ranks of armed warriors. In the rear wall is a niche for a statue of the dead man. – From this tomb an underground passage leads into the third tomb in the row, which belonged to *Tefyeb,* a Prince of the nome.

Continuing up the hill, passing a small Coptic *rock chapel* and rounding a spur of the hill, we reach a point from which there is a still wider *view of the extensive range of hills along the eastern edge of the Western (Libyan) Desert. – To the N of the ancient necropolis a larger ***Arab cemetery** extends far into the plain, with hundreds of domed tombs set amid palms.

At the foot of the hill is the badly ruined *Tomb of Hapidjefa III,* with harvest scenes painted on stucco and a decorated ceiling.

Some 4 miles/6 km S of the rock tombs we come to the Coptic Monastery of **Deir Rifa** *(El-Deir),* near which are several *rock tombs* of the Middle and New Kingdoms belonging to princes and dignitaries of Shes-hotep (Greek *Hypselis*), capital of the Hypselite nome, in which the ram-headed Khnum was revered. The town lay some $4\frac{1}{2}$ miles/7 km SE of Asyut at the village of Shotb, whose name preserves the ancient Egyptian name of the town.

SURROUNDINGS of Asyut. – To the N of the town, at the village of *El-Walidiya* on the W bank of the Nile, rises the imposing **Asyut Dam.** Built by a British firm to the design of British engineers in 1898–1902, at the same time as the first Aswan Dam, it serves to regulate the flow of water in the Ibrahimiya Canal, which starts here, and to irrigate more than 1,000,000 acres of land in the provinces of Asyut, El-Minya and Beni Suef. The dam, 40 ft/12·5 m high and 911 yds/833 m long, consists of 13 sections, the first of which (at the W end) has three arches and a lock to permit the passage of ships, while the others have nine arches each. The sluices, 111 in all, can be closed by iron gates.

El-Badari
See under Nile

El-Bagawat
See under Kharga Oasis

Bahr el-Ahmar
See Red Sea

Bahr el-Nil
See Nile

Bahriya Oasis

Western Desert. – New Valley Frontier District.

ACCESS. – By road from Cairo, 208 miles/334 km SW; macadamized, but in places covered with sand; cross-country vehicles only. Also accessible on difficult desert tracks from Medinet el-Fayyum, Beni Mazar or Samalut.

The *Bahirya (Northern) Oasis, also known as Wahet el-Bahnasa, the Oasis of Bahnasa, and to the ancients as the Little Oasis (Oasis Parva: in contrast to the Kharga Oasis) lies in latitude 28° 23 N and longitude 28° 19 E in a depression in the Western (Libyan) Desert, here hilly and very picturesque.

The oasis, 11 miles/18 km long by $5\frac{1}{2}$ miles/9 km across, has a population of some 6000, who live by the cultivation and export of high-quality dates, olives, citrus fruits and onions and by the rearing of poultry (mainly turkeys). A much-esteemed alcoholic drink is brewed from dates. It is planned to achieve a considerable increase in agricultural output by the drilling of wells. – A recent development is the opencast mining of iron ore at *El-Gedida*, some 25 miles/40 km NE of the oasis.

The main settlements are the neighboring villages of *El-Qasr* and **Bawiti**, the latter of which is notable for its characteristic whitewashed houses decorated with patterns in blue and red and for a 6th c. Coptic church. In the vicinity are remains of a *Temple of Amasis* with interesting bas-reliefs, a *Temple of Apries* and a *Catacomb of Isis* of the 26th Dynasty, which all remained open for worship into Christian times but are now largely covered by sand. There are also a *Temple of Alexander the Great,* a Roman *Triumphal Arch* (destroyed) and a necropolis, with only one tomb which can be entered – the *Tomb of Binati* (18th–19th Dynasty), with fine paintings. – Both villages have hot springs (79 °F/26 °C).

S of Bahriya is the small **Oasis of El-Hais**, surrounded by an area of black stones with a high iron content. There is a small Coptic church. Remains of a modest Roman settlement have been found here.

New Valley and **Western Desert**: see separate entries.

Behbeit el-Hagara

Lower Egypt. – Governorate: Daqahliya.
(i) **Tourist Information Office,**
Misr Travel Tower,
Cairo – Abbasia;
tel. 82 60 16.
Misr Travel,
Tourist Center,
Tanta;
tel. 22 12.

ACCESS. – $6\frac{1}{4}$ miles/10 km SW of El-Mansura by road.

The ancient site of Behbeit el-Hagara, the Iseum or Isidis Oppidum of classical times, lies near the provinoial oapital of El Mansura in the northern part of the Nile Delta. The modern name derives from the ancient Egyptian Hebet or Per-Ehbet, the "house of the god of Hebet" (i.e. Horus).

Lying within the Saite nome, the place was much revered by the kings of the 30th Dynasty, who stemmed from the neighboring town of Sebennytus, as a center of the cult of Isis, her brother and husband Osiris and their son Horus.

Within a precinct measuring 87 yds/80 m by 60 yds/55 m enclosed by brick walls, still well preserved on two sides, now used as a place of burial, rises a large heap of ruins – the remains of the once-splendid **Temple of Isis**. Built by Nectanebo II (30th Dynasty) and Ptolemy II Philadelphus, probably on the site of an earlier temple, it is now in a state of total collapse, either as the result of an earthquake or by deliberate demolition. It was built mainly of grey granite, with some red granite, which must have been transported here from a considerable distance. The ruins form a highly picturesque mass of blocks of stone, fragments of columns, broken architraves and other architectural elements, the original function and disposition of which can be established only by an expert.

The * reliefs, all dating from the time of Nectanebo I and II (both 30th Dynasty), Ptolemy II Philadelphus and Ptolemy III Euergetes I, are of high quality – far superior to those in the Graeco-Roman temples of Upper Egypt. One of them makes it possible to identify the position of the sanctuary. It depicts the King offering incense before the sacred barque of Isis, in a form otherwise preserved only in bronze. The boat resembles a two-storeyed house; above, the goddess, with the cow's horns and solar disc, seated on a lotus flower and flanked by two winged goddesses. To the W of this, near the original entrance, is a large slab of grey granite veined with red on which the King is depicted offering a gift of land to Osiris and Isis. To the N is an unusually large granite Hathor capital. All round are innumerable fragments of pillars, architraves, friezes with heads of Hathor and waterspouts in the form of crouching lions. Near by a section of staircase built into the walls can be seen.

The temple's sacred lake can still be identified in the village of **Behbeit**, NW of the ruins.

SURROUNDINGS of Behbeit el-Hagara. – Some 7½ miles/12 km SW of Behbeit, to the W of the little town of *Samannud* (pop. 15,000), are the scanty remains of ancient **Sebennytus** (Egyptian *Tyebnut-yer,* Coptic *Djebenuti*), the place of origin of the 30th Dynasty kings and the home of Manetho (3rd c. B.C.), the historian to whom we owe much of our knowledge of the rulers of ancient Egypt. On a hill are some remains of a *temple* dedicated to the local deity Onuris-Shu, probably dating from the time of Nectanebo II to Ptolemy II Philadelphus.

5 miles/8 km farther S, on a by-road, is the village of *Abusir,* occupying the site of the ancient *Djedu,* chief town of a nome, later known as *Per-Usir* ("House of Osiris") and to the Greeks as **Busiris**. This was revered as the place of burial of Osiris, the scene of an annual pilgrimage. Nothing remains of the ancient town nor of the Temple of Osiris which is mentioned by Herodotus.

Nile Delta: see separate entry.

Beit el-Wali
See under Kalabsha

Beni Hasan

Middle Egypt. – Governorate: El-Minya.

ACCESS. – By boat from El-Minya or Abu Qurqas.

The *rock tombs of Beni Hasan lie on the edge of the desert on the E bank of the Nile some 14 miles/23 km S of El-Minya and 22 miles/35 km N of Tell el-Amarna. The site takes its name from an Arab tribe which formerly lived in a number of neighboring settlements now ruined and abandoned and it now occupies the village of Beni Hasan el-Shuruq. The tombs were constructed during the Middle Kingdom (11th and early 12th Dynasties) for princes and dignitaries of the Oryx or Antelope nome, the 16th nome of Upper Egypt. The architectural features of the tombs and the important inscriptions and representations of scenes from everyday life which they contain make this the most important necropolis between Memphis and Asyut.

The quality of the later tombs is distinctly inferior to that of the earlier ones, reflecting a gradual decline in cultural standards during a period when there was no falling off in material prosperity. The mural decorations were painted on stucco in bright colors, but many of the scenes are damaged or, particularly in the later tombs, so faded that they can barely be distinguished. – The tombs, 39 in all, extend in a row along the rock face. Visitors whose time is limited should confine themselves to the four most important tombs (Nos 17, 15, 3 and 2); the others, less well preserved, are of interest only to specialists.

THE TOMBS. – From the valley a path leads up to Tomb 32. Turning left (N) here, we come to No. 17, the **Tomb of Kheti**, Nomarch of the Antelope nome (11th Dynasty). A doorway in the plain façade gives access into the rock-cut chamber, the roof of which was originally supported by six lotus cluster-columns with bud capitals, though only two of these, with their original coloring, are still standing. The wall-paintings are also well preserved. On the left-hand (N) wall are, in the upper rows, a hunt in the desert, in the lower rows male and female dancers, a statue of the dead man being transported to its place, carpenters, etc. On the rear (E) wall, above, are wrestlers in various attitudes; below, military scenes, including an attack on a fortress. On the right-hand (S) wall are, from left to right, the

Reliefs in the Beni Hasan necropolis

dead man and his wife; the dead man accompanied by his fan-bearer, sandal-bearer, two dwarfs and other attendants; and the dead man receiving various offerings (note the granary on the right).

The scenes on the entrance wall are poorly preserved.

Farther N, at the top of an ancient path ascending from the plain, is the *Tomb of Beket (No. 15), Kheti's father and also Nomarch of the Antelope nome (11th Dynasty). The two columns which supported the roof of the rectangular chamber are missing. In the SE corner is a small recess. On the left-hand (N) wall are, above, a hunt in the desert and a barber, laundrymen, painters, etc.; below, the dead man and his wife with four rows of women spinning and weaving, dancing-girls and girls playing with a ball; herdsmen bringing animals for sacrifice to the dead man; goldsmiths; a fishing scene; and various birds, with their names inscribed beside them. On the rear (E) wall, in the upper rows, are wrestlers; in the lower rows warlike scenes, as in Kheti's tomb. On the right-hand (S) wall is the dead man, in front of whom, in several rows, are men drawing a shrine containing his statue, while in front of this are female dancers and servants carrying ornaments, etc., for the statue; peasants driving in their flocks and herds, some of them being brought in forcibly to pay their taxes, while scribes record the amounts; potters at their wheels; men carrying wild-fowl they have shot; men gaming.

No. 3 is the **Tomb of Khnumhotep III**, son of Neheri, scion of a princely family with hereditary jurisdiction over the Antelope nome, with its capital at Menat Khufu (now El-Minya), and the Eastern Desert territories. Khnumhotep was invested with these territories by King Amenemhet II, and later married a daughter of the Prince of the Dog (Cynopolitan) nome, which then also passed to his son.

The *wall-paintings in this tomb have been cleaned and the colors freshened up by a new process on an experimental basis; if the results are satisfactory other tombs will be given the same treatment.

The *vestibule*, to the rear of an open court, has two 16-sided columns tapering towards the top. The cornice projects over the architrave, ostensibly supported on elegant laths which, like the rest of the structure, are hewn from the living rock, in a manner reminiscent of the mutules (blocks projecting below cornice) of the Doric Order. – The *main chamber* was divided by two pairs of columns into three aisles with flat-vaulted roofs. The scenes and inscriptions are much faded and difficult to distinguish. On the lower part of the walls is a long inscription cut in the rock in vertical lines 30 in/75 cm high, the characters being filled in with green coloring. The royal names were chiseled out of the rock in 1890 by some vandal hand.

On the *entrance wall* (to W) the statue of the dead man is being transported to the temple, with women dancing in front of it; below, the dead man watching carpenters at work. To the left (N) of the door is the dead man's estate office, with servants weighing silver, measuring grain and storing it in the granaries, while scribes seated in a pillared hall record the amounts. The next two rows, below, depict work in the fields (breaking up the ground, plowing, harvesting and threshing by cattle). The fourth row shows the dead man's mummy being conveyed to the Tomb of Osiris in Abydos. In the fifth row are scenes depicting the harvesting of grapes and figs and the cultivation of vegetables. The bottom row shows life by the river (cattle in the water, fishing). – The *left-hand* (N) *wall,* above, depicts the dead man hunting in the desert. Below, to the right, he is shown (a large figure) watching various activities in his nome. In the third row from the top two of his officials introduce a caravan of Asians – men, women and children – with their ibexes and donkeys, clad in gaily colored garments, their sharp features, hooked noses and pointed beards clearly identifying them as Semitic; the inscription describes them as 37 Amus (Semitic bedouin) bringing eye-paint to the Prince of the nome. The scribe is shown giving Khnumhotep a list of the strangers. The lower rows depict the dead man's cattle and poultry. – On the *rear* (E) *wall* the dead man is seen with his wife in a boat, hunting waterfowl with a throwing-stick; in the papyrus thicket are all manner of birds, flying about and nesting; in the water are fish, a hippopotamus and a crocodile; below is a fishing scene. To the right the dead man is shown catching two fish with his spear. In the middle is a niche which originally held a seated figure of the dead man. Above the door he is seen catching birds with a net. – On the *right-hand* (S) *wall,* to the left, he is depicted at table, with all kinds of sacrificial offerings heaped up in front of him; to the right servants and priests bring offerings; in the two lowest rows herdsmen bring cattle, gazelles, antelopes and poultry for sacrifice; slaughtering and cutting up of sacrificial animals. *Right-hand entrance wall* (to S of door): top row, laundrymen; second row, potters; men felling a palm; the dead man, in a litter, watching carpenters at work on a boat; third row, two boats carrying the dead man's family to the funeral ceremony at Abydos; fourth row, women spinning and weaving, bakers at work; bottom row, men building a shrine, a sculptor polishing a statue, etc.

No. 2 is the **Tomb of Amenemhet** or *Ameni,* Nomarch of the Antelope nome in the reign of Sesostris I.

In the *vestibule* are two octagonal columns supporting the flat-vaulted roof. On the uprights and lintel of the entrance door are prayers for the dead and the

Entrance to the Tomb of Amenemhet

titles of the dead man. On either side of the doorway is a long inscription of the 15th day of the second month of the inundation in the 43rd year of Sesostris I's reign glorifying Amenemhet's exploits in several military campaigns and the benefits he conferred on his nome. – The roof of the three-aisled *main chamber* is supported on four 16-sided, delicately fluted columns of Proto-Doric type. The wall-paintings are very similar to those in the Tomb of Khnumhotep. On the left-hand (N) entrance wall are various craftsmen, including shoemakers, carpenters, goldsmiths and potters, and agricultural scenes. On the left-hand wall, in the top row, is a hunt in the desert; second row, transport of the dead man's statue and ceremonial dances; below, right, the dead man receiving tribute from his estate; two lowest rows, his estate office. On the rear wall wrestlers and warlike scenes; bottom row, the dead man's mummy being conveyed to the Tomb of Osiris at Abydos. The niche in this wall contains badly damaged statues of the dead man, his mother and his wife. On the right-hand (S) wall, to the left, the dead man is seated at table with sacrificial offerings heaped in front of him, while priests and servants bring food and other offerings; below, slaughtering and cutting up of sacrificial animals; to the right, the dead man's wife Hetpet seated at table receiving sacrificial gifts.

Other tombs which can be visited if time permits: *Tomb 4,* belonging to Khnumhotep, son of the Khnumhotep III buried in Tomb 3. The vestibule has a Proto-Doric column; the main chamber is unfinished. – *Tomb 5,* with two pillars, unfinished. – *Tomb 13,* belonging to Khnumhotep II, predecessor of Khnumhotep III. – *Tomb 14,* belonging to Khnumhotep I, Prince of the nome in the reign of Amenemhet I. The main chamber had two plant columns, now broken off; the wall-paintings are badly faded. On the rear wall are warriors and a caravan of Libyans entering the dead man's nome along with their wives and children and their herds of livestock, the men with ostrich feathers in their hair, the women carrying their children in baskets on their backs. – *Tomb 18,* left unfinished, is of interest as showing the method of hewing the chambers from the rock; the floor in the front part of the chamber has not been completely excavated. To the rear are ten cluster-columns with bud capitals, five of them unfinished. – *Tomb 21,* belonging to Nakht, a Prince of the Antelope nome (12th Dynasty), is similar in layout to No. 15. – *Tomb 23,* belonging to Neternakht, Governor of the eastern districts, has wall-paintings of no particular interest; on the E wall is a Coptic inscription. – *Tomb 27,* belonging to Remushenti, a Prince of the Antelope nome. – *Tomb 28,* with two lotus columns, was converted into a church in Christian times. – *Tomb 29* belonged to *Beket,* a Nomarch of the Antelope nome. The doors opening into the adjoining Tombs 28 and 30 were made by the Copts. The wall-paintings are comparatively well preserved, but offer no new points of interest; note, in the western half of the S wall, the dwarfs following the dead man, and the wrestlers on the N wall. – *Tomb 33* belonged to Beket, a Prince of the Antelope nome, son of the Beket buried in No. 29; it has a number of wall-paintings. – Tombs 34 – 39 were left unfinished.

On the slopes below the tombs of these dignitaries are many smaller tombs belonging to less important officials and citizens of the Middle Kingdom.

Some 1¼ miles/2 km S of the Beni Hasan necropolis is the *rock temple of the cat-headed goddess Pakhet*, constructed during the joint reign of Queen Hat-shepsut and King Tuthmosis III (18th Dynasty), known to the Greeks as the **Speos Artemidos** ("Cave of Artemis") and to the Arabs as *Istabl Antar* ("Antar's Stable"), after an ancient hero. The names and representations of Hatshepsut were erased by Tuthmosis, and Sethos I (19th Dynasty) later replaced them by his own.

From the landing-place the road to the temple begins by running upstream, and then strikes off to the right towards the desert on an embankment running through fields. In the vicinity is the *Cats' Cemetery* in which the cats sacred to Pakhet, protective goddess of this region, were buried. Continuing SE, we come to a dry desert valley, from the mouth of which a *cemetery* of the 22nd–25th Dynasties extends towards the plain. In the valley itself are many ancient quarries. On the right-hand (S) side of the ravine, some 660 yds/600 m from its mouth, stands the rock temple.

The TEMPLE consists of a vestibule and an inner chamber connected with it by a short corridor. – Above the *entrance* is a long inscription glorifying the reign of Hatshepsut and inveighing against the mis-deeds of the Hyksos. – The *vestibule* originally had eight pillars, of which three remain, bearing on their sides the names of Tuthmosis III and Sethos I; the fronts were to be decorated with sistra, but these were left unfinished. On the rear wall, to the left of the door, is Sethos I between Amun-Re (enthroned) and the cat-headed Pakhet, with Thoth addressing the nine great gods of Karnak and the gods of Upper and Lower Egypt. To the right of the door are three reliefs: Sethos sacrificing to Pakhet, Sethos receiving from Pakhet the hieroglyphs for "life", hanging from two scepters, and Sethos being blessed by Thoth. – In the *corridor*, on the left, is a long inscription in the name of Sethos I and a representation of the King offering

wine to Pakhet; on the right, the King presenting a baboon to Pakhet. In the rear wall of the *inner chamber* is a niche for the goddess's statue.

To the W (right) of the Speos Artemidos is another *cave,* on the outside of which, at the entrance, are the names of Alexander II, son of Alexander the Great and Roxana; below are six small scenes depicting the King in the presence of various gods. The interior, which was supported by pillars, was never completed and is now in a state of ruin. – Near by are several rock tombs of the New Kingdom (rectangular chambers with deep shafts).

Some 1 mile/1·5 km E, at the end of the wadi (N side), is a *cult-niche* dedicated to Pakhet, also dating from the reign of Hatshepsut, with rich relief and painted decoration.

Kom el-Ahmar, *Mallawi, Roda and *Tell el-Amarna: see separate entries.

Beni Suef

Middle Egypt. – Governorate: Beni Suef.
Population: 150,000.
ⓘ **Tourist Information Office,**
Misr Travel Tower,
Cairo – Abbasia;
tel. 82 60 16.

ACCESS. – 80 miles/130 km S of Cairo by road or rail.

The provincial capital of Beni Suef, famed in the Middle Ages for its linen, lies on the W bank of the Nile, at the point where the valley is at its widest and a road goes off into the Fayyum. It is the economic center of the fertile surrounding region, with various processing industries (particularly cotton) and a large bazaar.

St Antony lived as a hermit in an abandoned fort in the hills opposite Beni Suef before withdrawing to the solitude of the Arabian Desert near the Red Sea, and a desert track still runs from the E bank of the Nile opposite the town to St Antony's Monastery (see that entry) and is used by the monks for obtaining the supplies they require; it is not suitable for cars. – On the edge of the desert are several ancient *alabaster quarries.*

SURROUNDINGS of Beni Suef. – Some 9 miles/15 km W, on the right bank of the Bahr Yusuf near the village of *Ahnasiya el-Medina,* popularly known as Ahnasiya Umm el-Kiman ("Hill of Potsherds"), is the huge accumulation of rubble, covering an area of $\frac{1}{2}$ sq. mile/1·5 sq. km, which marks the site of the ancient **Heracleopolis Magna**, capital of the 20th nome of Upper Egypt. Under the Old Kingdom the town was known as *Hatnen-nesut,* from which were derived the Coptic *Hnes* and the Arabic *Ahnas.* During the First Intermediate Period it was ruled by the Heracleopolitan princes, who succeeded in extending their power as far as Abydos. In Graeco-Roman times it was the capital of the Heracleopolitan nome and the chief center of the cult of the ram-headed god Herishef, whom the Greeks equated with Heracles. The ichneumon ("Pharaoh's rat", *Herpestes ichneumon*), a species of mongoose, was also worshiped here.

Nothing remains of the city's great temples, one dating from the Middle Kingdom and a new temple erected by Ramesses II. Four columns to be seen on the site probably belonged to a Byzantine church.

The necropolis of the ancient city is at *Sedment el-Gebel,* on the left bank of the Bahr Yusuf.

  * **Fayyum** and ***El-Lahun**: see separate entries.

Berenice

Eastern Desert. – Red Sea Frontier District.

ACCESS. – At the S end of the modernized road down the Red Sea coast.

The remains of the once-important port of Berenice lie in the same latitude as Aswan in a spacious bay in the Red Sea, the Halig Umm el-Ketef (the "unsafe bay"), which is enclosed on the N by the Ras Banas Peninsula and forms an excellent sheltered harbor.

HISTORY. – The town was founded by Ptolemy II Philadelphus in 275 B.C. with the object of reviving trade in the Red Sea and was given the name of his mother. Situated at the end of the great caravan routes from Coptos (Qift) and Edfu in the Nile Valley to the Red Sea, it was for four or five centuries one of the most important ports on the Red Sea coast, carrying on trade with India, Arabia and the E coast of Africa.

In the middle of the ancient site, now almost entirely covered by wind-blown sand, are the remains, discovered in 1873, of a **temple**. Facing ENE, it is preceded by a forecourt measuring 29 ft/8·75 m across and 12 ft/3·66 m from front to rear. The temple itself, 31 ft/9·50 m long, had two rows of chambers set behind one another. On the outer wall, to the left, is the figure of a Roman Emperor in the presence of a goddess, described in the accompanying inscription as the goddess of the "Green Mountain" (emerald-mine: see below).

Some $1\frac{1}{4}$ miles/2 km N of the site are the harbor, now of no importance, and the little fishing village of *Bender el-Kebir.* Linked with the project for the construction of a new road between Aswan and the Red Sea is a plan to build a modern port to the S of Ras Banas for the freight and pilgrim traffic to and from Jedda in Saudi Arabia.

Offshore lies the small island of *Topazos,* which has given its name to topaz and topazolite, a yellowish-green variant of andradite garnet. Both these minerals were found in abundance here, as was chrysolite, a type of olivine which was prized from ancient times as a gemstone.

SURROUNDINGS of Berenice. – The once-famous emerald-mines in the *Wadi Sakeit* (75 miles/120 km NW) and on *Gebel Zubara* (95 miles/150 km NW; 4465 ft/1361 m), the ancient Mons Smaragdus, were worked by the Arabs until 1370. In the 19th c. Mohammed (Mehmet) Ali attempted unsuccessfully to reopen the mines.

Red Sea: see separate entry.

Biban el-Harim (Valley of Queens)
See under Thebes

Biban el-Muluk (Valley of Kings)
See under Thebes

Bir el-Hammamat
See under Eastern Desert

Birket Qarun
See under Fayyum

Bubastis (Tell Basta)
See under El-Zagazig

Bur Safaga
See under Red Sea

Busiris (Abusir)
See under Behbeit el-Hagara

Cairo/Misr el-Qahira/El-Qahira

Lower Egypt. – Governorate: Cairo.
Altitude: 66 ft/20 m
Population: about 10 million; with surrounding built-up area over 13 million.

ⓘ **Tourist Information Office,**
Misr Travel Tower,
Abbasia;
tel. 82 35 10, 82 45 85, 83 13 53;
Heliopolis Airport,
tel. 96 64 75.
5 Adly St,
tel. 3 91 34 54;
Tourist Police,
5 Adly St.,
tel. 3 92 60 28;
Misr Station,
tel. 76 42 14;
Central Station,
tel. 75 35 55;
Heliopolis Airport,
tel. 62 25 84.
Automobile et Touring Club d'Egypte,
Shari' Qasr el-Nil 10,
tel. 74 33 55.
Misr Travel,
Shari' Talaat Harb 1,
tel. 75 00 10 and 75 01 68;
Shari' Qasr el-Nil 43,
tel. 91 41 88, 91 49 72 and 91 26 13.
American Express of Egypt,
Shari' Qasr el-Nil 15,
tel. 75 04 44;
Heliopolis Airport,
tel. (02) 67 08 95;

Marriott Hotel,
tel. 4 11 01 36;
Méridien Hotel,
tel. 84 40 17;
Nile Hilton Hotel,
tel. 74 33 83;
Ramses Hilton Hotel,
Corniche el-Nil 1115,
tel. 77 36 90;
Residence Hilton Hotel,
tel. 3 50 78 17.
Rail Information,
tel. 75 35 55

EMBASSIES/CONSULATES. – *United Kingdom:* Shari' Ahmed Raghab, Garden City; tel. 354 0850 and 354 0852. – *United States:* Shari Latin America 5, Garden City; tel. 355 7371. – *Canada:* Shari' Mohamed Fahmi el-Sayed, Garden City; tel. 354 3110.

HOTELS. – *Semiramis Inter-Continental* (28 floors), Corniche el-Nil, L, 1680 b.; *Ramses Hilton*, Corniche el-Nil 1115, L, 1600 b.; *Nile Hilton*, Corniche el-Nil/Midan Tahrir, L, 733 b.; *Cairo Sheraton*, Midan el-Gala 2 (left bank), L, 674 b.; *Meridien*, Corniche el-Nil, L, 588 b.; *Shepheards*, Corniche el-Nil, Garden City, L, 544 b.; *Sonesta*, Sharia el Tajaran, Nasr City, Heliopolis, L, 418 b.; *Marriot*, Gesira, L, 2500 b.; *ETAP Safir Cairo*, Midan el-Misaha 4, Dakki (near Botan. Gardens), I, 560 b.; *Sheherazade*, Sharia el-Nil, I, 376 b.; *Manial Palace Village* (Club Méditerranée), Kasr Mohamed Aly, El Manial; *Mohamed-Ali Palace*, I, 360 b.; *El-Nil*, Sharia Ahmed Ragheb 12, Garden City, I, 528 b.; *Green Pyramids*, Sharia Helejit el-Ahram 13, I, 152 b.; *El-Borg*, Sharia Sarai Gesira, I, 140 b.; *Cleopatra*, Sharia Abdel Saram Aref Bustan 2/Midan Tahrir, I, 164 b.; *Bel Air Cairo*, Mokattam, I, 520 b.; *Atlas Zamalek*, Sharia Gama Arabia, I, 204 b.; *Maadi Hotel*, in Maadi, I, 300 b.; *Care Kemet*, Midan Abbasia, II, 360 b.; *Continental Savoy*, Opera Square, II, 329 b.; *President*, Sharia Dr. Taha Hussein 22, II, 246 b.; *Indiana*, Sharia el-Sarai, II, 240 b.; *Khan el-Khalily*, Sharia el-Bosta 7, II, 240 b.; *Marwa Palace*, Sharia el- Kateeb 11, II, 236 b.; *Atlas*, Shari Mohamed Roushdy, Opera Square, II, 220 b.; *Victoria*, Sharia Gumhurija 66, Ranses Square, II, 200 b.; *Nabila Cairo Tower*, Sharia Gameet el-Dewal el-Arabia, II, 198 b.; *Elfara' ana*, Sharia Lotfy Hassuna 12, II, 192 b.; *Sphinx*, Sharia Magles el-Omma 8, II, 176 b.; *Cosmopolitan*, Sharia Ibn Taalab 1, II, 168 b.; *Rehab*, Sharia el-Fawakeh 4, II, 168 b.; *Raja*, Sharia Mohy-Eddin Abul-Ezz 34, II, 166 b.; *Residence*, in Maadi, II, 164 b.; *Al-Manar*, Sharia Abdel Hamid Lofty, II, 160 b.; *Concorde*, Sharia Tahrir 146, II, 144 b.; *Fontana*, Midan Ramses, II, 140 b.; *El-Aman*, Sharia Gisa 58, II, 132 b.; *Carlton*, Sharia 26 July 21, II, 120 b.; *Kanzy*, Sharia Abu Bakr el-Seddik 9, II, 117 b.; *Safa Inn*, Sharia Abbas el Akkad, II, 110 b.; *El-Tonsi*, Sharia el-Tahrir 143, II, 109 b.; *Windsor*, Sharia el-Alfi 19, II, 101 b.; *Cairo Crillon*, Sharia el-Montaser 19, II, 92 b.; *Salem*, Sharia Mohamed Kamel Morsi 12, II, 90 b.; *Horris*, Sharia 26 July, II, 86 b.; *Nile Savoy*, Sharia Sarai el-Gesira, II, 70 b.; *Odeon Palace*, Sharia Abdel Hamid Said, II, 60 b.; *Newstar*, Sharia Yehia Ibrahim 34, II, 56 b.; *Cairo Inn*, Sharia Syria 26, II, 50 b.; *Longchamps*, Sharia Ismail Mohamed 21, II, 48 b.; *New Horus House*, Sharia Ismail Mohamed 23, II, 48 b.; *El Kanter Chalets*, El-Kanter Gardens, II, 44 b.; *Arabia*, Sharia Abdel Aziz Seoud 13, II, 40 b.; *Sweet Hotel*, in Maadi, II, 12 b.; *Piccadilly*, Midan 26 July 19, III, 180 b.; *Grand Hotel*, Sharia 26 July 17, III, 179 b.; *Dreamers*, Sharia Gadda 5, III, 144 b.; *Hamburg*, Sharia el-Borsa 18, III, 138 b.; *Qasr el-Nil*, Sharia Qasr el-Nil 33, III, 124 b.; *International*, Sharia Abdel Asim Rashed 3, III, 120 b.; *Ommayad*, Sharia 26 July 22, III, 120 b.; *Scarabee*, Sharia 26 July 16, III, 117 b.; *Capsis Palace*, Sharia Ramses 117, III, 114 b.; *El-Hussein*, Midan Hussein, III,

The Egyptian Museum,

110 b.; *Lotus*, Sharia Talaat Harb 12, III, 110 b.; *New Hotel*, Sharia Adly 21, III, 106 b.; *Caroline Crillon*, Sharia Syria 49, III, 100 b.; *Zayed*, Midan Abul Mahasen el-Shazeli 42, III, 96 b.; *Tut-Ankh-Amon*, Sharia Abdel Rahim Sabri, III, 90 b.; *Garden Palace*, Sharia el-Muderija 11, III, 86 b.; *Amon*, Midan Sphinx, III, 84 b.; *Taher Touristic*, Sharia el-Yamani 12, III, 80 b.; *Tiab House*, Sharia Mahmud Khalaf, III, 75 b.; *New Rich*, Sharia Abdel Azaz 47, III, 74 b.; *Rose*, Sharia Iran 6, III, 73 b.; *Nooran*, Sharia Mahmud Khalaf 13, III, 70 b.; *Lo'lo'et el-Maady*, in Maadi, III, 60 b.; *Viennoise*, Sharia Mahamud Bassioni 11, III, 57 b.; *Cairo Commodore*, Sharia Fausi Ramah 10, III, 50 b.; *Holiday Home*, Sharia Hegaz 63, III, 50 b.; *El-Nil Garden*, Sharia Abdel Asis el-Saoud 131, III, 46 b.; *Green Valley*, Sharia Abdel Khalek Sarwat 33, III, 46 b.; *El-Nil Zamalek*, Sharia Maahad el-Swissri 21, III, 45 b.; *Tulip*, Midan Talaat Harb 3, III, 42 b.; *Happy Joe*, Corniche el-Nil, III, 30 b.; *Horus House*, Sharia Mahommed Mohamed, III, 24 b.; *National*, Sharia Talaat Harb 30, IV, 220 b.; *Central*, Sharia el-Bosta 7A, IV, 111 b.; *Nitocrisse*, Sharia Mohamed Farid 171, IV, 110 b.; *Tourist Palace*, Sharia el-Baidak 12, IV, 102 b.; *Big Ben*, Sharia Emad Eddin 33, IV, 82 b.; *Garden City*, Sharia Kamal Eddin Salah 23, IV, 75 b.; *Radwan*, Midan el-Azhar, IV, 75 b.; *Montana*, Sharia Sherif 25, IV, 67 b.; *Des Roses*, Sharia Talaat Harb 33, IV, 51 b.; *Tary*, Sharia Fom Bab el-Bahr 12, IV, 48 b.; *Cairo Palace*, Sharia el-Gumhurija, IV, 36 b.; *Blue Nile*, Sharia el-Hokama 4, IV.

IN HELIOPOLIS: *Heliopolis Sheraton*, Sharia el-Uruba, L, 1290 b.; *Meridien*, Sharia el-Uruba 5, L, 302 b.; *Hyatt el-Salam*, Sharia Abdel Hamid Badawy, L, 596 b.; *Baron Heliopolis*, Sharia el-Uruba, I, 252 b.; *Heliopark*, Sharia el-Hagaz 100, II, 194 b.; *Egyptel*, Sharia el-Marghani 93, II, 156 b.; *El-Horreya*, Sharia el-Horreya 14, II, 114 b.; *Beirut*, Sharia Beirut 56, II, 104 b.; *Aviation*, Sharia Ahmed Fuad, II, 46 b.; *Helio Cairo*, Sharia Abdel Hamid Badawi 85, III, 112 b.; *Egyptian Riviera Tours*, Sharia Mohamed Jussuf 23, III, 66 b.; *Ebeid House*, Sharia Gesir el-Suez, IV, 100 b.; *Champs Elysées*, Midan Salah Eddin, IV, 36 b. – AT THE AIRPORT: *Cairo Heliopolis Hotel Mövenpick* (formerly Cairo Concorde), L, 850 b.; *Novotel*, I, 412 b.; *Transit Airport Hotel Egyptair*, I, 150 b.

AT PYRAMIDS: see under Giza.

YOUTH HOSTELS. – *Garden City*, Shari' el-Ibrahimi; *El-Manyal*, Shari' Abdel Aziz 135, Roda. – CAMP SITE (with chalets) at Pyramids of Giza: see under Giza.

The Cairo Tower on the island of Gezira

RESTAURANTS with international cuisine in the hotels listed. – EGYPTIAN CUISINE: *El-Dahan*, Khan el-Khalili 4; *Ali Hasan el-Hati*, Midan Halim 8; *Filfila*, Shari' Hoda Shaarawi 15; *Arabesque*, Qasr el-Nil; *El-Leil*, Shari' el-Haram (Pyramid Road); *Sofar*, Shari' Adly 21; *Cairo Tower*, on 14th floor of Cairo Tower (view). – FAR EASTERN CUISINE: *Paxy's Korean Restaurant*, Midan 26 July. – *Pasticceria Groppi* (long-established), in the town centre.

The Egyptian capital of Cairo (Arabic El-Qahira or Misr el-Qahira), the largest city on the African continent and in the Islamic world, long known as the "Gateway to the East" and a mediator between Christianity and Islam, lies in latitude 30° 4′ N and longitude 34° 17′ E with the main part of the city on the right bank of the Nile, some 12½ miles/20 km S of the point where the river divides into the Rosetta and Damietta arms.

On the E side of the city rise the barren reddish rock walls of the Moqattam Hills, beyond which extends the Eastern (Arabian) Desert. To the S the city reaches out by way of Old Cairo to the suburb of Maadi; to the W the newer districts spread beyond the Nile into the Western (Libyan) Desert. Cairo is the seat of government, of the Egyptian Parliament and the various Government departments and the residence of the heads of the Islamic, Coptic and Catholic Coptic religious communities. It has several universities and colleges of high academic standing.

HISTORY. – From a very early period there was a town on the E bank of the Nile, opposite the Pyramids, which bore the name of **Khere-ohe**, or "place of combat", because Horus and Seth were believed to have fought here. The Greeks called it **Babylon**, and the Romans preserved this name when they built up the settlement into a fortress. – After the Arab Conquest in A.D. 641 the Caliphs built a new capital in the plain to the N of the Roman stronghold, naming it *Fustat*; and the name of Misr el-Fustat, or Misr for short, was thereafter applied both to the city and the land of Egypt.

After the fall of the Omayyads in 750 the entire town, with the exception of the Great Mosque, was destroyed by fire. A new capital was then established by the Abbasid governors in the *El-Askar* district, and at the end of the 9th c. the *El-Qatai* quarter, with the Ibn Tulun Mosque, was built. When Gohar, the general of the Fatimid Caliph Muizz, conquered Egypt in 969 he built a military settlement to the N of El-Qatai, naming it **Misr el-Qahira** (the "Victorious", after the Arabic name of the planet Mars, which was then at the meridian), and thus in effect founding the city of Cairo. In the 12th c. Saladin enclosed the two settlements of Fustat and El-Qahira within a single wall (never completed) and began to build the Citadel. Under the luxury-loving Fatimids the city was greatly enlarged and embellished, reaching its zenith in the 14th c. During this period, however, it was several times ravaged by plague, which carried off large numbers of people, and was frequently thrown into a turmoil by revolts, risings and bloody persecutions of Christians. – In 1517, after the Battle of Heliopolis, the Ottoman Sultan Selim entered the

Gold mask of Tutankhamun, Egyptian Museum

city. Although Cairo suffered from plundering and oppression under Turkish rule, it still remained a busy provincial capital with an active cultural life.

During his Egyptian expedition of 1798–99 Napoleon established his headquarters in Cairo. In 1805 Mohammed (Mehemet) Ali, as Pasha of Egypt, took possession of the Citadel, where in 1811 he treacherously massacred 480 leading Mamelukes whom he had invited to Cairo. Later in the 19th c., particularly after the opening of the Suez Canal, the city enjoyed a period of rapid economic development and grew considerably in size. Present-day Cairo is now an imposing modern city with streets and squares laid out on the European pattern and a sprinkling of high-rise blocks, in striking contrast to the over-populated Arab quarters and the bazaars, still retaining their medieval aspect. – On 27 September 1987 the first stretch (2½ miles/4·2 km below the city centre) of the Cairo *underground railway system* (the first "Metro" in Africa), mostly financed by France, was opened in the presence of the Egyptian president Mubarak and the French Minister Chirac. Work began in 1981 and its planned total length is 16 miles/25 km.

Museum Opening Hours

Agricultural Museum,
with *Cotton Museum,*
Shari Wazaret el-Ziraa,
Dokki;
in summer Sat.–Thu. 9 a.m.–2 p.m. Fri.
9–11 a.m. and 1–2.30 p.m.;
in winter Sat.–Thu. 9 a.m.–4 p.m., Fri.
9–11.30 a.m. and 1–4 p.m.

Center for Art and Life,
Manisterli Palace,
Roda;
Sun.–Thu. 9.30 a.m.–1.30 p.m.

Coptic Museum,
Old Cairo;
Sat.–Thu. 9 a.m.–4 p.m., Fri. 9–11 a.m. and
1–4 p.m.

Egyptian Antiquities Museum,
Midan el-Tahrir;
Sat.–Thu. 9 a.m.–4 p.m., Fri. 9–11.15 a.m. and 1.30–
4 p.m.

Ethnological Museum,
Shari' Qasr el-Aini 109;
Sat.–Thu. 9 a.m.–1 p.m.

Gayer-Anderson Museum,
adjoining Ibn Tulun Mosque;
Sat.–Thu. 9 a.m.–3.30 p.m., Fri. 9–11 a.m. and
1.30–3.30 p.m.

Geological Museum,
Shari' el-Sheikh Rihan;
Sat.–Thu. 9 a.m.–1.30 p.m.
closed Fri. and public holidays.

Gezira Museum,
with *Museum of Egyptian Civilization* and
Museum of Transport,
Gezira Exhibition Grounds;
Mon.–Thu. 9 a.m.–3 p.m., Fri. 9 a.m.–12 noon.

Gohara Museum,
on the Citadel;
daily 9 a.m.–4 p.m.

Khalil Museum,
Shari' el-Sheikh Marsafy;
Zamalek; Sat.–Thu. 9 a.m.–2 p.m., and 5–8 p.m.

Manyal Palace,
Shari' Sayyala;
daily 9 a.m.–2 p.m.

Mukhtar Museum,
Tahrir Gardens,
Gezira;
Tue.–Sun. 9 a.m.–1.30 p.m.

Museum of Islamic Art,
Midan Bab el-Khalk;
Sat.–Thu. 9 a.m.–4 p.m., (and Fri. 9–11 a.m.
and 1.30–4 p.m. in summer)

Museum of Modern Art,
Shari' Ismail Abdul Fetuh 18,
Dokki;
Sat.–Thu. 9 a.m.–1.30 p.m., Fri. 9–11.30 a.m.

Musaferkhana Palace,
Darb el-Tablawi;
daily 9 a.m.–4 p.m.

Palace of Art
(Mogamaa el-Fenun),
Shari' el-Maahad el-Swissry,
Zamalik;
Sat.–Thu. 9 a.m.–1 p.m. and 5–8 p.m., Fri.
9–11 a.m. and 5–8 p.m.

Postal Museum,
Head Post Office,
Midan el-Ataba;
daily 9 a.m.–1 p.m.

Railway Museum,
Central Station,
Midan Ramses;
Tue.–Sun. 9 a.m.–2 p.m.

Sightseeing in Cairo

The Modern City

The hub of the modern city of Cairo is the spacious **Midan el-Tahrir** (Liberation Square). Here all the city's main traffic arteries meet (underground railway station). – To the SW of the square are the *Ministry of Foreign Affairs* and the *Government Buildings*, to the SE the *American University* and the *National Assembly.*

Directly to the NW of the square is the large range of buildings (1897–1902) occupied by the ***Egyptian Museum**, which has the world's largest and finest

Midan el-Tahrir (Liberation Square)

collection of Egyptian and Graeco-Roman antiquities, founded in 1857 by the French Egyptologist Auguste Mariette (1821–81). – To do full justice to the Museum, which can display only a fraction of its total holdings, several days would be required. Visitors who are pressed for time will do well to confine themselves to the celebrated treasures of Tutankhamun and a selection of the Old Kingdom material.

Ground floor (major monuments ranging from the early Egyptian to the Graeco-Roman period). – *Rotunda:* recent acquisitions, special exhibitions. – *Grand Gallery:* stone sarcophagi of the Old Kingdom. – PYRAMID PERIOD OF THE OLD KINGDOM (3rd–6th Dynasties). – *Room 42:* diorite statue of

Entrance to the Egyptian Museum

Cairo

Egyptian Museum

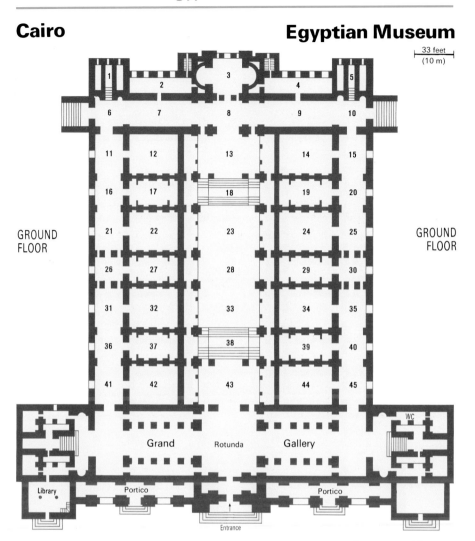

GROUND
FLOOR

GROUND
FLOOR

Chepren (JE 10062); wooden statue known as the Village Headman (CG 34); seated figure of King Djoser (JE 49158). – *Room 32*: limestone statue of the priest Ranufer (CG 3/4); painting on stucco of six geese (JE 34571); embossed copper statue of Phiops I (JE 33034); Seneb the dwarf and his family (JE 51280).

MIDDLE KINGDOM AND HYKOS PERIOD (11th–17th Dynasties). – *Room 26*: limestone statue of Amenemhet III. – *Room 22* (middle): tomb chamber of Harhotep, with pictures of the dead man's household goods; ten over-life-size limestone statues of Sesostris I (CG 411–420).

NEW KINGDOM (18th–24th Dynasties). – *Room 12*: Tuthmosis III as a young man, wearing the crown of Upper Egypt (JE 38234); inscription recording Tuthmosis III's victories (JE 88803), statue of Eset (Isis), mother of Tuthmosis III (JE 37417); Chapel of the goddess Hathor and statue of the Hathor Cow dedicated by Tuthmosis III (JE 38574/5); relief of the Punt expedition (JE 14276/JE 89661); statues of Amenophis II, stele of Amenophis III (JE 31409). – *Room 3* (Amarna period): colossal statues of Amenophis IV (Athenaten) from his temple at Karnak. – *Room 7*:

Tutankhamun's gold canopic shrine

Cairo   Egyptian Museum

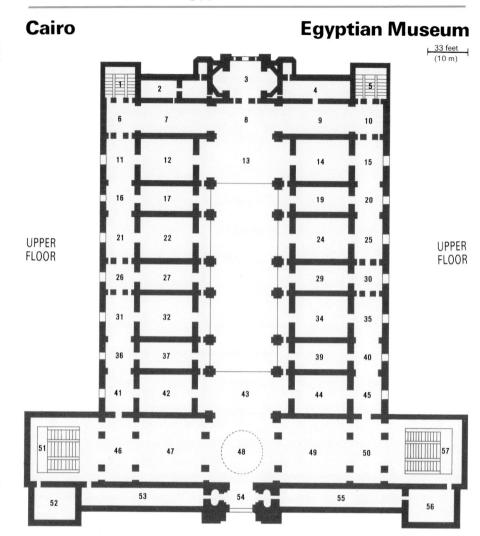

33 feet
(10 m)

sphinx with name of Queen Hatshepsut. – *Room 13* (N portico): stela of Amenophis III (Memnon) and Merneptah. – *Atrium* (Rooms 18, 23, 28 and 33): colossal group of Amenophis III with his wife and three daughters; painted pavement from palace at Tell del-Amarna; bier of Osiris. – *Room 20*: granite head of Ramesses II.

LATE PERIOD: *Room 24*: head of a high official (JE 36933). – *Room 25*: head of King Taharqa (Tirhakah of the Old Testament; CG 560); stool of Anchpachered (JE 36993); the "Pithom Stela" of Ptolemy II Philadelphus. – *Room 30*: alabaster statue of princess Amenirdis (JE 3420). – GRAECO-ROMAN AND COPTIC PERIODS. – *Room 34*: the trilingual Decree of Canopus (238 B.C.) in hieroglyphic, demotic and Greek scripts.

Upper floor. – *Rooms 4, 7–10, 15, 20, 25, 30, 35, 40 and 45:* the *treasures found in the tomb of **Tutankhamun**, son-in-law and successor of Amenophis IV (Akhenaten), who died at the age of 18. The tomb, discovered by Howard Carter in the Valley of the Kings (Thebes) in 1922, contained the largest and richest assemblage of grave-goods ever found intact in an Egyptian tomb, including some of the finest achievements of Egyptian artists and craftsmen. Particularly fine are the King's innermost mummiform *coffin, of solid gold, with the royal

insignia of the vulture and uraeus on the forehead (JE 60671), and the gold *portrait mask which lay within the gold coffin on the head of the mummy (JE 60672).

Ushabtis from Tutankhamun's tomb

Tutankhamun's gold throne

Room 13: sarcophagi and grave-goods from the Tomb of Yuya and Tuya, parents-in-law of Amenophis III. – *Room 12:* material from royal tombs at Thebes. – *Room 17:* material from the tomb of the fan-bearer Maherpra (18th Dynasty). – *Rooms 22, 27, 32 and 37:* sarcophagi and grave-goods of the Middle Kingdom. – *Room 14:* Roman coffins and mummy portraits. – *Room 19:* figures of gods and sacred animals. – *Rooms 24 and 29:* funerary papyri, drawings on limestone fragments, sculptors' models.

Room 52: **mummies, particularly mummies of Pharaohs, arranged in chronological order, followed by mummies of Queens. The X-ray photographs shown alongside the mummies have yielded information about their age, state of health and cause of death.

Room 2: furnishings of the Tomb of Queen Hetepheres, mother of Cheops. – *Room 3:* a magnificent collection of **jewelry, illustrating the development of the goldsmith's art from the earliest period (*c.* 3200 B.C.) to Byzantine times (A.D. 395–650). Of particular interest are four bracelets from the tomb of King Djer (1st Dynasty; Case 2), demonstrating the high degree of skill achieved even at this early period; a gold falcon's head (6th Dynasty; Case 3, No. 4010); the *Treasure of Dahshur, with outstanding examples of the work of the Middle Kingdom (12th Dynasty); the *jewelry of Queen Ahhotep, mother of King Amosis, who drove out the Hyksos (1580 B.C.; Case 10); a hoard of gold objects from Bubastis (19th Dynasty; Case 11); and the gold jewelry of Queens Tiy (18th Dynasty) and Tewosret (19th Dynasty). –

Just beyond the Egyptian Museum the ***Corniche el-Nil** along the bank of the Nile is lined by large modern hotels and prestige buildings. In Shari Qasr el-Aini, which runs S from the Midan el-Tahrir, is the *Ethnological Museum,* and in Shari el-Sheikh Rihan the *Geological Museum.* – To the NE of the Midan el-Tahrir are the main commercial and shopping districts of the modern city, which are entirely European in character. The goods sold in the shops here are marked with fixed prices, which cannot be reduced by bargaining like prices in the bazaars.

Another focal point of the city's life, now superseded by the Midan el-Tahrir, was the beautiful ***Ezbekiya Gardens** (formerly a lake) on the edge of the old Arab town, which are now traversed by Sharia 26 July. The gardens, laid out in 1870 under the direction of M. Barillet, a landscape-gardener from Paris, contain a

Statue of Ramesses II in Midan Ramses (Ramesses Square)

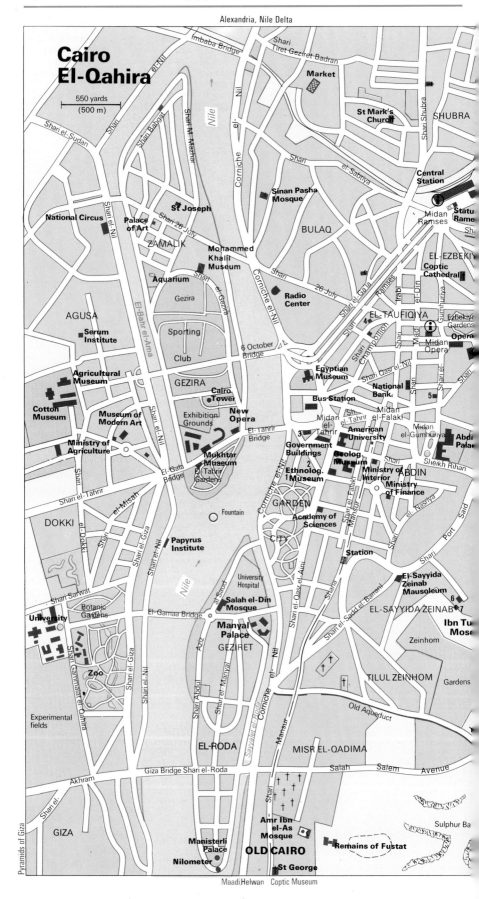

Cairo
El-Qahira

550 yards
(500 m)

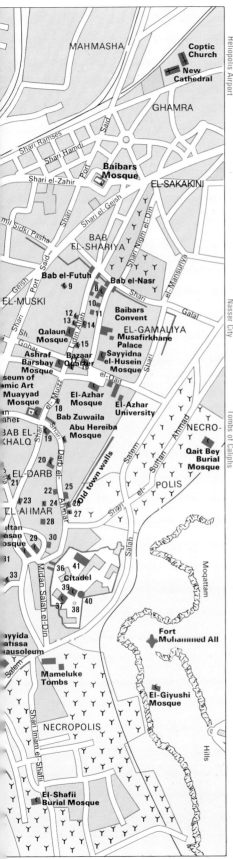

profusion of exotic bushes and plants, including an Indian banyan *(Ficus bengalensis)* whose aerial roots constantly form new trunks. – To the S of the gardens is Midan Opera (Opera Square), with the Opera House (burned down in 1971; new Opera House is on the island of Gezira), in which Verdi's ''Aida'' was performed for the first time in 1871, and an equestrian statue of Ibrahim Pasha (by Cordier). Near by is the **Head Post Office**, with the *Postal Museum*.

Shari el-Gumhuriya, on the W side of the Ezbekiya Gardens, runs N and comes in about 1100 yds/1000 m to **Midan Ramses** (Ramesses Square), with a 33 ft/10 m high * *statue of Ramesses II* from Memphis, set up here in 1955. On the N side of the square is the **Central Station**, with the *Railway Museum*. – Some 1100 yds/1000 m S of the Ezbekiya Gardens on Shari el-Gumhuriya stands the 19th c. **Abdin Palace**, formerly the residence of the King of Egypt, now *Palace of the Republic*. The former private apartments of the King are open to the public as a museum (pictures, tapestries).

Abdin Palace

1 United Kingdom Embassy	21 Rusun Mosque
2 United States Embassy	22 Sultan Shaapan Medrese
3 Foreign Ministry	23 Sulaimaniya Mosque
4 Supreme Court	24 Surdun Mosque
5 Gumhuriya Theater	25 Ibrahim Aga House
6 Emir Salar and Sanjar Mausoleum	26 Aq Sunqur Mosque
7 Qait Bey Mosque	27 Emir Khairbek Mosque
8 El-Hakim Mosque	28 El-Gei el-Yusufi Medrese
9 Abu Bekr ibn Muzhir Mosque	29 El-Rifai Mosque
10 Sabil Kuttab Wikala	30 Qani Bey Medrese
11 Beit el-Suheimi	31 Emir Taz Palace
12 Mohammed el-Nasir Mosque	32 Emir Sheikhu Convent
13 Barquqiya Mosque	33 Khushqadam el-Ahmedi Mosque
14 El-Aqmar Mosque	34 Beit el-Kiridliya
15 Salih Ayyub Mausoleum	35 Shagarat el-Durr Mausoleum
16 Khan el-Khalili	36 Mohammed Ali Mosque
17 El-Ghuri Medrese and Mausoleum	37 Bir Yusuf (Joseph's Well)
18 Fakahani Mosque	38 El-Nasir Mosque
19 Salih Talai Mosque	40 Moqattam Tower
20 El-Mardani Mosque	41 Military Museum

From the Ezbekiya Gardens the modern Shari 26 July, lined with shops and offices, runs W and then NW and crosses the Nile on *26 July Bridge* to reach the island of **Gezira** *(Gezira Bulaq)*, 3 miles/ 5 km long and just under 1100 yds/ 1000 m across. In the northern half of the island are the select residential district of ZAMALIK, with the Palace of Art (near the Zamalik Bridge, on the W side of the island), and an interesting *Aquarium* (fishes from the Nile) in the southern half are extensive sports grounds and public gardens (racing club, golf course, etc.) and Exhibition Grounds (El-Tahir Gardens). Also in the southern half of Gezira is the great landmark and emblem of the modern city, the 614 ft/187 m high **Cairo Tower** *(El-Burk)*, with observation platforms and a restaurant from which there are panoramic *views of the city. – Close to the tower a *cultural center* (with several museums) has recently developed around the ***New Opera House**, built in modern Islamic style with cupolas (opened in 1988). Off the southern tip of the island, in the middle of the Nile, a *fountain* forms a prominent feature in the landscape. – The S end of Gezira can be reached direct from the Midan el-Tahrir by way of the *El-Tahrir Bridge*.

Farther upstream is the smaller island of **Roda**, another residential area. Near the N end is the **Manyal Palace**, built in 1805–18 in the time of Mohammed (Mehemet) Ali, and which is now a museum. At the southern tip of the island is the *Nilometer*, constructed about 715 to measure the water-level of the Nile and much restored in later centuries; although it has now lost its original function it is still of great historical interest. To the N of this is the **Manisterli Palace**, with the *Center for Art and Life* (arts and crafts from Pharaonic times to the present day; exhibition and shop).

To the W of Gezira and Roda, on the left bank of the Nile, are the modern districts of DOKKI, with the **Agricultural Museum**, set in a beautiful park, and the *Museum of Modern Art,* and GIZA, with the extensive *Botanic Gardens,* the **Zoo** (African animals) and **Cairo University**.

The Old Town

The main thoroughfare of the old Arab town of Cairo is formed by ***Shari el-Muski**, a street laid out in the first half of the 19th c., and its continuation Shari Gohar el-Qaid, which leads SE from the Ezbekiya Gardens. Externally these streets, with their European-style shops, have lost their Oriental character, but they still present all the noise and bustle, the constant lively activity of the East.

To the E of Shari Port Said, which is laid out on the line of a former canal, extends the FATIMID TOWN founded by Gohar, which has preserved three of the old town gates in the second circuit of walls built from 1074 onwards (Bab el-Futuh and Bab el-Nasr on the N side and Bab Zuwaila on the S).

Illuminations on the Nile – the island of Gezira, with the Cairo Tower

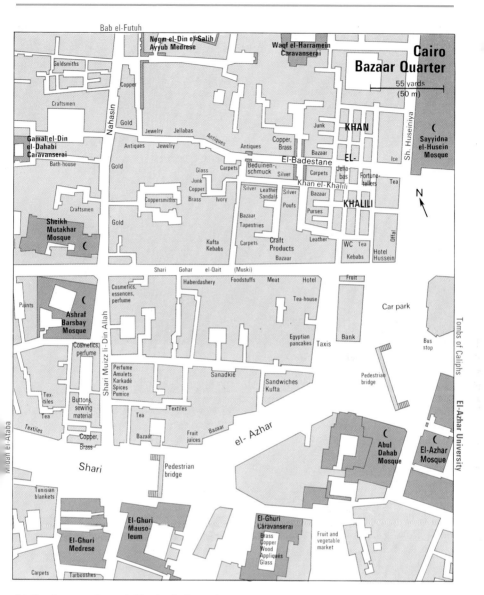

At the intersection of Sharia Gohan el-Qaid and the line of streets between Bab el-Futuh and Bab Zuwaila stands the **Ashraf Barsbay Mosque** (1425). Here we are already in the *Bazaar Quarter*, which with its large bazaars (Arabic *suq*) and teeming mass of humanity has an abundance of novelty and interest to offer the visitor.

Turning left at the intersection, we come to the *gold and silver bazaar* (filigree-work). – To the E of this is the large *Khan el-Khalili Bazaar*, established about 1400 on the site of a Fatimid castle, which has preserved its old-world character, although the shops now cater for the tourist trade (carpets, jewelry, antiques, perfume, etc.). – In a square in the bazaar quarter is the Neo-Gothic **Sayyidna el-**

Before you go **shopping in the bazaar** it is well to have some idea in advance of the level of prices for the goods you are interested in. It is normal to haggle, for the seller will always set his first price high enough to leave room for a substantial reduction. But though you may enjoy bargaining it should be remembered that with the low wage levels current in Egypt prices are likely in any event to be cheaper than at home, and that it becomes a visitor from a wealthier country not to press the bargaining too far.

Husein Mosque (1792), built in honor of the Prophet's grandson on the site of an earlier mosque. It claims to possess the skull of Husein, who was killed in the Battle of Kerbela (Mesopotamia) in 680. The mosque is richly decorated during the Ramadan feast.

Street scene in the bazaar quarter, Cairo

Turning right at the intersection, we soon come to the magnificent **Spa of Abd el-Rahman Katshuda** (1744–45). A short row of streets Sharia Darb Kirmis, recently restored with German assistance, branches off from here, with the **Tatar-el-Hidshansija Medrese** (14th c.). The main road ends S at Sharia el-Azhar which runs E from the Midan el-Ataba to the square in front of El-Azhar Mosque, where there are many bookshops.

The *El-Azhar Mosque** (the ''most blooming''), the finest building of the Fatimid period, was completed in 972 by Gohar, and in 988 was given the status of a university by Caliph El-Aziz. It was rebuilt after destruction by an earthquake in 1303, and thereafter the rulers and great ones of Egypt – including the wealthy Abd el-Rahman Kihya in the 18th c. and Said Pasha, Taufiq and Abbas II in more recent times – emulated one another in maintaining and enlarging this venerable building.

El-Azhar Mosque

The rectangular ground-plan of the original building is easily recognizable, however, in spite of later additions and alterations. The *El-Azhar University** is still the leading educational center of the Islamic World.

The main entrance is the *Bab el-Muzayyini* or ''Gate of the Barbers'', on the NW side of the building, adjoining the neo-Arab façade built by Abbas II. This leads into a small forecourt, on the right of which is the **El-Taibarsiya Medrese**, with a fine *mihrab (prayer-niche) of 1309, and on the left the 14th c. **El-Aqbughawiya Medrese**, now a library (60,000 volumes, 15,000 manuscripts). – Then through a handsome doorway into the *Main Court* (*Sahn*), with five minarets rearing above it. Round the court runs an arcade (restored by Taufiq) with keeled arches of Persian type, decorated with shallow niches and medallions and crowned by crenelations. The *liwans* on the NE and SW sides of the court are used as sleeping and working apartments for students *(riwak)*, distributed according to the countries and provinces from which they come. Adjoining the N liwan is the *Court of Ablutions*. – The **Main Liwan** or Sanctuary on the SE side of the court, with 140 marble columns (100 of them antique) and an area of almost 3600 sq. yds/3000 sq. m, is the principal lecture-hall. The lower front half, with four much-restored rows of arcading, is part of the original building; the higher rear part, with two prayer-niches, was added by Abd el-Rahman.

In the northern part of the Fatimid town are a number of notable examples of Mameluke architecture. NW of the Great Bazaar stands the little **Mosque of Sultan Barquq Qalaun**, its façade projecting into the street. This was part of a large hospital, now ruined, begun in 1284 by the Mameluke Sultan El-Mansur Qalaun; in the prayer-niche is a fine

El-Azhar Mosque   Cairo

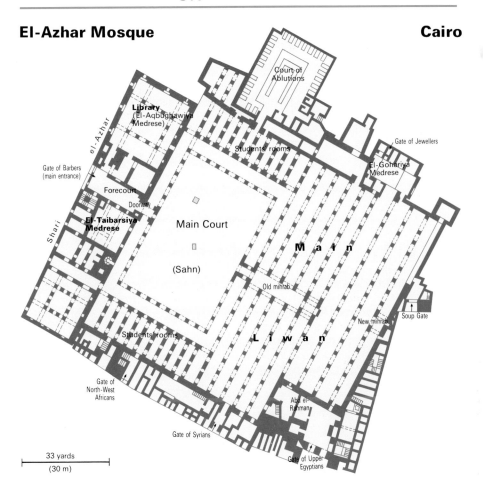

El-Azhar Mosque plan with labels: Court of Ablutions, Library (El-Aqbughawiya Medrese), el-Azhar, Students' rooms, Gate of Jewellers, Gate of Barbers (main entrance), El-Gohariya Medrese, Forecourt, Doorway, Shari, El-Taibarsiya Medrese, Main Court (Sahn), Main, Old mihrab, New mihrab, Soup Gate, Liwan, Students' rooms, Gate of North-West Africans, Abd el-Rahman, Gate of Syrians, Gate of Upper Egyptians, 33 yards (30 m)

Byzantine mosaic. On the right of the long corridor is the *Mausoleum of Qalaun, one of the finest Arab buildings in Cairo, completed in 1293 by Qalaun's son Mohammed el-Nasir; it has a richly ornamented prayer-niche and fine marble and mother-of-pearl mosaics. – On the N side of the Qalaun Mosque we come to the *Mosque of Mohammed el-Nasir (1304), one of the great masterpieces of Islamic architecture in Egypt. It is entered by a Gothic doorway from a church at Akka (Acre) in Syria. The beautiful minaret, the sanctuary (to the left) and the founder's tomb (right) preserve some of their original delicate plaster ornament. – The Barquqiya Mosque, a medrese built in 1386 by the Mameluke Sultan Barquq, is now a branch of the El-Azhar University. The *E wall of the sanctuary is strikingly beautiful.

Farther up the street which runs N through the old town to Bab el-Futuh, on the right, is the El-Aqmar Mosque, the "Grey Mosque", built in 1125 by the Grand Vizier of the Fatimid El-Amir. The hand-some façade, with tall pointed arches in rectangular frames, is the oldest mosque façade in Cairo. – Near by, in a side street to the right, can be seen the patrician house of Beit el-Siheimi (1648). – Almost at the end of the street, on the right, is the entrance to the *El-Hakim Mosque, begun in 990 by El-Aziz on a site outside the oldest town walls, on the model of the Ibn Tulun Mosque, and completed in 1012 by his son El-Hakim. The two minarets, standing on the second town wall, which at this point is well preserved, were originally round; their present square casing and the domed top section resembling an Arab incense-burner date from the rebuilding of the mosque after the 1303 earthquake. The Bab el-Futuh ("Gate of Conquests") at the end of the street and the Bab el-Nasr ("Gate of Victory"), with which it is connected by the old town walls, are similar in form to ancient Roman town gates. It is well worth while to climb up at the gates and walk along the walls, from which there are fine views of the city and surrounding area.

On the S side of the Fatimid town is the **Bab Zuwaila** (1091), a relic of the *first town wall*. On its two massive towers are the minarets of the dilapidated *Muayyad Mosque, also known as *El-Ahmar*, the "Red Mosque", which was begun in 1405 by Sheikh El-Mahmudi Muayyad and completed a year after his death (1410). The bronze gate at the entrance, the finest in Cairo, came from the Sultan Hasan Mosque. The magnificent three-aisled sanctuary has a beautiful painted wooden ceiling.

Outside the Bab Zuwaila Shari Darb el-Ahmar (to the left) and its continuation Shari Bab el-Wazir run SE and then S to the Citadel. – At the near end of the street, on the right, stands the *Salih Talai Mosque*, built in 1160 under the last Fatimid Sultan, with delicate plaster ornament on the arches of the sanctuary. – Farther down, also on the right, the *El-Mardani Mosque*, one of the largest in Cairo, was built in 1340 by the Cup-bearer of Sultan Mohammed el-Nasir. The prayer-niche beyond the modern concrete dome, borne on ancient Egyptian granite columns, is covered with costly mosaics. – Some distance beyond this, on the left, is the picturesque *Aq-Sunqur Mosque*, or Ibrahim Aga Mosque, built in 1346 and richly decorated in 1653 with blue wall-tiles which have earned it the name of the Blue Mosque.

From the Midan el-Ataba, immediately SE of the Ezbekiya Gardens, the wide Shari el-Qala runs SE in a dead straight line to the foot of the Citadel. – About a quarter of the way there it comes to the Midan Ahmed Maher, on the N side of which is the **Museum of Islamic Art**, founded by the German architect and scholar Franz Pasha (d. 1915), the finest collection of its kind in the world, with masterpieces from every Islamic country.

Vestibule and Room 1: chronology of the Islamic dynasties of Egypt; glass and pottery. – *Room 2:* applied art of the Omayyad period (661–750), including a richly decorated bronze vessel (8th c.) from Abusir. – *Room 3:* Abbasid (750–867) and Tulunid (668–905) periods: glazed pottery with stylized decoration; stucco-work from dwelling-houses; Late Sassanid metalwork; gravestones with Kufic inscriptions. – *Room 4:* utensils, textiles and jewelry in the vigorous style of the Fatimid period (969–1171); ceiling-paintings from a bath-house in Fustat, in Ayyubid style (1171–1250). – *Room 5:* Mameluke style (1250–1517): architectural elements and elaborate damascene-work from Cairo's artistic heyday. – *Room 6:* woodwork of the Fatimid and Ayyubid periods, including a door from the El-Azhar Mosque (1010). – *Rooms 7 and 8:* wood-carving, intarsia and inlay work of the Ayyubid and Mameluke periods. – *Room 9:* inlaid furniture and metalwork of the Mameluke period. – *Room 10:* 18th c. room with a fountain and a beautiful carved wooden stalactitic ceiling. – *Room 11:* metalwork of the Mameluke period. – *Room 12:* arms and armor. – *Room 13:* Egyptian faience, mainly of the Fatimid period; 18th and 19th c. tapestries. – *Rooms 14–16:* faience and porcelain from other countries. – *Room 17:* textiles (7th–17th c.). – *Court* (No. 18): inscriptions on stone in Kufic and Neshi script; stone-carving. – *Room 19:* Arabic books and manuscripts (book illumination). – *Room 20:* glass, pottery, metalwork and carpets from Asia Minor. – *Room 21:* glass; collection of glass lamps from mosques. – *Room 22:* a large collection of Persian pottery from the 8th to the 16th c.; Persian carpets (17–19th c.), metalwork, books and manuscripts, etc. – *Room 23:* temporary exhibitions of material from the Museum's reserves.

On the upper floor of the building is the *Egyptian Library* (entrance from Shari el-Qala), founded in 1869 by the amalgamation of a number of smaller

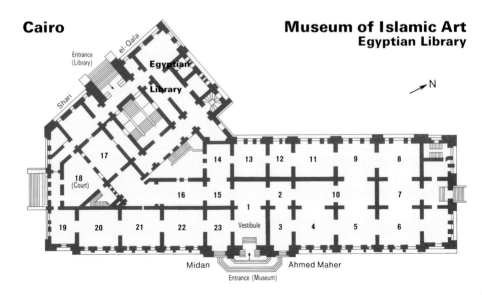

Cairo　　　　　　　　　　**Museum of Islamic Art**
Egyptian Library

Cairo Citadel from Midan Salah el-Din (Saladin Square)

libraries. It contains over 750,000 volumes, half in Oriental and the rest in European languages, including 2700 manuscripts of the Koran, papyri, Persian manuscripts and other written material from the 7th c. to modern times. In the exhibition rooms are displayed a selection of Arab coins and textiles from the Library's very extensive collection of some 5000 items.

Shari el-Qala ends in the spacious Midan Mohammed Ali, on the E side of which is the **El-Rifai Mosque**, built in 1912, on the model of the Sultan Hasan Mosque, to house the tomb of Khedive Ismail. The ex-Shah of Iran, Mohammed Reza Pahlevi (1919–80), is buried here. – On the W side of the square is the ****Sultan Hasan Mosque**, built in 1356–63, perhaps by a Syrian architect, for the Mameluke Sultan Hasan el-Nasir. Situated on a shelving rock below the Citadel, it is perhaps the finest example of Arab-Egyptian architecture. The exterior, with its large areas of stone, is reminiscent of an ancient Egyptian temple. The façades are crowned by a boldly projecting stalactitic cornice, the pinnacles of which have been restored. The wide wall surfaces are relieved by blind niches and twin round-arched windows. The mausoleum which projects from the SE front is roofed with 180 ft/ 55 m high dome of Arab-Turkish type (rebuilt in 18th c.). The massive *main doorway at the N corner is almost 85 ft/26 m high; and the *minaret at the S corner is the tallest in Cairo (267 ft/81·5 m). The ground-plan is in the form of an irregular pentagon covering an area of 9450 sq. yds/7900 sq. m, into which the cruciform shape of the original medrese has been very skilfully incorporated.

INTERIOR. – The *main doorway (the bronze door from which is now in the Muayyad Mosque) leads into a domed vestibule, beyond which are a small antechamber and a corridor leading into the open Court (Sahn; 115 ft/35 m by 105 ft/32 m), with a fountain for ablutions (hanafiya). The four liwans, with lofty barrel roofs, are all used as prayer-rooms; the teaching rooms are in the four small medreses. – The principal liwan has a carved stucco *frieze in Kufic lettering on a background of intricate arabesques. The rear wall with the prayer-niche is richly ornamented with marble. Of the once-sumptuous furnishings there remain only the dikka (a podium for the assistant officiants), the pulpit and the chains for the many

Fountain in the court of the Sultan Hasan Mosque

Cairo

Sultan Hasan Mosque

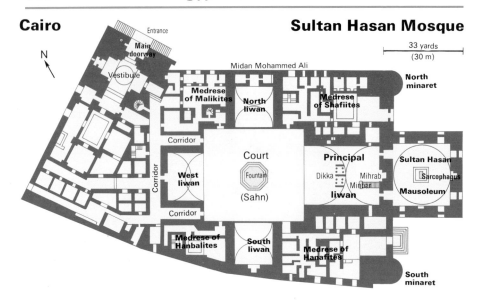

the main entrance. In the lane behind it the leaders of the Mamelukes were massacred on Mohammed Ali's orders in 1811.

hanging lamps; the lamps themselves are now in the Museum of Islamic Art. To the right of the pulpit is a *bronze door* with gold and silver inlays – The iron door to the left of the pulpit leads into the Sultan's **Mausoleum**, a square domed chamber measuring 69 ft/21 m each way and 92 ft/28 m in height. The stalactitic pendentives of the original dome still survive. In the center of the chamber is the simple sarcophagus.

To the S of the Sultan Hasan Mosque is a large elongated square, the *Midan Salah cd Din* (Saladin Square), where the caravans for Mecca used to assemble. On its E side is the Citadel, with a massive gate-tower, the **Bab el-Azab**, formerly

Commandingly situated at the foot of the Moqattam Hills, the **Citadel** was begun in 1176 by Saladin, who is said to have used stone from the small pyramids at Giza. Of the original structure nothing now remains but the outer walls on the E side and a few towers in the interior; and the two palaces of the Ayyubid period, which were already half destroyed at the time of Selim's entry into the city, have disappeared almost without trace. Long in military occupation and closed to visitors, the Citadel is now restored and opened to the public as a historical museum.

The Citadel is entered by the *Bab el-Gedid,* which leads into a courtyard and then through the *Bab el-Wastani* into the main courtyard. On the S side of this is the *Mohammed Ali Mosque, often called the *Alabaster Mosque,* one of the city's great landmarks with its tall and disproportionately slender minarets. It was begun in 1824 by Mohammed (Mehemet) Ali but completed only in 1857, under his successor Said. The architect was a Greek named Yusuf Boshna from Istanbul, who took as his model the Nuruosmaniye

Mohammed Ali Mosque at night

Dome, Mohammed Ali Mosque

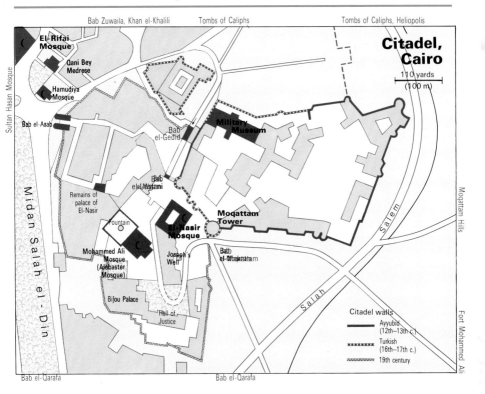

Bab Zuwaila, Khan el-Khalili | Tombs of Caliphs | Tombs of Caliphs, Heliopolis

Citadel, Cairo

110 yards (100 m)

El-Rifai Mosque
Qani Bey Medrese
Hamudiya Mosque
Sultan Hasan Mosque
Bab el-Asab
Bab el-Gedid
Military Museum
Bab el-Wastani
Remains of palace of El-Nasir
Fountain
Moqattam Tower
Mohammed Ali Mosque (Alabaster Mosque)
El-Nasir Mosque
Joseph's Well
Bab el-Moqattam
Bijou Palace
Hall of Justice
Midan Salah el-Din
Moqattam Hills
Salem
Salah
Fort Mohammed Ali

Citadel walls
━━━ Ayyubid (12th–13th c.)
▪▪▪▪ Turkish (16th–17th c.)
〰〰 19th century

Bab el-Qarafa | Bab el-Qarafa

Mosque in that city, itself modelled on the Hagia Sophia (Ayasofya).

The *forecourt* of the Alabaster Mosque, with a *fountain* for ablutions, is surrounded by vaulted galleries. Adjoining this on the E is the *prayer-hall*, with Byzantine-style domes resting on four square piers, impressive both for its size and for the manner in which it is lit. To the right of the entrance is the *Tomb of Mohammed Ali* (d. 1849).

From the W corner of the mosque there is an impressive *view of the grey city with its innumerable minarets and domes and, now, its high-rise blocks; in the distance can be seen the Pyramids of Giza.

Facing the Mohammed Ali Mosque, to the NE, is the **El-Nasir Mosque**, built in 1318–35 by Mohammed el-Nasir and incorporating various ancient architectural elements (columns, capitals, etc.). The two unusual minarets are crowned by bulbous domes with brightly colored faience decoration in the Persian style.

Just to the S of the El-Nasir Mosque can be seen *Joseph's Well* (Bir Yusuf), a square shaft 290 ft/88 m deep which probably dates from the time of Saladin, and has a spiral staircase running down the sides. Half-way down is a platform on which oxen formerly worked a wheel to bring up water. – NE of the well is the *Bab el-Moqattam*, the main S gate of the Citadel, from which a road runs SE to Fort Mohammed Ali in the Moqattam Hills. The *El-Gohara Palace* built 1811–1814 was restored in 1983 and contains the historic **Gohara Museum**.

From the Midan Salah el-Din Shari el-Saliba leads SW to the **Ibn Tulun Mosque*, the second oldest in Cairo. Built in 876 – 879 by Ahmed ibn Tulun on the 65 ft/20 m high rocky plateau of *Gebel Yashkur* and modelled on the Kaaba in Mecca, it was then the largest mosque in existence. The outer walls, almost without decoration, are topped by crenelations.

From the main entrance we enter the E forecourt and turn left through the sanctuary to reach the **Main Court** (*Sahn*), 295 ft/90 m square, with a fountain in the middle. This is surrounded by *liwans* with two rows of columns – five rows in the main liwan on the S side, the prayer-hall or sanctuary. The facades have pointed relieving arches above the columns and a frieze of rosettes along the top. The oldest parts of the decoration of the interior, in carved (not moulded) stucco and wood, are without the intricate interlace

Ibn Tulun Mosque Cairo

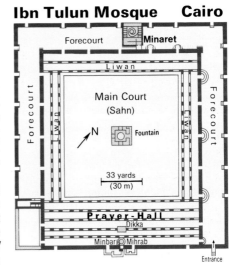

Forecourt | Minaret
Liwan
Forecourt
Liwan
Main Court (Sahn)
Fountain
N
Liwan
Forecourt
33 yards (30 m)
Prayer-Hall
Dikka
Minbar | Mihrab
Entrance

patterns of the later Byzantino-Arab style. – In the **prayer-hall** is a *prayer-recess (mihrab)* with elegant capitals and remains of gold mosaic decoration. Above the *dikka* are remains of the original wooden ceiling.

The 130 ft/40 m high *minaret in the N forecourt, with a fine horseshoe arch over the entrance and a spiral staircase in the interior, is modelled on the minarets of the Great Mosque of Samarra on the Tigris. From its platform (173 easy steps) there are superb *views, particularly in the evening, extending in the N over the sea of houses and the Nile Valley to the Delta, in the W and S to the Pyramids and in the E to the Moqattam Hills.

Immediately adjoining the Ibn Tulun Mosque, in a patrician house of the Mameluke period, the **Beit el-Kiridliya** (1631), is the *Gayer-Anderson Museum,* furnished in the style of an Arab house, with a variety of Islamic *objets d'art.*

The Necropolises and the Moqattam Hills

The cemeteries and necropolises which lay outside the old Fatimid town, to the E, have now been incorporated in the expanding city. Some of them are still in use; some, indeed, provide dwellings for the poorest of the living as well as for the dead.

Of particular interest are the so-called *Tombs of the Caliphs (reached from Bab el-Nasr or from the Citadel), most of which date from the time of the second, or Circassian, Mameluke dynasty (1382–1517). Of the various tombs in the northern group is the *Convent-Mosque of Sultan Barquq, a square structure measuring 240 ft/73 m each way with two minarets and two splendid domes (1400–05 and 1410). In the sanctuary is a fine stone pulpit of 1483. – Some 660 yds/ 600 m SW of the Barquq Mosque, in the southern group of mausolea, is the *Burial Mosque of Qait Bey (1474), perhaps the finest of them all. Notable features are the decoration of the walls in bands of different colors, the delicate reticulation of the dome and the elegant form of the 130 ft/40 m high minaret. The prayer-hall is floored with marble mosaic. Adjoining the splendidly colorful mausoleum, with a richly ornamented reading-desk, is a hall containing the tombs of the Sultan's four wives.

The **Tombs of the Mamelukes**, to the S of the Citadel, largely in a state of ruin. In

Tombs of the Caliphs Cairo
Heliopolis

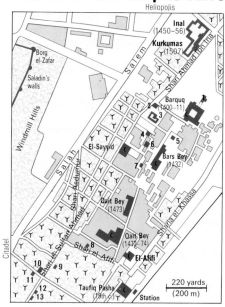

OTHER NOTABLE TOMBS
1 Anas (Barquq's father)
2 Asfur (1507)
3 Bars Bey el-Bagasi (1456) and Amir Suleiman (1544)
4 Seven Virgins (c. 1450)
5 Gani Bek el-Ashrafi (1427)
6 Rifai (mid 16th c.)
7 Khadiga Umm el-Ashraf (mother of Bars Bey)
8 Tashtimur (1334)
9 Guzal (Sidi Karkar: early 15th c.)
10 Umm Anuk (Princess Toghey: 1348)
11 Princess Tolbey (1363)
12 Nasrallah (1441)
13 Azrumuk (1503)

the southern part of this necropolis is the magnificent **Burial Mosque of Imam el-Shafii** (founder of the Shafiite school of Islam), built in 1211, with a massive dome.

An attractive trip (half-day) may be made from Cairo to the **Moqattam Hills**, or *Gebel Giyushi,* to the E of the city. From this 650 ft/200 m high range of hills of nummulitic limestone (fossils, including fossil trees) there are superb * *views; a particularly good viewpoint is the rocky spur to the S of the conspicuous *Giyushi Mosque* (1085). The area is sometimes closed to the public as a military zone;

Burial mosque in the Southern Necropolis, Cairo

care should be taken not to photograph military features. – A short distance NW of the mosque, picturesquely situated on the slopes of the hills, is the *Bektashi Convent,* belonging to a Turkish Order of Dervishes.

New Heliopolis and Nasser City

To the NE of Cairo is the modern suburb of NEW HELIOPOLIS (Arabic *Misr el-Gedida,* "New Cairo": for Old Heliopolis see separate entry). Built in 1905–06 on the initiative of a Belgian businessman, it occupies a site reclaimed from the desert under the name of the "Oasis of Heliopolis" which has a more agreeable climate than Cairo, lying as it does some 130 ft/40 m higher. It is laid out on a spacious plan, with hotels, sports grounds and places of entertainment, and is connected with Cairo by the suburban railway. – Farther NE, on the edge of the desert, is **Cairo International Airport**.

SW of New Heliopolis is the still newer suburb of NASSER CITY (Arabic *Medinet Nasr*), with the Cairo *Stadium,* extensive sports grounds and recreational facilities, the Exhibition Grounds, the offices of the

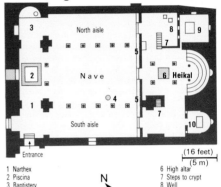

Coptic Church of St Sergius   **Abu Sarga, Old Cairo**

1 Narthex	6 High altar
2 Piscina	7 Steps to crypt
3 Baptistery	8 Well
4 Marble pulpit (on colonnettes)	9 St Michael's Chapel
5 Wooden screens	10 St George's Chapel

Department of Antiquities and a massive *War Memorial*; here, too, is the Tomb of President Sadat (assassinated October 6, 1981).

Old Cairo, Fustat and Maadi

There is much of interest to see in the southern district of *Old Cairo (Misr el-Qadima),* on the right bank of the Nile opposite the S end of the island of Roda. In the southern part of this district is the QASR EL-SHAMA quarter, mainly inhabited by Christians, which lies within the walls (still partly preserved) of the Roman fortress of Babylon.

The area of the fort is entered between two massive *Roman towers*. In a closely packed huddle of houses is the Church of *Abu Sarga (St Sergius),* founded in the 4th–5th c. and rebuilt in the 10th–11th c. According to tradition the Virgin and Child found refuge here for a month during their flight into Egypt.

The church represents the basic type of the Egyptian-Byzantine basilica of the early period, still favored by the Copts. It has a nave and aisles, with exposed roof beams over the nave, a raised transept (choir) and galleries in the flat-roofed aisles. The side walls of the nave consist of two rows of columns, one above the other, with keeled arches between the columns; the galleries are supported on alternate groups of two columns and a masonry pier. The marble columns, taken from ancient buildings, are used without regard to their diameter or architectural form.

The church is entered by a doorway at the SW corner. The three original doorways in the W front, now walled up, led into the *narthex,* which was occupied during services by catechumens (converts under instruction) awaiting baptism. The narthex is divided into three parts by wooden screens. In the middle section is an old *piscina,* used by the priest for washing the feet of male worshipers on the Feast of the

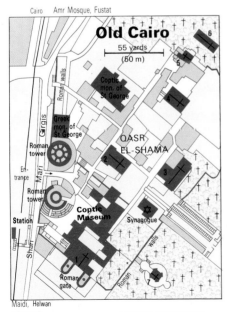

Cairo   Amr Mosque, Fustat

Maidi, Helwan

CHURCHES
1 El-Moallaqa (Coptic)
2 Abu Sarga (St Sergius: Coptic)
3 Sitt Barbara (St Barbara: Coptic)
4 Mari Girgis (St George: Coptic)
5 El-Adra (Church of the Virgin: Coptic)
6 Greek Orthodox church
7 St Elias (Greek Catholic)

Epiphany; the N section, with a recess, is the *Baptistery*. The narthex is separated from the nave by another wooden screen. – The *nave,* with an acute-angled timber roof, is traditionally reserved for men, while the women sit in the aisles. Steps lead up to the sanctuary and two side chapels, which are shut off by *wooden screens*, paneled and richly adorned with carvings in wood and ivory. In the sanctuary *(heikal)* are the canopied *high altar* and an apse with steps on which the priests used to sit. – Two flights of steps lead down from the side chapels into the oldest part of the church, the 5th c. **Crypt**, a small vaulted chapel with ancient marble columns separating the nave from the aisles. At the end of the nave is an altar in the form of an Early Christian tomb recess, said to mark the spot where Mary rested with the infant Jesus.

Crypt of Abue Sarga Church

Within the area of the Roman citadel are a number of other old Coptic churches. A few houses away from Abu Sarga is the Church of **Sitt Barbara** *(St Barbara),* founded in the 5th c. and rebuilt in the 10th–11th c. To the N are the churches of **Mari Girgis** *(St George),* founded in the 7th c., with a richly decorated nave, and **El-Adra** *(Church of the Virgin),* founded in the 9th c. and rebuilt in the 18th. In the **Synagogue** *(Keniset Eliahu;* until the 8th c. a Christian church), the largest in Egypt, Elijah is said to have appeared and Moses to have prayed.

At the SE corner of the citadel, on the E tower of the S gate, is the Metropolitan Church of *Sitt Miriam* (St Mary), known as **El-Moallaqa**, the "Hanging Church", which was founded in the 4th c. and rebuilt in the 9th c. and on a number of later occasions. It was originally much larger, probably built over both gate-towers. The narthex leads into the nave (divided into four aisles, but originally with at least five), with the pulpit. There are three chapels shut off by old carved screens; the central one (the *heikal* or sanctuary) is dedicated to Christ, the one on the N to St George, the one on the S to John the Baptist.

Attached to El-Moallaqa is the ****Coptic Museum**, founded in 1910 by Morkos Pasha Simaika, the largest and finest collection of Coptic material. The museum was erected at the beginning of the 20th c., using architectural elements from old Coptic buildings, and later extended. In addition to works of religious art it contains Coptic arts and crafts and everyday objects from the 3rd to the 18th c., particularly items of the early medieval period.

NE of the Coptic Museum is the **Mosque of Amr** *(Amr ibn el-As Mosque),* believed to be the oldest in Cairo; the present rather dilapidated building, however, dates mainly from the 18th c. On this site Amr ibn el-As, Caliph Omar's General, built the first mosque in Fustat in the year 642; it was soon considerably enlarged, but was destroyed during the Crusades. – Farther to the NW is the picturesque old Coptic Monastery of **Abu Seifein** *(St Stephen).*

To the NE of Old Cairo are the remains of **Fustat**. Numerous finds from the site are now in the Museum of Islamic Art and the Coptic Museum. – Between the Mosque

Interior of the Coptic Church of Abu Sarga, Old Cairo

Cairo – a panoramic view

of Amr and Fustat is the POTTERS' QUARTER, in which the popular big-bellied water-jars known as *kulla* are made.

4 miles/6 km S of Old Cairo in the direction of Helwan lies the residential suburb of MAADI *(El-Maadi)*, with modern houses and villas set in gardens (many the residences of foreigners) and a yacht club. Near Maadi a *prehistoric settlement* (probably of the 6th millennium B.C.), first discovered in 1930, has recently been excavated.

SURROUNDINGS of Cairo

The village of **Harrania**, a short distance SW of the city, is noted for its *woven carpets and rugs in naïve designs.

Some 8 miles/13 km NW of Cairo, at **Ausim**, is the site of ancient *Letopolis* (Egyptian *Khem*), capital of the 2nd nome of Lower Egypt, which is referred to in 4th Dynasty texts. The only remains so far discovered, however, date from the Late Period and Graeco-Roman times.

15 miles/25 km NW of Cairo, at the point where the Nile divides into two arms, is the **Nile Dam**, which at the end of the 19th c. ranked among the largest dams in the world. It was designed to keep the water-level in the Delta uniform throughout the year, so as to obviate the old methods of obtaining water for irrigation and to remove the difficulties of navigation during the three months when the water was at its lowest.

A plan for regulating the water-supply in the Delta had been put forward by Napoleon, but work on the construction of the dam began only in 1835, in the time of Mohammed Ali. Two competing proposals were put forward by two French engineers, Linant and Mougel. Linant's plan for constructing a dam farther N, where ground conditions seemed more favorable, was rejected as too costly, and Mougel's plan was

preferred. The cost of establishing foundations in the poor soil at the S end of the Delta, however, far exceeded the original estimate, and after more than 131,000 cu. yds/100,000 cu. m of building materials had been consumed the structure was found to be insufficiently secure, and in 1867 the project was abandoned. Finally it was successfully completed by Sir Colin Scott-Moncrieff in 1885–90 at the cost of a further huge expenditure of money. After a burst in the winter of 1909–10 extensive strengthening and rebuilding was required.

There are in fact two dams, one over the eastern (Damietta) arm of the Nile, the other over the western (Rosetta) arm. The eastern dam is 571 yds/522 m long and has 71 sluices; the western one is 494 yds/ 452 m

Rug from Harrania

long, with 61 sluices. The Taufiquay and Mahmudiya Canals are spanned by bridges with sluice-gates, at the end of which are spacious basins and passages for shipping, with swing bridges. A further dam, with a lock in the middle for traffic on the Menufiya Canal, runs between the bridges over these canals. The superstructures are in a medieval castellated style. – Some 240 yds/220 m downstream is the **Mohammed Ali Dam**, built in 1936–39 to improve irrigation of the land in this area.

Between the two arms of the Nile, in an area formerly occupied by fortifications, lies a beautiful landscaped garden laid out by an Englishman named Draper.

Some 22 miles/35 km N of Cairo, 2 miles/3 km SE of Shibin el-Kanatir, is **Tell el-Yahudiya** ("Hill of the Jews"), the site of ancient *Leontopolis*. Here Ramesses III built a temple faced with glazed mosaic tiles (most of which are now in the Egyptian Museum in Cairo). The technique of manufacture of the tiles is interesting, the coloring being produced partly by glazing and partly by inlaid pieces of glass. Later (170 B.C.) a Jewish High Priest named Onias, with assistance from Ptolemy VI Philometor, built a temple, modelled on Solomon's Temple, for the Jews who had been expelled from Jerusalem. There is little left to see on the site.

A further 12½ miles/20 km NE, just N of the provincial capital of **Benha** (pop. 40,000; production of attar of roses), on the right bank of the Damietta arm of the Nile, is *Kom el-Atrib*, a shapeless mound of rubble with the remains of ancient *Athribis*, capital of the 10th nome of Lower Egypt. The area has not yet been systematically investigated, but peasants digging for *sebbakh* (the rich soil found on ancient sites) have frequently made valuable finds, including a hoard of silver weighing almost 110 lb/50 kg.

Abu Gurab, Abu Roash, *Abusir, Beni Suef, *Dahshur, Eastern Desert, **Fayyum, **Giza, Heliopolis (Old Heliopolis), **Helwan, Ismailia Canal, **El-Lahun, Lisht, Meidum, *Memphis, *Nile, Nile Delta, **Saqqara, Tanta, *Wadi Natrun, Western Desert, El-Zagazig** and **Zawiyet el-Aryan**: see separate entries.

Crocodilopolis-Arsinoe

See under Fayyum

Dahshur

Middle Egypt. – Governorate: Giza.
(i) **Tourist Information Office,**
Misr Travel Tower,
Cairo – Abbasia;
tel. 82 60 16.

ACCESS. – By road (1¼ miles/2 km S of Saqqara). – Military installations in area: photography and use of binoculars prohibited.

The ***Pyramids of Dahshur** lie about 1¼ miles/2 km from the S side of the

Saqqara necropolis and the Mastaba el-Faraun. Scattered over an area some 2 miles/3 km long by 1 mile/1·5 km across on the edge of the desert are five pyramids and the remains of subsidiary tombs and temples.

Two large and prominently situated pyramids built of limestone rear up on the desert plateau at some distance from the Nile Valley, and near the edge of the desert stand two pyramids built of black bricks made from Nile mud (El-Ahram el-Sud, the "Black Pyramids") and a smaller stone-built pyramid with a brick core, now much weathered. The two large stone pyramids are believed to have been built by Snerferu (Snofru; 4th Dynasty), the other three by various kings of the 12th Dynasty (c. 1991–c. 1786).

THE SITE. – The **Northern Brick Pyramid** *(Black Pyramid)* is believed to be the tomb of Sesostris III (12th Dynasty). Its base length is 344 ft/104·9 m, its present height only 90 ft/27·5 m. It originally stood fully 215 ft/65 m high and was faced with marble slabs, none of which now remain. In the tomb chamber was found the Pharaoh's empty granite sarcophagus. – To the N of the pyramid, but still within the enclosure wall which originally surrounded it, were found two

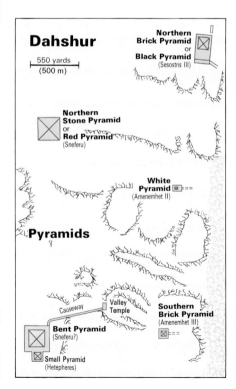

underground galleries containing tomb chambers belonging to female members of the royal family, with costly grave furnishings which can now be seen in the Egyptian Museum in Cairo.

SW of the Black Pyramid stands the imposing bulk of the *Northern Stone Pyramid or *Red Pyramid*, so called from the reddish tint of the horizontally coursed limestone blocks of which it is constructed; it is possible to climb to the top. With a base measurement of 700 ft/213 m and a height of 332 ft/101·15 m (angle of incline 43° 40), it is of approximately the same size as the Pyramid of Cheops at Giza. It is thought to have been built by Sneferu, founder of the 4th Dynasty and father of Cheops, who reigned gloriously for 24 years and conducted victorious wars in Libya and Nubia. The Red Pyramid is the oldest royal tomb in pure pyramid form, providing a model followed in later royal burials. From the entrance to the pyramid, at a height of 92 ft/28 m on the N side, a shaft leads down to three chambers in the heart of the structure, the third of which (30 ft/9·30 m long, 15 ft/4·50 m wide, 50 ft/15 m high) was the tomb chamber, although Sneferu was not in fact buried here.

To the SE of the Red Pyramid and S of the Pyramid of Sesostris is the much-ruined **White Pyramid** of Amenemhet II (12th Dynasty; *c.* 1929–*c.* 1895). The outer casing was filled with an unstable core of sand and bricks. The royal sarcophagus was found in the tomb chamber, and the female tombs on the W side of the pyramid contained valuable jewelry, now in the Egyptian Museum in Cairo. Three female mummies were discovered here in 1982.

Farther S is the imposing and enigmatic *Bent Pyramid. Like the Red Pyramid, this was built in the reign of Sneferu, probably before that pyramid, and apparently planned as a normal pyramid with straight sides and with the usual valley temple, causeway, subsidiary pyramid and enclosure wall. It has a base measurement of 619 ft/188·56 m and a height of 319 ft/97·26 m. The excellently preserved casing, constructed of slabs of Tura limestone slightly inclined downwards, gives a good idea of the original external appearance of other pyramids. The reason for the change of angle half-way up the pyramid, from 54° 31 in the lower part to 43° 21, is unknown. Two theories have

been put forward: either some unforeseen event may have made it necessary to complete the pyramid quickly, or – as plaster-filled cracks in the interior and traces of timber supports suggests – there were fears for the stability of the pyramid during its construction and the upper part was given a less steep angle to reduce the weight of stone.

The Bent Pyramid was first entered by an English traveler, M. Melton, as early as the mid 17th c. In 1860 Le Brun found a small chamber in the interior. This pyramid differs from the normal pattern in having an entrance on the W side as well as on the N. The N entrance (difficult to negotiate) runs down from a height of 36 ft/11 m to an underground chamber from which a passage leads to another chamber on a higher level. The W entrance descends from a height of 111 ft/33·9 m to a third chamber on the level of the pyramid's base, from which a shaft runs down to the two lower chambers. This shaft could be closed by monolithic slabs of limestone (portcullises). All three chambers have corbeled roofs formed of overlapping courses of stone which are well calculated to support the enormous superincumbent mass. Apart from some scanty remains of animal mummies in the passages, all the rooms were found empty. It may be that there are other chambers not yet discovered. The name of the builder of the pyramid is indicated only by two painted inscriptions dating from the time of construction and two stelae bearing cartouches.

On the S side of the Bent Pyramid is the so-called **Small Pyramid**, which has a base measurement of 180 ft/55 m and originally stood 105 ft/32 m high. Presumably built as the tomb of Hetepheres, Sneferu's wife and mother of Cheops, it has an entrance, with a small cult-niche, on the N side and an offering-table on the E side.

The **Valley Temple** of the Bent Pyramid, the only such temple surviving at Dahshur, is well preserved. Situated, unusually, in the desert some 765 yds/700 m NE, it is connected with the pyramid by an open causeway. It has an entrance hall flanked by two smaller chambers on each side, leading into a court lined by double colonnades, on the far side of which are six chapels. The remains of the temple's rich decoration of paintings and reliefs were detached and are now in Cairo. – Traces of another causeway running up from the Nile to the temple were also discovered here.

To the E of the Bent Pyramid and some 1½ miles/2·5 km S of the Black Pyramid, on the edge of the desert plateau near the village of *Minshat Dahshur*, is the **Southern Brick Pyramid**, which, like the Black Pyramid, was originally faced with slabs of Tura limestone. It is believed to have been built as the tomb of Amenemhet III (12th Dynasty; *c.* 1844–*c.* 1797), who irrigated and settled the Fayyum; but Amenemhet later built another pyramid at Hawara in the Fayyum and was buried there. – Practically nothing is left of the valley temple of this pyramid, which seems to have been symstematically demolished in the Ramessid period.

3 miles/5 km S of the Dahshur necropolis, near the village of *Mazghuna,* are the remains of two other pyramids, perhaps belonging to Amenemhet IV (12th Dynasty; *c.* 1798–*c.* 1790) and Queen Nefrusobek.

**Saqqara: see separate entry.

Dakhla Oasis

Western Desert. – New Valley Frontier District.

ACCESS. – 106 miles/170 km W of Kharga on a good road, occasionally blocked by dunes; cross-country vehicles only.

The *Dakhla Oasis (El-Dakhla, the Inner Oasis) lies in the Western Desert some 465 miles/750 km SW of Cairo, in latitude 25° 24′ N and longitude 28° 54′ E. Its lush green date groves and gardens are an attractive

El-Qasr, in the Dakhla Oasis

sight, contrasting strikingly with the ochre and pink rocks of the desert.

Dakhla is, after the Fayyum, the largest and most populous of the Egyptian oases, with some 20,000 inhabitants. It has large reserves of water, with more than 700 natural springs, lakes and ponds; but since the water of the springs is brackish it must be pounded and stored in a network of cisterns to allow the salt to settle. Like the other large oases in the Western (Libyan) Desert, Dakhla is being developed and enlarged under the New Valley land reclamation project. Deep bores have tapped underground water for use in irrigation and have made it possible to win new land for cultivation. The inhabitants of the oasis cultivate and export dates, citrus fruits, mangoes, apricots and vegetables, and also rear a certain amount of livestock (mainly poultry). In recent years increasing quantities of phosphate have been mined.

Excavations here have shown that Dakhla was inhabited at a very early stage. In antiquity there were many more springs and lakes than there are today, providing excellent conditions for the growing of vines and the rearing of livestock. The inhabitants of the oasis carried on an active trade with the people of the Nile Valley, but have preserved down to the present day their Berber inheritance.

The chief place in the NW part of the oasis is El-Qasr, with a picturesque old town, now abandoned, and a ruined castle. In the vicinity are the remains of a *Temple of Thoth* and a *cemetery* of the Graeco-Roman period. – To the SW, at *Amhada,* are tombs of the First Intermediate Period, and to the W, at *Qarct cl-Muzawaqa,* a cemetery of the Roman period with well-preserved painted tombs.

Some 6 miles/10 km SW of El-Qasr is the **Deir el-Hagär** ("Monastery of the Stone"), the sand-covered remains of a large Egyptian temple of the Roman Imperial period (1st c. A.D.) dedicated to Amun, Mut and Khons which was later occupied by Coptic monks. Surrounded by a strong brick wall (77 yds/70 m by 43 yds/39 m), it followed the classic pattern, with a pylon followed by a pillared court and a hypostyle hall with a vestibule and

sanctuary. The Roman Emperors Vespasian, Titus, Domitian and Nero are mentioned in inscriptions. There are fine reliefs of religious rituals and sacrifices. Near the remains are hot sulphur springs (108 °F/42 °C), with structures which appear to be of Roman date. In the surrounding area are numerous other ancient remains buried under the sand.

On the S side of the oasis, at **Mut el-Kharab,** are remains of temples and other buildings dating from the Third Intermediate Period. – NE of Mut, at *Smant el-Kharab,* are remains of a settlement and a temple of the Roman period.

The chief place in the eastern part of the oasis is the little town of **Balat,** which has the remains of a Temple of Mut dating from the New Kingdom, mastabas of the 6th Dynasty and the First Intermediate Period and tombs of the Graeco-Roman period. In this area, too, traces of Neolithic settlement have been found. – Some 9 miles/14 km SE of Balat lies the picturesque village of *Ezbet-Bashendi,* many of the houses in which are built with stones from ancient buildings.

New Valley and Western Desert: see separate entries.

Dakka
See under Wadi el-Sebwa

Damanhur

Lower Egypt. – Governorate: Buhayra.
Population: 200,000.
ⓘ **Tourist Information Office,**
Midan Saad Zaghlul,
Alexandria;
tel. 80 79 85.
Misr Travel,
Shari Salah Salem 33,
Alexandria;
tel. 2. 50 25.

ACCESS. – By road or rail, 37 miles/60 km SE of Alexandria.

Damanhur, chief town of the Governorate of Buhayra, which extends from the Rosetta arm of the Nile to the Western (Libyan) Desert, lies on the Mahmudiya Canal at the W

end of the Delta. It was the ancient Egyptian **Behdet**, later known as **Time-en-Hor** ("City of Horus"), from which its present name derives In Roman times it was named **Hermopolis Parva** and was capital of the 15th nome of Lower Egypt.

Damanhur is now an important railway junction, with several cotton-ginning plants. It is also the market town of the very fertile surrounding area and a major center of the rice trade. There are no remains of the ancient city.

SURROUNDINGS of Damanhur. – Some 13 miles/21 km SE, near the village of *El-Nebira* on the left bank of the old Canopic arm of the Nile, are two mounds, the *Kom el-Gief* and the *Kom el-Nikrash,* with the scanty remains of the old Greek trading town of **Naucratis**. Founded in the time of the 26th Dynasty by Greek settlers from Miletus, it was granted the monopoly of trade with Greece in the reign of Amasis and became capital of the 5th (Saite) nome of Lower Egypt. Until the foundation of Alexandria it was the center of trade between Greece and Egypt, and was also noted for the manufacture of faience. Its temples were mostly dedicated to Greek divinities, but it also had shrines of Amun and Thoth.

14 miles/22 km farther S, near the village of *Tod,* is the **Kom el-Hisn**, a mound of rubble which marks the site of *Imu,* the "House of the Mistress of the Trees", which under the New Kingdom displaced *Hutihit* (the site of which has not yet been located) as capital of the 3rd nome of Lower Egypt. Excavations here have brought to light the enclosure wall of a temple complex measuring 125 yds/115 m by 70 yds/64 m, probably dedicated to Sakhmet-Hathor, and several tombs of the Middle and New Kingdoms, notable for the number of weapons included in the grave-goods. – Some 550 yds/500 m S is the *Kom el-Dubbia,* with a large necropolis ranging in date from the Middle Kingdom to the Ptolemaic period. – A few miles NE the *Kom el-Firin* has remains of a temple built by Ramesses II.

Alexandria, Nile Delta, Sais and **Tell el-Faraun**: see separate entries.

Damietta/Dumyat

Lower Egypt. – Governorate: Damietta.
Population: 100,000.
(i) **Misr Travel,**
Corniche el-Nil;
tel. 28 84.

ACCOMMODATION. – IN GAMASA: *Hotel Amun,* II, 80 b.; *Beau Rivage,* 172 b, *Greenland,* III, 96 b.; etc.

ACCESS. – By road or rail from Alexandria (152 miles/245 km E) or Cairo (130 miles/210 km NE); by road from Port Said (28 miles/45 km SE).

Damietta (Coptic Tamiati, Greek Tamiathis, Arabic Dumyat), once a port of considerable importance, lies in the north-eastern part of the Delta some 9 miles/15 km S of the mouth of the **Damietta arm** (known in antiquity as the **Phatnitic arm**) of the Nile, on a narrow strip of land between the river and Lake Manzala.

Formerly a place of some consequence which rose to prosperity through its maritime trade and its craft industries, Damietta is now the chief town of a governorate, with silk-spinning mills and textile factories (cotton) and a lake harbor for small vessels. It has an Islamic university associated with the El-Azhar University in Cairo.

HISTORY. – The town, originally situated rather farther N, gained renown during the Crusades through its resistance to a siege by the forces of King John of Jerusalem in 1218. With the aid of an ingenious fortified double boat, designed by an engineer from Cologne named Oliverius, Frisian and German troops succeeded, after fierce fighting, in taking the tower from which a chain stretched across the river; and in spite of the intervention of the Papal Legate Pelagius Galvani and the vigilance of the Egyptian Sultan Malik el-Kamil the town itself finally fell. The victors gained much booty, sold the surviving inhabitants as slaves and converted the mosques into churches; but only three years later, in 1221, they were compelled to evacuate the town. In 1249 Louis IX of France occupied Damietta without striking a blow, the terrified defenders having hastily abandoned the place; but in the following year it was restored to the Muslims as part of the ransom for the King, following his capture at Mansura. The emirs then resolved to destroy the town and rebuild it on its present site on the E bank of the river. Thereafter Damietta rose to prosperity through its trade and its manufactures, becoming widely known for its leather goods and sesame oil, while its harbor was frequented by the ships of many nations. The construction of the Mahmudiya Canal deprived the town of much of its trade, and its decline was hastened by the rise of the ports on the Suez Canal.

Damietta has many handsome old houses, now rather down at heel, to bear witness to its former prosperity. Many of the houses have carved wooden oriel windows and lattice screens, usually very old, differing considerably in style from the mushrabiyas of Cairo. – Near the river is the *El-Madbuliya Mosque,* built by Qait Bey in 1475 together with its associated school, the Ashrafiya.

NE of the town, in the cemetery district of **El-Gabbana**, is the badly dilapidated *Abul Maata Mosque* (or Amr ibn el-As Mosque), which may date from the time of the old town. In the vestibule are Kufic inscriptions. Many of the columns in the interior are antique. In the SW corner are twin columns, set close together; and anyone accused of a crime who could squeeze between them was held to be innocent. In the same row is a column which is licked by sufferers from jaundice in the hope of a cure. On the minaret are the remains of early Arab ornamentation.

SURROUNDINGS of Damietta. – Some 7½ miles/12 km N of the town, on a peninsula on the W side of the Nile, is the modest resort of **Ras el-Bahr** (hotels: El-Shatte, IV, 189 b.; Marine Fuad el-Nil, IV, 157 b.; Marine Fuad el-Bahr, IV, 141 b.; El-Home, IV, 111 b.; etc.), with a beautiful beach of fine sand. – Farther W (reached by way of Kafr Saad; 28 miles/45 km) is another unpretentious resort, *Gamasa*, which also has a beautiful beach.

To the E of Damietta lies **Lake Manzala**, the largest of the lagoons along the N of the Delta (area 700 sq. miles/1800 sq. km). Here in ancient times the Mendesian and Tanitic arms of the Nile flowed into the Mediterranean, the former at El-Diba and the latter at the Eshtum el-Gamel Channel. Their courses can still be traced by the fluvial deposits and by the mounds of rubble which mark the sites of settlements built on their banks. – Between the lake and the sea is a very narrow spit of land along which a poor road (improvement planned) runs to Port Said. Two narrow passages, the Eshtum Hadawi and the Eshtum el-Gamel, link the lake with the sea. Lake Manzala – the area of which has been reduced by a third during the last 50 years by drainage and reclamation – is the haunt of great hosts of pelicans, great white egrets, storks, flamingos and other waterfowl. Only the northern part of the lake is navigable to any extent by flat-bottomed boats; the southern part consists of shallow brackish water and marshland. The lake yields sufficient fish only for the needs of the local people, the main center of the fisheries being the large village of **El-Matariya**, situated on a tongue of land some 37 miles/60 km SE of Damietta, which is linked with Damietta and Port Said by channels cut through the shallow marshy lake. The lake offers scope for attractive boat trips.

Nile Delta: see separate entry.

Deir el-Bahri
See under Thebes

Deir el-Medina
See under Thebes

Deir Mar Antonios
See St Antony's Monastery

Deir Mar Bolos
See St Paul's Monastery

Deir Sant Katerin
See St Catherine's Monastery

Delta
See Nile Delta

Dendera

Upper Egypt. – Governorate: Qena.
ⓘ **Tourist Information Office,**
Tourist Bazaar,
Luxor;
tel. 22 15.

ACCESS. – By taxi or horse-carriage from Qena.

The remains of ancient ✱✱Dendera (Greek Tentyris, Coptic Tentore) are prominently situated on the W bank of the Nile opposite the town of Qena, at a wide bend in the river. This was one of the most ancient and most famous of Egyptian cities, capital of the 6th nome of Upper Egypt. The Greek and modern Arabic names of the site are derived from its ancient designation of Yunet or Yunet Tantere ("Yunet of the Goddess", i.e. Hathor).

When, in ancient times, the economic center of the area and the bulk of the population moved from the W bank of the Nile to Qena on the E bank Yunet Tantere remained the principal center of the cult of Hathor, goddess of love and joy, who was equated with the Greek Aphrodite. The splendid temple in which she was worshiped together with her husband, the falcon-headed Horus of Edfu, and her youthful son Ihi (or Harsomtus), god of music, is one of the best preserved in Egypt. The principal ceremonies in her honor coincided with the great New Year festival.

THE SITE. – From the rest-house on the left bank of the river a road, once flanked by columns, leads to the N entrance to the temple precinct (315 yds/290 m by 305 yds/280 m), which is enclosed by a wall of bricks made from Nile mud, 33–39 ft/10–12 m thick at the base and well preserved to a height of some 33 ft/10 m.

The Temple of Hathor, Dendera

Within the enclosure are a number of other shrines in addition to the main temple. The monumental **gateway** dates from the reign of the Emperor Domitian (1st c. A.D.), who is named in an inscription with the style Germanicus. In inscriptions on the inner side the Emperors Nerva (also with the style Germanicus) and Trajan (who is given the epithet Dacicus as well as Germanicus) are also mentioned. Outside the gateway, to the right and left, are two Late Roman *wells*. There is a similar gateway on the E side of the precinct and a third, dating from the Imperial period, outside the walls to the E.

Ignoring for the moment the smaller buildings to the right of the entrance, we proceed straight ahead to the *Temple of Hathor, oriented approximately N and S. This was built during the reigns of the last Ptolemies and the Emperor Augustus (1st c. B.C.) on the site of an earlier temple traditionally believed to date from the Old Kingdom (at least 6th Dynasty) which was altered or added to principally by the kings of the 12th Dynasty and by the great rulers of the New Kingdom (in particular Tuthmosis III and Ramesses II and III). Some of the mural reliefs were executed at still later dates. The normal colonnaded forecourt and pylons at the N entrance were never constructed. The Dendera Temple lacks the magnificence of earlier temples like those of Abydos and Karnak, but it impresses the beholder with its fine proportions and dignified adaptation to its purpose. Although the profusion of reliefs and inscriptions on the walls cannot be compared with the master-works of the Old Kingdom or the reigns of Tuthmosis III and Sethos I they are, nevertheless, excellent examples of the Egyptian decorative art of the Late Period.

We come first into the large **Vestibule** or **Pronaos**, which has 24 sistrum columns with heads of Hathor. The façade is crowned by a massive cavetto cornice, in the middle of which is a winged solar disc. On the upper edge of the cornice is a three-line Greek inscription: "For the Emperor Tiberius Caesar, the new Augustus, son of the divine Augustus, under the prefect Aulus Avillius Flaccus, the governor Aulus Fulvius Crispus and the district governor Sarapion son of Trychambus, the people of the city and the nome dedicated the pronaos to Aphrodite, the great goddess, and her fellow gods in the ... year of the Emperor Tiberius."

The interior of the vestibule is shut off by six *screens* between the columns in the first row. On the interior walls are four rows of scenes depicting the Emperors Augustus, Tiberius, Caligula, Claudius and Nero as Pharaohs presenting votive offerings to Hathor and other deities. The reliefs on the screens between the columns, which related to the ceremonial entrance of the Pharaoh into the temple, have been chiseled out.

The reliefs on the screens to the right of the entrance depict the King, with the crown of Lower Egypt, leaving the palace, with his guardian spirit behind him and a priest with a censer in front of him; the falcon-headed Horus and the ibis-headed Thoth pouring the sanctifying water over the King, the water being represented by the hieroglyphs for "life"; and the protective goddesses of Upper and Lower Egypt blessing the King. On the screens to the left of the entrance are similar scenes with the King wearing the crown of Upper Egypt. On the left-hand (W) wall is a relief depicting the King being conducted into the presence of Hathor by Month and Atum, the gods of Upper and Lower Egypt.

The *ceiling* of the hall is divided by the architraves into seven bands, in which are depicted the following scenes (from left to right): 1. the sky goddess Nut, below her the signs of the zodiac and boats with personifications of the stars, and the sun shining on the temple, here represented by the head of Hathor; 2. deities of the stars and the hours of the day and night; 3. phases of the moon and the course of the sun during the 12 hours of the day; 4. flying vultures and suns; 5–7. scenes corresponding to 1–3.

The rear wall of the vestibule forms the façade of the temple proper; it is surmounted by a cavetto cornice and a round moulding. In the center is a door leading into the **Hypostyle Hall** ("Hall of Appearances"), the roof of which is supported by six columns with elaborate foliage capitals and Hathor heads. The base and the two lowest drums of the columns are of granite, the rest of sandstone. Light is admitted by eight square apertures in the roof. On the walls are four rows of reliefs depicting the deities of Dendera. Here, as in some other rooms in the temple, the King's name is missing, no doubt because the priests were uncertain, in the unsettled times when the temple was being built, which ruler should be selected for the honor.

Of particular interest are a number of reliefs in the bottom row depicting the ceremonies connected with the foundation of the temple. To the right of the entrance the King emerges from the palace wearing the Lower Egyptian crown, preceded by a priest offering incense; and to the left of this scene he is seen breaking up the soil with a hoe, with the goddess Hathor in front of him. To the left of the entrance are similar scenes in which the King is wearing the crown of Upper Egypt (on right he presents bricks to Hathor, representing the building material of the temple).

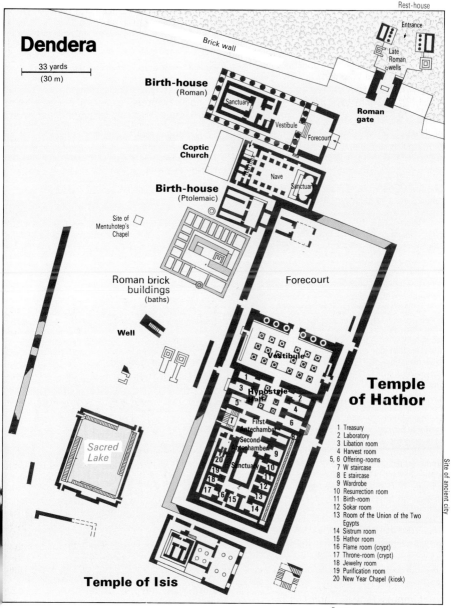

Dendera

33 yards
(30 m)

Rest-house

Entrance

Brick wall

Late Roman wells

Birth-house (Roman)

Sanctuary

Vestibule

Forecourt

Roman gate

Coptic Church

Nave

Sanctuary

Birth-house (Ptolemaic)

Site of Mentuhotep's Chapel

Roman brick buildings (baths)

Forecourt

Well

Vestibule

Hypostyle Hall

Temple of Hathor

First Antechamber

Second Antechamber

Sanctuary

Sacred Lake

New Year Chapel (kiosk)

1 Treasury
2 Laboratory
3 Libation room
4 Harvest room
5, 6 Offering-rooms
7 W staircase
8 E staircase
9 Wardrobe
10 Resurrection room
11 Birth-room
12 Sokar room
13 Room of the Union of the Two Egypts
14 Sistrum room
15 Hathor room
16 Flame room (crypt)
17 Throne-room (crypt)
18 Jewelry room
19 Purification room
20 New Year Chapel (kiosk)

Site of ancient city

Temple of Isis

E gate

On each side of the hall are three *chambers,* some dark and some lit by apertures in the roof, which may have served as a laboratory, treasure-rooms and store-rooms for votive offerings. The inscriptions and reliefs on the walls show the King in the presence of Hathor and other deities, including Horus of Dendera.

From the hypostyle hall we enter the **First Antechamber** or Hall of Offerings, which is lit by apertures in the roof and walls. The walls have four rows of reliefs depicting the King making offerings to Hathor and other deities. – To the right and left are passages leading to staircases up to the roof of the temple. Also on the left is a chamber used for sacrificial offerings.

The **Second Antechamber**, which is lit by openings in the side walls, also has four rows of reliefs. To the left is a small chamber used for storing unguents and the garments in which the divine images were dressed on festival occasions. – The door on the right leads into three chambers. The first, linked with the W staircase by a corridor, was a store-room. Beyond this, after crossing an open court and going up a (modern) flight of steps, we come to a charming *kiosk,* the roof of which is supported by two sistrum columns linked with the walls by screens rising to half the height of the columns. Here the priests assembled for the celebrations of Hathor's birthday and the New Year festival which followed. In the court were made the votive offerings which are depicted on the walls. On the walls of the kiosk are three rows of scenes depicting the King and various deities in the presence of the gods of Dendera; below is a procession of local gods (Upper Egyptian on the left, Lower Egyptian on the right) bearing votive offerings. On the ceiling is the sky goddess Nut bringing forth the Sun, whose rays shine on the Temple of Dendera, represented by the head of Hathor between two trees on a mountain. In the rear wall of the court are three windows separated by pillars bearing Hathor heads. From the court a staircase leads down to a *crypt.*

From the second antechamber we pass into the inmost part of the temple, described in an inscription as the "hidden secret chambers". – The central door leads into the dark **Sanctuary**, the "great seat", in which stood the sacred boats with the images of the gods. Only the King or a priest representing him was permitted to enter this chamber and hold converse with the deity, and even he might enter only during the New Year festival. The *reliefs* on the walls depict the ceremonies which had to be performed on entering the sanctuary and the presentation of offerings. The scenes are so arranged that each scene on the left-hand wall is followed by the corresponding scene on the right-hand wall, thus: the King ascends the steps leading up to the shrine (left); he removes the ribbon fastening the door (right); he removes the seal from the door (left) and opens it (right); he gazes upon the goddess (left) and prays to her with his arms hanging by his sides (right); he offers incense before the sacred barques of Hathor and Horus of Edfu (left) and of Hathor and her son Ihi (right). – On the rear wall, to the left, the King presents an image of the goddess Maat to Hathor and Horus of Edfu; in front of him is Hathor's young son with a sistrum and a rattle. On the right he performs the same action before Hathor and Ihi.

The sanctuary is surrounded by a *corridor* lit by apertures in the roof and walls and entered through two doors from the Second Antechamber. Along this corridor are 11 small chambers, used as chapels for various deities, as store-rooms or for other religious purposes. The last of these chambers, with reliefs similar to those in the sanctuary, was a shrine dedicated to Hathor. – From here a modern iron staircase leads up to a niche in the wall containing a relief of Hathor.

The subterranean chambers or crypts, which may have been used for storing cult vessels and divine images which were no longer required, are of interest both for their construction and for the fresh coloring of the paintings. There are altogether 12 such chambers, constructed at different levels in the thickness of the temple walls. The elaborate mural reliefs date from the reign of Ptolemy XII Neos Dionysos, and are thus the oldest as well as the best executed in the whole temple. – In the *crypt* reached through a square opening in the floor of Room 16 are a number of narrow chambers with representations on the walls of the objects which were kept in them. On the right-hand wall of the second chamber on the right is a fine relief depicting King Phiops (6th Dynasty) kneeling and offering a statuette of the god Ihi to four images of Hathor. – In the *crypt* reached from Room 17 Ptolemy XII is shown presenting jewelry and other offerings to the gods.

From the First Antechamber two *staircases* lead up to the roof. The E staircase, which is very dark, runs straight up to the roof, with easy steps; the one on the W is a kind of spiral staircase with ten right-angled bends, lit by windows with representations of the sun shining in. The *mural reliefs* in both staircases depict the solemn procession of the King and priests, some of whom wear the masks of lesser deities, during the New Year festival; on the left-hand side they are shown ascending to the roof of the temple with images of Hathor and the other gods of the temple, "so that the goddess might be united with the beams of her father Re", on the right-hand side they are seen descending after the ceremony. – The W staircase passes a small chamber (situated above the store-room adjoining the Second Antechamber) with three windows looking into the court. Higher up is a small (closed) court, adjoining which are two rooms

Reliefs on the outer wall of the Temple of Hathor

dedicated, like the chapel on the E side of the terrace, to the cult of Osiris; the reliefs in the second room depict the resurrection of Sokar-Osiris.

The *temple roof* is on several levels, the highest being over the pronaos. At the SW corner of the first (lowest) terrace is a small open *kiosk* with 12 Hathor columns. Adjoining the terrace on the N, above the chambers to the left of the hypostyle hall, is a small *Shrine of Osiris* dedicated to the cult of the slain and resurrected Isis, as is shown by the numerous inscriptions and scenes on the walls. On the ceiling of the second chamber, which is separated from the first (an open court) by pillars, is a cast of the famous "Zodiac of Dendera", the only circular representation of the heavens found in Egypt; the original was carried off to France in 1820 and is now in the Louvre. In the last room is a window with representations of Osiris lying dead on his bier and returning to life. – At the NW corner of the terrace a flight of steps leads up to the roof of the first antechamber, beyond which is the still higher roof of the hypostyle hall. From this a modern iron staircase continues up to the roof of the pronaos, from which there are superb panoramic *views of the Nile Valley and the hills of the desert.

Finally it is worth walking round the *outside walls* of the temple to see the inscriptions and reliefs with which they are covered. Those on the E and W sides date from the reigns of various Roman Emperors, in particular Nero. The large reliefs on the rear (S) wall depict Ptolemy XV Caesar (Caesarion), son of Julius Caesar and Cleopatra (VII Philopator), before the gods of Dendera, with the image of Hathor in the center. The faces are purely conventional and in no sense portraits. The projecting lions' heads on the sides of the building were designed to carry off rainwater.

To the right (SW) of the entrance to the temple precinct is the so-called **birth-house** *(mammisi)*, a small temple dedicated to the cult of the son of the two deities worshiped in the main temple, of a type found in all the larger temple complexes of the Ptolemaic period (e.g. Edfu and Philae). In this case the birth-house, built in the reign of Augustus and decorated with further reliefs in the reigns of Trajan and Hadrian, was dedicated to Harsomtus, son of Isis and Horus of Edfu. Along the two sides and the rear end runs a colonnade of flower columns, on the abaci of which are figures of Bes, the patron god of women in labor.

A ramp leads up to a spacious *forecourt,* with the ground-plan of a Late Roman building with three apses inscribed on the ground. From this we enter a *vestibule,* in the right-hand wall of which is the lower part of a staircase leading up to the roof; to the left are two doors, one leading into the colonnade, the other

into a small side chamber. The central door opens into a wide *transverse chamber,* beyond which is the long *sanctuary,* the birth-chamber proper, with reliefs depicting the birth and nursing of the divine infant; in the rear wall is a shallow door-recess. To right and left are small side chambers.

Immediately S of the birth-house we come to a large **Coptic church** of the late 5th c., an excellent example of the layout of an early Egyptian church. The entrance, at the NW corner, leads into a vestibule (with a round-headed recess) and beyond this into the narthex, which occupies the whole breadth of the church and has semicircular recesses at the N and S ends. To the W are a number of small chambers and a staircase. From the narthex three doorways lead into the nave, in the walls of which are rectangular recesses. At the far end is the trilobate sanctuary, with small rooms on either side.

The god Bes, Dendera

To the S of the church is an older *birth-house,* begun by Nectanebo I and completed in the Ptolemaic period. When the Temple of Hathor was built the wall of its forecourt (which was left unfinished) cut across the end of this birth-house and it was then abandoned and replaced by the later one to the N. From its E end a colonnade, with screens between the columns (here cut by the wall of the Temple of Hathor), leads through a Ptolemaic doorway into a transverse chamber with a door on the left leading out of the birth-house and three other doors in the rear wall. The middle door is the entrance to the sanctuary, with mural reliefs dating from the reign of Nectanebo and depicting the birth of the divine infant Ihi. The side doors lead into two rooms without decoration; from the left-hand one a staircase leads up to the roof. – The *brick *buildings* to the W and S of this birth-house date from the Roman period and were probably baths and well-houses.

At the SW corner of the Temple of Hathor is the *Sacred Lake,* a deep basin enclosed by walls of dressed stone, with flights of steps leading down into it at the four corners. Doorways on the N and S sides give access to staircases within the masonry of the walls leading down to water at a lower level.

On a high terrace at the S end of the Temple of Hathor is the **Temple of Isis** or "Birth-House of Isis", built in the reign of Augustus, using fragments of masonry from an earlier temple of the Ptolemaic period. It has the curious feature that while the main temple is oriented to the E its western half (destroyed), in which was the representation of the birth of Isis, is oriented to the N; the entrance is on the N side. – To the E of the Temple of Isis was another temple of some size, only the foundations of which are preserved, consisting of a forecourt, a hall with four columns and various subsidiary chambers.

Near this Sanctuary of Hathor were found remains of another temple complex, perhaps dedicated to Horus of Edfu, together with several tombs and mastabas (some of them of considerable size) belonging to high officials of the Old Kingdom and the First Intermediate Period. To the W of the ancient city, of which practically no trace remains, were animal cemeteries containing the mummies of dogs, birds and cows. – A small chapel of King Nebhepetre Mentuhotep II (11th Dynasty) which formerly stood to the W of the Temple of Hathor, within the temple precinct, is now reconstructed in the Egyptian Museum in Cairo.

Karnak, **Luxor, Qena** and **Thebes** (West): see separate entries.

El-Derr
See under Amada

Dimei
See under Fayyum

Djanet
See Tanis

Dra Abu el-Naga
See under Thebes

Dumyat
See Damietta

Eastern Desert/ Arabian Desert

The Eastern (Arabian) Desert is the great expanse of desert country which extends eastward from the Nile Valley to the Red Sea Rift, rising in the E to a formidable range of mountains (3300–6600 ft/1000–2000 m; Gebel el-Shayib, 7176 ft/2187 m) which descend in stages to the Red Sea. The hilly desert terrain is broken up by numerous wadis (dry valleys); and when rain falls in these valleys, and in the few small oases in the desert, an astonishingly luxuriant vegetation springs into life.

A trip through the Eastern Desert, particularly the southern part, is something of an adventure, but a very rewarding one, taking those who undertake it through magnificent scenery and offering an interesting change from the antiquities and museums they will have seen elsewhere in Egypt.

There were already a number of caravan routes across the desert between the Nile Valley and the Red Sea in ancient times, for the most part following the course of the wadis, with watering-points at regular intervals. These routes were used for trade with Sinai, Arabia, India and the E coast of Africa (Punt), and after the coming of Islam they were also followed by Egyptian pilgrims to Mecca. – There are now five asphalted roads connecting the Nile Valley with the main Red Sea ports.

Warning

A trip across the desert by car always holds certain dangers. Before setting out it is essential to make sure that you have sufficient supplies of water and gasoline (petrol), as well as spare parts for the car. The sensible plan is to drive in convoy. If you want to branch off the road, make sure that you have good maps, or preferably a knowledgeable local guide.

Across the Eastern Desert

Cairo to Ismailia (75 miles/120 km on a good asphalt road). – The road runs in a dead straight line across the flat northern fringe of the desert, offering a rapid but featureless route to the central part of the Suez Canal Zone.

Cairo to Suez (84 miles/135 km on an excellent asphalt road; bus service). – This route across the northern part of the desert – the most direct connection between Cairo and Suez – is easy and convenient, but without any features of tourist interest. It was the old caravan route and pilgrim route to Mecca, an important highway which was guarded by 16 watch-towers and in the 19th c. was developed by the British authorities into a modern post road. The pipeline from Suez to Cairo now runs along the N side of the road. – Half-way (37 miles/60 km) along the road, on a hill to the left, are the ruins of a *castle* built by Abbas II Hilmi (1892–94). – 3 miles/5 km farther on is a rest-house with a gasoline (petrol) station, near which is the Tomb of Sheikh el-Dakuri.

Qena to Bur Safaga (100 miles/161 km on a very good asphalt road; bus service; no petrol, water or food available anywhere on the route). – The road runs NE from Qena and then turns into the *Wadi Qena*, which it follows for a short distance. – 7½ miles/12 km: the ancient "Porphyry Road" (almost impassable in places) goes off on the left, at first following the Wadi Qena, then turning into the *Wadi el-Atrash* and continuing along the S side of **Gebel el-Dukhan** ("Smoke Mountain"; 4446 ft/1360 m), the ancient *Mons Porphyrites*, to reach the Red Sea. At the old Roman porphyry quarries on Gebel el-Dukhan are the ruins of an unfinished Ionic *temple* of the time of Hadrian, remains of an irregularly laid out settlement and two large cisterns. – 28 miles/45 km: **Bir el-Kreyya**, from which a track (barely passable) runs NE to the *Wadi Fatira*, below the S side of *Gebel Fatira* (4446 ft/1355 m), the ancient *Mons Claudianus*. ¾ mile/1 km S of the wadi are the granite quarries known as the *Umm Diqal* ("Mother of Columns"), which from the time of Nero, but principally in the reigns of Trajan and Hadrian, were worked by prisoners and condemned criminals to provide the much-esteemed Claudian granite for the buildings of Imperial Rome. Here can be seen the work-faces and roads for the transport of the stone, a number of unfinished columns and partly dressed stones, as well as Greek inscriptions. Near the quarries are the remains of the Roman settlement of *Hydreuma Iraiani*, including a fort some 245 ft/75 m square surrounded by granite walls and towers and, outside the walls, stabling for some 300 animals, silos for storing fodder, cisterns and other structures. Above the settlement are the ruins of a 2nd c. temple.
Farther along the track, before Bir Abd el-Wahab, a side track goes off and runs SE to rejoin the main road in the *Wadi Umm Taghir*.
Beyond Bir el-Kreyya the road ascends the Wadi el-Markh and after crossing the watershed descends the *Wadi Umm Taghir*. – 90 miles/143 km: the road enters the *Wadi Barud*. – 99 miles/160 km: **Bur Safaga** (see under Red Sea).

The old Roman roads and caravan routes from Qena and Qift (via Laqeita) and from Edfu to Berenice on the Red Sea, running through the territory of the Ababda bedouin, are not passable by car for the whole of their length and are now little used. Along both roads are the remains of ancient watering-points, listed as follows in the "Antonine Itinerary" (3rd c. A.D.), starting from Coptos (Qift), with the number of Roman miles between successive posts: Phienicon 24, Didyme 24, Afrodito 20, Kompasi 22, Jovis 23, Aristonis 25, Phalacro 25, Apollonos 23, Kabalsi 27, Kaenon Hydreuma 27, Berenice 18 – making a total of 258 Roman miles. – A third road, built in the reign of Hadrian, ran from Antinoupolis (between El-Minya and Mallawi) to the port of Myos Hormos on the Red Sea, continuing S along the coast to Berenice.

Qift to Quseir (the Wadi Hammamat road; 121 miles/194 km of asphalt road). – This well-built trunk road, running from ancient Coptos (Qift) to the port of Leukos Limen (Quseir), follows with only minor deviations the very ancient trade and caravan route through the *Wadi Hammamat*, with some very picturesque stretches of scenery. – The road branches off the road along the Nile ¾ mile/1 km S of Qift and heads straight into the desert. – 24 miles/39 km: *Laqeita*, a modest little village in a small oasis which in ancient times was an important caravan staging-point, located at the intersection of the desert tracks from Qena to Berenice and from Qus (Apollinopolis Parva) to Quseir. Near the principal well in Laqeita are the remains of a Greek inscription referring to the Emperor Tiberius. The village is inhabited by members of the Ababda tribe, many of whom still lead a nomadic life in the desert. Here they practice agriculture and stock-rearing. Their language is a curious mixture of Egyptian Arabic and East African (Hamitic) tongues. – 35 miles/56 km: *Qasr el-Benat* ("Castle of the Maidens"), an old Roman *hydreuma* (watering-station), now dry – one of the eight staging-points built by the Romans on this road, no doubt on the sites of earlier fortified Egyptian posts. The building, on a rectangular plan (125 ft/38 m by 102 ft/31 m), had an enclosure wall 6½ ft/2 m high constructed of sandstone blocks laid without mortar. Round an inner courtyard entered from the N are 20 small rooms. Near by is a picturesque sandstone rock, swept free of sand by the desert winds and covered with graffiti in Greek, Coptic, Arabic, Himyaritic and Sinaitic characters left by passing caravans. – Beyond Qasr el-Benat the road enters a winding defile, the *Mutraq el-Selam*. On a rock at the entrance, the Gebel Abu Ku ("Father of the Elbow"), are ancient inscriptions, one of which mentions the name of Amenophis IV.

Beyond the defile the road approaches the beautiful mountain region through which the second half of the Hammamat road runs. In the distance, to the right, can be seen the southern foothills of the scenically magnificent Hammamat Mountains, rising in terraces to a height of 4265 ft/1300 m; straight ahead, closer at hand, are the south-western spurs of the range. They consist of yellowish sandstones of the Upper Cretaceous, followed by the reddish "Nubian" sandstone, which belongs to the same system.

In the middle of the ranges of hills flanking the route, on the N side of the road, is another Roman station with a well which is now blocked by sand. – 48 miles/77 km: *Gerf el-Igul*, where the ancient Palaeozoic rocks of the Hammamat Mountains proper begin. The character of the scenery suddenly changes: the hard dark-coloured greywacke rears up in perpendicular walls, and the mountains take on a rugged Alpine aspect. – 56 miles/90 km: the *Wadi el-Hammamat*, known to the ancient Egyptians as the Rehenu Valley, which yielded the hard dark stone known as lapis niger or *thebaicus* (a greywacke with veins of more recent granites) used for statues and sarcophagi. – 59 miles/

95 km: **Bir el-Hammamat**, an old well, now dry, which gave its name to the whole area. In the vicinity are remains of a Roman wall and five unfinished and now broken sarcophagi. There are numerous Greek inscriptions in the quarries around here.

The earliest known expedition to Hammamat took place in the reign of King Isesi (5th Dynasty). Ramesses IV sent an army of 8368 workmen and soldiers to procure stone for the Temple of Amun at Thebes; and the quarries were still being worked in the time of Darius, Xerxes and Artaxerxes.

Just beyond the quarries the road turns sharply S and runs past ancient mine-workings. – 63 miles/102 km: *Bir Umm el-Fawakhir* (*fawakhir*="potsherds"). Remains of opencast workings and of deep underground shafts, now difficult of access, can be readily identified; and the foundations of hundreds of workers' houses, together with numerous Greek inscriptions, bear witness to the former importance of the settlement.

Beyond the pass (watershed between E and W) the road descends at *Wadi Abu Siran* to *Wadi Rosafa*. – 102 miles/164 km: *Bir Sijala* – 93 miles/150 km: an insignificant mountain track branches off NW to the coast road at Bir Safaga (53 miles/85 km). The road to Hammamat soon turns N towards the "Liteima" plateau which divides the central mountains from the coastal range; it is formed from chalk, sandstone and tertiary limestone. – 106 miles/170 km: **Bir el-Beda** or *Bir el-Inglis*, a cistern installed by British soldiers in 1800, but now dry. – 111 miles/178 km: *El-Ambagi* has a salt-water spring: further on the road crosses the railway line to Quseir several times. – 121 miles/194 km: Quseir (see under Quseir).

Edfu to Mersa Alam (143 miles/230 km on a moderately good asphalt road; no gasoline (petrol), no food). – The road begins at Edfu railway station, on the right bank of the Nile. The first half traverses a monotonous desert landscape, but the second half makes up for this by the beauty and variety of its mountain scenery.

12½ miles/20 km: *Bir Abbad,* in the *Wadi Miah.* At the point where the *Wadi Ammerikba* runs into the Wadi Miah are the remains of an ancient desert post with masons' marks.

31 miles/50 km: At an old watering-station is the *Temple,* discovered by Cailliaud in 1816, of *Redesiya* or El-Kanayis, built by Sethos I and dedicated to Amun-Re. The vestibule of the temple, made of sandstone blocks, has four columns with papyrus capitals and contains reliefs of the King depicted as victorious over Negroes (Kushites) and Asiatic warriors. The following chamber, hewn from the rock, has four square pillars, reliefs of the King offering sacrifices and long inscriptions recording the sinking of the well and the building of the temple. In the rear wall are three niches with statues of the King and the gods Amun-Re and Re-Harakhty. A small building adjoining the temple probably marks the position of the well. On a rock to the E are three inscriptions. One of these depicts an Asiatic goddess on horseback, with shield and spear; the second is by the official responsible for digging the well; and the third shows the Viceroy of Kush, Eni, kneeling before Sethos. Higher up on the rock are rude figures of gazelles, Greek graffiti and an inscription in the name of a certain Prince Mermes (reign of Amenophis III).

37 miles/60 km: *Bir el-Kanayis:* desert track on right to the emerald-mines in the Wadi Sakeit and Gebel Zubara (see under Berenice). – 68 miles/110 km: *Wadi Baramiya,* a mining settlement in a magnificent mountain setting. Here a track goes off on the right to the ancient gold-mines of Umm Rus and Sukkari (see under Red Sea), continuing to the Red Sea coast. – 75 miles/120 km: The road descends into the *Wadi Beiza,* with its beautiful acacias. On the rock faces are crude engravings and graffiti. – 130 miles/210 km: mountain track on right to the *Sukkari* gold-mines. – 143 miles/230 km: **Mersa Alam**, a small fishing village on the Red Sea (see under Red Sea).

Edfu/Idfu

Upper Egypt. – Governorate: Aswan.
Population: 35,000.
ⓘ **Tourist Information Office,**
Tourist Bazaar,
Aswan;
tel. 32 97.

ACCESS. – By car on the road along the Nile; by rail (station on the Nile Valley line).

The town of Edfu or Idfu, a market center with sugar factories and an old-established pottery industry, lies on a slightly raised site some 65 miles/100 km S of Luxor on the W bank of the Nile (now spanned by a bridge opened in 1969), at the point where the valley begins to open out. It was the ancient Egyptian Tbot, Coptic Atbo, from which the modern name is derived. The Greeks called it Apollinopolis Magna after the sun god Horus-Apollo, who was particularly revered here, and made

Pylon of the Temple of Horus, Edfu

Temple of Horus   Edfu

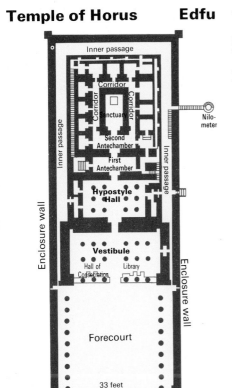

was begun in 237 B.C., in the reign of Ptolemy II Euergetes I and completed in 212 under his successor, Philopator. The decoration of the walls with reliefs and inscriptions, interrupted during the troubled reign of Epiphanes, was resumed by 176 by Philometor and finished in 147, during the reign of Euergetes II – i.e. exactly 90 years after the laying of the foundation-stone. Euergetes II also added the large vestibule (completed in 122) and decorated it with reliefs. During the reigns of Ptolemy IX Soter II and Ptolemy X Alexander I the forecourt with its colonnades, the enclosure walls and the pylon were built, but the pylon was decorated with reliefs only in the reign of Ptolemy XII Neos Dionysos. The building was finally completed in 57 B.C. The building material was sandstone. Some of the relief decoration was defaced in Christian times.

The temple was surrounded by a high brick wall, part of which survives. The main gateway was on the S, in the central axis of the temple, and there was a smaller gateway to the W.

The great **Pylon** originally stood within an inner enclosure wall of brick, and the entrance was closed by a double door. It is covered on all sides with reliefs and inscriptions. Particularly notable are the reliefs on the front: below, King Neos Dionysos smiting his enemies, whom he holds by the hair, with the falcon-headed Horus and Hathor looking on; in the top two rooms the King making offerings to Horus, to Hathor and Horus, "Uniter of the Two Lands", and to other divinities. On each side of the main entrance are two perpendicular recesses for flagstaffs, which were secured in position by clamps fastened to the holes still to be seen in the masonry directly above. The other small rectangular apertures are windows designed to admit light and air to the interior of the temple.

In each tower a passage leads to the outside of the enclosure wall, which is decorated with religious reliefs (Ptolemy X Alexander I before the gods of Edfu) and inscriptions, as well as the inscriptions relating to the temple itself which have already been referred to. In front of the pylon are two colossal falcons of black granite; in front of the left-hand one is the figure of a priest in Roman dress.

The colonnaded **Forecourt** between the pylon and the vestibule of the temple is paved with stone slabs and surrounded on three sides by a total of 32 columns. In the middle there once stood the great altar upon which offerings were made to the gods of Edfu in the presence of the assembled people. The *columns* have rich flower and palm capitals, and the incised reliefs show the King (whose name has been left blank in the inscriptions) before Horus and the other deities of Edfu. The rear walls of the colonnade are covered with three rows of large **reliefs** depicting the Pharaoh (Ptolemy IX Soter II or Ptolemy X Alexander I) holding converse with the gods or in the person of the victorious god Horus. Similar representations are repeated all over the temple. On the sides of the pylon the King is shown, with the Lower Egyptian crown on the W side and the Upper Egyptian crown on the E side, proceeding to the temple and being sprinkled

it the capital of the 2nd (Apollino-polite) nome of Upper Egypt.

Horus, who according to the myth fought one of his great combats with Seth here, was known as "he of Behdet" (Behdet being probably a district of ancient Edfu). He was represented as a flying falcon, in human form with a falcon's head or as the winged sun.

The 2000-year-old ****Temple of Horus**, almost perfectly preserved, creates an overwhelming impression. Built on the site of an earlier temple, it was dedicated to the sun god Horus, Hathor of Dendera and their son the youthful Harsomtus (Hersemtawi), "Uniter of the Two Lands". The history of its construction and a description of the whole structure are set forth in long inscriptions on the outside of the enclosure wall, particularly at the N end of the E and W sides. The rear part of the complex, the temple proper,

with the water of consecration by Horus and Thoth. – The doors to right and left of these reliefs lead to the staircases inside the pylon; the E and W exits are walled up. Outside the E exit are the remains of a building dating from the reign of Ramesses III.

At the far end of the forecourt is the handsome *façade of the vestibule,* topped by a cavetto cornice. Between the columns on either side of the large central doorway are low stone screens, on which King Euergetes II is depicted in the presence of the falcon-headed Horus (on the four outermost screens) and of Hathor (on the two middle screens) making offerings or standing with his arms hanging by his sides. To the left of the entrance is a colossal *Horus falcon wearing the double crown; the corresponding figure on the right lies on the ground.

The **Vestibule** has 12 columns with elaborate floral capitals. The ceiling is covered with astronomical representations, now blackened beyond recognition. On the walls are four rows of incised reliefs showing Euergetes making offerings to the gods or performing ritual acts (e.g. laying the foundation-stone of the temple, in the bottom row on the left-hand wall). Above are a band of astronomical representations and an ornamental frieze consisting of the names of the King guarded by two falcons. Below, just above the floor, are Euergetes, his wife Cleopatra and a long file of local gods bringing offerings to the three principal divinities of Edfu. The door in the E wall leads into the inner passage round the temple. – On each side of the entrance is a chapel. The one on the left (W) is the *Hall of Consecration,* as the reliefs on the rear wall (Horus and Thoth pouring the sacred water on the King) suggest; the one on the right was a *Library,* with a list of books it contained inscribed on the wall and, to the left, a figure of Seshat, goddess of writing. – On the architrave of the door leading into the Hypostyle Hall is an interesting relief of the solar barque, guided by two falcon-headed Horus figures, with the sun worshiped by Thoth and Neith. At the sides, in the attitude of prayer, are Ptolemy IV Philopator (left) and the Four Senses – to the right sight and hearing, to the left taste (symbolized by the tongue) and reason.

The **Hypostyle Hall**, the roof of which is supported by 12 columns with elaborate floral capitals, is lit by apertures in the walls and roof and has reliefs similar to those in the vestibule. There are two small chambers on each side. The nearer one on each side leads into the inner passage round the temple; the second on the left served as a laboratory; and the second on the right gave access to the E staircase up to the temple roof.

Beyond the hypostyle hall is the **First Antechamber**, with staircases on either side leading to the roof. As at Dendera, the mural reliefs depict the procession of priests, headed by the King, ascending (E side) and descending (W side). The rooms on the E side of the roof, probably serving the cult of Osiris, are of little interest. – On the E side of the **Second Antechamber** is a small Court of Offerings, and to the left of this an elegant little Kiosk, the roof of which is supported on two columns with floral capitals; on the ceiling is the sky goddess Nut, with the various figures of the sun in boats beneath her. On the other side of the Second Antechamber is a small room dedicated to the cult of the god Min.

In the **Sanctuary**, which is lit by three small square apertures in the roof, the most interesting reliefs are those in the bottom row on the right-hand wall. The King (Philopator) is depicted removing the lock from

In the Temple of Horus, Edfu

Horus's chapel; opening the door of the chapel; standing before the god in a reverential attitude with his arms hanging by his sides; offering incense to his deified parents, Euergetes I and Berenice; and offering incense before the sacred barque of Hathor. On the rear wall is a relic of the Pre-Ptolemaic temple, a granite shrine with a pointed roof dedicated to Horus by Nectanebo II. In front of this is a base of black granite (found elsewhere in the temple) intended to support the sacred barque, with an inscription indicating that it was presented by a private citizen.

Round the sanctuary runs a *corridor,* off which open ten small and poorly lit chambers decorated with reliefs (some with well-preserved colors) which served either as store-rooms for ritual utensils or for some cult purpose. In the two corner rooms are openings in the floor (formerly closed by stone slabs) leading down to the crypt.

Round the temple as a whole runs an *inner passage,* entered from the Hypostyle Hall, which is also decorated with reliefs and inscriptions. On the outside of the temple wall are lions' heads as waterspouts and four rows of religious reliefs. At the foot of the wall are the King, Queen and priests proceeding in procession into the presence of the three chief divinities of Edfu. On the inner side of the enclosure wall are (E wall) the King before the divinities of Edfu; (N wall) similar scenes and long hymns to the god of Edfu; and (W wall) striking reliefs depicting Horus's contests with his enemies, who are represented as crocodiles and hippopotamuses.

Particularly notable among the reliefs on the *W wall* are the following: (1st scene, below, right) the King tries to spear a hippopotamus, which turns aside; Horus does the same, holding a chain in his left hand and a spear in his right, with his mother Isis beside him and a small Horus at the helm of the boat to the rear; (2nd scene) the King stands on land, on the left, with two ships in front of him, in which are Horus and an attendant; Horus holds the hippopotamus with a chain and plunges his spear into its head; (5th scene) the hippopotamus lies on its back with its hind legs chained; (7th scene) Horus, in a sailing-boat, aims his spear at a hippopotamus, whose hind leg is tied in a

◀ **Horus falcon, Edfu**

Relief in the Temple of Horus, Edfu

the god Bes and consists of a vestibule flanked by two small chambers and the main chamber.

In the *main chamber,* on the right-hand wall (from left to right), are reliefs depicting Hathor of Dendera suckling Horus, with seven other Hathors playing musical instruments in front of her and her young son Ihi with a sistrum behind her; to the right Hathor giving birth, to the left the King with two sistra before seven Hathors suckling the infant; and the King before various deities and (left) before the sacred barque of Hathor. On the left-hand walls are reliefs relating to the birth of Harsomtus (Khnum shaping the child on the potter's wheel, etc.). – In front of the birth-house is a forecourt, originally enclosed by columns and stone screens. On the shafts of the columns are reliefs of goddesses playing musical instruments and Hathor suckling the infant Horus.

To the W of the Temple of Horus high mounds of rubble mark the site of the *ancient city.* A number of excavations have been carried out here in recent years. Under the houses of the Arab and Coptic periods are remains of the Graeco-Roman period. In the houses were papyri as well as a variety of domestic equipment.

Aswan, *Esna, *El-Kab, Kom el-Ahmar and ***Kom Ombo: see separate entries.

cord held by Horus and its head in a cord held by Isis, kneeling in the bow of the boat; the King, standing on the shore with two attendants, aims his spear at the animal's head; (farther left, opposite the pylon) the King, the ram-headed god Khnum, the falcon-headed Horus and the ibis-headed Thoth haul in a net in which are caught not only marsh birds, fish and a stag but also two Asiatics and a number of Negroes, Egypt's hereditary foes.

A subterranean staircase leads from the E side of the inner passage to an ancient **Nilometer,** a shaft outside the temple encircled by a spiral staircase which could formerly also be reached from outside. The scale on the wall of the shaft gives the depths in demotic characters. The Nilometer is no longer connected with the Nile.

An * ascent to the top of the pylon is very well worth the trouble. A staircase on the S side of the forecourt has 242 easy steps in 14 flights. The staircase and the small chambers which open off the landings are lit by windows. The staircases in the two towers are connected with one another by a passage running above the central doorway, and in each tower is a door giving access to the roof of the colonnades round the forecourt. On the roof of the W colonnade are workmen's drawings of the cavetto cornice on the pylon. From the platform there are extensive * views of the temple complex itself, the Nile Plain with its green fields and its villages fringed by palms and mimosas, framed by the desert hills in the distance.

To the W of the entrance to the temple is the **birth-house** *(mammisi),* built by Ptolemy VIII Euergetes II and decorated with reliefs by Ptolemy IX Soter II. It is surrounded by a colonnade of cluster-columns with floral capitals and figures of

El ...
See under the main element in the name

Elephantine
See under Aswan

Esna

Upper Egypt. – Governorate: Qena.
Population: 30,000.
ⓘ **Tourist Information Office,**
Tourist Bazaar,
Luxor;
tel. 22 15.

ACCESS. – 34 miles/54 km S of Luxor on the Nile Valley road; 30 miles/49 km NW of Edfu on an asphalted road. – By rail (station on E bank of Nile).

The little country town of *Esna straggles along the left bank of the Nile. It is connected with the main road on the E bank of the river by a road running over a large dam built by British engineers at the beginning of the 20th century.

Temple of Khnum, Esna

HISTORY. – In ancient times Esna, with the adjoining town of Enit or Yunit, was one of the most important places in Upper Egypt. Its Egyptian name was *Tesnet,* from which the Coptic *Sne* and Arabic *Esna* are derived. The Greeks called the town *Latopolis,* after the Nile perch *(Lates niloticus),* a fish here revered as sacred and buried in extensive cemeteries. – During the medieval period the town regained importance and a modest degree of prosperity as a caravan station and as a market for the agricultural produce of the area. – Esna is one of the main centers of the Coptic faith in Egypt.

SIGHTS. – In the center of the town, freed from the rubble of later centuries and now 30 ft/9 m below the present street-level, is the *Temple of Khnum, the ram-headed local god, and his associate goddesses Neith (equated by the Greeks with Athena) and Satet. Also associated with Khnum were the lion-headed goddess Menheyet and Nebtu, who corresponded to Isis. The temple was begun in the Ptolemaic period and extended and decorated with reliefs and inscriptions by various Roman Emperors.

Temple of Khnum   Esna

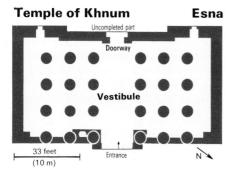

The *façade* of the temple, facing E, is 121 ft/37 m long and 49 ft/15 m high and is topped by a cavetto cornice bearing the names of Claudius and Vespasian on either side of a winged sun. On the architrave are inscriptions in the name of these Emperors, Vespasian being referred to as "ruler of the capital, Rome". On the stone screens between the front row of columns are reliefs depicting the Pharaoh being conducted into the temple by various deities; on the screen at the left-hand end Harsiesis and Thoth are shown pouring the consecrating water over the King, with the lion-headed goddess Menheyet standing on the right.

The seven-aisled **Vestibule**, the only part of the temple which was completed, dates almost entirely from the Roman Imperial period. Similar in layout to the vestibule of the Temple of Hathor at Dendera, it is 108 ft/33 m long by 54 ft/16·5 m deep. The roof is supported by 24 *columns,* in four rows, with elaborate floral capitals. The columns, 37 ft/11·3 m high and 18 ft/5·4 m in girth, are covered with reliefs and inscriptions. Over the broad central aisle the roof is decorated with two rows of flying vultures; over the lateral aisles are astronomical representations. – On the *walls* are four rows of reliefs depicting the Emperors, wearing the costume of a Pharaoh, making offerings to the various deities of Esna or performing other ritual acts relating to the building of the temple. In the middle of the rear (W) wall is a pylon-like *doorway* topped by a cavetto cornice, which would have led into the sanctuary (never built); it bears reliefs and inscriptions in the name of Ptolemy VI Philometor. At each end of the rear wall are smaller doors, now built up; to the right of the left-hand door Decius is depicted making an offering to the ram-headed Khnum. At the foot of the N wall the falcon-headed Horus, the Emperor Commodus and Khnum are shown drawing in a net full of waterfowl and fish; to the left stands the ibis-headed Thoth, to the right the goddess Sakhet. On the E wall, behind the screen immediately left of the entrance, is a small chapel.

The *outer walls* also bear reliefs and inscriptions by Roman Emperors. On the S side Domitian is depicted smiting his enemies in the presence of Khnum and Menheyet, and on the N side Khnum, with the goddess Nebtu standing behind him, presents Trajan, also shown smiting his enemies, with the sickle-sword.

Other relics of the Roman period in Esna are an ancient *quay* with fragments of inscriptions (cartouches of the Emperor Marcus Aurelius) and the remains of a *Nilometer*, also dating from Imperial times. Nothing remains of four other temples known to have existed here, including one in ancient Contra-Latopolis, on the E bank of the Nile at the village of el-Hilla.

SURROUNDINGS of Esna. – Around the town are the ruins of a number of Coptic monasteries and churches. 3½ miles/5·5 km S is the *Monastery of SS. Manaos and Sanutios*, said to have been founded by the Empress Helena, which has, in addition to its modern church, an ancient church decorated with frescos, now covered with whitewash. – 6 miles/10 km N is *Deir Amba Matteos*, the Monastery of St Matthias. – ¾ mile/1 km W is a rock-cut *church* with frescos.

On the E bank of the Nile, some 2½ miles/4 km SW of the railway station, lies the village of *Sarnikh*, where there are two important rock-cut stelae dating from the beginning of Amenophis IV's reign.

A temple of the Roman Imperial period has recently been excavated at *Kom Meir*, 7½ miles/12 km SE of Esna.

Edfu, Gebelein, *El-Kab* and **Kom el-Ahmar**: see separate entries.

Farafra Oasis

Western Desert. – New Valley Frontier District.

ACCESS. – Reached from Bahriya Oasis (106 miles/170 km NE) or Dakhla Oasis (130 miles/210 km SE) on desert tracks obstructed in places by sand-drifts; cross-country vehicle and adequate equipment and supplies essential. No accommodation, food or gasoline (petrol) available either at Farafra or on the road there.

The little Oasis of Farafra lies in latitude 27° N and longitude 28° E. Unlike the other Egyptian oases, it is not in a depression but on an apparently endless plain, surrounded by a sea of light-colored limestone rocks.

The 1000 or so inhabitants live by cultivating dates, olives and citrus fruits. Although Farafra was frequented by nomadic tribes as early as the Palaeolithic period and was settled in Early Dynastic times, developing into a place of some importance as a staging-point between Bahriya and Dakhla, it has practically no

ancient remains. The chief place, and indeed the only regular settlement, is **Qasr el-Farafra,** with the ruins of old town walls and picturesque winding lanes.

New Valley and **Western Desert**: see separate entries.

Fayyum

Middle Egypt. – Governorate: El-Fayyum.
Population: 1,300,000. – Area: 692 sq. miles/1792 sq. km.

ⓘ **Tourist Information Office,**
Misr Travel Tower,
Cairo – Abbasia;
tel. 82 60 16.

HOTELS. – *Auberge du Lac*, I, 104 b.; *Panorama*, Shakshouk, II, 66 b.; *Qarun-Village* (under construction), all next to Lake Qarun; *Ein El-Sellin*, in Fidimin, III, 48 b.; etc.

ACCESS. – By road: 56 miles/90 km SW of Cairo (leave on road to Pyramids) and 22 miles/35 km NW of Beni Suef; bus services. – By rail: Cairo to Medinet el-Fayyum via El-Wasta.

The **Fayyum (from Coptic Phiom, "the Lake"), the largest and economically the most important of the Egyptian oases, lies some 56 miles/90 km SW of Cairo in latitude 29° 29′ N and longitude 30° 40′ E. Lying in a large depression in the great plateau of the Western Desert, at up to 150 ft/45 m below sea-level, it has long been famed for its extraordinary fertility, and holds out great attractions to visitors in the tranquil beauty of its scenery and its remains of the past.

The Fayyum Oasis is in the form of a triangle with rounded corners and its point to the S, extending 40 miles/65 km from E to W at its widest part and 30 miles/50 km from N to S. Enclosed by low ranges of hills, it falls gradually from S to N. It is watered by the *Bahr Yusuf* ("Joseph's Canal"), which leaves the Ibrahimiya Canal (originally the Nile) at Deirut, cuts through the hills enclosing the Fayyum in a narrow passage at El-Lahun, spreads out over the oasis in many arms and ramifications and finally flows into the **Birket Qarun** (Lake Qarun), on the NW edge of the depression. – The Fayyum is noted for its agreeable climate.

HISTORY. – In prehistoric times the Fayyum Depression was probably still covered by the waters of an arm of the Nile dating from the Pliocene era which here formed an extensive lake and swamp area with

Oasis landscape in the Fayyum

luxuriant vegetation and abundant animal life. There must have been large numbers of crocodiles, which were worshiped as divinities from earliest historical times (Sobek, later known as Suchos; Crocodilopolis). The oldest traces of settlement date from the Neolithic and show affinities with the early cultures of the Nile Valley. By the beginning of the historical period the lake had shrunk in size and may have extended in the N as far as the little desert Temple of Qasr el-Sagha, in the S to Biahmu and the area between Abshawai and Agamiyin. It was known in ancient Egyptian as *Sha-resi* (the "Southern Lake") and later as *Mer-wer* ("Great Lake"), known to Greek travelers and geographers as *Lake Moeris*. According to Herodotus it had a circumference of 3600 stadia (445 miles) and covered an area of some 770 sq. miles – i.e about three-fifths of the present area of the oasis. It has been estimated that in ancient times the surface of the lake lay 74 ft/22·5m above the level of the Mediterranean (now 150 ft/45 m below). To the S of the lake was a narrow strip of cultivable land known as *Ta-she* ("Lake-Land"), with the chief town, *Shedet* (Crocodilopolis), which was protected against flood-ing by embankments. Several rulers of the 12th Dynasty established settlements at the E end of this area, and Amenemhet III in particular seems to have taken a special interest in it, undertaking large-scale reclamation of the swamps. Under the 18th Dynasty Amenophis III's wife Tiy had her residence at El-Lahun.

The Ptolemies, particularly Ptolemy II Philadelphus, reduced the size of the lake still further by the construction of dikes until it was about the dimensions of the present-day Lake Qarun. The draining of the swamps yielded new land on which Greek and Macedonian settlers were established; and the suc-cess of this program of land reclamation is demonstrated by the fertile fields and flourishing villages which have occupied the site of Lake Moeris over the past 2000 years. According to Strabo "Lake Moeris is capable, thanks to its size and depth, of taking in the surplus water during the inundation without flooding the inhabited and cultivated area, and later, when the water subsides, of returning the excess through the same canal (i.e. the Bahr Yusuf), while retaining sufficient to irrigate the land. At both ends of the canal there are lock-gates which enable the engineers to regulate the inflow and outflow of the water." It is not known how the distribution of the excess water was achieved. At present-day El-Lahun there is still a lock-gate. – Herodotus's statement that Lake Moeris had been artificially created was an error and is contradicted by Strabo's account.

In Ptolemaic times the Fayyum formed the Ar-sinoite nome, about which the Greek geographer *Strabo* (*c.* 63 B.C.–A.D. 20) has this to say:

"This nome is the most remarkable of all, on ac-count both of its scenery and its fertility and cultivation; for it alone is planted with large and excellent olive trees which bear fine fruit, and the oil is good when the olives are carefully gathered. Those who fail in this respect may indeed obtain oil in abundance, but it has a bad smell. Elsewhere in Egypt the olive tree is never seen except in the gardens of Alexandria, where under favorable circumstances it yields olives but no oil. In this region, too, vines, corn and pulses, together with many other plants, flourish in no small abun-dance."

The Fayyum is now a governorate with an area of 692 sq. miles/1792 sq. km and a population of 1,300,000. Olives are still grown here, together with cotton, sugar-cane, wheat, maize, rice, excellent fruit, wine, bananas and citrus fruits. Small livestock and poultry (dovecots) are also reared. Characteristic features of the landscape are the large undershot water-

Water-wheel in the Fayyum

district became known as the Arsinoite nome and the capital as the "city of the dwellers in the Arsinoite nome", or more briefly as *Arsinoe*. In its heyday Arsinoe had a population of more than 100,000.

The principal temple, dedicated to the cult of Sobek (Suchos), was at the N end of the site. It was already in existence in the time of the 12th Dynasty, and was later rebuilt by Ramesses II. Beside the temple was a sacred lake in which was kept a crocodile sacred to the god.

Some $4\frac{1}{2}$ miles/7 km N of Medinet el-Fayyum is the village of **Biahmu**, just N of which are two large structures of dressed stone, with the appearance of ruined pyramids, which are known to the local people as the *Kursi Faraun* ("Pharaoh's Chair") and *El-Sanam,* "The Idol". These were the bases of two colossal sandstone statues of Amenemhet III. The learned Father Vansleb of Erfurt saw the lower part of one of the figures in 1672, and Lepsius and Petrie found a few remaining fragments. Petrie estimated their original height at 40 ft/12 m. The bases were once washed by the waters of Lake Moeris, and there is little doubt that they are the two pyramids described by Herodotus as standing in the lake, each crowned by a colossal seated human figure.

wheels. Further land-reclamation projects are under way on the shores of Lake Qarun. – Among the urgent problems connected with the development of the Fayyum is the control of bilharzia, a troublesome disease transmitted by flukes parasitic on water-snails.

Sights of the Fayyum

The provincial capital of **Medinet el-Fayyum** (*El-Fayyum* or *El-Medina* for short; pop. 350,000) lies in the SE of the oasis on the Bahr Yusuf, which here divides into numerous arms. The town is the commercial and economic center of the oasis and the seat of the local government authorities. It has a number of mosques, including the Mosque of Qait Bey, which has an old doorway with bronze-mounted doors, and a large Coptic church.

To the N of the town rises the *Kiman Faris* ("Horseman's Hill"), with the remains of ancient **Crocodilopolis-Arsinoe**, one of the largest ancient sites in Egypt, with an area of 560 acres. Much of the mound has been removed by brick-makers or peasants digging for the fertile soil *(sebbakh)* found on ancient sites.

The ancient Egyptian name of the town was *Shedet*. It was the center of the cult of the crocodile-headed water god Sobek (Suchos), the protective deity of the whole of the lake area. His sacred animal was the crocodile, and the Greeks, therefore, called the town *Crocodilopolis*. Politically it never seems to have been a place of any consequence. By extending the town, building Greek temples and schools and introducing the Greek language Ptolemy II Philadelphus turned it into an essentially Hellenic city, of which he made his wife Arsinoe the protective goddess. Thereafter the

From Medinet el-Fayyum a charming road runs 9 miles/15 km N via the villages of *Beni Salih* and *El-Seliyin* and past *Fidimin,* picturesquely situated on a crag to the left of the road, to *Sanhur,* on the site of a considerable ancient town.

A road runs SW from Medinet el-Fayyum via *Itsa* ($5\frac{1}{2}$ miles/9 km) to *Abu Gandir* (14 miles/23 km), from which it continues S on an unsurfaced and sometimes difficult road, crosses the *El-Nasala Canal* and reaches the ancient site of **Medinet Madi**, on the SW edge of the oasis. The remains to be seen here are those of the Graeco-Roman settlement of **Narmouthis**, with a temple founded by Amenemhet III and completed by his son Amenemhet IV in honor of the crocodile god Sobek, his consort the snake goddess Renenutet (Thermouthis) and Horus. The temple, oriented from N to S, was extended under the Ptolemies by the addition of large halls and courts, and some smaller extensions were added in the Roman Imperial period.

The *Temple of Sobek lies in a large hollow in the hills on the edge of the desert, approached from the plain by a paved processional way flanked by lions and sphinxes. The core of the whole complex is the little *Temple of Amenemhet III* (12th Dynasty), which is of interest as one of the few surviving examples of Middle Kingdom religious architecture. It consists of a pronaos with two papyrus columns and the sanctuary, which has three niches, high up on the wall, for statues of the deities worshiped here. The walls are entirely covered with hieroglyphs and reliefs, unfortunately much damaged but sufficiently preserved to show their high technical and artistic quality. – A small Temple of Anubis was built on the rear of the main temple in Roman times.

The Ptolemaic extension at the S end of the temple has a number of remarkable inscriptions, the originals of which are in the Graeco-Roman Museum in Alexandria. The two pillars at the entrance to the vestibule of the first of the temple's three courts bear two dedicatory inscriptions in similar terms and four hymns, each of 40 lines, written in imperfect Greek and signed by their author, one Isidorus. The fourth hymn refers to the marvelous exploits of the Pharaoh Poremanre (i.e. Amenemhet III). All these texts reflect the variety of cultural influences to which Egypt was exposed during the Graeco-Egyptian period.

Some 9 miles/15 km SE of Medinet el-Fayyum, on the banks of the Bahr el-Gharaq at the village of *Umm el-Baragat,* are the remains of ancient **Tebtynis**, in the necropolis of which many papyrus rolls were found on crocodile mummies. The city, which may have originated in the Ramessid period and became a place of some consequence in the reign of Ptolemy I Soter, had a temple dedicated to the crocodile god Sobek, similar to the one at Medinet Madi, of which only scanty remains survive. Within the temple precincts were found many hieratic, demotic and Greek papyri, some of them with very informative texts, particularly in the fields of medicine and religion. – 2 miles/3 km SW of the site of Tebtynis, on the edge of the desert, are the rock tombs of *Kom Ruqayya,* probably dating from the 12th Dynasty.

Some 6 miles/10 km SE of Medinet el-Fayyum and 1 mile/1·5 km N of the village of *Hawaret el-Maqta,* on a plateau at the edge of the desert, stands the *****Pyramid of Hawara**, the Tomb of Amenemhet III, who did so much to develop the Fayyum – his second pyramid, for he had already built one at Dahshur (see that entry). The Pyramid of Hawara is constructed of sun-dried bricks made from Nile mud with an admixture of straw, and with its original limestone casing (which had already disappeared by Roman times) had a base measurement of 350 ft/106 m. At the core of the pyramid was an outcrop of natural rock 40 ft/12 m high. The entrance (now blocked) was on the S side and gave access to a complicated network of passages leading to the burial chamber.

Pyramid of Hawara, Fayyum

Adjoining the S side of the pyramid was Amenemhet's large mortuary temple, of which nothing is left but a large area covered with splinters of stone and fragments of fine granite and limestone columns, following its use as a quarry of building stone from Roman times onwards. Occasional fragments of walls can be seen in the sloping banks of the canal which traverses this area, the *Bahr Seila el-Gedid*. This structure was probably the famous **Labyrinth**, of which ancient travelers spoke with unbounded admiration.

Strabo, who had visited the Labyrinth, describes it in these terms:

"At the locks is the Labyrinth, a structure which vies in importance with the pyramids, and beside it is the tomb of the King who built it. After entering the canal and proceeding some 30 to 40 stadia [3½–4½ miles/5·5/7·5 km] along it you come to a table-like area in which are a small town and a large palace, consisting of as many separate palaces as there formerly were nomes. For there are that number of courts surrounded by colonnades, one adjoining another in a long row, so that all the courts seem to be built against a single wall. The entrances to the courts lie opposite this wall; but in front of the entrances are many long covered passages, which intersect with one another and form such a complicated path that a stranger cannot find his way into or out of the various courts without a guide. The remarkable thing is that the roof of each building consists of a single stone and that each group of passages is roofed with a single slab of extraordinary size. No wood or other building material is employed. When you climb to the roof, which is not of any great height since the building has only a single storey, you can see the great expanse covered by these huge slabs. On emerging from the passage you have a view of them extending in a long line, each of the 27 having a monolithic column to support the roof. At the end of the whole structure, more than a stadium [200 yds/180 m] in length, is the tomb, a square pyramid each side of which is 4 plethra [400 ft/120 m] in length, with a height also of 4 plethra. The dead man who is buried here is called Imandes. It is said that so many courts were built because it was the custom for the chief dignitaries of each nome to assemble here, together with priests and priestesses, to make offerings to the gods and deliberate on matters of particular importance. Each nome then occupied the court assigned to it."

To the N of the Pyramid of Hawara is a large *cemetery* in which the more prosperous citizens of Shedet-Crocodilopolis were buried during the Middle Kingdom. In 1956 the remains of a small *pyramid* containing the Body of Princess Neferuptah, Amenemhet III's daughter, were discovered 1¼ miles/ 2 km S of the Hawara Pyramid. It was previously believed that she had been buried in a small sarcophagus found in her father's tomb chamber. – To the E of the temple precinct are the remains of brick buildings belonging to a Roman village.

Market scene in the Fayyum

The NE part of the Fayyum Oasis is occupied by the **Birket Qarun**, the Lake of Qarun (the Korah of Numbers 16: 1), which is the surviving part of the much larger Lake Moeris of ancient times. It is almost 30 miles/50 km long from E to W, with a maximum width of 6 miles/10 m; the average depth is 13–16 ft/4–5 m, but in places the depth reaches 50–60 ft/ 15–18 m. The N side of the lake is barren and enclosed by hills rising to a considerable height; the S side is flat, and in many places intensively cultivated right up to the water's edge. The greenish water is slightly brackish and unsuitable for drinking. Bathing in the lake is not possible because of the thick layer of ooze on the bottom. There is a remarkable variety of bird-life around the shores of the lake, and it is well stocked with fish. Accordingly the local people gain much of their subsistence from wildfowling and fishing.

The boat trip across the lake from the *Auberge de Fayoum* or the fishing village of *Shaqshuq* – both on the lakeside road which branches off the main road to Cairo – takes about 2 hours. From the landing-stage on the N side a steep track climbs 2 miles/3 km to the top of the hill, on which are ruins of **Dimei**, the ancient *Soknopaiou Nesos* ("Island of Soknopaios"), a fortified caravan station and a place of some consequence. The ruins cover an area of about 125 acres/0·5 sq. km. A street 400 yds/370 m long, formerly flanked by figures of crouching lions, passes the well-preserved remains of houses to a platform on which are the ruins of a large *temple* of the Ptolemaic period dedicated to Soknopaios, a local form of the Fayyum deity Sobek or Suchos, and the "finely throned Isis". The temple, surrounded by a high enclosure wall of sun-dried brick, consisted of a number of chambers, the rooms to the rear being built of carefully laid limestone blocks, those in the front part of roughly hewn stone faced with stucco. Only a few reliefs survive; one of them depicts one of the Ptolemies (without cartouche) praying before a ram-headed god (probably Amun).

Some 5 miles/8 km N of Dimei, at the foot of a steep desert escarpment, is the small Temple of *Qasr el-Sagha*, probably dating from the Old Kingdom, which was discovered by Schweinfurth in 1884. Built of limestone blocks, it contains seven recesses and several other chambers, but no reliefs or inscriptions. Near by are the remains of an ancient quay.

At the SW end of the Birket Qarun is the site of **Qasr Qarun**, most conveniently reached on a moderately good road (22 miles/36 km) from Medinet el-Fayyum via *Ibshawai* and *El-Shawashna*. Qasr Qarun is a reasonably well-preserved temple of the Late Ptolemaic period, surrounded by the remains of an ancient city, probably *Dionysias,* on the extreme western verge of the Roman province. From here there was a caravan route to Bahriya, then known as the Oasis Minor. A circular foundation wall marks the position of an ancient cistern. The **Temple**, 63 ft/19·20 m wide across the façade and 89 ft/27 m long, is built of carefully dressed blocks of extremely hard sandstone. Like almost all the temples in the oases, it was dedicated to the ram-headed Amun-Khnum, of whom there are two representations at the top of the rear wall of the open top storey. Above every doorway of the temple is a winged sun. There are no ancient inscriptions.

The entrance, facing E, is reached by way of the *forecourt,* a high and well-built platform 43 ft/13 m from front to rear. On the façade of the temple, to the right (N) of the doorway, stands a huge half-column, a relic of the colonnade which once flanked the court. On the lower floor are the chambers dedicated to cult purposes: first three *antechambers,* the floors of which slope down towards the sanctuary, and the *sanctuary* itself, divided into three small rooms at the back. On either side of the sanctuary is a narrow corridor with three chambers opening off it. Over the doorways of the two antechambers and the sanctuary the usual cavetto cornice is replaced by a row of royal cobras. Flanking the antechambers are side rooms from which it is possible either to go down into the cellars or to climb two flights of stairs to the upper floor, on which there are various other chambers, and from there to the roof. From the roof there are extensive views of the sand-covered remains of the ancient city, the lake and the desert.

To the E of the main temple can be found two *smaller temples,* reasonably well preserved. One, on the same axis as the main temple, is a kiosk, similar in ground-plan to the Philae Kiosk. The other, 220 yds/200 m from the first, is larger, with walls of well-fired brick on stone foundations. At the far end of the sanctuary is an apse-like recess, and on the two side walls are two engaged half-columns, which the fragments lying around show to have been of the Ionic Order.

NW of the Qasr Qarun site are the remains of a Roman fort of the time of Diocletian. Defended by nine towers, it was constructed of kiln-fired brick with limestone blocks built in at certain points.

Some 9 miles/14 km SE of Qasr Qarun is **Qasr el-Banat**, with the remains of ancient *Euhemeria,* including a temple dedicated to Suchos and Isis. $4\frac{1}{2}$ miles/7 km W of Qasr el-Banat is *Watfa,* with the remains of ancient *Philoteris*; and 2 miles/3 km SE of this, at the village of *Harit (Batn Harit),* is the site of ancient *Theadelphia,* known as **Kharabet Ihrit**, with a temple dedicated to the crocodile god Pnepheros and a necropolis.

In the desert to the E of the Birket Qarun and NW of Tamiya is the hill of **Kom Aushim**, with the remains of the Greek city of *Karanis* which is frequently mentioned in the records, including a temple dedicated to Pnepheros and Petesuchos. – 7 miles/11 km E of Karanis is the hill of *Umm el-Qatl,* the ancient *Bacchias.*

On the E side of the Fayyum, $2\frac{1}{2}$ miles/4 km NE of **El-Roda**, are the remains of ancient *Philadelphia,* a Greek garrison town founded by Ptolemy II Philadelphus about 250 B.C.. Large numbers of mummy portraits were found in the necropolis here.

4 miles/6 km NW of El-Roda lies the well-fortified village of **Tamiya**, on the *Bahr Tamiya,* an arm of the Bahr Yusuf, also known as the *Bahr el-Wadi* or *Bahr el-Bats,* which is dammed at this point.

At the extreme eastern end of the Fayyum, on the railway line from Medinet el-Fayyum to El-Wasta in the Nile Valley, is **Seila**, with a small step pyramid which is thought to date from the 3rd Dynasty.

Beni Suef, * El-Lahun, Lisht, * Meidum and the Western Desert: see separate entries.

Feiran Oasis
See under Sinai

Gaza

Under Israeli military administration
Population: 120,000.
(i) **Israel Government Tourist Office,**
Rehov Hamelekh George 24,
Jerusalem;
tel. 23 73 11.

ACCESS. – By road (50 miles/80 km NE of El-Arish); Egyptian-Israeli frontier crossing.

The ancient and historic town of Gaza (Hebrew Azza, "strength, power"), surrounded by fertile arable land and fruit orchards, lies just off the Mediterranean coast some 50 miles/80 km NE of El-Arish, in the "Gaza Strip", a stretch of coastal plain well supplied with water from its many springs. Gaza is the headquarters of the Israeli military administration in the Gaza Strip. The population is almost exclusively Arab and Muslim.

HISTORY. – Gaza, one of the most ancient cities known to history, is referred to in Egyptian texts as early as about 2000 B.C. Tuthmosis III made it an Egyptian garrison town, a stronghold designed to guard against raids by Semitic and Asiatic peoples but also a base for Egyptian campaigns of conquest in the regions to the NE. – In the middle of the 17th c. B.C. Gaza was overwhelmed by the Hyksos, who then thrust into the Nile Valley, where they ruled for a hundred years.

In the 1st millennium B.C. Gaza was the most southerly and the largest city in the Pentapolis, a league of five towns (Gaza, Ashdod, Ascalon, Gath and Ekron) of the Philistines (Hebrew *pelishtim*), a Semitic people who established themselves from the 12th c. B.C. onwards in the low-lying country between Mount Carmel and the Egyptian border (Deuteronomy 2: 23). According to Amos 9: 7 they came from Caphtor (Crete?). The Philistines appear to have established a stable and well-organized State at an early date, and all accounts indicate that in cultural achievement they were far ahead of the Jews. They had the advantage over the Jews of possessing chariots and cavalry (1 Samuel 13: 5). Their heavily armed troops wore a round copper helmet, chain-mail and iron greaves, and were armed with a javelin and a long lance; and each man, like Homer's Greeks, had a servant to carry his weapons and his shield. Their light troops were archers. The Philistines established permanent camps, surrounded their cities with high walls and stationed garrisons to hold conquered territory. They carried on an active and far-flung trade both by sea and more particularly on land; and their wars with the Israelites stemmed partly from their need to keep the caravan routes, particularly the route to Damascus, open for their trade. – The principal deity of the Philistines was Dagon (Marnas), who, like the female divinity Dèrketo (Atargatis), had the form of a fish. Baalzebub

(Beelzebub) was revered as an oracular and prophetic god.

In the decades preceding the period of the Kings in Israel this warlike people vied with the Israelites for predominance in Palestine (Philistia), and indeed ruled over Israel for many years. The Danites in particular suffered at their hands. A lively account of the way in which this continuing war was carried on is given in the heroic tale of Samson (Judges 13 ff.). The Philistine domination was finally broken by the first Kings of Israel, Saul and David; but later Kings had repeatedly to contend with the Philistines.

During the war between Egypt and Assyria the Plain of Philistia, an area of great strategic importance, was constantly fought over, and most of the Philistines were driven out of their homeland. Thereafter the Philistine State disappeared from history, although the individual cities were able to maintain some degree of importance. In the time of Alexander the Great, however, the power of the cities was destroyed. During the wars between the Syrian and Egyptian contenders for Alexander's succession Philistia once again became the scene of bitter fighting. Under the rule of the Maccabees, who succeeded in gaining lasting control of the Plain of Philistia, there was fierce hostility between the Hellenized Philistine coastal cities and the Jews, and the new rulers could not overcome this national hatred: when Jerusalem was destroyed the Philistines with the other enemies of the Israelites took part in its destruction.

Tradition located in Gaza some of the exploits of the Israelite national hero Samson (Judges 16: 3 and 21–30). Thus Samson humiliated the Philistine city of Azza by tearing the town gates from their hinges and carrying them to the top of a hill near Hebron; then, after being betrayed by Delilah, thrown into prison and blinded, he pulled down the pillars of the Temple of Dagon during a great sacrifice, thus killing in his death more Philistines than he had killed during life.

Israelite rule extended as far as Gaza only at the time of its farthest expansion (1 Kings 4: 24). The town was now of considerable size, and was no doubt mainly of importance as a center of trade. Its port was *Maiumas Gazae,* which Constantine the Great raised to the status of a town under the name of *Constantia.* Herodotus calls it Kadylis. The town was taken by Alexander the Great after stubborn resistance. – Since Gaza had allied itself with the enemies of the Jews, Alexander Jannaeus captured the town and destroyed it in 96 B.C. In the time of Gabinius a new town was built on a site farther to the S, probably because of the proximity of more abundant supplies of water. Augustus presented the town to Herod, but after his death it reverted to the Roman province of Syria. As a Roman town Gaza enjoyed a period of peaceful development. Christianity came to the town relatively late, although traditionally Philemon, to whom Paul addressed his epistle, was the first Bishop of Gaza. In the time of Constantine it was still a stronghold of paganism, and it was not until A.D. 400 that the statues and temples of its god Marnas were destroyed by Imperial decree. On the site of the principal temple a large cruciform church was built at the expense of the Empress Eudoxia, wife of Arcadius. In the 5th and 6th c. the school of Christian sophists in Gaza achieved a great reputation, particularly under Procopius of Gaza.

In 634 the town was taken by Caliph Omar. It was a place of importance to the Muslims because Mohammed's grandfather Hashim, traveling to Gaza as a merchant, had died and been buried there. – The Crusaders found the place in ruins. In 1149 Baldwin II built a castle here and entrusted its defence to the Templars. Saladin plundered the town in 1170 but was unable to take the castle; finally in 1187 it fell into his hands, and Richard Cœur de Lion was able to reoccupy it only for a brief perod. In 1244 an army of Muslims and Christians, united in a common cause, were defeated by the Kharesmians near Gaza. Thereafter Gaza lost almost all its importance, though it continued to flourish as a market and trading center for the bedouin.

Napoleon took the town in 1799, and after his withdrawal it declined into complete insignificance. During the First World War it was a major base of the Turks and their German allies. After the war it enjoyed a revival of prosperity under the British Mandate. When the establishment of a new State of Israel was being contemplated Gaza became a center of Arab and Palestinian resistance. In 1948 Britain evacuated the area, whereupon Egypt occupied the town and made it a miltary base, directed against the Zionists, and the capital of the Gaza Strip.

During the Near Eastern War of 1956 Israel occupied the town, but was compelled by pressure from the United Nations, the United States and the Soviet Union to return it to Egypt a year later. In the Six Day War of 1967 Gaza was again occupied by Israeli troops, and since then the town and the Gaza Strip have been under Israeli military administration.

Warning. – In view of the tense political situation it is advisable to have an experienced guide when visiting Gaza and the Gaza Strip. It can be dangerous to speak favorably of the Israelis.

SIGHTS. – In the center of the town is the large Mosque of **Gami el-Kebir**, which stands on the foundations of an aisled 13th c. church dedicated to St John the Baptist. The mosque incorporates architectural elements from the church (e.g. the crosses on the pillars), including even older features which had been built into it. The Muslims added an aisle on the S side and destroyed three apses to make way for the minaret. The pointed vaulting of the nave is borne on three square pilasters and two semi-pilasters. The columns opposite the nave terminate in cushion capitals, above which are an upper row of columns with fine Corinthian capitals. The interior is lit by windows with pointed arches, protected by iron grilles. The W doorway is a fine example of Italian Gothic. On a column at the NE corner of the nave is a relief of a seven-branched candlestick, with Greek and Hebrew inscriptions, from a 3rd c. synagogue. – Near the mosque stands a *Greek Orthodox church,* built on the foundations of an earlier 5th c. building.

SW of Gaza rises a hill of sandstone, **Gebel el-Muntar** (272 ft/83 m), named after a popular local holy man. From here there is a magnificent view over the town in its verdant setting to the desolate sandy wastes of the desert. Visitors are shown the site of the Temple of Dagon which was destroyed by Samson. – Near the railway station is the supposed site of Samson's Tomb.

The remains of a *synagogue* or Jewish dwelling-house, believed to date from the 6th c., have recently been excavated to the S of the town. The mosaic pavements found here show Byzantine influence.

SURROUNDINGS of Gaza. – The town lies near the N end of the **Gaza Strip**, an area of mainly fertile land some 30 miles/50 km long and 4–6 miles/6–10 km wide (total area 140 sq. miles/360 sq. km). This band of low-lying land between the Mediterranean and the rocky hills of the Sinai Desert, well supplied with springs of fresh water, is bounded on the NE by the River Shiqma and on the SW by the River Bezor or Azza. A territory of great strategic importance in ancient times, lying as it did on the route (the Via Maris) from Egypt to Syria and Asia Minor, it was frequently the scene of bloody fighting, and it is now once again a bone of contention between the Egyptians and Palestinians and the Israelis. The present population of the Gaza Strip is some 450,000, including 350,000 Palestinian refugees (200,000 of them living in eight refugee camps). This area was excluded from the scope of the Camp David discussions between Egypt and Israel, and Israel is unwilling to contemplate its return to Egypt in view of its great strategic importance.

From Gaza a road, accompanied by a railway line (now closed), follows the course of the old Roman Via Maris through the sand desert of northern Sinai to the old caravan station of **Khan Yunis** (pop. 55,000), 14 miles/23 km SW, with the ruins of a 14th c. caravanserai. – 6 miles/10 km beyond this is **Rafah** (*Raphia*; pop. 50,000), which was a strong Egyptian fortress and trading-post in the 18th c. B.C. (referred to in the Tell el-Amarna Texts). At *Tell Rafah*, 3 miles/ 5 km NW, Antiochus III was defeated by Ptolemy IV Philopator in 217 B.C.

* **Sinai**: see separate entry.

Gebel el-Dukhan
See under Eastern Desert

Gebelein

Upper Egypt. – Governorate: Qena.
(i) **Tourist Information Office,**
Tourist Bazaar,
Luxor;
tel. 22 15.

ACCESS. – 14 miles/23 km N of Esna on a bad road. – By rail (El-Shaghab Station).

Gebelein ("Two Mountains") is the name of two hills separated by a saddle some 55 yds/50 m wide which lie 25 miles/40 km S of Thebes on the W bank of the Nile: a striking landmark which formerly marked the boundary between the 3rd and 4th nomes of Upper Egypt.

On top of the smaller eastern hill are the conspicuous **Tomb of Sheikh Musa** and remains of a *Temple of Hathor,* surrounded by a defensive wall. The temple, probably founded in the time of the 3rd Dynasty, was restored in the 11th Dynasty, enlarged in the reign of Tuthmosis, later destroyed and then rebuilt in the Ptolemaic period. A number of Greek and demotic papyri were found within the temple precinct. – In the plain W of the hill, near the village of Gebelein, are the remains of ancient **Crocodilopolis**, with a large *crocodile cemetery.*

On the eastern and northern slopes of the higher hill to the W are *cemeteries* dating from the Pre-Dynastic period (Naqada culture) to the end of the Middle Kingdom, but mainly from the First Intermediate Period. Near here was the town of Aphroditespolis or Pathyris (from Per Hathor, "House of Hathor"), which for a time was capital of a nome.

** **Karnak**, ** **Luxor** and ** **Thebes**: see separate entries.

Gebel Katerin
See under St Catherine's Monastery

Gebel Musa
See under St Catherine's Monastery

Gebel Silsila
See under Silsila

Gebel el-Teir
See under Nile

Geziret el-Faraun
See under Sinai

El-Ghardaka
See Hurghada

Giza

Lower Egypt. – Governorate: Giza.
(i) Tourist Information Office,
Tourist Police,
at the Pyramids;
tel. 85 02 59.

Pyramid of Cheops, Giza

HOTELS. – *Mena House Oberoi*, Sharia el-Haram, L, 1000 b.; *Holiday Inn Pyramids*, on the desert road to Alexandria, L, 1072 b.; *SIAG Pyramids*, on the road to Sakkara, L, 702 b.; *Ramada Renaissance*, on the desert road to Alexandria, 500 rooms with a congress centre; *The Oasis Hotel*, on the desert road to Alexandria, I, 520 b.; *Holiday Inn Sphinx*, on the desert road to Alexandria, I, 378 b.; *Pyramids Hotel*, Sharia el-Haram, II; *Lido*, Sharia el-Haram, II, 180 b.; *Sand*, Sharia el-Haram, II, 140 b.; *Vendôme*, Sharia el-Haram, 287, II, 132 b.; *Kino*, Sharia el-Haram, 383, III, 74 b.; *Abu el-Hoal Palace*, Sharia el-Haram, 161, III, 35 b.; *Lotus Hotel & Tourist Village*, Sharia Galal, 30 b, in chalets.

YOUTH HOSTEL: *Kohinoor*, Shari Shukri 8. – CAMP SITE (with chalets) at Pyramids.

ACCESS. – 6 miles/10 km SW of Cairo, road or rail.

The **Pyramids of Giza, the major tourist sight in the immediate surroundings of Cairo, are commandingly situated on the NE margin of the Plateau of the Western (Libyan) Desert. They are the largest and most imposing of the six groups of pyramids set along the edge of the desert over a distance of some 25 miles/40 km. They are approached by the Road to the Pyramids (Shari el-Haram), which runs SW from the Cairo suburb of Giza, increasingly flanked in recent years by high-rise buildings and blocks of flats.

HISTORY. – The Pyramids of Giza, built by rulers of the 4th Dynasty (*c.* 2600–*c.* 2500), rank among the oldest surviving structures erected by man. In Greek and Roman times they were marveled at as the first of the Seven Wonders of the World, and they still exert a

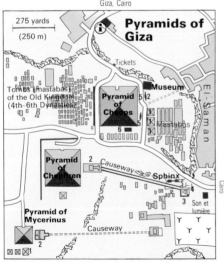

Giza, Cairo

Pyramids of Giza

275 yards
(250 m)

Tickets

Tombs (mastabas)
of the Old Kingdom
(4th–6th Dynasties)

Pyramid
of
Cheops

Museum

Mastabas

El-Saaman

Pyramid of
Chephren

Causeway

Sphinx

Son et
lumière

Pyramid of
Mycerinus

Causeway

Cairo

1 Queens' pyramids
2 Mortuary temple
3 Valley temple
4 Sphinx temple
5 Solar barques
6 Solar Barque Museum

Sections
(from W)

Pyramid of Cheops

Height
450 ft/137·2 m
(originally
481 ft/146·5 m)

H   G   H
F   E
D   B
C   A

Pyramid of Chephren
Height
448 ft/136·5 m
(originally
471 ft/143·5 m)

Pyramid of Mycerinus
Height 203 ft/62 m
(originally 218 ft/66·5 m)

PYRAMID OF CHEOPS
A Present entrance
B Original entrance
C Old tomb chamber
D Queen's Chamber
E Grand Gallery
F King's Chamber
G Relieving chamber
H Air-shafts

Solar Barque Museum

Trench for the solar barque, Pyramid of Cheops

powerful fascination, both as an extraordinary technical achievement and as a demonstration of the power of the Pharaohs, who could marshal tens of thousands of subjects and slaves to construct these colossal monuments. The question of the relationship between the size of a pyramid and the ruler for whom it was built is still unsettled; it seems probable, however, that the size depended on the Pharaoh's personal inclination, power and economic resources. It has not been possible to prove an alternative theory that the size of a pyramid might be increased in stages in the course of a lengthy reign. – Features common to all the pyramids are their situation on the edge of the desert to the W of the Nile and their structure, built up from huge blocks of the local (mostly nummulitic) limestone and enclosed in a casing, originally polished, of fine-grained white limestone or granite. Concealed within the great bulk of the pyramid (in the later period) or underground beneath its base (in the earlier period) were the relatively small tomb chamber, a chamber for the cult of the dead Pharaoh and other chambers for the grave-goods. Also common to all pyramids were the entrance on the N side and the mortuary temple on the E side, with a causeway (originally open, later frequently covered) leading up to it from a valley temple on the edge of the Nile Depression.

The ** **Pyramid of Cheops**, the largest of the group and indeed the most massive of all the Egyptian pyramids, was built by

Cheops or Khufu, and was known to the ancient Egyptians as *Ekhet Khufu* ("Horizon of Khufu"). According to Herodotus (ii, 124–125) 100,000 men worked on its construction for three months every year. The cubic content of this huge structure, excluding the rock foundation and the chambers in the interior, is 3 million cu. yds/2·3 million cu. m (originally 3·3 million cu. yds/2·5 million cu. m). The base measurement is 746 ft/227·5 m (originally 756 ft/230·38 m), the vertical height 450 ft/137·20 m

Pyramid of Chephren

(originally, including the apex, 481 ft/ 146·5m), the angle of inclination 51° 51'.

The ascent of the pyramid (permitted only exceptionally and with the help of a guide) is hazardous and extremely strenuous, since it is necessary to climb steps more than 40 inches/1 m high. From the platform on the top the * view extends W, S and NW over the yellowish-brown expanse of the desert, with the Sphinx, the smaller pyramids of Giza and the more distant groups of pyramids as far as Dahshur, while to the E are the cheerful green fields of the Nile Valley and, beyond the river, the Citadel of Cairo and the Moqattam Hills.

The INTERIOR of the pyramid can also be seen, but the visit is fatiguing (lack of fresh air) and not particularly rewarding. The entrance is by a passage on the N side which was cut by tomb-robbers some 50 ft/15 m below the original entrance. This narrow tunnel leads into the *Grand Gallery*, a long passage (28 ft/8·5 m high, 3–7½ ft/1–2·25 m wide, 154 ft/47 m long), a marvel of skilful masonry, beyond which is the *tomb chamber* (19 ft/5·75 m high, 34 ft/10·50 m long, 17 ft/5·25 m wide), containing the open, empty granite sarcophagus. The mummy has not been found. Further chambers were opened up by French and Japanese archaeologists in 1986–87.

On the E side of the pyramid are three *smaller pyramids* for queens and a

The Sphinx

Rear view of the Sphinx

daughter of the Pharaoh and a large *cemetery* for other relatives. On the S side is a row of large mastabas belonging to high dignitaries. – Excavations on the S and E sides of the pyramid in 1954 brought to light five long cavities for boats, with a *solar barque broken into more than a thousand pieces as a votive offering (now displayed in the new museum on the site). – To the W of the pyramid is the extensive *royal cemetery* for members of the Royal House and high State officials, established during the 4th Dynasty and used until the 6th. As on the E side of the pyramid, the mastabas here are arranged in straight lines.

Some 175 yds/160 m from the SW corner of the Pyramid of Cheops is the *Pyramid of Chephren**, known to the ancient Egyptians as *Wer-Khefre* ("Great is Chephren"). It stands higher than the Pyramid of Cheops and therefore appears larger. It has a vertical height of 448 ft/ 136·5 m (originally 471 ft/143·5 m), a base measurement of 691 ft/210·5 m (originally 706 ft/215·25 m) and an angle of 52° 20'. The total volume of masonry is 2·16 million cu. yds/1·65 million cu. m (originally 2·43 million cu. yds/1·86 million cu. m). A considerable section of the original casing has been preserved on the apex of the pyramid. – The layout of the mortuary temple on the E side of the pyramid can be clearly distinguished.

Immediately NW of the *Valley Temple of Chephren**, a simple but finely built granite structure, is the **Sphinx**, perhaps the most celebrated monument in Egypt after the Pyramid of Cheops: the figure of a recumbent lion hewn from the natural rock with the head of a Pharaoh (Chephren?) wearing the royal headcloth and cobra. The divine image on the breast and other royal insignia are missing. Weathering and deliberate mutilation

have wrought much damage over the course of the centuries. but in spite of this the Sphinx still conveys a powerful impression of majesty and artistic achievement. The total length of the figure is 241 ft/73·5 m, its height some 65 ft./20 m. Restoration work is in progress.

Some 220 yds/200 m SW of the Pyramid of Chephren is the smaller *Pyramid of Mycerinus** (Menkaure), which has a vertical height of 203 ft/62 m (originally 218 ft/66·5 m), a base measurement of 354 ft/108 m and an angle of 51°. The limestone blocks of which it is built are of unusually large size. – On the S side of the pyramid are three smaller pyramids, left unfinished, for relatives of the Pharaoh.

The pyramids and the Sphinx are floodlit at night. **Son et lumière** performances are given in the area to the SE of the Sphinx, along with occassional operatic performances. – A short distance E of the Sphinx is the **Cheops Papyrus Exhibition**, where the making of papyrus by hand is demonstrated and sheets of papyrus, with or without painting, are sold as souvenirs.

Cairo: see separate entry.

Goshen
See under Ismailia Canal

Hawara
See under Fayyum

Heliopolis
(Old Heliopolis)

Lower Egypt. – Governorate: Cairo,
ⓘ **Tourist Information Office,**
Misr Travel Tower,
Cairo – Abbasia;
tel. 82 60 16.

ACCOMMODATION: see under Cairo.

ACCESS. – 7½ miles/12 km NE of Cairo by road (bus services).

On the NE outskirts of Cairo, amid well-cultivated fields near El-Matariya, below the Hill of El-Hisn, are the remains of the ancient Egyptian town of Yunu, known in the Greek period as Heliopolis (not to be confused with the Cairo district of New Heliopolis), which is referred

to in the Old Testament under its Coptic name of On: thus in the Book of Genesis (41: 45) the father of Joseph's wife, Potipherah (Egyptian Pede-pre, "he whom Re has given"), is described as a Priest of On. Heliopolis-On, one of the oldest cities in Egypt, was capital of the 3rd nome of Lower Egypt and from the Old Kingdom onwards the spiritual and ecclesiastical center of the whole country.

HISTORY. – The local deities were the falcon-headed Re-Harakhty, the sun god, in whose honor the Greeks named the city Heliopolis ("City of the Sun"), and the human-headed Atum, with the sacred Mnevis bull. To these deities was dedicated the famous temple, the "House of Re", built by the 1st King of the 12th Dynasty, Amenemhet I, on the site of an earlier temple. Two large obelisks were set up in front of the temple by his son and successor Sesostris (Senwosret) I in celebration of his jubilee. Much of the religious literature of Egypt originated with the priests of Heliopolis, and their doctrines were widely disseminated throughout the country at a very early period, making Re-Harakhty one of the most highly venerated Egyptian deities. During the Greek period they still enjoyed a great reputation for wisdom: Herodotus conversed with them, and Plato is said to have spent 13 years with them.

Under the New Kingdom the Temple of Heliopolis was the largest and wealthiest in Egypt after the Temple of Amun at Thebes. When Strabo visited Egypt (24–20 B.C.) the city was destroyed and deserted, but the temple still stood intact apart from some minor damage attributed to Cambyses; even the priests' houses and the lodgings occupied by Plato and his friend Eudoxus were still shown to the traveler. The priestly school, however, had been closed, and only a few officiating priests and guides for visitors still lived there.

There are only scanty remains of the ancient city (estimated to have been some 1200 yds/1100 m long and 550 yds/500 m across) or of the Temple of Re-Harakhty, the buildings having been demolished to provide stone for the building of Cairo. The archaeological exploration of the site is made difficult, and sometimes impossible, by the extent to which the area has been built up. Scattered about in the fields are a few remnants of the double wall of brick which once surrounded the city. All that remains of the temple is a solitary **obelisk** (Arabic *El-Misalla*) of red Aswan granite, 67 ft/ 20·42 m high. Each of the four sides bears the same inscription in large hieroglyphic characters, recording that Senroswet (Sesostris) I, "King of Upper and Lower Egypt, lord of the diadems and son of the Sun, whom the (divine) spirits of On love" set up the obelisk on his first Sed festival (a kind of royal jubilee). The pyramidion at

the tip of the obelisk was originally gilded, as were the falcons at the beginning of the inscriptions. The counterpart of this obelisk (for the obelisks in front of temples always stood in pairs) fell in the 12th c. In addition to these two Heliopolis had many other obelisks, one of which now stands in the Piazza del Popolo in Rome. – It is known, in the light of modern research, that Heliopolis possessed at least ten temples, all probably associated with the principal temple or perhaps even forming part of it.

In the SE corner of the temple precinct tombs of High Priests of the 6th Dynasty were found, in El-Matariya tombs of the Late Period. 1 mile/1·5 km NE, at *Tell el-Tawil*, were bull burials. – In the desert some 3 miles/5 km E of the obelisk is the **Necropolis** of Heliopolis, dating from the Middle and New Kingdoms. A notable feature of the Middle Kingdom tombs was the large numbers of weapons found as grave-goods.

In front of the Chapel of the Virgin in the nearby village of **El-Matariya**, a popular place of pilgrimage in the Middle Ages, is the so-called *Virgin's Tree*, a sycamore planted in 1672 in replacement of an older tree. According to legend the Virgin and Child rested under the shade of a tree here during their flight into Egypt. The little garden in which the tree stands is watered from a spring, said to have been called into being by the infant Jesus, which yields good fresh water, whereas the water of all the other springs in the area is slightly brackish. The legend of the Virgin's tree links up with an older cult; for the ancient Egyptians venerated a tree in Heliopolis beneath which Isis was believed to have suckled the infant Horus.

New Heliopolis: see under Cairo.

Helwan

Lower Egypt. – Governorate: Cairo.
Population: 40,000.
ⓘ **Tourist Information Office,**
   Misr Travel Tower,
   Cairo – Abbasia;
   tel. 82 60 16.

HOTELS. – *Excelsior*, IV, 61 b.; *Evergreen*, IV, 43 b.; *Des Princes*, IV, 31 b.

ACCESS. – 16 miles/25 km S of Cairo by road (regular bus service); by rail from Cairo (Helwan line).

The spa of Helwan (Arabic Hamma-mat Helwan, French Hélouan-les-Bains), long a health resort of international reputation, lies some 16 miles/25 km S of Cairo on a plateau enclosed on the SW and SE by steep limestone hills and lying some 165 ft/50 m above the Valley of the Nile, 2 miles/3 km away. There are many viewpoints offering extensive prospects of the Nile Valley and the Pyramids of Saqqara, Dahshur and even Giza. On this favored spot, with its hot springs, its agreeable climate and its beautiful scenery, an artificial oasis was created in the second half of the 19th c. by Khedive Ismail and his son Taufiq, involving the transport of fertile soil from a considerable distance.

Helwan owes its reputation as a spa both to its sulphur and saline springs (91 °F/33 °C), probably already known in ancient times and brought into use again in 1871–72, and to its warm, dry desert climate. The springs, which are similar in chemical composition to those of Aix-les-Bains in France, are used in the treatment of rheumatic conditions, skin diseases and catarrhs. The climate, with little variation over the day, is beneficial to sufferers from lung and kidney complaints and in all cases where cold and damp must be avoided. In consequence of the stony soil and the strong sunshine the air is unusually pure and dust-free.

The rapid industrial development of the town and surrounding area in recent years has largely destroyed the image of the fashionable international spa of the turn of the century. The pattern of the area is now set by its large metalworking plants (aircraft and automobile assembly), factories producing cement, lime and fertilizers, a large power-station and a steelworks using iron from the opencast mines in the Bahriya Oasis.

SIGHTS. – The town is laid out on a regular plan. On the S side is the **Bath Establishment** (1899, rebuilt 1911), in Moorish style, which has a thermal swimming-bath and a variety of therapeutic facilities. To the E is the beautiful **Japanese Garden**. – NE of the town, on a rocky plateau (374 ft/114 m), is the *Observatory* and weather station.

SURROUNDINGS of Helwan. – 2 miles/3 km N are the **quarries** of *Masara* and *Tura*, which yielded the fine white limestone used for facing pyramids and mastabas and for other ancient buildings down to the Ptolemaic period. The quarries still in operation use opencast methods, but the quarrymen of the Pharaohs tunneled into the hillside and excavated large underground chambers at the points where they found good stone, leaving pillars of rock to support the roof. A few inscriptions recording the opening of new chambers, demotic graffiti and reliefs (in the names of Amenemhet, Amosis, Amenophis III and Nectanebo II) have been preserved. The Egyptian name of the quarries was Royu or Troyu, which the Greeks corrupted into *Troia* – believing, according to Strabo, that this area had been settled by Trojan prisoners who had followed Menelaus to Egypt and remained there.

An attractive excursion from Helwan is to the *Wadi Hof, 2 miles/3 km N, which is noted for its scenic beauty, its curious fossils (examples of which can be seen in the Cairo museums) and the desert vegetation which springs to life after rain. – At the near end of the wadi is the prehistoric settlement of *El-Omari,* the cemetery of which has been excavated. – If time permits it is well worth making a detour into the *Reil Gorge,* with grandiose scenery at the head of the valley.

2 miles/3 km of Helwan a 1st Dynasty *cemetery* (5000 burials) has been excavated.

Another worthwhile trip is to the **Wadi Risheid**, SE of Helwan (guide advisable). The valley gradually closes in to form a very picturesque gorge, at the end of which, lying at different levels one above the other, are several watering-points used by the bedouin.

Some 6 miles/10 km SE of Helwan is the **Wadi Gerawi**, a desert valley running E–W between steep limestone walls in which Schweinfurth discovered the remains of an ancient dam, the *Sadd el-Qarafa,* dating from the Early Old Kingdom (4th Dynasty?). The dam was designed to pound the water which flowed down the valley in rainy winters and so provide drinking-water for the workmen employed in the alabaster quarries 2½ miles/4 km to the E. Built of undressed stone with a facing of limestone blocks on the E side, it was 34 ft/10·25 m high, 150 ft/45 m thick and 72–87 yds/66–80 m long, traversing the whole width of the valley. NW of the dam, high up on the hillside, were found the remains of stone huts.

* * **Cairo**: see separate entry.

Heracleopolis Magna
See under Beni Suef

Hermopolis Magna
See under Mallawi

Hermopolis Parva

See Damanhur

Hibis

See under Kharga Oasis

Hieraconpolis

See Kom el-Ahmar

Hurghada/El-Ghardaka

Red Sea Frontier District.
Population: 5000.

ⓘ **Tourist Information Office,**
Misr Travel Tower,
Cairo – Abbasia;
tel. 82 60 16.

ACCOMMODATION. – *Sheraton*, Shira Giza 48 b.; Orman Tower Buildings, L, 161 b., seawater swimming-pool, beach. – *Club Magawish* holiday village, 9 miles/14 km away at Magawish, 408 b. in 204 chalets, L. – *Club Méditerranée*, El Samaka Village.

Sheraton Hotel

Magawish holiday village

It should be borne in mind that Hurghada lies on the edge of the desert and that there may be difficulty in the supply of services such as water and electricity, which may occasionally be cut off even in the luxury establishments listed. – On any excursion in the surrounding area it is essential to take sufficient water and fuel.

SPORT and RECREATION. – *Scuba diving (limited facilities for hire of equipment), snorkeling, fishing, sailing, wind-surfing, swimming, table tennis.

ACCESS. – Road from Suez along the Red Sea coast (245 miles/395 km); road from Qena, in the Nile Valley, across the Eastern (Arabian) Desert to Bur Safaga, then N along the coast (130 miles/210 km). – Bus services. – By air from Cairo (1 hour).

Hurghada – a distant view

Boats on Magawish beach

Half-way down the Egyptian Red Sea coast, on a promontory projecting into the sea, is the small but growing resort and water-sports center of *Hurghada (El-Ghardaka), chief town and administrative center of the Red Sea Frontier District.

Here beautiful and still-empty beaches of fine sand extend along the coast, against the magnificent backdrop of the desert hills, glowing red in the morning and evening sun. To the SW, farther away, is *Gebel el-Shayib* (7176 ft/2187 m), the highest peak in African Egypt (i.e. excluding Sinai). – With its perpetually warm and dry climate and its unique facilities for diving and snorkeling enthusiasts Hurghada is now attracting steadily increasing numbers of visitors both in summer and in winter.

Before the tourist trade reached this remote spot on the Red Sea coast it was the center of Egypt's principal oilfield, surpassed only quite recently by the still more productive oilfields in Sinai. The headquarters of the oil installations lie 2 miles/3 km NW of the harbor.

Lying off the *beaches are more than 30 small islands and islets and innumerable *coral reefs, some of them rising from great depths. With their abundance of marine plant and animal life these are a paradise for divers and fishermen. From the islands and reefs the visitors can observe, in the beautifully clear water, all the richness and variety of this underwater life. – Also popular are camping trips to the uninhabited islands (warm clothing should be taken).

6 miles/10 km N is an interesting **Oceanographical Institute**, with an *Aquarium* (Red Sea animal life) and a *Museum* containing, among much else, the last manatees caught in the Red Sea.

Red Sea, Suez, *St Antony's Monastery and *St Paul's Monastery: see separate entries. – Quarries on *Mons Porphyrites* and *Mons Claudianus*: see under Eastern Desert.

Iseum
See Behbeit el-Hagara

El-Iskandariya
See Alexandria

Ismailia

Lower Egypt. – Governorate: Ismailia.
Population: 180,000.
(i) **Tourist Information Office,**
Misr Travel Tower,
Cairo – Abbasia;
tel. 82 60 16.

HOTELS. – *ETAP Ismailia*, I, 286 b.; *El-Salam Touristic*, III, 103 b.; *Nefertari*, III, 56 b.; *El-Mossaferin*, IV.

ACCESS. – By road from Cairo (87 miles/140 km SW) along the Ismailia Canal, from El-Zagazig (50 miles/80 km W), from Port Said (50 miles/80 km N) or from Suez (53 miles/85 km S); bus services. – By rail from Cairo, Port Said or Suez.

The attractive town of Ismailia, headquarters of the Suez Canal Authority, a pilot station and a traffic junction halfway between Port Said and Suez as well as the seat of the faculties of Science and Medicine of the Suez Canal University, lies on the N side of Lake Timsah ("Crocodile Lake"). A town of shady avenues, flower-linked promenades and luxuriant parks and gardens, it was founded by Lesseps

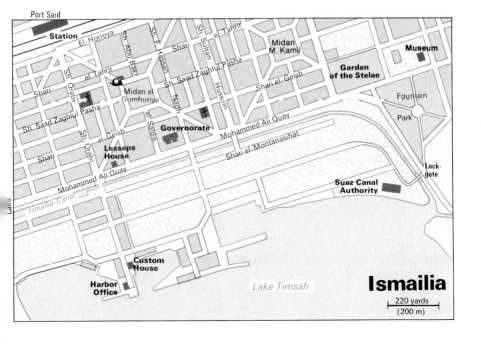

Ismailia

Street scene in Ismailia

in 1863 at the end of the Ismailia Canal (Freshwater Canal, constructed 1858–63 to provide a supply of drinking-water) as the main center of operations during the construction of the Suez Canal and named after Khedive Ismail. After the completion of the canal the town lost its importance but later enjoyed a revival as a British garrison town. In 1956, and again in 1967, Ismailia suffered severe damage during the military operations of those years, when most of the population had to be evacuated. The destruction caused by these wars has only partly been made good.

The town, laid out on a regular plan, lies to the N of the Ismailia Canal (see next entry), which, accompanied by the Mohammed Ali Quay, extends along the N side of the harbor with its port installations, turns down its E side and, after a lock-gate opposite the offices of the Suez Canal Authority, flows into Lake Timsah. – From the *railway station* Sharia Orabi leads S and crosses the canal to reach the harbor (Harbor Office; Custom House). – A busy shopping street runs SE from the station by way of the **Midan el-Gumhuriya** (gardens) to the Mohammed Ali Quay.

In the * **Garden of the Stelae** (admission only by special arrangement) are a number of large stelae from Tell el-Maskhuta. Of particular interest are a granite stela in the name of Ramesses II with a relief of the King offering an image of Maat, goddess of truth, to the falcon-headed Re-Harakhty and another relief of the King before Atum on the back;

Ramesses II between the gods Khepri and Atum; recumbent sphinxes, including one dedicated by Ramesses II to Atum and Harmachis; a fragment of a chapel dedicated by Ramesses II in the Temple of Tell el-Maskhuta; the black granite lid of a sacrophagus belonging to a high palace official from Tell el-Maskhuta; and a granite chapel from El-Arish with an inscription relating to the rule of the gods on earth.

To the E of the Garden of the Stelae is a small but very interesting **Museum** containing antiquities from the Canal Zone. So much destruction was caused by war and political disturbances that little material of the early period has survived. – Outside the entrance to the museum is a sphinx found during the construction of the Canal. On the walls of the museum are displayed a number of mosaic pavements, including one with representations of Phaedra and Hippolytus and the Dionysiac mysteries and with Greek verses, surrounded by birds. Other exhibits include Graeco-Egyptian terracottas and bronze figures (many of them from Tell el-Maskhuta). In the museum garden are fragments of a stela set up by Darius to commemorate the completion of the first freshwater canal 5 miles/8 km N of Suez, with a hieroglyphic inscription and cuneiform inscriptions in the Persian, Babylonian and Elamite languages.

SURROUNDINGS of Ismailia. – Some 14 miles/22 km W of the town, in the Wadi Tumilat (see under Ismailia Canal), is the **Tell el-Maskhuta**, the site of the Egyptian stronghold of *Tiyeku*, which was excavated by E. Naville in 1883. This is believed by many authorities to be the Biblical *Pithom* (Egyptian Per-Atum, "House of Atum"), one of the two cities which the Israelites were compelled to build for their Egyptian taskmasters (Exodus 1: 11), which became the capital of the 8th nome of Lower Egypt. The storerooms found near the temple – deep rectangular chambers without doors into which the grain was poured from above – are thought to date from the time of Ramesses II and may possibly be the "treasure cities" (storehouses) mentioned in the Bible. Alternatively it has been suggested that these structures were part of a fort.

** **Suez Canal**: see separate entry.

Ismailia Canal

Lower Egypt. – Governorates: Ismailia, Sharqiya and Cairo.

The Ismailia Canal or Freshwater Canal, constructed in 1858–63 to

supply the villages on the Suez Canal with drinking-water and enlarged in 1876, is to a large extent a modern replacement of an ancient canal dating from the Middle Kingdom which ran E from the Nile, watered the Biblical land of Goshen with its various branches and flowed into the Bitter Lakes, making them sweet (as Strabo tells us) and connecting them with the Red Sea.

The **Wadi Tumilat**, through which the Ismailia Canal runs over a considerable section of its course, can be regarded as the most easterly arm of the Nile. In the Early Historical Period it was already navigable during the Nile flood by boats of shallow draft, providing a means of transport for both people and goods to and from the E coast of Africa and Syria. It was much favored by the Pharaohs of the Middle Kingdom, who improved and deepened the channel. Ramesses II was particularly active in this respect, building on the banks of the canal the towns of Pe-Ramses and Pithom, which ranked with Bubastis as important trading and market centers. The remains of steeply battered masonry embankments show the canal to have been 150 ft/45 m wide and 16 ft/5 m deep. – In later times the canal fell into disrepair, and the frequent incursions into the Wadi Tumilat by warlike nomadic tribes made it unsafe. In the 7th c. B.C. Necho set about improving it, but according to Herodotus (ii, 159) abandoned the idea because of an unfavorable prophecy.

A century later Darius I completed the work begun by Necho and set up stelae along its banks commemorating this achievement; one such stela can be seen in the Ismailia Museum. Later the canal was restored by Trajan and became known as "Trajan's River" *(Amnis Traianus).* It retained its importance into the period of the Caliphs, who used it for transporting grain from the Nile Valley to Medina. In the 8th c., however, the canal was filled in for reasons of security, and thereafter it fell into oblivion until its rediscovery in 1798.

Although the present canal is navigable, it serves mainly to provide water for irrigation. It branches off the Nile at Cairo, runs between the Arabian Plateau to the N and the Land of Goshen to the S, just beyond Abu Hammad cuts across the old fresh-water canal coming from El-Zagazig and then continues E, parallel with this canal, along the Wadi Tumilat for rather more than 30 miles/50 km. At Nefisha a branch runs S to Suez, and at Moaskar-Ismailia another branch goes N to Port Said.

Ismailia and ****Suez Canal**: see separate entries.

El-Kab

Upper Egypt. – Governorate: Qena.
(i) **Tourist Information Office,**
Tourist Bazaar,
Luxor;
tel. 22 15.

ACCESS. – By road from Edfu (12½ miles/20 km S), Luxor (53 miles/85 km N) or Esna (19 miles/30 km N). – By rail to El-Mahamid Station, then 1½/2·5 km SE. – Nile cruise ships.

The remains of* El-Kab, the ancient Nekhab, lie on the E bank of the Nile between the railway and the river. In Pre-Dynastic and Early Dynastic times Nekhab was capital of the kingdom of Upper Egypt, and it continued to be one of the country's leading cities; in the Ptolemaic period it was capital of the 3rd nome of Upper Egypt, later the Latopolitan nome. The town goddess was Nekhbet, who was represented either as a vulture or as a woman with the crown of Upper Egypt. Corresponding to the cobra goddess Uto of Lower Egypt, she was the protective

The Biblical Land of **Goshen** lay to the S of the Ismailia Canal, roughly in the triangular area between El-Zagazig, Bilbeis and Abu Hammad. It is first mentioned in Genesis 45: 10, when Pharaoh says to Joseph: "And thou shalt dwell in the Land of Goshen, and thou shalt be near unto me, thou, and thy children, and thy children's children, and thy flocks, and thy herds, and all that thou hast." There are further references to Goshen in Genesis 46: 28–29 and 47: 1, 6 and 27; and Exodus 1: 11 names the cities in which the Israelites were compelled to work for Pharaoh: "Therefore they did set over them taskmasters to afflict them with their burdens. And they built for Pharaoh treasure cities, Pithom and Raamses." – The Land of Goshen was part of the old Egyptian province of Arabia. Its capital, *Persopt* (Greek *Pharcusa*) was discovered by the Swiss archaeologist E. Naville at *Saft el-Hina,* near *Suwa.* The remains have now completely disappeared, but a few ancient stones may be seen built into the walls of modern houses.

deity of the kingdom, the principal goddess of Upper Egypt and the goddess of childbirth. The Greeks, therefore, identified her with their goddess Eileithyia and named the town Eileithyiaspolis.

The *ruins of ancient Nekhab, lying close to the Nile, are surrounded by a massive *enclosure wall* of sun-dried bricks, probably dating from the Middle Kingdom, which has been destroyed by the river only on the SW side. The walls, of remarkable thickness (38 ft/11·50 m), enclose a rectangular area measuring 590 yds/540 m by 625 yds/570 m, with gates, approached by ramps, on the E, N and S sides. The wall on the N side cuts across an ancient necropolis. Within this enclosure, occupying only about a quarter of its area, is a smaller rectangular enclosure, also surrounded by a double wall (the line of which can be easily traced), containing the principal temples. Within the outer enclosure are a number of other temples, including the Temple of Nekhbet, which was frequently altered and rebuilt down to the time of the 28th Dynasty, together with a birth-house and a sacred lake, as well as temples of Tuthmosis III, Amenophis II and Ramesses II.

Outside the E gate in the outer wall are the remains of a small chapel built of sandstone which is ascribed to Nectanebo I or II. From here a path leads E ($\frac{1}{2}$ hour's walk) to a ruined *Chapel of Ramesses II*, known locally as El-Hammam, "The Bath". This was built by Setaw, Governor of Nubia, who is depicted on the entrance doorway and on the interior walls on each side of the entrance. On the side walls Ramesses II is seen in the presence of Thoth and Horus; on the rear wall are baboons (animals sacred to Thoth) and the figures of men in the attitude of prayer.

Farther E, roughly half-way between the Chapel of Ramesses and the Temple of Amenophis, which soon comes into view, two rocks rear up out of the plain. They bear many inscriptions and figures of animals, most of which are thought to date from the 6th Dynasty and were probably the work of priests. – Some 15 minutes' walk farther E is the charming little *Temple of Amenophis III, just over 50 ft/16 m long, which is dedicated to Nekhbet, "mistress of the entrance to the valley". It consists of a vestibule of the Ptolemaic period (now destroyed) and

the main chamber, the roof of which was borne on four 16-sided columns with Hathor heads. The names of Amenophis III, Amun and Nekhbet and several figures of gods were defaced in the reign of Amenophis IV and restored under Sethos I; many of them were again renewed in the Ptolemaic period.

On the doorway into the main chamber are a votive inscription and a figure of Amenophis III. The outer walls bear only a few later inscriptions and representations of ships. To the right of the door Khaemweset, Ramesses II's son, in the presence of his father, commemorating the King's 5th Jubilee, in the 41st year of his reign. A modern hieroglyphic inscription is dated in the "13th year of his majesty, the lord of the world, Napoleon III"; and even later is an inscription in the name of the Comte de Chambord, Pretender to the French throne (d. 1883). On the paving are representations of footprints scratched by pilgrims.

The coloring of the scenes inside the chamber is well preserved. To left and right of door Amenophis III and his father Tuthmosis IV are seen seated at table. – Left-hand wall: Amenophis III making offerings to the sacred boat, which is decorated with falcons' heads; Amenophis offering incense and water to Nekhbet; Amun (blue) embracing the King and holding the hieroglyph for "life" to his nostrils. – Rear wall, to the left and right of the niche: Amenophis III making offerings to Nekhbet. – Right-hand wall: the falcon-headed Horus presenting the hieroglyph for "life" to the King, who stands in front of him; the King offering two wine-jars to Nekhbet; the King sacrificing to the sacred boat. Beside these scenes are demotic inscriptions in red, written by visitors to the temple. – The frieze and the decoration of the architraves consist of Amenophis's names alternating with heads of Hathor. – At the base of the walls are bulls in a marsh.

From the Temple of Amenophis it is a 15-minute walk in the direction of the Nile to the **Rock Temple** on the right-hand side of the valley, recognizable from a distance by the long flight of steps leading up to it. The temple, also dedicated to Nekhbet, was built in the reign of Ptolemy VIII Euergetes II and decorated with reliefs and inscriptions in the reign of Ptolemy IX Soter II. The staircase has 41 steps hewn from the rock, flanked on each side by a massive balustrade.

From the platform at the top of the steps we pass through a doorway into a *vestibule* just under 33 ft/10 m wide, the roof of which was supported on columns with elaborate floral capitals. From here a door, the right-hand side of which is still standing, leads into a smaller *hall* 20 ft/6 m wide, which also had columns with screens between them; the floor is littered with fragments of stone. Beyond this is the *rock chapel,* originally a tomb chamber of the New Kingdom. It has a vaulted roof, in the middle of which are vultures hovering. Round the top of the walls runs a frieze consisting of the name of Ptolemy IX Soter II between heads of Hathor; below these are inscriptions and reliefs (largely destroyed) depicting the King and Queen in the presence of various deities.

Some 550 yds/500 m N of the site of Nekhab are a number of important *rock tombs, mostly dating from the early 18th Dynasty, which are of particular interest for their excellently executed reliefs depicting scenes of everyday life. Altogether there are 31 tombs, situated close together on the S side of the hill, but only six of them repay a visit.

The *Tomb of Pahery,* Nomarch of El-Kab, is recognizable from a distance by its wide entrance. It dates from the reign of Tuthmosis III, and is notable for the well-preserved coloring of the reliefs, which depict scenes from the life of the dead man. The faces of all the figures have been chiseled out.

In the platform in front of the entrance is a deep mummy-shaft. A badly ruined doorway leads into the *tomb chamber.* Entrance wall, to the left: the dead man with a long staff; above, a sailing-ship. – Left-hand wall: (above) the dead man watching harvesting operations (plowing, sowing, mowing with sickles, collecting and binding the sheaves, oxen treading out the corn, winnowing the grain, bringing in the crop in sacks); (below) the dead man inspecting his livestock (cattle, donkeys, etc.) and superintending the weighing of gold rings and the shipping of his grain; (beyond this, above) Pahery holding on his lap the young Prince Wedjmose, whose tutor he was; Pahery and his wife sitting in a kiosk receiving flowers and fruit; (above this) vintage scenes; (below) Pahery watching his fowlers and fishermen; the birds and fish being prepared for a meal; mending of the nets; (farther right, in five rows) burial of Pahery and funeral rites. – In the rear wall is a niche, with seated figures of Pahery with his wife and mother; on the side walls of the niche are various persons at table. – Right-hand wall: Pahery and his wife at a banquet (below the chair, a tame monkey), with their son officiating as priest; opposite them, relatives, also at table; (bottom row) a female harpist and flute-player; (farther right) Pahery and his wife praying and making offerings. In this wall is a later door opening into two other chambers.

To the right of Pahery's tomb is the *Tomb of Ahmose Pennekhbet,* who had a distinguished military career in the reigns of the first kings of the New Kingdom, from Amosis to Tuthmosis III. It consists of a single vaulted chamber, all the reliefs in which have been destroyed. In the doorway is an inscription giving the dead man's biography.

To the left of Pahery's tomb is the *Tomb of Setaw,* a High Priest of Nekhbet. It dates from the reign of Ramesses IX (20th Dynasty), and is thus 400 years later than the other tombs, though constructed on the same pattern and decorated in the same style as the others.

The left-hand wall is much damaged: nothing can now be distinguished but four sacred boats, apparently sailing to a royal festival. – Right-hand wall, to the left: Setaw and his wife at a meal; below the bench is a monkey; in front of them their son-in-law, in a panther skin, officiating as priest; opposite them, in rows, their relatives at table; below, the painter himself, identifiable by his palette. Part of this scene has been destroyed by a later door opening into a side chamber. Farther right, Setaw and his wife making offerings. – On the rear wall is a badly damaged stela.

Farther to the left is the *Tomb of Ahmose,* an Admiral, which is notable for a long inscription recording the dead man's exploits, in particular the part he played in the war of liberation against the Hyksos.

The tomb consists of a rectangular chamber with a vaulted roof and a side chamber, entered by a door in the right-hand wall, which contains the mummy-shaft. *Main chamber,* right-hand wall: the dead man, with staff and scepter, accompanied by his grandson Pahery, a painter, who constructed the tomb. In front of them is the inscription, which is continued on the entrance wall. The scenes on the left-hand wall are unfinished: note the grid of red lines used by the artist in setting out his work. The rear wall, with the dead man and his wife seated at a meal on the right and rows of relatives on the left, is badly damaged.

Farther W is the *Tomb of Reni,* a Nomarch and High Priest of the early 18th Dynasty. The reliefs are similar to those in Pahery's tomb but less finely executed.

Left-hand wall: harvest scenes; the dead man supervising the counting of livestock in his nome (including pigs – curiously, since the Egyptians abhorred pork); the dead man and his wife at a meal, with relatives opposite them. Right-hand wall: burial of Reni and funeral rites. In the rear wall is a niche with a seated figure of the dead man, now totally destroyed.

Still farther to the left, at the W end of the necropolis, are three *tombs* which probably date from before the New Kingdom. One of them, badly damaged, belonged to *Ahnofru,* a lady attached to the royal harem, and her husband. The second, a chamber with a vaulted roof, belonged to a man named *Debi* and his wife, who was also attached to the harem. The third, consisting of a vaulted main chamber with a finely decorated roof and a subsidiary chamber containing the mummy-shaft, dates from the reign of Sobkhotep II (13th Dynasty).

A short distance W of the hill containing the tombs is a small Temple of Tuthmosis III, now completely ruined.

Opposite El-Kab on the W bank of the Nile is the site of **Hieraconpolis** (see Kom el-Ahmar).

Edfu and *Esna: see separate entries.

New Kalabsha, seen from the High Dam, with Lake Nasser in the foreground

Kalabsha

Upper Egypt. – Governorate: Aswan.

(i) **Tourist Information Office,**
Tourist Bazaar,
Aswan;
tel. 32 97.

ACCESS. – By road from Aswan (8 miles/13 km N).

¾ mile/1 km S of the W end of the **Aswan High Dam, on the western shore of Lake Nasser, is the newly created archaeological site of New Kalabsha, on which the temples of Kalabsha, Beit el-Wali and Kertassi, saved from the rising waters of the lake by a rescue operation which attracted international support, have been re-erected.**

The large and picturesque *Temple of Kalabsha originally stood 30 miles/50 km farther S at the site of ancient Talmis,* now submerged under the waters of Lake Nasser. The most imposing monument in Nubia after the Rock Temple of Abu Simbel, it was built in the time of Augustus on the site of an earlier temple founded by Amenophis II and refounded by one of the Ptolemies. The decoration of the temple with reliefs and inscriptions was never completed; the reliefs that do exist are crudely executed and have frequently been misinterpreted. The temple was dedicated to the god Mandulis, but Osiris and Isis were also worshiped here. After the coming of Christianity it was converted into a church.

The temple, 243 ft/74 m long by 108 ft/33 m wide, is approached by a *causeway* of dressed stone, 104 ft/ 31·6 m long and 26 ft/8 m wide, which has a rectangular projection at its lower end. From the upper end a flight of low steps leads up to a long terrace in front of the pylon.

The **Pylon**, the main entrance to the temple precinct, is slightly askew to the axis of the causeway and the temple itself. It is excellently preserved, but has no

In the Kalabsha Temple

relief decoration apart from two figures of deities in the doorway. Each tower has a vertical groove for a flagstaff.

The **Court** between the pylon and the vestibule was surrounded on three sides by colonnades, now represented by four columns with elaborate floral capitals on the N and S sides. On the inner side of the S tower of the pylon are three doors, the two more northerly leading into two small chambers, the third giving access to a staircase which ascends in three flights to the roof. There is another staircase in the N tower. In the N and S colonnades are four doors leading into small chambers in the thickness of the walls; the N colonnade also has a fifth doorway giving access to the outer passage round the temple and to a crypt. On the rear side of the court is the imposing façade of the vestibule, which is entered by the large central doorway; between the columns of four stone screens.

On the first screen, at the left-hand end of the façade, Thoth and Horus are shown pouring the consecrated water, in the form of hieroglyphs for "life" and "well-being", over the King, with the god Harsiesis of Talmis seated on one side. – On the first screen on the right is a Greek inscription recording a decree by Aurelius Besarion, also named Amonius, Governor of Ombos and Elephantine, ordering the owners of pigs to drive them away from the temple. The decree is probably to be dated to A.D. 248–249. – On the second column on the right, between two Greek votive inscriptions, is a long inscription in Meroitic cursive script. – The most interesting inscription, however, is one at the right-hand end of the façade, the *memorial inscription of Silko*, who describes himself as King of the Nubians and all the Ethiopians (*c.* 5th c. A.D.) and celebrates, in bad Greek, his victory over the Blemmyes, whom he defeated "from Primis to Talmis, advancing as far as Taphis [Tafa] and Talmis".

The **Vestibule** has 12 columns with elaborate floral capitals. The roof has fallen in. Most of the reliefs depict the Emperor in the presence of the gods; two, on the rear wall to the left of the door, are particularly notable. One of these shows one of the Ptolemies presenting a field to Mandulis, Isis and a third deity; the other (to the right) shows Amenophis II, founder of the original temple, offering wine to Min and Mandulis. On the screens between the columns to the left of the entrance is a later Christian painting of the three youths in the fiery furnace.

Beyond the vestibule are *three rooms,* one behind the other, which contain reliefs depicting the Emperor in the presence of the gods of Talmis and other deities, with well-preserved colors. In the first room, at the foot of the walls, are local deities with their offerings. Many of the inscriptions are merely sketched in red. Smaller chambers are built into the left-hand (S) walls of the first and second rooms, and the S wall of the first room also has a staircase leading up to the roof of the third room, from which short flights of steps mount to the higher roofs of the front part of the temple. Another staircase leads from the roof of the second room to the outer wall; and from this a few steps on the left lead down to a *chapel* in the thickness of the wall, which has two chambers (the second one with a crypt) and was probably dedicated to the cult of Osiris.

From the court and the vestibule doors lead into the *inner passage* round the temple. On the outer walls of the temple are lions' heads (unfinished) as waterspouts. On the rear wall is a large relief of the Emperor

in the presence of the gods, with smaller reliefs below it; and opposite these, on the enclosure wall, are two representations of the god Mandulis, which were probably originally protected by a small wooden chapel. On the S side is a well-preserved *Nilometer.*

At the SW corner of the *outer passage* round the temple, the western wall of which was built into the rock, is a *chapel* (perhaps a birth-house) consisting of an open court (unfinished) enclosed by columns and stone screens and a rock-cut chamber, only the doorway of which has reliefs, depicting the Emperor in the presence of the gods. – At this NE corner is another well-preserved *chapel,* probably belonging to the earlier temple of the Ptolemaic period.

Temple of Kalabsha   ⟶ N

After the construction of the first Aswan Dam (see under Aswan) the Kalabsha Temple, like the one at Philae, was under water for most of the year, and the projected High Dam (Sadd el-Ali) threatened to submerge it permanently. It was resolved, therefore, to remove the temple to another site, and in a major rescue operation executed and financed by West Germany it was taken down and transported in 13,000 pieces to its present site, 30 miles/50 km farther N, where it was re-erected. During the demolition of the temple blocks belonging to a temple doorway of the Graeco-Roman period, decorated with reliefs, were found built into the fabric. This was reconstructed and presented to the Egyptian Museum in West Berlin as an expression of gratitude.

To the NW of the Kalabsha Temple is the *Rock Temple of Beit el-Wali* or

"House of the Wali" (holy man), also rescued from the rising waters of Lake Nasser with financial assistance from the United States. The temple, built by Ramesses II, consists of a vestibule, a transverse chamber and the sanctuary.

The lower walls of the *Vestibule,* hewn from the rock, are still standing; the upper parts, masonry-built, and the roof have disappeared. In Christian times the vestibule was used as a church, the nave and aisles of which were roofed with brick vaulting.

On the side walls of the vestibule are a series of lively *historical reliefs* (casts of which are in the British Museum). Particularly notable are two scenes on the left-hand wall depicting the King's triumph over the Kushites (who are represented as Negroes). In the first of these the King is sitting on the right under a canopy, while in front of him, in the lower row, high officials bring in tribute of various kinds, including in particular a tablet adorned with plants, from which are suspended hides and rings; behind them come two fettered Negroes, followed by other Negroes bearing offerings (monkeys, greyhounds, a leopard, a giraffe, an ostrich, cattle: one of the oxen has horns represented as arms, between which is the head of a Negro suing for mercy) and women with their children (one carrying her children in a basket held on her back by a strap round her forehead). In the upper row the tablet is set in front of the King, while the Governor of Nubia is rewarded with gold chains; here, too, are other articles presented as tribute (gold, rings, chairs, elephants' tusks, bows, shields, leopard skins, ebony, fans, etc.), and Negroes bring in cattle, gazelles and a lion. The second scene shows the King and his sons dashing in their chariots against the enemy, who flee to their village, situated among doum-palms. A wounded man is led by two comrades to his wife and children, who come to meet him, while another woman crouches over a fire cooking a meal.

The reliefs on the right-hand wall depict the wars against the Syrians and Libyans. The first scene on the right shows the King standing on two prostrate enemies and holding three others (Syrians) by the hair, while a Prince leads in fettered Syrian and Libyan prisoners. In the second scene the King is depicted outside a Syrian fortress, on the battlements of which are men and women begging for mercy (note the woman holding her child by the arm); the King seizes one of the enemy (who holds a broken bow) by the hair to kill him; below, one of the royal Princes is beating in the door of the fortress with an axe. The third scene shows the King in his chariot pursuing the fleeing Syrians; he kills two of the enemy, while two others are bound to the shaft of his chariot. Fourth scene: the King smites a Libyan, while his dog bites the fallen foe. Fifth scene: the King seated on the right under a canopy, with his lion at his feet, while Prince Amenherunanf leads in Syrian prisoners.

From the vestibule three doors lead into the rock-cut *Transverse Chamber,* which has two Proto-Doric columns with inscriptions on all four sides. The mural reliefs are well executed, but their subjects are of no particular interest: the King in the presence of the gods; to right and left of the side doors the King smiting enemies (a Syrian and a Kushite). The *Sanctuary,* which is decorated with similar reliefs, has three statues of gods, now defaced beyond recognition, against the rear wall. These rock-cut chambers were also converted for Christian use.

A little way N of the Kalabsha Temple is the small **Temple of Kertassi**, also transferred here from its original site, some 20 miles/30 km farther S. Only 25 ft/8 m square, it is very similar to the Kiosk at Philae. It is much ruined, preserving only two Hathor columns at the entrance (which faces N) and four other columns with elaborate floral capitals and a single monolithic architrave.

* *Aswan and * *Philae: see separate entries.

Kanat el-Suweis
See Suez Canal

Karnak

Upper Egypt. Governorate: Qena.
(i)**Tourist Information Office,**
Tourist Bazaar,
Luxor;
tel. 22 15.

ACCOMMODATION: see under Luxor.

ACCESS. – From Luxor either N along the Nile for 1½ miles/2·5 km, then a road on right (E) to the main entrance of the Temple of Amun, or via Sharia el-Markaz and Sharia el-Karnak 2 miles/3 km NE to the Gateway of Euergetes II on the SW side of the temple precinct.

SON ET LUMIÈRE performances several times every evening.

Kertassi Temple, New Kalabsha

The great ** temple complex of Karnak lies 2 miles/3 km NE of Luxor within the area of ancient Thebes, near the modern village of Karnak. Within its precincts are the Great Temple of Amun, the Temple of Khons and the Festival Temple of Tuthmosis III, as well as many other buildings; and ample time should be allowed for seeing all that this magnificent site has to offer.

From the Temple of Luxor a paved road, flanked on both sides by ram-headed sphinxes with the effigy of Amenophis III between their legs, ran N to the temples of Karnak. The *avenue of sphinxes* in front of the Temple of Khons is a relic of this old processional way. It leads to a *gateway* built by Ptolemy III Euergetes I, with a winged sun on the cavetto cornice, which is the SW entrance to the great walled ** **Temple Precinct** of Karnak. The reliefs on the gateway show Euergetes making offerings to the deities of Thebes.

Beyond the gateway another short avenue of sphinxes, set up by Ramesses XI, the last of the Ramessids, leads to the **Temple of Khons**, dedicated to the Theban moon god, son of Amun and Mut, a characteristic example of the architecture of the New Kingdom. The temple was built by Ramesses III, but the reliefs, apart from those in the innermost chambers, which were completed during his reign, were executed during the reigns of his successors Ramesses IV and XII and the priest-king Herihor, who also built the forecourt.

The temple is entered by a large *Pylon* 105 ft/32 m long, 33 ft/10 m deep and 59 ft/18 m high. Like the façades of other temples, it has four vertical grooves, with corresponding apertures in the masonry, for the fixing of flagstaffs. The reliefs on the towers depict a High Priest of the 21st Dynasty and his wife making offerings to various gods. In front of each tower stood a portico with a wooden roof; the bases of the columns are still *in situ*.

The central doorway, with reliefs of Alexander II, leads into the *Forecourt*, flanked on right and left by a double row of papyrus columns with closed capitals. On the smooth shafts of the columns and on the walls Herihor is depicted making offerings. Two doorways on each side lead out of the temple. – On the right-hand (E) wall is a relief of Herihor offering incense before the sacred barques of Amun (with a ram's head), Mut and Khons (with a falcon's head); to the

right is the façade of the temple, showing the pylon with its flagstaffs in place.

On the far side of the forecourt a ramp leads up to the *Vestibule* or *Pronaos*, with 12 columns. Beyond this is a transverse *Hypostyle Hall* with eight papyrus columns; the four columns flanking the central aisle have open capitals, while the columns between the lateral aisles (which are 5 ft/1·5 m lower than the central aisle) have closed capitals. On the walls and columns Ramesses XII and Herihor, High Priest of Amun, are depicted sacrificing to various gods.

The door in the middle of the rear wall leads into a larger hall in which is the *Chapel* (open at both ends), designed to house the god's sacred boat. The reliefs on the outer walls of the chapel depict the King (Ramesses IV or XII) in the presence of various gods. Built into the walls are blocks bearing reliefs and cartouches of Tuthmosis III.

On each side of the chapel are dark chambers with reliefs of Ramesses IV, and to its rear a doorway built by one of the Ptolemies gives access to a small chamber with four 16-sided columns, the reliefs in which show Ramesses IV and (to the right and left of the entrance) the Emperor Augustus in the presence of the Theban gods. Adjoining are seven small *chapels* with reliefs of Ramesses III and his successor. The colors are particularly well preserved in the reliefs in the two chapels on the right-hand (E) side. On the long N wall of the rear chapel the King, accompanied by Hathor, offers flowers to the falcon-headed Month of Thebes and to the goddess "Sun of the Two Lands, Eye of Re", who is seated in a chapel; on the W wall he offers incense and water to a lion-headed, ithyphallic god and to Khons. In another chapel at the NE corner of the temple which is dedicated to the cult of Osiris is a relief of the dead Osiris, with Isis and Nephthys mourning at his bier.

Adjoining the SW side of the Temple of Khons is a small **Temple of Osiris and Opet** (the hippopotamus goddess of childbirth and mother of Osiris) built by Euergetes II. It stands on a 10 ft/3 m high base topped by a cavetto cornice, with the main entrance on the W side. On the uprights of the doorway the King is depicted before Osiris and other deities.

The entrance, on the W side, leads into a *rectangular hall*, with a well-preserved ceiling supported on two columns with floral capitals and Hathor heads. High up on the S wall are lattice windows. To the right are three side chambers with crypts; the door on the left is walled up. Beyond this is a second hall, with mural reliefs depicting the King in the presence of various deities. Off this hall open two side chambers; in the left-hand one is a relief of the dead Osiris, with Isis and Nephthys standing by the bier, while the one on the right is dedicated to the birth of Horus. The relief above the door of this room shows Isis suckling Horus, surrounded by gods; to the left the King brings milk, to the right a length of cloth. On the lintel Harsomtus is depicted in a swamp in the guise of a falcon wearing the double crown, protected by the hippopotamus goddess Opet and a lion goddess.

A door with a figure of the goddess Opet on the right-hand upright leads into the *Sanctuary*, with a niche which originally held a statue of the goddess. The reliefs in the niche show the King in the presence of Opet, who is represented on the right as a post with a Hathor head, on the left as a hippopotamus. – In the E wall of the temple is a small *Chapel of Osiris* built by Ptolemy XIII, with its own entrance on the E side. To this temple belongs the shaft which stands in the Sanctuary of the Temple of Opet and may have contained a relic of Osiris.

Going S from the Temple of Khons in the direction of the Nile, we soon come to the first pylon of the Great Temple of Amun, which can also be reached direct on a road branching off the main Nile Valley road. – The rectangular terrace in front of the pylon was subject to flooding in ancient times, as it shows by the marks on its front recording the heights reached by the inundation under the 21st–26th Dynasties. On the terrace is a small *obelisk* erected by Sethos II; of the other one of the pair only the base is left. From here an *avenue of rams* dating from the reign of Ramesses II led to the temple. The ruins to the SW of the right-hand tower of the pylon belong to a *chapel* built by King Achoris and his successor Psammuthis; on the inside wall, to the right and left, Psammuthis is depicted offering incense to the sacred barque of Amun.

The****Great Temple of Amun**, founded at least as early as the beginning of the 12th Dynasty (*c.* 1991–*c.* 1785 B.C.), is not built to a single unified plan but represents the building activity of many successive rulers of Egypt, who vied with

I	First Pylon (Ethiopian period)
II	Second Pylon (Ramesses II)
III	Third Pylon (Amenophis III)
IV	Fourth Pylon (Tuthmosis I)
V	Fifth Pylon (Tuthmosis I)
VI	Sixth Pylon (Tuthmosis III)
VII	Seventh Pylon (Tuthmosis III)
VIII	Eighth Pylon (Hatshepsut)
IX	Ninth Pylon (Horemheb)
X	Tenth Pylon (Horemheb)

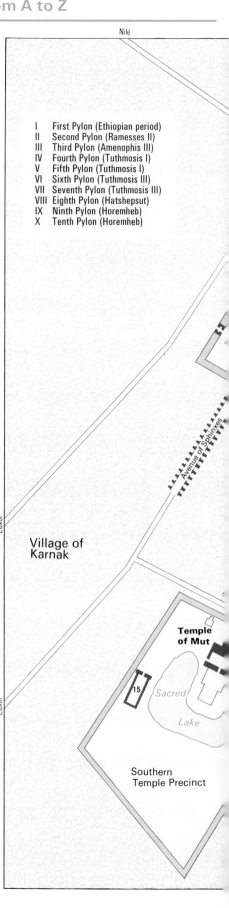

Nile

Avenue of Sphinxes

Luxor

Village of Karnak

Temple of Mut

15   Sacred

Lake

Southern Temple Precinct

Avenue of rams leading to temple precinct, Karnak

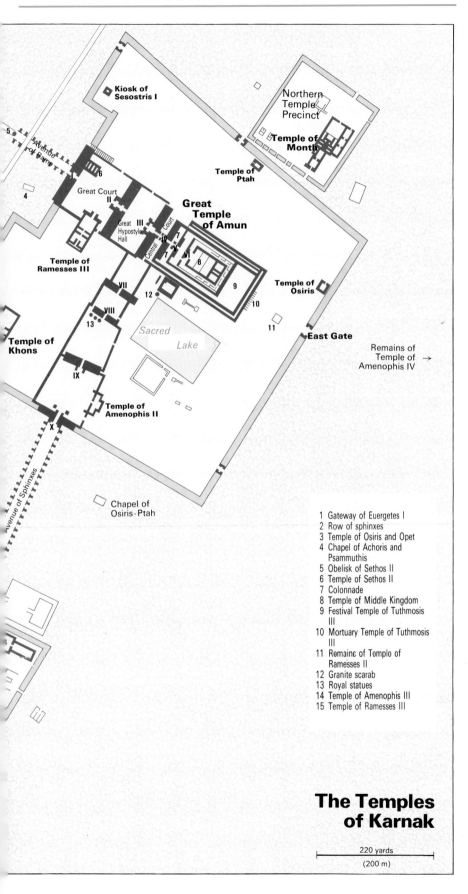

Kiosk of
Sesostris I

Northern
Temple
Precinct

**Temple of
Month**

Temple of
Ptah

**Great
Temple
of Amun**

Great Court

Great **III**
Hypostyle
Hall

Central Court

Temple of
Ramesses III

**Temple of
Osiris**

Temple of
Khons

Sacred
Lake

East Gate

Remains of
Temple of →
Amenophis IV

Temple of
Amenophis II

Avenue of Sphinxes

Chapel of
Osiris-Ptah

Avenue of Rams

1 Gateway of Euergetes I
2 Row of sphinxes
3 Temple of Osiris and Opet
4 Chapel of Achoris and
   Psammuthis
5 Obelisk of Sethos II
6 Temple of Sethos II
7 Colonnade
8 Temple of Middle Kingdom
9 Festival Temple of Tuthmosis
   III
10 Mortuary Temple of Tuthmosis
   III
11 Remains of Temple of
   Ramesses II
12 Granite scarab
13 Royal statues
14 Temple of Amenophis III
15 Temple of Ramesses III

The Temples
of Karnak

220 yards

(200 m)

one another in adding to and adorning this great national sanctuary. Amenophis I built a second temple alongside the main temple, but this was soon removed. When Tuthmosis I made Thebes capital of the New Kingdom the original modest temple no longer seemed adequate to the power of the god, and the King, therefore, added a large court bounded on the W by a Pylon (V) and surrounded by colonnades with Osiris pillars. Later he erected in front of this another Pylon (IV) with an enclosing wall, set up two obelisks in front of it and built a colonnade between the two pylons.

HISTORY. – In the reign of Hatshepsut various additions and alterations were made in the interior. In front of the temple of the Middle Kingdom, in Tuthmosis I's court, she built a special shrine and set up two obelisks between the Fourth and Fifth Pylons, besides rebuilding the colonnade itself. Hatshepsut's stepson, nephew, son-in-law and co-ruler Tuthmosis III continued to make alterations when he became sole ruler, pulling down most of the colonnades in Tuthmosis I's court and replacing them by rows of small chapels. The Sixth Pylon was now built, and the court between this pylon and Hatshepsut's shrine, which had been enlarged by the addition of a vestibule, was surrounded by colonnades. Tuthmosis I's colonnade between the Fourth and Fifth Pylons was extensively rebuilt, apparently with the object of concealing Hatshepsut's obelisks from view. In front of Tuthmosis I's obelisks two new ones were set up. Some 20 years later Tuthmosis III resumed his building activity, adding the two Halls of Records and the vestibules between the Fifth and Sixth Pylons as well as building the large Festival Temple at the E end. – On the main front of the temple Amenophis III built still another pylon (III).

All these 18th Dynasty buildings, however, were thrown into the shade by the work of the 19th Dynasty kings. Ramesses I erected the Second Pylon, and between this and the Third Pylon Sethos I and Ramesses II built the great hypostyle hall which has remained ever since one of the chief marvels of Egyptian architecture. Ramesses II also built a new enclosure wall. With this building of the great temple came, for the time being, to an end. The temples erected by Sethos II and Ramesses III were independent buildings outside the main temple.

Then the Libyan Kings of Bubastis (22nd Dynasty) revived the traditions of the earlier Pharaohs. In front of Ramesses I's pylon Sheshonq built a large court with colonnades along the sides, incorporating in it half of Ramesses III's temple and erecting a large pylon (I) on its W side. Later the Ethiopian ruler Taharqa (25th Dynasty) built in the center of this court a kiosk-like building with ten colossal columns. Thereafter the temple remained largely unaltered, apart from the addition of the granite Chapel of Philip Arrhidaeus; little building work was done by the Ptolemies. The decline and decay of the temple began in the Roman Imperial period.

The gigantic* **FIRST PYLON**, built in the time of the Ethiopian kings, is 370 ft/113 m wide, with walls 49 ft/15 m thick, and still stands 143 ft/43·50 m high. It was left unfinished, and indeed fragments of the scaffolding of sun-dried brick used during its construction

can still be seen. – High up on the right-hand side of the doorway is an inscription recording the latitude and longitude of the principal Egyptian temples as established by the French *savants* who accompanied Napoleon's expedition to Egypt in 1799, and opposite this on the left-hand side is an inscription by an Italian learned society recording the magnetic deviation (10′ 56″) as calculated by them in 1841. – There is a magnificent * view from the platform on the top of the pylon, which is reached by a staircase on the N tower.

Beyond the pylon is the * *Great Court,* which dates from the 22nd Dynasty. It is 338 ft/103 m wide by 276 ft/84 m deep, with colonnades on both sides. The S colonnade is interrupted by the front part of Ramesses III's temple.

In the N corner of the court is the small **Temple of Sethos II**, built on gray sandstone, with the exception of the door-frames and the lower part of the walls, for which a reddish quartzose sandstone was used. It consists of three chapels dedicated respectively (from left to right) to Mut, Amun and Khons, each with niches for the image of the deity. In the right-hand wall of the Chapel of Khons is a staircase leading up to the roof of the temple. – Along the NW side of the court are a number of *figures of rams*, which originally formed part of Ramesses II's avenue of rams and were stored here when they were removed to make way for the new buildings in the court.

The two pedestals in the middle of the court (only the base of the right-hand one being preserved) were intended for statues. Beyond them is the *Kiosk of Taharqa*. Of its original ten columns one, on the right, has survived complete with its open capital and abacus; the five on the left have been reconstructed. The kiosk had doorways on all four sides; in front of the W door, to the right, is a recumbent sphinx. – On the right-hand column (restored 1927) the name of Psammetichus II has been placed over that of the Ethiopian ruler Taharqa (25th Dynasty). Adjoining it is the name of Ptolemy IV Philopator, which also appears on the abacus. The shaft of the column is composed of 25 courses of carefully dressed stone, the capital of 5. The total height is 69 ft/21 m, the breadth of the capital $16\frac{1}{2}$ ft/5 m, the girth at the top of the column 49 ft/15 m. Between the columns were screens dating from the time of Ptolemy IV Philopator.

In the N colonnade is a doorway leading out of the court. The staircase to the top of the pylon can be reached by going through this door and turning left along the outside of the walls.

On the right-hand side of the court is the* **Temple of Ramesses III**, dedicated to Amun, which is perhaps the best example of a simple Egyptian temple built on a unified plan. It has a total length of 171 ft/52 m.

The *Pylon* of the temple, with the entrance doorway containing two statues of the King, had suffered much damage to the upper part (now restored). On the front of the left-hand (E) tower Ramesses, wearing the double crown, is shown holding his enemies by the hair and raising his club to smite them, while Amun hands him the sword of victory and delivers to him three rows of vanquished peoples (above from the S, below from the N). On the right-hand tower is a similar scene, with the King wearing the crown of Lower Egypt. On the left-hand side of the doorway Ramesses receives from Amun the sign for "life", etc.

Beyond the pylon is a *Court*, with covered passages on either side, the roofs of which are supported on eight Osiris pillars. – On the rear walls of the pylon towers Ramesses is shown receiving the sign for "jubilee" from Amun – signifying that he would celebrate many more jubilees. – The walls of the colonnades are decorated with reliefs – on the E side the procession of Amun's sacred barque, on the W side a procession with an ithyphallic statue of Amun borne by priests and accompanied by standard-bearers. – The votive inscriptions on the architraves record in florid style that Ramesses erected this monument to his father Amun. – A door in the left-hand (E) colonnade leads into the Bubastid Hall (see below); in the right-hand colonnade is a doorway, now walled up, which opened into the S colonnade of the Great Court.

On the far side of the court is the *Vestibule* of the temple proper, which stands on a higher level. Along the front are four Osiris pillars, while to the rear are four columns with closed capitals. The pillars are linked by screens (with reliefs).

From the vestibule a doorway leads into the *Hypostyle Hall,* which has eight columns with closed capitals. Beyond this are three *Chapels,* dedicated respectively to Mut (left), Amun (middle: with two lattice windows in the longitudinal walls) and Khons (right). In each chapel the King is depicted sacrificing to the sacred barque of the deity. Adjoining the Chapel of Khons is another small room; the Chapel of Amun has a room on either side; and beside the Chapel of Mut is a staircase.

The door on the E side of the court of Ramesses III's Temple leads into the *Bubastid Hall,* in the SE corner of the Great Court. The reliefs and inscriptions in this hall are by rulers of the 22nd Dynasty. The following reliefs are particularly notable: on the left (E; on the projecting wall), above, Amun presenting to Osorkon I the curved sword and palm branch, symbols of long life; below, Khnum holding the hieroglyph for "life" to

Columns in the Temple of Amun

the King's nostrils and Hathor suckling the King. On the right-hand (W) wall Takelothis II and his son Osorkon, High Priest of Amun, are depicted in the presence of the god; below is a long inscription.

The **SECOND PYLON**, built by Ramesses II, is badly dilapidated. The towers have been freed from the ruins of later buildings erected in front of them, using stone of the Amarna period. They have the usual four vertical grooves for flagstaffs. In the center is the huge *doorway,* formerly preceded by a kind of small vestibule flanked by two *statues of Ramesses II*: one of these (on the right) still stands, of the other only the legs are left. On the right-hand side of the vestibule Ramesses is depicted smiting his foes in the presence of Amun. In the doorway, which bears the cartouches of Ramesses I, Sethos I and Ramesses II, an intervening door was built by Ptolemy VI Philometor and Ptolemy IX Euergetes II during their joint reign; the lintel of this is missing but the jambs remain, with reliefs showing the King making offerings to the gods of the temple. The inner side of the earlier doorway has reliefs of the Ptolemaic period, with the same scenes on both sides. Below are the sacred barque of Amun and Ramesses III entering the temple; in the second bottom row Ramesses is depicted kneeling before Amun and holding the hieroglyph for "jubilee", behind him the goddess Mut, while Khons, wearing the lunar disc on his head, leads in Philometor; in the third row the King is seated under the sacred tree of Heliopolis, with the goddess Seshat inscribing his name on the leaves. This scene is evidently a restoration by Philometor of an earlier relief. In the other rows the King is shown in the presence of various gods.

Beyond the pylon is the ****Great Hypostyle Hall**, justifiably regarded as one of the wonders of the world. Although the work of the Egyptian Department of Antiquities in restoring it and stablizing its foundations has deprived it of the picturesqueness of its former ruinous state, this huge hall still exerts an overwhelming effect on the beholder. Measuring 338 ft/

Stone lattice window, Great Hypostyle Hall

103 m by 171 ft/52 m, it covers an area of 53,800 sq. ft/5000 sq. m (compared with the 87,400 sq. ft/8275 sq. m of St Paul's, London and the 163,200 sq. ft/15,450 sq. m of St Peter's, Rome). The roof was supported on 134 columns, in 16 rows. The two central rows, which are higher, consist of papyrus columns with open capitals, while the other rows have closed capitals. The roof of the central aisle, 80 ft/24 m high, rested on the two central rows of columns and on one of the lower rows on each side, the difference in height being made good by square pillars on top of the lower columns. Between these pillars were windows with stone lattice-work (one of which, on the S side, is almost perfectly preserved). The lateral aisles are 33 ft/10 m lower than the central ones.

The columns are built up from semi-drums $3\frac{1}{2}$ ft/1·10 m high and $6\frac{1}{2}$ ft/2 m in diameter, of reddish-brown sandstone. The 12 taller columns in the two central rows have a diameter of $11\frac{1}{2}$ ft/3·57 m and a girth of more than 33 ft/10 m – roughly the same as Trajan's Column in Rome and the Vendôme Column in Paris. The height of the columns is 69 ft/21 m, of the capitals 11 ft/3·34 m. The 122 columns of the lateral aisles have a height of 43 ft/13 m and a girth of $27\frac{1}{2}$ ft/8·40 m.

In the side walls of the hypostyle hall are doorways leading out of the temple. At the NW corner a door leads into a corridor, at the end of which is a staircase mounting to the roof of the N tower of the Second Pylon. At the NE corner a door gives access to a staircase which leads to the roof of the hypostyle hall. From another staircase to the left of the S doorway

there is a fine general view of the hypostyle hall. Beside the SE doorway is a staircase mounting to the roof of the Third Pylon.

To the right of the main entrance to the hypostyle hall is the frame, rather in the shape of a door, which once contained a memorial stela of Ramesses II. In front of it is an alabaster slab with a relief of prostrate enemies, and to the left of the door a colossal double statue of Amun and Ramesses II.

The walls of the hall, the shafts of the columns, the abaci and the architraves and covered with inscriptions and reliefs of kings making offerings, many of which have preserved their original coloring. Those in the northern half of the hall (as far as the tenth row of columns), which date from the reign of Sethos I, are in delicate low relief; those in the southern half, dating from the reign of Ramesses II, are in cruder sunk relief. Only one column, the first in the sixth row, bears the name of Ramesses I; later Ramesses III, IV, VI and XII also recorded their names.

Among the fine reliefs of Sethos I's reign the most notable are those on the N wall. To the left of the N side door, below: Sethos in front of the sanctuary, in which is the sacred barque of Amun; Sethos conducted into the temple by the falcon-headed Month and Atum; procession of the sacred barque; above, Sethos in presence of the gods of Thebes. To the right of the door, below: Sethos offering incense before the sacred barque, conducted into the temple, kneeling in the chapel before Amun and Khons and receiving the

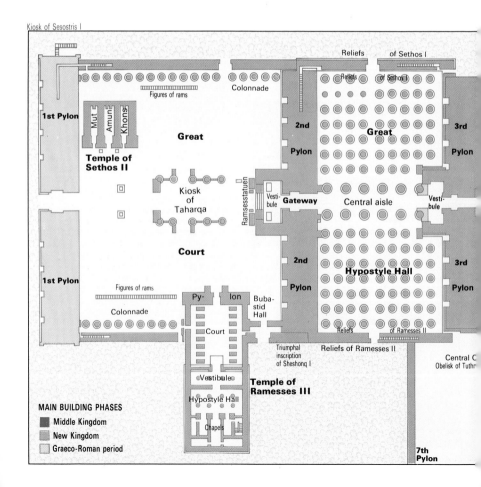

symbols of a long reign; above, Sethos making offerings to Amun in various forms; Sethos kneeling before the god Harakhty, who is seated under a canopy, and behind him the lion-headed goddess Werthekaw with a palm branch from which hang various symbols; to the left, the King kneeling under the sacred tree of Heliopolis, with Thoth inscribing his name on the leaves. – Among the mural reliefs of Ramesses II, probably connected with his visit to Thebes in the first year of his reign, those to the right and left of the S side door are of particular interest. To the right, Ramesses burning incense in front of the sacred barque of Amun, which is borne by priests (those in front with falcon masks, those to the rear with jackal masks); Ramesses beside the barque clad in a panther skin as a priest; behind, the barques of Khons and Mut, borne by priests. To the left, below, the King in front of the chapels containing the sacred barques of Amun, Mut and Khons; farther left, the King kneeling before Amun, Mut and Khons under the sacred tree of Heliopolis and receiving the symbols of a long reign, while Thoth inscribes his name on the leaves. – In the S aisle are two fine sandstone *statues of Sethos II* (headless).

The outer walls of the hypostyle hall have historical *reliefs depicting the victories of Sethos I (N wall) and Ramesses II (S wall) over the peoples of Palestine and Libya. They are best seen by afternoon light. E end of N wall, above: Sethos in Lebanon; the inhabitants, whose faces are sharply characterized, fell timber for him; below, a battle with the bedouin of southern Palestine; the King in his chariot launching his arrows against the enemy, with heaps of dead and wounded;

to the left, above, the Fortress of Canaan, the inhabitants of which beg for mercy and help fugitives into the fortress.

Round the corner, top row (partly destroyed), from the left: 1. Battle for Yenuam in Syria. The King in his chariot shoots arrows at the enemy, whose charioteers, cavalry and infantry flee in wild confusion. On the left, the Fortress of Yenuam, surrounded by water, with fugitives hiding behind the trees (some, unusually shown in full face). 2. The King binding Syrian prisoners. 3. The King, walking behind his chariot, leads two files of captured Syrians on ropes and holds two others in each arm. 4. The King leads two files of Syrian prisoners into the presence of Amun, Mut and Khons, to whom he presents costly vessels captured from the enemy. Lower row, left to right: 1. The King's triumphal progress through Palestine. Sethos, in his chariot, turns towards the defeated Princes of Palestine, who raise their hands in homage; behind the King are a fortress and the costly vessels taken in booty; above and below the horses are small castles built to protect watering-points. 2. Battle with the people of southern Palestine. The King, in his chariot, shoots arrows at the enemy, who flee into the hills; below, castles and wells, with the wounded lying beside them. 3. The King's victorious return. Sethos, in his chariot, preceded and followed by fettered prisoners. A canal, with reeds and crocodiles, marks the boundary between Egypt and Asia; at each end of a bridge is a fortified guard-house; on the Egyptian side (on the right) two rows of priests (with garlands of flowers) and dignitaries wait to welcome

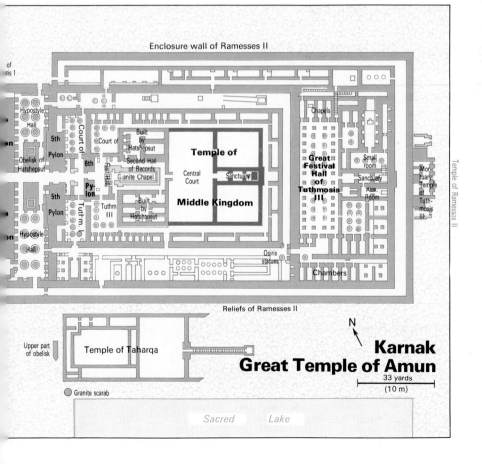

the King. 4. The King dedicates the captured Syrian prisoners and booty to Amun.

To the right and left of the doorway are two huge reliefs: Sethos I holding enemies by the hair, with his club raised to smite them; Amun, with several rows of captured nations and cities, presenting the curved sword of victory.

On the western part of the N wall the reliefs begin at the far end and go from right to left. Top row: the storming of Qadesh in the land of Amor (northern Palestine); the King (face missing) shoots arrows from his chariot, which has overturned an enemy chariot; to the right, on a tree-clad hill, the Fortress of Qadesh, the defenders of which are pierced by arrows; a herdsman and his cattle flee. Middle row: 1. Battle with the Libyans. The King, in his chariot, prepares to smite a Libyan, whom he holds with his bow; to the right, dead and wounded enemies. The Libyans are distinguishable by their long side pigtails and the feathers on their heads. 2. The King transfixes a Libyan with his lance. 3. The King in his chariot, with two rows of fettered Libyan prisoners in front of him. 4. The King dedicates the prisoners and booty to the divine triad of Thebes. Bottom row: 1. Battle with the Hittites in northern Syria. The King in his chariot shooting arrows at the enemy, who flee headlong, in chariots, on horseback or on foot. 2. The King, in his chariot, holding ropes to which are fastened several prisoners and two captured chariots; in front of him are two rows of Hittite prisoners. 3. The King dedicates the prisoners and booty to the divine triad of Thebes, here accompanied by the goddess of truth.

The reliefs on the outside of the S wall of the hypostyle hall can be seen by re-entering the hall and going out by the S doorway; alternatively they can be left until after the rest of the temple has been seen, leaving by the doorway at the Seventh Pylon. These reliefs depict in similar fashion Ramesses II's victories in Syria, chiefly over the Hittites. To the W of the reliefs, on the S end of the Second Pylon, is the **Triumphal Inscription of Sheshonq I**, the Shishak of the Old Testament. It celebrates the King's victory over Rehoboam of Judah, the son of Solomon. To the left is a large figure of Amun holding in his right hand the curved sword of victory and in his left cords binding five rows of captured cities, each represented by a circuit of walls bearing its name and the upper part of the body of a fettered prisoner. The hooked noses, prominent cheekbones and beards identify the prisoners as Semitic. Below Amun is the protective goddess of the Theban nome, with a club, bow and quiver, holding cords attached to five rows of prisoners. To the right the King (figure unfinished) holds a group of cowering Semites by the hair and smites them with his club.

These campaigns by Shishak are referred to in the Bible at 1 Kings 14: 25–26 and 2 Chronicles 12: 2–4 and 9. Only a few of the cities mentioned in the reliefs can be identified with certainty; these include Rabbath (last in the first row), Taanach, Shunem, Rehob, Haphraim, Mahanaim, Gibeon, Beth-Horon, Kedemoth and Ajalon (in second row). The inscriptions, in the usual bombastic style, give no further information on the campaign.

On the projecting wall to the E of the S doorway is an inscription recording the peace treaty with the King of the Hittites concluded by Ramesses II in the 21st year of his reign. – Beyond the projecting wall, at the end of the outer wall of hypostyle hall, a relief depicts Ramesses II leading two rows of prisoners into the presence of Amun. Below is the poetic account of the Hittite campaign known as the "Poem of Pentaur" (or Pentawer). Beyond this, round the corner beside the SE doorway (now closed) of the hypostyle hall, is a relief of Ramesses II presenting to Amun the prisoners and the costly vessels taken in the Syrian campaign.

The rear wall of the Great Hypostyle Hall is formed by the **THIRD PYLON**, built by Amenophis III (reconstructed), with its projecting vestibule. Incorporated in its structure were large blocks decorated with reliefs from 13 earlier temples. On the S tower is a long inscription (top part destroyed) detailing the gifts made by the King to Amun. On the N tower can be seen the last remnants of a relief depicting a ceremonial voyage on the Nile (the King on the sacred barque of Amun, with another vessel).

In the *Central Court* beyond the pylon there were formerly four *obelisks*, two of them set up by Tuthmosis I and two by Tuthmosis II. One of these is still standing, together with the bases of the other three. It is 71 ft/21·75 m high, on a base 6 ft/1·84 m square, and is estimated to weigh 143 tons. On each face of the obelisk are three vertical inscriptions, the central one being the dedicatory inscription by Tuthmosis I, the other two additions by Ramesses IV and VI. The obelisks erected by Tuthmosis I marked the entrance to the temple as it then was.

The *Kiosk of Sesostris I, re-erected to the N of the Temple of Amun from the blocks found built into the Third Pylon and its vestibule, is the oldest structure in the whole temple complex. It can be seen only by special arrangement. Built of fine limestone, it was erected to commemorate the King's Jubilee. It stands on a substructure and is approached by ramps on the E and W sides. The roof is borne on 24 pillars, which, like the outer walls, are covered with reliefs of excellent quality. In the interior is a base for the sacred barque of Amun.

The **FOURTH PYLON**, built by Tuthmosis I, is in a ruinous condition. The doorway, according to the

Seated figure of the goddess Sakhmet

relief inscription, was restored by Alexander the Great. – Beyond the pylon is a *Colonnade,* also ruined, which originally contained huge statues of Osiris set in niches and two obelisks of Aswan granite erected by Queen Hatshepsut, the tips of which were covered with electrum (an alloy of gold and silver). The right-hand (S) obelisk lies broken on the ground, its upper part on a heap of rubble to the right; on the base are long inscriptions celebrating the power of the Queen. The *left-hand obelisk* still stands erect to a height of 97 ft/29·50 m, with a diameter at the base of $8\frac{1}{2}$ ft/2·65 m and an estimated weight of 323 tons; it is exceeded in height only by the Lateran Obelisk in Rome (101 ft/ 30·7 m). On each of the four faces is a vertical inscription recording the dedication of the obelisks and the fact that they were constructed in only seven months. On the upper part are reliefs depicting Hatshepsut, Tuthmosis I and Tuthmosis III making offerings to Amun; the names and figures of Amun were defaced by Amenophis IV but restored by Sethos I. Against the wall to the left is a granite *statue of Tuthmosis III* kneeling and holding an altar in front of him.

The colonnade was much altered under the 18th Dynasty. As built by Tuthmosis I it had a timber roof borne on wooden columns, later replaced in stone; three stone bases still survive. Here Hatshepsut set up her two obelisks on the occasion of her Jubilee in the 16th year of her reign. Later Tuthmosis built a sandstone structure round them, concealing them to a height of some 82 ft/25 m; part of this structure can still be seen. The colonnade was then given a stone roof supported by two rows of papyrus columns (six on the N side, eight on the S), five of the older columns being retained. Niches were formed in the walls for statues of Tuthmosis I, which originally stood in the main court of the temple. The decoration of the S end of the colonnade was not completed until the reign of Amenophis II.

Beyond the **FIFTH PYLON**, built by Tuthmosis I, are two small *antechambers,* now in a state of ruin, built by Tuthmosis III in front of the Sixth Pylon. To the right and left are *courts* with colonnades of 16-sided columns and statues of Osiris – remnants of the large court built by Tuthmosis I round the temple of the Middle Kingdom. In the passage leading to the N court is a colossal *seated figure of Amenophis II* in red granite. – The **SIXTH PYLON** built by Tuthmosis III, the last and smallest of all, is also in a ruined state. On the walls to right and left of the granite central doorway are lists of the cities and tribes subdued by Tuthmosis III: to the right the peoples of the southern lands, to the left "the lands of the Upper Retenu [i.e. Syria] which his majesty took in the miserable city of Meggido "

Beyond this is the *First Hall of Records,* built by Tuthmosis III in a court which he had constructed some time previously. Here stand two **granite pillars** which once supported the roof, the one on the right (S) with the lotus, the one on the left with the papyrus, the emblems of Upper and Lower Egypt. Here, too, are the magnificent *colossal statues of Amun* (much restored) *and the goddess Amunet,* of reddish sandstone, dedicated by Tutankhamun, whose name was later chiseled out and replaced by that of his successor Horemheb.

To left and right of the Hall of Records is the *Court* constructed by Tuthmosis III, with a colonnade of papyrus cluster-columns with 16 shafts. On the rear side of the doorway leading to the southern part of the court are reliefs of Sethos II. In the E wall, on the façade of Hatshepsut's building, is a false door, once

Granite pillars in the First Hall of Records

lavishly adorned with gold and lapis lazuli. On the S side are five chapels dedicated to the cult of Amenophis I.

The granite chapel, still containing a base for the sacred barque, was built during the reign of Philip Arrhidaeus (323–317 B.C.), probably on the site of an earlier structure built by Tuthmosis III, fragments of which lie outside the chapel. Constructed of pink granite, it is divided into two parts, with the front chamber opening to the W and the rear one to the E. In the E wall of the rear chamber is a double window with four steps leading up to it. The front chamber is 20 ft/ 6 m long, the rear one rather over 26 ft/8 m; both are covered, internally and externally, with reliefs, some of them having well-preserved coloring.

Interior walls: in the front chamber, Philip making offerings to Amun in his various forms and performing other ritual actions (figures and inscriptions picked out with bluish-green pigment); rear chamber, Philip seated at table. The reliefs in the rear chamber are larger, but less well preserved, than those in the front chamber. – Outer walls, S side: front chamber, in four rows (the bottom one destroyed) 1. ceremonies at the King's entrance into the temple; 2. the sacred barque of Amun borne in procession by priests; 3. the procession returning. Rear chamber, four badly damaged scenes: the King making offerings to Amun in his various forms and performing other ritual actions. On the N wall of the front chamber the King is shown offering two small trees to Amun-Kamutef; rear chamber, foundation ceremonies and various offerings.

On the N wall of the *Second Hall of Records* of Tuthmosis III, which surrounds the chapel, are long inscriptions celebrating the King's military exploits. To the right of the black granite doorway, above the inscription, is a relief of Tuthmosis III presenting gifts (two obelisks, vases, necklaces, chests) to the temple. – The rooms on the N and S sides of the Hall of Records, now largely in ruins, were built by Queen Hatshepsut and decorated with reliefs, which were later chiseled out or replaced by the names of Tuthmosis II and III. On the S side are a room with a staircase leading to the roof and a chamber with a granite altar dedicated by Tuthmosis III. Here, too, is a *statue of Amenophis II.*

In a room to the N, closed off by a black granite door, are fine *reliefs,* with well-preserved coloring, dating from the reign of Hatshepsut. The left-hand wall, which originally adjoined the N wall of the Second Hall of Records, was removed and re-erected here. The reliefs of Hatshepsut were defaced and some of them replaced by poorly executed reliefs of Tuthmosis II and III. Note the fine figures of Amun of Karnak (depicted with a red skin) and Amun-Kamutef (with a black skin).

To the E of this, on a lower level, an area of rubble is all that remains of the earliest temple of the Middle Kingdom. The rooms built by Tuthmosis III can be identified on the N side; in front of them was a passage in which statues of high dignitaries especially deserving of honor were set up by the Pharaohs.

The **Great Festival Temple of Tuthmosis III** is entered by the main doorway at the SW corner, in front of which are the stumps of two 16-sided columns and two *statues* of the King as Osiris (only the left-hand one being preserved complete). From here we turn left through the antechambers into the *Great Festival Hall,* a five-aisled basilica 144 ft/44 m long and 52 ft/16 m deep. The roof of the three high central aisles was borne on two rows of ten columns and 32 square pillars. The tent-pole columns are unique, indicating that the central aisles were conceived by the builder as a large festal tent. The pillars, lower than the columns, supported, together with the side walls, the pentagonal roofing slabs of the lateral aisles, and also, with the addition of small pillars and architraves, helped to support the roof of the central aisles. The reliefs on the pillars show Tuthmosis III in the presence of the gods. In the hall are a number of torsos of statues which were found here.

At the SW corner of the hall is the chamber in which the "Tablet of Karnak" was found – a list of Egyptian rulers from the earliest times down to the 18th Dynasty, now in the Bibliothèque Nationale in Paris. The chamber was probably used for storing the statues of earlier kings which were borne in procession by the priests. – At the N end of the three central aisles are three *chapels,* in the most westerly of which is a *colossal group* of Tuthmosis III between Amun and Mut. – From the NW corner of the hall is an antechamber from which a doorway leads into a narrow *corridor.* On the N wall of the corridor are fine reliefs depicting Tuthmosis III offering incense to an ithyphallic Amun; the King pouring water over Amun, with priests and male and female singers coming in on the right; and the King pouring water on an altar and burning incense in the presence of Amun. – From the NE corner of the hall a staircase mounts within a tower-like structure to a room containing an *alabaster altar* which may have served some astronomical purpose. – The rooms on the E side of the hall are in a ruinous condition. To the NE is a chamber with two pillars, adjoining which is a chapel (ruined) with a large *granite altar.* – The central door in the E aisle leads to three rooms which have preserved only the lower parts of their walls. On the N side, reached by steps, is a small room, known as the *"Botanic Garden",* the roof of which was borne on four well-preserved papyrus cluster-columns with closed capitals; on the lower part of the walls are representations of plants and animals brought from Syria to

Egypt by Tuthmosis III in the 25th year of his reign. Steps to the S lead into the Sanctuary, adjoining which is the *Alexander Room,* built by Tuthmosis III, which in addition to a few reliefs dating from the reign of Tuthmosis contains inscriptions and reliefs in the name of Alexander the Great. Beyond this is a handsome hall which originally had eight 16-sided columns, seven of them still standing. To the E are rooms with two tiers of pillars and a corridor along the S side of the temple, off which open two small pillared halls and seven rooms with reliefs of Tuthmosis III.

The central and eastern parts of the Temple of Amun (from the Third Pylon) are surrounded by an **enclosure wall**, the surviving sections of which have reliefs of Ramesses II making offerings to the gods.

Just outside the enclosure wall, immediately E of the Festival Temple of Tuthmosis III, is another **Temple of Tuthmosis III**, probably a mortuary temple dedicated to the cult of the King and his aunt, stepmother, mother-in-law and co-ruler Hatshepsut. In the *central chapel* are colossal seated figures of the royal couple, and to the E of this is a *hypostyle hall* with six gigantic statues of the King as Osiris, later usurped by Ramesses II.

Farther E, beyond an unexcavated mound of rubble, is a badly ruined *Temple of Ramesses II* built on the same axis as the principal temple, which cuts across an older brick enclosure wall. The entrance doorway, on the E side, leads into a hall with eight columns and two Osiris pillars, behind which is a narrow hypostyle hall. In front of the doorway there was originally a hall dating from the reign of Taharqa, with 20 columns linked by screens. N of these structures are the remains of another *Temple of Ramesses II,* perhaps dedicated to the cult of King Mentuhotep III (11th Dynasty), which was restored in the time of the Ptolemies. – S of these remains, to the E of the Sacred Lake, are the remains of a brick building dating from before the Middle Kingdom.

Beyond this, to the E, we come to the well-preserved **East Gate** (now closed) in the brick enclosure wall which surrounded the whole temple precinct. Built by Nectanebo I, it stands 62 ft/19 m high. The distance from the First Pylon to this gate is 515 yds/470 m.

Built against the enclosure wall is a small *Temple of Osiris* erected by Osorkon III (22nd Dynasty), his son and co-ruler Takelothis III and his daughter Shepwepet. The front chamber was added by Amenirdis, sister of Shabaka (25th Dynasty) and mother-in-law of Psammetichus I. In the vicinity are a number of small chapels of the 26th Dynasty. – Outside the gate a ruined *Temple of*

Amenophis IV, with a hypostyle hall once contained colossal statues of the King. The mural reliefs in this temple were broken up and built into the Ninth and Tenth Pylons. – To the right (S) of the gate is a small building which bears the names of Ramesses III and IV.

Of the buildings to the N of the Temple of Amun only the Temple of Ptah is worth a visit; the others are so poorly preserved as to be of interest only to a specialist. – From the N door of the Great Hypostyle Hall an ancient paved road leads NE towards the Temple of Ptah, which is still within the precinct of the Temple of Amun. To the left of the road are a small brick-built fortress and three small *chapels* of the Late Period. The largest of these chapels, to the S, was built towards the end of the 26th Dynasty by Pedeneit, a Majordomo in the royal household. On the entrance doorway are reliefs of Psammetichus III and Queen Enkhnesneferebre in the presence of Amun and other gods. Beyond this is a brick-built hall with four stone columns. On the doorway into the sanctuary are depicted Nitocris, wife of Psammetichus II (right), and Amasis (left). – The central chapel was built by a Court official named Sheshonq in the reign of Amasis. On the left-hand jamb is a relief of the King, on the right-hand one Enkhnesneferebre, to whose household Sheshonq belonged. This chapel, too, is built of sun-dried brick; only the doorways, columns and sanctuary are of stone. – The third chapel, to the N, is the oldest of the three, built in the reign of Taharqa (25th Dynasty). It is decorated with reliefs of Princess Shepenwepet and the King.

The *Temple of Ptah, tutelary god of Memphis, was built by Tuthmosis III and enlarged and restored by the Ethiopian ruler Shabaka and some of the Ptolemies.

The temple is approached from the W through five successive *gateways*, the second and fourth of which were built by Shabaka (whose name has been erased), the others by the Ptolemies. Beyond this is a passage formed by four columns with rich foliage capitals, linked by screens. At the end of the passage is a small **Pylon**, with the names of Tuthmosis III (restored in the Ptolemaic period) on the doorway. This leads into a *Court*, on the rear side of which is a portico with two 16-sided columns. In the portico are two altar bases of red granite with dedications by Amenemhet I and Tuthmosis III. In the walls are six niches, and there is a staircase leading to an upper storey. In the center a door leads into the *Sanctuary*; on the doorway are reliefs (restored) dating from the reign of Tuthmosis III, while the sanctuary preserves original reliefs of that period. In the sanctuary is the

cult image of Ptah (now headless), which is lit, with magical effect, by an aperture in the roof. To the right is a room containing a *statue of the lion-headed goddess Sakhmet*, to the left another room with reliefs of Tuthmosis III.

SE of the Temple of Ptah, on the way to the Temple of Osiris, is a *storehouse* built by Shabaka, consisting of a single hall with 12 columns. Round the brick-built walls are stone tables on which offerings were laid.

From the Temple of Ptah a gateway in the N enclosure wall of the Temple of Amun gives access to the **Northern Temple precinct**, also surrounded by a brick wall. Within this enclosure is the **Temple of Month**, the war god and old local god of Thebes. It was built by Amenophis III (18th Dynasty), but was several times altered and enlarged down to the period of the Ptolemies. The temple is so badly ruined that it is difficult even to make out the ground-plan, but the older fragments of sculpture and architectural elements display a high standard of artistic skill. Outside the N entrance stood two obelisks of red granite, of which the bases and some fragments still remain. The N gateway of the temple precinct, of sandstone, was built by Ptolemy Euergetes. – In the enclosure wall to the S of the temple is a *gateway* with the name of Nectanebo II and the remains of a list of the peoples whom he subdued.

To the SW of the Ptolemaic gateway are the remains of a *temple* of the Ptolemaic period, and beyond this six small *chapels*, each with a sandstone gateway in the brick enclosure wall. The only considerable remains are those of the two chapels to the W, one of which bears the names of Amenirdis and her brother Shabaka. – Farther on towards the Nile are brick dwelling-houses, mostly in a state of ruin, and the remains of a small temple dedicated to Thoth by Ptolemy Philopator. – Still farther N, among the houses of Karnak village, can be found a small *temple* with palm columns built by Shepenwepet, daughter of the Ethiopian ruler Piankhi.

To the S of Ramesses II's enclosure wall round the Temple of Amun lies the **Sacred Lake** (Arabic *Birket el-Mallaha*, "Lake of the Salt-Pan"; the water of the lake is slightly saline). The walls encircling the lake are well preserved on the W, S and N sides, from which steps lead down to the water. On the N side is a structure built by Tuthmosis III. Near the NW corner are the ruins of a building erected by Taharqa, and on the edge of the lake is a large *granite scarab dedicated by Amenophis III to the sun god Atum-Khepri, who was represented in the form of a scarab.

Adjoining the S end of the central court of the Temple of Amun is a badly ruined court flanked by walls and bounded at the far end by the Seventh Pylon. In this court stood two temples, both demolished during the reign of Tuthmosis III; one dated from the Middle Kingdom, the other was built by Amenophis I. The fine limestone blocks from these temples, decorated with reliefs, were built into the Third Pylon erected by Amenophis III. Here, too, is the *favissa* or offerings pit (now filled in) in which a huge number of statues of many different periods (779 of stone and no fewer than 17,000 of bronze) were found between 1902 and 1909; most of them are now in the Egyptian Museum in Cairo. They came from the Temple of Amun, and were probably buried here when they were no longer required. – On the outside of the W wall of the court is inscribed Ramesses II's peace treaty with the Hittites. On the E wall is a long inscription about King Merneptah's battles with the Libyans and Mediterranean peoples (Etruscans and Achaeans), together with a relief showing the King smiting his enemies with a club in the presence of Amun.

The **SEVENTH PYLON** was built by Tuthmosis III, whose victories are celebrated on the front and rear faces. Like the Eighth Pylon, it lay on the S approach to the Temple of Amenophis I which was pulled down by Tuthmosis III. In front of the N façade are seven *colossal statues* in red granite of rulers of the Middle and New Kingdoms, in front of the S façade the lower parts of two colossal statues of Tuthmosis III, and in front of the more easterly of these figures the lower part of a large obelisk erected by Tuthmosis III (now in Istanbul).

On the E tower of the pylon is a *figure of Osiris* (on the front of which is a later inscription by Ramesses II) and *colossal statues of Tuthmosis III*. On the W tower, from left to right, are a *colossal statue of Tuthmosis III* wearing the double crown, an Osiris figure of Tuthmosis (the head of which has fallen off), a *seated figure* of a Pharaoh of the Middle Kingdom, a *seated figure of Sobkhotep*, a fine *statue of Amenophis II* and the left-hand half of an inscription in the name of Horemheb.

Beside the Seventh Pylon is a modern door by which visitors usually leave the temple to see the reliefs on the outside of the S wall of the Great Hypostyle Hall. – Abutting the left-hand (E) wall of the court between the Seventh and Eighth Pylons is a small, badly ruined *chapel* dating from the reign of Tuthmosis III. Farther along the wall are reliefs of Ramesses II making offerings to the gods.

The **EIGHTH PYLON** was built by Queen Hatshepsut and is thus the oldest in the whole temple complex; it

Temple precinct, Karnak: the Sacred Lake

is, however, relatively well preserved. Hatshepsut's names were erased from the reliefs by Tuthmosis II. Sethos I restored the reliefs after their destruction by Amenophis IV, in many cases inserting his own name in place of those of the earlier kings. – Of the reliefs on the N front the most interesting are the following. Left-hand (E) tower: above, Sethos I making offerings to various deities; farther right, Tuthmosis II (originally Hatshepsut) conducted into the temple by the lion-headed goddess Werthekaw, who is followed by Hathor, while behind the King priests bear the sacred barque of Amun; below, Tuthmosis I before the Theban divine triad, in front of the King an inscription relating to Hatshepsut's accession. Right-hand (W) tower, left to right: Sethos I (originally Hatshepsut) conducted into the temple by the falcon-headed god Month, who holds the hieroglyph for "life" to his nostrils, with priests bearing the sacred barque behind the King; upper row, right, Tuthmosis II (originally Hatshepsut) before Amun and Khons, behind him the goddess Werthekaw and Thoth, who inscribes his name on a palm branch; below, in two rows, Ramesses III before various gods. On the door-jambs are inscriptions in the names of Tuthmosis II (originally Hatshepsut) and Tuthmosis III.

On either side of the gateway Ramesses II is depicted in the presence of various gods. – The reliefs on the S front of the pylon show Amenophis II seizing fettered enemies by the hair and smiting them with his club; in front of him is Amun (added later by Sethos I). On the door-jambs are inscriptions in the name of Tuthmosis II (originally Hatshepsut) and Tuthmosis III. – Against the right-hand jamb leans a much-damaged red granite stela recording Amenophis II's campaigns in Asia. – On a side doorway on the E end of the E tower are reliefs and inscriptions by High Priests of Amun in the reign of Sethos II. – On the outside of the E wall of the court (facing the sacred lake) are reliefs showing the High Priest Amenhotep before Ramesses IX.

Of the four *colossal seated figures* of Kings in front of the S side of the Eighth Pylon the best preserved is that of Amenophis I (to W; limestone); the two figures of Tuthmosis II (the more westerly of siliceous sandstone; according to an inscription on the back, restored by Tuthmosis III in the 42nd year of his reign) lack the upper part of the body.

The **NINTH PYLON**, built by Horemheb, partly with stone from a Temple of Amenophis IV, is in a state of total ruin.

Beyond the pylon is a square walled court, on the E side of which are the ruins of a small **Temple of Amenophis II**, probably built on the occasion of his Jubilee. It stands on a base topped by a cavetto cornice, approached by a ramp on the W side. In front is a hall with 12 square pillars decorated with reliefs. From this a granite doorway leads into a large five-aisled hall, the ceiling of which was borne on 20 square pillars crowned by cavetto cornices. To the right is a smaller pillared room containing the lower part of a colossal alabaster statue; the corresponding room on the left is separated from the main chamber by a narrow corridor. The carvings on the walls and pillars

are mostly done in delicate low relief, with a few in sunk relief; much of the coloring is well preserved. The reliefs depict the King before various gods.

On the E wall of the court are a number of important reliefs of King Horemheb: the King conducting into the presence of the Theban divine triad prisoners from the Land of Punt bearing costly gifts and fettered Syrian captives. – On the rear side of the wall is a relief showing a procession of priests with the sacred barque. Beside this an inscription, dating from the time of the High Priest Pinudjem II, records the appointment of a priest in deference to an oracle of Amun.

The **TENTH PYLON**, which from the late 18th Dynasty onwards was the southern entrance to the precinct of the Temple of Amun, was built by Horemheb, using stone from a temple which Amenophis IV (Akhenaten) had erected in Karnak in honor of his new god. The reliefs on the central granite doorway show Horemheb making offerings to various gods and performing other ritual acts. – In front of the N face of the pylon are two headless *statues of Ramesses II*, of fine-grained limestone (with an adjoining figure of his wife), and the remains of a stele recording a declaration by Horemheb designed to restore order in the State. In front of the S face are the remains of two *colossal statues* of *Amenophis III* (E) and Horemheb (W); beside the statue of Amenophis is the lower part of a huge Osiris figure.

From the Tenth Pylon an *avenue of sphinxes* dating from the reign of Horemheb (in which stones from Amenophis IV's temple, formerly built into the Tenth Pylon, are now deposited) leads to a *gateway* built by Ptolemy II Philadelphus, with reliefs and long inscriptions, in the enclosure wall of the **Southern Temple Precinct**. To the E of the avenue is a *Chapel of Osiris-Ptah* built by the Ethiopian rulers Tanutamun and Taharqa (25th Dynasty), with well-preserved painted mural reliefs. – The gateway leads into an unexcavated area in which large figures of rams, sphinxes and a large alabaster stela of Amenophis III (usurped by Ramesses II) lie around.

To the E is a badly ruined *Temple of Amenophis III* dedicated to Amun-Re. Oriented from W to E, it consists of a colonnaded court, a hypostyle hall, two vestibules, the sanctuary and several subsidiary chambers.

Immediately S of the gateway is the **Temple of Mut**, also built by Amenophis III. In front of the entrance are pillars bearing figures of the god Bes. The doorway itself has long inscriptions of the Ptolemaic period (hymns to the goddess Mut) and an inscription of Ramesses III, who restored the temple.

The doorway leads into a large *Court,* across which a processional way flanked by columns led to the temple proper. In the court are numerous *seated figures of the goddess Sakhmet* dedicated by Amenophis III, on some of which his name has been replaced by that of Sheshonq I. To the left, lying on the ground, are two gigantic figures of Amenophis III (usurped by Ramesses II) which formerly stood before the entrance to the temple. – Beyond this is a *Second Court,* with colonnades along the sides, across which the processional way continued. Fragments of the Hathor capitals of the pillars and of statues of Sakhmet lie around. To the right of the entrance is a large *statue of Sakhmet,* to the left a black granite *statue of Amenophis III*. On the far side of the court are a hall with papyrus cluster-columns, the *Sanctuary* and other rooms, all in a ruinous state.

Beyond the temple lies the horseshoe-shaped *Sacred Lake,* at the W end of which are the remains of a small **Temple of Ramesses III**.

The entrance to the temple, at the N end, was formed by a **Pylon** (ruined) with two figures of the King. On the W outer wall are interesting reliefs celebrating the King's wars: 1. a battle in Syria; 2. Syrian prisoners brought before the King, heaps of severed hands being counted; 3. a battle with the Libyans; 4. the King's triumphal return, with a train of Libyan prisoners; 5. inspection of prisoners by the King; 6. a train of prisoners; 7. presentation of the booty to Amun and his fellow deities. On the S wall the King is depicted before Sakhmet, who leads Amun by the hand.

The excavation and study of the Great Temple of Amun and its subsidiary temples is still far from complete. Under the Akhenaten Temple Project at present in progress, begun by the University Museum of Pennsylvania and carried on jointly by the Egyptian Department of Antiquities and the Smithsonian Institution in Washington, D.C., computer analysis is being used to identify, date and classify architectural elements and stones bearing reliefs. It will thus be possible to reconstruct earlier buildings which had been pulled down and reused in the structure of later ones.

From Karnak an excursion can be made to the Temple of **Medamut**, only 5 miles/8 km away (see separate entry).

Luxor and **Thebes** (West): see separate entries.

Kelya
See under Wadi Natrun

Kerdasa
See under Abu Roash

Kertassi
See under Kalabsha

Kharga Oasis

Western Desert. – New Valley Frontier District.

ACCOMMODATION. – Government guest-house and a modest inn.

ACCESS. – 63 miles/100 km S of Asyut on a reasonably good asphalt road (adequate supplies and proper equipment for desert travel essential); bus service. – By rail (goods traffic only) from Oasis Junction at Nag Hammadi. – By air from Cairo.

The oasis town of Kharga

The *Kharga Oasis, known to the ancient Egyptians as the Southern Oasis and to the Romans as the Great Oasis (Oasis Magna: "great" compared with Dakhla), lies in latitude 25° 26′ N and longitude 30° 33′ E, extending some 125 miles/200 km from N to S with a breadth of 12–30 miles/20–50 km. Like almost all the Egyptian oases, Kharga is surrounded by a fairly steep chain of hills (Cretaceous limestones), which rise in stages to a height of 1410 ft/ 430 m. The lush green of the palm groves and walled fruit plantations makes an attractive and refreshing contrast with the ochre-yellow of the desert rocks.

HISTORY. – In ancient times, thanks to the many springs emerging from clefts in the Cretaceous marls, Kharga was a region of great fertility with many towns and smaller settlements, the remains of which –

sometimes excellently preserved – can still be seen. As an important staging-point on the "caravan route of the forty days" from Asyut to the Sudanese oasis of Darfur it developed a lively economic and cultural life. In the medieval period, however – no doubt because of a falling-off in the water-supply – the importance of the oasis was considerably reduced.

In recent years the New Valley development programme for the desert region between Kharga and Dakhla has been energetically pursued. The project also involves the oases of Bahriya and Farafra. Altogether an area of some 30,000 sq. miles/80,000 sq. km will be irrigated and made fertile by the drilling of wells to tap ground-water at depths of 3300–4900 ft/ 1000–1500 m. The plans provide for the improvement of the infrastructure (road-building, airfield) and of living conditions and for the resettlement in the New Valley of families from the over-populated Nile Valley. Impressive results have been achieved; but it is not yet certain whether the reserves of ground-water, which were left by a former arm of the Nile in the Tertiary era and in this arid region are not supplemented to any significant extent by rainfall, will be sufficient in the longer term to transform the desert into a garden.

The 15,000 inhabitants of the oasis, partly of Berber stock and partly incomers from Nubia, live from the produce of their large plantations of date-palms (some 200,000 in number) and from the cultivation of fruit, rice, corn and vegetables. In recent years the extraction of phosphates in the northern part of the area has made an increasing contribution to the economy.

The chief place in the oasis and in the New Valley Frontier District is the little town of **Kharga**, which has a population of some 9000. The old part of the town is a labyrinth of narrow lanes roofed over with palm-trunks and branches. From Kharga the ancient sites in the northern part of the oasis can be visited.

Some $2\frac{1}{2}$ miles/4 km N of the town, picturesquely situated in a palm grove, is the ***Temple of Hibis**, dedicated to Amun, which was built by Darius I (521– 486 B.C.), Nectanebo II (358–341 B.C.) and some of the Ptolemies. The remains were excavated in 1909–11 by an archaeological expedition from the Metropolitan Museum of Art in New York and restored by the Egyptian Department of Antiquities. The temple, measuring 138 ft/42 m by 66 ft/20 m, is oriented from W to E. It is approached by four gateways; on the right-hand side of the second gateway is a long Greek inscription (66 lines) recording a decree on the levying of taxes dated to the 2nd year of the reign of the Emperor Galba (A.D. 69).

Temple of Hibis

The temple is entered through a *portico* built by
Nectanebo II, with reliefs of Nectanebo I and II making
offerings and performing various ritual acts, accompanied by dedicatory inscriptions. Adjoining the
portico is a *colonnaded court,* on the rear wall of
which a winged, falcon-headed Horus is depicted
killing the Apophis snake. Beyond this is a *vestibule,*
with reliefs depicting the King in the presence of the
gods and mythological inscriptions, which leads into
a small *hypostyle hall* with four columns; to the left is
a staircase leading to a *Chapel of Osiris*. The *Sanctuary*
contains some interesting representations of deities
(Astarte on horseback, Astarte with bow and arrows,
etc.). To the left is a staircase mounting to the roof, to
the right a small chamber with a representation of the
god Khnum shaping the King on a potter's wheel.

A little way N of the temple are the ruins
of the Roman city of **Hibis** (Egyptian
Hibet), with some well-preserved remains
of houses.

On a ridge ¾ mile/1 km N of the temple
is the *Christian cemetery of El-
Bagawat**, with several hundred brick-
built tombs ranging in date from the Late
Empire to the Coptic period (4th–7th c.),
with a particular concentration of tombs
dating from the period when Athanasius
and Nestorius were banished to Kharga
(4th–5th c.). Mostly lying on either side of
a broad street, the tombs follow the
ancient Eastern and Coptic pattern of a
domed chamber, frequently with an apse
containing lateral niches on the E side and
preceded by a vestibule, which in the
larger tombs may become a regular little

basilica. The façades are frequently
decorated with pilasters and semi-
columns, and many have small triangular
niches for lamps. Little of the interior
decoration survives. In *Tomb 30* is a
representation of the Exodus (first half of
4th c.), while *Tomb 30* has a relief of
Daniel in the lions' den and other Biblical
scenes in Byzantine style (5th–6th c.). In
the middle of the cemetery is a ruined
church, probably dating from the 5th c.

¾ mile/1 km N of the cemetery is the
**Monastery of Qasr Ain Mustafa
Kashif**, a well-preserved brick structure
originally built in the 4th or 5th c. over the
tomb of a hermit, rebuilt in the 7th c. and
abandoned about the 10th c. The
entrance, on the N side, is protected by a
high square tower. On the W side are the
vaulted cells of the monks, in several
storeys; on the E side the refectory, the
assembly hall and the chapel. Just N of the
complex of buildings originally very
extensive, can be seen traces of the
gardens laid out round the well, which is
now dry.

Some 15 miles/25 km NE of Kharga can
be seen the remains of the **Roman Fort
of El-Deir**, a large structure with round
towers; on the N side is a temple. There are
other remains in the vicinity.

Christian cemetery, El-Bagawat

On a hill 1¼ miles/2 km SE is the **Temple
of Nadura**, surrounded by a high brick
wall, which dates from the reign of
Antoninus Pius (A.D. 138–161). The
pronaos, which stands on the W side of
the forecourt, with columns linked by
stone screens, is well preserved. – From
the triangulation point beside the temple
there is a fine *view of the northern part of
the oasis.

Roughly in the middle of the oasis is the
ruined Fort of **Qasr el-Ghueida**, near

which, enclosed within a high brick wall, are numbers of small brick-built houses and a red sandstone *temple* dedicated to the Theban deities Amun, Mut and Khons, with reliefs and inscriptions ranging in date from the 25th Dynasty to the Ptolemaic period. – $2\frac{1}{2}$ miles/4 km S is the ruined Fort of **Qasr Ain el-Sayyan**, with a temple of the Graeco-Roman period.

In the extreme S of the Kharga Oasis lies the large village of *Baris,* SW of which by way of *El-Maks* is **Qasr Dush** (ancient *Cysis*), with a large temple of the Roman Imperial period dedicated to Serapis and Isis. In the vicinity is another brick-built temple. – A few miles from Qasr Dush, at *Khams el-Dinei,* a 4th c. * church has recently been excavated – the earliest securely dated church in Egypt.

New Valley and **Western Desert**: see separate entries.

Kitchener's Island
See under Aswan

Kom el-Ahmar

Upper Egypt. – Governorate: Qena.
(i) **Tourist Information Office,**
Tourist Bazaar,
Luxor;
tel. 22 15.

ACCESS. – By road from Edfu ($12\frac{1}{2}$ miles/20 km S) or Esna (19 miles/30 km N).

On the W bank of the Nile opposite El-Kab, $\frac{3}{4}$ mile/1 km SW of the village of Muissat, is the Kom el-Ahmar ("Red Hill"), with the extensive remains and cemeteries of ancient Nekhen (Greek Hieraconpolis), one of the oldest cities in Egypt. The joint capital of Upper Egypt formed by the closely associated towns of Nekhab and Nekhen (El-Kab and Kom el-Ahmar) was the counterpart of the Lower Egyptian capital of Pe and Dep (Tell el-Faraun). The frequently occurring representations of the jackal-headed figures known as the "souls of Nekhen" are believed to date back to Pre-Dynastic times.

The town's protective god was a Horus with a high double feather whose sacred animal was the falcon: hence the Greek name of Hieraconpolis. Remains of temples, tombs and dwelling-houses extend for some 2 miles/3 km along the edge of the desert to the S and SW of Muissat. At the mouth of a wadi is a fortress-like structure of unknown function dating from the Early Old Kingdom, with a low outer wall and a higher interior wall built of sun-dried brick; the entrance was on the E side. – Near by, within the area of cultivation, are the scanty remains of the *Temple of Nekhen,* which was excavated by Quibell in 1897–99 and yielded important sculpture of the Early Old Kingdom (6th Dynasty), including copper figures of Phiops I and Merenre, a gold Horus head and the famous* *Palette of Narmer,* the only votive palette of this period to survive in relatively undamaged condition.

To the W of the brick-built "fort" is a hill containing *tombs* of the Old and Middle Kingdoms, in two of which are stucco reliefs and inscriptions. – $\frac{3}{4}$ mile/1 km farther W are **rock tombs** of the Early New Kingdom, similar in form to those of El-Kab. The most notable are the *Tomb of Dhuti,* dating from the reign of Tuthmosis I, and the *Tomb of Harmose,* High Priest of Nekhen, both of which have statues of the dead men and their wives in niches on the rear wall. – At the eastern end of the prehistoric cemetery area Quibell discovered during his 1897–99 campaigns the Pre-Dynastic tomb known simply as *Tomb 100,* richly decorated with mural paintings (animals, human figures, boats, etc.) which are now in the Egyptian Museum in Cairo.

* *Edfu, *Esna and *El-Kab: see separate entries.

Kom el-Hisn
See under Damanhur

Kom Ombo

Upper Egypt. – Governorate: Aswan.
ⓘ **Tourist Information Office,**
Tourist Bazaar,
Aswan;
tel. 32 97.

ACCESS. – By road (the road skirting the Nile) or rail from Aswan, 25 miles/40 km S.

The ancient Egyptian town of Ombos, whose name has been preserved in the present-day Kom Ombo ("Hill of Ombos"), probably owed its foundation to the strategic importance of its site, commanding the Nile and the routes from Nubia into the Nile Valley. Its heyday, however, was in the Ptolemaic period, when it was made capital of the Ombite nome and its magnificent temples were built.

HISTORY. – Of the temples of the earlier period practically nothing is left. The two principal gods of Ombos were the crocodile-headed Sobek (Suchos) and the falcon-headed Haroeris. With Sobek were associated Hathor and the youthful moon god Khons-Hor, with Haroeris Tsentnofret, the "Good Sister", a special personification of Hathor, and Penebtawi, "lord of the Two Lands". The remains of the town, now buried in sand, lie at the NE corner of the plateau. The temple complex, to the S, was excavated and restored by de Morgan in 1893.

The temple precinct, lying some 50 ft/15 m above the average level of the Nile, was enclosed by a brick wall, entered on the S side through a massive gateway built by Ptolemy XII Neos Dionysos. The left-hand (W) side of the gateway has been carried away by the Nile, but the right-hand half still stands. It has reliefs showing Neos Dionysos presenting various offerings to the deities of Ombos.

The great ***Temple of Suchos and Haroeris** was built to a unified plan, which in effect accommodated two temples in a single building, and embellished with reliefs by Philometor, Euergetes II and Neos Dionysos; the reliefs in the court and on the outer walls were added by various Roman Emperors, in particular Tiberius. The general plan is similar to that of other Ptolemaic temples (Dendera, Edfu, Philae); but since it was dedicated to two principal deities, each with his own rites and festivals, it was divided by an imaginary line along its longitudinal axis into two halves, each of which had its own gateways and doors and its own chapel. The right-hand (S) half belongs to Sobek (Suchos), the left-hand half to Haroeris.

The **Pylon** by which the court is entered had two gateways; but the left-hand half has completely disappeared and only the lower parts of the central pillar and the right wing survive. On the right-hand front wall are, from left to right, Sobek, Hathor and Khons, a hieroglyphic text of 52 lines and a relief of the Emperor Domitian, wearing the crown of Upper Egypt, and 14 deities making offerings to the two principal gods. Above this last scene, at the right-hand end of the pylon, are other reliefs: six spirits (the three to the rear being the dog-headed "souls of Hieraconpolis") bearing the newly crowned King (destroyed) in a throne to the palace, followed by the hieroglyphic signs for "life" and "well-being" borne by gods on long poles; and a large figure of the King making his way from the palace to the temple, preceded by a priest burning incense and followed by his *ka* bearing a scepter topped by a King's head.

Temple of Suchos and Haroeris, Kom Ombo

The **Court**, as at Edfu, was surrounded on three sides by colonnades, but only the lower halves of the 16 columns are left. The reliefs, which depict Tiberius making offerings, are remarkable for the freshness of their coloring. On the inner side of the right-hand wing of the pylon are two doors, one of which (nearer the entrance) leads into a small chamber, the other (at the corner of the court) to a staircase mounting to the roof. The ancient paving of the court, like that of the temple itself, is excellently preserved. In the center of the court is a square base, perhaps for an altar; and let into the pavement on either side of this are two small granite troughs. Along the far side of the court are stone screens, between which are two large and two smaller doorways. On the right-hand screen the falcon-headed Horus and the ibis-headed Thoth are depicted pouring the water of consecration over King Neos Dionysos, with the crocodile-headed Sobek, lord of the right-hand half of the temple, standing on the left. On the left-hand screen is the same scene, watched by the falcon-headed Haroeris (upper part of body destroyed), lord of the left-hand half of the temple. Along the tops of the screens are a row of serpents with solar discs on their heads.

The **Vestibule** has ten columns with rich foliage and palm capitals and is embellished with reliefs by Neos Dionysos (incised reliefs on the columns, bas-reliefs on the walls). On the shafts of the columns the King is depicted making offerings to the gods. On the ceiling over the two main aisles are flying vultures. On the underside of the architraves, which are borne on abaci, are astronomical representations (star gods in their boats, etc.). The grids used by the artists in setting out the picture can still be seen in some cases, as well as sketches which were never carried to completion. The mural reliefs are very fine, in particular the one to the left of the N doorway, which depicts Neos Dionysos, in the presence of Haroeris (on the right), being blessed by a lion-headed Isis and the falcon-headed Harsiesis (on the right) and by the goddess Nut and the ibis-headed Thoth (on the left).

If time permits it is worth while looking carefully at the other mural reliefs as well. On the rear side of the E screen between the court and the vestibule: the King being blessed by the tutelary goddesses of Upper and Lower Egypt, with the crocodile-headed Sobek and Hathor standing on the left. – Next to this, above the small doorway: Neos Dionysos making offerings to four fabulous beasts, including a four-headed winged lion (the animals have been obliterated). – On the opposite wall (the outer wall of the hypostyle hall): bottom row, on right, Euergetes II and Cleopatra VII (upper parts missing) in the presence of Suchos and his two fellow deities Hathor and Penebtawi, center, the King in the presence of the falcon-headed Haroeris and the "Good Sister"; on left, Euergetes presenting the Temple of Ombos to Sobek and Hathor; middle row, right, the King (missing) making offerings to Osiris, seated on a throne, to Isis and her young son and to Nephthys; centre, Euergetes presenting flowers to the earth god Geb and the sky goddess Nut; left, the King offering two jars of wine to Shu and the lion-headed Tefnut; top row, right, the King (missing) in the presence of Haroeris, the "Good Sister" and Penebtawi; center, the King presenting an ornament to Sobek and Khons-Hor; left, Euergetes II offering milk to Sobek and Hathor (badly damaged). – On the corresponding wall on the left-hand side are three rows of similar scenes.

Two doorways lead into the **Hypostyle Hall**, the roof of which (lower than that of the vestibule) was supported on ten papyrus columns with floral capitals.

Temple of Kom Ombo

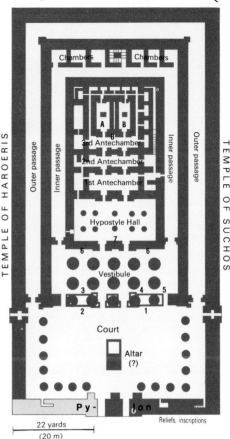

Reliefs, inscriptions

| 22 yards |
| (20 m) |

A Chapel of Haroeris   B Chapel of Suchos (Sobek)

RELIEFS
1 Horus and Thoth with Suchos
2 Horus and Thoth with Haroeris
3 King Neos Dionysos with Haroeris, Isis, Harsiesis, Nut and Thoth
4 The King blessed by the protective goddesses
5 Neos Dionysos making offerings to four fabulous beasts
6 Various offering scenes
7 Sacred crocodile of Ombos
8 Philometor and Cleopatra before Khons

On the column shafts Euergetes is depicted making offerings to various gods. The reliefs on the walls show him in converse with the gods. Note particularly the relief on the left-hand (N) wall: the falcon-headed Haroeris presenting to the King, behind whom are his sister Cleopatra VII and his wife Cleopatra, the curved sword of victory and the hieroglyph for eternal life. Between the doors from the vestibule is the sacred crocodile of Ombos. – Between the doors leading into the rear part of the temple are reliefs of Euergetes II's elder brother Philometor making an offering to the falcon-headed Haroeris.

The three **Antechambers** to the rear of the hypostyle hall, each slightly higher than the one before, also have fine reliefs. The small rooms on the left-hand side, which served as store-rooms, have almost completely disappeared. On the rear wall of the third antechamber, between two doors, is a fine relief of Philometor in a long white mantle, with Cleopatra behind him, standing before the falcon-headed moon god Khons, who is writing the King's name on a palm branch with the symbol for a long reign; to the rear are the principal gods of Ombos, Haroeris and Sobek.

Antechambers of the Kom Ombo Temple

The two doors in the rear wall of the third antechamber lead into the **Chapels** (only foundations preserved) of Haroeris (left) and Sobek (right). The black granite base in each chapel was for the sacred barque with the image of the god. Around the chapels were a number of smaller rooms with crypts.

From the vestibule two doors open into the *inner passage* round the temple, at the far end of which are seven small chambers. The unfinished reliefs in these chambers are of interest as showing different stages in the artists' work; there are also inscriptions sketched out but never completed. From the central chamber a staircase mounts to the upper floor.

The E walls of the *outer passage* round the temple are covered with reliefs depicting the Emperor Trajan making offerings to Egyptian gods. At the NE corner he is shown kneeling before two deities; beside this scene is a set of medical instruments.

On the terrace in front of the temple is a small, badly ruined **birth-house** *(mammisi),* built or restored by Euergetes II, the façade of which faced SE. Of the surviving reliefs one, on the W side, is worth notice: it shows Euergetes and two gods sailing in a boat through a papyrus swamp swarming with birds, with an ithyphallic Min-Amun-Re standing on the left. – On the S side is an underground staircase leading down to the river, on the banks of which are the remains of a *Nilometer* similar to the one at Edfu.

In the open space E of the birth-house and N of the temple are two large and handsome blocks from an architrave, one of them bearing the name of Neos Dionysos; the remains of several small structures, including a Roman doorway and a ruined chapel standing on a platform; two *wells,* one large and one small, with a water channel leading to a small pool in which young sacred crocodiles may have been kept; a small chapel dedicated to Suchos by Caracalla; a Coptic church, with only one column still standing; and a large Coptic house.

To the S of the temple court is a small *chapel* dedicated to Hathor, of red sandstone, built in the time of Domitian (unfinished). In one room of this are the mummies of sacred crocodiles found in the vicinity.

SURROUNDINGS of Kom Ombo. – The Temple of Suchos and Haroeris lies in the heart of the **Wadi Kom Ombo,** a valley some 37 miles/60 km long and 16 miles/25 km wide which opens out immediately S of the Silsila Gorge (see under Silsila). The chief place in the valley is the busy market town of Kom Ombo (pop. 25,000). This area of fertile alluvial soil, engulfed in the course of many centuries by the desert sand, has been irrigated and brought under cultivation since the beginning of the 20th c. by the privately owned Kom Ombo Company and now produces large quantities of sugar-cane (refined in a large local refinery) as well as cotton and vegetables. There has also been some development of stock-farming.

Relief in the Kom Ombo Temple

On the E side of the valley many of the Egyptian Nubians displaced by the construction of the Aswan High Dam (some 50,000 in all) have been resettled and provided with land. This area, now known as **New Nubia** *(El-Nuba el Gedida),* has been divided up into 40 rural districts or village territories with the same names as the 40 village units of "old" Nubia. The new villages are laid out on a regular plan and have all the necessary social services and cultural facilities. There have, however, been difficulties arising from the breaking up of established social structures and the sudden transfer of an exclusively rural population to a partly industrialized setting. It is planned to return part of the transferred population to the shores of Lake Nasser.

Aswan, **Edfu** and **Silsila**: see separate entries.

Kuban
See under Wadi el-Sebwa

El-Lahun (Illahun)

Middle Egypt. – Governorate: Fayyum.

(i) **Tourist Information Office,**
Misr Travel Tower,
Cairo – Abbasia;
tel. 82 60 16.

ACCESS. – By road from Beni Suef (11 miles/18 km SE) or Medinet el-Fayyum (10 miles/16 km NW).

The village of El-Lahun or Illahun, the Egyptian Ro-hent and Coptic Lehone ("Mouth of the Canal"), lies on the right bank of the Bahr Yusuf to the N of the point where it leaves the Nile Valley and turns into a narrow passageway through the desert mountains on its way to the Fayyum. At El-Lahun are two sluice-bridges regulating the flow of the Bahr Yusuf and the Giza Canal, successors to the massive ancient dams of the 12th Dynasty.

$1\frac{1}{4}$ miles/2 km NE of El-Lahun, in the desert, is the *Pyramid of Sesostris II (Senwosret), the structure of which is considerably different from that of earlier pyramids. Over a stone core some 30 ft/12 m high, which can be seen at several points, was built a framework of cross walls constructed of huge limestone blocks, the intervening spaces being filled by limestone bricks. Over this was a superstructure, also of brick. The whole pyramid had a casing of limestone, of which nothing now remains; the apex was faced with granite. The original base measurement was 351 ft/107 m. – The pyramid also differed from the normal pattern in having the entrance on the S side and not the usual N side. From the entrance two passages ran down, constantly changing direction, to the granite-clad tomb chamber containing the King's magnificent red granite sarcophagus and an alabaster offering-table.

N and NE of the pyramid are eight rock-cut *tombs* and the remains of the small *Queen's Pyramid.* – S of the pyramid are four *shaft graves* belonging to relatives of the King. In one of these, the Tomb of Princess Sat-Hathor-Yunet, daughter of Sesostris II, Flinders Petrie (who excavated the whole pyramid complex) found in 1914 the Princess's gold jewelry, a treasure of the highest artistic quality which is now shared between the Metropolitan Museum of Art in New York and the Egyptian Museum in Cairo.

The *Valley Temple* belonging to the pyramid lies $\frac{3}{4}$ mile/1 km E, on the margins of the cultivated land. Here, too, was the town of **Hetep Senwosret** ("Sesostris is content") or **Kahun**, founded by Sesostris II and occupied by workers, priests and officials. Laid out on a regular plan, it was inhabited only for a brief period during the 12th Dynasty, perhaps only during the construction of the pyramid. In the remains were found not only a variety of everyday objects but also numerous papyri (the Kahun Papyri) in hieratic script with mathematical, medical, legal, religious and literary texts. – Farther N is a *crocodile cemetery.*

2 miles/3 km SW of El-Lahun is the *Kom Medinet Gurab,* with the remains of a settlement dating from the late 18th and 19th Dynasties. It is still possible to identify dwelling-houses, two temples (one of them built by Tuthmosis III) and the necropolis. Much of the material found here referred to the reign of Amenophis III and his wife Tiy, suggesting that the town flourished particularly during his reign.

3 miles/5 km NE of El-Lahun, on the edge of the cultivated land, are the remains of the Coptic Monastery of *Deir el-Hammam,* with a church which dates from Early Christian times.

Beni Suef and the ****Fayyum**: see separate entries.

Lisht

Lower Egypt. – Governorate: Giza.

(i) **Tourist Information Office,**
Misr Travel Tower,
Cairo – Abbasia;
tel. 82 60 16.

ACCESS. – By road from Cairo (Giza), 43 miles/70 km S along the left bank of the Nile.

The pyramids and mastabas of *Lisht lie to the N of the village of that name, some 19 miles/30 km S of Dahshur. Amenemhet I, founder of the 12th Dynasty, moved his capital from Thebes to Lisht in order to establish firmer control over Lower Egypt, and near here, on the edge of the desert, he and his son Sesostris I, who for a time ruled jointly with

him, built their pyramids. The pyramids, now visible only as sand-covered mounds, were surrounded by smaller pyramids for female members of the royal family and hundreds of mastabas belonging to high State officials. A few ir-regularities in the ground on the edge of the cultivated land no doubt mark the site of the erstwhile capital of Itj-towy.

The smaller and more northerly of the two pyramids is the **Pyramid of Amen-emhet I**. This originally had a height of 190 ft/58 m and a base measurement of 275 ft/84 m and, as occasional fragments of inscriptions indicate, was partly built of stone from older tombs at Saqqara and Giza. As in most pyramids, the entrance is on the N side. From there a passage leads down to the tomb chamber, now flooded as a result of a rise in the water-table and, therefore, inaccessible. Within the en-closure wall lay a smaller pyramid for the Queen and, exceptionally, the *Tomb of Antefoker,* Superintendent of the Royal Tombs. Around the main pyramid were found numbers of lizard mummies. – The mortuary temple belonging to the pyramid lay on a lower rock terrace to the E. It was adorned with lively if sometimes rather coarsely executed reliefs.

1 mile/1·5 km S is the larger **Pyramid of Sesostris I**, which is very similar to the Pyramid of Amenemhet I. It, too, is built over a framework of retaining walls with a filling of sand and rubble (cf. the El-Lahun Pyramid) and a layout, with a mortuary temple, a valley temple and a causeway, which continues the 6th Dynasty tradition. The pyramid originally had a height of 200 ft/61 m and a base measurement of 345 ft/105 m, with a limestone casing which has now almost completely disappeared. It was sur-rounded by a double enclosure wall. Within the inner wall, which was built of Tura limestone with slabs bearing reliefs at regular intervals, lay the mortuary temple (on the E side) and, at the SE corner, a small subsidiary pyramid with its own cult chamber and small chapel. The entrance to the main pyramid was in the middle of the N side, with a small chapel built in front of it. A narrow passage faced with red granite led down to the tomb chamber, now filled with water and inaccessible. Within the outer enclosure wall, built of Nile bricks, were the temple forecourts

(on the E side) and, set around the enclosure, nine *small pyramids* for female members of the royal family, each with its own chapel on the E side, a chamber for offerings in front of the entrance and its own enclosure wall. The largest of these subsidiary pyramids, to the SE, belonged to Queen Neferu, the one immediately W of it to Princess Itakayt. No names were found on the other small pyramids.

From the *valley temple,* of which there are only scanty remains, a masonry causeway flanked by Osiris figures of the King led up to the mortuary temple. The line of this causeway can be traced at some points.

During excavations carried out by the Metropolitan Museum of Art of New York ten * seated figures of Sesostris I, finely carved from Tura limestone, were found in one of the subsidiary chambers of the mortuary temple. The excavators also found two painted wooden figures of the King, one of which, with the White Crown of Upper Egypt, is now in the Egyptian Museum in Cairo, while the other, with the Red Crown of Lower Egypt, is in the Metropolitan Museum of Art.

The most interesting of the tombs of high officials which surround the pyramid of Sesostris is the **Mastaba of Senwosret-ankh**, High Priest of Ptah in Memphis as well as the Royal Sculptor and Architect and thus the highest digni-tary in the realm. The size and appoint-ments of the tomb match the importance of its owner. It was surrounded by a double enclosure wall, an outer brick wall enclosing an area 305 ft/93 m long by 165 ft/50 m wide and an inner wall built of massive blocks of Tura limestone. On the E side of the mastaba was a *chapel,* on the N side the entrance, from which a narrow passage descended steeply to the rock-cut *tomb chamber*. The walls of the chamber are covered with hieroglyphic texts, in the manner of the rock tombs and pyramids of the Old Kingdom. On the E side is a cavity in the floor for the sarcophagus, originally covered by four stone slabs with slightly rounded upper surfaces; on the S side is a smaller cavity for the canopic chest.

Also of interest are the *mastabas* of Imhotep, High Priest of Heliopolis, and the Majordomo Sehetepobre-ankh.

Abu Gurab, Abu Roash,* Abusir,** Cairo,* Dahshur,** Fayyum,** Giza,* El-Lahun,* Meidum, Memphis,** Saqqara and Zawiyet el-Aryan: see separate entries.

Luxor

Upper Egypt. – Governorate: Qena.
Population: 60,000.

ⓘ **Tourist Information Office,**
Tourist Bazaar;
tel. 822 15.
Tourist Police,
Tourist Bazaar;
tel. 821 20.
Misr Travel,
Corniche el-Nil;
tel. 23 63.
American Express,
New Winter Palace Hotel;
tel. 8 28 62.

HOTELS. – *Sheraton, Corniche el Nil, L, 500 b.; *Isis, L, 300 b.; *ETAP, Crocodile Island, L, 240 b.; *Mövenpick-Hotel Jolieville, Shari el Nil, L, 640 b.; New Winter Palace, Shari el Nil, I, 520, b.; Akhenaton Village Club (Club Méditerranée), Shari Khaled Ibn El Walrd, I, 288 b.; Luxor, Shari Nefertiti, I, 170 b.; Windsor, opposite the temple, II, 108 b.; Philippe, II, 80 b.; Savoy, Shari Corniche el Nil, III, 440 b.; Ramosa, III, 96 b.; Mina Palace, III, 80 b.; Santa Maria, Shari Television, III, 72 b.; Pyramids, III, 56 b.; Sphinx, IV, 75 b.; Horus, IV, 71 b.; Nefertiti, IV, 54 b.; Venus, IV, 46 b. – YOUTH HOSTEL: Qasr el-Nil.

ACCESS. – By road and rail from Aswan, 125 miles/ 200 km S. – By air (flights several times daily from Cairo and Aswan).

The town of ** Luxor, the great tourist center of Upper Egypt, lies on the right bank of the Nile in an extensive depression bounded on the E by the rock walls of the Eastern Desert Plateau. The modern town occupies part of the area of the ancient Egyptian capital of Thebes, which extended much farther N beyond the temples of Karnak (see separate entry), with its necropolis (see under Thebes) on the W bank of the Nile reaching far into the hills of the Western Desert. The present name is derived from the Arabic El-Qusur (the "Palaces": plural form of El-Qasr) – referring to the mighty temple which was occupied until the end of the 19th c. by the houses of the village.

The town's main traffic artery is the Shari el-Bahr el-Nil, the corniche road, with the landing-stage used by the Nile cruise ships and the cross-river ferries, which runs N and S from the temple. Between the temple and the river are the remains of a Roman forum. To the S are the Winter Palace and New Winter Palace Hotels, and in the immediate vicinity of the temple the Tourist Bazaar, shops, banks and travel agencies. To the N of the temple are other hotels and the Museum. On the eastern outskirts of the town is the station; to the NE, outside the town, the airport.

To the N of Luxor is the great ** temple complex of Karnak, reached in ancient times through the streets of the city but now approached by a broad tree-lined avenue. Even in the time of the Pharaohs the Temple of Amun, the chief god of Thebes, was regarded as the finest creation of an age rich in architectural

General view of the Temple of Luxor, with the Abu el-Haggag Mosque

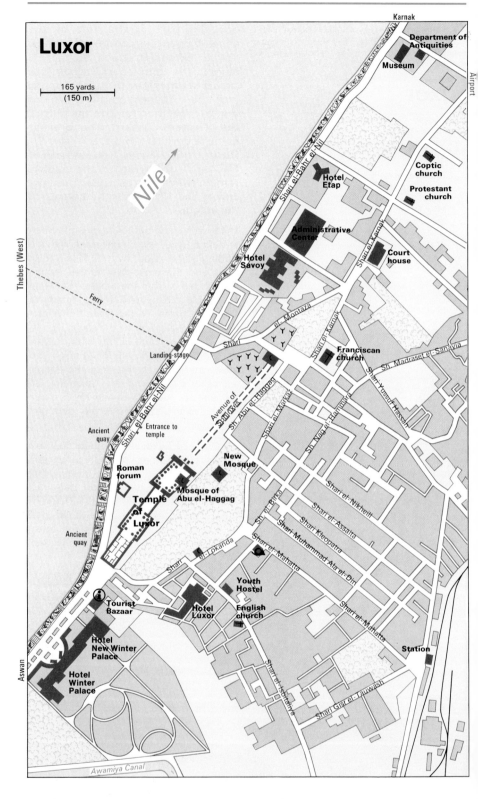

Luxor

165 yards
(150 m)

Karnak

Department of
Antiquities

Museum

Airport

Coptic
church

Protestant
church

Hotel
Etap

Administrative
Center

Court
house

Hotel
Savoy

Thebes (West)

Ferry

Franciscan
church

Sh. Madraset el-Sanavia

Landing-stage

Avenue of
Sphinxes

Entrance to
temple

New
Mosque

Ancient
quay

Roman
forum

Mosque of
Abu el-Haggag

Temple
of
Luxor

Ancient
quay

Youth
Hostel

Tourist
Bazaar

Hotel
Luxor

English
church

Station

Hotel
New Winter
Palace

Aswan

Hotel
Winter
Palace

Awamiya Canal

achievement. – To the N, at Medu,
present-day Medamut (see separate
entry), was another group of temples.

HISTORY: see under Thebes.

SIGHTS. – At the S end of the modern
town, close to the Nile, stands the
imposing **Temple of Luxor**, and
within to the NE, the little Mosque of Abu
el-Haggag, a much-revered Muslim holy

Luxor Temple

55 yards
(50 m)

N.B. During restoration of the S temple court in February 1989 several larger than life-size granite statues were uncovered; the first one to be discovered had the name Pharaos Amenophis III engraved on its base.

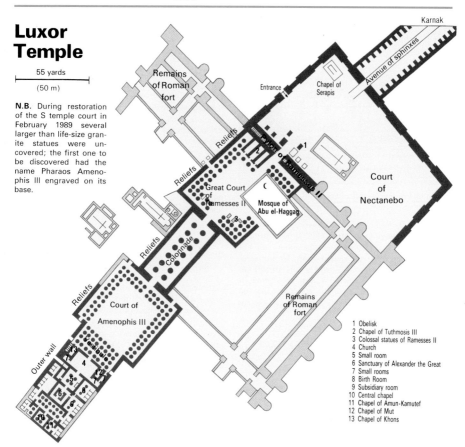

1 Obelisk
2 Chapel of Tuthmosis III
3 Colossal statues of Ramesses II
4 Church
5 Small room
6 Sanctuary of Alexander the Great
7 Small rooms
8 Birth Room
9 Subsidiary room
10 Central chapel
11 Chapel of Amun-Kamutef
12 Chapel of Mut
13 Chapel of Khons

man. The temple was built by Amenophis III on the site of an earlier sandstone temple and was known to the Egyptians as *Apet Amun resyet,* the "Southern Harem of Amun". It was dedicated to Amun, his consort Mut and their son the moon god Khons. Like all Egyptian temples, it comprised the chapels of the deities with their vestibules and subsidiary chambers, a large hypostyle hall and an open peristyle court, which was approached from the N by a great colonnade.

The temple was 623 ft/190 m long and 180 ft/55 m wide at its broadest part. Opposite the temple was a granite chapel built by Tuthmosis III. During Amenophis IV's religious revolution the figures and names of Amun were obliterated and a sanctuary of the Aten, the Sun, was built near the temple. When Tutankhamun moved the royal residence back to Thebes he had the walls of the colonnade embellished with reliefs, in which Horemheb later substituted his own names for those of his predecessor. The Temple of the Aten was destroyed, and in the reign of Sethos I the reliefs of Amun were restored. Ramesses II, the great builder, also extended the Temple of Luxor, adding a new colonnaded court at the N end, usurping Tuthmosis III's chapel and replacing the old reliefs by

new ones, and erected a massive pylon with its doorway adjoining Tuthmosis III's chapel. These later structures involved a slight displacement of the axis of the temple, and increased the total length to 583 ft/ 260 m. Thereafter the temple underwent little alteration. In Christian times it was converted into a church.

The old main entrance was formed by Ramesses II's huge **Pylon**, in front of which were six *colossal statues* of the King, two sitting and four standing; of these there survive the most westerly of the standing figures and the two seated figures, which are 46 ft/14 m high. In front of these two figures were obelisks of pink granite, erected on the occasion of a royal jubilee. The eastern **Obelisk** still stands on its original site; the smaller western one has stood since 1836 in the Place de la Concorde in Paris. The inscriptions refer to Ramesses, with many high-sounding titles, as the founder of the splendid building erected in the Southern Apet in honor of Amun.

On the walls of the pylon are incised *reliefs,* much damaged and now difficult to distinguish, depicting scenes from Ramesses II's campaign against the Hittites in the 5th year of his reign. On the right-hand (W) tower, to the left, the King is seen on his throne holding a Council of War with his Princes; in the middle is the camp, protected by a ring of shields, with the Hittites attacking; and on the right the King in his chariot dashes into the fray. The reliefs on the left-hand tower take us into the thick of the battle: the King in his chariot charges the enemy, launching his arrows against them; the field is strewn with dead and wounded; the Hittites flee in wild confusion to the

South end of the Temple of Luxor

Fortress of Qadesh, from which fresh troops advance against the Egyptians; farther left is the fortress, surrounded by water, with the defenders on the battlements; and on the extreme left, far from the battle, is the Prince of the Hittites in his chariot, turning fearfully towards the King. – The long inscription, in vertical lines, which begins on the W tower below the reliefs and is continued on the E tower is a poetical account of the battle.

On each of the pylon towers are two vertical grooves for flagstaffs, with square apertures for braces holding the flagstaffs in position and small windows to admit light and air to the rooms in the tower. The reliefs on the doorway depict Ramesses II in the presence of the gods of the temple. Those on the inner wall of the doorway, in fairly high relief, date from the reign of the Ethiopian King Shabaka.

Beyond the pylon is the **Great Court of Ramesses II**, 187 ft/57 m long by 167 ft/51 m wide. Owing to the presence of the *mosque* at the NE corner it has not been completely exposed. It was originally surrounded on all four sides by colonnades, with a total of 74 papyrus columns with bud capitals and smooth shafts. At the NW corner is the *chapel*, decorated with reliefs, which was built by Tuthmosis III and usurped by Ramesses II. Along the front of the chapel was a small colonnade of four elegant papyrus cluster-columns of red granite. It has three chambers, which housed the sacred barques of Amun (center), Mut (to the left) and Khons (to the right).

The walls of the court are covered with reliefs and inscriptions – representations of offerings, hymns to the gods, scenes showing conquered nations, etc. – mostly dating from the reign of Ramesses II. The relief on the SW wall shows the façade of the temple and the pylon with its flagstaffs, colossal statues and obelisks; from the right approaches a procession headed by the Princes and followed by garlanded sacrificial animals (continuation on W wall). – In the W wall is a doorway leading out of the court, in front of which are two *statues of Ramesses II* (upper parts missing).

On the S side of the court, between the front columns, are **colossal statues of Ramesses II**, with an average height of 23 ft/7 m, all of red granite except one which is of black granite. The finest of these figures, whose crown, carved from a separate block, has fallen off, was 17½ ft/5·30 m high; on the base and the apron are carved the King's names. On each side of the S doorway is a colossal seated figure of the King with the Queen seated on his right.

Adjoining the court on the S is the **Colonnade**, which is well preserved and makes a major contribution to the imposing effect of the ruins. Seven papyrus columns with open capitals, almost 52 ft/16 m high, still support heavy architraves borne on high abaci. They were erected by Amenophis III, but also bear the names of Tutankhamun, Horemheb, Sethos I, Ramesses II and Sethos II. The fine reliefs on the walls – the upper part of which is destroyed at some points – date from the time of Tutankhamun, whose name was later replaced by that of his successor Horemheb. They depict in vivid detail the great Opet (New Year) festival, when the sacred barques of the gods were taken out of the Temple of Karnak, sailed up the Nile to Luxor, where they were borne into the temple, and then returned to Karnak in the evening. The scenes, full of fascinating details, begin at the NW corner and end at the NE corner.

Beyond the colonnade lies the **Court of Amenophis III**, 148 ft/45 m long by 167 ft/51 m wide, which was surrounded on three sides by a double colonnade of papyrus cluster-columns. The columns and architraves on the E and W sides are excellently preserved. – On the fourth (S) side is the *Vestibule* or pronaos of the temple proper, the roof of which was borne by 32 (4 × 8) papyrus cluster-columns. On the E wall are reliefs showing Amenophis III in the presence of the gods of Thebes; below, personifications of the nomes of Egypt bearing gifts. On the S wall, to the right and left of the apse, is the coronation of Amenophis by the gods. To the left is an *altar* dedicated to the Emperor Constantine, with a Latin inscription. On the rear wall, to the right and left, are two small *chapels,* the one on the left dedicated to the goddess Mut, the one on the right to the moon god Khons, with a staircase (destroyed) adjoining it. – The central door in the rear wall leads into a smaller hall, originally with eight columns, which in Christian times was converted into a *church.* The old entrance to the inner rooms of the temple then became a kind of apsidal recess, flanked by two red granite Corinthian columns. At some points the later coating of

Street scene at the Temple of Luxor

whitewash has peeled off, revealing the fine reliefs of Amenophis III. Adjoining the church are a number of smaller rooms.

From the vestibule a door in the E wall leads out of the temple. Going out through this and turning right to re-enter the temple, we pass through three doors and come to the **Birth Room**. This room, with three cluster-columns, is named after the reliefs on the W wall referring to the birth of Amenophis III; those on the S wall depict his accession to the throne.

W wall, lower row, from left to right: 1. the god Khnum shaping two infants (Amenophis III and his guardian spirit) on the potter's wheel, with Isis seated opposite; 2. Khnum and Amun; 3. Amun and Mutemuia, mother of Amenophis III, seated on the hieroglyph for "sky" and supported by the goddesses Selkit and Neith; 4. Amun and Thoth; 5. the King and Amun (badly damaged); 6. Isis (destroyed) embracing Queen Mutemuia, with Amun on the right. Middle row: 1. Thoth foretells to Mutemuia the birth of a son; 2. Mutemuia, pregnant, conducted by Khnum and Isis; 3. confinement of Mutemuia, attended by Bes, Thoeris and other spirits; 4. Isis (destroyed) presents the newborn Prince to Amun; 5. Amun holds the infant, beside him Hathor and Mut. – Top row: 1. left, the Queen, with the goddess Selkit behind her; right, two goddesses suckling the Prince and his guardian spirit; below, the Prince and his guardian spirit suckled by two cows; 2. nine deities holding the Prince; 3. the god Hekaw (in blue) holding the Prince and his guardian spirit, behind him the Nile god; 4. Horus giving the infant to Amun; 5. Khnum and Anubis; 6. the Prince and his guardian spirit sitting and standing before Amun; 7. Amenophis as King.

Beyond the birth room is a side room with three columns and poorly preserved reliefs, from which an arched doorway inserted at a later date leads into the *Sanctuary of Alexander the Great*, a room largely rebuilt in the reign of Alexander. The four columns supporting the roof were replaced by a *chapel* for the sacred barque of Amun, the walls of which were decorated internally and externally with reliefs depicting Alexander in the presence of Amun and his fellow deities, while the walls of the original chamber still show Amenophis III in the presence of the various Theban gods. – A door in the N wall of the chamber leads into a small square room with four papyrus cluster-columns. The reliefs in this room, in three rows, show Amenophis III in the presence of the Theban deities, in particular Amun.

The rooms at the far end of the temple contain no features of particular interest. A gap in the wall of the Sanctuary of Alexander the Great leads into a hall with 12 columns, adjoining which are three chapels. The roof of the central chapel was supported by four papyrus cluster-columns. To the left is a relief showing the King being conducted into the sanctuary by Atum and Horus; the other reliefs show him in the presence of Amun. The S chapel, also accessible from outside the temple, was dedicated to the ithyphallic Amun-Kamutef.

On the way back to the pylon it is worth looking at the reliefs on the outer walls on the W side of the temple, which depict Ramesses II's campaigns in Asia. – On the outside of the SE wall of the Court of Ramesses II, in large vertical lines, is the famous "Poem of Pentaur" celebrating the King's war with the Hittites.

Ameneminet as a beggar (19th Dynasty)

Between the colonnade of the temple and the corniche road along the Nile are the remains of buildings of the Late Period, including a small *temple* with a few elegant columns still standing erect.

From the Temple of Luxor a paved road flanked on both sides by recumbent *figures of rams,* with the effigy of Amenophis III between their forelegs, led to the temples of Karnak (see separate entry). The avenue of sphinxes at the entrance to the Temple of Khons at Karnak is a relic of this.

On the corniche road $\frac{3}{4}$ mile/1 km N of the Temple of Luxor, half-way to the Karnak temples, is the *Museum of Ancient Egyptian Art**, opened in 1975, which is housed in a modern building designed by Mahmud El-Hakim. The collection consists primarily of the more recent finds from the Thebes area.

A number of items are displayed in the area in front of the museum, including a statue of Amenophis III from Qurna and a stela from Karnak with a figure of Amenophis II as an archer.
The *INTERIOR of the museum is attractively laid out on two levels, and the many valuable items in the collection are excellently displayed and lit. – In the entrance hall, on the right, is the *head of a colossal statue of Amenophis III in reddish granite (from Qurna). In the rotunda is the gilded *head of a cow

Lids of canopic jars

goddess (from the Tomb of Tutankhamun). From the entrance hall a short flight of steps leads to the *ground floor*. Notable items here include an * *alabaster group depicting Amenophis III under the protection of the crocodile god Sobek (from Dahamsha), a *head of Sesostris III in reddish granite (found at Karnak in 1970), a statue of Tuthmosis III in greenish greywacke (from Karnak), a bust of Amenophis II wearing the double crown (reddish granite; from Karnak), a large and historically important limestone *stela celebrating Kamose's victory over the Hyksos (from Karnak) and a squatting figure of Yamu-Nedjeh in black granite (from Qurna).

From the ground floor a *ramp* (on the wall Coptic tombstones, half-way up a niche from a Coptic church in the Luxor area, at the top a head of Tuthmosis I) leads to the *upper floor*. First come a number of cases containing small objects (amulets, jewelry, silver bowls, foundation deposits, coins, etc.), grave-goods and tomb furnishings, mythological papyri, votive tablets, dedicatory stelae, prehistoric pottery, etc., together with a chest containing canopic jars from Queen Hatshepsut's Temple at Deir el-Bahri. Other

items of interest include a seated figure of the Vizier Amenhotep (son of Hapu; 12th Dynasty) writing, a head of Amenophis IV (Akhenaten) in the Early Amarna style, reliefs from Hatshepsut's granite chapel in the Temple of Karnak (depicting musicians, dancers, acrobats, etc.), various small objects from the Tomb of Tutankhamun (including his sandals) and portraits and statues of the Roman period.

Also on the upper floor is the museum's *pièce de résistance*, the so-called * *Wall of Akhenaten**. 56 ft/ 17·17 m long and some 10 ft/3 m high, this consists of 283 sandstone blocks *(talatat)* covered with painted reliefs out of a total of 6000 such blocks, originally belonging to Akhenaten's Temple of the Sun at Karnak, which were found built into Horemheb's Ninth Pylon during restoration work in 1968–69. On the right-hand half of the wall temple servants are depicted at their everyday tasks; on the left-hand half Akhenaten, sometimes accompanied by his wife Nefertiti, is shown worshiping the Aten, the divine solar disc with rays ending in hands. – Altogether some 40,000 of such *talatat* have been recovered, coming from the various temples which were built by Akhenaten in honor of the sun god and which were later pulled down.

* *Dendera, Eastern Desert, * *Edfu, *Esna, Gebelein, *El-Kab, * *Karnak, Kom el-Ahmar, Medamut, *Nile, Qena, *Thebes (West) and Tod: see separate entries.

Maghara
See under Sinai

Maharraqa
See under Wadi el-Sebwa

Mallawi

Middle Egypt. – Governorate: El-Minya.

ACCESS. – By road or rail from El-Minya, 30 miles/ 48 km N.

The busy district capital of Mallawi lies on the W bank of the Ibrahimiya Canal in the extensive area of cultivated land between the Bahr Yusuf and the Nile. In spite of its rapid industrial development the town has preserved much of its old rural character. There is a colorful weekly market to which the people of the surrounding area flock to sell their produce.

SIGHTS. – Mallawi has an interesting **Museum** containing archaeological material from Hermopolis Magna and the

Amenophis II wearing the double crown

Statue of a baboon, Hermopolis Magna

Hermopolis Magna   Basilica

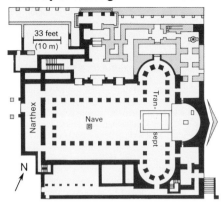

Tuna el-Gebel and Meir areas, including many mummies, sarcophagi and statuettes of ibises, which were worshiped here together with baboons as animals sacred to the god Thoth, and also glass, pottery, faience, domestic equipment and numerous papyri.

SURROUNDINGS of Mallawi. – 6 miles/10 km N, at the village of *El-Ashmunein,* are the extensive ruins and mounds of rubble which mark the site of the once-famous city of **Khmunu** (Coptic *Shmun*; the "City of the Eight Deities"), which from a very early period was the principal center of the cult of Thoth, the god of writing, of healing and of learning. In Egyptian belief this was the site of the primal hill on which Thoth created the eight primal gods of this world, who in turn engendered the egg out of which grew the sun. Khmunu was capital of the 15th nome of Upper Egypt, the Hare nome, whose Princes were buried during the Middle Kingdom at *Deir el-Bersha,* on the E bank of the Nile. – Later, for reasons that are not understood, the town declined, but under the Ptolemies it took on a fresh lease of life as a cult center and place of pilgrimage dedicated to the worship of Hermes Trismegistus, "thrice great Hermes", and under the name of *Hermoupolis* (to the Romans **Hermopolis Magna**) enjoyed its period of greatest prosperity. – After losing its importance as a cult center the town fell into decay, and for many centuries suffered devastation as a convenient source of building stone and *sebbakh,* the fertile soil found on ancient sites.

Of the ancient Egyptian Khmunu practically nothing is left, of the Greek Hermoupolis only a few ruins and mounds of rubble. A number of granite columns which were found here and have been re-erected belong to the **Agora**, with an Early Christian **basilica**. Immediately N of this was the temple precinct, which was surrounded by a brick enclosure wall of the 30th Dynasty. In the center of the precinct can be seen the

scanty remains of a *Temple of Thoth* built by Philip Arrhidaeus, Alexander the Great's half-brother; two rows of columns belonging to this temple were still standing at the beginning of the 19th c. – SW of this temple are the remains of the *pylon* and *hypostyle hall* of a 19th Dynasty temple. On the outside of the E wall of the N pylon tower is a long inscription by Merneptah; the reliefs on the inside walls of the pylon date from the reign of Sethos II. – To the S of the Temple of Thoth were found the remains of a *pylon* erected by Ramesses II, in the foundations of which were more than 2000 blocks from temples built by Akhenaten at Tell el-Amarna (see separate entry); most of the pylon had been removed by stone-robbers. – Other remains dating from the Middle Kingdom are a *temple entrance* of Amenemhet II and the first *pylon* of a 19th Dynasty Temple of Amun.

$4\frac{1}{2}$ miles/7 km W of El-Ashmunein, beyond the Bahr Yusuf, is the necropolis of **Tuna el-Gebel**, the burial-place of Hermopolis, lying under the plateau of the Western Desert. Here, too, are two badly weathered rock-cut stelae in the name of Akhenaten, marking the boundary of the territory controlled by Tell el-Amarna. The cemetery itself dates back to the 5th c. B.C. In an extensive system of catacombs were found many ibis and baboon burials and Aramaic papyri dating from the time of Darius.

The most important monument in the necropolis is the *Funerary Temple of Petosiris, a leading citizen of Hermopoulis and High Priest in the Temple of Thoth, who built this family mausoleum about 300 B.C. It consists of a vestibule dedicated to the memory of Petosiris – a later part of the structure – and an almost square chapel, with four pillars, which Petosiris dedicated to the cult of his father and his elder brother. Both chambers were decorated by Egyptian artists with reliefs of great interest for the history of Egyptian art, some of them with well-preserved coloring. While the religious scenes, particularly in the chapel, are in purely Egyptian style, apparently following 18th Dynasty models, the secular ones depicting events from everyday life in the vestibule and on the lower part of the chapel walls are in a hybrid Egyptian-Greek and sometimes in a purely Greek style.

The temple, surrounded by mounds of rubble, is approached by a paved road some 22 yds/ 20 m long and 13 ft/4 m wide, on the left-hand side of which is an *altar,* 8 ft/2·40 m high, with four horn-like projections at the corners. The facade of the temple has four columns with elaborate foliage capitals and a *doorway* in the middle. Between the columns are high stone screens, which, like the pilasters at the sides, are adorned with reliefs depicting Petosiris making offerings and praying to the gods of his nome. – The reliefs on the back of the screens – the N wall of the *vestibule* – are on secular themes, depicted in a hybrid Graeco-Egyptian style. To right of the entrance: metalworkers making a variety of articles; a man working on the centerpiece for a table; metal being weighed; the finished articles being packed for dispatch. To the left of the entrance: two uppermost rows, the preparation of unguents; two lower rows, carpenters at work; two men working with a lathe (the earliest known representation); making of a four-poster bed. – East wall, in three rows (from the bottom row upwards): plowing; the flax harvest; the corn harvest, the corn being threshed with sticks. South wall: to the left of the door, Petosiris's sons with their parents; at the foot of the wall, men carrying offerings; to the right of the door, Petosiris's daughters with their parents; at the foot of the wall, mourning women and an offering scene, in purely Greek style. On the side pilasters, above, the dead man playing a board game. – West wall: in the two upper rows cattle-herds in the fields, in the bottom row vintage scenes, a wine-press, delivery of the jars of wine.

Funerary Temple Tuna el-Gebel of Petosiris

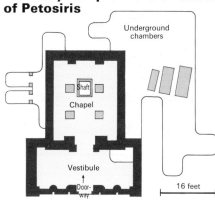

In the *chapel* the four pillars are covered with long inscriptions and reliefs showing the dead man at prayer. – North wall, right-hand (E) side: the goddess Nut dispensing water from a tree to Petosiris's parents; below, Petosiris in prayer before his father; base of the wall, cattle driven through a marsh. – East wall: Petosiris's funeral procession, with men, women and gods (the four sons of Osiris), some with votive gifts, accompanying the coffin to the tomb; on the right the mummy in front of the tomb, with a priest pouring the water of consecration over it. On the lower part of the walls offering-bearers. – South wall (divided into three parts by stucco projections), to the left: Petosiris's father before nine gods adoring the sun; Djed-Dhutefonkh, his brother, with his children, praying before his father; below, a marsh landscape with cattle. Center: Es-Shu (left), Petosiris's father, and Djed-Dhutefonkh praying to Osiris and Isis and to Nephthys; below, the snake and vulture goddesses protecting with their wings Osiris in the form of a scarab; to the right and left Isis and a soul-bird perched on a false door; on the base of the wall, water being dispensed to the soul. On the right: above, Djed-Dhutefonkh praying to nine divine beings; below, Petosiris before his brother; on the base of the wall a marsh landscape with hippopotamuses

and crocodiles. – West wall, top row (from left to right): Djed-Dhutefonkh praying to nine baboons, to 12 snakes and to sacred bulls and gods; Djed-Dhutefonkh conducted before Osiris; Djed-Dhutefonkh in prayer. Middle row: the dead man praying to various gods (18th Chapter of the "Book of the Dead"). Bottom row: offering-bearers, some reliefs being in Greek style. – North wall, left-hand (W) side: the dead man before the offering-table; below, Petosiris before his dead brother; on the base of the wall, men in boats driving oxen and calves across a river. – The shaft in the middle of the chapel (closed) leads down to the tomb chamber, in which Petosiris, his wife and one of his sons were buried. His coffin is now in the Egyptian Museum in Cairo.

Tomb of Isidora, Tuna el-Gebel

To the S of Petosiris's tomb is a **necropolis** of the Graeco-Roman period, with a number of two-storey tombs in Graeco-Egyptian style. The finest is the *Tomb of Isidora,* a young woman who was drowned about 120 B.C.

Opposite Mallawi on the E bank of the Nile, some distance from the river, lies the Coptic village of **Deir el-Bersha,** with an old church. To the E of the village, at a Coptic cemetery, is the mouth of a ravine running from NW to SE, the *Wadi Nakhla* of *Wadi Deir el-Bersha,* in the steep sides of which are many quarries and ancient tombs. The valley is chiefly noted for the rock tombs of the Middle Kingdom in its northern slopes, belonging to Princes of the 15th nome of Upper Egypt, the Hare nome. The only tomb worth a visit is No. 2, the **Tomb of Thuthotep,** son of Kai, Prince of the Hare nome in the reigns of Amenemhet II and Sesostris II and III. The tomb is similar in form to the tombs of Beni Hasan (see separate entry). The vestibule, originally with two palm columns, has fallen in.

From the vestibule a door leads into the *inner chamber,* partly collapsed, decorated with mural reliefs (some destroyed). The relief on the left-hand wall depicts the transport of a colossal statue of the dead man from the quarries of Hatnub (see under Tell el-Amarna) to a temple. The accompanying inscriptions tell us that the statue was of alabaster and measured 12 cubits (about 21 ft/6 m) in height. It is fastened with ropes to a wooden sledge drawn by a total of 172 men, in four files. A priest precedes the statue, scattering incense, and a man standing on the front of the sledge pours water on the ground to reduce the friction. Another man, on the knees of the statue, claps his hands to give the time to the men harnessed to the sledge, who sing as they pull. Below are workmen carrying water and a wooden beam, and behind the statue are foremen and other officials. In the top row are companies of people with branches in their hands hastening to meet the procession. Far left is Thuthotep, followed by his bodyguard, watching the progress of the work.

Below the Middle Kingdom tombs are tombs of the Old Kingdom, shaft tombs of the Middle Kingdom and numerous tombs of the Ptolemaic period. – Opposite the tombs, on the S side of the valley, is a large *quarry* from which, according to an inscription which is now destroyed, stone was taken in the first year of Amenophis III's reign for building the Temple of Hermoupolis. Farther up the valley are quarries used in the reign of Nectanebo I.

*Asyut, *Beni Hasan, *Nile, Roda and *Tell el-Amarna: see separate entries.

Manfalut
See under Nile

Lake Manzala
See under Damietta

El-Mansura

Lower Egypt. – Governorate: Daqahliya.
Population: 280,000.
(i) **Misr Travel,**
Tourist Center,
Tanta;
tel. 22 12.

HOTEL. – Hotel *Cleopatra Touristic*, III, 100 b.

ACCESS. – By road or rail from Cairo, 75 miles/120 km S.

The important commercial and industrial city of El-Mansura, chief town of the Governorate of Daqah-liya and the seat of a university associated with the University of Cairo and of a college of technology, lies in the eastern half of the Nile Delta on the right bank of the Damietta arm (in classical times known as the Phatnitic arm) of the Nile, from which the Bahr el-Sughayyar branches off here to flow into Lake Manzala.

The city has an entirely European aspect, with modern buildings in Western style in addition to many mosques of little architectural interest. It is a market and processing center for the agricultural produce of the Delta, with several large cotton factories, and also has metalwork-ing industries.

HISTORY. – El-Mansura (the "Victorious") was founded by Sultan Malik el-Kamil in 1221 to replace Damietta, which had fallen to the Crusaders. In 1249 a Crusading army led by Louis IX of France suc-ceeded, after hard fighting, in crossing the Ushmum Canal (now the Bahr el-Sughayyar) to El-Mansura, but were then surrounded and defeated by the young Sultan El-Moazzam Turanshah. Their fleet was destroyed, their supplies were cut off and finally, after great slaughter, Louis himself was taken prisoner in April 1250, and was released (on May 6, 1250) in return for a heavy ransom and the surrender of Damietta.

Visitors are still shown a small house near the Mosque of El-Muwafiq which is said to be *Louis IX's prison,* and a spot near the point where the Bahr el-Sughayyar branches off the Nile is reputed to be the site of the Crusaders' camp.

SURROUNDINGS of El-Mansura. – Some 6 miles/10 km SE, at the village of *El-Baqliya,* is *Tell el-Naqus,* on which are the scanty remains of *Hermopolis Parva,* the ancient Egyptian *Bah,* capital of the 15th nome of Lower Egypt in the Graeco-Roman period. – In the same area, 6 miles/10 km NE of the modern town of *El-Simbillawein,* are two rubble mounds separated by the village of *Tmei el-Amdid* and a canal, **Tell el-Rub,** the site of ancient *Mendes,* to the N and **Tell el-Tmei,** with the remains of ancient *Thmuis* – two cities which were successively capital of the 16th nome of Lower Egypt in the Graeco-Roman period. The remains of a temple dating from the reign of Amasis and the massive sarcophagi of the sacred rams which were venerated here can still be seen.

Damietta, Nile Delta and **Tanta:** see separate entries.

Marsa Alam
See under Red Sea

Marsa Matruh
See Mersa Matruh

Medamut

Upper Egypt. – Governorate: Qena.
(i) **Tourist Information Office,**
Tourist Bazaar,
Luxor;
tel. 22 15.

ACCESS. – Track (usable by cars) from Luxor, 5 miles/8 km SW.

5 miles/8 km NE of Luxor, amid the houses of a village in the cultivated land, are the ruins of the Temple of

Medamut, the ancient Egyptian town of Madu which was the northern neighbor of Thebes.

During the Old Kingdom there was a temple here dedicated to the falcon-headed war god Month and his sacred bull. Under the Middle Kingdom it was enlarged and rebuilt by the Kings of the 12th and 13th Dynasties, in particular by Sesostris III, and this process continued under the New Kingdom – reflecting the increasing importance of the deity honored here.

THE SITE. – The remains of the **Temple** as we see it today date from the Ptolemaic period (3rd c. B.C.) and Roman Imperial times. Oriented from W to E, the temple differs in many respects from other Ptolemaic temples. The precinct, enclosed by a brick wall, was entered by a gateway built in the reign of Tiberius, now collapsed. In front of the pylon-like main front of the temple were three curious kiosks from which doors gave access to the large colonnaded court decorated with reliefs of Antoninus Pius. On the far side of the court was the façade of the vestibule or pronaos, five columns of which are still standing; the two middle columns, flanking the doorway, have elaborate foliage capitals, while the other three are papyrus cluster-columns with closed capitals. Beyond the vestibule are a small hypostyle hall, two antechambers and the sanctuary, adjoining which are several chapels, Beyond the temple proper, which had corridors along the N and S sides, was a separate shrine for the sacred bull. Along the base of the outer walls on the N, E and S sides is a relief depicting a procession of Nile gods advancing from S to N with gifts. On the S side is an *inscription* depicting a Roman Emperor making an offering to the sacred bull, with a reference to the presence of an oracle in the temple.

165 yds/150 m W of the entrance to the temple can be seen an ancient *quay*, similar to the one at Karnak, which originally had two obelisks. On the paving are scratched footprints and demotic inscriptions left by visitors to the temple.

* * **Karnak**, * * **Luxor** and * * **Thebes** (West): see separate entries.

Medinet el-Fayyum
See under Fayyum

Medinet Habu
See under Thebes

Meidum

Middle Egypt. – Governorate: Beni Suef.
ⓘ **Tourist Information Office,**
Misr Travel Tower,
Cairo – Abbasia;
tel. 82 60 16.

ACCESS. – By road (the main Nile Valley road) from Beni Suef, 28 miles/45 km S.

The *Pyramid of Meidum, 6 miles/ 9 km SW of the village of that name, stands on the edge of the Western Desert Plateau, near the middle road into the Fayyum. It is believed to have been begun by Huni, the last King of the 3rd Dynasty, and completed by his successor Sneferu, founder of the 4th Dynasty and the immediate predecessor of Cheops, but was probably never used as a burial-place. It is so different from all other pyramids that it is known as El-Haram el-Kaddab, the "False Pyramid". Although a variety of theories and speculations – some of them decidedly far-fetched – have been put forward about the history of the pyramid, it has never been systematically investigated.**

THE PYRAMID. – The *Pyramid of Meidum was built in three phases, which can still be clearly identified. The earliest structure, at the core of the pyramid, was a seven-stepped *mastaba* modeled on the older Pyramid of Djoser at Saqqara and built over a knoll of rock which is still visible to a height of 130 ft/40 m. The first step, still exposed, is 37 ft/11·20 m high; the second is 32 ft/9·90 m; and the third, largely destroyed, is 22 ft/6·85 m high. The pyramid was faced with polished limestone slabs, inclined slightly inwards (angle 74° 10'). This first structure was later increased in size by the application of an additional 16 ft/5 m of masonry to each

Pyramid   Meidum

Section

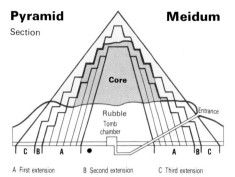

A First extension   B Second extension   C Third extension

of the steps and possibly by the addition of an eighth step. Finally Sneferu had it converted into a "true" pyramid by filling in the steps with a packing of local stone and giving the whole structure a smooth facing of Tura limestone. Its total height must then have been about 300 ft/92 m, its base measurement 470 ft/144 m and its angle of inclination 51° 51′. What caused the collapse of the outer casing, which now lies in a heap of rubble around the foot, is not known. – Difficult access.

On the N side of the pyramid a section of the old casing, with the entrance, is exposed. A passage 187 ft/57 m long cuts down obliquely into the rock, runs horizontally for a short distance and then rises to enter the *tomb chamber*, 20 ft/6 m long by 8½ ft/ 2·60 m across and faced with limestone slabs. The cedar-wood beams which are still to be seen may have served to support the structure in some way, or alternatively may have been used in the transport of some heavy item such as a sarcophagus. The tomb was plundered by tomb-robbers during the 20th Dynasty, entering by the hole in the S wall. – On the E side of the pyramid is a well-preserved small **mortuary temple** built of limestone, with two bare chambers and an open offerings court containing two uninscribed stelae.

To the N and E of the pyramid are mastabas belonging to dignitaries of the 4th Dynasty, among them the famous *Double Mastaba of Prince Rahotep,* son of Sneferu and High Priest in Heliopolis, and his wife Nofret, in which were found the painted limestone figures of the couple now in the Egyptian Museum in Cairo. Here, too, is the *Double Tomb of Nefermaat* and his wife Itet, which yielded the magnificent frieze of geese now in the Egyptian Museum, one of the few examples of independent painted decoration in the territory of Memphis.

Beni Suef, **Fayyum, *El-Lahun and *Lisht: see separate entries.

Memphis

Lower Egypt. – Governorate: Cairo.
ⓘ **Tourist Information Office,**
Misr Travel Tower,
Cairo – Abbasia;
tel. 82 60 16.

ACCESS. – By road from Cairo, 14 miles/22 km N. – A visit to Memphis can conveniently be combined with a visit to the tombs and pyramids of Saqqara.

The very modest remains of the once-splendid capital city of Memphis, of whose wealth and magnificence ancient writers give such

Memphis – excavation site at Mit Rahina

glowing accounts, are scattered about amid the houses, palm groves and fields in the fertile land on the E bank of the Nile opposite the cemeteries of Saqqara. As was the general practice from the Old Kingdom right through to the Roman Imperial period, dwelling-houses and other secular buildings were constructed of sun-dried brick and were thus relatively impermanent. Limestone and granite were used only for temples and occasionally for royal palaces; but these buildings were pulled down in later periods and the stones reused in new construction.

HISTORY. – The story of Memphis reaches back to the very beginnings of Egyptian history. Menes, the first historical Egyptian ruler, is credited with the building of the "White Walls", a fortress established on land reclaimed from swamp on the borders between the two ancient kingdoms of Upper and Lower Egypt, in order to keep the conquered inhabitants of Lower Egypt in subjection. To the S of the town he erected a temple dedicated to the town's patron god Ptah, who during the Greek period was identified with Hephaestus. The new foundation rapidly prospered, becoming capital of the 1st nome of Lower Egypt, and the kings of the early dynasties from time to time established their residence in the town.

Under the 6th Dynasty a new district of the town grew up, in which King Phiops (Pepi) I took up his residence, building his pyramid in the vicinity of the town. The pyramid was given the same name as the King, *Men-nefru-Mire,* "The beauty of Mire [i.e. Phiops] remains"; and this name, later contracted to Menfe (Greek Memphis) was applied to the town as a whole.

The city's most flourishing period was during the Old Kingdom, whose rulers had their royal residence either in Memphis or in the vicinity, at Giza or Abusir. It was scarcely less important, however, under the Kings of the Middle and New Kingdoms, when Thebes became the center of Egypt and the Theban god Amun the principal Egyptian deity. In the time of the 20th Dynasty the Temple of Ptah at Thebes was still the third largest in the country.

Later, during the recurring struggles for control of Egypt from the 22nd Dynasty onwards, the Ethiopians, led by Piankhi, and the Assyrians captured the town. Cambyses, the first ruler of the Persian dynasty, took it by storm after defeating Psammetichus II at Pelusium in 525 B.C. Even after the foundation of Alexandria in 331 B.C., however, Memphis seems to have retained its importance. Still later, in the time of Augustus, it was a large and populous city, although its palaces, built on higher ground, were by then destroyed. Of its temples there still remained the Temple of Ptah, a temple dedicated to Apis and another dedicated to a female divinity, perhaps the Greek Aphrodite. Towards the end of the 4th c. the temples were destroyed under an edict issued by the Emperor Theodosius (A.D. 379–395). Under the later

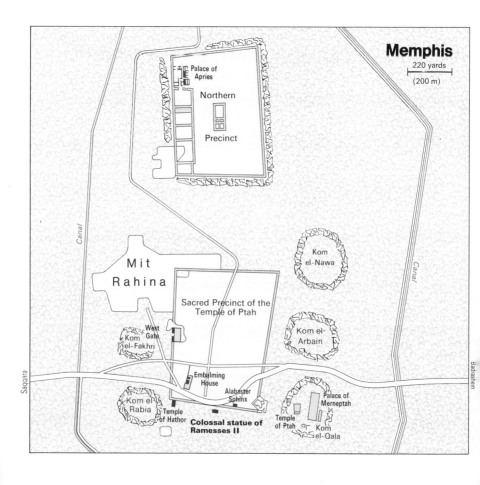

Colossal figure of Ramesses II

Alabaster sphinx

Byzantine Emperors the Monophysite heresy appears to have had many adherents in the town.

When the Arabs arrived Muqauqis, leader of the Copts, negotiated with Caliph Omar's general Amr ibn el-As from his residence at Memphis. The Muslim conquerors established their capital on the right bank of the Nile opposite the N end of Memphis, and used dressed stone from Memphis for building their palaces, fortresses and mosques in Cairo. Much later, however, the ruins of Memphis still excited the admiration of visitors: the Arab writer Abdellatif (1162–1231), for example, reported that the profusion of marvels to be seen at Memphis bewildered the mind and baffled description. Thereafter the town seems to have fallen into complete ruin and been forgotten.

THE SITE. – A little way SE of the village of *Mit Rahina,* within a modern building erected to protect it, lies a *colossal figure of Ramesses II which once stood outside the entrance to the temple. It was discovered by Caviglia and Sloane in 1820. Carved from hard fine-grained limestone, it was probably more than 43 ft/13 m long when complete – a figure which is in broad agreement with Herodotus's statement that it measured 30 cubits (52 ft/16 m). The ear alone measures fully 20 inches/50 cm. The King's handsome face and mild expression are excellently rendered; on the chin is a stylized beard. In the King's belt is a dagger decorated with two falcons' heads. His name is inscribed on the right shoulder, the breast and the belt. On a piece of stone between the legs is incised the figure of Bent-Anat, his wife. –

Another colossal statue of Ramesses, which also stood at the entrance to the temple and was found in 1888, now stands in Ramesses Square in front of Cairo's main railway station. – In the building containing the prostrate statue and behind it are various fragments of statues found on the site.

Immediately NE of the building containing the statue is a large and well-preserved alabaster *Sphinx, excavated in 1912, which may have stood outside the S entrance to the Temple of Ptah. It is 26 ft/ 8 m long and 13 ft/4 m high and weighs 80 tons. On stylistic grounds it is dated to the 18th or 19th Dynasty. – Beside the sphinx is a *stela,* originally found close to the second of the colossal statues of Ramesses II, recording a decree issued by King Apries, in the rounded pediment of which are figures of Ptah (left) and the falcon-headed Sokar (right). The inscription lists the lands and personnel belonging to the Temple of Ptah and grants them exemption from tax.

To the N of the sphinx is the *Sacred Precinct of the Temple of Ptah,* of which so far only the dimensions have been established and part of the *West Gate* excavated. At the SW corner of the precinct are the remains of the *Embalming House,* with huge alabaster tables, weighing up to 50 tons, for the embalming of the sacred Apis bulls. One of these tables has an inscription referring to Necho (26th Dynasty). – Outside the SW corner of the precinct are traces of a small *Temple of Hathor* dating from the reign of Ramesses II and tombs belonging to High Priests of the 22nd Dynasty. Farther W are tombs of the First Intermediate Period and Middle Kingdom.

On the *Kom el-Qala,* SE of the Temple of Ptah, are the scanty remains of a *Palace of Merneptah* and a smaller *Temple of Ptah.*

Abu Roash,* Abusir,** Cairo,* Dahshur,** Giza, Helwan,** Saqqara and Zawiyet el-Aryan: see separate entries.

Mersa Alam
See under Red Sea

Mersa Matruh/ Marsa Matruh

Lower Egypt. – North-West Frontier District. Population: 20,000.
(i) Tourist Information Office, Midan Saad Zaghlul, Alexandria; tel. 80 79 85.

HOTEL. – *Beau Site*, Shari el Shates, II, 66 b.; *Rommel House*, Shari Gallaa, III, 120 b.; *Reem*, III, 116 b.; *Marine Fouad*, III, 60 b.; *Arouss el-Bahr*, III, 44 b.; *Riviera*, market area, IV, 64 b. – CAMP SITE: 12½ miles/20 km W.

SPORT AND RECREATION. – Swimming, diving.

ACCESS. – Coast road and railway from Alexandria, 145 miles/230 km E; bus service.

The port of Mersa Matruh (Marsa Matruh), the ancient Paraetonium from which Alexander the Great set out on his historic journey to the Siwa Oasis and now a seaside resort much frequented by the people of Alexandria, lies in a large lagoon bounded on the seaward side by a line of reefs, some 105 miles/170 km W of El-Alamein and 135 miles/220 km E of the Libyan frontier.

Now the principal resort on the stretch of coast known, by virtue of its mild climate, picturesque rocky * coves, fascinatingly hued sea and superb * beaches of fine white sand, as the "Egyptian Riviera",

Mersa Matruh was already a popular summer resort in ancient times. The harbor provided a base for Cleopatra's fleet during the conflict with Augustus; and remains of ancient quays, traces of settlement and the ruins of an Early Christian church have been brought to light. Mersa Matruh is now the administrative center of the North-West Frontier District and the base of the Egyptian sponge-fishing fleet, and is also a busy trading center for the bedouin of the Western (Libyan) Desert, who bring to market here their sheep, wool and agricultural produce (barley, dates, olives, excellent melons).

SIGHTS. – Near the harbor is a *cave* which was occupied for a time by General Rommel during the Second World War. – There are attractive, though strenuous, walks along the beach, particularly to the so-called *"Bath of Cleopatra"*, a natural basin at the foot of a 165 ft/60 m high cliff.

SURROUNDINGS of Mersa Matruh. – A fascinating expedition from Mersa Matruh (at present permitted only exceptionally with special authority) is a trip to the Siwa Oasis (see separate entry) on the* desert road. – The coast road continues W from Mersa Matruh to the little fishing port and market town of *Sidi Barani* (85 miles/136 km; gasoline (petrol) station) and Sollum, a place of some consequence in antiquity under the name of *Banaris*. During the Second World War, in 1940–42, it was the scene of bitter fighting, lying as it did 6 miles/10 km E of the frontier between Egypt and the then Italian colony of Cyrenaica (now part of Libya).

* El-Alamein,** Alexandria, Qattara Depression,* Siwa Oasis and Western Desert: see separate entries.

El-Minya
See under Nile

Misr el-Qahira
See Cairo

Mons Porphyrites
See under Eastern Desert

Nag Hammadi
See under Nile

Narmouthis
See under Fayyum

Lake Nasser
See under Aswan

Naucratis
See under Damanhur

Nekhab
See El-Kab

New Abu Simbel
See Abu Simbel

New Amada
See Amada

New Heliopolis
See under Cairo

New Kalabsha
See Kalabsha

New Sebwa
See Wadi el-Sebwa

New Valley/Wadi el-Gedid

Western Desert. – New Valley Frontier District.

The New Valley Frontier District (Wadi el-Gedid) occupies an area of some 145,000 sq. miles/376,000 sq. km in the SW of Egypt. It consists predominantly of desert; the population is concentrated in the oases of Bahriya, Dakhla, Farafra and Kharga.

Since the late 1950s, under the New Valley development project, considerable effort has been devoted to winning new land for cultivation. Artesian wells have been sunk in the oasis depressions to tap underground water-supplies and thus make possible the cultivation of fodder plants, grain and date-palms. Problems

The dunes of Abu Muharriq in the Western Desert

Mummified cow on a desert track

have, however, been caused by the increasing salt content of the soil.

*Bahriya, *Dakhla, Farafra, *Kharga and *Siwa oases and Western Desert: see separate entries.

River Nile/Bahr el-Nil

Total length: 4145 miles/6671 km.
States: Burundi, Uganda, Ethiopia, Sudan and Egypt.

The *Nile is the longest river in Africa and, after the Mississippi-Missouri river system, the longest watercourse in the world. Garnering great masses of water from the Ethiopian Highlands and rain-rich tropics, it traverses the very different world of the NE African desert plateau to end in the Mediterranean after a course of 4145 miles/6671 km. In striking contrast to the green valley bottom are the yellow and reddish scarps of the desert plateau through which the river has carved a passage: and along the verges of the plateau stand the temples and pyramids which bear witness to an age-old culture.

The Nile (Bahr el-Nil) rises at Rutana in BURUNDI as the River Kagera, which flows through UGANDA into Lake Victoria, to emerge from the N end of the lake as the Victoria Nile. After a course of 242 miles/389 km it flows through Lake Albert and then, as the Mountain Nile (Bahr el-Gebel), cuts its way through rocky hills to enter the SUDAN, where it spreads out again as it flows through the 470 mile/756 km long swamp region of the Sudd. Thereafter it is joined by three tributary rivers, the Bahr el-Ghazal, the Bair el-Zeraf and the Sobat, and, considerably augmented by the abundant flow of the Sobat, continues N as the White Nile (El-Nil el-Abyad).

At Khartoum the White Nile is joined by the Blue Nile (Bahr el-Azraq), coming from Lake Tana in the Highlands of ETHIOPIA, which owes its name to its turbid water, heavily laden with sediment. Over the rest of its course to the Mediterranean it receives only one other tributary,

Cataract on the Nile at Aswan

the *Atbara*. Passing over a total of six *cataracts*, several of them now engulfed by the waters of artificially created lakes, and varying in width from 550 yds/500 m to 1000 yds/900 m, it now cuts its way through the desert plateau of NE Africa in a bed 350–1150 ft/100–350 m deep, a wide ribbon of water which brings life to the swathe of green fringing its banks; then, N of Cairo, it forms a wide fan-shaped *delta* (area 9000 sq. miles/23,300 sq. km) flanked by many lagoons and spits of land, splits into two arms, the *Damietta* and *Rosetta* arms – in ancient times there were seven arms – and finally reaches the Mediterranean.

In the course of its long journey the river loses more than half its water by evaporation, mainly in the swamps of the Sudd; but the mass of water is so large (an annual average of 120 billion cu. yds/92 billion cu. m) that what is left is still sufficient to transform the almost rainless Nile Valley into a green and fertile oasis.

With the beginning of the monsoon rains in the Ethiopian Highlands the Blue Nile and the Atbara swell rapidly in size from June to September, carrying down an immense volume of mud and suspended matter which over many millennia has been deposited in the Nile Valley in the form of fertile soil. Accordingly the mouth of the river has been gradually advancing into the Mediterranean, creating new land comparable with the polders of Holland. The swelling waters of the Blue Nile pen up the water of the White Nile as they sweep past the confluence, so that during August and September the waters of the Mountain Nile and the Sobat are dammed up in the Valley of the White Nile and make only a small contribution to the **Nile inundation**. The height of the inundation thus depends mainly on the amount of rainfall in the Ethiopian Highlands. It begins at Khartoum in mid May, arrives at Aswan at the beginning of June and reaches its highest point at both places in the first weeks of September.

Since the earliest times the inundation has come at the same time every year and has accordingly determined the annual rhythm of agriculture – the tilling of the land, the harvest, the fallow period. In ancient Egypt the beginning of the inundation was marked by a great festival, for on the height it reached depended the prosperity or penury of the coming year.

Nowadays the ancient traditional methods of supplying water to the cultivated land in the Nile Valley have largely been superseded by modern techniques of irrigation. The water of the inundation is now pounded by **dams** and made available for use throughout the year. As a result considerable areas of new land have been brought under cultivation, and it is now possible to take two or even three crops off the land every year.

The first major dam on the lower course of the Nile was the *Aswan Dam, built between 1898 and 1912 (see under Aswan). Between 1960 and 1968 President Nasser carried through his ambitious project, the **High Dam (Sadd el-Ali), 4½ miles/7 km farther S, forming a large new lake which was named *Lake Nasser (see under Aswan). – Farther downstream, there are dams at *Esna, Nag Hammadi* and **Asyut** (see under Esna and Asyut). – 15 miles/25 km N of Cairo is the **Nile Dam**, built in the mid 19th c., and farther downstream is the *Mohammed Ali Dam*, built in 1936–39 (see under Cairo, Surroundings). The Damietta and Rosetta arms of the Nile, in the Delta, are also regulated by dams.

The water stored in the artificial lakes and reservoirs created by the dams is distributed to the fields through a network of *canals* more than 12,500 miles/20,000 km long. The canals are now fed chiefly by modern **pumping-stations**, but to some extent also by old-established traditional devices – the *saqiya* (an undershot water-wheel), the *shaduf* (a bucket pivoting on a weighted pole) and the *tanbur* (Archimedean screw).

The Nile Valley from Cairo to Aswan

By rail 548 miles/882 km; by road 587 miles/944 km; by boat 600 miles/960 km. – The distances shown below are by rail: for travel by car or by boat add roughly 10%.

Places which are the subject of a separate entry in this Guide are marked by an asterisk before the name.

On the outskirts of Cairo *Old Cairo* and beyond this the *Moqattam Hills*, with the Citadel, are seen on the E bank, the *Pyramids of Giza* on the W bank. – Then on the E bank the suburbs of *Maadi, Tura* and *El-Masara*, with the large quarries in the hills (see under Helwan); on the W bank the pyramids of *Abusir, *Saqqara and *Dahshur.

21 mi (33 km)	*Badrashein*, a railway station on the W bank from which *Memphis and *Saqqara, can be visited; on the E bank the town of *Helwan. Then on the right the Pyramids of Dahshur.
28 mi (45 km)	*Mazghuna* (W bank), from which Pyramids of *Dahshur can be visited.
35 mi (57 km)	*Bahbit* (W bank). Near the village are remains of a Temple of Isis.
37 mi (59 km)	*El-Ayyat* (W bank), with the remains of ancient quays.
40 mi (65 km)	*El-Matanya* (W bank). To the W, on the edge of the desert, are the Pyramids of *Lisht. On the E bank is the little town of *El-Saff*.
45 mi (73 km)	*Kafr Ahmar* (W bank). 1¼ miles/2 km SW of the station, beyond the Bahr el-Libeni

(canal), is *Kafr Tarkhan,* where Flinders Petrie excavated a large cemetery of the Early Historical period in 1911–12.

52 mi   *El-Riqqa* (W bank), a place of some size
(84 km)   with a large brickworks and cement factory, from which the *Pyramid of Meidum* can be visited. – On the E bank, some 2 miles/3 km from the river, is the village of *Atfih*, with the scanty remains of ancient *Aphroditopolis.* The ancient Egyptian name of the town was *Tep-yeh* or *Per-Hathor nebt Tep-yeh* ("House of Hathor, Mistress of Tep-yeh"), from which the Coptic *Petpeh* and Arabic *Atfih* derive. The Greeks equated Hathor with Aphrodite. According to Strabo a white cow sacred to Hathor was worshiped here. In Christian times (*c.* A.D. 310) Aphroditopolis gained celebrity from St Antony, who lived as a hermit in the hills E of the town but was compelled to retreat farther into the mountains to escape from the pilgrims who flocked to his cell.

56 mi   Side road (2½ miles/4 km NW) to the
(90 km)   *Pyramid of Meidum.*

57 mi   *El-Wasta* (W bank), a road junction at the
(92 km)   entrance to the *Fayyum.* Beyond El-Wasta the hills recede from the W bank, while on the E bank they advance in many places to the edge of the river, rearing steeply up from the banks to a considerable height. On the E bank is the Monastery of *Deir Mar Antonios,* with a dome topped by a cross, from which there is a desert track to the Red Sea.

65 mi   *El-Maimun* (W bank), with the *Qosheisha*
(104 km) *Dam* (said to date from the time of the founder of the Egyptian kingdom, Menes), which pounds the surplus water of the Bahr Yusuf.

67 mi   *Ashmant* (W bank). Some 3 hours NW is
(108 km) the village of **Abusir el-Melek**, known to the Egyptians as the "Abydos of Lower Egypt", with large ancient cemeteries. Near here is the Tomb of Merwan II (744–750), the last Omayyad ruler.

72 mi   *Bush* (W bank), a village mainly inhabited
(116 km) by Copts.

77 mi   **Beni Suef** *(W bank).
(124 km)

91 mi   *Biba* (W bank), a district capital and market
(146 km) town, with a conspicuous Coptic church. – 14 miles/22 km NW, beyond the Bahr Yusuf, on the edge of the desert, is the village of **Dishasha**, with the tombs of 5th Dynasty nomarchs of this area. The tombs of Inti and Shedu contain interesting mural reliefs (battle scenes, the siege of a Syrian town, etc.). – Beyond Biba are a number of large islands in the Nile.

99 mi   **El-Fashn** (W bank). – On the E bank,
(160 km) some 3 miles/5 km above El-Fashn, is the village of **El-Hiba**, nestling amid palms,

with the remains of the Greek city of *Ancyronpolis.* The well-preserved town walls, several yards thick, date from the 21st Dynasty. Within the walls, among the palms, are the remains of a Temple of Amun built by Sheshonq I (22nd Dynasty).

112 mi   **Maghagha** (W bank), a district capital,
(180 km)   with a sugar factory. On the E bank of the Nile, in which there are many islands at this point, is the village of *Qarara*, the ancient *Phylace Hipponos*, near which are Coptic cemeteries (8th c.). Some 1½ miles/2·5 km N of this, at the village of *Awlad el-Sheikh*, is a cemetery of the Early Historical period (*c.* 3000 B.C.). – 12–15 miles/20–24 km E of the Nile, near the wide *Wadi el-Sheikh*, are prehistoric flint factories discovered by H. W. Seton-Karr in 1896.

115 mi   *Sharuna* (E bank). Near here, on the E side
(185 km)   of the Hill of *Kom el-Ahmar,* is a rather dilapidated rock tomb of the late 6th Dynasty, the owner of which is named as Peponkh. It consists of a wide vestibule (reliefs of the dead man catching birds and spearing fish) and three small chambers, one of which has reliefs and inscriptions. – Farther S are the remains of a temple built by Ptolemy I and rock tombs of the Late Period belonging to the town of *Hatnesut* in the Cynopolitan nome.

122 mi   **Beni Mazar** (W bank). 1½ miles/2·5 km
(197 km)   SW is the village of *El-Qeis,* the ancient Egyptian *Kais,* whose local divinity was the dog-headed Anubis. This was probably the site of the Greek *Cynopolis,* capital of the nome. – Some 9 miles/15 km W of Beni Mazar, on the Bahr Yusuf, is **Bahnasa**, with the mound of rubble which marks the site of ancient *Oxyrhynchus* (Egyptian *Permedjed,* Coptic *Pemje*), once capital of a nome, where the Oxyrhynchus fish (Arabic *mizda*) was worshiped. Plutarch tells us that there was a war between Cynopolis and Oxyrhynchus, settled only after Roman intervention, because the people of each town had eaten the sacred animal of the other. After the introduction of Christianity Oxyrhynchus became a great monastic center, with 12 churches within the town and many monasteries and nunneries round it. In the 5th c. the diocese of Oxyrhynchus is said to have contained 10,000 monks and 12,000 nuns. In the Mameluke period the town was still a place of some consequence, but thereafter it declined. Excavations by Grenfell and Hunt from 1897 onwards yielded large quantities of Greek, Coptic and Arabic papyri. Remains of colonnades and a large theater of the Roman period were also brought to light. – From Bahnasa there is a desert track to the *Bahriya Oasis.*

129 mi   **Matai** (W bank).
(208 km)

134 mi   In the Nile is the large *island of El-Siriya.*
(215 km)   Opposite, on the E bank, is the village of *El-Siriya,* to the N and S of which are ancient quarries, with a Chapel of Hathor built by

Bird's-eye view of the ribbon of cultivation along the Nile

Merneptah (reliefs of offerings). On the rock face Ramesses III is depicted between Hathor and a god.

139 mi   **Samalut** (W bank), a district capital on the
(223 km) Ibrahimiya Canal, with a Coptic church and a sugar factory. – Soon after this, at the mouth of a side valley on the E bank, is seen a steep rocky hill, the **Gebel el-Teir** (Bird Mountain), on the flat top of which is the Coptic Monastery of *Deir Gebel el-Teir,* also known as *Deir el-Bayara* or *Deir el Adra* (Monastery of the Virgin). A steep flight of steps runs up to the top of the hill. The monastery, surrounded by a wall of dressed stone dating from the Roman period, consists of a group of very modest buildings now mainly inhabited by peasants. The church is said to have been founded by the Empress Helena over a cave in which the Holy Family rested during their flight into Egypt. The sanctuary is hewn from the rock, with a doorway, now half-buried in rubble, decorated in Byzantine style. From the top of the hill there is a fine view of the Nile Valley with its fields of cotton and sugar-cane plantations.

144 mi   *Tihna el-Gebel* (E bank). S of the village
(232 km) (along the banks of the river, then over a narrow canal and through fields) is a low ridge (65–80 ft/20–25 m) containing Egyptian rock tombs which were reused in the Greek period. Here, too, is a temple of the Roman Imperial period, half hewn from the rock and half in masonry, with limestone columns; and on the river side of the hill is a chapel with a relief of a bald-headed man in Roman dress before Egyptian gods. – To the N, towards the village, are the remains of brick buildings belonging to the ancient town of **Tenis** or *Acoris,* in the Hormopolitan nome. – Half an hour's walk S, buried under fallen rock, are three rock tombs of the Old Kingdom with interesting inscriptions (testaments). Carved on the rock face is a colossal figure of Ramesses III making offerings to Sobek (Suchos) and Amun. – In the valley on the far side of the hill, to the N of a Muslim cemetery, are Graeco-Roman and Christian necropolises.

153 mi   **El-Minya** (W bank; Hotels Lotus, III, 44
(247 km) b.; Ibn Khasib, IV, 20 b.), chief town of a governorate (pop. 150,000) and a considerable commercial town, situated between the Nile and the Ibrahimiya Canal, with a museum. This is a good base from which to visit *Beni Hasan, Hermopolis Magna* (see under Mallawi) and *Tell el-Amarna.* – Opposite the town, on the E

bank of the Nile is the *Kom el-Kefara,* with tombs of the Middle Kingdom. – 4$\frac{1}{2}$ miles/ 7 km farther S, at the village of *Zawiyet el-Mayyetin,* is the modern cemetery of El-Minya, with many small domed tombs and chapels. Faithful to ancient traditions, the people of the town still ferry their dead across the river to be buried and take them annual gifts of fruit and palm branches. – Still farther S is a great mound of rubble, the *Kom el-Ahmar* ("Red Hill"), on the far side of which are the rock tombs, now half buried, of the princes and dignitaries of the ancient city of *Hebenu,* mainly dating from the end of the Old Kingdom. – At the village of *Nueirat,* father to the S, are more rock tombs of the Old Kingdom.

167 mi   **Abu Qurqas** (W bank), a small district
(268 km) capital, with a sugar factory. On the E bank of the Nile are the rock tombs of * *Beni Hasan.* – 9 miles/15 km W of Abu Qurqas, on the Bahr Yusuf, is the village of *Balansura,* which occupies the site of the ancient Egyptian *Nefrus.*

178 mi   * **El-Roda** (W bank), from which *Her-*
(286 km) *mopolis Magna* and *Tuna el-Gebel* (see under Mallawi) can be visited.

183 mi   * **Mallawi** (W bank).
(295 km)

186 mi   *Deir Mawas* (W bank), from which * **Tell**
(306 km) **el-Amarna** can be visited.

196 mi   **Deirut** or *Deirut el-Mahatta* (W bank), a
(316 km) district capital situated at the point where the Bahr Yusuf branches off the Ibrahimiya Canal (dam with sluice-gates). – 2 miles/3 km N is *Deirut el-Sherif,* to the W of which, on the edge of the desert, is the village of *Bawit,* with the ruins of the Coptic Monastery of *Apa Apollo.*

205 mi   *Nazali Ganub* (W bank). Beyond the rail-
(330 km) way and the Ibrahimiya Canal is the town of **El-Qusiya,** the ancient *Cussae,* in which, according to Aelian, Aphrodite Urania (i.e. Hathor), mistress of the heavens, and a cow were worshiped. The ancient Egyptian name of the town was *Kis.* It was the capital of the Lower Sycamore nome of Upper Egypt. – 3 miles/ 5 km W of Nazali Ganub is *Meir,* and some 4$\frac{1}{2}$ miles/7 km beyond this is the **necropolis** of Kis, with *rock tombs belonging to dignitaries of the 6th and 12th Dynasties and their relatives. Of particular interest are the tombs of Senbi, son of Ukh-hotep (reign of Amenemhet I) and his son Ukh-hotep (reign of Sesostris I), with reliefs (some of them in naturalistic style) which are among the best of their kind in the Middle Kingdom. – SW of Nazali Ganub, on the fringes of the desert, is the large Coptic Monastery of *Deir el-Maharraq,* traditionally the most southerly point at which the Holy Family rested on their flight into Egypt.

Opposite Nazali Ganub on the E bank of the Nile, surrounded by beautiful palm groves, is the village of *Quseir el-Amarna,*

near which are rock tombs of the 6th Dynasty. The tomb of Khunukh has some scanty painted decoration; the larger tomb of Pepionkh is unfinished.

210 mi   In the Nile are the islands of *El-Hawata* and
(340 km) *El-Mandara.* Beyond them the hills of the Arabian Desert come close to the river in **Gebel Abu Foda.**

217 mi   **Manfalut** (W bank), a district capital
(350 km) situated between the Nile and the Ibrahimiya Canal, the market town for the surrounding area and the seat of a Coptic Bishop. – 4$\frac{1}{2}$ miles/7 km SW, on the edge of the Western Desert, is the *Kom Dara,* with traces of prehistoric settlement, a necropolis of the Early Historical period and a Coptic cemetery.

Opposite Manfalut on the E bank of the Nile lies the village of *El-Maabda,* NE of which, in the hills, are Old Kingdom tombs. – 4 miles/6 km NE, on the plateau of the Arabian Desert, is the *Crocodile Cave,* with scanty remains of crocodile mummies. – S of El-Maabda is *Gebel Qurna,* with a quarry which was worked in the reign of Sethos II (inscription). – 3 miles/5 km E, at *Arab el-Atiyat,* are ancient tombs and quarries. 2 miles/3 km E of this in the Coptic Monastery of *Deir el-Gabrawi* a Greek dedication by the Lusitanian Cohort to Zeus, Heracles and Nike dating from the reign of Diocletian, was discovered. – Some distance farther away is *Gebel Marag* (* view), with many rock tombs of the Late Old Kingdom belonging to princes and dignitaries of the Snake Mountain nome. The tombs are divided into a northern and an older southern group; the most interesting tombs are those of Djaw and Ebe, Princes of the Snake Mountain and Abydos nomes, which contain reliefs of various craftsmen, harvest scenes, fishing and hunting, etc.

235 mi   * **Asyut** (W bank).
(378 km)

250 mi   **Abutig** (W bank), a considerable market
(403 km) town (cotton-ginning factory), which in ancient times lay in the Hypselite nome.

256 mi   *Sidfa* (W bank), with a number of pictur-
(412 km) esque dovecots. – On the E bank, some 1$\frac{1}{4}$ miles/2 km from the Nile, is the district capital of **El-Badari,** near which, in 1924–25, were found the prehistoric tombs which gave their name to the Badarian culture.

262 mi   **Qaw** (E bank), in a fertile plain surrounded
(421 km) by a semicircle of hills. At *El-Hammamiya,* on the edge of the desert, are three rock tombs (reliefs) of high officials of the early 5th Dynasty. Some 1$\frac{1}{4}$ miles/2 km SE of this are large rock tombs, laid out on terraces, belonging to Princes of the 10th (Aphroditopolitan) nome of Upper Egypt (Middle Kingdom) and the extensive necropolis of *Antaeopolis,* with tombs of the Late Period. A short distance away are quarries with demotic inscriptions and two

curious painted figures of the god Antaeus and the goddess Nephthys. – The name Qaw is derived from the ancient Egyptian *Tu-kow* (Coptic *Tkow*); the Greeks called the town *Antaeopolis*, after a local god whom they equated with Antaeus. According to the myth Antaeus was a Libyan King celebrated for his physical strength who challenged all visitors to his kingdom to wrestle with him and after defeating them killed them and used their skulls to build a temple to his father Poseidon; he was finally defeated and slain by Heracles. – According to Diodorus this was the scene of the decisive struggle between Horus and Seth. In Roman times Antaeopolis was capital of the Antaeopolitan nome. The last remains of a Temple of Antaeus built by Ptolemy Philometor and rebuilt by Marcus Aurelius and Lucius Verus in A.D. 164 were swept away by the Nile in 1821.

265 mi (427 km) *Mishta* (W bank). 3 miles/5 km W is the village of *Kom Ishqaw,* the ancient *Aphroditopolis.*

272 mi (438 km) *Tahta* (W bank), a district capital with a noted livestock market. – On the E bank the hills come close to the river.

280 mi (451 km) **El-Maragha** (W bank).

292 mi (470 km) *Sohag (W bank). – On the E bank is *Akhmim.

301 mi (485 km) *El-Minsha* (W bank), a large village on the mound marking the site of *Ptolemais Hermiou,* a city founded by Ptolemy I which in the time of Strabo was the largest in the Thebaid and not inferior in size to Memphis, with a constitution on the Greek model. Its Coptic name was *Psoi.* – Some $7\frac{1}{2}$ miles/12 km W, at the village of *El-Kawamel,* are large cemeteries of the earliest period.

On the E bank is the village of *El-Ahaiwa,* with cemeteries of the earliest period and the New Kingdom. On the hill, near a sheikh's tomb, are the remains of an ancient Egyptian brick-built fort.

Beyond El-Minsha the hills on the E bank come close to the river in *Gebel Tukh.* Stone for the building of Ptolemais came from the large quarries (Greek, Latin and demotic inscriptions) in this area, particularly in the vicinity of *Sheikh Musa.*

314 mi (505 km) **Girga** (W bank), a district capital with attractive brick houses (many of them decorated with glazed tiles), mosques and a Coptic monastery on the outskirts of the town. – 4 miles/6 km NW is the village of *El-Birba,* perhaps occupying the site of ancient *This,* the place of origin of the 1st and 2nd Dynasties and capital of the Thinite nome. – 4 miles/6 km W of Girga, at *Beit Khallaf,* is a large brick mastaba built in the reign of Djoser (3rd Dynasty) which was frequently taken for the tomb of Djoser himself (see under Saqqara). Here and at the neighboring village of *Mahasna* are cemeteries of the Early Old Kingdom.

Opposite Girga on the E bank, at *Nag el-Deir,* are a number of cemeteries, some of them dating from prehistoric times. – Near by is the old Coptic Monastery of *Deir el-Malak,* with a large cemetery in which the Christian inhabitants of Girga are still buried. Beyond the village the hills of the Eastern Desert approach close to the river. Among the many tombs in the hills are four Old Kingdom tombs, situated high up on the slopes of a hill, belonging to dignitaries of the city of This: only scanty remains of reliefs and inscriptions survive. – 3 miles/5 km farther S, in the village of *Mesheikh,* which occupies the site of ancient *Lepidoptonpolis,* are the remains of a temple built by Ramesses II and rebuilt by Merneptah. Above the village are rock tombs, including one which belonged to a High Priest of This, Enhermose, in the reign of Merneptah (19th Dynasty).

324 mi (521 km) *El-Balyana* (W bank), from which *Abydos can be visited.

329 mi (529 km) *Abu Shusha* (W bank), the ancient Egyptian *Per-djodj.* – 3 miles/5 km SE is the village of *Samhud,* built on mounds of rubble marking an ancient site.

345 mi (556 km) *Nag Hammadi* (W bank; Hotel Alamoniom, III, 150 b.). District capital with a sugar factory and aluminium foundry. The main road and railway now cross to the E bank, which they follow to Aswan.

348 mi (560 km) **Hiw** (W bank), a large village situated at one of the Nile's sharpest bends. A short distance above the village, on the banks of the river, is the Tomb of Sheikh Selim (d. 1891), who spent most of his long life sitting naked on this spot and was revered as the helper of boatmen on the river. Near

A *shaduf* near Abydos

Hiw are the sparse remains of ancient *Diospolis Parva*, with large Early Christian cemeteries.

350 mi *El-Daba* (E bank). N of the railway station,
(564 km) near some large quarries in the hills of the Eastern Desert, are the tombs of *Qasr el-Sayyad* (ancient *Chenoboscion*), belonging to Princes of the 7th nome of Upper Egypt under the 6th Dynasty. The Tomb of Tjawit consists of two chambers, the walls between which have almost completely disappeared; the barrel-vaulted roof, hewn from the rock, has survived intact. The tomb has much-damaged reliefs (boats, men bearing offerings, etc.). To the S is the Tomb of Idu, consisting of a single transverse chamber. Here, too, little is left of the inscriptions and reliefs (the dead man going after wildfowl, offering scenes, etc.). Inscriptions in the tomb chambers show that they were occupied by monks during the Early Christian period.

357 mi **Faw Qibli** (E bank), the Coptic *Phbow.*
(575 km) This was the site of a large monastery founded by Pachomius at which monks from all the Egyptian monasteries used to meet twice a year. A short distance to the S was *Tabennese*, where Pachomius founded the first coenobitic monastery about 320.

361 mi **Dishna** (E bank), on the site of an ancient
(581 km) town.

370 mi *Awlad Amr* (E bank). The ruins of the
(596 km) Temple of *Dendera now come into sight on the W bank.

380 mi *Qena (E bank). – Beyond Qena the river
(612 km) turns S and flows past a number of islands. – On the W bank, in the district known to the Greeks as *Typhonia* (sacred to Typhon, i.e. to Seth), lies the village of *Ballas,* with deposits of clay used in making the pottery of Qena (the jars known as *balalis,* singular *ballas*).

393 mi **Qift** (E bank), on the site of ancient
(633 km) *Coptos,* which developed into a great trading town at an early period and in Graeco-Roman times was still an important entrepôt on the trade route from Arabia and India. The town's protective divinity was the ithyphallic harvest god Min (Pan), the patron of desert travelers. Coptos was the starting-point of the expeditions which set out on the journey from the Nile Valley across the desert to the Red Sea, heading for the Sinai Peninsula and for the Land of Punt (probably on the coast of present-day Somalia), which supplied Egypt with incense, ivory, ebony, panther skins and other precious wares and, like India, was a land of fabulous wonders. The Egyptians also went to the desert Valley of the *Wadi el-Hammamat* (see under Eastern Desert) for the sake of its hard stone, much prized for use in sculpture.

During the great rising in Upper Egypt in A.D. 292, in the reign of Diocletian, Coptos

Sunset over the Nile (West Thebes)

was besieged and destroyed. It made a rapid recovery, however, and was still a populous and prosperous town in the time of the Caliphs.

400 mi **Qus** (E bank), a busy district capital on the
(643 km) site of ancient *Apollinopolis Parva*, where the god Haroeris (one of the forms of Horus) was worshiped. In later times, according to the 14th c. traveler Abulfida, the town was second in size only to Fustat (Cairo) and was the chief center of the trade with Arabia. Nothing is now left of the ancient city but heaps of rubble and a few inscribed stones built into houses. The El-Amri Mosque, one of the few notable examples of Muslim architecture in Upper Egypt, has a fine pulpit of 1155 and a basin made from a single ancient stone bearing the name of Ptolemy II Philadelphus.

On the W bank, opposite Qus, is the village of *Tukh,* to the NW of which, on the edge of the desert, are the remains of ancient **Ombos**, which was capital of Upper Egypt in very early times and had Seth as its protective deity. Near by are large prehistoric cemeteries. Farther S, also on the W bank and reached from Tukh, is *Naqada,* a Coptic village, to the N of which, on the fringes of the desert, is a badly ruined brick mastaba dating from the time of Menes, legendary founder of the Egyptian kingdom. – Between Naqada and *Qamula,* along the edge of the desert, are several old Coptic monasteries which are said to date from the time of the Empress Helena. The largest of these, *Deir el-Malak,* stands in the Coptic cemetery of Naqada. Built of sun-dried brick, it has four adjoining churches, the largest of which is dedicated to St Michael. The monastery, which has no fewer than 28 domes, is now unoccupied, being used only on certain feast-days when priests come from Naqada. To the W are the ruins of the *Monastery of St Samuel.*

354 mi (569 km) *Khizam* (E bank), with an ancient necropolis. – On the W bank can be seen the ruins of Thebes (West), and near the railway line the imposing Temple of **Karnak.**

419 mi (674 km) *Luxor (E bank) and *Thebes (West).

431 mi (694 km) *Armant* (W bank: see under Tod).

436 mi (702 km) *El-Shaghab* (E bank), from which *Gebelein* can be visited.

447 mi (720 km) *El-Matana* (E bank). – On the W bank is the village of *Asfun el-Matana,* the ancient *Asphunis* (Egyptian *Hesfun*).

452 mi (727 km) *Esna (W bank).

470 mi (757 km) *El-Mahamid* (E bank), from which *El-Kab* can be visited. – Behind the railway station are quarries, and on top of the hill a conspicuous white sheikh's tomb. To the right are the old town walls of Nekhab (see under El-Kab).

On the W bank, opposite El-Mahamid, is the *Pyramid of El-Kula,* which now has the appearance of a step pyramid as a result of the loss of the filling-in material.

484 mi (779 km) *Edfu (E bank). – The area of cultivated land now becomes wider.

489 mi (787 km) *El-Redesiya* (E bank), a modest little town which has given its name to the Rock Temple of Sethos I in the *Wadi Miah* (see under Eastern Desert).

494 mi (795 km) On the Hill of *El-Sirag* (E bank) are the picturesque ruins of a Late Byzantine fortified town, with a church and monastery, perhaps the ancient *Thmuis.* In the vicinity are old quarries with inscriptions (including one in the name of Tuthmosis III). The nummilitic limestone of the hills now gives place to sandstone, the material used in most of the monumental buildings of Upper Egypt.

503 mi (809 km) *Silwa* (E bank). – On the W bank is the village of *El-Hosh,* near which, on *Gebel Abu Shega,* are ancient quarries, with Greek inscriptions dated to the 11th year of the reign of Antoninus Pius (A.D. 149) recording that stone was hewn here for a Temple of Horus (Apollo), probably in Edfu. – A short distance upstream is the Valley of *Khor Tangura.* Some 2 miles/3 km up the valley, on a rock face on the right-hand side, are fine prehistoric engravings (elephants, antelopes, giraffes, a boat, etc.). There are similar engravings on a rock on the edge of the Nile, S of the valley. – Farther S, below *Silsila, on the left-hand side of a rock face a few yards from the river-bank, is a curious relief known as the *Shatt el-Rigal.* This depicts a petty King called Entef doing homage to King Nebhepetre Mentuhotep II (11th Dynasty) and the Queen Mother Yoh, with an official named Kheti standing behind Entef. On the same rock face, higher up, are other inscriptions and reliefs of the Middle Kingdom and Early New Kingdom.

507 mi (816 km) *Kagug* (E bank), the station from which the *Silsila quarries can be visited.

513 mi (825 km) **Gebel el-Silsila** (E bank: see under Silsila).

521 mi (838 km) *Kom Ombo (E bank).

The island of Elephantine at Aswan

525 mi *Daraw* (E bank), a large village which was
(845 km) once a famous camel market on the route
from Egypt to the Sudan. – On the W bank,
near *Rakaba,* are the remains of ancient
Contra-Ombos. – Beyond this, still on the
W bank, is the village of *El-Kubaniya,* near
which are early Egyptian cemeteries. –
Then (E bank) *Gebel el-Hammam,* with
quarries which provided stone during the
reign of Hatshepsut (18th Dynasty) for the
older Temple of Ombos of which nothing
now remains.

541 mi *El-Khattara* (E bank). The Aswan granite
(870 km) now appears for the first time in the cliffs
flanking the Nile. – The large island of
Bahrif is passed. Opposite the island on
the W bank is *El-Waresab,* where there are
quarries with graffiti. – Beyond this, on
the W bank, the hill containing the picturesquely situated rock tombs of Aswan
comes into view.

548 mi **Aswan* (E bank).
(882 km)

Village, with dovecot, in the Nile Delta

Rosetta arm to the W and the **Damietta
arm** to the E, both of which flow through
the middle third of the Delta, whereas in
ancient times the Pelusiac and Canopic
arms reached the sea at the extreme E and
W ends of the area.

Nile Delta

Area: 9000 sq. miles/23,300 sq. km.
Population: over 30 million.
Governorates: Alexandria, Buhayra, Cairo,
    Daqahliya, Damietta, Gharbiya, Ismailia, Kafr el-
    Sheikh, Minufiya, Port Said, Qalyubiya,
    Sharqiya and Suez.

The huge triangle of the Nile Delta
extends to the N of Cairo between
Lake Mareotis in the W and the Suez
Canal in the E, forming a wide arc
along the Mediterranean coast bordered by lagoons and sand-spits.
Formed over millions of years by the
deposits of mud brought down by
the regular annual inundation of the
Nile, it marks the end of the river's
long journey, when, emerging from
its narrow bed at the edge of the
desert plateau, it breaks up into
separate arms which pursue their
meandering courses towards the
sea.

While the course of the Nile from the
cataracts in the S to the point some $12\frac{1}{2}$
miles/20 km N of Cairo where it splits into
its separate arms has remained practically
unchanged through historical times, the
pattern of the Delta has changed considerably. In antiquity there were seven
arms – the Pelusiac, the Tanitic, the
Mendesian, the Bucolic or Phatnitic,
the Sebennytic, the Bolbitine and the
Canopic. There are now only two, the

Although the ancient remains in the Delta
cannot compare with those to be seen in
Middle and Upper Egypt, this does not
mean that the region was of less importance in antiquity. Long before the
unification of Egypt the sand-hills between the arms of the Nile, winding their
way to the sea through impassable
papyrus swamps, were settled by peoples
of semi-peasant culture very different
from those of the Nile Valley and organized in their own independent principalities. These Delta peoples traded with the
inhabitants of the Nile Valley from an early
period; but on occasion there were wars
as well as peaceable exchanges between
them.

With the unification of the kingdom (1st
Dynasty) the Delta was incorporated in
the Pharaonic Empire as the most northerly part of Lower Egypt, with the royal
symbols of the Red Crown and the
papyrus. The old territorial divisions or
nomes, however, remained as relatively
independent administrative units, although in the course of the centuries they
underwent some changes.

The bringing into cultivation of the Delta
swamps cost the inhabitants enormous
effort over a long period; but the ampler
space available in this region offered
much better conditions for agriculture
than the Nile Valley, which at some points
was very narrow indeed and in total
possessed only half the cultivable area of

the Delta. Thus in the course of many centuries – indeed almost 2 millennia – Lower Egypt increased steadily in importance, and in the Age of the Ramessids, who themselves stemmed from the Delta, gained mastery over the whole of Egypt. During the last 1500 years of ancient Egyptian history several ruling houses came from the Delta, where they built mighty royal residences (Pi-Ramesse, Tanis). In the absence of any large quarries of stone in the region they caused palaces and temples in other parts of Egypt to be pulled down and reused the stones in their own sumptuous buildings. It is not clear why all these buildings have disappeared, leaving only the characteristic *tells* and *koms* to relieve the otherwise level and featureless landscape; but undoubtedly peasants digging for *sebbakh,* the fertile soil found on ancient habitation sites, played a considerable part in the process of destruction.

Nubian musicians

The Nile Delta is still Egypt's major agricultural region, with the associated industrial (foodstuff industries, textile factories) and commercial activities. Its largest and most important city and the main center of attraction for tourists in Lower Egypt is the port of **Alexandria**; the principal center of commerce and communications, situated in the heart of the Delta, is **Tanta**; and other major towns are *El-Mansura, Damanhur, El-Zagazig* and *Benha,* together with *Port Said, Ismailia* and *Suez* on its eastern margins.

*Abu Mena, Abu Roash, **Alexandria, Behbeit el-Hagara, **Cairo, Damanhur, Damietta, Heliopolis (Old Heliopolis), Ismailia, Ismailia Canal, Mansura, *Nile, Port Said, Rosetta, Sais, Suez, **Suez Canal, *Tanis, Tanta, Tell el-Faraun, *Wadi Natrun and El-Zagazig: see separate entries. – **Nile Dam and Benha**: see under Cairo, Surroundings.

Nubia

States: Egypt and Sudan.
Egyptian governorate: Aswan (Lower Nubia).
ⓘ **Tourist Information Office,**
Tourist Bazaar,
Aswan;
tel. 32. 97.

Nubia (Arabic El-Nuba, formerly Bilad el-Barabra, ''Land of the Berberines'') extends S from the First Cataract at Aswan, reaching far into the Sudan, beyond the Fifth Cataract, to the 18th degree of latitude. Lower Nubia, as far as the Second Cataract at Wadi Halfa, belongs to Egypt; Upper Nubia, beyond Wadi Halfa, is Sudanese territory. Lower Nubia was known to the ancient Egyptians as Wewet, while the regions on the Upper Nile, to the S of the Second Cataract, were grouped together as the Land of Kush, the Cush of the Old Testament. The Greeks and Romans called the inhabitants of these territories Ethiopians.

HISTORY. – In prehistoric times – on which some light has been thrown by the archaeological work of the last few decades, particularly by the Unesco-sponsored campaign for rescuing the Nubian monuments and the excavations which accompanied these operations – Lower Nubia was occupied by the same population of Mediterranean type as Egypt proper, and the cultural pattern was broadly similar from the Delta to the Second Cataract. But from the beginning of the Historical period (c. 3000 B.C.), marked by the unification of the two parts of the country, Egypt developed a rich culture which reached a peak of material prosperity and artistic achievement, while Nubia remained as it was. All cultural links with Egypt were broken off, and the burials of the period reflect the acute poverty of the population.

In the earliest Egyptian texts Lower Nubia is mentioned as the land through which the Egyptians obtained the products of the Sudan – ebony, ivory, leopard skins and a variety of resins. Under the 6th Dynasty mercenary troops were enlisted in this region, and the Princes of Elephantine dispatched great trading expeditions to the lands of the Upper Nile. – In the First Intermediate Period between the Old and Middle Kingdoms, towards the end of the 3rd millennium B.C., there was a sharp change in the population of Lower Nubia. Nubian tribes thrust up from the S and took possession of the territory between the Second and the First Cataract, bringing with them their own African culture; but this culture assimilated local traditions and practices, as well as some influences from Egypt, to evolve into a characteristic Nubian culture which reached its peak during the Middle Kingdom.

During this period, however, political conflicts arose between Egypt and Nubia. The rulers of the 11th Dynasty sought to subdue Lower Nubia and gain control of the important route into the Sudan, but it was left to the Kings of the 12th Dynasty to achieve the *conquest of Nubia* and advance the Egyptian frontier to Semna, below the Fourth Cataract. In order to secure the newly acquired territory against enemy incursions a series of forts was constructed in the rocky Valley of the Batu el-Hagar, with its many rapids, between Wadi Halfa and Semna.

The decline of Egypt during the Hyksos period enabled Nubia to recover its independence, but at the beginning of the New Kingdom it returned to Egyptian control. The Pharaohs of the 18th Dynasty pushed farther S and conquered the Land of Kush as far as Napata, which now became the southern frontier of the kingdom. The conquered regions were combined with the most southerly Egyptian province (El-Kab: see that entry) to form a new territory ruled by a dignitary who bore the title of "Prince of Kush and Governor of the Southern Lands". Under stable Egyptian Government Nubia enjoyed a period of material prosperity. Egyptian culture, which had reached Nubia and been adopted by the native population before the time of the 18th Dynasty, increasingly pervaded the region under the New Kingdom, steadily displacing the Nubian culture of the Middle Kingdom. Under the 18th Dynasty Nubia was completely Egyptianized. All over the country, particularly on the W bank of the Nile, which was safe from attack by bedouin from the E, temples were built which rivaled those of Egypt proper in size and splendor. Most of these temples were dedicated to the great Egyptian gods Amun, Re-Harakhty and Ptah; but other Egyptian gods, particularly Isis, were also worshiped, as well as the local Nubian god Dedun, the deified Sesostris III – the first Egyptian ruler of Nubia, who had become a King of protective divinity – and sometimes also the reigning king and queen. The inscriptions in the temples were written in the Egyptian language and script; for Egyptian had now become the official language, although the great mass of the population still spoke their native Nubian tongue.

Until about 1100 B.C. Nubia remained a political and cultural dependency of Egypt; but when Egyptian power declined under the 21st Dynasty Nubia shook off this alien rule, and an **Ethiopian (Kushite) kingdom** was established with its capital at *Napata*. Its culture was still Egyptian; and indeed its kings, who were much dependent on the priesthood, believed themselves to be the true guardians of the Egyptian religion and the legitimate rulers of Egypt. About 730 B.C. the Ethiopian King *Piankhi* temporarily overran the whole of Egypt, and soon afterwards an Ethiopian (Kushite) dynasty (the 25th) established itself firmly on the Egyptian throne. In 663 B.C., however, the Ethiopian Pharaohs were forced to give way to the superior power of Assyria and were restricted to Nubia. The frontier between Egypt and Nubia now lay at the rocky islet of Konosso, just N of Philae.

Much is known about the kings of the immediately subsequent period, with their capital at Napata; and we know also of the unsuccessful campaign by Psammetichus II in Lower Nubia (*c.* 590 B.C.) and of the attempted conquest by Cambyses (525 B.C.). Thereafter, however, the historical sources dry up almost completely. Around 300 B.C. the capital was transferred from Napata to *Meroe*, although a branch of the Royal House continued for a time to rule the northern part of Kush from Napata.

Egyptian culture in Nubia now gradually declined. The Egyptian hieroglyphic script became corrupt, and new Meroitic hieroglyphic and cursive scripts were developed, which at the beginning of the Christian era began to be used for writing the native Nubian language even in official documents.

Nubian village on the island of Elephantine, Aswan

During the Ptolemaic and Roman periods the Egyptian frontier was near Hierasycaminus (latitude 23° N), and for a time apparently farther S, at Primis (Qasr Ibrim); but the Ethiopian kings occasionally extended their power as far N as Philae, and perhaps even into part of Upper Egypt. At the beginning of the Roman period the Kushite Queen *Candace* launched an attack on the Roman province, but was repulsed by the Governor, Petronius, in 23 B.C. About this time, too, the nomadic **Blemmyes** of the Eastern Desert regions, who had previously acknowledged Ethiopian suzerainty, became more aggressive, harassing the northern part of Lower Nubia and even raiding Roman territory in Upper Egypt. In the end the Romans gave up the attempt to subdue them: about A.D. 300 Diocletian withdrew from Nubian territory, and thereafter Roman rule was confined to Egypt proper, with the frontier at Philae. The Blemmyes, in alliance with the Nubians, continued their incursions into Upper Egypt; but in A.D. 451 they were defeated by Marcian, who concluded a peace treaty with them. A century earlier, about A.D. 350, the Abyssinian kings of Aksum had conquered the Upper Nile Valley and put an end to the kingdom of Meroe.

Christianity reached Philae in the 4th c. and from there extended into Nubia, the Egyptian temples being converted into churches. In A.D. 640 the Upper Nile Valley fell into the hands of the Arabs together with the rest of Egypt. Caliph Omar's great general Amr advanced as far as Dongola and levied tribute on the Nubians, but the Arabs did not establish permanent control over the territory. In 1173 Saladin's brother Shams el-Dola captured the Fortress of Qasr Ibrim and plundered the church treasury. Christianity yielded to **Islam** only gradually, and a Christian kingdom was able to maintain itself at Soba on the Blue Nile into medieval times.

Little is known about the Islamic principalities which were established at *El-Derr* (see under Amada), *Dongola, Sennar* and elsewhere in Nubia. In 1821 the whole of Nubia was conquered by Ismail Pasha and incorporated in the Egyptian kingdom of his father Mohammed Ali, and since then Lower Nubia has shared the destinies of Egypt.

The construction of the first Aswan Dam (1898–1912) led to the flooding of large areas of the Nile Valley in Lower Nubia and to a considerable reduction in the amount of land available for cultivation. Many villages had to be evacuated and their inhabitants resettled on higher ground. Thereafter such major monuments as the temples of Philae and Kalabsha were partly under water for most of the year. The building of the High Dam (Sadd el-Ali), however, meant that the last remaining habitable areas in Lower Nubia as well as much of Upper Nubia were doomed to disappear beneath the rising water. The whole population of some 80,000 people were moved to new homes, mostly in the area around Kom Ombo (see that entry) which is now known as *New Nubia* (El-Nuba el-Gedida). It is planned to resettle them on the shores of Lake Nasser.

The building of the High Dam also threatened the tombs, rock temples, forts and other major monuments in the Nubian part of the Nile Valley; and accordingly a rescue operation was launched under the aegis of Unesco in order to save for posterity at least the most important of these remains of the past. They were removed from their original sites – either in one piece where this was practicable or sawn into blocks of convenient size where it was not – and re-erected on new sites at a safe height above the water.

In gratitude for the international help, both financial and technical, which made the operation possible the Egyptian Government presented a number of small temples and other monuments to various foreign museums, where they were re-erected and put on display.

The Temple of Kalabsha, the Kertassi Kiosk, the Rock Temple of Beit el-Wali and the Rock Stela of Qasr Ibrim were re-erected at **New Kalabsha**, a short distance S of the W end of the High Dam; the Temple of Isis on the island of **Philae** was moved to the neighboring island of Agilka; at **New Sebwa**, above the drowned Wadi el-Sebwa, are the rock temples of Wadi el-Sebwa, Dakka and El-Maharraqa and the reliefs from the memorial niches of Qasr Ibrim; the temples of Amada and El-Derr and the Rock Tomb of Pennut formerly at Aniba are at **New Amada**, to the N of the drowned site of Amada; and the two rock temples of Abu Simbel now stand at **New Abu Simbel**, above their original site.

Of the monuments presented to other countries in gratitude for their help the **Temple of Debod** (2nd c. B.C.), dedicated to Amun and Isis, is now in the Parque de la Montaña in Madrid; the southern temple from **Tafa** (whose northern neighbor disappeared at the end of the 19th c.) is in the Rijksmuseum van Oudheden in Leyden; the **Temple of Dendur** (dedicated by Augustus to the local deities Pediese and Pahor) is in the Metropolitan Museum of Art in New York; and Tuthmosis III's rock chapel from **Ellesiya** is in the Museo Egizio in Turin.

The Temple of **Gerf Husein** and innumerable cemeteries, rock tombs, cult-niches, chapels, remains of houses, forts and Coptic churches with frescos could not be saved and were engulfed in the waters of Lake Nasser.

New Nubia: see under Kom Ombo.

**Abu Simbel, *Amada, **Aswan, *Kalabsha, *Nile, **Philae and *Wadi el-Sebwa: see separate entries.

Oxyrhynchus
See under Nile

Philae

Upper Egypt. – Governorate: Aswan.
ⓘ **Tourist Information Office,**
Tourist Bazaar,
Aswan;
tel. 32 97.

ACCESS. – By road from Aswan to landing-stage 4 miles/6 km S; then boat (individually hired or group excursion) to the island to Agilka.

Once renowned as the "pearl of Egypt" by virtue of its rich vegetation and its magnificent assemblage of temples, the island of Philae now lies beneath the waters of Lake Nasser; but fortunately, thanks to a spectacular rescue operation carried through with financial and technical assistance from Italy and West Germany, it was possible to save at least the most important **monuments and re-erect them on the higher neighboring island of Agilka.

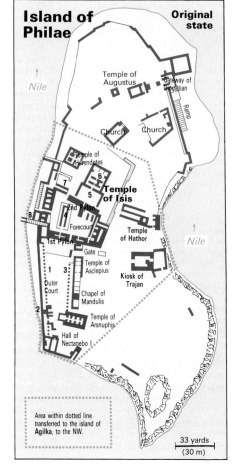

Island of Philae — Original state

Temple of Augustus
Gateway of Diocletian
Nile
Ramp
Church   Church
Temple of Harendotes
7   6   **Temple of Isis**
5
2nd Pylon
8
Forecourt   Temple of Hathor
1st Pylon
Gate   Nile
1   3   Temple of Asclepius
Outer Court   Kiosk of Trajan
2   Chapel of Mandulis
Temple of Arsnuphis
Hall of Nectanebo I

Area within dotted line transferred to the island of **Agilka**, to the NW.

33 yards
(30 m)

1 W Colonnade   5 Vestibule
2 Small Nilometer   6 Sanctuary
3 E Colonnade   7 Gateway of Hadrian
4 Birth-house   8 Nilometer

HISTORY. – The ancient Egyptian name of Philae was **Pi-lak**, from which the Greek and Latin **Philae**, the Coptic *Pilakh* ("corner") and the Arabic *Bilak* were derived. It was known to the local people as *El-Qasr*, the "Castle", or as *Geziret Anas el-Wogud*, after the hero of one of the tales in the "Arabian Nights" who traced his beloved to the island, where she had been locked up by her father, only to find that she had escaped: whereupon further adventures and further trials followed before the lovers were reunited.

Herodotus, who visited Elephantine about 450 B.C., makes no mention of Philae. The oldest surviving temple buildings date from the time of Nectanebo I (*c.* 370 B.C.), but there were undoubtedly earlier temples on the site. The principal deity was Isis, but Osiris, Nephthys, Hathor and the cataract gods Khnum and Satet were also venerated here. The imposing buildings now to be seen were erected by the Ptolemies in the last two centuries B.C. and by the Roman Emperors in the first three centuries A.D. Many inscriptions show that pilgrims flocked to Philae in Greek and Roman times to pay homage to the mysterious and benign Isis, goddess of healing. She was also revered by the predatory Nubians and

First Cataract   Aswan

Philae

Aswan Dam
Nile
Shash
456 ft (139 m)
Boats to Agilka
541 ft (165 m)
Awad
Konosso
Agilka
525 ft (160 m)
Bigga   Philae
High Dam, Airport
Western (Libyan) Desert
Eastern (Arabian) Desert
El-Heisa
443 ft (135 m)
528 ft (161 m)
Nile
⅓ mile
(1 km)

High Dam

Agilka: new site of Philae temples, above highest level of water

Philae: original site of the temples, partly under water

Blemmyes, whose priests were still permitted, even after their defeat at the hands of the Emperor Marcian in A.D. 451, to make offerings to Isis together with the Egyptian priests and on special occasions to retain the image of the goddess in their keeping. Long after the introduction of Christianity the Nubians remained faithful to the cult of Isis, and it was only in the time of Justinian (527–565) that the temples were closed and some of their chambers converted for use in Christian worship. From then until the coming of Islam a Coptic town flourished on the island.

Until the construction of the first Aswan Dam the island ranked as one of the most beautiful places in Egypt and attracted large numbers of visitors every year. Thereafter it lost much of its charm, since it was under water for the greater part of the year and the temples were accessible only between August and December. Then, more recently, the High Dam project threatened to engulf them for good. They were saved from this fate by the great international rescue operation sponsored by Unesco and carried out between 1972 and 1980. The island of Philae was surrounded by a coffer-dam and the area within this was drained; then a new site was prepared on the neighboring island of **Agilka**, the temples were broken up into sections, which were carefully numbered, and they were then re-erected in the same relative positions on

The Temple of Philae before removal

The Temple of Philae within its coffer-dam

Agilka. The gray coloring of the lower part of the walls and columns still shows the effect of their annual immersion over the period between the construction of the two dams, and the vegetation on Agilka is very sparse; but the imposing and magnificently preserved temples of Philae still retain their power to impress.

THE TEMPLES. – The great ****Temple of Isis** is oriented from S to N, the main entrance to the temple precinct being at its S end, through the *Hall of Nectanebo I*. This was originally the vestibule of a temple dedicated by Nectanebo to "his mother Isis, mistress of Philae, revered in the Abaton Shrine", and to Hathor of Senmet which was soon afterwards swept away by the inundation of the Nile and was later completely rebuilt by Ptolemy II Philadelphus. This elegant structure had 14 columns with varying floral capitals surmounted by sistrum capitals. Only six

columns remain, and nothing is left of the roof. Between the columns are screens some 6½ ft/3 m high topped by cavetto cornices and a frieze of royal cobras and decorated with reliefs of Nectanebo making offerings; at three points there were doorways through the screens.

On the river front of the temple are two *obelisks* (unusually, of sandstone and not the normal granite) set on rectangular bases. The one on the W, which has one Greek and several Arabic inscriptions, is still standing, though it has lost its apex; only the base of the other one remains.

The Hall of Nectanebo leads into the large **Outer Court** of the temple, bounded on the N by the first pylon and on the E and W by colonnades; it dates from the end of the Ptolemaic period or the reign of

The Temple of Philae re-erected on the island of Agilka

Outer court of the temple, from the S

Augustus. Here can be seen a section of the solid embankment wall which presumably enclosed the main part of the island and was interrupted at several points by steps leading down to the water.

The *West Colonnade*, which runs along the river side of the court, is 305 ft/93 m long and has 31 (originally 32) plant columns 17 ft/5·10 m high, with capitals of very varied form. Most of the columns have reliefs showing the Emperor Tiberius making offerings to the gods. The roof of the colonnade, part of which has collapsed, is decorated with stars and flying vultures. On the rear wall are two rows of reliefs depicting the Pharaoh, usually Augustus or Tiberius, dedicating gifts to the gods. – From the colonnade a subterranean staircase leads down to a small *Nilometer*.

The *East Colonnade* is unfinished, only six of the planned 16 columns having been completed. The others are only rough-hewn and the capitals have been left unfinished. In the rear wall are five doors which led into various chapels.

Adjoining the S end of this colonnade is the badly ruined **Temple of Eri-hems-nufer** (Arsnuphis),

built by Philopator and his Nubian contemporary Ergamenes and enlarged by Epiphanes. – Practically nothing is left of a small *chapel* dedicated to the Nubian god Mandulis which stood behind the central part of the colonnade; but at the N end of the colonnade is a well-preserved little *Temple of Asclepius* (Imhotep) built by Philadelphus.

The *Temple of Isis, the principal temple of Philae, dedicated to Isis and her son Harpocrates, probably occupies the site of an earlier temple. It was begun by Ptolemy II Philadelphus and substantially completed by Euergetes I, although the embellishment of the temple with reliefs and inscriptions was a very gradual process which was never quite completed.

The **First Pylon** 150 ft/45·5 m wide and 60 ft/18 m high, consists of two towers and a central doorway, which was decorated with reliefs by Nectanebo. On the front of the E tower is a huge figure of Ptolemy XII Neos Dionysos grasping a band of enemies by the hair and raising his club to smite them, with Isis, the falcon-headed Horus of Edfu and Hathor on the left. Above are two reliefs of Neos Dionysos presenting the crowns of Upper and Lower Egypt to Horus and Nephthys (right) and offering incense to Isis and Harpocrates (left). There are similar reliefs on the W tower; at the foot are demotic and Greek inscriptions. A doorway in this tower, with reliefs by Philometor, leads directly to the entrance to the birth-house (see below). In front of the pylon there originally stood two granite obelisks erected by Euergetes II and two granite lions.

Adjoining the E tower an elegant *gateway* has reliefs by Ptolemy II Philadelphus (on the lintel) and the Emperor Tiberius (on the jambs). The gateway, built by Philadelphus, originally stood in a brick wall. – The *ascent of the pylon is well worth the effort; there is a winding staircase at the SE corner of the forecourt beyond the pylon. The rooms in the interior are undecorated and dark.

Detail of E colonnade

First pylon from the N

First and second pylons of the Temple of Philae after re-erection on Agilka

The central doorway, within which (on the right) is a French inscription ("an 7 de la République") commemorating Napoleon's campaign and the pursuit of the Mamelukes by General Desaix in 1799, leads into the *Forecourt,* between the first and second pylons. On the rear wall of the first pylon are four priests with the sacred barque of Isis, preceded by the King burning incense. On either side of the forecourt are small buildings fronted by colonnades. The one to the W, the **Birth-House** (*mammisi*), was dedicated to Hathor-Isis in honor of the birth of her son Horus. It is surrounded on all four sides by colonnades, the columns in which have foliage capitals surmounted by sistrum capitals. The walls, columns and screens between the columns are covered with reliefs and inscriptions, mostly by Euergetes II, Neos Dionysos, Augustus and Tiberius. Of particular interest are the reliefs in the last chamber, which depict scenes from the childhood of Horus, including Horus as a falcon in the swamps of the Delta, Isis suckling Horus in the swamps, etc.

The small building to the E, opposite the birth-house, contained rooms for the priests and others which served some scientific purpose. The plant columns in the vestibule are notable for their elegant proportions. The reliefs and inscriptions are by Neos Dionysos, the dedicatory inscription on the architrave by Euergetes II. On the N side of the vestibule a door, approached by steps, gives access to the inner passage round the temple. The reliefs depict Neos Dionysos in presence of the gods.

The **Second Pylon** is 105 ft/32 m wide and 40 ft/12 m high. The reliefs on the central doorway are by Euergetes II. On the lower part of the E tower is a large figure of Neos Dionysos dedicating the slaughtered sacrificial animals to Horus and Hathor. Above are two small reliefs depicting the King presenting a garland to Horus and Nephthys (right) and offering incense to Osiris, Isis and Horus and pouring water on the altar (left). The natural granite at the foot of the tower has been smoothed to form a stela, with a six-line inscription and reliefs relating to a grant of land made by Philometor in the 24th year of his reign (157 B.C.).

In front of it are the foundations of a small *chapel.* – The W tower has similar reliefs, which have been deliberately defaced. – The second pylon can be climbed by a staircase on the N side of the W tower, from the top of which it is possible to cross the central doorway to the E tower. – Within the central doorway (on the right, above) are some much-faded Early Christian paintings.

Beyond the second pylon stands the **Temple of Isis** proper, which consists of a court, a vestibule, several antechambers and the sanctuary, together with some subsidiary chambers. The walls are covered, inside and out, with reliefs and inscriptions depicting various Ptolemies (Philadelphus, Euergetes II, etc.) and Roman Emperors (Augustus, Tiberius, Antoninus Pius) making offerings or performing other ritual acts. They are very similar to the reliefs in other temples of the period, particularly those of Dendera and Edfu.

On each side of the *Court* was a small colonnade with a single column. The court could be shaded from the sun by an awning; the holes for the cords can be seen on the upper part of the cavetto cornice facing the second pylon.

The *Vestibule,* with eight columns, was originally separated from the court by screens between the columns on the front. The conversion of the vestibule and court into a Christian church is recalled by Coptic crosses incised in the walls and a Greek inscription that "this good work" was done in the time of Bishop Theodore (during the reign of Justinian). Above the door is an inscription commemorating the archaeological expedition sent to Philae in 1841 by Pope Gregory XVI.

A number of antechambers flanked by dark side chambers lead into the **Sanctuary**, lit by two small windows, with a base (presented by Euergetes I and his wife Berenice) for the sacred barque bearing the image of Isis. – To the left of the first antechamber is a small room with reliefs of the King in the presence of Isis. On the W side of this room is a door leading out

Kiosk of Trajan re-erected on Agilka

of the temple; on the N side is a staircase leading to the roof of the sanctuary.

From the roof steps lead down to the *Osiris Chambers*, which contain fine reliefs relating to the death of Osiris. Vestibule, left-hand wall: the northern Nile god offers a libation of milk to the soul of Osiris, sitting before him in the form of a bird; the falcon-headed Harendotes pours the water of consecration over the falcon-headed mummy of Osiris; behind, the god's sisters; four demons, the god Shu and the Emperor Antoninus Pius (who built this chamber) before Osiris and his sisters Isis and Nephthys. Small main chamber, opposite door, middle row (from left to right): Isis and Nephthys at the bier of Osiris Onnophris (who is naked); the tomb of Osiris (head missing), with two kneeling goddesses; the doorway of the tomb, with a lion; four demons carrying the falcon-headed mummy of Osiris. Lower row (left to right): the frog-headed Heqet and the falcon-headed Harsiesis at the bier of Osiris, under which are the canopic jars for his entrails; the body of Osiris among swamp plants, with a priest pouring the water of consecration; the dog-headed Anubis at the bier of Osiris, with Isis and Nephthys kneeling beside it.

NW of the second pylon is the small **Gateway of Hadrian**, in the old enclosure wall of the temple. This,

Detail of the Kiosk of Trajan

together with a much-ruined vestibule, was built in the reign of the Emperor Hadrian and decorated with reliefs by Hadrian, Marcus Aurelius and Lucius Verus. The gateway presumably led to the Sanctuary of Abaton on the neighboring island of Bigga, where there was a Tomb of Osiris, and accordingly the reliefs relate to the cult of Osiris. On the lintel Hadrian is depicted making offerings to Osiris, Isis and Harsiesis and to Osiris, Nephthys and Harendotes; on the left-hand jamb is the sacred relic of Abydos, on the right-hand jamb the *djed* pillar of Osiris (the sacred emblem of Busiris). Within the gateway, on the right (above), Marcus Aurelius is depicted in the presence of Osiris and Isis (note the guide-lines for the artist); (below) Marcus Aurelius making offerings of food, including grapes, and flowers to Isis.

The reliefs in the *Vestibule,* left unfinished and now ruinous, are of particular interest. Over the door in the S wall, above: Horus seated on a bench, with Nephthys and Isis presenting the crowns of Lower and Upper Egypt; Thoth (left) and Seshat, goddess of writing (right) inscribing the King's name on a palm branch; behind Thoth sits the air god Shu, holding a sail, and behind him again another god and a goddess playing a lyre. Below: the tomb of Osiris at Abaton, with the body of Osiris borne by a crocodile; to the left Isis; above, the sun between mountains; and above the whole scene the sun, crescent moon and stars. All this lies within a small temple with a door on the left, in front of which are one small and two large pylons; to the right are rocks. To the left of the door are unfinished reliefs showing the King making grants of land; above are three lines in Meroitic cursive script. – On the right-hand wall (second top row) is a famous relief depicting the source of the Nile: the god of the Nile, with a snake entwined round his body, pours water from two jars under a rocky crag on which are perched a vulture and a falcon. To the right of this is the soul of Osiris in the form of a bird within the sacred grove, worshiped by Hathor (left) and by Isis, Nephthys, Horus and Amun (right).

SW of Hadrian's Gateway is a *Nilometer* (inaccessible), which has the scale marked in hieratic and demotic as well as in the usual Coptic characters. – NW of the gateway can be seen the foundations of a *Temple of Harendotes* built by the Emperor Claudius.

Some 55 yds/50 m E of the Temple of Isis we find the little *Temple of Hathor*, built by Philometor and Euergetes II in honor of Hathor-Aphrodite; the vestibule and the sanctuary (destroyed) were added by Augustus. The columns of the vestibule are decorated with charming reliefs: flute-players and harpists, Bes with a tambourine, Bes dancing and playing a harp, monkeys playing the lyre, priests bearing an antelope, etc. On the screens between the columns Augustus is depicted making offerings to various personifications of Hathor. The best-preserved part of the structure is the main temple chamber, on the front of which are two plant columns linked to the walls by screens.

SE of the Temple of Hathor, on the bank of the river, is the most attractive little building on the island, the *Kiosk of Trajan*. As its name implies, it dates from the Roman Imperial period, but was left unfinished: the capitals of the plant columns were intended to be surmounted by sistrum capitals.

Various structures at the N end of Philae – in particular two Coptic churches and the remains of a Coptic monastery, the ruins of a Temple of Augustus dating from the 18th year of the Emperor's reign and the large Roman town gate to the NE – were left where they stood and not transferred to Agilka. It is hoped to recover them at a later date.

From the rocky neighboring island of **Bigga** (ancient Egyptian *Senmet*) there is a good * view of Agilka and the temples of Philae. The principal deities of Bigga were the fire goddess Ups and Hathor. There are the remains of a colonnaded court belonging to a temple built by Ptolemy XII Neos Dionysos, with plant columns linked by screens. On the E side is a doorway with an apse built into it. – On this island there once stood the famous Abaton, the sacred shrine containing the Tomb of Osiris.

* *Aswan and* * *Kalabsha: see separate entries.

Port Safaga
See under Red Sea

Port Said/Bur Said

Lower Egypt. – Governorate: Port Said.
Population: 280,000.
ⓘ **Tourist Information Office,**
Shari Palestina,
tel. 218 87.

HOTEL. – *ETAP*, Sharia Tarh el-Bahr, I, 116 b.; *Holiday*, Sharia Gumhurija, II, 180 b.; *Crystal*, Sharia Mohammed Mahmud 2, III, 154 b.; *Riviera*, Sharia Ramses 30, III, 100 b.; *Abu Simbel*, Sharia Gumhurija 15, III, 93 b.; *Savoy*, Sharia Mohammed Ali, III, 54 b.; *New House*, Sharia Orabi, IV, 102 b.; *El-Merryland Touristic*, Sharia Dagla, IV, 96 b.; *Lootas*, Sharia Babel, IV, 96 b.; *El-Ghazl*, Sharia 23 July, IV, 82 b.; etc.

ACCESS. – By road from Cairo (125 miles/200 km SW), crossing the Eastern Desert to Ismailia, then N along the W side of the Suez Canal. – By rail from Cairo in 4¼ hours. – By air from Cairo, Alexandria or Suez.

Port Said (Bur Said; named after Viceroy Said, 1854–63), chief town of a governorate, Egypt's fourth largest city and after Alexandria its largest port, lies in a barren and desolate setting on a narrow strip of land – which is gradually increasing in width by the deposit of silt – between Lake Manzala and the N

Souvenir-dealers in Port Said harbor

entrance of the Suez Canal, to which the town owed its foundation in 1859.

In November 1956 much of what was then a thriving town was destroyed by air bombardment during the Suez War. It made a rapid recovery, but suffered another severe blow when the Suez Canal was closed to traffic in 1967 and the Sinai Peninsula was occupied by Israeli forces, some 70% of the population being evacuated. Reconstruction has been under way since 1974, and it is planned to develop the port and airport.

Apart from commerce and shipping the main elements in the city's economy are foodstuffs and chemical industries and the production of salt.

SIGHTS. – Port Said is a town of European-style architecture with a regular layout in the form of a right-angled triangle, which has little in the way of tourist attractions apart from its fascinating mixture of races and the lively and colorful Oriental bustle of its streets.

The large **Harbor** (570 acres) and the northern entrance to the Suez Canal are protected by two long *piers*. The W pier, continuing the line of the harbor quay for some $2\frac{1}{2}$ miles/4 km, is designed to prevent the silting up of the channel by the deposit of mud carried down by the Nile. At its near end there formerly stood an imposing statue of Ferdinand de Lesseps (1805–94), constructor of the Suez Canal, but this was pulled down by Egyptian nationalists in 1956. To the S, on the harbor quay, is a 175 ft/53 m high **lighthouse**, with a light visible 23 miles away. The E pier is almost $1\frac{1}{4}$ miles/2 km long.

The town has recently been considerably extended on the N and W, where new land has been reclaimed from the sea.

Opposite Port Said, on the E side of the Suez Canal and the harbor, is the suburb of PORT FUAD (Bur Fuad: ferry service),

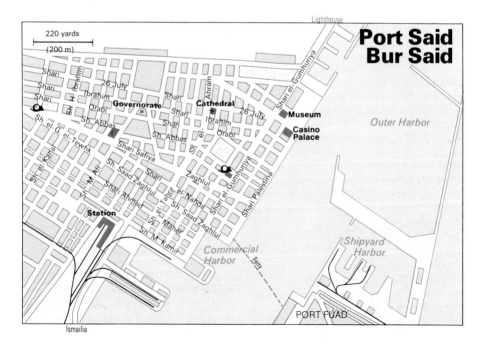

Martyrs' Memorial, Port Said

established in 1926 (and named after the then reigning King) by the Suez Canal Company, with their headquarters and housing for their employees. It has attractive parks and gardens and good beaches.

SURROUNDINGS of Port Said. – To the W of the town is the great expanse of **Lake Manzala** (see under Damietta), mainly consisting of marshland and reed-beds, with great numbers of water-birds.

Damietta, Ismailia, El-Mansura, Nile Delta, * **Sinai,** ** **Suez Canal,** * **Tanis** and **Tell el-Faraun**: see separate entries.

El-Qahira

See Cairo

Qara Oasis

See under Qattara Depression

Lake Qarun

See under Fayyum

Qasr Ibrim

See under Wadi el-Sebwa

Qasr Qarun

See under Fayyum

Qattara Depression

North-West Frontier District.
Administrative center: Mersa Matruh.

ACCESS. – 37 miles/60 km S of El-Alamein Station on a desert track passing through the small uninhabited oasis of El-Mefara. Special authorization required.

The Qattara Depression, the largest and most northerly of the Egyptian oasis depressions, is a deep wide rift in the gently undulating plateau of the Western (Libyan) Desert, lying within the triangle formed by El-Alamein, Mersa Matruh and the Siwa Oasis. Its rugged northern and north-western edges, with their steep fissured rock walls, have long been regarded as an insuperable natural obstacle, which played an important part in the battles of the Second World War.

The depression, filled with impassable and treacherous salt swamps (*sebkha*), is some 175 miles/280 km long and up to 90 miles/140 km wide, with a total area of

The eroded landscape of the Qattara Depression

some 6950 sq. miles/18,000 sq. km, and at its lowest point lies 440 ft/134 m below sea-level. It owes its origin to wind erosion, which at some points has gouged out the surface as far down as the water-table.

The only inhabited oasis is **Qara**, on the W side of the depression, with a settlement of some 150 inhabitants perched on a picturesque crag. The main source of income is the cultivation of dates. Alexander the Great stayed here on his return journey from the Siwa Oasis (see that entry), and the place is referred to by ancient authors as "Alexander's Camp". The Negroid element in the population

The so-called **Qattara Project** has been the subject of repeated study and investigation since 1916. The idea is to cut a 37 mile/60 km long canal from the Mediterranean and channel sea-water into the depression. With a difference in level of some 177 ft/54 m when the basin was full it would then be possible to harness the water for the production of electric power and perhaps also to operate a plant for the desalination of sea-water. The inland sea thus created, with an area of 4650 sq. miles/12,000 sq. km, would probably exert a moderating influence on the climate of the surrounding area and might lead to an increase in rainfall. Carrying out the project would involve a number of nuclear blasting operations. Although the scheme is technically feasible its realization seems likely to give rise to difficulties and problems, and for the time being at any rate the plan, which was vigorously espoused by President Sadat, has been put into suspense.

The desert village of Qara

Salt deposits in the Qattara Depression

ACCESS. – By road (the main Nile Valley road) from Aswan (170 miles/275 km S), Luxor (39 miles/62 km S) or Cairo (300 miles/480 km NW). – By rail from Aswan via Luxor or from Cairo.

The busy provincial capital of Qena, the ancient Cainepolis, lies on the E bank of the Nile, a mile or so from the river. The town itself has no features of tourist interest, but it is the nearest place to the Temple of Hathor at Dendera.

Qena is noted for its pottery, in particular the porous water-bottles (*kulal,* singular *kulla*) made from the local clay which are sold all over Egypt. Evaporation keeps the water in these bottles 9–11 °F/5–6 °C below the outside temperature.

From Qena a road crosses the **Eastern Desert** (see that entry) to *Bur Safaga* on the Red Sea.

Abydos, **Dendera, **Karnak, **Luxor and ****Thebes (West): see separate entries.

reflects the importance of Qara as a center of the medieval slave-trade.

In recent years there have been intensive investigations into the possibility of the economic development of the area. Test drillings for oil (at the end of the 1950s by the Soviet Union, since 1979 by the Royal Dutch Shell group) have so far yielded no result. – During the past 20 years water forced up by artesian pressure at the old well known as *Qifar 1* has formed a considerable lake, now surrounded by reeds and frequented by migratory waterfowl.

*El-Alamein, Mersa Matruh, *Siwa Oasis and **Western Desert**: see separate entries.

Qaw
See under Nile

Qena

Upper Egypt. – Governorate: Qena.
Population: 60,000.
ⓘ **Tourist Information Office,**
Tourist Bazaar,
Luxor;
tel. 22 15.

HOTEL. – *New Palace,* IV, 120 b.

Qift
See under Nile

Qurna
See under Thebes

Qurnet Murai
See under Thebes

Qus
See under Nile

Quseir

Red Sea Frontier District.
Population: 3000.
ⓘ **Tourist Information Office,**
Tourist Bazaar,
Luxor;
tel. 22 15.

ACCOMMODATION. – *Government Rest-House,* 15 b.; tent hotel.

ACCESS. – By the road down the Red Sea coast from Suez (339 miles/545 km) or on the Hammamat road from Qift or Qena in the Nile Valley (121 miles/194 km).

The quiet little port town of Quseir lies in a small inlet on the Red Sea coast at the mouth of the Wadi el-Ambagi, sheltered by a coral reef. A center of bedouin life with plenty of local color, it is little visited by tourists.

HISTORY. – This port at the end of the ancient caravan route through the Wadi Hammamat from Qift or Qena in the Nile Valley was highly valued in antiquity, since it offered a safe landing-place even during the monsoon. The Egyptian name was *Tjau*; the trade route from the Nile Valley then ended rather farther N, at the mouth of the Wadi el-Gasus. In the time of the Ptolemies it was known as the *Leukos Limen* ("White Harbor"), from which the produce of the Nile Valley (particularly corn) was shipped and to which cargoes of precious wares came in from distant lands. From medieval times until the 19th c. this was the port most favored by pilgrims on their way to Mecca, who took ship here for Jedda; and the town has a number of caravanserais (still functioning) built to serve this traffic.

Quseir now ships phosphates from the nearby mines, which are linked with the port by an industrial railway line. The headquarters of the Phosphate Company are in the town.

SIGHTS. – The harbor, with its pier, is dominated by the old **Fort** of Sultan Selim (16th c.), which after falling into a state of dilapidation was rebuilt by the French in 1798. – Picturesque features of the town are the two modest *mosques* and the *bazaar*. – Attractive boat trips on the Red Sea.

SURROUNDINGS of Quseir. – 6 miles/10 km N is the site of the ancient port of *Quseir el-Qadim* (Old Quseir), of which only scanty remains survive. There is a beautiful sandy beach.

Some 60 miles/100 km W of Quseir are the ancient quarries of **Bir el-Hammamat** (see under Eastern Desert). – 180 miles/290 km S are the remains of the ancient port of **Berenice** (see that entry), largely covered by sand.

Eastern Desert and **Red Sea**: see separate entries.

Ramesseum
See under Thebes

Ras el-Bahr
See under Damietta

Ras Gharib
See under Red Sea

Rashid
See under Rosetta

Ras Muhammad
See under Sinai

Ras Zafarana
See under Red Sea

Red Monastery
See under Sohag

Red Sea/Bahr el-Ahmar

The Red Sea (Bahr el-Ahmar in Arabic), known in Roman times as the Sinus Arabicus or Mare Erythraeum, and later as Mare Rubrum, branches off the Indian Ocean between Egypt and the Arabian Peninsula and thus forms the boundary at this point between the continents of Africa and Asia. With a total length of 1390 miles/2240 km and a greatest width of 220 miles/355 km, it has a total area of 177,600 sq. miles/460,000 sq. km. Its greatest depth, reached around the latitude of Jedda, is 8544 ft/2604 m (average depth 1610 ft/490 m). At its northern end it is divided by the Sinai Peninsula into two long inlets, to the W the Gulf of Suez, which is linked with the Mediterranean by the Suez Canal, to the E the Gulf of Aqaba (Eilat). At its southern end is the Bab el-Mandeb ("Gate of Lamentation"), a strait 16 miles/26 km wide which gives access to the Gulf of Aden and thence to the Indian Ocean.

The Red Sea occupies a Tertiary rift valley running from NW to SE through the tableland of North Africa and Arabia, continued to the N by the Jordan Valley and to the S by the rift system of East Africa. The whole region shows the volcanic phenomena characteristic of recent fault zones. – Reflecting its geological origin, the coast falls steeply down, with few intermediate steps or shelves. The coastline is relatively feature-less, with only a few inlets usable as harbors. On both sides are mighty mountain ridges rising to 6560 ft/2000 m. The coasts are fringed by long coral banks and reefs which constitute a hazard for shipping.

As a result of the meagre inflow of fresh water and the high rate of evaporation the *salt content* of the water is considerably higher than in other seas, ranging from 4·2% in the Gulf of Suez to 3·65% off the island of Perim in the Bab el-Mandeb. In general the salt content increases from the surface towards the bottom. – An unusual phenomenon, discovered by a scientific expedition in 1964, is a body of water of exceptionally high salinity, 3–6 miles/5–10 km long and 330 ft/100 m thick, lying at a depth of over 6560 ft/2000 m in latitude 21° 30′ N and longitude 38° 6′ E; the salt content, at a temperature of 140 °F/60 °C, was no less than 33%.

The *marine currents* in the Red Sea, flowing N on the Arabian side and S on the African side, are subject to the influence of the monsoon. Counter-currents at different levels carry highly saline deep water into the Indian Ocean and surface water of low salinity from the Indian Ocean into the Red Sea. – There is a tidal movement averaging 24 inches/0·6 m at the N end of the Red Sea, rising to 83 inches/2·1 m at the spring tides.

The Red Sea is the warmest of all seas, with a *water temperature* on the surface of up to 95 °F/35 °C, with a constant 71 °F/21.5 °C at greater depths. – The color of the water normally ranges between deep blue and greenish blue, though there may be variations caused by the presence of minerals or algae.

The *climate* is hot, with only scanty and sporadic rainfall. The high rate of evaporation produces a relatively high air humidity. At the height of summer temperatures regularly rise above 104 °F/40 °C in the shade, but during the winter months the heat is tempered at the N end of the sea by the strong northerly and north-westerly winds then prevailing in this area. In the S the monsoon winds, blowing from the N in summer and from the S in winter, bring a measure of relief.

The name "Red Sea" (Latin *Mare Rubrum,* a name found only in the Late Roman period) has been variously interpreted, being explained by reference to the reddish color of the rocks along its shores, or to the reddish coloring imparted to the water at certain points by algae (*Trichodesmium erythraeum*), or again to the ancient designation of NE Africa as the land of the "red tribes".

In antiquity the northern part of the Red Sea was the principal route for trade between Asia and North Africa. In the Middle Ages the maritime trade of the great European commercial cities (Venice, Pisa, Genoa, etc.) with the East Indies passed through the Red Sea. After the discovery of America and of new routes to East Asia, however, the importance of the Red Sea route – which in any case might on occasion be interrupted by political circumstances – suffered a rapid and lasting decline, to recover only with the opening of the Suez Canal in 1869. – Although in ancient times the Red Sea was one of the world's most important and busiest seaways, its coasts, with their lack of fresh water, offered little scope for permanent human settlement. Only a few ports and trading-posts, mostly quite small, were established in these inhospitable regions where the desert reached right down to the coast. In recent years, however, the Red Sea coast with its beautiful empty beaches and magnificent diving grounds has begun to be cautiously developed for the tourist trade, and modern holiday colonies have been established at Ain Sukhna and Hurghada.

Down the Red Sea Coast

Suez to Berenice (519 miles/835 km; a good asphalt road for most of the way to Quseir, deteriorating later). – The road runs SW from Suez below *Gebel Ataqa* (2858 ft/871 m), through modern industrial installations. – 11 miles/18 km: *El-Adabiya*, a small naval harbor established by Britain during the Second World War, sheltered by the *Ras el-Adabiya*. – 27 miles/43 km: *Bir Udeib*, where a desert track branches off to *Maadi* (71 miles/115 km). – 34 miles/55 km: **Ain Sukhna** ("Hot Springs"), a seaside resort in a charming setting at the foot of the desert plateau, which here advances to the coast. With its hot sulphur spring, still preserving some of the ancient marble basin, its beautiful flat sandy beach and its modern tourist facilities, it is a very pleasant winter resort.

Beyond Ain Sukhna the road follows a winding and very picturesque course above the coast. – 59 miles/95 km: *Ras Abu Darag*, an outlier of the northern *Galala Plateau*, with a lighthouse and a few houses. – 81 miles/130 km: *Ras Zafarana*, a small port (lighthouse) at the mouth of the *Wadi Araba*. A desert track runs up the wadi to St Antony's Monastery (31 miles/50 km: see that entry) and to the Nile Valley. – 96 miles/155 km: desert track up the Wadi Deir to St Paul's Monastery (9 miles/15 km: see that entry). – 146 miles/235 km: **Ras Gharib** (pop. 12,000), a modern town (gasoline/petrol station, rest-house) in the middle of a large oilfield (150 bores). To the SW is the *Gebel Gharib* Massif (5745 ft/1751 m). – 166 miles/267 km: *Ras Shukheir* (off the road to the left), with an oilfield and a lighthouse. – The road now turns away from the sea to pass the promontory of *Gebel el-Zeit* (1499 ft/457 m). – 204 miles/329 km: *Ras Gemsa* (oilfields, phosphate-mine), at the mouth of the Gulf of Suez, with a view of many coral islands and the S tip of the Sinai Peninsula. – 239 miles/384 km: *Abu Shar el-Qibli*, at the foot of the Abu Shar Plateau, with the remains of the ancient port of *Myos Hormos*, now silted up. 3 miles/5 km E are the remains of a Roman fort. – From Abu Shar el-Qibli there is a desert track, the old *Porphyry Road*, to the ancient quarries on the *Mons Porphyrites* (Gebel el-Dukhan: see under Eastern Desert), continuing to *Qena* (see that entry) in the Nile Valley. – 245 miles/395 km: **Hurghada** (see that entry).

286 miles/460 km: **Bur (Port) Safaga** (pop. 3000; Safaga Hotel, II), a small port at the end of a narrow-gauge railway from the phosphate-mines. Offshore is

the small island of *Safaga*. From here a road runs W to Qena in the Nile Valley (100 miles/161 km: see under Eastern Desert). – 297 miles/470 km: The road passes through *Mersa Gasus el-Foqani*, the ancient *Philotheras*, at the mouth of the Wadi Gasus. There are ancient Egyptian remains in the vicinity. – 339 miles/545 km: **Quseir** (see that entry). From here the "Hammamat road" (121 miles/194 km: see under Eastern Desert) runs W to Qift in the Nile Valley. – 388 miles/625 km; *Mersa Umbarek*, a small port at the mouth of the *Wadi Umbarek*, at the end of which (4¼ miles/7 km) are the old gold-mines of *Umm Rus*, with the extensive remains of the Graeco-Roman settlement of *Nechesia*, established to house the labor force.

429 miles/690 km: **Mersa Alam**, a fishing village with offshore coral reefs which are a happy hunting ground for snorkelers and scuba divers (underwater fishing club, with guest-house). From here a road runs W to *Edfu* (140 miles/225 km: see under Eastern Desert). 465 miles/748 km: desert track to the emerald-mines of *Nasib el-Mandara*, in the *Wadi Gemal*. – 519 miles/835 km: **Berenice** (see that entry). From here there are old Roman and caravan routes to *Qena* (Qift), *Edfu* and *Antinoupolis* (see under Eastern Desert).

Warning. – In view of the large numbers of sharks and other dangerous predatory fish in the Red Sea swimmers should never venture beyond the coral reefs fringing the coast.

El-Roda

Middle Egypt. – Governorate: El-Minya.

ACCESS. – By road from Mallawi (6 miles/9 km S) or El-Minya (23 miles/37 km N).

The large village of El-Roda, with several mosques, a palace built by Khedive Ismail (now a school) and a large sugar factory, lies on the W bank of the Nile, a short distance away from the river. From here a number of important ancient sites can be visited.

Opposite El-Roda on the E bank of the Nile, set among palms, is the village of *Sheikh Abada*, to the E of which are the remains of **Antinoupolis** or *Antinoe*, the "City of Antinous" built by the Emperor Hadrian in A.D. 130 to commemorate his favorite Antinous. The handsome young man whose features are known to us in many ancient works of sculpture is said to have drowned himself here in order to avert any worse misfortune from the Emperor, who an oracle had foretold would suffer a great loss. There was an earlier settlement here with a *Temple of Ramesses II*, the remains of which, with

the columns of the forecourt and the hypostyle hall emerging from a mound of rubble, can be seen to the N of Sheikh Abada. When Napoleon's Egyptian expedition passed this way they saw a triumphal arch, a theater and various colonnades which have now almost completely disappeared. The site is littered with broken granite columns and capitals. On a track running E from the mosque, beside the scanty remains of a large building, lies a broken limestone basin which must have had a diameter of some 10 ft/3 m. The Roman and Christian cemeteries have been much damaged and plundered in modern times.

To the S of Sheikh Abada, by the site of an ancient Christian settlement known as *El-Medina*, is the village of **Deir Abu Hennes** (St John's Monastery), or *El-Deir* for short, which is inhabited by some 2000 Copts. On the N side of a ravine in the hill beyond the village are many ancient quarry holes or caves which in Christian times were converted into chapels or occupied by hermits. The largest of the chapels, which is said to date from the time of the Empress Helena, contains many poorly preserved wall-paintings of New Testament scenes and figures of saints. Of more interest are the paintings in a neighboring chapel, in particular the "Raising of Lazarus" and the "Marriage at Cana". – Half an hour away from Deir Abu Hennes is *Deir el-Bersha* (see under Mallawi).

Some 4 miles/6 km W of El-Roda, at the village of *Ashmunein*, are the remains of the once-famous city of *Khmunu*, the Greek *Hermoupolis*. Farther W is the necropolis of *Tuna el-Gebel*. (For both these sites see under Mallawi.)

*Beni Hasan, *Mallawi and *Tell el-Amarna: see separate entries.

Rosetta/Rashid

Lower Egypt. – Governorate: Buhayra.
Population: 40,000.
ⓘ **Tourist Information Office,**
Midan Saad Zaghlul,
Alexandria;
tel. 80 79 85.

ACCESS. – By road or rail from Alexandria (35 miles/56 km SW) or Damanhur (31 miles/50 km S).

The once-important port and commercial town of Rosetta (Rashid) lies 9 miles/15 km above the mouth of the Rosetta arm of the Nile, probably on the site of ancient Bolbitine, after which this westerly arm of the river was known in antiquity as the Bolbitine arm.

HISTORY. – Founded in A.D. 870, in the time of the Caliphs, Rosetta was from medieval into modern times the principal Egyptian port and a major center of Mediterranean trade. After the construction of the Mahmudiya Canal, however, it was rapidly overshadowed by Alexandria, which was developed by Mohammed Ali and took the place of Rosetta as a port and commercial center. Rosetta is still an important center of the rice trade, with several rice-mills, and also has foodstuff, tobacco and textile industries.

SIGHTS. – Rosetta preserves many handsome old **houses** of the 17th–19th c., which bear witness to the prosperity and high standards of comfort and good taste of its citizens in the town's heyday. These tall buildings of four or five storeys have brick-built façades in mosaic patterns of black and red, often with ancient stone built into the walls; the windows have richly decorated lattice screens (*mushrabiyas*). The following houses are particularly fine: *El-Fatari* (1620), *Arab Keli* (18th c.: now a museum) and *El-Amaciali* (early 19th c.).

The mosques of Rosetta differ from other Egyptian mosques in the simplicity and clarity of their structure and their restrained decoration: only the doorway and the mihrab have the lavish ornament of the Arab-Egyptian style, often using fine faience. – At the end of the main street, which runs S from the railway station, with the picturesque covered *bazaars*, stands the large **Zaghlul Mosque**, a combination of two older mosques which achieves an astonishing harmony. It has more than 300 columns from various earlier buildings, their varying heights adjusted by the removal or duplication of capitals. – To the E of the Zaghlul Mosque, near the river, is the *Mohammed el-Abbasi Mosque* (1809), with a handsome minaret. – Outside the town, 3 miles/5 km S, is the *Abu Mandur Mosque*. From the nearby hill of the same name there is a fine view.

Some of the fortifications to the N and W of the town date from the 16th c. 2 miles/ 3 km N is **Fort Rosetta**, formerly known as *Fort Saint-Julien*, where the famous

The Rosetta Stone (British Museum)

Rosetta Stone (now in the British Museum), with a trilingual inscription which led to the decipherment of the Egyptian hieroglyphs, was discovered during restoration work in 1799.

*Alexandria, Damanhur and **Tell el-Faraun**: see separate entries.

Sadd el-Ali (Aswan High Dam)
See under Aswan

St Antony's Monastery/Deir Mar Antonios

Red Sea Frontier District.
ⓘ **Tourist Information Office,**
Misr Travel Tower,
Cairo – Abbasia;
tel. 82 60 16.

ACCOMMODATION. – Guest-house (men only), 8 b.; no food.

ACCESS. – 31 miles/50 km from Ras Zafarana, on the Red Sea coast, on a desert track along the Wadi Araba.

St Antony's Monastery, in the Eastern Desert

*St Antony's Monastery, the oldest and largest Coptic monastery in Egypt, lies in a desert setting at an altitude of 1345 ft/410 m in the wide Wadi Araba, at the foot of the southern Galala Plateau, which rises to a height of 4803 ft/1464 m.

HISTORY. – **St Antony the Great** is regarded as the founder of Christian monasticism. According to the account of his life – partly legendary and partly historical – given by St Athanasius (*c.* 295–373) he was born at Coma (near Beni Suef) in 250, the son of well-to-do parents. While still a youth he distributed his inheritance to the poor and withdrew into the wilderness to devote himself to prayer and asceticism. During the persecution of Christians in the time of Maximinus Daia in 311 he went to Alexandria to declare his faith publicly. Later he retired to the total solitude of the desert hills on the Red Sea, where he lived in a cleft in the rock. The fame of his sanctity and his ascetic life soon spread and attracted thousands of disciples, who later formed communities of hermits and monks. The legend asserts at the age of 90 Antony traveled to the cell of the dying St Paul of Thebes and buried him with the help of two lions. Antony himself died at the great age of 105 and in accordance with his wishes was buried by his disciples in an unmarked grave.

Antony is regarded as the patron saint of domestic animals, and is frequently depicted with a pig. He was invoked against the medieval ailment known as St Antony's Fire (ergotism or erysipelas) and also in case of fire. He is often represented with the T-shaped "St Antony's cross" or Egyptian cross; his feast-day is January 17.

The monastery was founded by Antony's disciples at the end of the 4th c., on a site by the spring below the cave in which Antony had lived as a hermit. Remains of buildings dating from the original foundation can be seen here and there, but the monastery was much altered and enlarged in later centuries. By careful husbanding of the water of the spring the monks created in the midst of the desert a fertile little oasis

which was tended and maintained by the occupants of the monastery down the centuries. The remoteness of the monastery's situation preserved it from Arab and Muslim influence, and it developed into a flourishing center of spiritual and cultural life, particularly between the 12th and 15th c. The monks devoted themselves during this period to the translation of works of scholarship and theology from Coptic into Arabic, and decorated their churches and chapels with frescos of notable quality, a few of which have been preserved.

All this came to a sudden end in 1483, when Muslim bedouin plundered the monastery and killed or expelled the monks. For 70 years the monastery stood empty and in ruins, and it was unable thereafter to regain its former importance. It is now occupied by some 30 monks, who live a largely self-sufficient life in their little oasis. They provide accommodation for

In St Antony's Monastery

male visitors in a modern guest-house; but guests must bring their own food.

THE MONASTERY. – The monastery covers an area of some 15 acres. The buildings, irregularly planned, are surrounded by a *defensive wall* (wall-walk for part of the way) 1225 yds/1120 m long, $6\frac{1}{2}$ ft/2 m thick and up to 40 ft/12 m high, originally built in the 10th c. and rebuilt and strengthened in the 16th and 19th c. The monastery could originally be entered only by means of a hoist, which can still be seen; the present entrance, approached by steps, dates from a more recent period.

Within the walls the monastic town is traversed from N to S by a narrow main street, giving access to an intricate network of lanes in which are the seven churches and chapels, the various offices and workshops, the communal facilities and the low two-storey buildings containing the monks' cells, each with its own entrance. To the W is the small cemetery. On the S side of the enclosure wall is the slightly brackish spring which, together with a few smaller springs in the immediate vicinity, supplies water to the monastery's luxuriant vegetable garden, orchard and vineyard and to the groves of olives and palms.

Prominent among the buildings within the walls is the massive square *watch-tower* (1560; originally 10th c.), from which there is a good view of the monastery as a whole. It contains the now-abandoned St Michael's Chapel.

At the end of the main street stands *St Antony's Church, the oldest intact Christian church in Egypt, probably built in the 6th c. – according to tradition, on the spot where Antony was accustomed to celebrate Mass. The present building dates mainly from the 10th c., with later alterations. The church (65 ft/20 m by 20 ft/6 m), with three modern domes, has a sanctuary preceded by a vestibule and flanked by two chapels, a square narthex, with a chapel attached to it, on the right-hand side and a vaulted choir. The walls of the narthex chapel and the choir are covered with excellent frescos (renewed in the 13th c.) of knights depicted in vivid colors and ascetics, hermits and saints in more muted tones. In the vestibule leading into the sanctuary are fine figures of the Archangels Michael and Gabriel (10th c.) which are among the oldest Coptic frescos in Egypt. The frescos in the sanctuary itself are blackened almost beyond recognition. In the small side chapels adjoining the sanctuary are figures of early Patriarchs of Alexandria (11th–13th c.). – To the E of St Antony's is the *Church of SS. Peter and Paul* (18th c.).

St Mark's Church, which contains the Tomb of St Mark, a disciple of St Antony much revered in Egypt, not only by Copts, draws large numbers of pilgrims during Holy Week.

The *Refectory* (7th c.) is probably the oldest surviving building in the monastery. It is no longer in use, but the stone tables, benches and abbot's chair can still be seen. – In the same building as the refectory are the little Chapel of the Virgin, which is still in use, and the Library, which lost its oldest and most valuable contents as a result of the bedouin raid in 1483 and the neglect of later centuries.

Also within the walls of the monastery are two unfinished and nameless churches, the more recent of which (1930) has prominent white towers. Other features of interest include the old oil-press, the grain-mill and the bakery.

Some 890 ft/270 m above the monastery is *St Antony's Cave, in which the Saint lived for 20 years, resisting all temptations and assaults by the Devil.

Eastern Desert and *St Paul's Monastery: see separate entries.

Road to the Mount Sinai Airport

St Catherine's Monastery/Deir Sant Katerin

Sinai Frontier District.
Altitude: about 4925 ft/1500 m.
(i) **Tourist Information Office,**
   Misr Travel Tower,
   Cairo – Abbasia;
   tel. 82 60 16.

ACCOMMODATION. –

HOTELS. – St Catherine Tourist Village, Wadi el Raha, I, 140 b.; El Salam, Shari Abdel Hamid Badawi, Heliopolis, II, 140 b.

ACCESS. – Air services from Cairo and from Israel to Mount Sinai Airport; transfer from there by Egyptian companies. – By road from Suez to the Airport (see under Sinai); from there transfer by Egyptian companies.

The world-famed **St Catherine's Monastery lies at an altitude of some 4925 ft/1500 m in the Wadi Shuaiba (or Wadi el-Deir, "Monastery Valley"), at the foot of the steep granite walls of Gebel Musa (Mount of Moses; 7497 ft/2285 m), also known as Mount Sinai. According to tradition this was the site of the well

St Catherine's Monastery, Sinai

at which Moses watered the flocks of his father-in-law Jethro and the spot where he saw the burning bush. The fortress-like exterior of the monastery still preserves, in spite of later alterations, essentially the same appearance as when it was originally constructed.

HISTORY. – The present monastery occupies the site of an earlier fortified monastery founded by Justinian about A.D. 530 as a place of safety for the hermits and anchorites of southern Sinai. Justinian granted the monks 100 Roman and 100 Egyptian slaves, with their wives and children, whose work contributed to the prosperity of the monastery and whose descendants, the Muslim Gebeliye or Tuarah, still live in the neighboring mountains. The monastery was able to maintain itself in spite of the advance of Islam thanks to its great hospitality to Muslim as well as Christian travelers and to its care for Muslim shrines. Most of the monks came, and still come, from Crete and Cyprus. Their numbers, which about the year 1000 were between 300 and 400, have now shrunk to about 50, of whom only 20 live in the monastery itself, the remainder in dependent houses. The rules of the Order are extremely strict. The monks are forbidden to eat meat or drink wine, though they do drink a pleasant date brandy (*araki*, "juice"). The order is headed by an Archbishop, who is normally resident in Cairo and is, therefore, usually represented by a Prior, the Dikaios. The monastery's affairs are managed by an administrator, the Oikonomos.

THE MONASTERY. – Roughly square in plan, the monastery measures 93 yds/85 m by 83 yds/76 m and is surrounded by walls $5\frac{1}{2}$ ft/1·65 m thick and 39–49 ft/ 12–15 m high. The walls on the S and W sides date from the original foundation;

those on the E and N sides were destroyed by an earthquake in 1312 and later rebuilt.

The focal point of the monastery is the *Church of the Transfiguration, with a *bell-tower* which dominates the whole complex. Its bells waken the monks every morning with 33 strokes, symbolizing the 33 years of Christ's life.

The church, the floor of which is some 13 ft/4 m below present ground-level, is entered through a modern porch, from which a flight of steps (the top ones inscribed with the Greek letters spelling the Greek name Iakobos, or James) leads down to the *Narthex*, with an elaborately carved wooden door (6th c.) which gives access to the three-aisled **interior** of the basilica.

The walls of the nave, rising above the aisles and lit by windows, are borne on sturdy granite columns with richly decorated foliage capitals. The aisles, with pitched roofs, are lit by five Byzantine windows on each side. The floor is paved with marble. On the left is a marble *pulpit* (1787), on the right the *Bishop's throne*, with an interesting painting of the monastery in the 18th c. by an Armenian artist. Between the columns are crudely carved choir-stalls. – In the aisles are side chapels, mostly dedicated to saints of the Orthodox Church.

The choir is separated from the nave by a richly painted and gilded **iconostatis** (Cretan work 1612). On the conch of the apse are magnificent *mosaics,* probably the work of Western artists, dating from about 565 and excellently preserved. The Transfigured Christ is depicted in an almond-shaped mandorla, surrounded by medallions with figures of Prophets, Apostles and saints. In the choir are a marble *sarcophagus* containing the remains of St Catherine,

Sinai

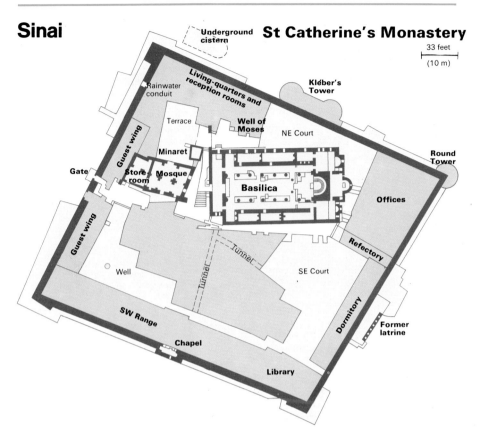

St Catherine's Monastery

a precious *reliquary* and a coffin-like shrine (presented by Empress Catherine of Russia) with an embossed silver-gilt figure of the Saint.

Beyond the apse, on a still lower level than the nave, is the **Chapel of the Burning Bush**, probably the oldest part of the church (shoes should be taken off before entering). The walls are clad with blue Damascene faience. A silver plate marks the spot where God is said to have appeared to Moses.

Opposite the church is a simple *mosque* with a separate minaret, built in the 12th c. on the site of an earlier 6th c. guest-house, for the use of Muslim travelers.

The monastery *Library is one of the largest and most interesting collections of Arabic and Turkish writing in existence, most of it not properly arranged. The large

numbers of valuable old manuscripts (more than 2000) also include works in Greek, Syriac, Persian, Amharic and Russian. The library's most valuable possession, now in the British Museum, was the Codex Sinaiticus, a Greek text of the Bible dating from about A.D. 400 which was found by the German scholar Konstantin von Tischendorf in 1844. – The monastery has an *Icon collection* consisting of c. 2000 pictures as well as a valuable *Treasury* (gold and silver articles), individual items from which are displayed in the museum beyond the library.

Outside the monastery walls, to the NW, are the beautiful monastery *gardens,* shaded by tall cypresses, which have their finest show of blossom in March and

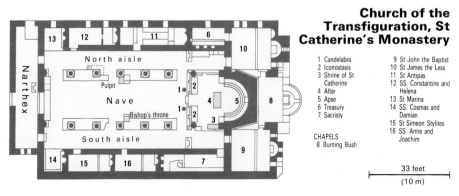

Church of the Transfiguration, St Catherine's Monastery

1 Candelabra
2 Iconostasis
3 Shrine of St Catherine
4 Altar
5 Apse
6 Treasury
7 Sacristy

CHAPELS
8 Burning Bush

9 St John the Baptist
10 St James the Less
11 St Antipas
12 SS. Constantine and Helena
13 St Marina
14 SS. Cosmas and Damian
15 St Simeon Stylites
16 SS. Anne and Joachim

33 feet
(10 m)

April. The gardens are laid out in terraces and well watered, and in addition to the flowers produce a variety of fruit and vegetables. – Also outside the walls can be seen the pilgrims' cemetery and, in the *crypt* of *St Tryphon's Chapel,* the charnel-house, which is also the place of burial of the monks.

SURROUNDINGS of St Catherine's Monastery

A very rewarding expedition from the monastery is the ascent of **Gebel Musa**, the Mount of Moses (7497 ft/2285 m), on which Moses is said to have received from God the Tables of the Law. There are two main routes, the more strenuous of which is the pilgrims' route, believed to have been established as early as the 6th c., which involves climbing some 2500 steps, passing on the way the simple *Chapel of St Elias* (Elijah; 6880 ft/2097 m). The alternative route is by way of the unfinished Abbas Pasha Road. For those who feel unable to tackle the ascent on foot there is also the possibility of hiring a camel. Whichever method is chosen the trip takes at least 3 hours there and back.

On the summit of the mountain are a small *chapel* (built in 1930 on the site of an earlier chapel which had been destroyed) and a small *mosque* which is much revered by Muslims. At the NE corner of the crag on which the chapel stands visitors are shown a hollow in which Moses stood when God appeared to him. Beside the mosque is a cistern-like cavity in which, according to Muslim tradition, Moses lived for 40 days, fasting, while writing down the Law on two tablets. – From the summit of Gebel Musa there are breath-taking * *views of the wild and desolate surrounding country, extending SW beyond the highest peaks of Sinai to the Red Sea and the Gulf of Aqaba and NW over the hills of southern Sinai to the lower country in the N.

From a level area planted with cypresses half-way between the monastery and Gebel Musa an easy path (45 minutes) runs between two lush green depressions (in the first of which is an old Chapel of St John the Baptist) to the foot of **Ras el-Safsaf** ("Hill of the Willow"), with a ruined Chapel of the Virgin's Girdle. Here visitors are shown the ancient willows from which Moses is said to have cut his rod. The first part of the ascent of Ras el-Safsaf (6542 ft/1994 m) is facilitated by rock-cut steps, but the ascent beyond this is for experienced climbers only.

Another rewarding excursion (4 hours) is to the **Wadi el-Leja**, which flanks the W side of Gebel Musa and contains many places revered as sacred and visited by pilgrims. Before reaching the mouth of this valley, in the *Wadi el-Raha*, visitors are shown the spot where Korah and his followers were swallowed up by the earth (Numbers 16) and the cavity in the rock in which the golden calf was cast. – At the entrance to the Wadi el-Leja, on the right, are the ruins of the huts in which SS. Cosmas and Damian lived as hermits and a chapel dedicated to the Apostles but never used; on the left is the ruined Monastery of *El-Bustan*. Beyond this can be seen the *Stone of Moses* (Hagar Musa), from which Moses drew water by striking it with his rod (Numbers 20: 8 ff.). It is a 12 ft/3·6 m high block of reddish-brown granite (about 120 cu. yds/100 cu. m), divided into two parts by a 16 inch/40 cm thick vein of porphyry on the S side. The water is said to have flowed from 12 cavities in the porphyry, one for each of the tribes of Israel (two of the cavities are now missing). On the rock are a number of Sinaitic inscriptions.

Some 1¼ miles/2 km S of the Stone of Moses is the **Deir el-Arbain**, the Monastery of the Forty Martyrs (killed by the Saracens). It is an unpretentious building with a large garden, in the rocky upper part of which is a spring, and near this a cave in which St Onuphrius is said to have lived as a hermit. The monastery was abandoned in the 17th c., but is still occasionally occupied by a few monks.

The ascent of **Gebel Katerin**, St Catherine's Mount (8668 ft/2642 m), is more strenuous than that of Gebel Musa, requiring a full day. The route to the summit from the Deir el-Arbain is marked by cairns set up by pilgrims. – There are three peaks – *Gebel Katerin*, the highest summit in the Sinai Peninsula, *Gebel Sebir* and *Gebel Abu Rumel*. It can be very cold on the top, and snow lies in crevices in the rock right into summer. On the summit are a modest little chapel and some irregularities in the ground, explained by the monks as the marks left by St Catherine's body, which is said to have lain here after her execution for 300 (some say 500) years before being revealed by the light radiating from it. – From the summit there are magnificent *views, interrupted only by the massive bulk of Gebel Umm Shomar (8449 ft/2575 m) to the SW. To the SE can be seen the broad Wadi Nasib and the Gulf of Aqaba, the Arabian Mountains and, in good weather, Ras Muhammad at the southern tip of Sinai. To the W and SW is the arid El-Qaa Plain, ending at El-Tor. To the N rear up to the peaks of Gebel Serbal and Gebel el-Banat, and farther N can be seen the light-colored sandy plain of El-Ramle and the long ridge of Gebel el-Tih.

*Sinai: see separate entry.

St Menas, City of
See Abu Mena

St Paul's Monastery/Deir Mar Bolos

Red Sea Frontier District.
(i) **Tourist Information Office,**
Misr Travel Tower,
Cairo – Abbasia;
tel. 82 60 16.

ACCOMMODATION. – Guest-house (men only), 6 b.

ACCESS. – On the Red Sea coast road to 12½ miles/20 km S of Ras Zafarana; then a difficult track up the Wadi Deir (9 miles/15 km) to the head of the valley.

*St Paul's Monastery, the oldest Coptic monastery in Egypt after St Antony's, lies in a magnificent mountain setting in a cirque at the head of the Wadi el-Deir, which in places contracts into a narrow gorge. It is similar in general plan to St Antony's Monastery, but is considerably smaller and more modest and looks older. Its grandiose situation, however, makes it in some respects more impressive than St Antony's.

HISTORY. – **St Paul of Thebes**, also known as St Paul the Hermit, is honored as the patron saint of hermits. His life, richly embroidered with legend, was written by St Jerome (347–419/420) in his "Vita Pauli". According to this account Paul was born about 228, the son of well-to-do parents, and received a good education. During the persecutions of Christians in the time of Decius, fearing that his father would denounce him in order to gain control of his property, he withdrew at the age of 16 into the solitude of the Lower Thebaid, and later into the Eastern Desert, in order to pursue an ascetic life. There, it is said, he at first lived on dates from the palms, and later was fed by a raven which brought him bread every day. In 340 he was visited by St Antony, who found him dying and after his death buried him with the help of two lions which dug his grave. St Paul, however, never achieved the same celebrity or attracted such a host of disciples as St Antony. He is depicted with a palm and a raven, or sometimes two lions, and frequently appears with St Antony; his feast-day is on January 15.

By about 460 a church had been built over the Saint's grave, and in the 6th c. this became a place of pilgrimage.

The monastery buildings date mainly from the medieval period. Laid out in the form of a rectangle, they cover an area of 3¾ acres and have widely scattered plots of land and plantations. There are some 20 monks.

THE MONASTERY. – The walls surrounding the monastery, with a total length of 490 yds/450 m, were originally built in the 5th c. and were rebuilt during the Middle Ages. From the top of the walls there is a magnificent view, extending as far as Gebel Musa in Sinai. In the massive **watch-tower** (third storey) is the *Chapel of the Virgin.* Immediately adjoining this stands the large **St Michael's Church** (17th c.), with an icon said to have been painted by St Luke the Evangelist.

The main entrance, on the S side (there are two other gates on the E side), leads into a small square, in which are the *guest-house* (for men only) and **St Paul's Church**, built over the hermit's cave in the 6th and 7th c. From the narthex steps lead down to the *Lower Church,* which contains the Saint's marble sarcophagus and three sanctuaries. In the domes and on the walls are medieval frescos which were restored in rather amateurish fashion by a monk and are accordingly in poor condition. In the dome over the staircase the military saints George, Theodore, Victor and Michael are shown fighting the Devil and against temptation; on the walls of the lower church are archangels and saints, including Paul with the lion, Antony and the Virgin and Child; and in the dome of the left-hand side chapel are Christ with the Four Evangelists and the 24 Elders of the Apocalypse. – Near St Paul's Church can be seen the Church of **St Mercurius** (*Abu el-Sefein; c.* 1800).

St Paul's Church stands at the end of a street lined with two-storey buildings containing the monks' cells, each with its separate entrance. – On the W side of the wall is a domed *fountain- and wash-house.* The oasis is supplied with water by three springs. – The **gardens**, which occupy roughly a quarter of the monastery precinct, are separated from the living-quarters and offices by a wall. Within this area are the old oil-press and the grain-mill.

Eastern Desert and *St Antony's Monastery: see separate entries.

St Simeon's Monastery
See under Aswan

Sais/Sau

Lower Egypt. – Governorate: Gharblya.
ⓘ **Tourist Information Office,**
Midan Saad Zaghlul,
Alexandria;
tel. 80 79 85.
Misr Travel,
Tourist Center,
Tanta;
tel. 22 12.

ACCESS. – Road from Tanta to Basyun (15 miles/24 km NW), then track to Sa el-Hagar, 4 miles/6 km NW.

The site of the ancient Egyptian city of Sau, later known as Sais, lies near the village of Sa el-Hagar on the right bank of the Rosetta arm of the Nile. It was the chief center of the cult of the goddess Neith and

the residence of the kings of the 24th and 26th Dynasties.

The existence of the town is attested from the beginnings of Egyptian history, and in the Early Period it was a political and religious center of the Delta. The principal temple was dedicated to the goddess Neith (Nereth, the "Fearsome One"), who was venerated as the mother of the sun god, a war goddess with a bow and arrows as her attributes and one of the four protective goddesses of the dead. As the incarnation of the power of Lower Egypt she wore the Red Crown. – After the unification of the two kingdoms the political importance of Sais rapidly declined. It now became the chief town of the 5th nome of Lower Egypt, with a territory which until the time of the 12th Dynasty extended over the area of the later 4th nome.

HISTORY. – The rising of Saite local Princes against Ethiopian and Assyrian rule towards the end of the 8th B.C. brought the town back into the politcal limelight. Bocchoris and his son Tefnakhte made it the capital of their ephemeral kingdom of Lower Egypt and founded the 24th (1st Saite) Dynasty. Later it became the capital of Psammetichus I and his successors of the 26th (2nd Saite) Dynasty.

Herodotus gives detailed accounts of the ceremonies in honor of Osiris which were celebrated here and of the splendid buildings erected by Psammetichus and Amasis. A representation of the royal burial-place, which, as at Tanis, was in the principal temple, has also come down to us.

Practically nothing is left of the ancient city, and the site has little to interest the ordinary visitor. Considerable remains of brick masonry were still standing in the 19th c., but these have been almost completely removed by peasants digging for *sebbakh,* the fertile soil found on ancient sites. The stone had long been robbed for reuse in later buildings. There is an astonishingly large number of statues, architectural fragments and sarcophagi from Sais in museums all over the world.

* * **Alexandria, Damanhur, Nile Delta** and **Tanta:** see separate entries.

San el-Hagar
See under Tanis

Saqqara

Middle Egypt. – Governorate: Giza.
ⓘ **Tourist Information Office,** Misr Travel Tower, **Cairo – Abbasia;** tel. 82 60 16.

ACCESS. – By road from Giza (12½ miles/20 km N).

The vast** necropolis of Saqqara, the cemetery area of ancient Memphis, lies on the edge of the Western (Libyan) Desert, on the W bank of the Nile, some 9 miles/15 km S of the Pyramid of Cheops. Extending over an area of almost 4½ miles/7 km from N to S and 550–1650 yds/500–1500 m from E to W, it contains tombs from almost every period of Egyptian history. The whole necropolis has been repeatedly prospected and plundered from an early period down to modern times, notably under the Byzantine Emperors and the Caliphs. Nevertheless modern scientific excavations, most recently those directed by Walter B. Emery in 1936–56 and by the Egyptian Department of Antiquities since 1965, have still been able to recover much new material which has made important contributions to knowledge.

The most conspicuous landmark of Saqqara is the** **Step Pyramid** (Arabic *El-Haram el-Mudarrag*), the tomb of the 3rd Dynasty ruler Djoser or Zoser, which is probably the earliest major stone structure erected in Egypt. The form of the pyramid can be explained as a development of the large mastabas of the 1st and 2nd Dynasties, the six steps, each smaller than the one below, having been produced by the addition to the original mastaba of successive new layers of masonry, accompanied by the enlargement of the lower stages. Detailed examination of the pyramid has made it possible to identify six changes of plan during its construction. – The building of the pyramid is ascribed to Imhotep, who according to Manetho (*c.* 280 B.C.) devised the method of construction with dressed stone. It is remarkable for the complete mastery of the technique shown even at this early stage in its use.

The Step Pyramid stands some 200 ft/60 m high, with a base measurement of 397 ft/121 m by 358 ft/109 m. It is built of locally quarried clayey sandstone of poor quality. The entrance to the burial chambers, which are below ground-level, is on the N side of the lowest

Remains of enclosure wall, Step Pyramid of Djoser, Saqqara

step. The chambers and passages in the interior of the pyramid served partly for the burial of close relatives of the King, in particular those of his sons who died in childhood, and partly for storing grave-goods for the use of the dead. Large numbers of costly vessels for foodstuffs were found in these store-rooms. Some of the passages and chambers were due to the work of tomb-robbers and to later attempts at restoration. Fragments of the King's mummy were found in the main tomb chamber, 92 ft/28 m below the base of the pyramid. In another chamber constructed at an earlier date the walls were faced with tiles of bluish-green faience imitating plaited reed mats (now in the Egyptian Museum in Cairo).

In front of the entrance to the pyramid are remains of the *mortuary temple*. In a sealed chamber (*serdab*) on the E side of the temple, connected with the outside world only by two "peepholes", was found the life-size statue of Djoser which is now also in the Egyptian

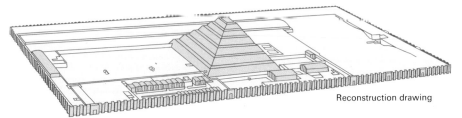

Reconstruction drawing

Saqqara   Pyramid of Djoser

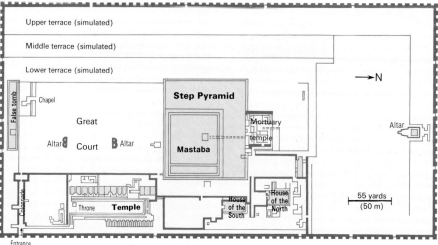

Step Pyramid of Djoser

Museum, with a copy on the original site. – To the N of the pyramid, within the enclosure wall, was found a rock-cut altar which had originally been faced with marble.

At the NE corner of the pyramid are the so-called *House of the North* and *House of the South,* each with a chapel and an open court. These buildings are interpreted as symbolic palaces referring to Djoser's role as ruler of Upper and Lower Egypt. Their façades have fluted engaged pillars and columns with papyrus capitals. – To the SE of the pyramid is a **temple,** probably erected on the occasion of the King's Sed festival (commemorating the 30th year of his reign). Adjoining the temple are a number of chapels, on the façades of which are colonnettes simulating wooden posts. Staircases lead up to an upper floor. In the court is a stone base approached by steps, probably for the King's throne.

The *enclosure wall round the pyramid precinct, with towers, niches and false doors, originally stood 34 ft/10·50 m high and was faced with limestone. The SE section, with the original main entrance, still stands to a considerable height and has been partly reconstructed. The wall enclosed a rectangular area

NE corner of Step Pyramid

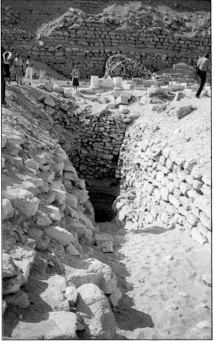

Entrance to Step Pyramid

measuring 595 yds/544 m by 303 yds/277 m. – The entrance leads into a large *Colonnade,* originally divided into three aisles by 48 pillars arranged in pairs; the pillars, topped by engaged cluster-columns, had an original height of over 16 ft/5 m. At the E end are curious false doors simulating open double doors. – At the far (W) end of the colonnade is a small *transverse chamber* with four pairs of pillars, from which a doorway, also with false doors, leads into the court on the S side of the pyramid.

The *Great Court* is bounded on the E and W sides by finely built stone walls and on the N side by the pyramid. In the middle are the bases of two altars, probably representing the two lands of Upper and Lower Egypt. Under the S side of the pyramid was another altar approached by a small ramp. – At the W end of the S enclosure wall is a *false tomb* of the 3rd Dynasty discovered by Cecil Firth in 1927. Staircases and underground passages lead to antechambers containing large alabaster jars and two chambers faced, like the chamber under the pyramid, with tiles imitating reed mats. In the second chamber are three false doors with magnificent relief figures of Djoser. – The *chapel* on the NW side of the tomb has a fine cobra frieze (partly restored).

Outside the enclosure wall, to the S, are several **mastabas** of the 3rd–6th Dynasties. Particularly notable is one which was originally constructed for an official named *Ikh* but was later used for the burial of Princess Sesh-seshet or *Idut.* It is decorated with reliefs with well-preserved coloring, including one of a genet and an ichneumon robbing birds' nests in a papyrus swamp, and has a number of underground store-rooms, originally containing baskets of fruit and grain, which were sealed with the seals of Kings Khasekhemwy and Djoser.

To the E of this mastaba is the *Mastaba of Mehu,* a 6th Dynasty Vizier, with excellently preserved paintings in unusually vivid colors depicting the dead man and his wife in scenes of everyday life. On the side wall of the entrance Mehu is depicted as a corpulent elderly man.

First side chamber, on the right, husband and wife hunting and fishing; on the left, kitchen scenes and bird-catching. – Doorway into passage, left, work in the bakery; right, agricultural scenes. – S wall of passage, top row, funeral procession on the Nile, with the mummy in the first boat; middle row, work in the field; bottom row, 39 women and one man, representing the estates managed by Mehu. – W wall, vintage scenes. – N wall, in three rows, Mehu hunting and supervising work in the fields; to right of door into court, goldsmiths at work. – The court is divided into two unequal parts by pillars, on which Mehu is depicted with his name and titles. – S wall of small pillared hall, Mehu's son Hetepka at table; N wall, sketches for paintings which were not completed.

The passage leads into an offering-chamber with representations of various rites connected with the cult of the dead. In the main cult chamber, to the N, are more ritual scenes, exceptionally well preserved. On the W side of the offering-chamber is the cult chamber of one Merire-ankh, with paintings of similar scenes, inferior in style and less well preserved.

SW of the Step Pyramid is the ***Pyramid of Unas** or Onnos, last King of the 5th Dynasty. **The exterior of the Pyramid of Unas has collapsed, resembling a large pile of rubble, with the stone steps, one attached so neatly, threatening to slide down the sides. The interior is interesting but the extremely low entrance to the tomb chamber makes access quite difficult.**

The INTERIOR of the pyramid, which was opened in 1881, is open to visitors. From the N side a sloping passage, the entrance to which was originally concealed under the paving, leads to an *antechamber,* from which a horizontal corridor, originally barred by three trapdoors at the far end, continues to a *central chamber.* To the right (W) of this is the *tomb chamber,* which, like the central chamber, has a pitched roof; to the left is a small chamber with a flat roof and three niches, which was originally closed by a stone slab. The walls of the central chamber and the tomb chamber are covered with inscriptions – the "Pyramid Texts", the oldest known Egyptian religious texts, relating to the life after death – in which the incised hieroglyphs are filled in with blue pigment. Against the W wall of the tomb chamber is the King's sarcophagus, with alabaster false doors to the right and left.

On the E side of the pyramid is the small *Mortuary Temple,* badly ruined. It had a court with palm columns, fragments of which can still be seen. At the foot of the pyramid, probably on the site of the sanctuary, are remains of a granite false door.

On the S side of the Pyramid of Unas are three **shaft tombs of the Persian period**, all broadly similar in layout. A square vertical shaft descends to the tomb chamber, constructed of stone blocks, at the foot of a larger shaft sunk during the building of the chamber and later filled in. The tombs are now accessible by a spiral staircase and are connected with one another by tunnels.

The descent to the tombs is not easy. The shaft, 82 ft/ 25 m deep, leads by way of a 16 ft/5 m long corridor to the vaulted *Tomb Chamber of Psamtik,* a physician who lived in the reign of Darius I. The walls are covered with religious texts. The lid of the large limestone coffin, which, like the coffins in the other tombs, is let into the ground, is raised, and the device for lowering it can be seen; it originally contained a smaller basalt coffin. – To the W, reached through a modern tunnel, are the shaft and *Tomb Chamber of Djenhebu,* a Royal Admiral, both with finely incised inscriptions. – To the E, down some steps, are the shaft, 90 ft/27·5 m deep, and *Tomb Chamber of Pedeese.* The walls are decorated with inscriptions in fine low relief, with well-preserved colors, and with representations of votive offerings. The vaulted roof is painted with colored stars on a white ground.

To the NE of the Pyramid of Unas is the large **Double Mastaba of Nebet and Khenut**, Unas's wives, which originally covered an area of 161 ft/49 m by 72 ft/22 m and stood 13 ft/4 m high. Both tombs have the same ground-plan and layout, reflecting the equal status of the two occupants. Khenut's tomb, to the W, is much ruined, but Nebet's is well preserved and worth close inspection.

The entrance, on the SE side, leads into an *antechamber* of some size, the walls of which are decorated with reliefs of the dead Queen sailing in a boat through the marshes, etc. To the left (W) of this chamber is a spacious open court, without decoration, and straight on is a second, smaller, antechamber with highly unusual mural reliefs showing Nebet with servants bringing in food and sledges laden with large winejars; one of the women of the harem is a dwarf. On the N wall, above the door, Nebet is shown seated in front of votive offerings. – From the second antechamber the door in the N wall leads into two small chambers, probably store-rooms; the door on the left (W) side opens into a long *corridor* covered with reliefs, on the right-hand side of which are four other undecorated store-rooms. Between and over the doors Nebet is depicted with her daughters receiving votive offerings, particularly livestock. – The corridor leads into a *chapel* with four niches for statues of the Queen. Opposite these, on the E wall, are reliefs depicting votive offerings. – At the N end of the offering-chamber is a small room with the representation of a man, evidently a commoner, and his children: perhaps a relative of the Queen, and thus giving an indication of her non-noble origin. – To the S of the chapel are two chambers, one behind the other; the first has the usual representations of the dead Queen at table, while on the walls of the second are four large unguent vessels.

To the W of the Pyramid of Unas is the large precinct, now buried in sand, of the unfinished *Step Pyramid of Sekhemkhet*, Djoser's successor, who died young.

On either side of the causeway leading up to the Pyramid of Unas are *mastabas* and *rock tombs* of the 5th and 6th Dynasties, discovered in 1844 and subsequently excavated.

Some 330 yds/300 m E of the Pyramid of Unas is the small *Tomb of Nefer-her-ptah*, Overseer of the Palace, Royal Wigmaker and confidant of an unidentified King. It consists only of an entrance corridor and a single chamber, but contains preliminary drawings of high artistic quality for reliefs which were never executed. They depict scenes from everyday life, farming and hunting.

To the E is the rock-cut **Tomb of Iru-ka-ptah Khenu** (5th Dynasty), Superintendent of the Royal Slaughterhouses. This, too, has a single chamber at the end of a narrow corridor. On the left-hand and rear walls of the chamber are ten figures of the dead man carved from the rock in high relief. On the right-hand wall are similar figures of three young men and a woman who were also buried in the tomb, together with a false door. In the floor are five tomb-shafts. The painted reliefs on the N and E walls depict the usual scenes from everyday life, the dead man at table, and religious themes. – Immediately W is the *Mastaba of Akhet-hotep*, in which many wooden statues were found. Little is left of the tomb itself or of a third tomb which adjoins it.

Some 55 yds/50 m farther E, on the S side of the causeway leading to the Pyramid of Unas, is the *Tomb of Nefer and Companions* (5th Dynasty), probably the family or communal tomb of a guild of singers. It has a single chamber 26 ft/8 m long, with nine tomb-shafts. In one of these was found the mummy of a naked man, adorned only with a necklace of blue beads, lying on his side with his legs slightly bent, as if asleep. The walls, faced with plaster, display a rich variety of reliefs. On the left-hand (E) wall are five rows of scenes from everyday life, including woodworkers, farming scenes and – a rare and informative scene – the launching of a boat. – On the right-hand wall the dead men are depicted with their wives at a funeral banquet. – On the S wall, from left to right, are Nefer and his wife Khonsu receiving votive gifts, a man leaning on his staff accompanied by his wife and Nefer at table eating the funeral meal.

To the E of this tomb, under the causeway (which was constructed over it), is the **Double Tomb of Ni-ankh-khnum and Khnum-hotep** (5th Dynasty), two friends or relatives who were priests of Re in Niuserre's Sun Temple (see under Abu Gurab) and Court manicurists. The tomb is partly hewn from the rock, partly masonry-built, and the front part is faced with fine-grained limestone. The rich decoration of painted reliefs is well preserved in the stone-built front part; in the rock-cut chambers to the rear, however, it is in poor condition as a result of the friability of the rock.

On the walls of the **portico** are reliefs depicting funeral rituals, and on both sides of the entrance are the dead men with their eldest sons. – Within the doorway the mummy is seen being conveyed to the tomb, accompanied by offering-bearers; below, the catching of the sacrificial ox for the evening and morning meals. – The portico leads into an *antecham-*

ber, with excellently preserved reliefs in five rows, alternately referring to Ni-ankh-khnum and Khnum-hotep. On the N and E walls are scenes of farming life and of the dead men's professional activities. – On the S wall are depicted various methods of catching fish and birds. – In the W wall is a door leading into the undecorated court; in the doorway, on the left and right, dead men in litters borne by donkeys. – Adjoining this room is the vestibule to the tomb chamber.

The reliefs in the rock-cut main chamber are poorly preserved. – N wall: winnowing of grain; corn being taken into the granary, with scribes recording the quantity. – E wall: the dead men supervising work in the fields and, accompanied by their sons, inspecting workshops. – S wall: banquet, with music and dancing (the figure of Ni-ankh-khnum's wife defaced). – Between the two doors: the dead men, with their children but without their wives, embracing and touching one another with their noses (i.e. kissing). – W wall: scenes of everyday life. – The chapel is divided equally between the two men, the S side being assigned to Ni-ankh-khnum, the N side of Khnumhotep. In each half is a false door, and between the doors the two men are depicted embracing one another. On the walls are scenes from the funeral banquet.

To the E of this tomb is the Double Tomb of Nefer-seshem-ptah and Sekhen-tiu. From here a path leads S to the nearby ruins of the **Monastery of St Jeremias** (Jeremiah), excavated by J. E. Quibell in 1907–09. Founded in the second half of the 5th c. and destroyed by the Arabs about 960, the monastery buildings include two churches (fine capitals and reliefs from which are now in the Egyptian Museum in Cairo), a refectory, a bakery, an oil-press, a wine-press and other offices, the room occupied by St Jeremias and cells for the monks, each with a niche in the E wall, many of which had frescos of the Virgin, the Archangels and the founder of the monastery; the frescos are now also in the Egyptian Museum.

To the S of the tombs flanking the causeway to the Pyramid of Unas and to the W of the Monastery of St Jeremias is an area containing tombs of the New Kingdom, only a few of which have been excavated. Here was unexpectedly discovered in 1975 the *Tomb of Horemheb, Tutankhamun's General and Co-ruler, reliefs from which had previously been removed by 19th c. tomb-robbers and had found their way into various museums. Horemheb, the "general of generals", built this tomb before his accession to the throne, but later had another tomb constructed in the Valley of the Kings, where he was buried. The *reliefs in the Saqqara tomb, in both raised and sunk relief, are the finest examples of the art of Memphis under the influence of the Amarna style,

showing its characteristic smooth and flowing lines and its plastic and realistic handling of its themes. They depict with consummate skill and in great variety the Mannerist spirit of the time, shown for example in its leaning towards such fashionable externals as ever-changing wigs, elaborately draped garments and luxuriously furnished rooms.

The entrance to the tomb, flanked by pillars and preceded by a paved forecourt, is on the E side. It leads into the first colonnaded court, which was surrounded by a wall 10 ft/3 m high, built of brick with a cladding of limestone slabs. The painted reliefs, now largely replaced by copies or much restored, depict scenes from the dead man's career, including the presentation of a gold collar of honor by the King and Queen, a celebrated relief of which the original is in the Museum van Oudheden in Leyden. At the NW corner of the court is a tomb-shaft. – Beyond the court is the hall of statues, which contains statues of Horemheb and Anubis. At the entrance are representations of Horemheb at the offering-table, to which offerings are being brought. On the door-jambs are the name and titles of the dead man. – The walls of the adjoining second colonnaded court are decorated with painted reliefs: on the N wall and N end of the E wall are Horemheb in the presence of Osiris and a procession of offering-bearers; on the S end of the E wall, Horemheb receiving representatives and prisoners from foreign lands. The maltreatment of the prisoners, dragged in by the hair or at the end of a rope, is depicted with striking realism. The original of a scene depicting captured Negroes (Kushites) being registered by Egyptian officials is now in the Museo Civico in Bologna. On the S wall: Horemheb receiving offerings. – On the W side of the court is the chapel, with a statue of Horemheb and his wife (?). On both sides are further chapels and tomb-shafts.

NE of the Step Pyramid of Djoser is the mound of rubble which represents the Pyramid of Userkaf, founder of the 5th Dynasty. It was relatively small, with an original base measurement of some 245 ft/75 m, and lay within a correspondingly small precinct. The mortuary temple was on the S side; and to the SW of this are the remains of a subsidiary pyramid. – In the area S of Userkaf's Pyramid and E of Djoser's are mastabas of the Old Kingdom.

Some 550 yds/500 m NE of Djoser's Pyramid is the mound of earth which marks the site of the Pyramid of Teti, founder of the 6th Dynasty. On its E side are the scanty remains of the mortuary temple, remains of an alabaster altar and many table-like statue bases. Farther E is a confused tangle of structures excavated by the Egyptian Department of Antiquities and ranging in date from the Old Kingdom to the Ptolemaic period. The oldest are two large stone mastabas of the Old Kingdom, on top of which brick tombs were built during the Middle Kingdom. The brick enclosure walls, 30–33 ft/ 9–10 m thick, date from the Greek period. – Farther NW is a *cemetery* with brick-built mastabas of the 2nd and 3rd Dynasties.

At the NW corner of the Pyramid of Teti we find the* **Tomb of Mereruka** or Meri, a priest attached to the pyramid. Dating from the early 6th Dynasty, it is the largest structure of its kind in the Old Kingdom – 130 ft/40 m by 80 ft/24 m, with a total of 31 rooms and passages. It is divided into three parts, belonging respectively to Mereruka, his wife Her-watet-khet (to the left of the entrance) and their son Meriteti (to the rear). A tablet at the entrance records that the tomb was excavated in 1893.

To the right and left of the entrance: Mereruka and his wife (who is on a smaller scale). Within the entrance, right-hand side: the artist (probably Mereruka himself) sitting at an easel and painting the three seasons, which are represented by gods; in one hand he holds a shell containing paint, in the other a pen, while other writing materials hang from his shoulder; in front of him is his son Khenu. Left-hand side: Mereruka, before whom is his small son Meriteti, holding a lotus stem and a bird; behind him his wife and rows of servants. – *First room,* N wall: Mereruka, in a papyrus boat with his wife, spearing fish; men in two small boats harpooning three hippopotamuses; in the reeds are birds, in the river fish. S wall: the dead man, in a boat with his wife, hunting in the marshes. The scene is full of fascinating detail – birds, fish, etc., a hippopotamus biting a crocodile; below, left, cattle being driven through a river; above, cattle thrown to the ground for slaughter (note the accurately observed attitudes of the cattle); gardens being watered. – To the right of the first room is a small side chamber with a mummy-shaft.

Adjoining the first room on the N is an almost exactly *square room*. E wall: Mereruka and his wife (to left)

inspecting various operations, depicted in six rows. Two lowest rows: goldsmiths making necklaces and various vessels. Third row: three statues being drawn to the tomb, while a priest burns incense. Fourth row: carpenters making beds. Fifth and sixth rows: manufacture of stone vessels. W wall: Mereruka and his wife, accompanied by servants, watch hunters in the desert; desert animals; a hound seizes an antelope; a lion devouring a bull; hedgehogs and hares. – Beyond this is a *long room.* E wall: on the right Mereruka and his wife, followed by servants, watching fishermen; Mereruka's stout brother, in a boat, drinking from a cup; on the left Mereruka and his wife, preceded by servants, one of whom leads a monkey and two hounds on a leash. W wall: on the left the estate office, a hall with columns in which the clerks sit, while the village elders are dragged in to pay their taxes, some being cudgeled, while one is stripped, tied to a post and beaten; on the right Mereruka and his wife watching offerings being made to his statue. – Immediately left of the entrance to this room is a door into another long room, without decoration.

At the NE corner of the long room a door leads into a *hall* with four pillars supporting the roof, on which are sunk reliefs of the dead man. W wall (from the left): bedroom scenes; Mereruka and his wife watching as the canopied bed is prepared; the dead man and his wife, who is playing a harp, sit on a large couch with lions' feet, under which are two rows of vases; Mereruka, seated in an armchair, receiving gifts (vases, wooden chests, etc.) brought by servants. N wall: priests of the mortuary cult bring in food and drink for the dead man. E wall: Mereruka and his wife, with servants; servants bringing in votive offerings; male and female dancers (bottom two rows). S wall: the dead man receiving votive offerings.

Beyond the long room is a transverse room in which only a few reliefs are preserved, together with a false door at the W end, with the *serdab.* In the floor is a shaft leading to the *tomb chamber,* which was closed by a stone slab running in vertical grooves. The walls of the chamber are covered with reliefs depicting votive offerings and lists of offerings, and have magnificent false doors. Against the rear wall is the huge stone sarcophagus. – Adjoining the E end of the transverse room is a *smaller room* with reliefs depicting the bringing of offerings and scenes from everyday life. N wall: the dead man receiving offerings; second bottom row, ten store-rooms; bottom row.

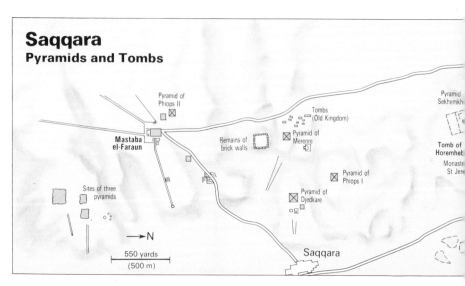

Saqqara
Pyramids and Tombs

Pyramid of Phiops II

Tombs (Old Kingdom)

Pyramid Sekhemkh

Mastaba el-Faraun

Remains of brick walls

Pyramid of Merenre

Tomb of Horemheb

Sites of three pyramids

Pyramid of Phiops I

Monaste St Jere

Pyramid of Djedkare

→N

550 yards
(500 m)

Saqqara

treading grapes and pressing the trodden grapes in a sack. On the other walls the dead man is shown having food and drink brought to him.

Immediately N of the transverse room is the large *sacrificial chamber,* the roof of which is borne on six square pillars, on which Mereruka is represented standing erect. In the middle of the room is a stone ring for tethering the sacrificial ox. In the N wall is a niche containing a statue of Mereruka, with an offering-table in front of it. Reliefs on the N wall (left to right): Mereruka inspecting domestic animals, etc.; top row, boatbuilding; four lower rows, gazelles, antelopes, cattle; bottom row, feeding tame hyenas; the aged Mereruka conducted by his two grown-up sons; Mereruka carried in a litter, with a large retinue, including two dwarfs leading dogs. W wall (badly damaged): boats. S wall (only bottom row preserved): the funeral; entrance to the tomb, in front of which stand priests and dancing-girls; farther left, men carrying a large chest; votive offerings; four boats, with several men in the water; funeral procession, with women mourners; to the left of the door, the dead man, accompanied by two women, sailing through the marshes, with crocodiles and fish in the water. E wall: on the right Mereruka with his wife and mother watching harvesting operations; on the left Mereruka and his wife playing a board game. Above and beside the door at the NE corner which leads into Meriteti's part of the tomb: Mereruka with his wife and mother watching dancers and female musicians; various games.

The doorway into **Meriteti's tomb** is of later construction. – *Vestibule,* E wall: on the right a poultry-yard in which geese are being fattened, on the left cattle and antelopes. N wall: Meriteti receiving offerings from servants. W wall: Meriteti watching a hunt in the desert; the bag of gazelles and antelopes is presented to him. S wall: servants with votive gifts (poultry, fish). There are no reliefs in the small room to the left. – Beyond the vestibule is a *transverse room.* E wall: two lowest rows, cattle being slaughtered; upper rows, servants bringing in cattle, gazelles, etc. N and S walls: Meriteti at table, with servants bringing votive gifts. On the W wall is a false door, on which the dead man's name has been substituted for an earlier one; in front of it an offering-table. – To the N is a *second transverse room.* E wall: men bringing Meriteti (on the left) large chests containing garments and vases. N wall: in the middle Meriteti, with servants to the left and right bringing him jars and chests; to the right, large jars being brought in on sledges. W wall: servants with votive gifts (crude and unfinished); square opening into *serdab.* S wall: similar to N wall (unfinished).

From the NW corner of Mereruka's sacrificial chamber a passage leads to a number of undecorated *store-rooms.* Passing through the one immediately on the left, we come into a long room on the W side of the sacrificial chamber. W wall: Mereruka and his wife, to the left and right servants bringing lengths of cloth, jars of sacred oil, boxes of clothing and jewelry; a sledge with three large jars. E wall: similar scenes.

Immediately S of this room is a *transverse room* with a false door, in front of which stood the offering-table. – Beyond this is a *second transverse room.* W wall: poultry (pigeons, geese, cranes) being fed; a narrow cleft in this wall leads into the *serdab,* in which a painted statue of Mereruka was found. S wall: to the left, cattle, antelopes, etc., being brought to the dead man, with scribes recording the numbers; to the right, peasant women bringing votive gifts, with the names of the villages from which they come. N wall: to the left, cattle being slaughtered, to the right Mereruka watching fishermen.

From the vestibule of Mereruka's tomb a door on the left leads into **Her-watet-khet's tomb**. The first room is a *pillared hall.* N and S walls: Princess Her-watet-khet, Mereruka's wife, receiving votive gifts from servants. W wall: to the right, the dead woman with her son and daughter; four maids bearing a litter adorned with lions; to the left fishermen; above, capture of wild bulls. – Beyond the hall are two smaller rooms. *First room,* N wall: dancing-girls. Other walls: servants bringing in food and driving in cattle. *Second room,* W wall: in the center an elaborate false door, in front of which is a square block, the base of an offering-table; to the right and left, the dead woman at table, with servants bringing food, flowers, etc. N

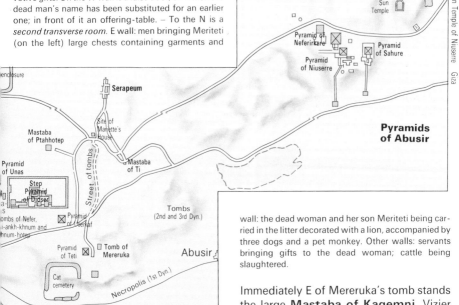

wall: the dead woman and her son Meriteti being carried in the litter decorated with a lion, accompanied by three dogs and a pet monkey. Other walls: servants bringing gifts to the dead woman; cattle being slaughtered.

Immediately E of Mereruka's tomb stands the large **Mastaba of Kagemni**, Vizier and Judge under three kings of the 5th and 6th Dynasties, which was also discovered in 1893.

The entrance is at the S end of the E front, which has an inscription giving the name and titles of the dead man. It leads into a *vestibule,* with reliefs of fishermen and offering-bearers, beyond which is a *hall* with three pillars containing an attractive series of scenes: dancing-girls; hunting in the marshes; a farmyard; boats; cattle crossing a ford; boys feeding a puppy; court scene. To the left is a *corridor,* off which open five store-rooms (originally probably two-storeyed). – To the N of the pillared hall is the *first chamber.* Left-hand wall: Kagemni inspecting his cattle and poultry; tame hyenas and poultry being fed; bird-catching. Right-hand wall: Kagemni watching fishermen; the catch is recorded and carried away. Above the door into the next room: the dead man carried in a litter. To the W of this room is the *serdab* (inaccessible). – *Second room*: the dead man receiving votive gifts from servants. To the left is a room in which two figures of the dead man have been obliterated. – *Third room,* on longitudinal walls: Kagemni, seated on a chair, receiving votive gifts. In the end wall is a false door, in front of which stood the offering-table, approached by steps. – *Fourth room*: two figures of Kagemni, standing, while attendants bring in votive gifts; tables, with various vessels on them; large jars of unguents being brought in on sledges.

From the vestibule a door on the N side leads into a hall from which a staircase mounts to the roof of the mastaba. On the roof were two rooms 36 ft/11 m long, probably for the solar barques.

A short distance E of Kagemni's tomb, to the N of the Pyramid of Teti, we come to a **street of tombs**, with some interesting 6th Dynasty tombs, which was excavated by Loret in 1899 but is now partly covered by sand. The first of the tombs to be encountered is the badly ruined *Tomb of Nefer-seshem-re* or Sheshi, a Judge and Vizier, the chief remains of which are a hall with six square pillars, each bearing a figure of the dead man, and an elegant false door.

The first tomb on the left is the * **Tomb of Ankh-me-hor** or Sesi, also known as the "Tomb of the Physician" because of the surgical operations depicted in its reliefs. The upper part of the walls has been destroyed.

First room, on the wall to left of the entrance: harvest scenes; below, cattle being driven across a river. – *Second room,* left-hand wall: the dead man watching the catching of birds. Rear wall: statues being carved for the tomb, etc. In the doorway to the next room: sacrificial animals being slaughtered (on the right, an ox being thrown to the ground for slaughter). – The three following rooms have the usual scenes of the presentation of offerings to the dead man, the slaughtering of cattle, etc.

Adjoining the first room is a *hall*, the roof of which was borne by five pillars. In the doorway, on the right, are depicted two surgical operations – circumcision and

an operation on a man's toe. On the entrance wall of the hall: to the right, servants and women mourning the dead man; to the left, dancing-girls.

Next comes the *Tomb of Uze-he-teti* or *Nefer-seshem-ptah,* also known as Seshi, "the first next to the king".

From the vestibule a door (reliefs of sacrificial animals in the doorway) leads into a *second chamber,* with fine reliefs. Right-hand wall: wild ducks being caught with a net; above, a poultry-yard, catching of fowls, fattening of geese. Other walls: servants with votive gifts, some of them in boats. – *Last room,* W wall: false door, from which the dead man is twice represented as emerging; above, a window, from which the dead man looks out; in front the offering-table. Other walls: the dead man at table, servants with votive gifts, slaughtering of sacrificial oxen.

To the E of the Pyramid of Teti and the street of tombs are the unexcavated remains of a *pyramid,* usually ascribed to a King Merikare of the Heracleopolitan period (9th and 10th Dynasties).

Some 550 yds/500 m NW of the Step Pyramid of Djoser is the ** **Mastaba of Ptahhotep**, a high dignitary under the 5th Dynasty.

The entrance, on the N side, leads into a *corridor,* the walls of which are covered with interesting sketches for reliefs and unfinished reliefs (right) and empty royal cartouches (left). To the right is a large square *hall* with four pillars, from which a door at the SE corner leads through a vestibule into the **offering-room**, with **mural reliefs which are among the highest achievements of Egyptian art at its zenith, some of them surpassing even the reliefs in the Mastaba of Ti (see below). The colors are well preserved. The roof of the chamber is decorated with imitation palm-trunks.

In the doorway: servants with votive gifts. N wall: above the door, Ptahhotep at his morning toilet, with greyhounds under his chair and his pet monkey held by a servant; in front of him harpists and singers, dwarfs stringing beads (upper row); officials seated on the ground (next two rows); harpists and flute-players, with a singer beating time (bottom row); to the left of the door, servants with votive gifts, sacrificial animals being slaughtered. W wall: at each end a false door; the right-hand one is highly elaborate, perhaps representing a palace façade; on the left-hand one the dead man is depicted sitting in a chapel (below, right) and in a litter carried by servants (left); in front is the offering-table. The reliefs depict Ptahhotep (on the left) at a richly furnished table; in front of him (top row) priests making offerings and (three lower rows) servants with various votive gifts; above, a list of the dishes.

On the S wall is a similar scene: the dead man at the funeral banquet; in front of him (top row) peasant women with gifts (mutilated); second row, cutting up of sacrificial animals; two bottom rows, servants with various gifts. – The finest and most interesting reliefs are on the E wall. To the right the dead man is seen inspecting gifts and tribute from "the estates of the north and the south"; top row, boys wrestling and seven boys running (the first having his arms tied); second and third rows, the spoils of the chase, with four men pulling two cages containing lions, another with young gazelles in a litter, another with a cage of hares and hedgehogs; fourth row, herdsmen and cattle in the fields, the calves being tethered to pegs; next two rows, cattle being brought for inspection (note the herdsman with a broken leg leading a bull with a neck ornament); bottom row, poultry. To the left the dead man contemplates "all the pleasant diversions that take place throughout the country"; top row, a herd of cattle being driven through a marsh, and men gathering papyrus, tying it in bundles and carrying it away; second row, boys playing; third row, the vintage (vines growing on trellises, a man watering them, others gathering the grapes, treading them and pressing them in sacks); fourth and fifth rows, animal life and hunting in the desert; sixth row, men working in the marshes, gutting fish, making rope and constructing papyrus boats; seventh row, men catching birds with nets, putting them in crates and carrying them away; bottom row, peasants in boats on the Nile, with plants and fish (some of the peasants are fighting). In the boat on the left is a sculptor named Ni-ankh-ptah with a boy giving him a drink – probably the artist responsible for the reliefs in the tomb.

From the pillared hall a door in the W wall leads into the *offering-chamber of Akhethotep,* Ptahhotep's son. To the right and left the dead man is shown at a banquet, with servants bringing him votive gifts. On the W wall is a false door with a large offering-table.

Some 275 yds/250 m N of the Tomb of Ptahhotep is the site of *Mariette's House,* built by the French Egyptologist Auguste Mariette when excavating the Serapeum as a site office and museum. The new building begun in the 1960s remains unfinished and ruined, a conspicuous landmark.

550 yds/600 m W of this is the *Serapeum, with the rock-cut underground burial chambers of the Apis bulls. Apis, the sacred bull of the god Ptah, was worshiped in a temple of his own, and after his death was embalmed and buried with great pomp. From the time of Amenophis III, and probably earlier, the

Apis tombs consisted of an underground chamber entered by a sloping shaft, over which was a chapel, as in the tombs of high dignitaries. In the reign of Ramesses II Prince Khaemweset constructed a common burial-place for all the Apis bulls, consisting of an underground corridor 110 yds/100 m long flanked on both sides by chambers in which the wooden coffins of the bulls were enclosed. Psammetichus I added, at right angles to this, a much larger and more carefully constructed complex of chambers, which was enlarged at various times down to the Ptolemaic period. Altogether there were some 380 yds/350 m of corridors, 10 ft/ 3 m wide and 18 ft/5·5 m high. Over these subterranean chambers was built a large temple.

The Egyptians believed that, like men, the bulls were united with Osiris after death, and the dead bull was given the name of Osiris-Apis (Egyptian Oser-hapi, Greek Osorapis) and became a kind of god of the dead, known, like Osiris, as "Lord of the Western Land". Great numbers of pilgrims visited the tombs of the bulls and left votive offerings – usually small memorial tablets set into the walls of the underground corridors. When the cult of the foreign god Sarapis (Serapis), introduced in the reign of Ptolemy I, became popular in Egypt Sarapis was identified with Osorapis and venerated with him in the ancient temple in the necropolis of Memphis, which came to be known as the Sarapeion or Serapeum.

Opposite the temple built over the burial-place of the Apis bulls a second Temple of Osorapis was erected by Nectanebo II. On the walls flanking the path between the two temples were Greek statues, some of which are still *in situ,* though now covered with sand. The great avenue of sphinxes which ran W from the cultivated land through the necropolis to the Serapeum ended in a semicircular open space adorned with statues of Greek philosophers.

When visiting the Serapeum it is advisable to take a good electric torch, since the lighting system does not always work. – The entrance leads into a room of some size, with niches in the limestone walls in which many votive tablets and tombstones of dead bulls were

Saqqara
Serapeum

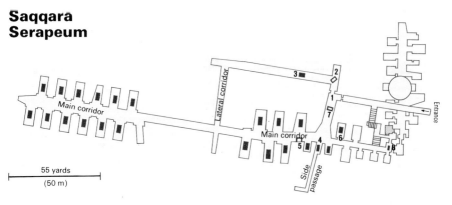

1 Vestibule	3 Sarcophagus	5 Lid of sarcophagus (No. 4)	7 Lid of sarcophagus (No. 6)
2 Lid of sarcophagus (No. 3)	4 Sarcophagus of Khabbash	6 Sarcophagus of Amasis	8 Sarcophagus of Cambyses

found. Turning right, we come in a few yards to a huge *sarcophagus lid* of black granite and, some 20 yds/ 18 m beyond it (on left) the *sarcophagus* to which it belonged, almost filling the corridor – both perhaps left lying here, on their way to a tomb chamber, when the cult of Apis was abandoned. Near the end of the corridor a lateral corridor goes off on the left towards the *main corridor*, which runs parallel with the first. The chambers on either side of this corridor, in which the mummies of the Apis bulls were buried in huge stone sarcophagi, average 26 ft/8 m in height; their pavements and vaulted roofs are faced with Moqattam stone. Twenty of the chambers still contain their *sarcophagi* of polished black or red granite, each hewn from a single block. They average some 13 ft/4 m in length by 7½ ft/2·30 m in width and 11 ft/3·30 m in height and are estimated to weigh 65 tons. Many of the lids have been pushed aside; five of them are constructed of separate pieces of stone cemented together. When found the sarcophagi had already been plundered and emptied of their contents, apart from two which still contained a few trinkets and other grave-goods. Three of them have inscriptions, one in the name of Amasis, the second in the name of Cambyses and the third in the name of Khabbash, the last native ruler before Alexander the Great's conquest. The finest of the sarcophagi is the last one on the right-hand side, to which a flight of steps descends. Of finely polished black granite, it is covered with inscriptions and door-shaped ornaments.

Near the E end of the main corridor a side passage 22 yds/20 m long goes off on the right to another corridor running parallel with the main one (now walled up). Going N from here and stepping over the lid of Amasis's sarcophagus, we return to the vestibule at the end of the entrance passage.

Just N of the Serapeum is a tent where refreshments may be obtained.

NE of the Serapeum is one of the principal sights of Saqqara, the ** **Mastaba of Ti**, belonging to a high Court official and wealthy landowner of the early 5th Dynasty. A tablet at the entrance records its discovery and excavation by Mariette and its restoration by the Egyptian Department of Antiquities. Its mural reliefs are among the finest and best preserved of the Old Kingdom as well as the most interesting in terms of subject-matter.

The entrance opens into a small *vestibule* with two pillars (upper parts restored), on the front of which Ti is depicted wearing a long wig and a short, wide apron and holding a long staff in one hand and a kind of club in the other. E wall: women, representing the villages owned by Ti, bringing food to the tomb. S wall: poultry-yard, feeding of pigeons. The other reliefs are obliterated.

A doorway flanked by figures of the dead man and inscriptions leads into a large *pillared hall*, with a modern timber roof borne on 12 square ancient pillars (restored), in which offerings were presented. In the center is a flight of steps leading into a low sloping passage which runs the whole length of the building to an antechamber and beyond this the *tomb chamber*. The *sarcophagus*, now empty, completely fills the recess in which it stands.

Entrance to Mastaba of Ti, Saqqara

The reliefs in this hall are badly weathered, some of them being quite unrecognizable. N wall: Ti watching the sacrificial animals being slaughtered and cut up; servants with votive gifts. Behind this wall was the *serdab* containing a statue of the dead man. E wall (left-hand side only): Ti carried in a litter, preceded by servants with fans, boxes and chairs. W wall (right to left): Ti and his wife watching the fattening of geese and the feeding of cranes; a poultry-yard; Ti receiving the accounts of his officials, who stand in a pillared building; Ti (upper part of figure destroyed) watching his ships coming in and herds of livestock being driven towards him; false door for Ti's son.

A door at the far corner (on either side three figures of Ti, each time in different garb, walking towards the entrance) leads into a *corridor*, with reliefs of servants bearing gifts of all kinds into the tomb. On the right-hand wall is a false door for Ti's wife Neferhotpe. – Another door opens into a *second corridor*. Left-hand wall, bottom row: sacrificial animals being slaughtered; above, statues of the dead man being conveyed to the tomb on sledges, with a man in front of them pouring water. Right-hand wall: arrival of the ships in which Ti has inspected his estates in the Delta (note the curious steering-gear). Above the entrance door: Ti and his wife in a boat in a thicket of papyrus. Over the door into the chapel: female dancers and singers. – A door on the right leads into a *side room*, in which the colors of the reliefs are excellently preserved. On the upper part of the left-hand door-jamb a piece

Stone sarcophagus in Serapeum, Saqqara

of the sycamore wood to which the door was attached is still in place. Right-hand wall: Ti, on right, receiving votive gifts (flowers, cakes, poultry, etc.) from servants; top row, tables with votive offerings. Rear wall, upper rows: potters, bakers and brewers; below, a man measuring corn, with scribes recording the quantity. Left-hand wall: Ti; to right, servants with votive gifts; above, tables and vessels of various kinds. Entrance wall: tables, with various vessels.

Returning to the corridor, we now turn right through a door flanked by figures of Ti to enter the *chapel*, 16 ft/5 m wide, 23 ft/7·20 m long and 15 ft/4·50 m high, the roof of which is borne on two sturdy square pillars painted to resemble red granite. On the pillars are inscribed Ti's names and titles. The**mural reliefs** in this chamber, with well-preserved colors, repay detailed examination.

On the E side, to the left of the entrance, Ti (on the right), with his wife kneeling beside him, watches harvesting operations; in front of him are ten rows of harvest scenes (from top to bottom): the flax harvest; corn being cut with sickles, packed in sacks and loaded on donkeys, which take it to the threshing-floor; oxen and donkeys treading out the corn; the threshed grain along with the chaff is piled in a great heap with three-pronged forks, then sifted and winnowed with two small boards; a woman fills a sack of corn.

To the right are two well-preserved and several damaged shipbuilding scenes: shaping the tree-trunks; sawing them into planks; construction of the ship, with workmen using adzes, mallets and crowbars and others fitting the planks together; Ti standing in one of the ships, inspecting the work. The simple tools used by the workmen (saw, axe, adze, drill) are of great interest.

There are numerous reliefs on the S side of the chapel (upper rows damaged). To the left, above, is a figure of Ti, below which is a narrow opening leading into a second *serdab* in which one intact and several broken statues of Ti were found. To right and left of the opening are two men offering incense to Ti. Ti and his wife watch their workmen, who are depicted in four rows (from top to bottom): men blowing through long tubes into a furnace in which gold is being smelted; sculptors and makers of stone vessels; carpenters polishing a door and a box (left), sawing planks, polishing a bedstead, under which lies a head-rest, and working with drills; leather-workers and a market scene (one man has a wineskin and two jars of oil for sale, another a wallet, for which he is being offered a pair of sandals in exchange); a stamp-cutter making a stone seal; a man selling sticks. - In the center, above, Ti, with his wife sitting at his feet, watches as peasants from his estates bring various animals (antelopes, gazelles, goats, deer, cattle, etc.) as funeral offerings; against each animal is inscribed its name. Below, in three rows: cattle are led in; three village elders are forcibly brought into the estate office to account for their taxes; bottom row, a variety of poultry (cranes, geese, pigeons, etc.). - To the right, above, Ti seated at table, with servants bringing funeral offerings; below, servants with gifts and musicians (harpists and flute-players); sacrificial animals slaughtered and cut up.

On the W side of the chapel are two large false doors marking the entrance to the Realm of the Dead. In front of the left-hand one is a stone offering-table. In the center of the wall: slaughtering of sacrificial animals and presentation of offerings (damaged); above, tables.

The reliefs on the N side of the chapel depict life in the marshes of the Delta. On the left (from top to bottom): Ti watching bird-catchers and fishermen; a hut containing the birds and fish that have been caught; two men cutting up fish at a small table; (below) cattle grazing; a cow calving and another being milked, with an overseer leaning on his staff and a herdsman holding the calf to prevent it from running to its mother; (left) calves tethered to stakes try to break loose, while others graze peacefully; (right) herdsmen in small papyrus boats driving cattle across a river in which two crocodiles are lying; (left) two dwarfs with their master's pet monkey and greyhounds. In the center of the wall: Ti sailing through the marshes in a papyrus boat; in front of him another boat whose crew are hunting hippopotamuses with harpoons; a hippopotamus biting a crocodile; to the rear a small boat with a man who has hooked a catfish; birds nesting and fluttering about in the papyrus thicket. To the left: harvesting papyrus and building papyrus boats; boatmen quarrelling and fighting; fishing (a fisherman putting the fish he has caught into his fish-trap into a basket); tilling the ground (one man plowing) with two oxen - note the form of the plow - while another spurs them on; another breaks up the clods, while another sows the seed, with a scribe looking on); rams are driven over the newly sown ground to tread in the seed, while to the right are men hoeing; cattle returning from pasturage in the Delta are driven through the water; in front a herdsman carrying a young calf on his shoulders.

A narrow strip running along the foot of the N wall depicts 36 peasant women bearing offerings of meat, poultry, vegetables, fruit and drink from Ti's various estates, the names of which are given.

In the northern part of the Saqqara necropolis are cemeteries of the Early Period. On the edge of the desert are *rock tombs*, some of them with brick super-structures, of the 1st Dynasty; farther W are tombs of the 2nd and 3rd Dynasties. – Some 275 yds/250 m farther W large *animal cemeteries* have been excavated since 1965. They were associated with a large temple of the Late and Ptolemaic periods which was replaced in Christian times by a church. The intricate system of underground galleries and passages in which the animal mummies were buried was entered from the temple terrace.

The **worship of animals** was practiced in Egypt from early times, but developed on a considerable scale in the Late Period. The animals venerated as sacred were kept and reared for the specific purpose of being mummified and buried in specially constructed burial complexes. Burial-places of this kind have been found for ibises, falcons, baboons, dogs, jackals, crocodiles, rams, bulls, cows, fish, ichneumons, cats and other animals. It was regarded as meritorious for a pilgrim visiting a particular shrine to acquire one of the animals sacred to the divinity and to have it mummified, elaborately painted and decked with ornaments, and then buried in a stone or wooden coffin (or in the case of a bird a pointed pottery vessel).

Ti sailing through the papyrus marshes

Carpenters at work

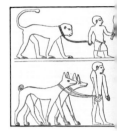

Dwarfs with a monkey and greyhound

Donkey carrying grain

Peasant women with offerings

Emptying a fish-trap

Cattle being driven across a river

Shaping a tree-trunk

On the way to the estate office

Shipbuilding

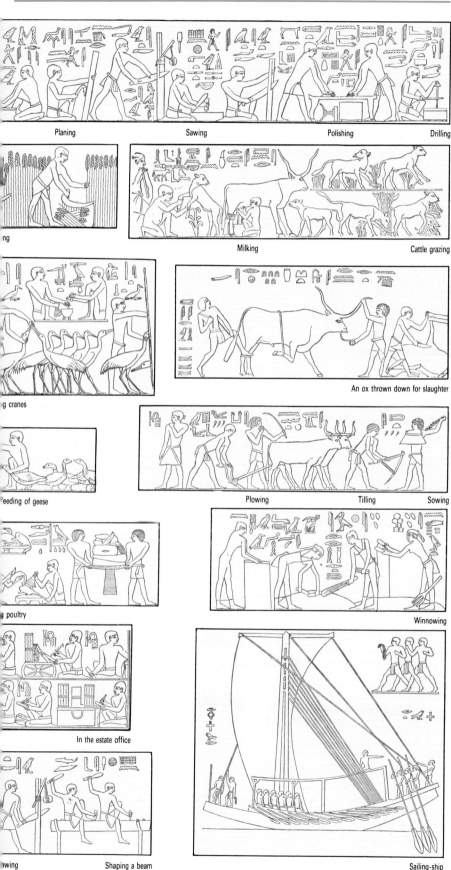

Planing

Sawing

Polishing

Drilling

ng

Milking

Cattle grazing

g cranes

An ox thrown down for slaughter

eeding of geese

Plowing

Tilling

Sowing

poultry

Winnowing

In the estate office

wing

Shaping a beam

Sailing-ship

The animal cemeteries of Saqqara comprise a *burial gallery for the "Apis mothers"* (the Iseum; only partly accessible), the counterpart of the Serapeum, in which the sacred cows were buried in stone sarcophagi; a *baboon gallery,* on two levels, with over 400 coffins; an *ibis gallery,* in which more than 2 million ibis mummies buried in pointed jars have so far been found; and a *falcon gallery* which contained a variety of cult vessels and equipment and yielded much valuable information.

If time permits the **Southern Necropolis** of Saqqara can also be visited. For this purpose a donkey should be hired at the Tourist Center near the site of Mariette's house. It takes about 1½ hours to reach the cemetery area. – The track runs due S, passing close to a large court or enclosure some 440 yds/400 m square, bounded on three sides by massive walls, now ruinous, and on the S by the hills of the desert. – Farther on, to the left, are the remains of the *Pyramids of Phiops (Pepi) I, Djedkare and Merenre,* in a much-dilapidated state as a result of their use as convenient quarries of building stone. Some 440 yds/400 m farther S is the *Pyramid of Phiops (Pepi) II,* also much ruined. The structure and decoration of all these pyramids follow the pattern introduced by Unas.

SSE of the Pyramid of Phiops II is the **Mastaba el-Faraun**, the most important monument in the southern group. Originally 330 ft/100 m long and 240 ft/73·5 m wide, it is in the form of a gigantic coffin with a barrel roof, built of massive blocks 2–2½ ft/1·5–2 m thick and faced with Tura limestone. it is the Tomb of Shepseskaf, last King of the 4th Dynasty.

The layout of the passages in the interior is similar to that of the pyramids of Unas and his successors. From the entrance, on the N side, a very narrow passage, only 4¼ ft/1·30 m high and 65 ft/20 m long, originally faced with granite slabs, descends to the chambers 23 ft/7 m below the base of the mastaba. Built entirely of granite, these were closed off by three stone portcullises. The tomb chamber had been thoroughly ransacked by tomb-robbers and yielded only a few fragments of the sarcophagus.

The *mortuary temple* on the E side of the mastaba was also used as a quarry of building stone, and scarcely a trace survives. Nothing is left of the valley temple, which stood on the outskirts of the village of Saqqara. The causeway, however, can

be traced for part of its course. – The Mastaba el-Faraun is easy to climb and affords an excellent* view from the top.

Abu Gurab, Abu Roash, *Abusir, **Cairo, *Dahshur,** **Giza, Helwan,** *Memphis, **Western Desert** and **Zawiyet el-Aryan**: see separate entries.

Sau
See Sais

Sebennytus
See under Behbeit el-Hagara

Sebwa
See Wadi el-Sebwa

Sharm el-Sheikh
See under Sinai

Sheikh Abd el-Qurna
See under Thebes

Sidi Abd el-Rahman
See under El-Alamein

Silsila

Upper Egypt. – Governorate: Aswan.
ⓘ **Tourist Information Office,**
Tourist Bazaar,
Aswan;
tel. 32 97.

ACCESS. – Road from Kom Ombo (12½ miles/20 km S) or rail to Kagug Station.

Some **12½ miles/20 km N of Kom Ombo the hills come close to the river in Gebel Silsila ("chain of** hills"), forming a defile with many eddies and shallows, long a place of worship of the god of the Nile.

On the E bank of the river, 4 miles/6 km below the narrowest point, are the large **Silsila quarries**, worked particularly under the New Kingdom. In the reign of Ramesses II some 3000 workers were employed here in quarrying stone for the Ramesseum alone; and an inscription of Amenophis III records the transport of stone on the Nile for a Temple of Ptah. At the N end of Gebel Silsila are the scanty remains of the ancient town of *Khenit* and its temple (fragments of inscriptions in the name of Ramesses II). Near the river are the ruins of modern quarry-workers' houses. To the E, high up on the N side of the rock, is a *Stela of Amenophis IV* (numbered 37) recording that he had caused an obelisk for the Temple of the Sun at Karnak to be quarried here. To the right, lower down, are prehistoric rock-engravings, and at the foot of the hill are a number of small rock-cut tombs.

Following the hills S, we come first to a large cave facing W formed by quarrying, with pillars left to support the roof. Beyond this are a small empty quarry and, higher up, a huge unfinished *Sphinx* (no. 40). Then comes a larger quarry, on the N-facing wall of which are incised pylons, indicating that stone for a temple pylon was quarried here. A modern inscription records that stone from this quarry was used in the construction of the Esna Dam in 1906–09. At the entrances to other quarries are inscriptions in the name of Sethos I. The largest of the quarries, to the S, is now closed by a railing. On the N side of its narrow entrance is an engraving of an obelisk.

To see the more important monuments, which are on the W bank, take the ferry across the river and turn N. The well-beaten track runs along the Nile, past tomb-recesses and memorial inscriptions and through quarries, to a **Rock Chapel**, built during the reign of Horemheb (18th Dynasty) and adorned in subsequent centuries with reliefs and inscriptions, some of them of high artistic quality and great historical interest, in honor of kings and high dignitaries. The façade, with five doorways separated by pillars of varying width, is topped by a torus and cavetto cornice. On the lintel of the central doorway, now the only entrance to the chapel, are a winged solar disc and the names of Horemheb. The interior consists of a wide but shallow vaulted hall, to the rear of which is a smaller oblong chamber. All the walls are covered with reliefs and inscriptions.

On the left-hand end wall is a fine relief of a goddess offering the breast to King Horemheb. Behind her is the god Khnum, behind the King Amun-Re.

On the rear wall is * *Horemheb's triumphal procession* after his Nubian campaign. The Pharaoh, seated on his throne, is borne by 12 soldiers adorned with feathers. He is preceded and followed by a soldier with a long-handled fan. In front is a priest, offering incense, with a train of captured Nubians and three rows of soldiers, including a trumpeter. To the left are the King and Amun, standing on prostrate Negroes (Kushites). Under the main scene is a niche, to the left of which are Negro prisoners, to the right Egyptian soldiers marching off fettered captives. The "barbarians" are depicted in a free style, without the usual stiffness of Egyptian drawing. Poetic inscriptions above both reliefs extol the King as victor over the people of Kush: "Hail to thee, king of Egypt: thy name is great in the land of the Nubians. . . ."

To the right is a niche with the full-face figure, in high relief, of Khai, an official under Ramesses II. Above is an inscription with a representation of King Siptah bringing flowers to Amun, while an official named Bai stands behind him with a *flabellum* (fan); below, Horemheb shooting arrows at an enemy. – Then follows a stela dated in the 2nd year of King Merneptah depicting the King presenting an image of the goddess Maat to Amun-Re and Mut; behind him are Queen Astnefert with the sistrum and his Vizier Penehsi with a flabellum. – In the next niche is a high-relief figure of a man holding his left hand in front of his breast. – Then a stela commemorating Ramesses II's 4th Jubilee, set up by his son Khamweset. To the right of the doorway into the rear chamber is a similar inscription by Khamweset. – Small relief figure of a man named Moi praying. – Niche with a large figure of Khamweset in high relief. – Badly damaged figure of Khamweset receiving votive offerings. – Stele commemorating Ramesses II's Jubilee, set up by his Fan-bearer Moi, who is depicted kneeling on the left; above, Ramesses II presenting an image of Justice to Amun, Harakhty, Maat, Ptah and Sobek, the local god of Silsila. – Relief of a Vizier; below, a representation of a column with a palm capital. – Stela dedicated in the 45th year of Ramesses II's reign by a high official, who is depicted kneeling below, with a flabellum; above, the King offering an image of Justice to Amun, Mut, Khons, Harakhty and Sobek (head destroyed). – At the end of the wall, three men praying.

In the right-hand end wall is a niche with six figures in high relief. – There are also many memorial inscriptions at the N end of the entrance wall and on the pillars between the doorways. On the left-hand wall of the doorway into the inner chamber Horemheb is depicted making offerings to the sun god Harakhty and the goddess Eusos of Heliopolis; on the right-hand wall he is in the presence of Amun and Mut.

On the side walls of the inner chamber are representations of various deities. In the rear wall is a niche containing seven badly damaged *seated figures of gods* (in the middle Amun).

The road continues S along the banks of the Nile, passing old quarries which were probably worked in Roman times, *rock* inscriptions and **funerary niches**. – On the next rock, on the side facing the river, are three inscriptions: to the left Ramesses III before Amun, Mut and Khons; in the middle Sheshonq I is conducted by the goddess Mut into the presence of Amun, Harakhty and Ptah, with his son Yewpet, High Priest of Amun-Re and General-in-Chief, behind him; to the right Ramesses IX praying before Amun, Mut, Khons and Sobek.

Beyond this is a niche with a painted ceiling, on the left-hand side of which, praying, is a clerk of the treasury named Tuthmosis. Another niche with a ceiling finely painted in spiral patterns bears on the lintel the names of Tuthmosis III and Hatshepsut (destroyed).

Farther on, close to the river, are three other niches. The one farthest to the right (N) has a fine relief on the left-hand wall depicting the dead man, Nekhetmin, Royal Scribe and Overseer of the Granaries of the South and the North, seated at table with another man; on the right-hand wall are three seated figures. – The niche next to this has fine reliefs with well-preserved colors: rear wall, Amenemhet, Priest of Amun, with servants bringing in food and drink; side walls, Amenemhet and his wife Mimi, etc.

Continuing along the river for another 15 minutes, we come to the *southern group of monuments,* of which there is a picturesque *view from the bank of the river. The main feature is two large *funerary niches* (cenotaphs), some 6½ ft/2 m deep, lying close together. The entrances are flanked by cluster-columns supporting an architrave with a cavetto cornice and royal cobras. The one on the right dates from the 1st year of Merneptah's reign, the other from the 1st year of Ramesses II. The reliefs are well preserved only on the rear walls of these niches; they depict the King making offerings to Harakhty, Ptah and the god of the Nile (on the right) and to Amun, Mut and Khons (on the left); below are a long hymn to the Nile and lists of offerings to be made to the river god. Between the two niches is a door-shaped stela dedicated by the Vizier Penehsi to Merneptah and depicting the King presenting an image of the goddess Maat to Amun. Farther S is a similar inscription dedicated to Merneptah by Roi, a Priest of Amun.

On a curiously shaped sandstone rock to the right is a *stela* of the 6th year of Ramesses III's reign depicting the King making offerings to Amun, Harakhty and the god of the Nile. On the same rock, to the left, is the figure of a priest adoring the names of Sethos I. – A few paces farther S, lower down, is a third niche, badly damaged, dating from the reign of Sethos I. On the river-bank are the remains of ancient steps leading down to the river.

**Aswan, *Edfu and *Kom Ombo: see separate entries.

Sinai

Sinai Frontier District.
Area: 18,900 sq. miles/49,000 sq. km (peninsula proper 9650 sq. miles/25,000 sq. km).
Altitude: sea-level to 8668 ft/2642 m.
Population: 180,000.

ACCESS. – By road from Ismailia or Suez. – By air to Mount Sinai Airport; scheduled services from Cairo and (until further notice) from Israel.

The *Sinai Peninsula, bounded on the W by the Gulf of Suez, on the S by the Red Sea and on the E and SE by the Gulf of Aqaba (Eilat), is generally thought of as forming part of Asia. With an area of some 9650 sq. miles/25,000 sq. km, it is roughly the same size as Sicily. Together with the strip of territory to the N extending along the Mediterranean from the Suez Canal to the Israeli frontier it forms the Sinai Frontier District, with a total area of almost 19,300 sq. miles/50,000 sq. km. Sinai is a scantily populated region consisting mainly of steppe and desert, with cultivable land only in the northern coastal strip and a few small oases; but its rugged mountain country, with its picturesque rock scenery, remote valleys and magnificent and constantly changing views, forms one of the most spectacular and impressive landscapes in Egypt.

Northern Sinai is an undulating tableland of Cretaceous and Tertiary limestones and sandstones, rising gradually from N to S and reaching heights of about 3900 ft/ 1200 m in the *Gebel el-Tih* Range, which is dissected by the widely ramifying (and at certain points cultivable) *Wadi el-Arish.* The southern part of the peninsula is

Gebel Musa, the Mount of Moses, in Sinai ▶

Bedouin camp in the Sinai Peninsula

occupied by the great massif of **Mount Sinai**, built up of archaic crystalline rocks (gneiss, granite, porphyry, metamorphic schists). Its highest peaks, *Gebel Katerin* (8668 ft/2642 m), *Gebel Musa* (7497 ft/ 2285 m) and *Gebel Serbal* (6749 ft/2057 m), reach up almost to the line of eternal snow and ice. – Throughout their long geological history these majestic peaks have escaped all tectonic change, though in the course of millions of years the Red Sea coast along the foot of the massif has acquired a broad fringe of coral reefs, which are still continuing to grow.

The Sinai Frontier District has a population of some 180,000, including an estimated 50,000 bedouin, some of whom are said to be descended from the 200 Roman and Egyptian slaves presented to St Catherine's Monastery by its founder, the Emperor Justinian. – The major settlements in Sinai are on its coasts: in the N *El-Arish* and *Gaza* on the Mediterranean and the ports of *Suez* and *El-Tor* on the Gulf of Suez, in the extreme S *Sharm el-Sheikh* (Ras Nasrany) and, at the N end of the Gulf of Aqaba, the Jordanian port of *Aqaba* and the Israeli holiday resort of *Eilat* (Elat).

The mineral resources of this inhospitable region, which include manganese, copper and phosphates, have recently been substantially augmented by the discovery of large reserves of oil and natural gas on the W side of the peninsula.

HISTORY. – From the earliest times (7000–3300 B.C.) nomadic peoples ranged over the Sinai Peninsula, and the northern coastal strip was already of the greatest importance in Pre-Dynastic times as a link between Egypt and Palestine or Syria and a major commercial and military route (the later Via Maris of the Romans) along the Mediterranean. – The copper of western Sinai was already much sought after by the Pharaohs of the 1st Dynasty, and in later periods was frequently the occasion of bloody conflicts with the bedouin. Malachite and turquoise mined in Sinai filled the treasuries of Memphis. The peninsula also enjoyed

great religious veneration in ancient Egypt: here, it was believed, Isis had sought the corpse of her husband Osiris; and Hathor was known as the "Mistress of Sinai".

The "Sinai Inscriptions" – more than 30 rock inscriptions in a Cananaean script which was a forerunner of our present alphabetic script – were found in the old malachite-mines of the Wadi Maghara and the ruins of the Temple of Hathor at Serabit el-Khadim in 1868 and from 1927 onwards. The mines are now, with a few exceptions, totally worked out.

We lack precise evidence on the Sinai of the Old Testament. It has not been possible to establish exactly where the Israelites crossed the Red Sea, nor is it certain that the Mount Horeb on which Moses received the Tables of the Law was really Mount Sinai: there are good reasons for believing that this lay E of the Gulf of Aqaba. – Pilgrimages to Sinai, as one of the holy places of the Old Testament, are attested from the 3rd c. Veneration for this area led many hermits and monks to settle in southern Sinai, forming communities and living lives of great poverty and sanctity. They were exposed to bloody raids by Saracens, and it was to provide protection against these attacks that, in the mid 6th c., Justinian built a fortified monastery with a church dedicated to the Virgin, in the immediate vicinity of the legendary site of Moses's burning bush.

Although the Crusades ravaged much of Sinai, in particular the coastal towns, the holy places on Mount Sinai remained undisturbed. After several rebuildings and enlargements Justinian's monastery was dedicated in the 12th c. to St Catherine of Alexandria, a Saint much venerated by the Orthodox Church. Legend asserts that after her martyrdom her body was deposited on the hill named after her, Gebel Katerin. Muslim pilgrims on their way to Mecca also visited the holy place, receiving hospitality in the monastery, in which a small mosque was built for their use.

During the recurrent wars between Egypt and the State of Israel part of the Sinai Peninsula was occupied by the Israelis in 1948 and the whole of it in 1956 and 1968 (the Six Day War). The Camp David Agreements of 1979 provided for the phased return of the peninsula to Egypt, and the process was completed in 1982.

The main center of attraction in the Sinai Peninsula is ** **St Catherine's Monastery** (see separate entry), where there is now an airport (Mount Sinai Airport) served by scheduled flights from Cairo and (until further notice) from Israel. A longer and more strenuous but very rewarding route is by road from Suez, following the line of an old caravan route.

From Suez to St Catherine's Monastery

Distance: about 185 miles/300 km.
Sufficient food, water and gasoline (petrol) should be taken, since there are very limited facilities for obtaining them *en route*.
It is essential to have a cross-country vehicle.

The road runs N from Suez and at El-Kubri crosses to the E side of the Suez Canal through the **Ahmed Hamdi Tunnel**. – 15 miles/24 km: *Port Taufiq*. – 22 miles/35 km: side road on right to the Springs of Moses (see under Suez). The main road then crosses the *Wadi el-Iran* and runs through flat country, with fine views – to the right over the Gulf of Suez to the Ataqa Hills, to the left of Gebel el-Raha and later Gebel el-Tih. – 42 miles/68 km: *Ras el-Sudr* (oil). – 48 miles/77 km: the road crosses the *Wadi Werdan*. Between here and the sea are very productive oilfields. – 65 miles/105 km: **Wadi Gharandal**, a valley flanked by steep rock walls, with a number of springs which have an abundant flow after rain and give rise to a small oasis. The water is not drinkable.

In 12½ miles/20 km the road skirts **Gebel Hammam Faraun** ("Mountain of Pharaoh's Bath"; 1568 ft/478 m), which has the shape of a truncated pyramid. On the rugged slopes facing the sea are seven hot sulphur springs, which the bedouin believe to be good for the treatment of rheumatism. – 83 miles/134 km: **Abu Zenima** (rest-house, with overnight accommodation; gasoline (petrol) station), an industrial town (oil, magnesium) and the most considerable place on the W coast of Sinai. Some 5 miles/8 km S of the town is the site of the ancient Egyptian port of *Magara*, attested from about 1500 B.C., from which the copper and turquoise of the nearby mines were shipped. Some remains of the ancient town have been excavated. – 91 miles/147 km: *Abu Rudeis*, a settlement founded by an oil company for workers in the local oilfield, with a military camp.

From Abu Rudeis an ancient track runs 15 miles/25 km E into the hills to the *turquoise-mines of Magara. This is a rewarding excursion which should not be omitted.

As early as the 1st Dynasty these mines were of great importance to the Pharaohs and were worked by their agents. The reliefs and inscriptions on stelae and on the rock faces have yielded valuable information about ancient Egyptian mining techniques. Among the scenes depicted are the subjugation of the local tribe, the Mentu, and the procurement of the necessary supplies for the mine-workers. The Pharaoh, depicted on a large scale, is seen holding the defeated natives by the hair and raising his weapon to smite them. There are representations of offerings being presented and references in the inscriptions to festivals and visits by highly placed mine inspectors. The earliest King mentioned is Sneferu, first ruler of the 4th Dynasty, who is followed by Khufu or Cheops (also 4th Dynasty) and various kings of the 5th and 6th Dynasties. There is also a stela bearing the name of Ramesses II.

The brown and brick-red sides of the valley rise steeply to a considerable height; some of the slopes are sandstone, others are granite. In the sandstone rocks on the NW side of the valley the entrances to the mine-shafts are some 150 ft/45 m above the valley bottom. The shafts run far into the rock; of some width at the mouth, they become steadily narrower as they go in. Every now and then pillars are left for the support of the roof. The ancient chisel-marks are still visible. At many points in the reddish stone can be seen small bluish-green turquoises, which can be extracted with a penknife; they are impure and of little value, and their color usually fades after a few years. – From the mouth of the shaft there is a view of a hill some 200 ft/60 m high on which are the remains of a fort, workshops and small workers' houses of the Pharaonic period. On the top of the hill a variety of flint implements lie around,

particularly pointed instruments which may have been used for incising inscriptions.

Beyond the junction of the *Wadi Sidri* with the Wadi Magara the track turns S towards the wide *Wadi Moqattab*, the "Valley of Inscriptions". On the W side of this valley is *Gebel Moqattab* (2379 ft/725 m), at the foot of which are numbers of sandstone blocks, many of them bearing inscriptions – the "Sinaitic Inscriptions" – in Nabataean, Greek and, more rarely, Coptic and Arabic script, scratched by passing travelers of the 1st–6th c. A.D. – The track continues through the Wadi Moqattab to join (26 miles/42 km from Abu Rudeis) the track into the Wadi Feiran.

The still larger turquoise-mines of **Serabit el-Khadim** lie farther N in a side valley of the Wadi Sidri and are also approached by a difficult hill track. They were of such importance in ancient times that during the 12th Dynasty a Temple of Hathor, "Mistress of the Turquoises", was built there (discovered by Carsten Niebuhr in 1762, excavated by Flinders Petrie in 1904. Here were found some 400 inscriptions, some of them written in a proto-Cananaean script similar to that of the Wadi Magara inscriptions; the importance of this script in the development of our modern alphabetic scripts is still matter for scholarly argument.

From Abu Rudeis the coast road continues S. – 111 miles/179 km: track on left (mostly very poor) which follows the **Wadi Feiran**, through magnificent mountain scenery, to St Catherine's Monastery. – The Wadi Feiran, the largest valley in the Sinai Peninsula, runs down from the foot of Gebel Serbal, above the Feiran Oasis. The lowest section is relatively wide; farther up the valley the granite walls flanking it draw close together at some points and then open out again. The rock – gray, with veins of reddish-brown porphyry and black diorite – is shaped into picturesque forms, and the scenery, set against the backdrop of the great bare peaks to the S, is of striking magnificence. – 125 miles/201 km: junction with a track from Abu Rudeis through the Wadi Sidri (turquoise-mines) and Wadi Moqattab. – 144 miles/231 km: *Feiran Oasis, the "pearl of Sinai", which is by far the most fertile area in the whole peninsula. Here palms, maize and corn are grown, and there are large numbers of tamarisks, the trees which are believed to have supplied the manna of the Bible.

The Feiran Oasis is referred to by Eusebius (4th c. A.D.) as the scene of the Israelites' battle with the Amalekites

Wadi Feiran

Pharaoh's Island in the Gulf of Aqaba, with its Crusader castle

(Rephidim; Exodus 17: 8). The Greek geographer Ptolemy (2nd c. A.D.) mentions the town of *Pharan*, which later became the see of a bishop and a great center of hermit life. Both here and on the rocky slopes of Gebel Serbal are remains of old monasteries and hermits' cells. There is evidence that in the 4th c. the town was governed by a senate. About A.D. 400 the name of the Bishop is given as Nathyr; the Council of Chalcedon raised the see to the status of an archbishopric; and in 454 one Macarius is referred to as Bishop of Pharan. The well-defended oasis town was left undisturbed by the Blemmyes and Saracens, although it was required to pay tribute to them. Theoretically within the Roman Empire, it was in practice controlled by the Saracen Princes, one of whom, Abocharagor, presented it to Justinian, who thereupon made him Phylarch (Governor) of the Palestinian Saracens. Early in the 5th c. the monks of Pharan fell into heresy and were censured by Orthodox councils and Emperors as Monothelites and Monophysites.

Half-way up Gebel Musa, probably on the site of the present Chapel of St Elias, Justinian (527–565) founded a church dedicated to the Virgin, and at the foot of the mountain, where St Catherine's Monastery now stands, he built a strong fortress. It was no doubt the protection afforded by this fortress that gradually drew the hermits, and with them all the Christian legends, from Gebel Serbal to Gebel Musa. – The

spread of Islam finally put an end to monastic life in this area.

A few miles beyond the Feiran Oasis the track turns into the *Wadi el-Sheikh.* – 169 miles/272 km: *Watiya Pass* (4023 ft/1226 m), flanked by majestic granite peaks. In the valley beyond the pass is the *Tomb of Nebi Salih,* a prophet mentioned in the Koran and much venerated by the bedouin, of whom it is reported that as proof of his divine mission he conjured a camel out of the rock and caused the Thamudites to be killed by a thunderstorm when they remained unbelieving and hamstrung the camel. Here annual festivals are celebrated – a minor one after the date harvest and a major one in May – which reach their climax with the making of offerings on Gebel Musa. – 177 miles/285 km: side road (last section asphalted) to the Mount Sinai Airport, the starting-point of the conducted visit to St Catherine's Monastery. It is not permitted to drive up to the monastery.

Beyond the Wadi Feiran track the coast road continues SE through desert country to the little port of **El-Tor**, the ancient *Raithu* (168 miles/271 km; lighthouse; offshore oil installations), and the southern tip of the peninsula, where (215 miles/346 km) a track branches off on the right and comes in 14 miles/23 km to the southernmost point, **Ras Muhammad**, from which there is a superb** view of the Red Sea, the two gulfs opening off its northern end and the mountains along their shores, with Saudi Arabia to the E.

Beyond the turn-off for Ras Muhammad the road continues to **Sharm el-Sheikh** (231 miles/371 km), recently renamed *Ras Nasrany*, a port and military base, with a beautiful beach, and then runs N through the hills bordering the E coast to the seaside resorts of *Nuweiba* and *Neviot* (339 miles/545 km). It then continues along the coast to the **Israeli frontier** SW of Eilat.

A few miles before the frontier, off the coast in the Gulf of Aqaba, lies the islet of *Geziret el-Faraun (Pharaoh's Island), a granite rock fringed by coral measuring 350 yds/320 m by 165 yds/150 m. On the S side is a small sheltered harbor, identified by some authorities with the Old Testament port of *Eziongeber*. The island seems to have been inhabited under the 20th Dynasty and to have acquired some importance as a port for the shipment of copper from the Wadi Araba and the Wadi Timna (now in Israel). It is crowned by the conspicuous ruins of a *Crusader castle*.

El-Arish, Gaza, Ismailia, Port Said, Red Sea, **St Catherine's Monastery (with Gebel Katerin and Gebel Musa), **Suez** and ****Suez Canal**: see separate entries.

Siwa Oasis

North-West Frontier District.
Population: 5500.

ACCESS. – Reached from Mersa Matruh. Special authorization and permission to spend the night must be obtained from the Governor in Mersa Matruh or the Frontier Corps in Cairo. Travel in convoy of at least two vehicles obligatory; sufficient supplies of gasoline (petrol) and water must be carried; guide advisable. – The desert track follows the caravan route used by Alexander the Great, through the *Wadi el-Raml* to *Bir Goaiferi*, then over the *Kanayis Pass* and past a number of wells to *Ras el-Hamraya* and *Siwa*. – Another caravan route, now little used, runs from Cairo via *Abu Roash* to the *Monastery of St Macarius* in the *Wadi Natrun*, then W to the uninhabited *Moghara Depression*, and from there by way of the small oasis of *El-Qara* (Qaret Umm el-Zughayyar), which has a population of some 60, to Siwa. – From Alexandria a caravan route runs SW via Abu Mena to *Moghara*, where it joins the track from Cairo.

The Oasis of *Siwa, lying in latitude 29° 12′ N and longitude 25° 20′ E in a wide depression in the Western Desert, 65 ft/20 m below sea-level, is the most westerly of the Egyptian oases. Thanks to its remote and isolated situation it has preserved many old customs and characteristics.

Siwa is an attractive island of green under a sky that is always cloudless. The inhabitants are Berbers, with a mingling of bedouin and Sudanese slaves acquired in the course of the centuries. They speak their own Berber dialect, and usually

Arabic as well. The oasis owes its fertility to its 200 or so springs, 80 of which are used for irrigation; in ancient times there were said to be a thousand springs. The main crops grown in the oasis are dates (200,000 palms), olives (50,000 trees) and citrus fruits, with some wine.

In 331 B.C. *Alexander the Great* traveled to Siwa – the first King of Egypt to do so – and was received as the son of Zeus-Amun and crowned with the ram's horn crown.

The chief place in the oasis is the little town of **Siwa** (pop. 5000), perched on a rocky hill. The ancient town was 2 miles/3 km W, at the village of *Aghurmi* (pop. 350); only a few remains survive, apart from the conspicuous and well-preserved Temple of Amasis (26th Dynasty), the presumed site of the oracle consulted by Alexander the Great. – Near by, at *Umm el-Ebeida*, are the remains of a Temple of Nectanebo II. At *Qaret el-Musabberin* (Gebel el-Mota) are rock tombs of the 26th–30th Dynasties, with interesting reliefs.

Mersa Matruh, Qattara Depression and **Western Desert**: see separate entries.

Sohag

Upper Egypt. – Governorate: Sohag.
Population: 50,000.

ACCESS. – By road (the main Nile Valley road) from Cairo (292 miles/470 km N). – Railway station.

The provincial capital of Sohag lies on the W bank of the Nile, here spanned by a large bridge (one section of which is a swing bridge), at the point where the Sohagiya Canal branches off the river.

Sohag has cotton-weaving factories and other textile industries, a busy *bazaar*, several mosques of no particular interest

White Monastery Deir el-Abyad

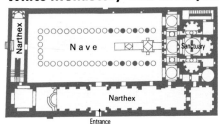

and a large Coptic **Cathedral** of the early 20th c.

SURROUNDINGS of Sohag. – Some 15 miles/25 km NNW of the town, on the edge of the desert hills, is the ancient *White Monastery (*Deir el-Abyad*), also known as *Deir Amba Shenuda* after its most notable Abbot, Shenute.

The monastery, centered on the **church** (built 440), is surrounded by a high *wall* of white limestone blocks which gives it something of the aspect of a fortress. The wall and the entrance gateway on the S side have the cavetto cornice familiar in Egyptian temples. The church, entered through a narthex with an apse at the W end, is an aisled basilica with a trilobate sanctuary, consisting of a square domed central area and three apses with semi-domes. In the sanctuary and the nave are columns from the nearby ancient city of Atrepe (Athribis). The apses have two rows of five niches alternating with columns. Some of the ceiling-paintings are well preserved. – At the W end of the church is a second narthex with a pillared apse at the N end. The many treasures once contained in the monastery library are now in European collections.

Red Monastery   Deir el-Ahmar

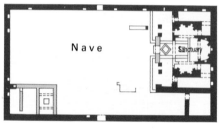

Nave   Sanctuary

4 miles/6 km W of the White Monastery is the **Red Monastery** (*Deir el-Ahmar*), also known as *Deir Abu Bshoi,* now enclosed on two sides by modern buildings. The *church*, built at the same time as the White Monastery, was originally an aisled basilica with finely carved capitals. The sanctuary has apses, columns and poorly preserved ceiling-paintings.

Opposite Sohag on the E bank of the Nile is **Akhmim** (see that entry).

Sollum
See under Mersa Matruh

Speos Artemidos
See under Beni Hasan

Suez/El-Suweis

Lower Egypt. – Governorate: Suez.
Population: 380,000 (including Port Taufiq).
ⓘ **Tourist Information Office,**
   Port Taufiq;
   tel. 2 11 41.

HOTELS. – *Red Sea,* II, 54 b.; *White House,* III, 84 b.; *Beau Rivage,* III, 32 b.; *Summer Palace,* III, 31 b.; *Misr Palace,* IV, 101 b.

ACCESS. – Good road from Cairo (83 miles/134 km W), running across the Eastern Desert, with the oil pipeline on its N side. The railway line runs parallel to the road 5 miles/8 km N.

The provincial capital of Suez (Arabic El-Suweis), which was badly damaged and for a time almost completely evacuated during the war with Israel in 1967, is beautifully situated at the S end of the Suez Canal, which here projects into the shallow northern waters of the Gulf of Suez, and of the southern branch of the Ismailia Canal coming from Ismailia. Reconstruction is still continuing on a considerable scale, with financial assistance from Saudi Arabia. Part of the Suez Canal University is found here.

The town, founded in the 15th c. on the site of ancient *Clysma,* was a modest little township, a staging-point for pilgrims traveling to Mecca, until the construction of the Suez Canal, which gave it great importance as a transit port in the trade with East Asia and in passenger traffic, particularly to and from Mecca. It is now mainly an industrial city, with oil-refineries, petrochemical and ironworking industries and factories producing artificial fertilizers. It has no particular features of interest for the tourist. It is planned to rebuild the Museum of Antiquities, which was destroyed during the Six Day War; it contained material from the area around the Suez Canal.

SE of the old town are the more modern quarters, built on land reclaimed from the sea. To the SW lies the industrial zone. – To the N of the city is the *Kom el-Kolzum,* a mound of rubble which probably marks the site of the Graeco-Roman town of Clysma and a still earlier settlement.

Farther N the Ismailia Canal flows into the Gulf of Suez. Its water-level is $6\frac{1}{2}$ ft/2 m higher than that of the Red Sea, the difference in level being accommodated by a lock. On either side of the canal are luxuriant gardens.

Since the Gulf of Suez ends in a shoal at its northern end which is dry at low tide a channel 2 miles/3 km long was cut to bring the entrance to the Suez Canal to the edge of deeper water. A stone causeway 50 ft/15 m wide connects the town with

Port Taufiq, at the mouth of the Suez Canal

the island of **Port Taufiq** (*Bur Taufiq*), created by the accumulation of the great masses of soil dredged out of the sea. On the SW side of the islands are the port installations of *Port Ibrahim.*

SURROUNDINGS of Suez. – Some 12½ miles/20 km SW of the town, bounded on the S by the *Ras el-Adabiya,* is **Adabiya Bay**, where new port installations are under construction. – Half way there is the beach of *Cabanon.*

7 miles/11 km SE of the town, on the E side of the gulf, are the **Springs of Moses** (*Ain Musa*), a group of hot springs (70–84 °F/21–29 °C), some sweet and some bitter, which form a small fertile oasis. One of the springs is said to be the bitter spring of Marah which Moses made sweet by casting a tree into it (Exodus 15: 23 ff.). From this side of the gulf there are fine [*] views of the sea and the heights of the Gebel Ataqa Range to the W.

From Suez down the W side of the Red Sea to *Ain Sukhna,* [*]**Hurghada, Quseir** and **Berenice:** see under Red Sea (and entries for *Hurghada, Quseir* and *Berenice*).

Eastern Desert, Ismailia, Red Sea,[*] **St Antony's Monastery,** [*]**St Catherine's Monastery,** [*]**St Paul's Monastery,**[*] **Sinai** and[**] **Suez Canal:** see separate entries.

Suez Canal/Kanat el-Suweis

Lower Egypt and Sinai.
Governorates: Port Said, Ismailia and Suez;
Sinai Frontier District.

(i) Tourist Information Office,
Port Taufiq,
Suez;
tel. 2 35 89.
Shari Palestina,
Port Said;
tel. 31 00.

ACCESS. – By road from Cairo to Suez (83 miles/134 km) or Ismailia (75 miles/120 km). – By rail from Cairo to Suez or from Alexandria via Tanta and el-Zagazig to Ismailia.

The[**] **Suez Canal (Arabic Kanat el-Suweis), which cuts through the 70 mile/112 km wide isthmus between the great land masses of Africa and Asia, links the Mediterranean with the Red Sea and thus opens up the longer route between the North Atlantic and the Indian Ocean.**

HISTORY. – The idea of cutting a channel through this neck of land goes back a very long way. The earliest authenticated attempt to connect the Red Sea with the Nile, and thus with the Mediterranean, was made by the Pharaoh *Necho* about 600 B.C. The canal he began was completed a century later by *Darius* (522–486 B.C.). It broadly followed the line of the present Ismailia Canal, which runs through the Wadi el-Tumilat from Cairo to Ismailia. To commemorate the completion of the great work Darius set up stelae

The Suez Canal

alongside the canal, and remains of some of these have been found.

By the 1st c. B.C. the canal had fallen into disrepair, and *Trajan* (A.D. 98–117) seems to have restored it about A.D. 100: at any rate a waterway from near Cairo to the Gulf of Suez, the exact course of which cannot be determined but which probably followed the line of the old canal for at least part of the way, was known as *Amnis Traianus* ("Trajan's River"). Later the Arabs used the canal for the transport of goods between their capital, Fustat, and the Arabian Peninsula. – From the 8th c. the canal again fell into disrepair, and all later plans for cutting a new canal fell through; while a miscalculation by Napoleon's engineer Lepère, who estimated the Red Sea to be some 33 ft/10 m higher than the Mediterranean – both seas are in fact about the same level – threw doubt on the feasibility of the whole enterprise.

The practicability of constructing a canal was demonstrated by *Ferdinand de Lesseps* (1805–94), who came to Cairo in 1836 as a young French diplomat and had his attention drawn to Lepère's memoir on the subject. Exact measurements in 1841 and 1847 by Linant Bey, the Government Water Engineer, Robert Stephenson (son of the inventor Robert Stephenson), the Austrian Alois von Negrelli and the Frenchman Bourdaloue finally disproved Lepère's calculations, and in 1854 Lesseps submitted a carefully considered plan to the then Viceroy, Said, who formally granted permission to begin the work on January 5, 1856.

As a result of difficulties thrown in the way of the enterprise by the British Government and other obstacles there was some delay in raising the necessary capital, and work was begun only on April 25, 1859. Subsequently the Viceroy made more money available and provided 25,000 workmen, to be paid at modest rates and relieved every three months. Until the completion of the Ismailia Canal even the supply of water, which had to be transported on camels, was a considerable undertaking. From 1864 onwards, however, the number of native laborers was reduced, skilled European workers were brought in and increased use was made of modern machinery.

On March 18, 1869 the water of the Mediterranean was at last allowed to flow into the nearly dry, salt-encrusted basins of the Bitter Lakes, the northern parts of which lay 25–40 ft/8–12 m below sea-level; the southern parts required extensive dredging. The canal

was finally opened with great pomp and circumstance on November 17, 1869.

The cost of constructing the canal, about £19 million, was raised by the issue of shares, most of which were held in the early years by the British, French and Egyptian Governments. Ownership of the canal, until its sudden nationalization by President Nasser in 1956 (instead of the previously planned date of 1968), was vested in the Compagnie Universelle du Canal Maritime de Suez (Suez Canal Company).

The Suez Canal is now under exclusively Egyptian sovereignty and ownership. A declaration by the Egyptian Government in 1957 transferred to the State all the obligations of the old Suez Canal Company, which stemmed mainly from the Convention of Constantinople of 1888. This provided that the canal should be a neutral zone through which merchant ships and warships of all nations had the right of free passage both in peace and in war.

As a result of the war between Egypt and Israel the canal was blocked by wrecks from 1967 to 1975. The resultant lengthening of the route between the Indian and Atlantic oceans led to the building of huge tankers and other vessels which were too large to pass through the canal after its reopening in 1975. It is hoped to counter the threatened reduction in the canal's importance to international sea traffic by widening and deepening operations during the 1980s.

The Suez Canal, which has no locks at any point in its course, has a total length of 106 miles/171 km including the piers projecting into the Mediterranean and the shallow Gulf of Suez. Its depth, originally 26 ft/8 m, is now 36–49 ft/11–15 m, its width 310–460 ft/95–140 m (on the bottom 150–260 ft/45–80 m). Ships pass through the canal in convoys of 20 or more. There are passing-places at intervals of 6 miles/10 km, and there is also room for two-way traffic on **Lake Timsah** ("Crocodile Lake"), roughly half-way along the canal, and in the **Great** and **Little Bitter Lakes**.

At the N end of the canal lies the important port of **Port Said** (*Bur Said*: see separate entry). At the S end is the attractively situated town of **Suez** (*El-Suweis*: see separate entry), which suffered severe damage during the war with Israel, with the oil and industrial port of **Port Taufiq** (*Bur Taufiq*: see under Suez) on the opposite bank of the canal.

About half-way between Port Said and Suez, on the N side of Lake Timsah, is the town of **Ismailia** (see that entry), built during the construction of the canal as the base and starting-point of the whole huge operation.

There is no permanent bridge over the Suez Canal. The first regular link between the Delta and the Sinai Peninsula was provided by the opening of the **Ahmed Hamdi Tunnel**, 7½ miles/12 km N of Suez, at the end of 1980. A joint Egyptian and British enterprise, this is a road tunnel 1¾ miles/2·8 km long, passing under the canal at a depth of up to 167 ft/51 m, and which also carries water-mains and power-lines supplying the Sinai Peninsula. It is named after an Egyptian General killed in the October War with Israel in 1973. – A further tunnel is under construction near Ismailia.

The area on both sides of the Suez Canal is to be developed over the next 20 years into one of Egypt's largest industrial zones. The towns of Port Said, Ismailia and Suez are all expected to have populations of over a million by the year 2000 – Port Said and Suez as industrial and commercial cities of international standing, Ismailia as the cultural and administrative center of the region. The basis for this optimism is provided by the established and recently discovered new oilfields on both sides of the Gulf of Suez and the substantial deposits of phosphates, manganese, chromium, tin, wolfram and asbestos along the Red Sea coast.

Through the Suez Canal from Port Said to Suez

The canal, with the railway and road to Ismailia on its W bank, runs in a dead straight line across the E end of Lake Manzala. The section of the lake to the E of the canal and part of the area to the W have been drained. This was once one of the most fertile regions in Egypt, traversed in ancient times by the Pelusiac, Tanitic and Mendesian arms of the Nile. Of the many large settlements here the towns of *Tanis* (see that entry) and *Tennis* were the most important. – 9 miles/14 km: *Ras el-Eish*. – 27 miles/44 km: **El-Qantara**, at the SE end of Lake Manzala. Along the isthmus between Lake Manzala and the Ballah Lakes ("Date Lakes"), now drained, ran the ancient military highway from Egypt to Syria. El-Qantara is the starting-point of the Palestine Railway, constructed during the First World War and now closed. The canal is crossed on a pontoon-bridge.

Some 5 miles/8 km NW of El-Qantara, on the road to El-Arish (see that entry), is *Tell el-Ahmar* ("Red Hill") or *Tell Abu Sefe*, with the ruins of a Temple of Ramesses II and remains of the Graeco-Roman period. – Some 12¼ miles/20 km E, to the N of the road, are two rubble mounds, **Tell el-Farama** and *Tell el-Fadda*, which mark the site of ancient **Pelusium**, the "key to Egypt" and its most easterly port.

31–38 miles/50–61 km: bypass canal (constructed 1949–51), through an area once occupied by the Ballah Lakes. – 43 miles/70 km: *El-Gisr*, a low range of hills (52 ft/16 m) which cuts across the isthmus and was the most serious obstacle encountered during the construction of the canal, calling for the removal of

Offices of the Suez Canal Authority, Ismailia

more than 18 million cu. yds/14 million cu. m of earth. On top of the hill is the abandoned village of *El-Gisr*, with a ruined mosque and a chapel dedicated to the Virgin of the Desert. A flight of steps ascends the hill from the canal. From the top there are extensive *views embracing a large area of the isthmus; to the S are the Gebel Ataqa Hills, to the E and SE the mountains of Sinai.

50 miles/80 km: **Ismailia** (see that entry), at the N end of Lake Timsah ("Crocodile Lake"). Before the construction of the canal the lake (area 6 sq. miles/15 sq. km) was a shallow expanse of brackish water with a dense growth of reeds. The dredged channel is lined by markers. – After leaving Lake Timsah we pass (on right) *Gebel Maryam*, in Arab legend the place where Moses's sister Miriam spent seven days outside the camp of the Israelites when smitten with leprosy for disapproving of her brother's marriage with an Ethiopian woman (Numbers 12). – 54 miles/87 km: *Tusum*, identifiable by the whitewashed dome of a sheikh's tomb. Excavations in this area yielded fossil remains of large animals of the Miocene (Tertiary) era and pieces of fossilized wood. – 57 miles/92 km: cutting through the rocky *Serapeum* ridge. Here one of the stelae marking Darius's canal was found.

61 miles/98 km: the canal enters the shimmering bluish-green waters of the **Bitter Lakes**, which are identified with the Biblical *Marah* (Exodus 15: 23: "And when they came to Marah, they could not drink

The Suez Canal at El-Shallufa

of the waters"). The shores are flat and sandy; to the SW are the hills of the *Gebel Geneifa* Range. The channel and passing-places in the Bitter Lakes are indicated by markers. – 76 miles/121 km: *Kabrit* signal station, at the end of the Great Bitter Lake. The bed of the Little Bitter Lake consists entirely of shelly limestone. – 84 miles/135 km: *Geneifa* signal station, at the end of the Little Bitter Lake. – 90 miles/145 km: *El-Shallufa,* where 46,000 cu. yds/35,000 cu. m of limestone had to be removed during the construction of the canal. The stone, colored reddish brown by iron compounds, contained the fossil teeth and vertebrae of sharks (*Carcharodon megalodon* Ag.), bivalve shells and remains of bryozoans. In the bed of sandstone over the limestone were found crocodiles' teeth and the remains of hippopotamuses and other large quadrupeds. There was one of Darius's stelae at El-Shallufa. – 98 miles/158 km: *El-Kubri,* where the **Ahmed Hamdi Tunnel** runs under the Canal. 1¾ miles/2·8 km long and running at a depth of up to 167 ft/51 m below the bottom of the canal, it accommodates a two-lane carriageway 25 ft/7·5 m wide, pedestrian walkways and power- and water-mains. – 106 miles/170 km: *Port Taufiq,* adjoining **Suez** (see that entry) at the N end of the Gulf of Suez, which at this point is so shallow that, but for the canal, it could be crossed on foot at low tide. Here, too, there are several islands.

Ismailia, Ismailia Canal, Nile Delta, Port Said, Red Sea, *****Sinai** and **Suez**: see separate entries.

Tanis/Djanet

Lower Egypt. – Governorate: Sharqiya.
(i) **Tourist Information Office,**
   Misr Travel Tower,
   Cairo – Abbasia;
   tel. 82 60 16.

ACCESS. – From El-Zagazig 23 miles/37 km NE via Abu Kebir to Faqus, then N via El-Huseiniya to San el-Hagar (total distance 46 miles/74 km).

The remains of ancient* Tanis (Egyptian Djanet, Coptic San, the Zoan of the Old Testament), capital of the Tanite kings of the 21st and 22nd Dynasties and later chief town of the 14th nome of Lower Egypt, lie in the NE of the Delta at the modest village of San el-Hagar, still partly buried under a ridge of hills 2 miles/3·5 km long and 1 mile/1·5 km wide which rises to a height of 115 ft/35 m above the flat and desolate plain bordering Lake Manzala. The excavated remains are the most important and most discussed in the Delta, full of interest for the archaeologically inclined.

The rubble mound of **San el-Hagar** was first investigated in 1825. The first systematic excavations were carried out by Mariette between 1860 and 1880, and

Flinders Petrie worked on the site in 1883–84. Excavation was resumed between 1929 and 1951 under the direction of P. Montet, yielding new finds of the greatest interest.

HISTORY. – The town of *Tanis,* situated on the right bank of the Tanitic arm of the Nile, on the edge of the marshes bordering Lake Manzala (which then reached farther S), was probably founded during the 6th Dynasty. After the fall of the Ramessids and their capital Pi-Ramesse Tanis became the residence of the Kings of the 21st and 22nd Dynasties. The excavations yielded material from almost every period of Egyptian history, but objects from the Ramessid capital founded by Ramesses II were of particularly frequent occurrence, leading Montet to the conclusion that San el-Hagar was actually the site of Ramesses's town. It is now established that after becoming capital Tanis was considerably enlarged and embellished, using stones and architectural elements from other sites, particularly the nearby royal residences of Pi-Ramesse and Avaris. – The site, which covers some 75 acres, has not yet by any means been fully explored, so that further discoveries are still to be expected.

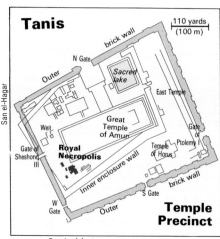

Temple of Anat

THE SITE. – From the road to San el-Hagar a track leads up to the excavation headquarters, from which there is a good general view of the **temple precinct** and the surrounding mounds of rubble.

The most striking feature is a *brick wall* 50 ft/15 m thick, probably with an original height of some 33 ft/10 m, enclosing a trapezoid area 470 yds/430 m by 405 yds/370 m. Within this area was a smaller enclosure built by Psusennes (Pinudjem) I. At the W end, where the two enclosure walls coincide, is a monumental *gateway* built by Sheshonq III. Within the inner enclosure stood the **Great Temple of Amun** built by Ramesses II and rebuilt by Pinudjem I. It was oriented from SW to NE and was some 820 ft/250 m long. The temple is now completely destroyed, leaving only scattered architectural fragments, the most important of which are now in the Egyptian Museum in Cairo.

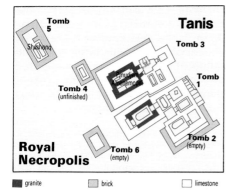

Tanis

Tomb 5
Sheshonq

Tomb 3

Tomb 4 (unfinished)

Tomb 1

Pinudjem / Amenemope

Royal Necropolis

Tomb 6 (empty)

Tomb 2 (empty)

■ granite   ■ brick   □ limestone

The small *East Temple,* built entirely of black granite, is also totally destroyed. The handsome monolithic columns date from the Old Kingdom but bear the cartouches of Ramesses II and Osorkon II. – In the SE corner of the outer enclosure wall are the remains of a small *Temple of Horus* of the 30th Dynasty (Nectanebo II and Ptolemy II Philadelphus).

In the SW corner of the inner enclosure Montet discovered in 1939–40 a *royal necropolis of the 21st and 22nd Dynasties. The tombs were originally vaulted underground chambers, but are now partly above ground.

Tomb 1 is the **Tomb of Osorkon II** (or III?). It has one chamber faced with granite and four faced with limestone, and has sunk reliefs (originally painted in vivid colors) in the style of the royal tombs of Thebes. In a sandstone sarcophagus of the Middle Kingdom was found the mummy of Takelothis II; the mummy of Osorkon III was in a granite sarcophagus, and another sarcophagus contained the mummy of a Prince. – *Tomb 2* was found empty, and contained no indication of its original occupant. – *Tomb 3,* the **Tomb of Pinudjem (Psusennes) I** (21st Dynasty), is the best preserved in the necropolis. The four burials in this tomb were found intact, with grave furnishings of high artistic quality and historical interest. In the antechamber was the silver sarcophagus of Hedjkheperre Sheshonq, now in the Egyptian Museum in Cairo; in the N chamber, faced with granite, was the mummy of Pinudjem, occupying the usurped sarcophagus of Merneptah; and in the S chamber, also granite-clad, was Amenemope. The grave-goods included costly jewelry and ornaments – necklaces, bracelets, pectorals and gold mummy masks. – *Tomb 4* was intended for Amenemope but was left unfinished. – *Tomb 5,* to the W, was the *Tomb of Sheshonq III,* whose massive sarcophagus had been hewn from an architrave of the 13th Dynasty. – *Tomb 6* was found empty and anonymous.

To the SW, outside the outer enclosure wall, was a **Temple of Anat**, a Syrian goddess who was identified with the Egyptian goddess Mut, with her companion the youthful Khons.

SURROUNDINGS of Tanis (San el-Hagar). – 8 miles/ 13 km SE of Tanis is **Tell Nabasha** (also known as *Tell Faraun* and *Tell Bedawi*), a rubble mound which contains the remains of the ancient Egyptian *Yemet.* The site was excavated by Flinders Petrie in 1886, revealing the remains of a temple apparently built by Ramesses II and other Ramessids, using stone from earlier buildings, and a temple dedicated by Amasis to the local goddess Buto. In the cemetery were found Egyptian tombs of the 19th Dynasty and the tombs of Cypriot mercenaries who were stationed here in the reign of Amasis. – SE of the temple precinct are the scanty remains of a town of the Graeco-Roman period.

Some 9 miles/15 km SW of Tell Nabasha, at the villages of *El-Khatana* and *Kantir,* are irregularities in the surface of the otherwise level plain which are thought to mark the sites of the Hyksos capital of Avaris and the Ramessid residence of Pi-Ramesse. This remains to be established by excavation.

Ismailia, El-Mansura, Nile Delta, Port Said and **El-Zagazig**: see separate entries.

Tanta

Lower Egypt. – Governorate: Gharbiya.
Population: 300,000.
ⓘ **Misr Travel,**
Tourist Center;
tel. 22 12.

HOTEL. – *Arafa,* II, 80 b.

ACCESS. – By road or rail from Cairo (57 miles/92 km S), Alexandria (77 miles/124 km NW) or Ismailia (85 miles/136 km E).

Tanta, the lively capital of the Governorate of Gharbiya, within the Rosetta and Damietta arms of the Nile, lies between Cairo and Alexandria in the heart of the Nile Delta. The principal commercial center of the Delta (particularly for cotton), it is also one of the most important traffic junctions in Egypt.

Tanta has cotton-ginning factories and textile industries, and is also a university town, with an institute attached to the El-Azhar University in Cairo and a medical school associated with Alexandria University, as well as the seat of a Metropolitan of the Coptic Church.

SIGHTS. – The town's most notable building is the 19th c. **Mosque of Sheikh el-Said Ahmed el-Bedawi** built by Abbas I and Ismail Pasha on the site of an earlier mosque. It stands over the tomb of a much-revered and very popular Egyptian holy man, and attracts large numbers of pilgrims, particularly on his birthday in August. Ahmed el-Bedawi, born in Fez in the 12th c., settled in Tanta on his way back from a pilgrimage to Mecca. Frequent miraculous cures are said to have been wrought at his tomb. The celebration of his birthday is a lively and colorful popular festival and fair.

SURROUNDINGS of Tanta. – Some 15 miles/25 km E is the **Zifta Dam** on the Damietta arm of the Nile, built in 1903, with 50 sluice-gates 16 ft/5 m wide. Very similar in construction to the Asyut Dam, it regulates the irrigation of the governorates of Gharbiya, Daqahliya and Sharqiya in the eastern Delta.

Some 25 miles/40 km SE of Tanta and 6 miles/10 km S of *Mit Ghamr,* in one of the most beautiful parts of the Delta, on the right bank of the Damietta arm of the Nile, is **Tell Mokdam**, a massive rubble mound marking the site of *Leontopolis* ("Lion City"), a town mentioned by Strabo which in the Ptolemaic period was the flourishing capital of the 11th nome of Lower Egypt. The buildings, including a temple erected by Osorkon II (22nd Dynasty), were almost completely demolished in later times for the sake of their stone. Excavation has brought to light many statues of lions and the local lion god Mahes. The discovery of the Tomb of Kamama, mother of Osorkon IV, indicates that Leontopolis was the residence of a collateral line of the 23rd Dynasty. There may well be other royal tombs of the same period awaiting discovery.

Damanhur, El-Mansura, Nile Delta, Sais, Tell el-Faraun and **El-Zagazig**: see separate entries.

Taposiris Magna
See under Alexandria

El-Tarif
See under Thebes

Tebtynis
See under Fayyum

Tell Basta (Bubastis)
See under El-Zagazig

Tell el-Amarna

Middle Egypt. – Governorate: El-Minya.

ACCESS. – By road or rail from Mallawi to Deir Mawas, 7 miles/11 km S of Mallawi; then by car (taxi) to the ferry crossing to the right bank of the Nile. It is advisable to hire a donkey for the tour of the site.

The site of *Tell el-Amarna, with its rock tombs and other remains, lies some 9 miles/15 km SE of Mallawi at the mouth of a valley on the E bank of

the Nile. This is all that is left of the city of Akhetaten ("Horizon of the Aten"), the new capital founded by Amenophis IV, who later took the name of Akhenaten, and dedicated to the Aten or Sun God. The present name comes from that of a local bedouin tribe, the Amra.

When Amenophis IV/Akhenaten became devoted to the exclusive worship of the Sun and abjured the ancient gods of Egypt he withdrew from the old capital at Thebes and established his residence in an area in the Hermopolitan nome lying on both sides of the Nile. The boundaries of his new capital are still marked by 14 stelae carved on rock faces at El-Hawata, close to the southern and northern cemeteries of El-Amarna, at Sheikh Said on the right bank and at Tuna el-Gebel, Dirwa and Gilda on the left bank. The royal residence was on the right bank, where a new town rapidly sprang up. Temples and palaces were built, the mansions of high dignitaries clustered around the sumptuous Royal Palace, and magnificent tombs were constructed for the King and his favorites in the hills to the E.

When the old religion was re-established after Akhenaten's death his next-but-one successor Tutankhamun moved the Court back to Thebes and the new city rapidly decayed. It had had a life of no more than 30 years, and its site was never afterwards built on: hence the excellent preservation of the old street pattern and the comparative ease with which archaeologists have been able to reconstruct some of the buildings.

The reign of Akhenaten saw not only a religious but also an artistic revolution, reflected in the emergence of the *Amarna style* which continued to be influential during the reigns of his successors Smenkhkare, Tutankhamun and Ay. Under the new creed the artists

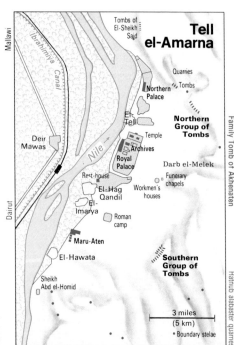

of the period enjoyed greater freedom in their treatment of ancient traditions, and the previous stylized and symbolic presentation gave place to an artistic realism and idealism which sometimes – particularly in depicting the emaciated figure of the King himself – fell into exaggeration. Characteristic of this period are the many representations of nature, which in Akhenaten's monotheist and universalist religion and philosophy was venerated as divine. – The finest examples of this important new artistic trend are provided by the reliefs in the tombs of El-Amarna.

THE SITE. – From the landing-place it is an hour's ride to the extensive remains of the city and Akhenaten's **Royal Palace** at El-Tell, the fine stucco pavements in which were ruthlessly destroyed in 1912 (fragments in the Egyptian Museum, Cairo). To the S of the palace are the remains of brick pillars, perhaps belonging to the palace vineyard. – To the E of the palace were the **Archives**, in which large numbers of clay tablets with Babylonian cuneiform inscriptions (now in the Egyptian Museum in Cairo, the British Museum in London and museums in West and East Berlin) were found in 1888 – letters from Babylonian and other kings of western Asia and Syrian and Phoenician vassals to Amenophis III and IV which are of the greatest historical importance.

N of El-Tell was the **Northern Palace**, dating from the end of Akhenaten's reign. – The Sikket el-Sultan, the track which runs S from El-Tell to El-Hag Qandil, leads to the excavated part of the ancient city, which was traversed by three main streets running N–S and a number of cross-streets. The ground-plans of many houses can still be clearly identified. Particularly notable are the *House of the Vizier Nakht*, the *House of the High Priest Pewoh*, a very typical example of the house of a high official, and the *House of the Sculptor Tuthmosis*, with workshops, in which many fine pieces of sculpture were found (now in the museums of Cairo and East and West Berlin). Here, too, was found the famous painted limestone **bust of Nefertiti, Akhenaten's beautiful Queen, which is now in the Egyptian Museum in West Berlin. Many of the houses have large gardens. – At the SW end of El-Hag Qandil, still partly concealed under the houses of the village and a sheikh's tomb, are the remains of a temple. – At *El-Hawata*, 1 mile/2 km SW of El-Hag Qandil, are the remains of the **Maru-Aten**, Akhenaten's summer palace.

From the ruins of the main Royal Palace it is a 45-minute ride NE, past the site of the large temple adjoining the palace, to the ***Northern Group of Tombs**. – The rock tombs of Tell el-Amarna are similar in form to those of Abd el-Qurna in western Thebes. In front of each tomb is a forecourt, which in most cases was probably enclosed by a brick wall. The wide doorway frequently opens into a pillared chamber, from which a doorway or passage leads into a narrow antechamber, beyond which is a chamber containing a statue of the dead man. Many tombs were left unfinished when the capital was moved back to Thebes. The tombs are numbered in black from 1 to 25, going from N to S.

No. 1 is the **Tomb of Huye**, Superintendent of the Royal Harem and Steward to the Queen Mother, Tiy.

In the entrance is a figure of the dead man praying. The main chamber had originally two cluster-columns, one of which is still standing. Right-hand entrance wall: the King and Queen seated at table; below the Queen, two Princesses sitting opposite one another; to the right, guards, etc.; above the royal couple (as in all similar representations in the tombs of El-Amarna), the sun, with rays ending in hands; below, girl musicians, a table with offerings, servants bowing, soldiers, etc. Right-hand end wall: the Temple of the Sun, with the large altar in a colonnaded court and statues; on the right the King conducting the Queen Mother to the mortuary temple of his parents Amenophis III and Tiy, accompanied by guards behind and below them; above, the sun, with its rays ending in hands. On the rear wall, to the right and left of the door, are two matching representations (much damaged) of Amenophis III and IV and their wives. Left-hand end wall: the King being carried in a litter to a reception hall (on right) to receive tribute from subject nations, accompanied by a large retinue. Left-hand entrance wall: similar to the right-hand one. On both walls of the doorway into the next chamber the dead man is shown in prayer. – In the following room (unfinished) is the mummy-shaft, surrounded by a parapet hewn from the rock. – In the last chamber, the shrine, is a niche containing an over-life-size *seated figure* of the dead man (face mutilated). On the walls are burial scenes, mourning women, men carrying votive gifts, a carriage, chairs, etc.

No. 2, the **Tomb of Merire II**, who was also Superintendent of the Royal Harem, is of particular interest because work on the tomb continued during the reign of Akhenaten's son-in-law and successor Smenkhkare.

Only the main chamber, with two columns, is completed. Left-hand entrance wall: the King seated under a canopy holding a bowl into which the Queen is pouring water, with three Princesses in attendance. Right-hand entrance wall: the King and Queen, on a balcony, handing down gold ornaments to the dead man; in the forecourt of the palace (on the right), the

Queen Nefertiti (from Tell el-Amarna: Egyptian Museum, West Berlin)

royal chariot and fan-bearers, together with Merire's officials and servants; below, Merire being welcomed on returning to his house. Right-hand end wall: the King and Queen seated under a high canopy receiving tribute from Asiatics (on the left) and Negroes (on the right); other prisoners doing homage to the King.

The next tombs lie 15 minutes' ride SE, in the side of another hill. – No. 3, the **Tomb of Ahmose**, "Fan-bearer on the right hand of the King", can be omitted if time is short.

Above the entrance the dead man is depicted worshiping the names of the sun; in the doorway, to the right and left, he is seen praying, wearing his official costume, with fan and axe. Main chamber, left-hand wall: the royal family at table in the palace; above, four rows of soldiers with shields, spears, etc., marching to the temple, followed by the royal chariot (merely sketched in). In side chambers on the left and right are two mummy-shafts, with false doors on the wall behind. In the last chamber is a statue of the dead man.

No. 4, the **Tomb of Merire I**, High Priest of the Sun, is one of the largest and most interesting in the group. The reliefs are very dark and require good lighting (powerful torch advisable).

In front of the tomb is a spacious forecourt. The doorway, topped by a cavetto cornice and with figures of the dead man in prayer on the inner walls, leads into an antechamber, on the right-hand and left-hand walls of which are false doors, with Merire praying in front of them; behind him a large bunch of flowers in the shape of a column. The other walls are covered with inscriptions. – The main chamber, beyond, originally had four columns, of which two are left. In the doorway are figures of the dead man (right) and his wife (left) in prayer. Left-hand entrance wall: the King at a window in the palace presenting gold to Merire. Left-hand wall: the King in his chariot driving from the palace (above, left) to the Temple of the Sun (below); in front of him his bodyguard, behind him the Queen, the Princesses and retinue, in chariots and on foot. The scene continues on the left-hand half of the rear wall: priests and girl musicians awaiting the King at the entrance to the temple. Right-hand wall, continuing on right-hand half of rear wall: the King visiting the temple; below, Merire is presented with gold chains by the King and Queen; on left, the royal barns and store-rooms. Right-hand entrance wall: the King and Queen, with two Princesses, making offerings to the sun; at the altars Merire and another priest; below, the royal retinue and priests (note, bottom right, the fine representations of blind singers). – The two rear chambers are unfinished.

No. 5, the **Tomb of Pentu**, a physician, is much damaged. In the entrance doorway, on the right and left, the dead man is shown at prayer; in front of him an inscription (a hymn to the sun). On the left-hand wall of the first chamber the King and Queen are depicted praying to the sun, above the pylon of the temple. In a side passage on the right is a deep mummy-shaft. The statue of the dead man which stood in the rear chamber has been chiseled away

To the SE, a short distance away, is No. 6, the **Tomb of Penehse**.

In the entrance doorway, on the left: the King and Queen, followed by three Princesses and the Queen's sister, praying to the sun; below, a row of servants, fan-bearers and other attendants; at the foot, the dead man praying. Similar scene on the right-hand side. The main chamber originally had four papyrus columns with closed capitals, two of which remain. In the rear wall is a false door, converted into a font when the tomb was used as a church. – Steps on the right lead into the tomb chamber. Left-hand entrance wall: the King and Queen presenting Penehse with gold ornaments from a window in the palace. Left-hand wall: above, left, the Temple of the Sun, with the King praying at an altar in the forecourt. Right-hand entrance wall: the dead man and his retinue bringing votive gifts to the King and Queen, who are accompanied by four Princesses. – A door with figures of the dead man and his sister leads into a second chamber with four columns, containing a niche for the statue of the dead man (which has been chiseled away).

Half an hour's ride E of Tomb 6, carved on a rock face, is one of the 14 stelae which marked the boundaries of the city of Akhetaten.

Half-way between the Northern and Southern groups of Tombs, outside the city on a spur of the hills to the E, are the remains of a walled settlement in which the workmen constructing the tombs and looking after the cemetery were housed. Near by is a *cemetery* with brick-built chapels.

A good hour's ride S of the Northern Group of Tombs, in the lower slopes of *Gebel Abu Hasah*, is the *Southern Group of Tombs*.

No. 8 is the **Tomb of Tutu**.

On the door-jambs the dead man is depicted in prayer; above him his names and titles. In the doorway, on the right, the King and Queen making offerings to the sun, with the dead man kneeling in prayer below; on the left, the dead man in prayer. The main chamber originally had 12 columns, in two rows, of which eight remain. The columns in the rear row are linked by screens, and between the two middle columns is a low doorway, of a type usually found only in the Ptolemaic period. Steps on the left lead into the tomb chamber. In the two end walls are small unfinished niches containing statues. Right-hand entrance wall: the King and Queen look out of a palace window as Tutu is decorated with gold chains; below, the dead man in prayer. Left-hand entrance wall: the King and Queen seated in the palace, with Tutu and other courtiers in respectful attitudes before them; below, the dead man praying. – The corridor is unfinished.

Immediately adjoining is No. 9, the **Tomb of Mahu**, a high military officer.

A short flight of steps leads down to the entrance. In the doorway, on the left, are the King, holding the hieroglyph for "truth" towards the sun, the Queen and a Princess, with sistra, in the presence of the sun; below, the dead man kneeling, with the text of his prayer in front of him; on the right, the dead man praying. – Main chamber, left-hand entrance wall: the King at a window in the palace (preliminary sketch in black pigment). Left-hand end wall: a round-topped gravestone, approached by two steps; above, the King and Queen; below, the dead man praying. To the right (continued on the left-hand half of the rear wall), people in front of the Temple of the Sun; bottom row, the dead man kneeling and offering thanks for the King's goodness. Right-hand half of the rear wall (continued on the left half of the end wall): above, the King and Queen driving out of the palace to inspect the defences of the City of the Sun, with men running ahead; below, their return. In the center of the right-hand end wall is a door-shaped tombstone. Right-hand entrance wall: bottom row, left, Mahu setting out in his chariot; to the right, Mahu bringing prisoners to the Vizier, who is accompanied by his retinue; second bottom row, on the left Mahu leaning on a staff with his subordinates in front of him, on the right a chariot and soldiers running. The upper rows are poorly preserved. – The second chamber has a false door on the rear wall; on the right a winding staircase of 46 steps leads to a chamber containing the *mummy-shaft.*

No. 10, the **Tomb of Epei**, is unfinished. In the entrance doorway, on the left, the King and Queen present two pictures to the Sun, the King's picture showing two Princesses worshiping the names of the sun, while the Queen presents her own portrait worshiping the names of the sun, behind them three Princesses with sistra; the sun's rays shining down on an altar laden with food and drink.

No. 11 is the **Tomb of Ramose**. In the entrance doorway, on the left, the King and Queen, accompanied by a Princess, receive the hieroglyph for "life" from the hands of the Aten. In the niche are seated figure of the dead man and his wife.

Nos. 12 and 13 are unfinished. They show how these tombs were hewn out of the rock.

No. 14 is the **Tomb of Mei**, "military commander and Fan-bearer on the right hand of the King"; Mei's name has everywhere been carefully obliterated, while the names of the King and Queen have been left untouched. The tomb is unfinished. On the right-hand entrance wall is a preliminary sketch of the harbor quay of the City of the Sun, with ships, gardens and the palace in the background. – *No. 17* is a handsome tomb, but has no reliefs or inscriptions. No. 19, the *Tomb of Suti,* is only just begun.

No. 23, the **Tomb of Enei**, a Steward and Scribe in the royal household, differs in form from the other tombs.

A flight of limestone steps leads to the entrance, which has a cavetto cornice and was planned to have a colonnade in front of it. On the lintel, to the right and left, are the King and Queen and three Princesses praying to the sun. In the doorway, on the left, the dead man is shown praying, with the text of his prayer in front of him; on the right the dead man with a staff and a bunch of flowers (painted on stucco). The walls of the main chamber have a coating of stucco, but apart from the cavetto cornice at the top are unpainted. In the niche is an over-life-size *statue* of the dead man; right-hand wall, the dead man and his wife seated, with a praying man in front of them; left-hand wall, the dead man seated at table, with a priest offering him flowers. These scenes are painted on stucco, but are much faded.

Farther S is No. 25, the **Tomb of Ay**, Tutankhamun's successor as King. Like many other tombs, it was left unfinished when the capital was moved back to Thebes (where Ay had a new tomb constructed for him).

On the door-jambs, on the right and left, Ay and his wife are depicted kneeling (below); above, inscriptions. In the entrance doorway, on the left, the King and Queen, accompanied by courtiers, praying to the sun, whose rays, ending in hands, reach down to the altar; below, Ay and his wife Tiy in prayer; right, Ay, in official costume, and his wife praying, their prayers inscribed beside them. – The main chamber was to have 24 papyrus columns with closed capitals, but only 15 were rough-hewn and only four completed; the others, to the S, have merely been begun in the rock at the top. On three of the columns the dead man and his wife are depicted worshiping the names of the sun god and the King and Queen. In the center of the rear wall is an unfinished doorway; at the NE corner is a flight of steps designed to lead to the tomb chamber, which is not even begun; and at the NW corner is an unfinished doorway. On the left-hand entrance wall is an interesting relief, the only one completed: to the left are the King and Queen throwing down ornaments to Ay and his wife (upper parts of bodies in Egyptian Museum, Cairo) from a palace window; beside the Queen are her three small daughters, the one in front stroking her mother's chin; above, the sun. In the courtyard of the palace the royal retinue (charioteers, scribes, fan-bearers, soldiers), raise their hands in homage; note the curious bent attitudes of the courtiers. Below are boys capering in delight. On the right Ay is seen leaving the palace and receiving the congratulations of his retainers, who raise their hands in exultation; servants carry the gifts away; and in the top row the palace doorkeepers with some small boys observe the scene.

Some 7 miles/11 km from Tell el-Amarna, in the *Darb el-Hamzawi* or *Darb el-Melek,* a valley running E between the Northern and Southern Groups of Tombs, are a number of rock tombs without reliefs or inscriptions and one (No. 26) which has interesting reliefs but is unfortunately much damaged. This is the **Family Tomb of Amenophis IV/Akhenaten**, long thought, erroneously, to be the tomb of Akhenaten himself, who was buried in the tomb of his mother Tiy in the Valley of the Kings (see under Thebes).

A flight of 20 steps, with a ramp in the middle for the sarcophagus, leads to the doorway, from which a sloping corridor and another flight of 16 steps lead to an antechamber with a mummy-shaft, now filled in, and badly damaged mural reliefs. Beyond the shaft is the tomb chamber, which once contained a sarcophagus. All the pillars but one have disappeared. The mural reliefs were incised on stucco. The best preserved are those on the left-hand entrance wall (the King and Queen and Princesses praying to the sun) and the left-hand side wall, which depict the King and Queen, a Princess and women mourners at a bier (?). In the right-hand wall is a small niche.

Returning towards the entrance, we enter (to the left of the steps) three rooms with reliefs and inscriptions, perhaps the funerary chapel of Princess Meketaten. Both the main walls of the first room show almost the same scene: the King and Queen, four Princesses and the royal retinue praying and presenting offerings to the sun, which is seen rising over the hills behind the temple; at the foot of the hills are various animals. To the left (on the left-hand entrance wall and on the rear wall between the doors) a variety of people, including Negroes and Asiatics in their distinctive garb, worship the sun. On the right-hand entrance wall, in the bottom row, the dead Princess is seen on her bier, with the King and Queen and women mourners standing by it; in the upper row are the King and Queen, a nurse with a little Princess, and women mourners lamenting the dead Princess. – The second room has no reliefs. – Third room, rear wall: to the left, the dead Princess standing under a canopy; in front of her, mourning, the royal family and their retinue. This scene is continued on the right-hand wall. Left-hand wall: the mummy lying under the same canopy, with the royal family mourning in front of her; farther right, a wet nurse with an infant Princess at the breast. Entrance wall: representations of tomb furnishings (mirrors, spoons, caskets, etc.; badly damaged). – Nearer the entrance a corridor leads to a sloping passage ending in an unfinished chamber.

In the hills around the wide valley in which Tell el-Amarna lies are many limestone and alabaster quarries. The largest are the *Hatnub alabaster quarries*, some 5 hours away on a track to the S of the Southern Group of Tombs. Inscriptions indicate that they were worked in the Old Kingdom and Early Middle Kingdom.

*Asyut, *Beni Hasan, *Mallawi and Roda: see separate entries.

Tell el-Faraun

Lower Egypt. – Governorate: Kafr el-Sheikh.
ⓘ **Tourist Information Office,**
Midan Saad Zaghlul,
Alexandria;
tel. 80 79 85.

ACCESS. – By road from Damanhur (20 miles/32 km S) via Desuq.

Between the villages of Ibtu and Shaba are the large rubble mounds of Tell el-Faraun ("Pharaoh's Hill"), which mark the site of ancient Buto (from Per Uto, "House of the Goddess Uto"), capital of Lower Egypt, which was discovered and identified by Flinders Petrie in 1886.

Before the unification of the two kingdoms Buto seems to have been the political center of Lower Egypt, but later lost this position to Abydos. However it remained the chief town of the 6th nome of Lower Egypt and the principal center of

the cult of the Lower Egyptian cobra goddess Uto (or Buto), whose counterpart in Upper Egypt was the vulture goddess Nekhbet of El-Kab and who was venerated along with Nekhbet as the protective goddess of the kingdom. The falcon-headed "souls of Pe" which are associated with Uto may possibly be symbolic representations of Lower Egyptian territorial units of a very early period.

According to tradition the city of Buto originally consisted of two parts, *Pe* and *Dep*. Excavations have so far identified three areas of occupation (two settlements and a temple precinct), but no material has yet been found dating from the earliest period, when for many centuries the town was a major cult center. What has been found so far dates from the time of Ramesses II and later. – Excavations are still in progress, but there is little to interest the ordinary visitor.

SURROUNDINGS of Tell el-Faraun. – 7½ miles/12 km SW, on the right bank of the Rosetta arm of the Nile (here spanned by a railway bridge), is the little town of **Desuq,** to which there is a great pilgrimage on the birthday of a local holy man, Ibrahim el-Desuqi, founder of the Burhamiya Dervish Order. The mosque which he founded (rebuilt 1885), with a medrese built by Sultan Qait Bey, is now an Islamic university.

**Alexandria, Damanhur, Nile Delta, Rosetta, Sais and Tanta: see separate entries.

Terenuthis
See under Wadi Natrum

Thebes

Upper Egypt. – Governorate: Qena.
ⓘ **Tourist Information Office,**
Tourist Bazaar,
Luxor;
tel. 22 15.

ACCOMMODATION: see under Luxor.

ACCESS to Luxor. – By road from Cairo (416 miles/ 670 km N) or Aswan (130 miles/210 km S). – Railway station. – By air (several flights daily from Cairo and Aswan).

The ancient city of **Thebes, under the Middle and New Kingdoms (12th–21st Dynasties) the magnificent and widely famed capital and religious center of Egypt, extended over the territory of present-day Luxor and Karnak and reached out on

to the W bank of the Nile and far into the valleys of the Western Desert with its vast necropolises and great mortuary temples.

HISTORY. – The history of Thebes during the Old Kingdom is veiled in obscurity. The Egyptian name of the town was **Weset** or, more shortly, *Newt* ("the City"), which gave the Biblical No or No-Amon ("City of Amun"). The W bank was known as "the West of Weset". It is not known what led the Greeks to call it **Thebai** (Thebes), the name of a number of Greek cities; they and the Romans also knew it as *Diospolis* (the City of Zeus, who was equated with Amun), or more specifically as *Diospolis he Megale* or *Diospolis Magna* (Diospolis the Great) to distinguish it from Diospolis Parva (Hiw), some 60 miles/100 km NE. Weset was the chief town of a nome and was ruled by its own Princes, whose burial-place during the 6th Dynasty was at Dra Abu el-Naga, on the W bank of the Nile. The town's protective deity was the falcon-headed war god Month, who was also worshiped in the neighboring towns of Medu and Hermonthis (Armant: see under Tod).

Thebes gained in importance when, during the Middle Kingdom, the Princes of Thebes assumed the dignity of King, and at the same time the god Amun of Karnak, previously of little consequence, rose to a position of central importance. The greatness of Thebes, however, really began under the Early New Kingdom. The struggle against the Hyksos and the unification of Egypt were spearheaded by Thebes, and thereafter the city remained for many centuries the splendid capital of the Pharaohs, into which flowed the immense treasures won from conquered nations in booty or in tribute. Much of this wealth was bestowed on Amun, and the huge temples dedicated to him date from this period. The existing Temple of Epet-esowet at Karnak was enlarged, and the new Temple of Apet-resyet was built at Luxor. The great ones of the kingdom considered it an honor to be priests of Amun; the temple schools flourished; and the Kings offered their richest gifts to the god. Thebes was now renowned throughout the Eastern World, a city of which the Prophet Nahum said that "Ethiopia and Egypt were her strength, and it was infinite" (Nahum 3: 9). Homer, too, refers to "Egyptian Thebes, where the houses are rich in treasures; with a hundred gates, from each of which two hundred warriors sally forth with chariots and horses" (*Iliad* 9: 381–384; perhaps an interpolation). Later classical writers (Diodorus, Strabo, Pliny, Stephanus of Byzantium) also refer to the great "hundred-gated" city.

The hostility shown to Amun by Amenophis IV/Akhenaten and the temporary transfer of the capital to Tell el-Amarna (see that entry) did little to diminish the splendor of Thebes. Under Horemheb, Sethos I and Ramesses II the images and inscriptions that had been destroyed were restored and the wealth of the temples still further increased. We are told that in the reign of Ramesses III more than two-thirds of the landed property held by the temples of Egypt belonged to Amun and that three-quarters of the gifts lavished on the gods by the King fell to Amun: thus of 113,433 slaves presented to the temples 86,486 went to Amun. The High Priests thus increasingly came to feel themselves to be leading figures in the State, and sometimes even acceded to the throne.

When the capital of the kingdom was transferred to the Delta under the 21st Dynasty, however, the city lost much of its importance. Nevertheless Thebes and much of Upper Egypt long remained a distinct political entity governed by the High Priests of Amun and more or less independent of the Kings reigning in the N. In the 7th c. B.C. the city was plundered by Assyrian armies. The Ethiopian rulers of Egypt made Thebes their capital and honored Amun with temples and inscriptions. The rulers of the 26th Dynasty, however, transferred the capital to Sais (see that entry). The armies of Cambyses, which advanced into Upper Egypt, appear to have done little or no damage to Thebes. Nectanebo II, one of the native rulers who for a time shook off Persian rule, erected a handsome doorway in the Temple of Month. In the time of Alexander the Great and the Ptolemies the city declined, and although the buildings erected in the Ptolemaic period show that it was still held in respect it now had to contend with a dangerous rival in the new capital of Ptolemais founded by Ptolemy I.

When a rebellion broke out in Upper Egypt in the reign of Epiphanes against Macedonian domination Thebes, though now politically and economically weakened, once again achieved independence under native Princes; but the rising was soon repressed, and Thebes was reduced to the status of a provincial town, which gradually broke up into a series of separate villages. Under Ptolemy IX Soter II there was a further rising, which ended when the town was captured after a three-year siege; and when it took part in an insurrection against high Roman taxation it was utterly destroyed by the Roman Governor, Cornelius Gallus. Strabo, visiting Egypt in 24–20 B.C., found only a few scattered villages on the site. In the Roman Imperial period Thebes is mentioned only as a place visited by curious tourists, attracted by the temples and the colossi of Memnon.

After the introduction of Christianity and the Edicts of Theodosius many pagan statues were destroyed and many inscriptions obliterated. The Nile, which annually flooded the Temple of Karnak, and saline exudations from the soil wrought much damage. Many tombs were used as dwellings by the local peasants; temples were converted into churches and monasteries; houses were built within the Great Temple of Luxor; and much stone was burned to produce lime.

The main features of interest on the E bank of the Nile – **Thebes (East)** – are the great temples of ****Luxor** and ****Karnak** (see those entries).

Thebes (West): the Necropolis of Thebes

From Luxor there is a ferry to the W bank, where a taxi or bus can be taken to the various features of interest (which are some distance apart). An electric torch should be taken.

The **** NECROPOLIS OF THEBES** on the W bank of the Nile contains, in addition to the tombs, many temples, mostly dating from the New Kingdom, dedicated not only to Amun but also to the cult of the various Kings after their death. Associated with the temples were dwellings for the priests, libraries and

The natural pyramid above the Valley of the Kings

schools, together with sacred groves and lakes, granaries, stalls for the sacrificial animals, barracks for the guards and prisons. Close by were the villages occupied by the large numbers of workmen employed in the necropolis – masons, painters, builders and above all the embalmers who prepared the bodies for burial. A whole town gradually grew up here, like the district around the tombs of the Mamelukes in Cairo. Under the New Kingdom its administration was in the hands of a special official, the "Prince of the West and Commander of the Mercenaries of the Necropolis".

All the temples on the W bank of the Nile are sited with the end containing the entrance facing the river. Their longitudinal axes accordingly run from SE to NW. For the sake of simplicity, however, the following descriptions refer to the E and W ends and N and S sides.

Qurna, Dra Abu el-Naga and El-Tarif

Some 2½ miles/4 km N of the landing-stage is the *Mortuary Temple of Sethos I at **Qurna**, dedicated to Amun and to the cult of the King's father Ramesses I. Left unfinished by Sethos I, it was adorned by Ramesses II with reliefs and inscriptions, which vie in quality with the contemporary work at Abydos (see that entry). The temple was originally 519 ft/ 158 m long, but all that now remains is the sanctuary with its various halls and chambers (154 ft/47 m deep) and some scanty fragments of the courts and pylons.

The *Colonnade,* which preserves nine of its original ten papyrus cluster-columns with closed capitals, bears on the architrave a dedicatory inscription by Ramesses II. On the rear wall, flanking the central doorway, are reliefs of men and women bearing votive offerings; those on the left have lilies on their heads, representing Upper Egypt, those on the right the papyrus of Lower Egypt. Above, left, the King offering incense in the presence of the sacred barque of Amun, borne by priests; right, the King before various deities.

The central door leads into the *Hypostyle Hall,* which has six papyrus columns with closed capitals. On the roof slabs over the central aisle are the winged solar disc, flying vultures and the names of Sethos I, enclosed by snakes and flanked by two rows of hieroglyphics. The low reliefs on the walls depict Sethos I and Ramesses II making offerings to various gods; to the left Mut, to the right Hathor of Dendera, who is suckling Sethos.

Of the six *side chambers,* most of them with well-preserved roofs, one is destroyed. The fine reliefs show Sethos I making offerings to various gods and performing ritual acts. In the third chamber on the left,

on the left-hand wall, is Thoth in front of the King's sacred barque; on the right-hand wall, to the left, the King at table with the goddess of the temple behind him; to the right, the King in priestly vestments performing ceremonies in front of himself; on the rear wall, the King as Osiris seated in a chapel, with the gods of Thebes (Amun and Mut) on his left and the gods of Memphis (Ptah and Sakhmet) on his right. In the first chamber on the right are sunk reliefs of Ramesses II pacing out the precincts of the temple in the presence of Amun, Khons and Mut (right) and offering incense to these gods (left). – Beyond the hypostyle hall is a transverse *antechamber* on a higher level, with five chambers opening off it. The central chamber is the *Sanctuary,* which still preserves the base for the sacred barque of Amun and has mural reliefs of Sethos I burning incense in front of the barque. – Beyond the sanctuary is a room with four pillars and low reliefs of Sethos I, on either side of which are badly ruined side chambers.

The ruinous part of the temple to the right consists of the long *Hall of Ramesses II,* with an *altar* and a number of subsidiary chambers, now destroyed. The sunk reliefs, depicting Ramesses II making offerings to various gods, are inferior in quality to those in the central and left-hand parts of the temple.

Entering the left-hand part of the temple from the colonnade, we come first to the *Chapel of Ramesses I,* a small room with two columns. On the right-hand and left-hand walls are low reliefs, apparently usurped by Ramesses II; on the right he is seen kneeling before Amun, Khons and the deified Sethos, with the goddess Mut behind him. – Off the chapel open three *chambers.* On the right-hand and left-hand walls of the central chamber Sethos I is depicted burning incense before the barque of Amun and anointing the statue of his father, Ramesses I, with his finger; on the rear wall is a double false door with a representation of Ramesses I's Osiris coffin, on which is perched Isis in the form of a falcon. The other two chambers, built by Ramesses II, have reliefs of poor quality. – A door on the left of the chapel opens into a narrow corridor, the left-hand wall of which is destroyed down to the lowest courses of masonry. From this steps lead down to two underground chambers. At the far end of the corridor, on the right, is a room containing sunk reliefs dating from the reign of Ramesses II which depict Ramesses and his father Sethos making offerings to the gods and performing other ritual acts.

From the temple a road runs W to the village and **Necropolis of Dra Abu el-Naga**, among the lower slopes of the desert hills, with rock tombs of the New Kingdom. The most interesting tombs are those noted below.

No. 17, the *Tomb of Neb-Amun,* Royal Physician (18th Dynasty): on the rear wall of the vestibule, figures of Asiatics; fine ceiling decoration. – No. 20, the *Tomb of Mentu-her-khopshef,* Royal Fan-bearer, with funeral scenes. – Adjoining is No. 24, the *Tomb of Neb-Amun,* a high official under Tuthmosis III, with charming stucco reliefs (funeral scenes, fields of the blessed, banquet) and ceiling decoration; on the end wall a stela with a long inscription. – No. 13, the *Tomb of Shuroi* (20th Dynasty), with fine funeral scenes.

No. 19, the *Tomb of Amenmose,* High Priest of a Temple of Amenophis I (early 19th Dynasty). Roughly half the reliefs in the chamber have been preserved. They depict the funeral procession and the ceremonies at the tomb; on the right-hand side of the rear wall the sacred barque with the image of Amenophis I is seen being carried out of the temple of which the dead man was High Priest. – No. 115, the *Tomb of Antef* (18th Dynasty). The vestibule, which is now roofed over for protection, was originally open, with seven pillars. On the rear wall are the remains of stucco reliefs: on the left the dead man, with his wife, receiving a variety of gifts; on the right vintage scenes, treading and pressing of the grapes, dispatch of jars of wine; above, far right, remains of a hunting scene, with a hippopotamus. On the right-hand end wall are remains of the stela. The inner rooms are badly ruined.

Rather higher up is the *Tomb of Roi (No. 255), a Royal Scribe and Steward, which was excavated by Carter. Left-hand entrance wall: work in the fields. Left-hand (S) wall: above, the dead man and one of his relatives, each accompanied by a woman, praying to various gods; the dead man and his sister led by the falcon-headed Horus to the scales on which their hearts are to be weighed; they are conducted by Harsiesis into the presence of Osiris; below, the burial. Right-hand wall: the dead man, his sister and various relatives receiving an offering from a priest clad in a panther skin.

To the N of the Mortuary Temple of Sethos I are the **royal and princely tombs of El-Tarif** (11th Dynasty). These are very large structures with courts up to 330 yds/300 m long and 66 yds/ 60 m wide hewn from the rock. The row of simulated pillars along their rear façades has led them to be called *saff tombs* (from Arabic *saff*, "row"). The rooms in the interior are small and the decoration (where it has been preserved) modest. The best preserved are the tombs of Kings Antef I, II and III.

Valley of the Kings

From the Mortuary Temple of Sethos I a good road runs 3 miles/5 km SW to the ****Valley of the Kings (Biban el-Muluk)**, above which rears a rocky peak in the shape of a pyramid. The valley takes its name from the sumptuously furnished tombs constructed here for kings of the 18th, 19th and 20th Dynasties. In contrast to the pyramid tombs which had previously been favored, these tombs consist of a series of passages and chambers hewn from the rock. Like the chambers within the pyramids, these were intended only for the reception of the sarcophagus: the temples dedicated to the cult of the dead kings were built in the plain. The tombs usually have a succession of three corridors leading into their innermost recesses. The first corridor sometimes has small side chambers opening off it; in the second and third are

niches for grave-goods. The third corridor leads into an antechamber, beyond which is the main chamber, its roof often supported by pillars, with a cavity in the floor in which the heavy granite sarcophagus was deposited. Adjoining the main chamber are various subsidiary chambers. Since it was believed that the dead man, accompanied by the sun god (or perhaps having become one with the sun god), sailed through the Underworld at night in a boat, the walls of the tombs were frequently adorned with texts and scenes depicting this voyage and giving the dead man instruction on its course.

The scenes and texts were chiefly taken from two books closely related to one another. The first is the "**Book of what is in the Underworld**", which has 12 chapters, since the Underworld (Duat) was thought of as being divided into 12 parts or caverns, corresponding to the 12 hours of the night. In the center of each of these scenes is a river on which the ram-headed sun god and his train are sailing in the solar barque, briefly dispensing light and life. The banks of the river, above and below, are populated by spirits, demons and monsters which greet the sun god as he passes and fend off his enemies.

The second book is known as the "**Book of the Gates**", which also deals with the sun's nocturnal voyage through the 12 parts of the Underworld. Between these various parts are massive gates guarded by giant snakes, whose names the dead man must know. Two gods and two fire-breathing snakes guard the approach and greet the sun god. In other respects the conception of the Underworld is similar to that of the first book.

A third work can be called "**The Sun God's Journey through the Underworld**". It depicts the sun god addressing the spirits and monsters of the Underworld, who are exactly portrayed in long rows.

Other texts used in decorating the walls of the tombs were the "**Praising of Re**" (or "Litany of Re") and the "**Book of the Opening of the Mouth**". The former, which appears in the first two corridors, contains a hymn to the sun god, whom the dead man had to invoke under 75 different names when he entered the Underworld in the evening. The latter teaches the various ceremonies which had to be performed in front of the statue of the dead man so that it could eat and drink what had been set out for it in the tomb.

Strabo knew of 40 tombs which he described as worth seeing; the English traveler Richard Pococke (1737), who wrote the first account of the valley in modern times, describes 14; the number now known is 62. – Pausanias, Aelian, Heliodorus, Ammianus Marcellinus and other ancient writers, as well as the Greek inscriptions in the tombs themselves, call them "shepherd's pipes", from the resemblance of the long corridors to the reeds of a pipe.

A visit to the Valley of the Kings is one of the high spots of any tour of Egypt; but the swarms of visitors

Wall-painting in the Tomb of Ramesses IX, Valley of the Kings

and the great heat, particularly during the summer, make the trip quite a demanding one. There is, however, a rest-house where refreshments can be obtained. Since the order in which the tombs are visited may vary according the waiting time involved, and since some tombs are opened and closed in rotation, they are described here in numerical order. The entrances to the various tombs open to visitors can be reached on easy paths.

No. 1, the *Tomb of Ramesses VII*. A Greek inscription shows that this tomb was known and accessible during the Greek period.

No. 2, the **Tomb of Ramesses IV**. An ancient staircase, with a ramp in the middle, leads to the entrance. On the lintel of the door are Isis and Nephthys worshiping the sun, within which are the ram-headed sun god and a scarab. On the right-hand entrance wall are two figures of Copts raising their hands in prayer; according to an inscription one of them is "Apa Ammonios the martyr". The scenes and inscriptions were painted on stucco, almost all of which has fallen away. In the main chamber is the King's granite sarcophagus ($10\frac{1}{2}$ ft/3.2 m long, 7 ft/2.1 m wide, 8 ft/2.5 m high), with inscriptions and reliefs.

To the left of the path is No. 3, originally intended for Ramesses III, half filled with rubble. – No. 4, the *Tomb of Ramesses XI*, last of the Ramessids, is unfinished and undecorated. – Beyond this, on the left, is No. 5, with a door opening into a corridor.

Rest-house in the Valley of the Kings

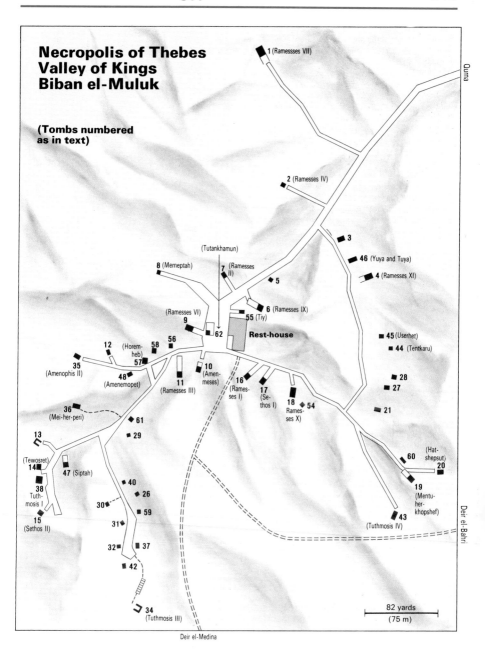

**Necropolis of Thebes
Valley of Kings
Biban el-Muluk**

**(Tombs numbered
as in text)**

1 (Ramessses VII)

2 (Ramesses IV)

3

46 (Yuya and Tuya)

4 (Ramesses XI)

5

(Tutankhamun)

8 (Merneptah) 7 (Ramesses II)

6 (Ramesses IX)

55 (Tiy)

(Ramesses VI) 9

62

Rest-house

45 (Userhet)

44 (Tentkaru)

12 (Horem-heb) 58 56

57

35 (Amenophis II)

48 (Amenemopet)

10 (Amen-meses)

11 (Ramesses III)

16 (Rames-ses I)

17 (Se-thos I)

18 Rames-ses X)

54

28

27

21

36 (Mei-her-peri)

61

29

13

(Tewosret) 14

47 (Siptah)

38 Tuth-mosis I

40

26

30

59

15 (Sethos II)

31

32 37

42

34 (Tuthmosis III)

60 (Hat-shepsut)

20

19 (Mentu-her-khopshef)

43 (Tuthmosis IV)

82 yards

(75 m)

Deir el-Medina

Qurna

Deir el-Bahri

No. 6, the **Tomb of Ramesses IX** (Neferkare), is approached by a flight of steps with a ramp in the middle. On the right-hand side of the staircase is an unfinished inscription in Ramesses's name. On the lintel of the doorway: the sun worshiped by the King and Isis (left) and by the King and Nephthys (right).

In the *first corridor*, at the near end, on left, is a chapel, beside which the King is depicted in presence of Harakhty and Osiris. Farther along, above the doors of two small undecorated chambers, is a text from the "Praising of Re". Just beyond the second chamber is a text from the 125th Chapter of the "Book of the Dead" which contains a declaration by the dead man of his freedom from sin; below, a priest in the costume of the god Hor-en-metef pours the hieroglyphs for "life", "constancy" and "wealth" over the King, who is clad like Osiris. – On the right-hand wall, opposite the chapel, the King is depicted in a chapel in the presence of Amun and the death goddess Mertseger. Above the doors of the side chambers are representations of snakes and dog- and bull-headed spirits, with an inscription giving the beginning of the "Sun God's Journey through the Underworld".

At the near end of the *second corridor*, on the left, is a snake rearing up in a vertical position; to the right of this and in the niche are figures of gods (from the "Praising of Re"); below the niche is the King, followed by the goddess Hathor. Beyond this, on the left, texts from the "Book of the Dead"; then the King in the presence of the falcon-headed Khons-Neferhotep, with a falcon hovering over his head. On the right-hand wall is another erect snake; beyond the niche, figures of demons and spirits (many of them enclosed within oval frames). – On the ceiling are stars.

Third corridor, left-hand wall: the sun's journey during the second hour of the night and the beginning of the third. Right-hand wall: the King presenting an image of Maat to Ptah, before whom the goddess herself is standing; beyond this, the King's resurrection (his mummy lying on a hill with his arms raised above his head; the erect phallus chiseled away), with a scarab and the sun above the mummy. Then come three rows of demons: top row, eight suns, in each of which is a black man standing on his head; middle row, snakes pierced by arrows, praying women and a scarab in a boat with snakes' heads at both ends; bottom row, demons mounted on snakes and four men, bent backwards, spitting out scarabs. *First chamber,* rear wall: on each side of the door a priest wearing a panther skin and side-lock making an offering before a standard. – The roof of the *second chamber* is supported on four pillars. From here a short passage runs down to the *tomb chamber,* which contained the sarcophagus. On the wall are figures of gods and spirits. On the vaulted ceiling are two figures of the sky goddess, representing the morning and evening sky; below her are constellations, stellar barques, etc.

Opposite No. 6, on the right of the path, is No. 7, the *Tomb of Ramesses II.* The tomb was plundered in antiquity, and the mummy was then removed to Deir el-Bahri. – On both sides of the entrance corridor, in raised hieroglyphs, are texts from the "Praising of Re"; to the left, the King in presence of the sun god Re-Harakhty and the image of the sun with the ram-headed sun god and a scarab. The scenes and inscriptions in low relief are badly damaged.

No. 8, the *Tomb of Merneptah.* Above the entrance, Isis and Nephthys worshiping the sun, within which are the ram-headed sun god and a scarab.

The *entrance corridors,* with texts from the "Praising of Re" (on the left a very fine painted relief of the King before Re-Harakhty) and scenes from the Realm of the Dead (from the "Book of the Gates"), run fairly steeply down to an *antechamber* containing the granite lid of the outer coffin. From here steps lead down to a three-aisled *hypostyle hall* with a barrel vault over the central aisle and flat roofs over the side aisles. In this chamber is the *lid of the royal sarcophagus,* on which is a recumbent figure of the King. The lid, which, as usual, is in the form of a royal cartouche, is beautifully carved in pink granite; the King's face is particularly fine. The rooms adjoining the hypostyle hall are of no interest, and are in any event inaccessible.

No. 9 is the *Tomb of Ramesses VI* (Nebmare), named by the French expedition the *Tombe de la Métempsycose* and by British archaeologists the *Tomb of Memnon,* following the Roman tradition (on the ground that Ramesses had the same praenomen as Amenophis III, who was known to the Greeks as Memnon). The tomb – originally begun for Ramesses V – is notable for the excellent preservation of its painted sunk reliefs (though they are inferior in style to those of the 19th Dynasty).

Three corridors lead into an antechamber, beyond which is the *first pillared chamber,* with which Ramesses V's tomb ended. Left-hand wall: the sun's journey through the Underworld according to the "Book of the Gates". Right-hand wall: other scenes and texts relating to the life beyond the tomb. On three of the four pillars the King is depicted making offerings to the gods of the dead. On the ceiling are astronomical figures. – Two *corridors,* with scenes from the

Wall-painting in the Tomb of Ramesses VI

sun god's journey through the Underworld according to the "Book of what is in the Underworld", lead into another *antechamber,* the walls of which are covered with texts and scenes from the "Book of the Dead" (on the left-hand wall the 125th Chapter). Beyond this is the *second pillared chamber,* still containing remnants of the great *granite sarcophagus.* On the walls are texts relating to the Underworld; in the rear wall is a niche. On the vaulted ceiling are two figures of the sky goddess, representing the day sky and the night sky, with the hours. – The tomb contains numerous Greek and Coptic graffiti.

No. 10, the *Tomb of Amenmeses,* one of the claimants to the throne at the end of the 19th Dynasty, with his mother Takhat and his wife Beket-werer. The inscriptions and figures on the walls have been deliberately destroyed.

No. 11 is the **Tomb of Ramesses III**, called by Bruce the *Harper's Tomb,* which is exceeded in size only by Nos. 17 and 14. As far as the third chamber the tomb was constructed by Ramesses's father Sethnakhte, whose names are still to be seen in various places where the later stucco has fallen off. Peculiar to this tomb are the side chambers opening off the two corridors. The sunk reliefs are not particularly well executed, but they are notable for their variety and the excellent preservation of the colors.

On each side of the entrance, which is approached by a flight of steps with a ramp in the middle, are two pilasters adorned with cows' heads. On the door-lintel are the usual representations of Isis and Nephthys worshiping the solar disc, within which are the sun god and a scarab.

First corridor, to the right and left of the entrance: the goddess Maat kneeling, sheltering with her wings those who enter the tomb; on the left-hand wall, the King before Harakhty; beyond this the title-picture of the "Praising of Re", the sun between a snake, a crocodile and two gazelles' heads; then the text of the

Thebes (West)   Valley of Kings

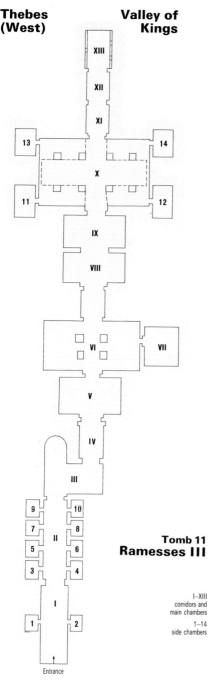

XIII

XII

XI

13   14

X

11   12

IX

VIII

VI   VII

V

IV

III

9   10

7   II   8

5   6

3   4

I

1   2

↑
Entrance

**Tomb 11
Ramesses III**

I–XIII
corridors and
main chambers

1–14
side chambers

cobras wearing aprons and two fertility gods. Upper row (much damaged), left: the Nile god of Upper Egypt presenting gifts to ten clothed royal cobras; right, the Nile god of Lower Egypt before Napret and three cobras. – The *fourth side chamber*, on the right, was the King's armory. Left-hand entrance wall: the sacred black bull Meri on the "Southern Lake". Right-hand entrance wall: the black cow Hesi on the "Northern Lake". Left-hand wall, above: standards, with pictures of sacred animals, heads of the goddess Hathor, etc. Rear wall, above: bows, arrows, quivers. Right-hand wall, above: standards, with gods' heads; lower row destroyed.

Fifth side chamber, on the left: upper row, various local divinities, alternately hermaphrodites (with pendulous breasts) and goddesses, bringing offerings; lower row, kneeling Nile gods. – The *sixth side chamber*, on the right, was the King's Treasury. On its walls are depicted various vases, jars and bottles (including the stirrup-jars imported into Egypt from the Greek islands), elephants' tusks, necklaces and beds with head-rests and steps leading up to them. – *Seventh side chamber*, on the left: entrance wall, to the right and left, the King's guardian spirit holding a staff topped by a King's head; other walls, in two rows (lower row destroyed), snakes, sacred bulls and cows. – *Eighth side chamber*, on the right: work in the sacred fields (plowing, sowing, reaping); the King sailing on a canal. – *Ninth side chamber*, on the left: left, a harpist singing before the god Enhuret and the falcon-headed Harakhty; right, a similar scene, largely destroyed. The text of the songs is inscribed on the entrance walls. *Tenth side chamber*, on the right: 12 different figures of Osiris.

The *third chamber* is deflected to the right in order to avoid the adjoining tomb, No. 10. On the rear wall is a goddess, representing the South, raising a water-jar; on the other walls the King is depicted making offerings to various gods. – *Fourth corridor*: on the left-hand wall the sun's journey during the fourth hour of night, on the right-hand wall during the fifth hour (both from the "Book of what is in the Underworld"). *Fifth chamber*: figures of gods.

The *sixth chamber* is a sloping passage with side galleries and four pillars, on which the King is depicted in the presence of various gods. Walls on the left (beginning on the entrance wall): the sun's journey through the fourth part of the Underworld ("Book of the Gates"); in the bottom row representatives of the four chief races of man known to the ancient Egyptians. Walls on the right: the sun's journey through the fifth part of the Underworld ("Book of the Gates"). Rear wall, to the right and left: the King before Osiris. – *Seventh chamber*: right-hand entrance wall, the King conducted by Thoth and the falcon-headed Harkhentekhtai; left-hand entrance wall, the King presenting an image of Truth to Osiris; other walls, scenes from the "Book of what is in the Underworld" (gods felling trees, etc.).

The other rooms are much damaged and of little interest. In the tenth room, a *pillared chamber*, stood the King's sarcophagus. His mummy was found at Deir el-Bahri and is now in the Egyptian Museum in Cairo.

No. 12, a tomb without inscriptions.

No. 13, low and filled with debris, is not a royal tomb. It apparently belonged to Bai, Chief Minister to King Siptah (19th Dynasty).

"Praising", which is continued on the right-hand wall. – *First side chamber*, on the left: bakers, slaughtermen and cooks at work. – *Second side chamber*, on the right: two rows of ships, the upper row with sails set, the lower row with sails furled.

Second corridor (with niches on the right and left): on both sides the continuation of the "Praising", with the appropriate figures of the sun god approaching Isis on the left and Nephthys on the right. – *Third side chamber*, on the left: upper row, to the left of the entrance, a kneeling Nile god bestowing gifts on seven fertility gods (with ears of corn on their heads); to the right of the entrance a Nile god before the snake-headed goddess Napret ("corn"), five royal

Wall-painting in the Tomb of Ramesses I

No. 14, *Tomb of Queen Tewosert* (Tausert), wife of Siptah; later appropriated and enlarged by King Sethnakhte, when the Queen's names and figures were covered over with stucco.

No. 15, *Tomb of Sethos II,* with good reliefs in the first corridor.

No. 16, the *Tomb of Ramesses I**. A wide flight of steps leads to the entrance.

A sloping corridor and a steep staircase lead down to the *tomb chamber,* in the middle of which is the open coffin of the King, of red granite, with pictures and texts painted in yellow. The walls of the chamber are covered with colored scenes and inscriptions on a gray ground.

Entrance wall: to left, Maat and Ramesses I before Ptah, behind whom is an Osiris pillar; to the right, Maat and the King offering wine to Nefertum, behind whom is the symbolic knot of Isis. Left-hand wall: to the left of the door into a small side chamber, Ramesses I conducted by the dog-headed Anubis and the falcon-headed Harsiesis; to the right of the door and above it, the third section of the "Book of the Gates". First comes the gateway, guarded by the snake Zetbi; then the journey through the third division of the Underworld; in the middle the boat is being drawn by four men towards a long chapel, in which are the mummies of nine gods; then follow 12 goddesses representing the hours of the night, divided into two groups by a snake, ascending a mountain below which is a pond (indicated by zigzag lines). – In the rear wall is a door leading into a small chamber, on the rear wall of which Osiris is depicted between a ram-headed god and a sacred snake. Above the door are dog-headed and falcon-headed demons (the souls of Pe and Nekhen); to the right of the rear wall, Ramesses I dedicating four packages to the beetle-headed sun god Amun-Re-Khepri; Harsiesis, Atum and Neith conducting the King to the throne of Osiris. On the right-hand wall, in which is a door into a small undecorated side chamber, has scenes and texts from the second section of the "Book of the Gates".

No. 17, the **Tomb of Sethos I**, also known as *Belzoni's Tomb* after its discoverer (October 1817). Like Nos 11 and 14, it has a total length of some 330 ft/100 m. The reliefs are far superior in quality and state of preservation to any others in the Valley of the Kings, rivalling those of Abydos. A flight of wooden steps descends to the entrance.

First corridor, left-hand wall: the King in the presence of the falcon-headed sun god Harakhty; the title-picture of the "Praising of Re" (the sun, with a scarab and the ram-headed sun god, between a snake, a crocodile and two cows' heads); the text of the

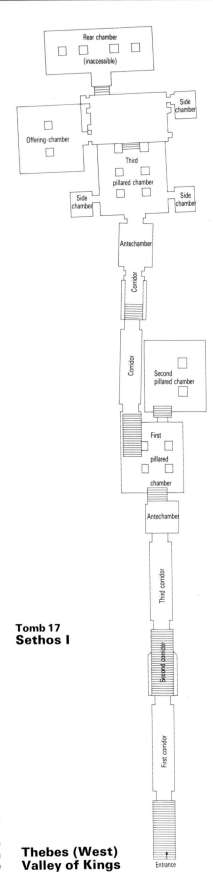

Tomb 17
Sethos I

**Thebes (West)
Valley of Kings**

Entrance

"Praising", which is continued on the right-hand wall. On the ceiling are hovering vultures. – *Second corridor* (staircase), left-hand wall: above, in a niche, the sun god in 37 different forms (from the "Praising of Re"); below the niche, texts from the "Book of what is in the Underworld", continued on the right-hand wall; on the right and left of the staircase Nephthys and Isis. – *Third corridor*, left-hand wall: the sun's journey during the fifth hour of night (5th part of the "Book of what is in the Underworld"); right-hand wall, the sun's journey during the fourth hour of night (4th part of the "Book of what is in the Underworld"). – *Antechamber*: the King in presence of various gods.

First pillared chamber, left-hand walls: the sun's journey through the fourth division of the Underworld (4th part of the "Book of the Gates"). At the beginning is the fourth gateway, guarded by the snake Tekehor; then, in the middle row, the solar barque drawn by four men; in front of it spirits with a coiled snake, three ibis-headed gods and nine other gods ("the spirits of men who are in the Underworld"); on the right a god with a scepter. Upper row: men greeting the god, with others holding a coil of rope. Bottom row: left, Horus; in front of him representatives of the four chief races of men known to the Egyptians – four Egyptians, four Asiatics with pointed beards and colored loincloths, four Negroes (Kushites) and four Libyans, identified by the feathers on their heads and tattooed bodies; farther along genii with a snake bearing the hieroglyph for "time", etc.

Right-hand walls: the sun's journey through the fifth division of the Underworld (5th part of the "Book of the Gates"). In the middle row is the solar barque drawn by four men and preceded by demons. Upper row: 12 gods with forked sticks, 12 gods with a snake from which human heads project and 12 gods with a cord attached to a mummy. Bottom row: a god leaning on a staff, 12 mummies on a bier in the form of a snake, etc. In the center of the rear wall is Osiris enthroned; in front of him the King conducted by the falcon-headed Horus, behind him Hathor. On the pillars the King is depicted in presence of various deities.

A short flight of steps leads into the *second pillared chamber*, with two pillars. The scenes and inscriptions in this room are merely sketched out in red and black on stucco. On the pillars the King is depicted before various deities. Left-hand walls: the sun's journey during the ninth hour of night (9th part of the "Book of what is in the Underworld"). Middle row: the solar barque; in front of it 12 star gods with oars; three sacred animals (a cow, a ram, a human-headed bird); a mummy standing upright, the guardian god of the offerings. Upper row: 12 genii crouching on curious stands and 12 women. Bottom row (partly destroyed): fire-breathing snakes; men with sticks; a mummy.

The scenes on the rear wall, continuing on part of the right-hand wall, show the sun's journey during the tenth hour of night (10th part of the "Book of what is in the Underworld"). Middle row: the solar barque, preceded by various deities, including a falcon perched on a snake with two heads and four legs; four spirits with solar discs in place of heads carrying arrows, four with lances and four with bows. Upper row: a god with a scepter; a scarab holding the hieroglyph for "land" in its forelegs; the protective goddesses of Upper and Lower Egypt seated beside two erect snakes bearing the solar disc; two goddesses beside the hieroglyph for "god", on which rests the sun; lion-headed and human-headed goddesses, etc. Bottom row (partly destroyed): Horus, leaning on a staff, watches 12 damned souls swimming in the waters of the Underworld; four goddesses with snakes; the head of the god Seth on a scepter.

The scenes on the right-hand entrance wall, continuing on the right-hand wall, show the sun's journey during the eleventh hour of night (11th part of the "Book of what is in the Underworld"). Middle row: the solar barque; in front of it 12 men bearing a snake; two snakes, on the backs of which are the two Egyptian crowns, with heads projecting from them; four goddesses. Upper row: a two-headed god; a snake (the god Atum); the tortoise constellation, in the form of a snake on which a god is seated; a two-headed god; four goddesses, each sitting on two snakes; etc. Bottom row: the damned (the enemies of the sun god being burned in curious furnaces under the supervision of the falcon-headed Horus, on the right; goddesses holding swords and breathing fire; in the last furnace four corpses standing on their heads; other deities).

From the first pillared chamber a flight of 18 steps, on the left, lead down by way of two corridors with representations of the "opening of the mouth" ceremony into an *antechamber, with fine reliefs of the King in the presence of various gods of the dead (Osiris, Isis, Harsiesis, Hathor, Anubis, etc.). – Beyond this is the *third pillared chamber*, from which a ramp flanked by steps leads down to the mummy-shaft. This consists of a front portion, with six pillars, and a rear portion, with a vaulted roof, on a lower level. In the front section are scenes in the realm of the dead from the "Book of the Gates". In the rear section was the King's alabaster sarcophagus, now in the Soane Museum in London. The King's mummy was found at Deir el-Bahri and is now in the Egyptian Museum in Cairo.

On the left-hand wall of the rear part of the chamber, above the doorway, the King is depicted offering a libation of wine to Harakhty. Beyond this, in four rows, the sun's journey during the first hour of night (1st part of the "Book of what is in the Underworld"). Two middle rows: above, the solar barque, adorned with a mat, in which are the ram-headed sun god, seven other gods and the "mistress of the boat"; in front of it several deities, including two goddesses of truth, Osiris and the lion-headed Sakhmet; below, in a boat, the sun god in the form of a scarab worshiped by two figures of Osiris; in front, three snakes and several deities. Top and bottom rows (representing the banks of the river), in small square panels: spirits in human and animal form (including baboons and fire-breathing snakes) greeting the god and driving away his enemies. – At the end of the left-hand wall is a niche, in which the dog-headed Anubis is depicted performing the ceremony of the "opening of the mouth" on Osiris.

The rear wall depicts the sun's journey during the second hour of night (2nd part of the "Book of what is in the Underworld"). Middle row: the solar barque, with the sun god and other deities, including Isis and Nephthys in the form of cobras; in front of it four small boats, in the first of which are three armless deities, in the second a crocodile with a human head on its back, in the third (which is adorned with two gods' heads) a sistrum, two goddesses and a scarab, in the fourth (with two gods' heads) a god holding a large ostrich feather, the symbol of justice and the moon on a head-rest. Top and bottom rows: various spirits and demons protecting the sun god.

Wall-painting in the Tomb of Sethos I

The right-hand wall shows the sun's journey during the third hour of night (3rd part of the "Book of what is in the Underworld"). Middle row: the solar barque, with three smaller boats in front of it and four gods with draped arms coming to meet them. Upper and lower rows: various spirits (a ram with a sword, five bird-headed demons, four enthroned figures of Osiris, etc.) greeting the procession. On the vaulted roof are constellations and other astronomical figures.

Side chamber to the left of the front portion of the pillared chamber: the sun's journey through the third division of the Underworld ("Book of the Gates"). – *Side chamber* to the right: texts relating a very ancient myth of a rebellion by mankind against the sun god, their punishment and the eventual rescue of the survivors. On the rear wall is a scene from this myth: the celestial cow, supported by the god Shu and other spirits, with two solar barques sailing on its body.

Off the rear part of the pillared chamber opens the *offering-chamber*, which has two pillars; on the left-hand one the King is depicted in the presence of Ptah and Osiris. Round the three main walls runs a bench with a cavetto cornice, originally supported on small pillars (now destroyed) and decorated with reliefs which are almost entirely obliterated. The walls to the left depict the sun's journey during the seventh hour of night ("Book of what is in the Underworld"). Middle row: the sun god in the solar barque, on the prow of which is Isis, driving away evil spirits with her spells; in front, the goddess Selkit and a god, who have subdued a large snake; farther along, four goddesses with swords, and the tombs, adorned with human heads, of the gods Atum, Khepri, Re and Osiris. Upper row: spirits and demons; a human-headed snake; a god ("Flesh of Osiris") sitting on a throne under a snake; three enemies of Osiris beheaded by a lion-headed god; a god holding a rope binding three prostrate enemies; three birds with human heads, crowned; a god borne by a snake. Bottom row: Horus, preceded by the 12 star gods who conduct the sun on its nightly journey; 12 star goddesses approaching the Tomb of Osiris, on which a crocodile is lying, with the god's emerging from the burial mound.

The rear wall depicts the sun's journey during the eighth hour of night ("Book of what is in the Underworld"). Middle row: the solar barque, drawn by eight men; in front, nine attendants on Re, represented by the hieroglyph for "follow", on which is a head; at the head of the procession four rams (forms of the god Tatjenen). Top and bottom rows: the dwellings of the dead, their doors opening at the approach of the sun god and revealing the spirits and gods now brought back to life; in each house in the top row three gods (beginning with the nine gods of Heliopolis), in the bottom row snakes and other spirits.

Walls to the right: the sun's journey during the sixth hour of night ("Book of what is in the Underworld"). Middle row: the solar barque; in front of it Thoth enthroned (with the head of a baboon, his sacred animal), holding an ibis (another sacred animal), and a goddess holding the pupils of Horus's eyes; 16 spirits and the god Khepri, encircled by a five-headed snake. Four of the spirits represent the Kings of Upper Egypt, four the Kings of Lower Egypt; the others are in the guise of mummies. In the top and bottom rows are various spirits (among them a snake with the heads of the four genii of the dead on its back and nine fire-breathing snakes with swords), whose function is to destroy the sun god's enemies. – The second side chamber on the right is undecorated, as is the chamber to the rear (inaccessible).

No. 18, *Tomb of Ramesses X* (Khepermare).

No. 19, *Tomb of Prince Mentu-her-khopshef* (late 20th Dynasty); rear part unfinished.

No. 20, **Tomb of Queen Hatshepsut**, without inscriptions or reliefs. The corridors of this tomb have a total length of 233 yds/213 m and go down to a depth of 320 ft/97 m. The sarcophagi of the Queen and her father Tuthmosis I were found in the tomb chamber and are now in the Egyptian Museum in Cairo.

No. 21, without inscriptions.

Nos 22–25 lie in the western valley of the Biban el-Muluk, which is known locally as the **Gabanet el-Qurud** ("Monkeys' Cemetery"). – No. 22 is the *Tomb of Amenophis III*. It is entered by the W, but after a short distance the corridor turns N at right angles and later turns E again. – No. 23, the *Turbet el-Qurud* or Monkey's Tomb, occupies a very secluded situation. It belonged to King Ay, whose coffin is now in the Egyptian Museum in Cairo. – Nos 24 and 25 are uninscribed.

Nos 26–33 are of no interest.

No. 34, the **Tomb of Tuthmosis III**, is in a narrow and steep-sided gully some 275 yds/250 m S of the tomb of Ramesses III.

A sloping corridor down to a staircase, with wide niches on the right and left, beyond which a further corridor leads to a square shaft 16–20 ft/5–6 m deep, probably intended to deter tomb-robbers; it is now crossed by a footbridge. The roof has white stars on a blue ground.

Beyond the shaft is a *chamber* with two pillars (undecorated). The ceiling is covered with stars. On the walls are lists of 741 different deities and demons. – At the left-hand end of the rear wall a staircase leads down to the *tomb chamber*, which has the oval shape of a royal cartouche. The ceiling, with yellow stars on a blue ground, is supported on two square pillars. The walls are covered with excellently preserved scenes and texts from the "Book of what is in the Underworld". Those on the pillars are of particular interest. On one side of the first pillar is a long religious text; on the second side are Tuthmosis III and his mother Eset in a boat (top), the King suckled by his mother in the form of a tree (below), and the King followed by his wives Merit-re, Sat-yoh and Nebt-khru and Princess Nefreterew; and on the third side are demons. On the front of the second pillar is a long text, with demons above it; and on the other sides are further figures of demons.

Pillar in the Tomb of Amenophis II

dead; on the walls are finely executed scenes and texts from the "Book of what is in the Underworld", on a yellow ground imitating papyrus. In the crypt is the King's sandstone *sarcophagus*, in which the mummy of Amenophis II was found intact, with a bunch of flowers and garlands. – On each side are two chambers, in which many mummies, no doubt brought here to be safe from tomb-robbers, were found, including those of Tuthmosis IV and Amenophis III (18th Dynasty) and Siptah and Sethos II (19th Dynasty).

No. 36, the *Tomb of Mei-her-peri*, a Fan-bearer.

No. 37, without inscriptions.

No. 38, the **Tomb of Tuthmosis I**, the oldest royal tomb in the Valley of the Kings, in the steep slope at the head of the valley, between Tombs 15 and 14.

A steep flight of steps descends to an antechamber, from which another flight leads down to the roughly hewn tomb chamber, the roof of which was originally supported on a column. The painted stucco which covered the walls has disappeared. The handsome *sarcophagus* of red sandstone has figures of Isis (at foot), Nephthys (at head), various gods of the dead (on sides) and the sky goddess Nut (interior). – Adjoining is a small side chamber.

No. 39, of no interest.

Nos 40 and 41: no inscriptions.

No. 42 (perhaps the tomb of Tuthmosis II), of no interest.

No. 43, the *Tomb of Tuthmosis IV*, unfinished. In two of the rooms the King is depicted in the presence of various gods.

No. 44, the *Tomb of Tentkaru*, of no interest.

No. 45, the *Tomb of Userhet*, of no interest.

No. 46, the *Tomb of Yuya and Tuya*, parents-in-law of Amenophis III; without inscriptions.

No. 47, the *Tomb of King Siptah* (19th Dynasty), which has some good scenes (the King before Re-Harakhty; the sun between two hills; the body of Osiris, attended by Isis, Nephthys and Anubis). The royal sarcophagus is still in the tomb.

No. 48, the *Tomb of Amenemopet*, a Vizier (18th Dynasty): without inscriptions.

Nos 49–54, without inscriptions.

No. 55, *Tomb of Queen Tiy*, mother of Amenophis IV/Akhenaten. Akhenaten himself may also have been buried in this tomb. No inscriptions.

No. 56, without inscriptions.

No. 57, the *Tomb of Horemheb* (see also under Saqqara), with some excellent paintings. The tomb chamber still contains the sarcophagus.

Nos 58–61, without inscriptions.

No. 62 is the **Tomb of Tutankhamun**, son-in-law of Akhenaten, who died (in circumstances unknown) in his 18th or 19th year. The tomb was discovered by Howard Carter on November 4, 1922 and opened by Carter and Lord Carnarvon on November 26. Although the tomb had been broken into soon after

The *sarcophagus* is of red sandstone, with painted scenes and inscriptions. It was empty when the tomb was opened, but the mummy was found at Deir el-Bahri. The grave-goods from the four small side chambers are now in the Egyptian Museum in Cairo.

No. 35, the **Tomb of Amenophis II**, is some 165 yds/150 m W of the tomb of Ramesses III.

From the entrance steep flights of steps and sloping corridors descend to a shaft (now bridged over), at the foot of which is a small room, and beyond this the *first chamber* (undecorated) with two pillars. At the left-hand end of the rear wall is a flight of steps leading down to a sloping corridor, at the end of which is the *second chamber*, with six pillars. – To the rear of this chamber, on a lower level, is a *crypt*. On the pillars the King is depicted in the presence of the gods of the

Thebes (West)   Valley of Kings

Tomb 35
Amenophis II

33 feet
(10 m)

1 Shaft
2 Side chamber
3 First chamber
4 Second chamber
5 Crypt with sarcophagus
6–9 Side chambers

Innermost gold coffin of Tutankhamun

coffins inside the sarcophagus. The mummy is still in the sarcophagus, but the inner coffins are now in the Egyptian Museum in Cairo, where they rank among the museum's principal treasures. The four gilded wooden shrines which stood around the sarcophagus are also in the museum. – On the E side of the tomb chamber is a small store-room. On the walls of the chamber are painted scenes, rather hastily executed: E wall, funeral scenes; N wall, King Ay, Tutankhamun's successor, performing the "opening of the mouth" ceremony on the mummy, and Tutankhamun making offerings to various gods.

If time permits it is well worth while to return to the plain by the hill path which runs direct from the Valley of the Kings to Deir el-Bahri. The walk, strenuous but not difficult (stout footwear needed), takes about 45 minutes. It affords magnificent *views – at first down into the desolate Valley of the Kings and then, from the crest of the ridge and on the way down, into the curiously shaped amphitheatre in which Deir el-Bahri lies, enclosed within steeply scarped hills, and over the fertile green plain on both sides of the Nile, with its palms and massive temple ruins, to the buildings of Karnak and Luxor on the E bank of the river.

the King's burial it remained almost intact, together with its rich furnishings. These furnishings, the famous **"Treasures of Tutankhamun" (mostly now in the Egyptian Museum in Cairo), were the largest and most valuable find of grave-goods ever made in Egypt, giving an overwhelming impression of the splendor of a royal burial in Pharaonic times.

A flight of 16 steps leads down to the entrance, on the E side of the tomb. The doorway opens into a narrow passage 25 ft/7.50 m long, at the far end of which another door gives access to an *antechamber*, the largest chamber in the tomb (26 ft/8 m by 12 ft/3.60 m), which was found filled to overflowing with grave-goods of all kinds. At the SW corner (far left) is a side chamber. The N wall, against which, flanking the doorway, were found two life-size wooden statues of the King, has been removed and replaced by a railing which enables visitors to look into the *tomb chamber*. In the middle of the chamber is the *sarcophagus*, of yellowish crystalline sandstone. Its sides are covered with religious scenes and texts, and at the corners are four relief figures of goddesses with wings protectively outspread. The King's mummy was contained within three richly decorated wooden

Deir el-Bahri

The great **Temple of Deir el-Bahri** is magnificently situated at the foot of the sheer cliffs fringing the desert hills, the light-colored, almost white, sandstone of the temple standing out prominently against the golden yellow to light brown rocks behind.

HISTORY. – The temple was built at the beginning of the New Kingdom, in the reign of Queen **Hatshepsut**, who was at once aunt, stepmother and mother-in-law of Tuthmosis III and Co-ruler with him. It encroached on the court of the 11th Dynasty temple, laid out in terraces and richly adorned with statues, reliefs and inscriptions, which adjoins it on the S, and incorporated architectural elements from that temple. When Tuthmosis III became sole ruler he caused all statues of the Queen to be removed from the temple and had her name and figure erased from all reliefs and inscriptions, replacing them by his own. In the reign of Amenophis IV/Akhenaten the figures and names of the god Amun were obliterated, but they were later restored, rather clumsily, during the reign of Ramesses II. – In subsequent centuries the temple suffered little change. Minor alterations and additions were made by *Ptolemy VIII Euergetes II* (146–117 B.C.), but these did not affect the main structure. – After the introduction of Christianity the temple was occupied by monks, who converted it into a monastery – known in Arabic as **Deir el-Bahri**, the Northern Monastery – and defaced the pagan scenes depicted on the walls.

Mariette carried out some minor excavation of the site; then in 1894–96 it was cleared of rubble and sand by

Thebes (West)

Valley of Kings

Store-room

Tomb 62 Tutankhamun

Tomb chamber

Ante-chamber

Passage

Steps

Side chamber

33 feet

(10 m)

Edouard Naville on behalf of the Egypt Exploration Fund; and later it was carefully investigated and made structurally safe by an expedition from the Metropolitan Museum of Art, New York. In recent years restoration work has been carried out by Polish archaeologists, and these are still in progress.

> In examining the wall-paintings and reliefs it should be borne in mind that Queen Hatshepsut, as if to demonstrate that as ruler of Egypt she possessed all the authority of a king, had herself represented with the attributes (the beard and short apron) of a Pharaoh, normally appropriate to a man.

The temple was dedicated to Amun of Thebes, but the goddess Hathor and Anubis, god of the dead, also had their own chapels here, and there were also chambers set apart for the mortuary cult of the Queen, whose tomb was in the Valley of the Kings, on the main axis of the temple. – The temple complex is laid out on three terraces rising from the plain, linked by ramps which divide it into a northern and a southern half. Along the W side of each terrace is a raised colonnade. The terraces were hewn out of the eastern slopes of the hills, with retaining walls of the finest sandstone along the sides and to the rear. The temple itself was also partly hewn from the rock.

An avenue of sphinxes originally led up from a valley temple (now disappeared) in the plain, ending at a

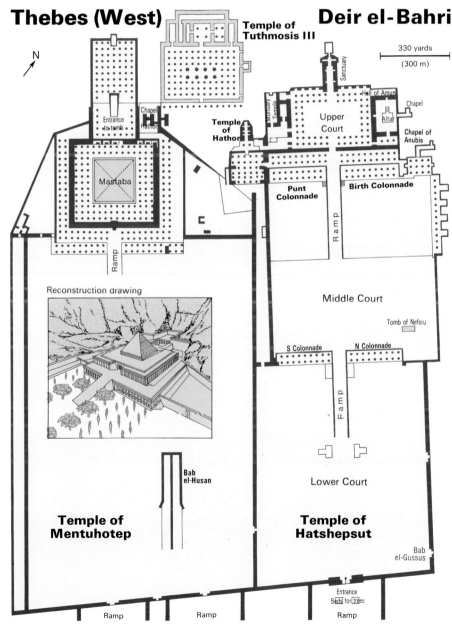

gateway (also almost totally destroyed) at the entrance to the temple precinct. In front of the gateway, in square masonary enclosures, were two persea trees (*Mimusops schimperi*), the stumps of which still remain.

We first enter the **Lower Court**, at the farther (W) end of which is a ramp leading up to a colonnaded terrace. On either side of the ramp is a balustrade; on the left-hand side, at the foot, is a lion couchant. Each half of the colonnade had two rows of 11 pillars, those in the rear row being 16-sided, those in the front row square, adorned at the top with falcons, vultures and snakes. Little is left of the inscriptions and reliefs on the walls.

On the rear wall of the *northern colonnade* are remains of a relief depicting a pond on which waterfowl are being caught with nets. Rear wall of *southern colonnade* (right to left): the Queen (figure obliterated) making an offering to an ithyphallic Amun; erection and dedication of the temple obelisks; ships and soldiers on their way to a festival; ships transporting two obelisks from the Aswan quarries to Thebes. – In front of the ramp are two cavities in the rock in which papyrus plants were grown; there were also round holes for flowers.

From the lower court there is a good view of the fine masonry of the southern *retaining wall,* built of carefully dressed limestone blocks with simple but effective decoration, echoing that of the pillars in the colonnade.

Continuing up the ramp, we reach the **Middle Court**, which, like the lower one, is bounded on the W by a colonnaded terrace: to the right the Birth Colonnade, to the left the Punt Colonnade. – The **Birth Colonnade** has two rows of 11 pillars supporting the roof, with the same scenes on all four sides of the pillars: Amun laying his hands in blessing on the shoulders of the Queen (whose figure is invariably obliterated) or Tuthmosis III. The inscriptions and reliefs on the walls relate to the procreation and birth of the Queen (note the two fine figures of her mother Ahmes: in one she is conducted while pregnant into the presence of the ram-headed Khnum and the frog-headed Heqet, in the other she stands opposite the ibis-headed Thoth). – Two steps at the N end of the colonnade lead down into a *Vestibule* with 12 16-sided columns and fine mural reliefs.

In the S wall of the vestibule is a small niche with representations of the Queen (figure obliterated) before Usiris. To the left of the niche is Anubis, originally with the Queen behind him; to the right Nekhbet and Harakhty, between whom the names of the Queen were originally inscribed. – Above the niche in the N wall is Tuthmosis III making a libation of wine to the falcon-headed god of the dead Sokar; to the right of the niche Anubis and the Queen (obliterated); to the left the Queen (obliterated) standing in a chapel in front of the symbol of Emewet. Rear (W) wall: left, the Queen (obliterated) making an offering to Amun, with votive gifts heaped up in front of him; right, a similar scene with Anubis.

From the rear of the vestibule three steps lead into the *Chapel of Anubis,* which consists of three chambers with vaulted roofs. On the walls are paintings with well-preserved coloring, depicting the Queen (always obliterated) in the presence of various gods, in particular Anubis. On the E wall of the second chamber Tuthmosis III is depicted once, pouring out water in the presence of Sokar. – The colonnade along the N

In the Chapel of Anubis, Deir el-Bahri

side of the terrace, with 15 16-sided columns and four rear chambers (now walled up), was left unfinished.

On the S side of the ramp is the **Punt Colonnade**, which is identical in plan to the Birth Colonnade.

The* reliefs, some of which are unfortunately much damaged, depict a trading expedition to Punt (on the Somali coast) in the reign of Hatshepsut. On the S wall is a village in the Land of Punt, with beehive-shaped huts set among palms and incense trees on the coast and entered by ladders. In the lower row, to the right, the Egyptian Envoy and his retinue are received by the Prince of Punt; above, the Envoy in front of his tent looking at the gifts that have been heaped on him. – The W wall shows (on the left) the arrival of the Egyptian vessels at Punt, where they are laden with merchandise; on the right, the voyage home; above, the people of Punt and the Egyptians with their gifts, while dignitaries prostrate themselves in homage to the Queen; beyond this, the Queen (obliterated), accompanied by her guardian spirit, dedicating to Amun the valuable wares brought back from Punt (note the cattle grazing under the trees); gold and other precious metals being weighed, with the goddess Seshat keeping a record; Horus operating the scales, with the Nubian god Dedun behind him; below, incense being measured, with Thoth noting down the quantities; seven incense trees in tubs, brought back from Punt; Tuthmosis III offering incense to the barque of Amun, which is borne by priests; the Queen in the presence of Amun (a long inscription between them obliterated). – On the N wall the Queen (obliterated) seated under a canopy with her guardian spirit behind her; in front are various dignitaries, whom she is addressing, and a long inscription.

On the N side of the Colonnade of Punt is a **Temple of Hathor**, tutelary goddess of the Theban necropolis, which was originally also entered from

◀ **The temples of Deir el-Bahri**

below by a flight of steps. Of its two colonnades, now in ruins, one had 16-sided columns and square pillars with Hathor capitals, the other (on a slightly higher level) round Hathor columns and 16-sided columns. – The *second colonnade* has preserved some reliefs. N wall: Tuthmosis III, holding an oar, in presence of a goddess; on the right, a procession, with two ships in each of the three upper rows and soldiers with standards and axes in the bottom row (on right two soldiers dancing to the sound of castanets). S wall (much dilapidated): an offering scene; a Hathor cow in a boat, with Hatshepsut drinking from the udder. – W wall: on the right Tuthmosis II (replacing the Queen), with an oar and a builder's square, in the presence of Hathor (figure obliterated by Amenophis IV); the King, with the Hathor cow licking his hand; on the left similar subjects.

From the second colonnade two steps lead up to the rock-cut *Chapel,* which has three chambers, one behind the other and each one step higher than the preceding one; in each chamber are several niches. The first chamber has two 16-sided columns and a ceiling decorated with stars on a blue ground. The mural reliefs show Hatshepsut (obliterated) or Tuthmosis III before various deities. – The second chamber has *mural reliefs of great beauty: the Queen (obliterated) making an offering to the Hathor cow, which stands in a boat under a canopy, with Hatshepsut (remains of defaced figure) drinking from its udder; in front of the Queen the naked figure of Ihi, Hathor's young son, with a sistrum. – The third chamber is roofed with a parabolic vault. On the side walls are two fine representations of Hatshepsut drinking from the udder of the Hathor cow, in front of which is a small figure of Amun; on the rear wall the Queen between Hathor and Amun, who holds the hieroglyph for "life" to her nostrils; above the niches Hatshepsut and Tuthmosis III offering milk and wine to Hathor.

At the NE corner of the middle court is the entrance to the *Tomb of Queen Neferu* (11th Dynasty: torch

In the Deir el-Bahri Temple

necessary). From the court a ramp leads up to a badly ruined colonnade, the roof of which was supported by pillars (originally colossal statues of Hatshepsut, which were removed by Tuthmosis III and reshaped into pillars) and 16-sided columns. From here a granite doorway opens into the **Upper Court**. In the middle of this there originally stood a large hypostyle hall, now totally ruined, on the walls of which were reliefs of a solemn procession (largely destroyed by

Hathor columns in the Temple of Hatshepsut, Deir el-Bahri

Coptic monks). – A doorway at the NE corner of the court leads into a *vestibule* which has three 16-sided columns supporting the roof. Opposite the entrance is a niche with well-preserved figures of the Queen. On the rear wall Hatshepsut (obliterated) is depicted in the presence of Amun; on the side walls the Queen (here left undamaged) is seated at table, with a priest (defaced by Amenophis IV) in front of her.

Beyond the vestibule is an open court, in the center of which, approached by ten steps, is an *altar dedicated to the sun god Re-Harakhty, one of the few altars found on their original sites. In the W wall of the court is a niche in which the Queen (obliterated) is depicted making offerings.

In the N wall is a doorway into a *chapel* consisting of two chambers. With only a few exceptions the reliefs on the walls have been chiseled away either by Tuthmosis III or by Amenophis IV. First chamber, side walls: the Queen making offerings to various deities, in particular the gods of the dead (Anubis, Sokar, Osiris, Emewet) but also Amun. Rear wall, above the bench: Hatshepsut and Tuthmosis I in front of the symbol of Emewet. Second chamber, right-hand wall: Tuthmosis I (originally Hatshepsut) and his mother Seniseneb making offerings to Anubis. Left-hand wall: the Queen and her mother Ahmes making offerings to Amun. Rear wall: Hatshepsut and Anubis. On the ceilings are representations of stars in the night sky.

At the S end of the upper court are several ruined chambers and the well-preserved vaulted **Mortuary Chapel of Hatshepsut**, which is decorated with reliefs. To the right and left of the entrance: the slaughtering and cutting up of sacrificial animals. Side walls: three rows of priests and officials bringing votive gifts to Hatshepsut; above, various offerings; the Queen (obliterated) seated with a list of the offerings in front of her, with priests burning incense and performing other ritual acts. On the rear wall is the door leading into the realm of the dead.

In the W wall of the large hall which stood in the middle of the court are niches of varying size with representations of Tuthmosis III and Hatshepsut in the presence of various gods; in the larger niches there were originally statues of the Queen. In the center is the entrance to the sanctuary. At the left-hand end is a small chamber; at the right-hand end is the so-called Hall of Amun. – The left-hand chamber has a well-preserved roof. On the right-hand wall Amun-Re is depicted in front of an offering-table, which has been inserted in place of the obliterated figure of the Queen; behind the table is her guardian spirit. Rear wall: Tuthmosis III and Tuthmosis I (substituted for the Queen) making an offering of garments to Amun. Left-hand wall: Tuthmosis II (substituted for the Queen) offering sacred oils to an ithyphallic Amun. – The *Hall of Amun* has preserved only part of its roof, which was decorated with stars on a blue ground. Left-hand wall: Hatshepsut pacing out the temple precinct in the presence of Amun, before an ithyphallic Amun-Min and before Amun enthroned. Right-hand wall: Tuthmosis III before the same deities. Rear wall: Tuthmosis III (originally Hatshepsut) and Amun. The figures of the gods were defaced by Amenophis IV and not replaced.

The **Sanctuary**, entered by way of a balustraded passage and a granite doorway of the 18th Dynasty, has three badly ruined chambers. The first two have vaulted roofs and niches in the walls. In the first chamber Hatshepsut and Tuthmosis III are depicted making offerings to various divinities, including the deified Tuthmosis II. The third chamber, built during the reign of Euergetes II, was dedicated to Imhotep and Amenhotep, who were much venerated during the Ptolemaic period; the inscriptions and reliefs of this late period are much inferior to the fine work of Hatshepsut's reign. – On the right-hand wall of the first chamber, above: Hatshepsut, Tuthmosis III and Princess Neferure making offerings to the sacred barque of Amun, behind which stood Tuthmosis I, his wife Ahmes and their small daughter Bitneferu. On the left-hand wall, above the first niche, was a similar scene, in which only the kneeling figure of Tuthmosis III and Princess Neferure can still be distinguished.

Immediately adjoining the Temple of Hatshepsut, to the S, is the *Mortuary Temple of Mentuhotep II**, the best-preserved example of the architecture of the Early Middle Kingdom. Originally consisting of a terrace with a hypostyle hall and a pyramid (though the remains are sometimes differently interpreted) built over the tombs of the King and his family, it was much altered and extended in the course of Mentuhotep's long reign. It is the oldest Theban temple known to us, and is of particular interest for the simplicity of its architecture. It was excavated by the Egypt Exploration Fund in 1905–07, and since then has been thoroughly investigated by an expedition from the Metropolitan Museum of Art in New York (1922–25) and recently by German archaeologists.

From the cultivated land, where there are the remains of a temple of the Ramessid period and a brick building associated with the tomb of one of the Sheshonqs, a wide avenue led up to the large temple forecourt, which was planted with trees (set in holes which can still be seen). The temple itself was laid out in terraces. From the *Forecourt,* bounded on the W side by two colonnades with square pillars bearing Mentuhotep's name (Nebkhru-re), a ramp leads up to the main *Terrace* on which the mortuary temple and pyramid stood. Beyond the scanty traces of a vestibule aligned from N to S is the main structure, a large colonnade of 140 eight-sided pillars which surrounded the sub-structure, faced with fine limestone slabs, of the royal pyramid. In the W wall of this colonnade were the mortuary chapels of the favorites of the royal harem. Beyond this is a colonnaded court, in the pavement of which is the entrance to a sloping passage 165 yds/150 m long leading down to the King's subterranean burial chamber. On the E side of the court are openings giving access to the shaft tombs of the royal favorites. To the rear of the court are a large pillared hall (with only the bases of its 80 octagonal pillars remaining) and the rock-hewn *Sanctuary.*

To the N of Mentuhotep's Temple was a Temple of Hathor built by Tuthmosis III but now destroyed. Its rock-hewn sanctuary, with the image of the goddess, is now in the Egyptian Museum in Cairo.

In the forecourt of Mentuhotep's Temple is the subterranean tomb, known in Arabic as *Bab el-Husan,* of Mentuhotep I Nebhepetre (11th Dynasty), which was excavated by Howard Carter in 1900.

Other major discoveries have been made in the Valley of Deir el-Bahri. In 1881 a number of royal mummies, including those of Amosis I, Tuthmosis III, Sethos I and Ramesses II, were found in a shaft in a small valley S of the mortuary temple – brought here during the 21st Dynasty to protect them from tomb-robbers. In 1891 a mass tomb of Theban priestly families was found immediately N of the lower court (material in Alexandria and Cairo museums).

To the E of Deir el-Bahri is the *El-Asasif* Valley, in which is a large *Necropolis*, mostly dating from the Saite period (25th and 26th Dynasties). Notable among the remains of brick-built tombs is the large gateway of a mortuary chapel belonging to a Theban prince named Mentemhet. The tombs consist of a superstructure enclosed within brick walls, with an entrance pylon on the E side, and the subterranean burial chambers, entered by a doorway on the N side.

An interesting example of a tomb of the Saite period is the *Tomb of Pabasa* (No. 279), Steward of Princess Nitocris, Psammetichus I's daughter (*c.* 610 B.C.). The superstructure is much ruined.

The entrance, on the N side, leads down by way of a brick-walled ramp and a steep flight of steps to an *antechamber,* with reliefs and inscriptions (on the left-hand and rear walls the dead man at table, with his son and a priest in front of him; below, the mummy's journey to Abydos). Beyond this is an *offering-court,* at the foot of a 46 ft/14 m deep shaft, the lower part of which is hewn from the rock, the upper part lined with brick. On the E and W sides of the court are narrow colonnades with four pillars. On the architraves are detailed Pabasa's styles and titles. On the walls are sunk reliefs of offering scenes and the dead man at table. On some of the pillars, in addition to representations of the usual offerings, are wine-making, fishing and bee-keeping scenes; the charming decorative patterns on the ceiling are well preserved. On the S wall, to the right of the door into the next chamber, Nitocris, accompanied by Pabasa, makes libations of wine to Osiris, Isis and Horus; to the left, Psammetichus, followed by Nitocris (with sistrum) and Pabasa, offers milk to Re-Harakhty. The reliefs and inscriptions in the main chamber, which has eight pillars, are badly damaged. Adjoining are other chambers with tomb-shafts.

Also of interest is the **Tomb of Ebe** (No. 36), an official in the service of Nitocris, which has reliefs imitating Old Kingdom models. A flight of steps leads down to an antechamber, in which the dead man is depicted sitting at the offering-table receiving votive gifts. In a room on the right are fine reliefs of craftsmen at work and dancers. Beyond the antechamber is what was originally an open court with colonnades along the sides (mural reliefs of offerings and a fine hunting scene). Adjoining is a colonnade leading to other chambers.

Among other tombs of the same period are the *Tomb of Mentemhet* (No. 34), a Theban Prince of the

time of Taharqa (25th Dynasty), and the *Tomb of Peteamenopet* (No. 38), a high official of the 26th Dynasty. The latter tomb (288 yds/263 m long, with an area of 2710 sq. yds/2266 sq. m) exceeds in size even the royal tombs in the Valley of the Kings. The inscriptions and reliefs, almost all relating to the life beyond the tomb, are finely executed but badly damaged and blackened.

Ramesseum

The ****Ramesseum**, the great mortuary temple built by Ramesses II and dedicated to Amun, lies on the edge of the cultivated land on the W bank of the Nile, some 1 mile/1·5 km S of Deir el-Bahri. It is probably the Tomb of Ozymandias mentioned by the historian Diodorus (1st c. B.C.) – the name Ozymandias being apparently a corruption of Ramesses II's praenomen User-Maat-Re. Although only about half of the original structure survives it is still a highly impressive monument.

The temple is entered at the E end by a large *Pylon* 220 ft/67 m wide, the exterior of which is badly ruined. The reliefs on the inner side are in a fair state of preservation; they are best seen by afternoon light, preferably with the aid of field-glasses. They relate to Ramesses's Syrian campaigns, in particular his war with the Hittites in the fifth year of his reign.

On the *North Tower,* to the extreme left, are depicted the Syrian fortresses (originally 18, of which 13 can still be distinguished) destroyed by Ramesses in the eighth year of his reign, each inscribed with its name. Prisoners are seen being led away. – In the middle section of the wall are scenes from the war with the Hittites (continued on the S tower): below, the Egyptian army on the march; above, the Egyptian camp, enclosed within a ring of shields; the chariots stand in long rows, with the unharnessed horses beside them; heavy baggage-wagons with their teams, the King's lion, donkeys enjoying their freedom; soldiers taking their ease, one drinking from a wineskin, others quarrelling and fighting; to the right, above, a sudden attack by the Hittites. – At the right-hand end the King is seen holding a Council of War with his Princes; below, captured spies being beaten.

On the *South Tower* the whole of the left-hand half of the wall is taken up by the Battle of Qadesh: Ramesses in his chariot dashing against the Hittites, who are killed by his arrows or flee in wild confusion and fall into the River Orontes; behind the King are other chariots; on the right, the Hittite Prince; above (barely distinguishable), the enemy fleeing into their fortress. – The right-hand half of the wall has the familiar representation of the King grasping his enemies by the hair and smiting them; farther right he is depicted with a long staff, accompanied by a fan-bearer.

On the inside of the *doorway* are the usual scenes showing Ramesses making offerings to various gods. On the jambs, above, he is seen pacing out the precincts of the temple (part of the foundation ceremony); below are various deities.

The **First Court** is totally ruined apart from fragments of the W wall, in front of which lie the remains of a

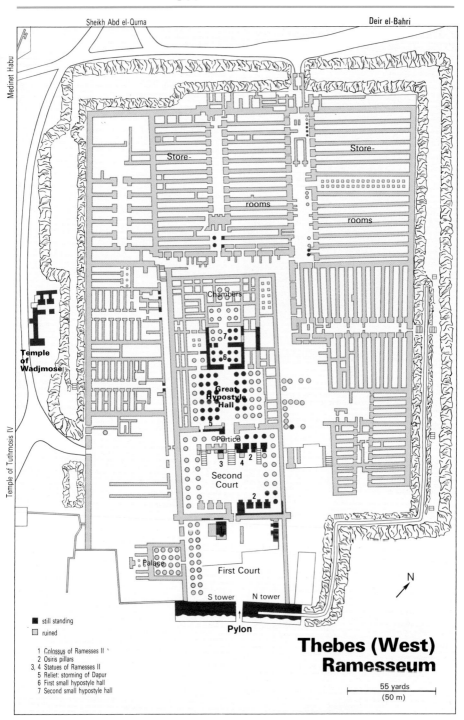

Sheikh Abd el-Qurna   Deir el-Bahri

Medinet Habu

Temple of Tuthmosis IV

Store-

Store-

rooms

rooms

Chambers

7

6

Temple
of
Wadjmose

Great
Hypostyle
Hall

5

Portico

3   4   2

Second
Court

2

Palace

First Court

S tower   N tower

N

■ still standing
□ ruined

1 Colossus of Ramesses II
2 Osiris pillars
3, 4 Statues of Ramesses II
5 Relief: storming of Dapur
6 First small hypostyle hall
7 Second small hypostyle hall

Pylon

Thebes (West)
Ramesseum

55 yards
(50 m)

colossal figure of Ramesses II, whose name appears in well-preserved hieroglyphs on the upper arms and seat of the statue. The surviving parts (breast, upper arms, one foot, etc.) bear witness to the care with which this gigantic monument was carved and polished. The ear is 41 in./1·05 m long, the torso from shoulder to shoulder measures 23 ft 4 in./7·11 m, the girth of the arm at the elbow is 17 ft 6 in./5·33 m, the index finger is 40 in./1 m long, the breadth of the foot across the toes is 55 in./1·40 m. The figure is estimated to have had a total height of 57 ft 5 in./17·50 m and to have weighed over 1000 tons. – The head of another

colossal statue of the King was found in 1816 and is now in the British Museum.

On the S side of the court was a colonnade (now totally destroyed) fronting a royal palace of which only a few fragments remain.

A gap in the wall to the right of the broken colossus gives access to the **Second Court**, which is better preserved than the first. It was flanked on right and left by double colonnades, now almost completely destroyed: along the front square pillars with statues

Broken statue, Ramesseum

of Osiris, to the rear a raised terrace with Osiris pillars and columns with bud capitals. Four *Osiris pillars* are still standing in both the front and the rear rows, together with the shafts of columns, which have reliefs of Ramesses making offerings. The *Osiris figures*, most of which have lost their heads, also represent Ramesses. These are no doubt the "caryatides" referred to by Diodorus in his description of Ozymandias's tomb.

On the surviving part of the front wall are fine reliefs, with traces of coloring, which can be distinguished with the aid of binoculars. The lower row celebrates once again the Battle of Qadesh: on the left the King,

Court in the Ramesseum

depicted on a much larger scale than the other figures, dashes in his chariot against the enemy; the Hittites, pierced by his arrows or trampled by the horses, fall in confused heaps or are plunged into the River Orontes; farther right is the battlemented Fortress of Qadesh, with the river flowing round it; beside it, on the far side of the river, are Hittite troops, some of them reaching out to help their drowning comrades. The upper row depicts the festival of the harvest god Min, which was celebrated on the King's accession: on the left the King awaits a procession headed by priests carrying images of his ancestors; in front of the King are two tall poles bearing the god's head-dress; priests send off four carrier-pigeons to carry news of the King's accession to the four quarters of the world; on the right the King cuts a sheaf with a sickle for presentation to the god. – The second court also contained colossal *statues of the King*. There are still some fragments of a black granite figure, in particular the head, well preserved apart from the nose. On the throne are the names of Ramesses II, beside which the 19th c. Egyptologist Giovanni Battista Belzoni inscribed his own name.

Three flights of steps, the most northerly of which is well preserved, lead up to the *Portico* on a raised terrace. Of the rear wall only the southern part survives, with three rows of reliefs: bottom row, eleven sons of the King; middle row, the King conducted into the temple by Atum and the falcon-headed Month, who holds the hieroglyph for "life" to his nostrils; to the right the King kneeling before the three chief Theban gods, behind him Thoth inscribing his name on a palm branch; top row, the King making an offering to Ptah (left) and burning incense before an ithyphallic Min and a goddess.

Beyond the portico originally entered by three doorways, is the **Great Hypostyle Hall**, which, like the hypostyle hall at Karnak, is divided into three higher central aisles and six lower lateral aisles. The central aisles, which have preserved part of their roof, have six couples of taller columns with calyx capitals and six couples of lower columns with bud capitals, topped by a wall, with pillars and window-openings, reaching to the same height as the taller columns; 11 columns of each type are still standing. The lateral aisles had columns with bud capitals, of which there remains 11 on the left-hand side, together with a section of the roof. On the shafts of the columns Ramesses is depicted making offerings to the gods. On the wall to the left of the entrance, below, is a relief depicting the storming of the Hittite fortress of Dapur: to the left is the familiar figure of Ramesses in his chariot, with the enemy fleeing on foot, on horseback and in chariots; on the right the Egyptians are seen mounting the walls of the fortress on scaling-ladders, while others advance under the protection of storming-sheds and their shields; the King's sons, taking part in the battle, are identified by their names. Above are several reliefs showing the King sacrificing to various gods. West wall: below, the King's sons; above, the King before Amun and Khons, with the lion-headed goddess Sakhmet behind him, and the King, followed by a goddess, in the presence of Amun and Mut.

Beyond the Great Hypostyle hall is the *first small hypostyle hall*, which has eight columns with bud capitals supporting the well-preserved roof, adorned with astronomical representations and scenes showing the King in the presence of the gods. – The mural reliefs are of some interest. E wall: priests bearing the sacred barques of Amun, Mut and Khons, each decorated with the head of its deity. W wall, N end: the

King seated under the sacred tree of Heliopolis, with Atum (left, enthroned) and the goddess Seshat and Thoth (right) inscribing his name on its leaves.

Of the following *second small hypostyle hall* only the right-hand (N) half, with four columns, remains. The representations of offerings on the walls are of little interest.

To the NW, beyond the main temple, are extensive remains of brick buildings, some of them (as the stamps on the bricks show) built in the reign of Ramesses II. They have well-built vaults, originally covered by a platform, which, to judge from the fragments of wine-jars and stoppers found here, were presumably **store-rooms**. Here, too, is an *altar* similar to the one at Deir el-Bahri. To the W, adjoining the vaulted brick buildings, are the ruins of a large rectangular hall with 32 columns supporting the roof; 12 stumps of columns remain.

Some 550 yds/500 m NE of the Ramesseum, within a modern enclosure wall, is the **Mortuary Temple of Tuthmosis III**. The ancient enclosure walls are partly hewn from the rock and partly built of sun-dried brick. The interior is in a very dilapidated condition, but it is possible to identify remains of hypostyle halls, brick-built rooms, etc. Many of the bricks bear the stamp of Tuthmosis III. – Between the Ramesseum and this temple lay the *mortuary temples* of *Amenophis II* (18th Dynasty) and *Siptah* (19th Dynasty), the scanty remains of which were discovered by Flinders Petrie in 1896. – To the NE, near Qurna, are the remains of the *Mortuary Temple of Amenophis I*.

To the S of the Ramesseum were the *mortuary temples* of Prince *Wadjmose* (18th Dynasty), King *Tuthmosis IV*, Queen *Tawosret*, Siptah's wife, and King *Merneptah*, all of which were excavated by Flinders Petrie; there are only scanty remains.

Sheikh Abd el-Qurna

The****rock tombs of Sheikh Abd el-Qurna**, the hill to the N of the Ramesseum, together with those of El-Khokha to the E, form the largest and most important assemblage of **private tombs** in the Theban cemeteries, built by great dignitaries, priests, high officials and others of lesser account during the New Kingdom. In the southern part of the area are the tombs in the Hill of Qurnet Murai and the Valley of Deir el-Medina; to the N those in the long slopes of Dra Abu el-Naga. The total number of tombs of some

consequence, as recorded by the Department of Antiquities, is at present 414, but this figure can be expected to increase.

The tombs normally consist of a forecourt, a main chamber, frequently with columns or pillars supporting the roof, and a corridor ending in a niche for statues of the dead man and his favorite relatives; there may also be a small chamber on either side of the corridor. The funeral offerings to the dead were made in the forecourt. Since the local limestone is of poor quality and unsuitable for relief sculpture, most of the decoration consists of paintings, the walls having been prepared by the application of a coating of Nile mud covered with whitewash. Many of these paintings, which throw a flood of light on life in the New Kingdom, are perhaps the finest of their kind in Egyptian art.

The end walls of the hall usually imitate the form of huge gravestones, one of them normally inscribed with prayers for the dead man, the other recording his biography; the longitudinal walls show him engaged in his everyday activities; while in the corridor are depicted the funeral ceremonies.

The tombs of Abd el-Qurna fall into four separate groups:
1. Those in the eastern and northern slopes of the hill, to the W of the road from the Ramesseum to Deir el-Bahri, which are enclosed within a low stone wall. This *Upper Precinct*, as it is called, has two entrances, one on the S side, near Tomb 100, and one on the N, near Tomb 68.
2. Those in the *plain* between the Ramesseum and the Upper Precinct.
3. The tombs in the so-called *Lower Precinct*, between the NE side of the hills of Sheikh Abd el-Qurna and El-Khokha, to the E of the road from the Ramesseum to Deir el-Bahri. The entrance is opposite the northern entrance to the Upper Precinct.
4. The tombs of El-Khokha, to the NE of the Lower Precinct.

UPPER PRECINCT. – This is reached by going N from the Ramesseum along the E side of the hill. The precinct is entered by the S gate, from which there are paths to the various tombs.

Opposite the entrance is the **Tomb of Rekhmere** (No. 100), a Vizier under Tuthmosis III and Amenophis II. It consists of a forecourt and a wide chamber, from which a long corridor of some height, gradually becoming higher towards the far end, runs into the rock, ending (18 ft/5·50 m above ground-level) in a small recess, originally closed by a false door and intended to contain a statue of the dead man (the *serdab*).

In the *main chamber*, on the left-hand entrance wall, Rekhmere (on right) is depicted sitting in his audience hall receiving petitioners; to the left, people bringing tribute. On the rear wall he is seen receiving gifts from foreign people, depicted in five rows (from top to bottom): the people of Punt; the Princes of Keftiu (Crete) and the Aegean islands, bringing costly vases;

Nubians, with a panther, a giraffe, gold and skins; Syrians, with chariots, horses, an elephant, a bear and costly vases; the people of the south (men, women and children). – *Corridor*, left-hand wall (left to right): Rekhmere supervising the delivery of tribute (corn, wine, fabrics) to the royal store-rooms; watching craftsmen at work (carpenters, leather-workers, goldsmiths, potters); below, the building of a pylon and sculptors polishing statues; funeral rites. Right-hand wall (left to right): the dead man at table; below, a statue of Rekhmere being towed in a boat; a banquet, with musicians and singers; ships.

In the hill above Rekhmere's Tomb are the *Subterranean Chambers of Sennofer** (No. 96B), a Prince of Thebes and Overseer of the Gardens of the Temple of Amun in the reign of Amenophis II. The paintings in this tomb are notable for their freshness and beauty. The upper chambers are of no interest. – A steep flight of steps descends to an antechamber and the main chamber, which has four pillars. The mural decorations are all on religious themes.

The ceiling of the *antechamber* is painted to resemble an arbor, with vines and dark-colored grapes. Left-hand wall: Sennofer, seated, with his daughter (partly destroyed) and ten priests presenting offerings. Right-hand wall: Sennofer with his daughter behind him and servants bringing the tomb furnishings; to the right, Sennofer entering and leaving the tomb. Rear wall, to the right and left of door: the dead man and his sister worshiping Osiris, who is depicted on the lintel. – The ceiling of the *pillared chamber* is decorated with vines and interlace patterns; there are also vines in the frieze on the walls. Above the door are two crouching dogs (Anubis); below and on the door-jambs the usual prayers for the dead. Left-hand entrance wall: the dead man and his sister Merit coming out of the tomb; beyond this, the same couple seated on a bench. Left-hand wall: the funeral ceremonies, watched by Sennofer himself (on the left). Rear wall: the dead man and his sister (destroyed) at a meal, with priests performing the funeral sacrifice; farther right, the ships taking the body to Abydos and bringing it back for burial. Right-hand wall: the dead man and his

sister, in a vine arbor, praying to Osiris and Anubis; religious scenes and texts (in the middle Anubis at the bier of Osiris); a priest pouring the purifying water over the dead man and his sister. Right-hand entrance wall: the dead man and his sister at a meal; a priest making offerings to them. The dead man and his sister are also frequently depicted on the pillars.

From Sennofer's tomb steps lead farther up the hill to the **Tomb of Kenamun** (No. 93), Chief Steward of Amenophis II. This is one of the largest and finest tombs in the cemetery, but it is badly dilapidated, and little is left of the superb decoration, painted on stucco on a yellow ground.

From the spacious forecourt we enter the wide *main chamber*, with ten pillars. Right-hand entrance wall: the dead man (his name and figure everywhere obliterated) receiving tribute of cattle. Left-hand entrance wall: the funeral rites (men drawing statues of the dead man to the tomb, women, ships, slaughtering of sacrificial animals). Rear wall: the King on his nurse's lap, in front of him girl musicians, etc. (on the right); on the left, Amenophis II, enthroned under a canopy, receiving from the dead man New Year gifts (statues of the King and the Queen Mother Hatshepsut, ornaments, furniture, weapons, etc.). – In the barrel-vaulted *corridor*, right-hand wall (right to left): the bag of a desert hunt (ostriches, an ibex with a dog, jackals, etc.); a hunt in the marshes; the funeral meal. In the *niche*, to the right and left, the dead man and his wife at table; on the rear wall, the dead man praying to Osiris (left) and Anubis (right).

Up the hill from Sennofer's tomb, to the right, is No. 84, the **Tomb of Emunedjeh**, an official under Tuthmosis III. In the first chamber are representatives of the lands of the South and the North bringing tribute to the King; in the second chamber (on the right) the dead man hunting.

Farther to the right is No. 85, the **Tomb of Amenemheb**, an officer in the service of Tuthmosis III.

Pillared chamber, to the left of the entrance: the dead man superintending the distribution of food (bread and meat) to his troops. On the pillars: Amenemheb and his wife Bek. Above the two central pillars (rear side): hyena-hunt. Fine ceiling decoration. Rear wall, to the right: the King sitting under a canopy, in front of him Amenemheb giving an account (in a long inscription written in blue characters on a white ground) of his part in the King's campaigns in Asia; below the inscription, Syrians bringing tribute, wearing white garments with colored borders. – *Corridor*, left-hand wall: Amenemheb receiving from the King furnishings for his tomb (vases, caskets, sandals, shields, etc.). *Side chamber on the left*: funeral rites, etc. – *Side chamber on the right*: to the left, the dead man and his wife (destroyed) at table; to the right, a banquet, with servants bringing in flowers; two guests in easy-chairs and three on ordinary chairs are served with drink; below, women, with blossoms in their hair, while a servant carries staffs wreathed with flowers; at the foot, a male harpist (seated), a female harpist (standing), a female flute-player (standing) and a female lute-player (standing). Rear wall: catching wildfowl. – Far end of *corridor*, on the left, funeral rites, presentation of offerings; on the right, Amenemheb's garden, with a fish-pool in the middle and (to the left) flowers being brought to Amenemheb, who is sitting on a chair with his wife.

Farther up the hill is No. 86, the **Tomb of Menkheperre-seneb**, High Priest of Amun in the

Wall-painting in the Tomb of Sennofer

reign of Tuthmosis III. The only paintings are in the first transverse chamber. Right-hand entrance wall: carriage-builders, herds of cattle being brought in. Left-hand entrance wall: harvest scenes. On the wall to the right of the door into the corridor: Asiatics bringing tribute, including a Keftiu (Cretan) with a curious goblet.

Uphill again to No. 82, the **Tomb of Amenemhet**, Granary Superintendent, Scribe and Steward to User, Vizier under Tuthmosis III. On the rear wall, to the left, is a fine painting of a banquet, with musicians; below, a bull-fight. Corridor: left-hand wall, funeral rites, the mummy's journey to Abydos; right-hand wall, funeral banquet, with musicians and offering-bearers.

Beyond this is No. 81, the **Tomb of Enene**, Prince and Overseer of the Granaries of Amun, who flourished in the Early New Kingdom and had charge of the building of Tuthmosis I's tomb. The tomb has an unusual layout, with a main chamber which is open in front, with a pillared façade. The paintings depict the dead man's life.

On the *pillars* (left to right): fishing; harvest scenes (a woman gleaning, three men reaping); work in the fields; Enene at table; Enene's garden, with (below) his house and granary, surrounded by a wall; hunting scene (a hyena, hit by an arrow in the mouth, rears up, while a dog leaps at it); a hare, ibexes and gazelles. – *Main chamber*, rear wall, on either side of the door: on the right, peasants bringing tribute; Enene hunting in the marshes and spearing fish; on the left, Enene receiving tribute (top row, dark-brown Nubians, including two women carrying children in baskets on their backs); Enene receiving tribute from peasants (note the lines drawn to help the artist); Enene receiving tribute (only the two bottom rows remain, in one of which are necklaces, in the other incense being weighed). – *Corridor*, left-hand wall: the funeral, with women mourners; the dead man in the Temple at Abydos (left); farther right, Enene and his wife, seated. – In the niche are four *statues* (the dead man, two women and another man). The shaft in front of the niche has been filled in.

Above the hill from Enene's Tomb is the highest row of tombs. There is a fine * view from the top of the Ramesseum and the Colossi of Memnon, extending across the Nile to Luxor and Karnak; to the left are the desert hills, with the temples of Deir el-Bahri at their feet.

In the highest row is the **Tomb of Horemheb** (No. 78), a General in the service of Tuthmosis IV.

First transverse chamber, on the walls to the right and left of the entrance, is a banqueting scene, with female lute-players. Rear wall, to the left: Horemheb presenting to the King contributions from peasants; above, enlistment of soldiers. Rear wall, to the right: tribute being brought to the King by Syrians and Kushites (depicted as Negroes, among them Negresses with pendulous breasts). – *Corridor*, left-hand wall: funeral procession, with costly grave-goods reminiscent of those found in the Tomb of Tutankhamun; the mummy's journey to Abydos; judgment of the dead (damaged). Right-hand wall: right, funeral rites; left, hunting in the marshes (various birds, with curious and interesting details); below, bird-snaring (note the pelicans). – Both the transverse chamber and the corridor have finely decorated ceilings. The corridor leads to a broad pillared chamber (unfinished).

Close by, to the N, is the much-mutilated **Tomb of Tjenen** (No. 76), "Fan-bearer on the right hand of the King" (Tuthmosis IV). On the rear wall, to the right, the dead man is depicted conducting into the presence of the King representatives of Asiatic nations bringing tribute. – A breach in the wall leads from this tomb into the **Tomb of Amenhotep** (No. 75), Second Prophet of Amun in the reign of Tuthmosis IV. On the wall to the left of the entrance are craftsmen working for the temple and surveyors; on the opposite wall gifts made to the Temple of Amun (statues, a harp, a pillared hall, vases); to the right of the entrance the funeral banquet; on the opposite wall the dead man escorted to the Temple of Amun at Karnak (the façade of which, with flagstaffs and statues, is shown on the right) and greeted by the priestesses of Amun, his relatives.

From the crest of the hill we descend towards the N to No. 74, the **Tomb of Tjenen**, "Chief Scribe of the soldiers" in the reign of Tuthmosis IV. On the rear wall of the first chamber, to the right, the dead man is seen inspecting various tributes brought to him; in the lower row, horses; to the left, the dead man reviewing his troops (including drummers with their drums on their backs).

A little way N is No. 71, the **Tomb of Senmut**, Chief Architect and favorite of Queen Hatshepsut, who was responsible for building the great Temple at Deir el-Bahri. This tomb, of great historical interest, is unfortunately in an advanced state of ruin. At the right-hand end of the rear wall, under a protective roof, are three Keftiu (Cretans) carrying curiously shaped vases; above, a frieze of Hathor heads.

Farther N, downhill, is No. 60, the **Tomb of Entefoker**, Vizier in the reign of Sesostris I (12th Dynasty). This is the oldest tomb in the cemetery. A long corridor leads into a chamber containing a niche, in front of which is a badly damaged life-size statue of Senet, the dead man's wife. The paintings on the walls of the corridors show the old-fashioned style of the Middle Kingdom to which they belong. Right-hand wall: catching birds in a net; hunting in the desert; cooks, bakers and brewers at work; the dead man and his wife inspecting New Year gifts brought to them. Left-hand wall: the mummy's journey to Abydos; funeral rites; dancing-girls and musicians.

Lower down is No. 65, the **Tomb of Imesib**, an official of the Temple of Amun at the end of the 20th Dynasty. The tomb was originally constructed during the 18th Dynasty, but Imesib had the old reliefs covered over with stucco on which new scenes were painted.

From the forecourt we enter a transverse chamber with six 16-sided pillars, from which a long vaulted corridor leads to the niche for the dead man's statue. The paintings in the main chamber, which are much faded, depict festal barques bearing the name of Ramesses IX, gold utensils and (on the left-hand wall) the King making offerings to the sacred barque of Amun and the statues of his ancestors. Fine decorated ceiling.

Still lower down, near the N gate of the precinct, is No. 69, the * **Tomb of Menne**, Land Steward and Estate Inspector under the 18th Dynasty.

First chamber; right-hand entrance wall: the dead man and his wife receiving votive offerings; relatives bringing flowers and food. Left-hand entrance wall: the dead man, in his official capacity, superintending work in the fields; above, the field being measured with a cord (very fine details). Right-hand rear wall: the dead man and his relatives at table. Left-hand end wall: the dead man and his wife praying to Osiris. – *Second chamber,* left-hand wall: funeral scenes; Osiris judging the dead. Right-hand wall: the dead man hunting in the marshes; the mummy's journey to Abydos; ceremonies over the mummy. Fine ceiling decoration.

TOMBS IN THE PLAIN. – Some of the finest tombs in the whole cemetery lie in the desert plain to the W of the road to Deir el-Bahri, amid the rubble mounds between the Ramesseum and the Upper Precinct.

The largest of these tombs, and the most interesting from the historical and artistic points of view, is No. 55, the **Tomb of Ramose,** Governor of Thebes and Vizier under Amenophis IV. Constructed at the beginning of the heretic King's reign, it is one of the few monuments dating from the period of transition from the old religion to the exclusive veneration of the sun. The tomb was left unfinished when the capital was transferred from Thebes to Tell el-Amarna. Most of the decoration, some of it in delicate low relief, show the old style of Amenophis III's reign, but there are also a number in the new Amarna style.

From the forecourt we enter a large *hypostyle chamber,* the roof of which is borne on four rows of eight columns. On the left-hand (N) half of the E wall are delicate reliefs in the style of Amenophis III's reign (from left to right): Ramose and his wife, followed by officials, presenting votive gifts; above, the dead man, with his wife Merit-ptah behind him and his three daughters in front of him; below, the purifying water being poured over the dead man; Ramose and his wife, along with another couple, receiving votive gifts brought by servants; below, Ramose and his wife, with Amenhotep, "Chief Steward of the King in the nome of Memphis", and his wife, seated at table, with a priest wearing a panther skin performing rites in front of them. On the S wall are vividly colored paintings of funeral scenes (note the fine group of women mourners in the lively Amarna style); below, right, Ramose entering the palace. At the far end of the wall a sloping shaft leads into the *tomb chamber.* On the left-hand half of the W wall is Amenophis IV, still depicted in the old conventional manner, seated under a canopy with Maat, goddess of truth, with Ramose (twice) standing in front of them. On the right-hand half of the wall (in Amarna style) the King, his unattractive figure depicted with great naturalness, and his beautiful wife are seen on a balcony of the palace, watching Ramose (figure merely sketched in) being adorned with the gold chain they have thrown down to him; above them, the sun, its rays streaming down, behind them the royal bodyguard; farther right, Ramose leaving the palace with his decoration and receiving congratulations.

In the passage leading to a chamber on a lower level: on the left, Ramose and his wife (only partly preserved) praying; on the right, Ramose and his wife entering the tomb. – The lower chamber, with eight papyrus cluster-columns, is unfinished and undecorated. Beyond it is a small chamber with unfinished niches.

Close by, to the S, is No. 56, the **Tomb of Userhet,** which dates from the reign of Amenophis II. It has fine wall-paintings and attractive ceiling decoration.

Right-hand half of the rear wall: the dead man presenting gifts to the King; to the left, store-rooms with different kinds of bread; below, left, barbers at work. Left-hand wall of the corridor: the dead man in his chariot hunting gazelles and in the marshes; below, catching fish and making wine. Right-hand wall: funeral scenes.

Immediately adjoining is No. 57, the **Tomb of Khaemhet,** Superintendent of the Royal Granaries under Amenophis III, which has fine low reliefs.

In the forecourt are remains of the funerary stela. In the entrance doorway, on the left, the dead man is depicted with his arms raised in prayer to the sun god. In the first wide *chamber,* on the left, is a niche with two much-mutilated *statues* of Khaemhet and his relative Imhotep, a Royal Scribe, who was buried in an adjacent (inaccessible) tomb. On the wall to the right of the entrance: the dead man making an offering of two brace of geese; above, left (two rows), surveying the fields; below, lively harvest scenes. Rear wall, to the left: Khaemhet reports on the harvest to Amenophis III, who is enthroned under a canopy; at the foot of the throne, nine captured tribes. To the right, similar scenes: the King is seated on a splendid throne, on which he is depicted as a sphinx; behind Khaemhet are two rows of his officials in respectful attitudes; top row, Khaemhet is arrayed with ornaments and anointed. – In the long *corridor* are badly damaged scenes and inscriptions relating to the life beyond the tomb. In the side chambers and the niche in the rear wall of the corridor are large and finely polished *statues.* Beside the niche is a door leading into a small undecorated chamber.

To the W of the tomb of Ramose is No. 139, the **Tomb of Pere,** Priest of Amun, perhaps in the reign of Tuthmosis IV, which has a number of well-preserved paintings.

Right-hand entrance wall and facing the rear wall: the dead man and his wife receiving votive gifts. End wall: the dead man and his wife, followed by their family, praying to Osiris; below, in three rows, funeral rites (funeral procession, the mummy's journey to Abydos, "opening of the mouth" ceremony).

To the E of the tomb of Khaemhet, close to the road, is a court round which are four tombs. On the S side is No. 50, the *****Tomb of Neferhotep,** a Priest in the reign of Horemheb. The sunk reliefs in this early 19th Dynasty tomb have already lost the liveliness of 18th Dynasty art.

The first wide *chamber* has fine and well-preserved ceiling-paintings. Left-hand end wall: the dead man is decorated with chains of honor in the presence of the King. Rear wall, to left of the door into the corridor: the dead man and his family, with a son bringing in food; below, left, a harpist, with the text of the song he is singing in front of him. The song is repeated on the right-hand wall of the *corridor,* on which the dead man and his wife are depicted seated at the offering-table. In the niche are statues of the dead man and his family.

On the N side of the court is No. 51, the **Tomb of Userhet,** First Prophet of Tuthmosis I. The tomb was constructed in the reign of Sethos I. On the right-hand end wall is a charming scene: the dead man and two women seated under a tree, accompanied by their souls in the form of birds; in the tree are other birds, and there are many other attractive details; on the right a goddess dispensing water to the dead man. Rear wall, to the right of the door (now blocked) into the corridor: above, the dead man and his sisters making offerings to Osiris; below, the dead man and his sisters in the presence of Tuthmosis (who is depicted with a black skin).

On the E side of the court is No. 111, the **Tomb of Amenwesu**, a painter, who himself executed the paintings and inscriptions on religious themes. The tomb dates from the reign of Ramesses II. – On the W side of the court is the Tomb of Khensumose (No. 30), which is almost totally ruined and inaccessible.

The most northerly of the tombs in this area, near the N gate of the Upper Precinct, is No. 52, the **Tomb of Nakht**, an official and Priest of Amun under the 18th Dynasty.

Wall-painting in the Tomb of Nakht

Only the *first chamber* has paintings, which are excellently preserved. The name of Amun was obliterated wherever it occurred during the reign of Amenophis IV. Left-hand entrance wall: below, the dead man supervising work in the fields (plowing, digging, sowing); two men breaking up the clods with hammers; on the left, a laborer drinking from a water-skin hanging from a tree; a man felling a tree; above, Nakht supervising harvest operations, in three rows (below, three men reaping with sickles, followed by a woman gleaning, two men putting the grain into a basket and two women plucking flax; middle row, the threshed corn being measured; above, winnowing the grain); to the left, the dead man and his wife making an offering. – On the left-hand end wall is a false door, painted to imitate granite; above, the dead man and his wife at table; beside the door, servants with votive gifts; at the foot of the door, a heap of offerings, with two tree goddesses and two servants standing beside them (note the grapes). – Left-hand rear wall (less well preserved): below, to the right, the dead man and his wife (badly damaged) at table, seated on a bench, below which is a cat eating a fish; their son bringing them flowers and geese, three women musicians; to the left, relatives seated in two rows; above, only the left half is preserved (a blind harpist, women seated on the ground conversing). Right-hand rear wall: below, the dead man and his wife seated in an arbor, with servants bringing them flowers, grapes, poultry, fish, etc.; to right, birds being caught in nets and plucked; above, the grape harvest and wine-pressing; above, left, the dead man and his wife, seated; right, the dead man spearing fish and fowling. – Right-hand end wall (unfinished): the dead man and his wife at table, with relatives bringing them offerings. – Right-hand entrance wall: the dead man and his wife, followed by three rows of servants, making offerings.

LOWER PRECINCT. – There are a number of interesting tombs in this precinct, which is most conveniently reached from the Tomb of Nakht or the Tomb of Menne.

No. 106, the **Tomb of Peser**, Vizier of Sethos I. In the forecourt are a fine stela and statues of the dead man. In the entrance doorway and on the pillars Peser is depicted in his official costume with his wife.

No. 41, the **Tomb of Amenemopet**, Chief Steward of Amun in the early 19th Dynasty. On the pillars of the first chamber are statues of the dead man; on the walls are inscriptions and religious scenes.

No. 42, the **Tomb of Amenmose**, Governor of the northern subject territories (18th Dynasty). On the left-hand rear wall and end wall of the first pillared chamber the dead man is seen presenting tribute from the Asiatic peoples to the King.

No. 23, the **Tomb of Tjai**, an official in the Archive Office (reign of Merneptah, 19th Dynasty).

A flight of steps, originally preceded by a colonnade, leads down into the open *forecourt*, which was also surrounded by colonnades (now restored). At the E end of the S colonnade are scenes depicting the work of the "Foreign Office". Beyond this is a *transverse chamber*, the paintings in which mostly show offering scenes; on the right-hand entrance wall Tjai is seen receiving gold chains of honor from the King, seated on his throne. In niches in the rear wall are two life-size half-length statues of the dead man. – *Corridor*, left-hand wall: the burial and the judgment of the dead (partly destroyed). Right-hand wall: presentation of various offerings; the dead man, sometimes accompanied by his wife, praying to the gods of the dead. – In the chamber beyond this is the granite *sarcophagus*. In a niche in the rear wall are half-length *statues* of Osiris, Isis and Horus.

No. 38, the **Tomb of Djeserkereseneb**, Clerk in the Granaries of Amun in the reign of Tuthmosis IV. On the right-hand rear wall of the first chamber is a fine banqueting scene, with female musicians and dancers performing in presence of the dead man and his sister.

Wall-painting in the Tomb of Djeserkereseneb

TOMBS OF EL-KHOKHA. – Among the tombs on the S side of the Hill of El-Khokha and in the hill itself the following are of particular interest.

No. 178, the **Tomb of Neferronpet**, also named Kenro, an official in the Treasury of Amun-Re in the reign of Ramesses II. The well-preserved wall-paintings and ceiling decoration in the two chambers of the tomb are characteristic examples of the art of the Ramessid period. In the first chamber are burial scenes; on the rear wall of the second chamber four statues.

No. 48, the **Tomb of Surer** (full name Amenemhet), which lies E of No. 178, near the NW corner of the precinct of Tuthmosis III's Temple. It is a large tomb of the reign of Amenophis III, similar to the Tomb of Ramose, with magnificent reliefs in the best style of the period. Adjoining the open forecourt is a transverse chamber with fluted columns, on the right-hand rear wall of which the King is seen enthroned; farther right, statues being drawn to the tomb; a large, badly damaged, stela. The main chamber, hewn from the rock, has a vaulted roof supported by papyrus columns; it was left unfinished and is badly ruined.

No. 181, the **Tomb of Nebamun and Ipuki**, two sculptors of the late 18th Dynasty, which is situated on the S side of the hill, has fine paintings with well-preserved colors.

Transverse chamber, left-hand entrance wall (W half of S wall): Nebamun and his wife making offerings; a banquet; below, Ipuki and his wife receiving votive offerings from relatives. Right-hand entrance wall (E half): the dead man praying to the deified Amenophis I and Queen Nefertari; below, the dead man, seated, supervising the work of his craftsmen (carpenters, goldsmiths, jewelers). Right-hand end wall: the dead man praying to Osiris and the four sons of Osiris; below, two seated couples. Left-hand rear and end walls: the burial and the funeral rites.

No. 39, the **Tomb of Puyemre**, Priest of Amun in the reign of Tuthmosis III, lies on the NE side of the hill. Badly ruined, it was restored from very many fragments by Norman de Garis Davies. It has fine reliefs, some of them with well-preserved coloring.

From the large forecourt, along the rear wall of which were a colonnade and six stelae, a central doorway leads into a transverse chamber, from which three doors open into chapels. – *Transverse chamber,* right-hand entrance wall: above, hunting in the marshes; below, bringing in tribute from the marshlands (poultry, cattle); wine-making; fishing and bird-catching; gathering papyrus. Left-hand entrance wall: the workshops of the Temple of Amun (carriage-builders, goldsmiths, jewelers, carpenters, makers of stone vessels). Right-hand end (N) wall: hunting in the desert. Rear wall: receiving tribute from the northern lands and the countries on the Red Sea (the best-preserved reliefs are to the right of the central doorway). *Right-hand (N) chapel*: funeral rites, the journey to Abydos, the dead man at table. *Central chapel*: slaughtering of sacrificial animals; the dead man receiving offerings. In the adjoining niche (the ceiling of which has a door-shaped ornament): S wall, the dead man and his wife at table; on the rear wall was a stela, now in the Egyptian Museum in Cairo. The surviving scenes in the *left-hand chapel* show the dead man and his wife receiving offerings and seated at table.

No. 188, the **Tomb of Prennufer**, Royal Steward at the beginning of Amenophis IV's reign, lies to the W of No. 39. The Amarna style reliefs in the transverse chamber are much damaged and difficult to distinguish.

Deir el-Medina and Qurnet Murai

In a barren ravine $\frac{3}{4}$ mile/1 km W of the Ramesseum, on the way to the Valley of the Queens, is the little *Temple of Deir

Temple   Deir el-Medina

West Chapel

Central Chapel

East Chapel

Pronaos

Floral columns

Vestibule

Entrance

N

10 feet
(3 m)

el-Medina, surrounded by a high wall of sun-dried bricks laid in undulating courses with a stone gateway at the SE corner. The temple, begun in the reign of Ptolemy IV Philopator and completed under Philometor and Euergetes II, was principally dedicated to Hathor and the goddess of truth, Maat. It is an elegant structure of dressed stone, on the smooth façade of which, topped by a cavetto cornice, are numerous Greek and Coptic graffiti. In Christian times it was occupied by monks, who mutilated many of the reliefs and inscriptions. On the left-hand side is a brick arcade.

From the *Vestibule,* the roof of which was supported on two floral columns, we enter the small *Pronaos* or antechamber, which is separated from the vestibule by two columns with elaborate floral capitals and two pillars with Hathor heads. Between the columns, which bear figures of the deified sage Amenhotep and the god Imhotep, was a door, open at the top. Of the screens between the columns and pillars only the one on the left survives. On the walls are sunk reliefs depicting the King making offerings to various gods. Near the top of the left-hand wall is a handsome window, originally lighting a staircase. On the rear wall, above the cavetto cornice of the doorway into the central chapel, are seven Hathor heads. – Three doors lead into the three chapels.

In the *Central Chapel* Philopator, sometimes accompanied by his sister Arsinoe, is depicted making offerings to various gods. On the jambs of the doorway are four gods with bulls' heads. – On the left-hand wall of the *West Chapel* are fine reliefs depicting the judgment of the dead: on the right, Osiris enthroned, in front of him the symbol of Emewet, the four genii of the dead on a lotus flower, the "Devourer of the Underworld" in the form of a hippopotamus and Harpocrates, leaning on a crooked staff; the ibis-headed Thoth writing down the judgment; farther left, Anubis and Horus weighing the dead man's heart; two goddesses of truth with feathers on their heads conducting the dead man into the judgment hall; above, the dead man praying to the 42 judges of the dead. Rear wall: Philopator offering incense to Osiris and Isis. Right-hand wall: on the left, the sacred barque of Sokar-Osiris on a pedestal, beside it standards, etc.; on the right, the King offering incense to Anubis, who holds a disc, and the ithyphallic Min. On the lintel of the doorway is a four-headed ram (the god of the winds), above which is a flying vulture, worshiped by four goddesses. On the jambs are the King and three falcon-headed and three dog-headed genii. – The *East Chapel* has excellent reliefs depicting the King before various gods.

To the S of the temple, in the valley between the western hills and the Hill of *Qurnet Murai,* are the remains of a settlement occupied during the New Kingdom by artists and workmen engaged in the construction of the royal and private tombs. On the W side of the valley is the **Cemetery of Deir el-Medina**, with many rock tombs, mostly belonging to officials of the necropolis during the 19th and 20th Dynasties, together with a few dating from the 18th. In the tombs of the Ramessid period the scenes of everyday life which are the great attraction of the 18th Dynasty tombs are almost wholly absent, giving place to conventional representations of offerings and funeral rites and scenes from the "Book of the Dead".

Going up the hill from the valley bottom, we come to No. 1, the **Tomb of Sennutem**, of the Ramessid period, with a vaulted tomb chamber. It has reliefs and paintings on religious themes, including a fine representation of a funeral banquet. The rich contents of the tomb, which was discovered in 1886, are now in the Egyptian Museum in Cairo.

Wall-painting in the Tomb of Sennutem

Close to No. 1 are Nos. 218–220, the **Tombs of Amennakht, Nebenmaat and Khaemtore** (a father and his two sons), of the Ramessid period.

A flight of steps leads into a vaulted chamber decorated with religious scenes; above the entrance is the Hathor cow. Beyond this is an antechamber (undecorated), from which steps on the left lead to the *Tomb of Nebenmaat*. Right-hand wall: Anubis by the bier. Rear wall: funeral rites at the tomb; from behind a pyramid a goddess presents the sun, which has emerged from the hill. Left-hand wall: the dead man and his sister pray to Osiris, the deified Amenophis I and Queen Nefertari. – To the right of the antechamber is the *Tomb of Khaemtore*, the reliefs in which have been destroyed. – A second flight of steps leads into the *Tomb of Amennakht*, with scenes and texts from the "Book of the Dead" (the dead man and his sister in the fields of the blessed; left-hand end wall, Anubis by the bier).

Higher up are Nos. 2 and 2B, the **Tombs of Khonsu and Khabekhnet**, sons of Sennutem (No. 1). In No. 2B a steep flight of steps leads down to the chamber, on the left-hand wall of which is a curious scene showing Anubis at the bier of Osiris, who is represented as a fish. No. 2 is of no interest. To the N is No. 250, the **Tomb of Neferhotep** and his wife **Mutemuia** (Ramessid period), with well-preserved paintings. Right-hand wall: the dead man with his wife and family praying before the Hathor cow, which is emerging from the rocks. Rear wall: above, right, the dead man praying to Osiris; left, his wife praying to Amenophis I; below, funeral procession and offerings to the mummies at the tomb.

No. 290 is the **Tomb of Erenufer** (Ramessid period). A flight of steps runs down to an antechamber, in which is a tomb-shaft. Beyond this is a vaulted chamber with excellently preserved texts and scenes from the "Book of the Dead". On the left-hand entrance wall are Erenufer and his parents (with gray hair) praying to Ptah. – Adjoining is No. 291, the **Tomb of Nu and Nakht-Min**. – The vaulted chamber, entered from a small forecourt, has fine ceiling decoration. On the left-hand wall are the funeral procession and burial rites, painted in white on a gray ground. The other walls show offerings to various members of the family and to Osiris and Hathor.

To the N of No. 291, close behind the Temple of Deir el-Medina, is No. 5, the **Tomb of Nefrabet**, which is also of the Ramessid period.

A flight of steps leads into a vaulted chamber, on the walls of which the dead man and his relatives are depicted worshiping the Hathor cow emerging from the hill (right) and the Horus falcon (left). Another flight of steps descends to a second chamber decorated with religious scenes: Horus and Thoth pouring the purifying water over the dead man; Amenophis I praying to the snake-headed goddess of the dead Meresger and to Hathor; the sun, borne by two lions. On the rear wall, above the mouth of the shaft, are depicted the mummies of the dead man and his wife.

To the S, up the hill, is No. 8, the **Tomb of Kha** (reign of Amenophis II). The vaulted chamber has an attractively decorated ceiling. The rich grave-goods found in this tomb are now in the Museo Egizio in Turin.

Farther S is No. 3, the ***Tomb of Peshedu** (Ramessid period).

A steep flight of steps leads down to a number of outer chambers, from which a low vaulted passage (on the right and left, representations of a chapel with the Anubis jackal lying beside it) leads into the *tomb chamber*. Right-hand entrance wall: the dead man lying in prayer under a palm. Right-hand wall: above, a small figure of the dead man praying to Osiris and other gods of the dead; below, the dead man and his small daughter before Re-Harakhty, Atum, Khepri, Ptah and the sacred Osiris pillar. Against the rear wall stood the sarcophagus, constructed of limestone masonry; above, Osiris and the Hill of the Dead. Left-hand wall, continuing on the left-hand entrance wall: above, Osiris and his associated deities; below, texts from the "Book of the Dead"; the dead man and his family, headed by his white-haired father, worshiping the Horus falcon.

Close to No. 3 is No. 340, the **Tomb of Amenemhet**, an official of the necropolis at the end of the 18th Dynasty.

Steps lead down to the vaulted entrance into the small chamber, with excellently preserved paintings on a yellow ground. Left-hand rear wall: above, the dead man praying to Anubis (left) and Osiris (right); below, the dead man and his wife at the offering-table with their sons and daughters on the left, attended by servants. Rear wall, to the right and left of the small niche: the dead man and his wife at table. Right-hand end wall (unfinished): above, the same scene as on the left-hand wall; below, in two rows, the funeral ceremony. The ceiling is decorated with square panels containing grapes and vine leaves.

A short distance farther on is No. 335, the **Tomb of Nekht-Amun**, a sculptor. A steep staircase descends to an upper chamber, off which is a small side chamber with fine paintings (the dead man worshiping his protective god Thoth, etc.). From here another flight of steps runs down to a lower chamber with vigorously painted family scenes; on the right-hand end wall, Anubis at the bier. – At the same level on the hillside, farther S, are Nos 4 and 9, the tombs of a sculptor named Ken and an official of the necropolis named Amenmose (both of the Ramessid period), with reliefs in a fair state of preservation.

To the N, in the highest row of tombs, is No. 217, the *Tomb of Ipuy, a sculptor (19th Dynasty). On the right-hand end wall are interesting scenes depicting the preparation of a tomb (carpenters at work on two chapels). On the right-hand entrance wall are scenes from everyday life (a wine-press, craftsmen at work, fishing).

The Hill of **Qurnet Murai**, which lies between the Deir el-Medina Valley and the cultivated land, is occupied by the huts of the local fellahin and crowned by the ruins of a brick-built monastery. Most of the 18th Dynasty rock tombs in the slopes of the hill are of no interest.

One tomb which is worth a visit, however, is No. 40, the **Tomb of Huy** (Amenhotep), Governor of Ethiopia (Nubia) in the reign of Tutankhamun.

Entrance wall: to right, Huy being ceremonially installed as Governor in the presence of the King and receiving the congratulations of his relatives and officials; to the left, Huy and his relatives with two richly decorated Nile boats in front of them, and beyond this Huy as Governor, with five rows of people bringing tribute. – Left-hand end wall: the dead man making offerings to the dog-headed Anubis (left) and

Osiris (right). – Rear wall: the Governor, with the fan and crook which are the emblems of his dignity, and three rows of Nubian chiefs; behind him the tribute they have brought, including a Nubian landscape (in the center a conical hut, flanked by doum-palms, giraffes and Negroes) standing on a table covered with panther skins and fabrics; above, bowls of precious stones, gold rings, sacks of gold-dust, gilded shields covered with colored skins, chairs, ebony benches, a chariot, etc.; the Nubian chiefs, almost all dressed in the Egyptian fashion, being received by Huy and his brother Amenhotep. In the top row, behind the chiefs, is their Princess in an ox-cart, shaded by a parasol; she is followed by chieftains wearing ostrich feathers in their plaited hair and by two Negresses with pendulous breasts, one with an infant on her back and both holding a small boy by the hand. In the second and third rows are Nubians bringing gold, panther skins, a giraffe and oxen; between the horns of the oxen are Negroes' heads, and on the tips of the horns are Negroes' hands, raised in an appeal for mercy. Farther left are five rows of ships (the bottom rows much damaged); in the second boat are five Negro Princes, in those in the lower rows cattle and other goods. On the other side, near the corner pillar, Huy is seen presenting to the King the tribute from Syria, in particular costly gold vases. The other scenes are almost completely destroyed. – On the right-hand end wall, to the right and left, offerings are being presented to Huy; the inscription which would have occupied the intervening space was never executed. The rest of the decoration is destroyed.

Below No. 40 are two tombs of the Ramessid period, Nos. 227 and 278. No. 227 is the **Tomb of Amenemonet**, a Priest, with funerary scenes (ships carrying the dead man's shrine; women mourners; statues of Amenophis III and Queen Tiy being conveyed to the tomb on sledges; a tomb topped by a pyramid, with a large stela in front, against the background of the desert cliffs). No. 278, the **Tomb of Amenemheb**, is decorated with religious scenes (the Hathor cow emerging from the hill, etc.); the ceiling has spiral patterns following Cretan models.

Valley of the Queens

If time permits the Queens' tombs in the *Valley of the Queens (Biban el-Harim, "Place of Beauty"; actually the Wadi el-Malikat) are well worth seeing. An old footpath from Deir el-Medina (1 mile/1·5 km) over a low hill passes a number of stelae, formerly in niches. On the first of these Ramesses III is depicted in the presence of Amun and Ptah. On the next one Meresger, goddess of the West, offers Ramesses III her breast, with the sun god Re-Harakhty standing behind; to the right Amun presents the King with the curved sword of victory; the inscription relates to Ramesses's military campaigns. The path then continues up a valley flanked by picturesque limestone cliffs, on which are inscribed prayers to the deities of the Underworld, and joins the modern road from Medinet Habu. The road ends in

Valley of the Queens

an enclosed valley, the Valley of tho Queens, which is of great beauty, though less imposing than the Valley of the Kings. There are magnificent **views, particularly from the head of the valley, of the Theban Plain and the Colossi of Memnon.

The tombs in the Valley of the Queens mostly belong to the 19th and 20th Dynasties. A total of almost 80 tombs are now known, most of them excavated by an Italian expedition led by E. Schiaparelli (1903–05; commemorative plaque). Many of the tombs are unfinished and without decoration, resembling mere caves in the rocks. There are few incised inscriptions or reliefs; such decoration as there is consists of paintings on stucco. – The following tombs are worth a visit:

No. 43, the **Tomb of Prince Seth-her-khopshef**, a son of Ramesses III. Two narrow corridors lead to a rather wider chamber, off which opens a smaller chamber. The reliefs, once brightly colored but now blackened, depict the dead man and the King praying to various gods and performing other ritual acts. In the last chamber Osiris is depicted on the rear wall, to the right and left; on the side walls are two rows of various deities.

No. 44, the **Tomb of Prince Khaemweset**, also a son of Ramesses III, with well-preserved painted reliefs. First chamber: the dead man and his father before various gods. In the two side chambers: the Prince before various gods; on the rear wall Isis and

Nephthys before Osiris. In the corridor beyond the first chamber the King and Prince are shown in front of the gates of the Fields of the Blessed and their guardians. In the last chamber the King is depicted in the presence of various gods.

From No. 44 the route continues past No. 51, the *Tomb of Queen Eset* (mother of Ramesses VI), to No. 52, the **Tomb of Queen Titi**. This consists of an antechamber, a long corridor and a chapel of some size, with smaller chambers opening off the rear and side walls.

At the near end of the *corridor,* to the right and left, are figures of the goddess Maat, her wings outspread to protect those entering the tomb. Left-hand wall: the Queen before Ptah, Re-Harakhty (the morning sun), the two genii of the dead, Imsety and Duamutef, and the goddess Isis. Right-hand wall: the Queen before Thoth, Atum (the evening sun), the two genii of the dead, Hapi and Qebhsenuef, and Nephthys, sister of Isis. At the far end are Selkit (with a scorpion on her head) and Neith, the "Lady of Sais". – *Chapel*: figures of gods and demons. – *Side chamber on S,* rear wall: left, Hathor (in the form of a cow) in a mountain landscape, in front of her a sycamore from which Hathor (in human form) pours out Nile water to refresh the Queen. – In the *side chamber on the N* is the mummy-shaft. – *Rear chamber,* rear wall: Osiris enthroned, in front of him Neith and Selkit, behind him Nephthys and Isis (side by side) and Thoth. Other walls: genii of the dead and gods seated at tables, with the Queen worshiping them.

A short distance farther on is No. 55, the ****Tomb of Prince Amen-her-khopshef**, another son of Ramesses III. The colors of the paintings are well preserved.

First chamber, left-hand wall: the King embraced by Isis; the King, accompanied by the Prince, offering incense to Ptah; various deities (Ptah, Tatjenen, the dog-headed Duamutef and Imsety, guardian spirits of the dead, and Isis) holding the King by the hand. Right-hand wall, similar scenes: the King embraced by Isis; the King and Prince offering incense to the god Shu; Qebhsenuef, Hapi and Isis holding the King by the hand. The side chambers are undecorated. – The *corridor* beyond the first chamber has the same scenes as the corridor in Tomb 44. – At the end of the corridor is the *tomb chamber,* with the granite *sarcophagus.*

Next to No. 55 is No. 66, the ****Tomb of Queen Nefertari**, wife of Ramesses II, which is different in form from the other Queen's tombs. It has magnificent painted stucco reliefs, executed with the utmost delicacy, which have unfortunately been damaged by the infiltration of water; particularly fine are the figures of the Queen. The ceiling is painted with stars in imitation of the night sky.

A flight of steps descends to the *first chamber,* along the left-hand walls of which runs a bench for the reception of offerings, topped by a cavetto cornice. The inscriptions are from the 17th Chapter of the "Book of the Dead". The accompanying reliefs depict the Queen sitting under a canopy and playing a board game; the Queen's soul, in the form of a bird with a human head; the Queen kneeling in adoration of the sun, which is borne by two lions; the god Thoth in the form of an ibis; the mummy on its bier; and various deities. Right-hand walls: the Queen, in presence of Osiris, praying to the sun god Harakhty and the goddess of the West; far right, the Queen, followed by Isis, before the scarab-headed Khepri; on the opposite

side the goddess Selkit. – *Side chamber* (right to left): the god Khnum, accompanied by Isis and Nephthys; the Queen worshiping the sacred bull and seven sacred cows; the Queen before Atum; the Queen before Osiris; the Queen presenting writing materials to Thoth and making an offering to Ptah. – On the side walls of the staircase leading out of the first chamber, above, the Queen is depicted in the presence of various divinities; below, Isis and Nephthys kneeling and protecting those entering the tomb. On the architrave of the doorway is the goddess Maat with outspread wings. – The *pillared chamber* at the foot of the staircase was intended for the Queen's sarcophagus. The mural reliefs in this chamber and the three small side chambers opening off it are largely destroyed.

Medinet Habu

Prominently situated in the plain to the SE of the Valley of the Queens, against the backdrop of the desert hills, is the most southerly temple complex in the Theban necropolis, **Medinet Habu**. It takes its name ("City of Habu") from a Christian village, now abandoned, which grew up within the area of the temple from the 5th c. onwards and was named after the wise Amenhotep, son of Habu. The complex consists of a small older *temple* of the 18th Dynasty which was enlarged in the Late Period and the great ***Temple of Ramesses III**, associated with a royal palace, which was surrounded by a battlemented enclosure wall 13 ft/4 m high.

Just inside the gate in the outer wall (13 ft/4 m wide, with porters' lodges on either side) is the **High Gate**, formerly called the Pavilion of Ramesses III, a massive structure which here replaces the normal pylon and gateway. This lay on the line of the great inner wall of brick enclosing a rectangular precinct within which were the temple complex and the royal palace. It was in fact part of the palace, which lay some distance away, and its rooms were occasionally occupied by the Pharaoh and his harem and were decorated accordingly. Two high *towers* with almost imperceptibly inclined walls, resting on the E side on a sloping foundation wall, enclose a narrow court which contracts towards the back, where there is a gateway linking the two towers. On the front of the towers are reliefs. Right-hand tower: the King smiting his enemies in the presence of Re-Harakhty; below, in chains, seven Princes of conquered peoples – the Kheta (Hittites), Emor, Zakari, Shardana (Sardinians), Shakalasha (Sicilians), Tuirsha (Tyrrhenians, Etruscans) and Peleste (Philistines). Left-hand tower: the King smiting Nubians and Libyans in the presence of Amun-Re.

In the court between the two towers are two seated figures of the lion-headed goddess Sakhmet in black granite which were found in front of the gate. On the walls, between the first and second storeys, are curious brackets adorned with four busts of enemy prisoners, which formerly supported statues of the King. The reliefs on the walls (numbered as in the plan on p. 343) mainly depict offerings. – 1. the King making offerings to Seth (obliterated) and Nut; below, the King leading two rows of prisoners before Amun. – 2: above, the King offering wine to Atum and a goddess; below, offering flowers to Enhuret and a goddess. – 3: the gods Month (destroyed) and Atum conducting the King into the presence of Amun. – 4: above, the King presenting an image of Amun to Harakhty and Maat; below, the King presenting two rows of fettered prisoners to Amun (note the Libyan depicted full-face in the lower row). – 5: above, the King offering incense to the moon god and Seshat; below, presenting an image of Maat to Ptah and Sakhmet; on the second storey is a window with attractive ceiling decorations. – 6: the King in the presence of Amun, with Mut and Thoth behind him.

In the *gateway* leading into the temple forecourt the King is depicted leading two rows of fettered prisoners into the presence of Amun (left) and smiting a band of enemies, whom he grasps by the hair (right).

A modern staircase in the S tower leads up to two *rooms, one above the other, in the middle part of the structure; the floor between them has been destroyed. The mural reliefs in the lower room (in which visitors stand) have disappeared, but those in the upper room, depicting the King with the ladies of the harem, can still be distinguished. From the windows there are good views of the temple and the remains of the town to the W and of the plain to the E. There are also reliefs in other rooms (inaccessible) depicting the King with his favorites and his children. Note the curious coiffures of the ladies of the harem.

Some of these reliefs can be seen from below. On the W wall of a room on the top storey of the N wing, visible from the entrance, is a scene showing the King seated on a chair with five girls standing round him. On the upper storey of the N wing, to the right and left of two windows, is another scene (visible from the NE corner of the forecourt) depicting the King surrounded by girls (on the right he strokes a girl's chin). Farther right, beside a gap in the wall, the King is depicted with a girl standing in front of him; to the left, the lower halves of two other female figures, one kneeling and one standing. Below is a narrow window, with vases of flowers above it and to the right the King listening to girl musicians. – On this side of the N wing can be seen the cavities in the walls for the rafters supporting the two upper floors.

In the spacious *Forecourt* between the High Gate (on the rear side of which are reliefs of the King in various postures as the vanquisher of his enemies) and the main temple is a small *gateway* built by Nectanebo I. To the right of this is the 18th Dynasty temple, to the left the **Mortuary Temple of Amenirdis**, a Princess who was the ecclesiastical ruler of Thebes under the last Ethiopian kings and Psammetichus I. – On the doorway (left and right, above) Amenirdis is depicted making an offering to Amun; below she is seen (left) before Amun and Mut, holding two sistra, and (right) making an offering to a goddess. – From the forecourt, which had a colonnade supported by two columns on either side, we enter the vaulted *sanctuary*, which is surrounded by a corridor. To the right are three *chapels*, dedicated respectively to Nitocris (daughter of Psammetichus I), Shepenwepet (daughter of the Ethiopian King Piankhi) and Mehtwesekhet (wife of Psammetichus I). Under the last chapel is a crypt (visible through the broken floor) covered with inscriptions.

The main temple, the *****Temple of Ramesses III**, was built exactly on the model of the Ramesseum and, like the Ramesseum, was dedicated to Amun. On the front of both towers of the large *First Pylon* are reliefs celebrating the King's military successes. On the right-hand tower he is depicted, in the presence of Amun Re-Harakhty, grasping his enemies by the hair and smiting them with his club, while the falcon-headed god presents him with the curved sword of victory and leads in on a cord the conquered lands, represented in the usual way by their names enclosed within a circle of walls; below, two other rows of vanquished peoples; farther left, between two grooves for flagstaffs, a similar but much smaller scene and, below it, a long inscription celebrating in bombastic terms the King's victory over the Libyans in the 11th year of his reign. At the foot, on the left, is the seated figure of Amun, with Ptah behind him inscribing the years of the King's reign on a palm branch; the King kneeling before Amun under the sacred tree and receiving from him the symbols for a long reign, suspended from a palm branch; Thoth inscribing the King's name on the leaves of the tree, with the goddess Seshat standing beside him. To the right of the doorway, below, is a door-shaped stela dated in the 12th year of Ramesses III's reign recording the gifts made to Ptah – copied from the inscription by Ramesses II at Abu Simbel (see that entry). – On the left-hand tower are similar

First Pylon of the Temple of Ramesses III, Medinet Habu

Relief in the Temple of Ramesses III, Medinet Habu

scenes, depicting Ramesses III in the presence of Amun-Re.

Through the central doorway (on both inner and outer walls, reliefs of the King worshiping various gods) we enter the *First Court,* which is roughly square, measuring 115 ft/35 m each way. The reliefs on the rear side of the first pylon relate to the Libyan War: to the S (on the left when entering) a battle, in which the Egyptians are supported by mercenaries from the Shardana tribe (Sardinians), distinguished by their round helmets with horns; to the N, prisoners marshaled before the King and an inscription. – The court is flanked on the right and left by covered *colonnades.* The roof of the right-hand colonnade is supported on seven square pillars, against which stand colossal *Osiris figures* of the King. The left-hand colonnade has eight papyrus columns with open capitals. This colonnade was the façade of the royal palace which adjoined the S side of the temple and communicated with the first court by three doors and a large balcony-window. To the right and left of the window the King is depicted smiting his foes, standing on a bracket formed of their heads. Below the window are scenes of dancing, singing and jubilation, representing thè crowds who would greet the King's appearance on the balcony. On the rear walls of both colonnades there are further reliefs depicting the King's battles and victories and the prisoners captured; on the end walls he is seen (depicted on a large scale) on his way to the festival of Amun, attended by fan-bearers.

The inscriptions and reliefs on the *Second Pylon* are of still greater interest. On the right-hand tower is a long inscription celebrating the King's victory, in the 8th year of his reign, over a league of Mediterranean peoples who menaced Egypt by sea and by land from Syria. On the left-hand tower the King is seen leading into the presence of Amun and Mut three rows of prisoners, representing the peoples conquered in this campaign. They are depicted as beardless, wearing curious caps adorned with feathers and loincloths

with tassels, hanging down in a point in front. The inscription indicates that they are Danawa (Danai) and Peleste (Philistines). – A ramp leads up to the granite gateway of the pylon.

The *Second Court,* which is similar in layout and to some extent in decoration to the second court of the Ramesseum, but is better preserved, is 125 ft/38 m long by 138 ft/42 m wide. It is surrounded on all four sides by colonnades. Those on the N and S sides have columns with closed capitals; the one on the E side has pillars with Osiris figures; and the one on the W side, forming a raised terrace, has eight Osiris pillars in front and eight columns to the rear. On both the columns and the pillars the King is depicted making offerings to various gods. In Christian times the court was converted into a church, but most of the remains of this have been removed. – On the walls of the colonnades are reliefs depicting events in Ramesses's life, in particular great festivals and military exploits. In the following description the reliefs are numbered as in the plan on p. 343.

North Colonnade and adjoining part of *East Colonnade,* rear wall, above: the *festival of the harvest god Min, which was celebrated as a coronation festival. – 1: the King being borne out of the palace on a richly decorated litter under a canopy which is carried by Princes (names missing); he is followed by courtiers and preceded by priests bearing censers, a lector priest and soldiers, each wearing two feathers on their heads (note in the upper row trumpeters and drummers, in the lower row men with castanets). – 2: the King making offerings and burning incense before the image of Min. – 3 (continued on E wall): the festival procession; the image of Min is carried on a litter by priests, flanked by fan-bearers and followed by priests carrying shrines; in front is the King, who is preceded by a white bull (the god's sacred animal), the Queen and a long train of priests carrying standards, temple utensils and images of the King and his predecessors; on the right, the King awaiting the procession, with two emblems in front of him; priests release four carrier-pigeons. – 4: the King cuts with a sickle the sheaf presented to him by a priest (as in the Ramesseum); the lector priest recites a hymn to Min, while another priest presents the sheaf to the god; the Queen, above, looks on; the white bull in front of the King, below it a series of images of the royal ancestors. – 5: the King offers incense to Min, standing under a canopy.

The lower rows are of less interest. 1: the King making offerings to the sacred barques of Khons, Mut and Amun. – 2: the barques are borne out of the temple by priests, while the King, behind a fourth barque, advances to meet them.

Door-lintel in the Temple of Ramesses III

S end of *East Colonnade* and *South Colonnade*, above: scenes from the festival of Ptah-Sokar. – 6: procession of priests carrying sacred barques, images of gods, standards and temple utensils; behind them the King and dignitaries. – 7 (on S wall): the sacred emblem of the god Nefertum (son of Ptah) borne by 18 priests. – 8: the King holding a cord which is pulled by 16 high dignitaries; in front of the King two priests

burning incense. – 9: the barque of Sokar carried by 16 priests, followed by the King. – 10: the King making offerings to the sacred barque of Sokar; the King before the ram-headed Khnum and two other gods and before the falcon-headed Sokar-Osiris, to whom he presents a platter with bread. – Below are military scenes. – 6 (right to left): the King and other charioteers dashing against the Libyans and slaying

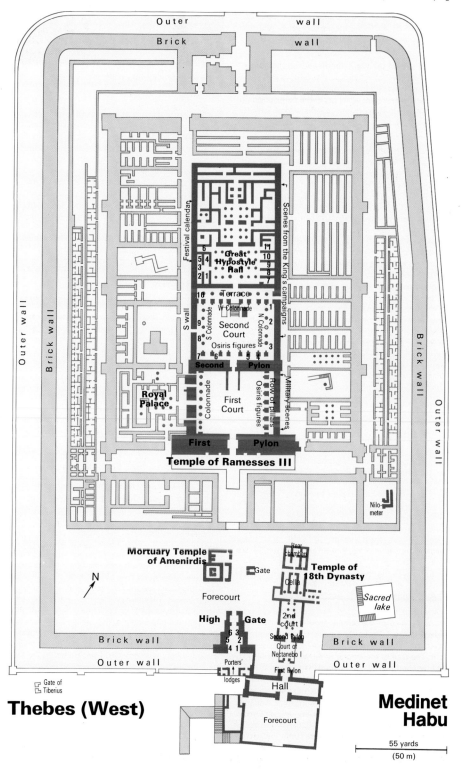

Thebes (West)

Medinet Habu

55 yards
(50 m)

them with his arrows; foot-soldiers fighting in wild confusion; the King returning from the battle in his chariot, with three rows of fettered Libyan captives in front of him and two fan-bearers behind him; the King presenting the Libyan prisoners to Amun and Mut. – 7 (on S wall): the King seated in his chariot, with his back to the horses, receiving Libyan prisoners (with light red skin) brought in by the Princes and other dignitaries in four rows; the severed hands and phalluses of the slain being counted. Most of the wall is occupied by a 75-line inscription celebrating the victorious war.

The rear wall of the *West Colonnade,* on the terrace, has three rows of reliefs: in the two upper rows, Ramesses III in the presence of various deities; bottom row, Princes and Princesses (as in the corresponding position in the Ramesseum; names added later by Ramesses VI).

Beyond the second court only the lower parts of the walls and columns are preserved. – We come first into the *Great Hypostyle Hall,* the roof of which was supported by four rows of six columns, the central columns being considerably higher than those on either side. On the walls the King is depicted in the presence of various gods (note particularly the magnificent gold vessels he presents to Amun, Mut and Khons on the S wall). – Beyond this are three smaller chambers, the first two with two rows of four columns, the third with four pillars. The only features of any interest are two statues of red granite in the second chamber, one (on the left) of Amun and Maat, the other (on the right) the King and the ibis-headed Thoth. – The other chambers to the rear of the temple were dedicated to various gods; those to the left of the pillared chamber to Osiris (including one with a vaulted roof decorated with astronomical representations). – There were other rooms on the upper floor, reached by a staircase from the first of the three chambers to the rear of the hypostyle hall.

On either side of the hypostyle hall are a series of small rooms. Those on the left-hand side were evidently used for storing the temple treasures, as the scenes on the walls indicate (numbers as in the plan on p. 343). – 1: the King presents to Amun papyrus-holders borne by royal lions or kneeling figures of the King. – 2: the King presenting to Amun costly vessels and boxes with lids in the form of sphinxes, rams and the heads of rams, falcons and the King himself. – 3: the King presenting bags of precious stones to Amun. – 4: the King making offerings of costly table ornaments, jewelry and piles of gold, silver and lead. – 5: the King offering great heaps of gold and other precious metals. – In rooms 6–11 the King is depicted making offerings to various gods. – In the second last room on the right (No. 10) is a *colossal statue* (headless) of Ptah, in alabaster, dating from the reign of Amenophis III.

On the S side of the temple are the remains of the **Royal Palace.** In the throne room can be seen the dais for the throne, with three shallow steps leading up to it. The roof of the throne room was borne on two columns and two pillars engaged in the rear wall (built of brick). To the left is a second dais, to the right a large bathroom. In a room to the W (perhaps the Queen's throne room) is a third dais; adjoining is a room for ablutions. – To the W of the palace is a *well,* with steps leading down to it. At the sides of the steps are reliefs of the Nile gods dispensing water, Thoth and Horus sprinkling Ramesses III with water, and the King before Khons-Neferhotep.

In the Temple of Ramesses III, Medinet Habu

Finally there is a series of interesting **reliefs,** mainly devoted to Ramesses III's military exploits, on the **outer walls** of the temple. – *South wall,* at the first pylon: fine hunting scenes; above, the King hunting mountain goats and wild asses; below, the King and his retinue hunting wild bulls in a marshy area abounding in fish and waterfowl. – W end of wall: a long *festival calendar,* listing the appointed sacrifices from the 16th day of the month of Pakhon (the day of Ramesses III's accession) to the 19th day of the month of Tybi. Below is a procession of priests carrying loaves and other food. – To right and left of the palace balcony (which is approached by a flight of steps) the King is depicted slaying enemy prisoners. In the embrasure of the window the King and his retinue are seen approaching the balcony.

The *west wall* has scenes from a war with the Kushites (Negroes) and the beginning of the series on the Libyan War. – S end of wall: the King in battle; triumphal procession with captured Kushites; presentation of prisoners to Amun. – N end of wall (Libyan War): the King in the presence of Amun and Khons, with Thoth behind him; the King with the falcon-headed Month behind him and four priests carrying divine images on poles in front of him; the King in his chariot, accompanied by his bodyguard.

The *north wall* continues the record of the Libyan War and celebrates a victory over the northern peoples in ten scenes at the W end, followed by five scenes devoted to the Syrian Wars.

W end of N wall. – 1: the King's departure for the war, with a lion beside his chariot; in another chariot in front is the standard of Amun-Re with a ram's head. – 2: a battle with the Libyans. – 3: the King addressing his troops, in five rows, with Libyan prisoners; the severed hands, etc., are counted (the total is given as 12,535). – 4: the King watches the mustering of troops from the palace balcony; standards are brought out and weapons distributed. – 5: the King departing for Syria, preceded by soldiers with lances and below bows; below, Shardana mercenaries. – 6: battle with the northern peoples in Palestine; the King in his chariot launching arrows at the enemy, identifiable as Zakari by their curious caps; children sitting in ox-carts. – 7: the King hunting lions; in the thicket a wounded lion, with another dying under the horse's feet; below, a parade of Egyptian troops and mercenaries. – 8 (seen properly only in slanting light): *naval battle with the northern peoples,* whose fleet is annihilated at one of the mouths of the Nile; from the shore the King shoots arrows at the enemy; below, one of the enemy ships has capsized; the Egyptian ships are distinguishable by the lions' heads on their prows (one vessel with many oarsmen – below, right – contains Zakari prisoners); bottom row, other prisoners being marched away; the King trampling on prisoners, in front of him archers, hovering above him the goddess of Lower Egypt in the form of a vulture. 9: the King, on the palace balcony, receiving dignitaries who bring in the Zakari prisoners; bottom row, the severed hands being counted; left, the royal chariot; above, the "castle of Ramesses", perhaps the Palace of Medinet Habu. – 10: the King conducting two rows of prisoners (above Zakari, below Libyans) into the presence of the gods of Thebes (Amun, Mut and Khons).

E end of N wall (first court), upper row (left to right). – 1: the King storming a Syrian fortress. – 2: the King, having alighted from his chariot after the victory, pierces a Syrian with his lance. – 3: the King receiving the prisoners. – 4: the King presenting the prisoners to Amun and Khons, together with costly vessels. – Lower row (left to right): the King in his chariot attacking a Libyan stronghold; bringing in Libyan prisoners; receiving three rows of prisoners brought in by officers; returning home with prisoners and being greeted by dignitaries; and presenting the captured Libyans to Amun and Mut.

First Pylon, above, the King storming a Hittite fortress; below, a battle with the Libyans; the King alighting from his chariot and binding two captured Syrians.

On the N side of the temple forecourt, between the High Gate and the main temple, is the oldest part of the whole temple complex, the elegant little **18th Dynasty Temple** (peripteral), which was begun during the joint reign of Hatshepsut and Tuthmosis III and completed after Tuthmosis became sole ruler. Here as elsewhere Hatshepsut's inscriptions and her figure were obliterated or replaced by others. The divine images and names which were destroyed by Amenophis IV/Akhenaten were restored in the reigns of Horemheb and Sethos I. – The original entrance was on the E side; but the alterations and additions made by later Pharaohs (particularly by Ramesses III, who was also responsible for the reliefs on the outside walls) and during the Ptolemaic and Roman periods make it difficult to distinguish the original plan.

A gateway to the N of the High Gate leads into the second court of the temple, which lies to the left. It consists of a cella surrounded by a colonnade (added by Tuthmosis III) and six chambers to the rear, the oldest part of the building. Along the outside of the colonnade runs a parapet from which rise square pillars supporting the roof. The 16-sided columns within the colonnade were added later to prevent the collapse of the roof. – The reliefs depict Tuthmosis III (in the rear chambers also Tuthmosis I and II, replacing Hatshepsut) making offerings to various gods and performing other ritual acts. On the pillars to the right and left of the entrance are inscriptions by Horemheb, Sethos I and Pinudjem recording the building work done by them. The cella, with reliefs restored after their earlier destruction, had doors (restored by Euergetes II) at both ends. In the last room on the right is an unfinished shrine in red granite. – The structures on the N and S sides of the front colonnade are later additions, the one on the N side incorporating stones from earlier buildings (bearing the names of Ramesses II, Pinudjem and Achoris); note the small lattice windows and the rings on the upper parts of the columns.

The Second Court, to which we now return, dates from the Saite period, the granite gateway to the N from the early 26th Dynasty. At its E end is the Second Pylon, built by the Ethiopian ruler Shabaka and restored by Ptolemy IX Soter II, with a relief of Taharqa

grasping his enemies by the hair and smiting them. – The adjoining Court of Nectanebo I had four cluster-columns with closed capitals, linked by screens, along each side (two columns restored) and a gateway at the E end. Some 13 ft/4 m E of the gateway is the large First Pylon, built in the Ptolemaic period and incorporating many stones from earlier buildings (particularly the Ramesseum). In the central doorway Ptolemy IX Soter II and Ptolemy XII Neos Dionysos are depicted worshiping the gods.

Along the E side of the pylon, facing the First Court (130 ft/39·60 m long, 83 ft/25·40 m wide), was a colonnade, which had columns with rich floral capitals and high screens. Only the two central columns have been preserved. In front of one of the screens is a false door of red granite dating from the time of Tuthmosis III which was found in the pavement of the first pylon. The gateways into the court are now walled up; on the one to the S is an inscription in the name of the Emperor Antoninus Pius.

At the NE corner of the temple precinct lies the Sacred Lake, 60 ft/18 m square, with two flights of steps. – Some 45 yds/40 m NW of the lake is a Nilometer. A doorway inscribed with the name of Nectanebo I leads into a room beyond which is a corridor with a staircase descending to a depth of 65 ft/20 m. – Between the 18th Dynasty temple and the Nilometer is a small gateway with inscriptions in the name of the Emperor Domitian. It was rebuilt here – the original site is unknown – from stones which had been reused in a Coptic building.

Some 200 yards S of the High Gate is a small Ptolemaic **Temple of Thoth**, now known as the Qasr el-Aguz. It was dedicated by Euergetes II to a deity named Teephibis who was equated with Thoth, but was never completed. It consists of a wide vestibule and three chambers, one behind the other. On the left-hand entrance wall of the second chamber the King is depicted making offerings to Thoth, Imhotep and the deified sage Amenhotep. Only the lower row of reliefs was completed; the upper row was merely sketched in.

$\frac{3}{4}$ mile/1 km SE of Medinet Habu are the remains of a royal city founded by Amenophis III, with a large palace known as the "House of Joy", which contained the royal apartments and reception rooms, the dwellings of courtiers, the harem, the residence of Queen Tiy, a large festal hall dedicated to the celebration of the King's 2nd Jubilee, workshops, etc.

To the S, on the road to Armant (footpath from Medinet Habu, 50 minutes), is a well-preserved **Temple of Isis** of the Roman period, now known as the Deir el-Shelwit. It dates from the reigns of Hadrian and Antoninus Pius, and the ruined pylon has inscriptions in the names of Vespasian, Domitian and Otho. The

Colossi of Memnon

cella is surrounded by a number of smaller chambers, in one of which (far left from entrance) is a staircase leading to the roof.

Colossi of Memnon

Beside the road which runs from the Valley of the Queens and Medinet Habu towards the Nile are two prominent landmarks visible from a long way off, the famous *Colossi of Memnon. These two gigantic statues, carved from a very hard yellowish-brown sandstone quarried in the hills above Edfu, represent Amenophis III seated on a cube-shaped throne. They stood at the entrance to the King's temple, of which only scanty traces are left. In Roman Imperial times they were taken for statues of Memnon, son of Eos and Tithonus, who was killed by Achilles during the Trojan War.

The **South Colossus** is better preserved than the one to the N. It stands 64 ft/19·59 m high; the figure alone measures 52 ft/15·95 m, while the base (partly buried under the sand) is 13 ft/3·97 m high. With the crown, long since vanished, which it originally wore the total height must have been some 70 ft/21 m. The legs, from the sole of the feet to the knees, measure 20 ft/ 6 m; the feet themselves are 10½ ft/3·20 m long. The breadth across the shoulders is 20 ft/6·17 m, the length of the middle finger on one hand 4½ ft/1·38 m, the length of the arm from the finger-tips to the elbow 15½ ft/4·76 m.

On the left-hand side of the **North Colossus** is a smaller figure of Amenophis's mother Mutemuia, on the right his wife Tiy; a third figure between the legs is no longer distinguishable. On each side of the

throne are figures in sunk relief of two Nile gods twining the traditional symbols of Upper and Lower Egypt, the lotus and the papyrus, round the hieroglyph meaning "unite", symbolizing the unity of the kingdom. This is the famous "musical statue" which attracted many visitors in Roman Imperial times. It was observed that the statue emitted a musical note at sunrise, and this gave rise the the myth that Memnon was greeting his mother Eos (the dawn) with this soft and plaintive note, whereupon his mother's tears (the morning dew) fell on her beloved son. Strabo expresses doubts on the subject, but Pausanias and Juvenal (2nd c. A.D.) accept the phenomenon as a fact. If the sound was not heard, it was taken as a sign that the god was angry. The sound ceased to be heard after the Emperor Septimius Severus, perhaps to propitiate the god, had the upper part of the statue rather clumsily restored. No satisfactory scientific explanation of the phenomenon has ever been put forward.

Numerous Greek and Latin inscriptions, in prose and verse, cover the legs of the northern colossus up to the height a man standing at the foot of the statue can reach, suggesting that it was this colossus that gave out the musical sound. The earliest inscription dates from the 11th year of Nero's reign, the latest from the reigns of Septimius Severus and Caracalla; most (27) date from the reign of Hadrian. There is only a single inscription by an Egyptian, in demotic script. Most of the inscriptions are dated. Among the travelers (sometimes alone, sometimes with their wives) who have immortalized themselves in this way are eight governors of Egypt, three epistrategi (military governors) of the Thebaid and two procurators. If the figure remained mute visitors frequently stayed on until the sound was heard; some were not content until they had heard it several times. In A.D. 130 the Emperor Hadrian, with his wife Sabina and a large retinue, stayed here for some days. From his reign date numerous Greek verses on the legs of the statue, most of them by the Court Poetess, Balbilla. One of her effusions, on the left leg, relates in 12 hexameters that Memnon greeted the Emperor before sunrise "as well as he could", but that at the second hour a clear note, as if from a copper instrument, was heard, followed later by a third note, so that all the world could see how dear Hadrian was to the gods. The best verses are those by the "Imperial procurator and poet" Asclepiodotus on the front of the base: "Sea-born Thetis, learn that Memnon did not die. When his mother's beams bathe him in a warm radiance then his cry is heard in the Libyan mountains, separated by the Nile from hundred-gated Thebes. But thy son, ever eager for battle, now rests in Troy and Thessaly, eternally mute."

Karnak and Luxor: see separate entries.

Tod

Upper Egypt. – Governorate: Qena.
ⓘ **Tourist Information Office,**
Tourist Bazaar,
Luxor;
tel. 22 15.

ACCESS. – Road from Luxor (12½ miles/20 km N). – Railway Station at Armant.

The village of Tod, the ancient Egyptian Djerti and Graeco-Roman Tuphium, lies on the E bank of the Nile 12½ miles/20 km S of Luxor. It contains the picturesque remains of a large temple of the Ptolemaic and Roman Imperial periods dedicated to the war god Month.

HISTORY. – There seems to have been a temple here as early as the reign of Userkaf (5th Dynasty). It was rebuilt during the Middle Kingdom, in the reigns of Mentuhotep II and III (11th Dynasty) and Sesostris I (12th Dynasty), and thereafter embellished and much enlarged during the New Kingdom, in the reigns of Tuthmosis III and Amenophis II (18th Dynasty), Sethos I (19th Dynasty), the 19th Dynasty usurper Amenmesses, and Ramesses II and IV (20th Dynasty). Ptolemy VIII Euergetes II added a further temple and a sacred lake. – In the vicinity was a kiosk of the Roman period, and just outside the temple precinct were Roman baths.

Much of the **Ptolemaic temple** was later used as dwelling-houses, and a Coptic church was built on the site, so that in the course of the centuries the original structure has been considerably altered. The remains still visible include a wall, the stumps of four columns belonging to a colonnade of the Roman period, part of another colonnade and a chapel of the Theban goddess Tenenet, with a store-room for the temple treasures.

In the ruins of the 12th Dynasty temple was found the *"Treasure of Amenemhet II", a hoard of costly gold and silver articles and finely wrought metal utensils contained in four copper chests, most of them votive gifts from Mesopotamia. They are now in the Egyptian Museum in Cairo and the Louvre in Paris.

SURROUNDINGS of Tod. – 2 miles/3 km W, on the left bank of the Nile, is the town of **Armant**, which has a large sugar factory. It occupies the site of the ancient Egyptian *On,* known as the "Upper Egyptian On" to distinguish it from Heliopolis-On and also as *Per-mont* ("House of Month"), after the falcon-headed war god Month who was particularly venerated here. From Per-mont came the Greek name of *Hermonthis.* This is believed to have been the place of origin of the 11th Dynasty. In Roman Imperial times On was the chief town of a nome. 1¼ miles/2 km NE are the scanty remains of a temple built in the early 11th Dynasty and altered and extended by Nectanebo II and the Ptolemies, in particular Cleopatra VII and Ptolemy XV Caesarion, which continued in use into Roman times. Stones from the temple, much of which was still standing in the 19th c., were used in the construction of the sugar factory and the quay along the river front.

N of Armant, on the edge of the desert, was found the **Bucheum**, the local counterpart of the Serapeum of Memphis (see under Saqqara). This was the burial-place of the Buchis bulls sacred to Month, which were interred here from the time of Nectanebo II to the reign of Diocletian. The associated burial-place of the sacred cows, the "mothers of the Buchis bulls", was also found.

Tuna el-Gebel
See under Mallawi

Valley of Kings
See under Thebes

Valley of Queens
See under Thebes

Wadi Feiran
See under Sinai

Wadi el-Gedid
See New Valley

Wadi Natrun

Lower Egypt. – Governorate: Mudiriya el-Tahrir.
Population: 20,000.

ⓘ **Tourist Information Office,**
Misr Travel Tower,
Cairo – Abbasia;
tel. 82 60 16.

ACCOMMODATION. – *Rest-house*, with overnight
accommodation, in Bir Hooker, II, 24 b.

ACCESS. – Side road branching off the desert road
from Cairo to Alexandria at Bir Hooker, about half-
way between the two cities.

The *Wadi Natrun (Natron Valley),
the Greek region of Nitria and the
Roman Scythiaca, is a 20 mile/32 km
long depression in the Western
Desert between Cairo and Alexandria, some 50–55 miles/80–90 km
from each city. Strung along the
valley are 12 salt lakes, linked with
the Nile by underground channels,
which dry up almost completely in
summer. The deposits in the lake
basins and the surrounding area
yield salt and natron, used for
bleaching cloth and in the manufacture of soap and glass.

In the Deir Amba Bshoi

The Wadi Natrun is famous for the
hermitages and monasteries which were
established here from the 4th c. onwards
and, together with the other desert
monasteries (St Antony's, St Paul's and St
Catherine's), had great influence on the
development of Christianity. They were
repeatedly raided, plundered and
destroyed by Berber hordes, particularly in
the 9th c., so that out of more than 50
monasteries which once flourished here
there now remain only four houses
occupied by Coptic monks. None of these
monasteries have preserved their original
aspect, and only a few scanty remains
survive from the period of their foundation. They are all surrounded by defensive
walls and have a watch-tower or keep

(*qasr*), entered by a drawbridge, in which
the monks could take shelter in case of
attack. – In order to protect the monks'
seclusion only one monastery, the Deir
Amba Bshoi, was open to visitors. Nowadays foreign visitors are allowed in to all
the monasteries which can all be reached
by asphalted roads.

The ***Deir el-Suryan** (Monastery of the
Syrians) is a sombre-colored building
surrounded by palms. It was founded in
the 6th c. and purchased in the 8th c. by a
wealthy and pious Syrian merchant
named Tekrit for monks from Syria. Like
the other monasteries in the Wadi Natrun,
it was several times devastated by Berber
raiders in the 9th c., and in the 14th c. it
was visited by a devastating plague. In the
16th c. the monastery, then almost totally

Monastery of the Syrians, Wadi Natrun

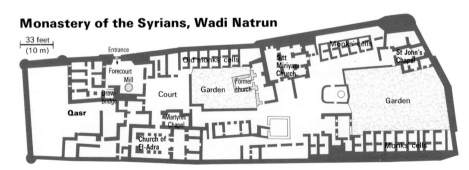

abandoned, was taken over by Coptic monks, who still occupy it.

The monastery has two churches and a small chapel. The large **Church of el-Adra** dates in part from the 10th c. The excellent frescos in the choir, the carved wooden choir-screen and a number of stucco reliefs show techniques and ornament characteristic of Eastern (and Islamic) art in the medieval period. The church has many icons depicting saints of the Wadi Natrun, a fine iconostasis and a doorway with ivory inlays.

At one end of the monastery is the **Qasr** (Keep), with monks' cells, store-rooms and a kitchen for use in the event of a siege. From the top there is a fine* view of the Deir Amba Bshoi. – The **Sitt Miriyam Church** (St Mary's) has a number of fine icons. – The monastery's valuable library, which contained early Syriac manuscripts and important Arabic and Coptic works, was dispersed in the mid 19th c. to Britain, the Vatican and Cairo.

$\frac{3}{4}$ mile/1 km SE of the Deir el-Suryan is the **Deir Amba Bshoi**. It was found at the end of the 4th c. by a hermit named Bshoi who had withdrawn to the solitude of the desert at an early age. Like the other monasteries, it is surrounded by a high and massive wall and has a church, monks' cells, various offices and a garden. It is occupied and managed by some two dozen monks.

6 miles/10 km NW of the Deir el-Suryan, in a totally isolated situation, is the **Deir Amba Baramus**, said to have been founded by Maximus and Domitius, sons of the Emperor Valentinian (364–375). The monks in this monastery observe a very strict rule. Within the walls (built in the 9th c. after a devastating Berber raid) are four churches. The large *Church of the Virgin* has a fine painted iconostasis. The smaller *Church of St Macarius* has a 13th c. pulpit. The monastery also has a qasr, the usual monks' cells and offices and a garden.

$4\frac{1}{2}$ miles/7 km SE of the Deir Amba Bshoi, at the SE end of the Wadi Natrun, is the **Deir Abu Makar** (Monastery of St Macarius), founded in the 4th c. by St Macarius the Great (c. 300–c. 380/390), in which Patriarch Theodosius I sought refuge in the 6th c. Apart from the three churches and the qasr, the buildings are modern. The principal church, and the oldest in the monastery, is the *Church of St Macarius,* which has an iconostasis dating in part from the 4th and 5th c. and fine frescos of the 10th–11th c. The old qasr has been converted into three chapels, one above the other, dedicated respectively to the Virgin, St Antony and the Archangel Michael; the frescos date from the 14th c.

SURROUNDINGS of the Wadi Natrun. – 2 miles/3 km W of the Deir Amba Baramus is the end of the *Bahr Belama* ("River without Water"), an old river-bed, perhaps a former arm of the Nile but now filled with sand, which runs N from the Dakhla and Bahriya oases (see those entries) into the Wadi Natrun. At this point it is 7½ miles/12 km wide. Evidence of the erstwhile fertility of the valley is provided by petrified tree-trunks 26–33 ft/8–10 m long.

Scattered about in the desert some 30 miles/50 km NW of the Wadi Natrun, on the road to the City of St Menas, are about 700 hermitages and monasteries of the 5th–7th c., abandoned at various times down to the 15th c. and now covered by sand. The area, known

Monastery of St Macarius, Wadi Natrun

as **Kelya** (from Latin *cella*, "cell"), was rediscovered and partly excavated in 1964 during the construction of irrigation works. Of particular interest are the ruins of a 7th c. monastery with fine frescos.

Some 37 miles/60 km from Giza on the desert road from Cairo to Alexandria and 12½ miles/20 km before the turning for the Wadi Natrun a road goes off on the right and runs NE towards the Delta, coming in 14 miles/22 km to the Rosetta arm of the Nile. A short distance to the N is the *Kom Abu Billo*, the site of ancient **Terenuthis**, where remains of a temple dedicated to Hathor, "Mother of the Turquoises", and a cemetery used from the time of the 6th Dynasty to the 4th c. A.D. have been discovered. A distinctive feature of the late tombs is the occurrence of grave-stones (known as Terenuthis or Kom Abu Billo stelae) on which the dead man is depicted lying on a bier with his arms raised, with demotic or Greek inscriptions.

Alexandria, Cairo and **Western Desert**: see separate entries.

Wadi el-Sebwa

Upper Egypt. – Governorate: Aswan.
(i) **Tourist Information Office,**
Tourist Bazaar,
Aswan;
tel. 32 97.

ACCESS. – Only by boat (inquire in Aswan).

Some 87 miles/140 km S of Aswan, in the Wadi el-Sebwa ("Valley of Lions"), is the well-preserved *Temple of Sebwa, in Egyptian Per-Amun ("House of Amun"), now re-erected at New Sebwa, 2½ miles/ 4 km W of its original site. It was built by Ramesses II on the same plan as the Temple of Gerf Husein, now engulfed by the waters of Lake Nasser, and was dedicated to Amun and the sun god Re-Harakhty, and also to the cult of the deified Ramesses himself.

THE SITE. – The *temple lies within a brick enclosure wall, part of which is destroyed.

A stone *gateway*, in front of which, to right and left, are a statue of Ramesses II and a royal sphinx, leads into the *First Court*, traversed by an avenue with three *lion-sphinxes* wearing the double crown on either side (from which the place takes its name). Behind these are stone purification basins. Passing through a ruined brick pylon, we come into the *Second Court,* on either side of which are two fine falcon-headed *sphinxes*, representing the sun god Re-Harakhty. To the left of this court is a small brick temple, in the main chamber of which is an *altar* dedicated to Amun-Re and Re-Harakhty; adjoining is a room containing two circular grain-stores.

From here a flight of steps leads up to a terrace on which stands the **Temple** proper. The entrance is formed by a well-preserved stone *Pylon* 65 ft/20 m high and 80 ft/24·50 m wide, in front of which stood four *colossal statues* of the King. One of these (to the left), holding a staff with a ram's head (the symbol of Amun-Re), is still erect; another (to the right), holding a staff with a falcon's head, lies on the ground. On the towers are badly weathered reliefs of the King smiting his enemies in the presence of Re-Harakhty and Amun-Re. The central doorway, with reliefs of the King making offerings to the gods, leads into the *Main Court,* 65 ft/20 m square, flanked by colonnades of five pillars, against which stand *colossal statues* of Ramesses II. The reliefs on the walls are poorly executed and of little interest (the usual offering scenes). To the left of the court is a slaughter-court, which has stones pierced with holes for tethering the sacrificial animals.

From the court another flight of steps leads up to a narrow terrace. Here, passing through double doors inserted in Christian times into the ancient doorway, we enter a large *Pillared Chamber* (41 ft/12·40 m long, 52 ft/15·70 m wide, 19 ft/5.90 m high), partly hewn from the rock. The roof is supported on six pillars which originally bore statues of the King and six plain pillars. Like many other Egyptian temples, the temple was converted in Christian times into a church, oriented from W to E; and the apse and the *altar* in front of it are still preserved. Most of the reliefs were covered over during this period. – Beyond the pillared chamber is a rock-cut *transverse chamber,* to the right and left of which are other rooms. The reliefs in this chamber show Ramesses II making offerings to various gods and to his own image. – On the rear wall are three *chapels*, the one in the center being the *Sanctuary.* Right-hand wall: the King presenting flowers to the sacred barque of Re-Harakhty, which is decorated with falcons' heads. Left-hand wall: the King making an offering to the barque of Amun, decorated with rams' heads. Rear wall: above, the solar barque, in which the ram-headed sun god Re-Harakhty is sitting under a canopy, worshiped by the King (left) and by three monkeys (right); below, a niche with statues (chiseled away) of the three deities worshiped in the temple, Amun, Ramesses and Re-Harakhty; to the right and left, the King making an offering of flowers. A figure of St Peter with a large key has been painted over the middle statue.

Also re-erected at New Sebwa was the **Temple of Dakka**, originally situated 25 miles/40 km farther N. The oldest parts of the temple, which was built on the site of an earlier temple, probably of the New Kingdom, and was dedicated to Thoth of Pnubs (an Ethiopian town), who was known to the Greeks as Paotnuphis, date from the time of the Ethiopian ruler Ergamenes and his contemporary Ptolemy IV Philopator. The pronaos was added by Euergetes II, and with the building of the sanctuary and the pylon in Roman Imperial times the temple reached its present form. It is aligned from N to S and thus, unlike most Nubian temples, lies parallel to the river.

The temple is entered by a well-preserved *Pylon* in the outer enclosure wall. The towers of the pylon each have a groove for a flagstaff; they bear a few reliefs and many Greek and some demotic and Meroitic inscriptions by visitors to the temple. On the left-hand wall of the doorway the King is depicted making offerings to Thoth, Tefnut and Hathor (above) and to Isis (below).

It is well worth while climbing to the top of the pylon. In each tower is a staircase leading up from the porter's lodge through three rooms on successive floors to the platform. In the W tower are inscriptions left by visitors and scratched footprints marking the spot where the worshippers stood. From the W tower the roof of the central doorway can be reached.

No trace now remains of the court between the pylons and the pronaos. The *Pronaos* or Vestibule has two plant columns linked with the side walls by screens. The mural reliefs show the King in the presence of the various deities worshiped at Dakka. Particularly notable is a relief on the W wall in which he is presenting to Thoth a palette, borne by Isis and Nephthys, which is probably a symbol of Osiris. On the rear wall (to left, above) are reliefs depicting an Ethiopian ruler. The pronaos was later converted into a church and decorated with religious paintings, some remnants of which can still be seen. – The door in the rear wall was originally the entrance to the older temple. On the left jamb Philopator is depicted in presence of Re, Khnum and Isis, on the right-hand one before Amun-Re, Re-Harakhty, Harendotes and Isis. Within the doorway an Emperor is seen presenting an image of Maat to Thoth of Pnubs and the lion-headed goddess Tefnut.

Beyond the pronaos is a *transverse chamber,* from which a staircase of the Roman Imperial period leads up to the roof of the temple. At the top is a crypt in the thickness of the wall. – Beyond this again is the *Chamber of Ergamenes,* which has only one relief of interest (right-hand wall), depicting the King making a libation of wine to a god described as the "Pharaoh of Senmet" (Bigga) and the goddess Anuket. – In the E wall is a doorway of later construction giving access to two rooms. On the rear wall of the second room are two lions sitting face to face; above them is a baboon (Thoth) worchiping a lioness (Tefnut); higher still are two ibises.

A little way S of the original site of the Dakka Temple was the village of **Kuban**, with remains (now lost under the waters of Lake Nasser) of the ancient settlement of *Beki,* which commanded the road to the gold-mines of Umm Garayat.

Some 30 miles/50 km N of Abu Simbel, on a crag close to the Nile, there formerly stood the picturesque ruin of the ancient Fortress of **Qasr Ibrim**, the Roman *Primis.* Its situation made this the most important strategic point in Nubia. From the early 16th c. the fort and surrounding area were held by Bosnian mercenaries originally sent by Sultan Selim I to conquer Nubia. In 1812 it was taken by the fleeing Mamelukes, but was recaptured and destroyed by Ibrahim Pasha later that year. The ruins of Qasr Ibrim are now drowned in Lake Nasser; but before it disappeared under the water a number

of reliefs in memorial niches below the fortress were cut out of the rock and set up at New Sebwa. The site was also carefully investigated and important texts and other remains were recovered.

The little **Temple of Maharraqa** (or *Ofeduina*), originally situated near the villages of Ofeduina and Birba, 30 miles/ 50 km N of the Wadi el-Sebwa, was also brought to New Sebwa before it disappeared under Lake Nasser. It stood on the site of ancient *Hierasycaminus,* the "city of the sacred sycamore tree", which in Ptolemaic and Imperial Roman times lay on the southern frontier of Egypt. The temple, dedicated to Sarapis, was built in Roman times but was left unfinished. Entered on the E side, it has an open court bordered on three sides by covered colonnades. The columns on the S side are linked by screens, with a doorway in the middle leading into the main chamber. At the NE corner is a spiral staircase of dressed stone leading up to the roof of the colonnade.

**Abu Simbel, Amada and Aswan: see separate entries.

Wadi Tumilat
See under Ismailia Canal

Western Desert/ Libyan Desert

North-West and New Valley Frontier Districts.

The Western (Libyan) Desert, the north-eastern part of the Sahara extending E to the Nile Valley, is an almost entirely empty and barren region of rocky, stony and sandy desert with a total area of almost 772,000 sq. miles/2,000,000 sq. km, of which some 266,400 sq. miles/ 690,000 sq. km are within Egypt and the rest in Libya and Sudan.

This desert – one of the most inhospitable regions in the world – came into being over a period of some 600 million years through the build-up of alternate layers of marine deposits and continental sediments which were convulsed by upthrusts and subsidences of the earth's

The Western Desert – view from St Simeon's Monastery, Aswan

crust and reshaped into a huge plateau. This was then broken up by further subsidence, folding and erosion into ridges and shelves, great terraces and wide basins. These basins reach down in the N to well below sea-level (Qattara Depression −440 ft/−134 m, Wadi Natrun −80 ft/−24 m); farther S they are only just above sea-level and are enclosed by steeply scarped hills.

Imprisoned within the layers of sediments are large underground stores of water left over from ancient seas. In the depressions the water occasionally finds its way to the surface or can easily be tapped by sinking wells, making possible the development of luxuriant oases. Strung across the desert in a wide arc are the oases of Kharga, Dakhla, Farafra and Bahriya, and in the extreme NW of Egypt, near the Libyan frontier, is the great Oasis of Siwa. Between these major oases are a number of small oases and watering-points, of importance only as staging-points for caravans. In a different category is the Fayyum Oasis, which is supplied not by fossil water but by water from the Nile.

In particularly low-lying areas salt-water from the Mediterranean seeps into the ground-water; and in such depressions (e.g. in the Qattara Depression) the high rate of evaporation and absence of leaching by rain lead to the formation of extensive salt-marshes.

The higher regions of the desert are for the most part without water or vegetation, covered by gravel or pebbles. The water-less depressions are frequently traversed by sand-dunes 100–200 ft/30–60 m high, driven by the trade winds into a NNW–SSE alignment. – The arid climatic conditions, interrupted only by occasional cloudbursts, and the wide temperature variations over the day lead to a very rapid erosion process.

Erosional formations

Sea of sand – a bird's-eye view

The Western Desert near the Fayyum Oasis

HISTORY. – Abundant finds of fossils show that in the course of the earth's history the Western Desert, like the Sahara as a whole, has experienced several pluvial periods, broadly corresponding to the glacial periods of more northerly regions, during which it had abundant plant and animal life. The last of these rainy periods ended more than 20,000 years ago, giving place to the aridity which determines the aspect and the life of the region today. – Archaeological evidence shows that the oases were settled from the Palaeolithic onwards by semi-nomadic tribes who practiced a primitive kind of agriculture in these fertile spots. The shallow artesian wells of these early days, however, soon dried up, and the population declined. Thereafter the oases were of importance only as bulwarks against the repeated penetrations by the Libyans into the Nile Valley; and from the time of Ramesses II onwards fortresses were built to provide protection along the edge of the desert bordering the Mediterranean. During this period, too, the remoteness and inaccessibility of the oases made them places of refuge for those fleeing from persecution and places of banishment for political opponents.

In the 6th c. B.C. the Persians introduced new techniques of well construction into Egypt, and these were subsequently refined, making it possible to draw ground-water from greater depths. The oases enjoyed a heyday in Graeco-Roman times, when new towns and other settlements were established, with magnificent temples the remains of which are still impressive. During the medieval period, however, they declined into insignificance; the wells dried up and the population shrank to a fraction of what it had once been.

In our own time the oases of the Western Desert can look forward to a fresh period of prosperity. Minerals (phosphates, iron, oil) have been discovered in considerable quantities and are in process of being developed. At the same time a great agricultural redevelopment programme is in progress. It is planned by deep boring (down to 4900 ft/1500 m) for fossil water and the use of modern irrigation techniques minimizing evaporation to bring into cultivation, as the "New Valley", the valley between the Kharga, Dakhla, Farafra and Bahriya oases and to resettle it with fellahin from the Nile Valley and Nubians. Although the first results of this program have been encouraging, it seems likely that the limited reserves of ground-water, with little rainfall to replenish them, will set natural limits to its development.

> **Warning**
>
> The desert holds serious hazards for drivers. Before setting out on a journey across the desert make sure that you have sufficient supplies of water and gasoline (petrol); important spare parts should also be taken. It is advisable to drive in convoy. Do not leave the main road or track unless you have an adequate map – or preferably an experienced guide.

ROUTES THROUGH THE DESERT. – ROADS (sometimes subject to sand-drifting): from Cairo (Giza) to Farafra and Medinet el-Fayyum; from Beni Suef to Medinet el-Fayyum; from Asyut (Manqabad) via Kharga to Dakhla; (under construction) from Dakhla to Farafra. – DESERT TRACKS: from Mersa Matruh to the Siwa Oasis; from El-Alamein to the Qattara Depression. – CARAVAN ROUTES: from the western oases to the Darfur Oasis in western Sudan, an ancient route (now known as the Darb el-Arbai, "Road of 40 Days"), which after the introduction of the camel in the 6th–5th c. B.C. became a major trade route and is still in use today; from Cairo (Giza) via El-Maghra, Bir Abu Gharadik and the Qattara Depression to the Siwa Oasis; from Bahriya via the Sitra Oasis or from Farafra via the El-Bahrein Oasis to the Siwa Oasis; from Sollum or Sidi Barani to the Siwa Oasis (closed military area).

*Bahriya, *Dakhla, Farafra, *Fayyum, *Kharga and *Siwa oases and Qattara Depression: see separate entries

White Monastery
See under Sohag

El-Zagazig

Lower Egypt. – Governorate: Sharqiya.
Population: 205,000.
ⓘ **Tourist Information Office,**
Misr Travel Tower,
Cairo – Abbasia;
tel. 82 60 16.

ACCESS. – By road from Cairo (53 miles/85 km SW) via Bilbeis.

The rising provincial capital of El-Zagazig lies on the Muweis Canal (Bahr Muweis), the ancient Tanitic arm of the Nile, from which the Mashtul Canal branches off here. The chief center of the Egyptian cotton and corn trade, with large cotton-ginning factories, it is a town of largely Western aspect.

There is a small *Museum* containing archaeological material from the surrounding area.

On the south-eastern outskirts of the town is the Hill of **Tell Basta**, with the extensive remains of ancient **Bubastis** (Egyptian *Per-Bastet*), capital of the Bubastite nome. The walls of some ancient brick buildings survive to a considerable height. Below the SW side of the hill, usually lying in water, are the remains (granite blocks, columns, architraves and other architectural fragments, some of them with inscriptions and reliefs, and a few statues) of the *Temple of Bastet*, the town's tutelary goddess, which was excavated by the Egypt Exploration Fund in 1887–89; they are likely, however, to be of interest only to specialists. The temple was begun by Cheops and Chephren, underwent much alteration at the hands of Ramesses II and other later kings and was given its final form by the 22nd Dynasty rulers who had their

---

The **festival of Bastet** was described by *Herodotus* (*c.* 490–*c.* 420 B.C.) in the following words:

"When the Egyptians travel to Bubastis they do so in the following manner. Men and women sail together, and in each boat there are many persons of both sexes. Some of the women make a noise with rattles, and some of the men play pipes during the whole journey, while the other men and women sing and clap their hands. When they come to a town on the way, they lay to, and some of the women land and shout and mock the women of the place, while others dance and get up to mischief. They do this at every town lying on the Nile; but when they come to Bubastis they begin the festival with great offerings and sacrifices, during which more wine is consumed than during the whole of the rest of the year. The Egyptians say that some 700,000 men and women make this pilgrimage every year."

The prophet Ezekiel, in his prophecy on the desolation of Egypt, refers to Bubastis under the name of **Pi-beseth** (Ezekiel 30: 17).

---

capital at Bubastis and by Nectanebo II (30th Dynasty). It then consisted of four large halls with a total length of 600 feet in which the festivals of Bastet were celebrated.

Nile Delta: see that entry.

Zawiyet el-Aryan

Middle Egypt. – Governorate: Giza.
ⓘ **Tourist Information Office,**
Misr Travel Tower,
Cairo – Abbasia;
tel. 82 60 16.

ACCESS. – By road from Giza (3 miles/5 km N).

The two unfinished pyramids of Zawiyet el-Aryan, dating from the 3rd and 4th Dynasties, lie on the edge of the Western Desert 3 miles/5 km S of the Pyramids of Giza.

The **Northern Pyramid**, lying farther into the desert, is known as the *Shughl Iskandar* ("Alexander's Excavation") after its excavator, Alexander Baranti. It is believed to have been destined for the burial of a King of the 4th Dynasty but to have been abandoned at a very early stage in its construction. The pyramid was apparently planned on a considerable scale, with a base measurement of 590–660 ft/180–200 m. A rock-cut ramp 28 ft/8·50 m wide and 360 ft/110 m long runs down to a depth of 82 ft/25 m, leading to a square shaft in which the tomb chamber was to have been constructed. The foundations and paving of the chamber, in red granite, were completed, and in it stands the finely worked royal sarcophagus of pink granite, which was to have been set into the pavement.

1 mile/1·5 km to the SE is a low mound of rubble marking the site of a stone **Step Pyramid** which is ascribed to King Khaba (3rd Dynasty). The exterior was apparently completed, with five steps and a base measurement of 272 ft/83 m, but the interior was left unfinished. – In an early tomb in the immediate vicinity was found a seal impression with the name of the Pre-Dynastic or Early Dynastic King Narmer, whose dates have not been precisely established.

****Giza**: see separate entry.

Practical
Information

Visitors to Egypt will find it very different from the countries of the West. The differences are particularly marked in the fields of culture and religion, as well as in social structure, economic life and mental attitudes, and set up considerable barriers to understanding for those unfamiliar with the country. Accordingly the best plan, at any rate on a first visit, is to join one of the many organized tours that are now available and thus be spared all the trouble of making your own arrangements. It is sometimes difficult for individual travelers to secure accommodation and arrange for excursions on their own: nor should the advantage of having competent guides and couriers be underestimated.

When to go, Weather
Time, Electricity
Travel Documents
Inoculations, etc.
Customs Regulations
Currency
Postal Rates
Getting to Egypt
Travel in Egypt
Language
Accommodation
Food and Drink
Health
Manners and Customs, Tipping
Spas
Water sports, Diving
Golf, Entertainment
Calendar
Shopping and Souvenirs
Opening Times
Information
Museums with Egyptian Material

Queen Nefertiti (*c.* 1350 B.C.) ▶

When to Go

The best time to visit Egypt is the winter season, from about the end of October to the end of April. The summer, particularly in Upper Egypt, is very hot and extremely dry.

Weather

The moderating influence of the Mediterranean is felt to any degree only in the coastal regions, where most of the rainfall is in winter. The rest of the country has a desert climate with very little rain and considerable variations in temperature over the day. During the winter months there can be night frosts in the desert, while the day temperature may rise to around 86 °F/30 °C.

For a more detailed account of climatic conditions in Egypt, see pp. 12–13.

Time

Egypt observes **Eastern European Time**, which is 2 hours ahead of Greenwich Mean Time and 7 hours ahead of Eastern Standard Time. From March to September, Egypt operates daylight saving hours, when local time is 3 hours ahead of Greenwich Mean Time.

Electricity

The voltage is normally 220 volts A.C., occasionally 110 volts. Power sockets are of the circular, two-pronged European continental type. Razors and other appliances should be adjusted to the appropriate voltage, and a suitable adaptor should be taken.

Since the electricity supply is occasionally unreliable, it is advisable to take a powerful pocket-torch. This is also essential when visiting underground chambers in tombs, temples, etc., where the lighting may not be good.

Travel Documents

Visitors to Egypt must have a **passport** valid for at least 6 months beyond the date of entry. A *visa* is also required: although it can be issued at the point of entry, visitors will be well advised to get it in advance by applying in plenty of time to the nearest Egyptian embassy or consulate. Children under 16 must either be entered in their parents' passport or have one of their own. A visa is normally valid for three months from the date of issue, with a stay of one month from the date of arrival; but this can be extended to six months when in Egypt.

Visitors must report to the local passport authorities within one week of arrival. If staying in a hotel, the hotel will do this for you.

Car-drivers must have an **international driving license**. If they are bringing a car into Egypt with them they must have a *carnet de passage en douane*, and if they are not the owner of the car must have a written authority from the owner. The international insurance certificate ("green card") is not valid in Egypt, and short-term **insurance** must therefore be taken out when entering the country; third-party insurance is compulsory, but it is strongly recommended to have *comprehensive insurance*. Foreign vehicles must bear the oval *nationality plate*, and are given *Egyptian number plates* for the duration of their stay, which can be up to 90 days without liability for tax.

Inoculation certificates (see below).

It is essential to take out short-term **medical insurance** to provide cover in case of illness. If you are traveling on a package tour this insurance (and other insurance cover, e.g. against loss of baggage) can normally be obtained through the travel firm.

For visitors leaving Egypt by air an *airport tax* is payable.

Inoculations, etc.

Visitors arriving from a cholera or yellow fever infected area must produce a certificate of inoculation. – Precautions against *malaria* (pills) are strongly recommended for visits to the Delta, the Fayyum and other oases, and parts of Upper Egypt between June and October. The prophylactic treatment should begin some 48 hours before arrival and continue for 28 days after departure. Immunisation against cholera, polio and typhoid are recommended.

Customs Regulations

On entering the country visitors must complete a *customs declaration* (Form D) listing articles they have brought in with them, in particular cameras, binoculars, tape-recorders, radios, typewriters, sports equipment, jewelery, etc., and all forms of foreign currency. They will be given a copy of the completed declaration, and must produce this when leaving Egypt. Personal effects, 2 litres of spirits, 1 litre of perfume, 200 cigarettes or 25 cigars or 200 grams of tobacco, and gifts up to a total value of 500 Egyptian pounds can be taken into the country duty-free. Visitors should note that they have access to the duty-free shop upon arrival in Egypt, before going through customs, as well as on departure.

On leaving the country visitors must present their copy of Form D, and must show that they are taking out again all the items listed on it. They may take out a reasonable quantity of articles purchased in Egypt; the export of antiquities, however, is permitted only with special authority.

Currency

The unit of currency is the **Egyptian pound** (£E) of which there are 100 *piastres* (PT). There also used to be *milliomes* (of which there were 1000 to the pound). Although no longer in circulation, prices sometimes show three figures after the decimal point, *eg* 8.400 is eight pounds, four hundred milliemes.

There are *banknotes* for 1, 5, 10 and 20 pounds and 5, 10, 25 and 50 piastres and also *coins* in denominations of 5 and 10 piastres (silver in colour). Some old coins of other values are still in circulation and are becoming collector's items, it is up to you whether you spend them or keep them.

Tourist exchange rates (approximate)

£E1 = £0·25 sterling
              £1 sterling = £E4·00

Import and export of currency. – The import and export of Egyptian currency is restricted to £E20. There are no restrictions on the amount of foreign currency that may be brought in, but all cash, travelers' checks and other forms of currency must be entered on the customs declaration (see ''Customs Regulations'' above). Foreign currency may be taken out up to the amount entered on the customs declaration less any amounts changed into Egyptian money.

Changing money. – The formerly fixed exchange rate of Egyptian currency is now officially set at regular intervals (sometimes daily). The Egyptian authorities are seeking to combat the flourishing black market in foreign currency. It is generally more favorable to change money in the country itself, where the currency is weak.

Foreign currency can be changed only at banks and authorized exchange offices, and each transaction must be noted on the Customs declaration form: this is important when it comes to changing money back on departure. It is advisable to ask for some small notes and coins. – Eurocheques are accepted only by a few of the larger banks. The most convenient places to change money are the offices of American Express or Thomas Cook. The compulsory exchange of a certain sum of ''hard'' currency by individual tourists was dropped in the autumn of 1987.

In order to re-exchange any unused Egyptian currency at the time of your departure you will need to produce receipts of all transactions during your stay.

Postal Rates

Letters (up to 10 g) to Europe 30 PT, by air 40 PT.

Postcards to Europe 25 PT, by air 30 PT.

Air mail takes 3 days to Europe and 10 days to the U.S.A.

Getting to Egypt

The most convenient way of getting to Egypt is *by air* (direct flights from London to Cairo and from New York via Paris). – There are passenger and car *ferry services* from Italy: Venice (either direct or with intermediate ports of call) and Ancona, summer only, (via Piraeus or Heraklion) to Alexandria. – It is occasionally possible to get a passage on a *cargo ship* from a North Sea port or from Venice; but this method of transport is only for those who have plenty of time at their disposal.

Travel in Egypt

By Road

International road routes run along the Nile River Valley and along the northern and Red Sea coasts. The only part of the country with a relatively dense network of roads is the Delta area, between the Mediterranean coast and Cairo, where most of the population is concentrated. The condition of the roads, apart from the main roads into the cities, is moderate to poor. The desert tracks to the oases are of sand consolidated by the passage of traffic, and are frequently uneven and corrugated.

Driving on desert tracks calls for a sturdy and well-equipped vehicle. A full set of tools should be taken, together with a selection of essential spare parts and an extra spare wheel. An ample supply of drinking-water – at least 8 or 9 pints/5 litres per person per day – is a "must". Always travel in a convoy of at least two vehicles. Take a local guide if you possibly can, and inform the police in advance of your proposed route (this is obligatory in some cases). If you have a breakdown do not leave your vehicle, since it is easier for a search-party to find a vehicle than an individual; and never venture off the marked track. Stretches of corrugated track should be taken either at a very low speed (under 20 m.p.h/30 km.p.h) or sufficiently fast to carry the vehicle over the bumps without falling into the hollows. This is, of course, very hard on the vehicle, and may loosen nuts or even break welded joints. The resistance offered by the rough road surface and the need to drive in low gear lead to a considerable increase in gasoline (petrol) consumption: it is absolutely essential, therefore, to make sure that you have sufficient supplies of fuel. Vehicles which become bogged down in sand may have to be winched out. – The fine sand will find its way into the vehicle through the smallest cracks; cameras and other apparatus should, therefore, be protected against it.

Vehicles travel on the right, with passing (overtaking) on the left. At junctions between roads of equal status traffic coming from the right has priority. In practice, however, traffic regulations are very frequently disregarded, so that visiting drivers should exercise extreme care

and watchfulness. In Cairo and Alexandria the traffic is very heavy and, by European or North American standards, chaotic; and in the country the local people pay very little attention to motorized traffic. Moreover, since direction signs are normally written only in Arabic, foreign drivers may have difficulty in finding their way.

Night driving should be avoided except in major cities; and indeed some roads (such as the road from Suez to Hurghada on the Red Sea) are closed at night. For a trip of any length it is beter to join an organized tour.

A foreigner involved in an accident, whether he is the guilty party or not, should go immediately to the nearest police post and report the accident, since the reaction of the local people who will rapidly appear on the scene is unpredictable.

Travel near the Libyan border is restricted by the government for military reasons. In other security areas a permit is required: applications to the Ministry of Interior, the corner of Sharia Sheikh Rihan and Sharia Nubar (Cairo).

Speed limits: in built-up areas **31 m.p.h./50 km.p.h.**, with trailer **18½ m.p.h./30 km.p.h.**; outside built-up areas **50 m.p.h./80 km.p.h.**, with trailer **31 m.p.h./50 km.p.h.**

In the event of an accident or breakdown, recovery or roadside aid is carried out by the Traffic Police, or on the main trunk roads in the Delta, by the *Automobile et Touring Club d'Egypte* (see "Information" section for addresses).

Egyptian standard gasoline (petrol or *benzene*) has poor anti-knock qualities and is unsuitable for European and American engines. It is advisable to fit a gasoline (petrol) filter. Higher grade gasoline and diesel are available.

Gasoline (petrol) stations are plentiful in Cairo and Alexandria, but outside of main towns they are scarce, make sure you have information about the location of fill-up stations before starting a long journey.

Car rental. – The big international car rental firms have offices in Cairo and Alexandria, where cars can be rented with or without driver.

By Air

The principal international airport in Egypt is Cairo (Heliopolis), to which there are direct flights from London. Cairo Airport is also of importance for its services to the Arab countries and the Near East generally, and as a staging-point for pilgrims on their way to Mecca and Medina.

In addition to its international services the national airline, **Egypt Air**, also flies domestic services to Alexandria, Abu Simbel, Aswan, Hurghada, Luxor and Kharga in the New Valley. For these services advance booking is advisable.

Air Sinai flies from Cairo to the principal places in Sinai and to Eilat in Israel. *Nifertiti Airlines* fly services between Cairo and Tel Aviv.

By Rail

There are a number of railway lines in the Delta serving the main towns in this area, between Alexandria, Port Said, Suez and Cairo. The main east–west route runs from the Delta along the northern coast to

**Tourist
High Spots
of Egypt**

* Sights of major interest

** Sights of outstanding interest

Mediterranean

**Alexandria
*El-Alamein
*Abu Mena
*Wadi Natrun
*Tanis
**Suez Canal
*Siwa
**Giza
*Abusir
**Saqqara
*Dahshur
*Lisht
*Meidum
**Fayyum
*El-Lahun
**Cairo
*Memphis

Sinai
Peninsula

St Antony's
* Monastery
St Paul's
* Monastery
**St Catherine's
Monastery
Gulf of Suez

*Bahriya
*Beni Hasan
*Mallawi
*Tell el-Amarna
* Asyut
Eastern
*Hurghada
Western
*Sohag
**Abydos
**Dendera
Red
Sea
**Dakhla
** Thebes
(West)
**Karnak
**Luxor
*Kharga
Desert
Nile
*Esna
*El-Kab
**Edfu
Desert
*Kom Ombo
**Aswan
* Kalabsha
**Philae
* Wadi el-Sebwa
*Amada
Lake
Nasser
**Abu Simbel

Under
Sudanese
administration

Sallom, on the Libyan border. The most important line in the country is the one between Cairo and Alexandria, on which there are frequent services (at intervals of between 1 and 2 hours). There is also a line along the Nile from Cairo via Luxor to Aswan, mainly used by tourists, with air-conditioned sleeping-cars and restaurant cars. Inclusive tickets with reduced hotel charges are available for Aswan and Luxor. In view of the great demand for seats advance booking is essential. First-class travel is recommended on all services for a comfortable journey.

By Bus

Most of the regular bus services are in the Nile Delta and to the Suez Canal. A fairly comprehensive network of long distance buses covers the rest of Egypt, some are air-conditioned and well-organised but the standards of comfort and punctuality of others leave much to be desired. The excursion coaches run by the Government travel agency, *Misr Travel*, are comfortable and reliable; for the most part they cater for organized groups. There are other buses, and fixed-route shared taxi and minibus services run by private operators. Vehicles normally wait at city terminals until full, but there are frequent departures.

By Boat

There are comfortable *passenger ships* on the Nile, running very popular cruises lasting from four to fifteen days. They normally ply between Aswan and Luxor, but some also sail from Cairo. The organized cruises include excursions to sights near the river; beds and meals are provided on board. – There are also *sailing-boats* (feluccas) plying between Luxor and Aswan; simply equipped, with accommodation for some 15 passengers (no beds, but sleeping bags on deck), they serve meals of standard Egyptian type. They are not recommended for merely traveling between towns.

There are occasionally also organized cruises through the Suez Canal and in the Red Sea.

From the Aswan High Dam there are sometimes *hydrofoil* services to Abu Simbel. There is also a regular steamer service (2nd and 3rd class only) on Lake Nasser to Wadi Halfa (just over the border in Sudan).

Language

The official language of Egypt is **Arabic**, which belongs to the Semitic language family. Northern Arabic spread with Islam over large territories in North Africa and the Near East, forming many different dialects, among which *Egyptian Arabic* occupies a special place.

The foreign languages most commonly spoken by educated Egyptians are French and English; in recent years increasing attention has also been paid in Egyptian schools to German.

Arabic is fundamentally different from the Indo-European languages, not only in grammatical structure but also in the *script* it uses. Running from right to left, the Arabic script is essentially concerned with the consonantal structure of words, which determines their semantic content. Since the numerous dialects of Arabic differ mainly in their use of vowels, a consonantal script of this kind is much more widely applicable than a fully developed phonetic alphabet would be.

The 28 characters of the Arabic alphabet vary considerably according to whether they occur at the beginning, middle or end of a word (initial, medial and final positions) or stand by themselves (independent position). No generally agreed system of transcription into the Latin alphabet has yet been devised; and since Arabic has some sounds which have no equivalent in that alphabet a word will appear in different forms in an English, a French or a German transcription. The pronunciation followed in this book is essentially that of the Lower Egyptian dialect as spoken in Cairo. The table on p. 363 gives the formal transcription of the characters, with numerous diacritic (distinguishing) marks; in the Arabic vocabulary given in the following pages, however, a simpler form of transcription is used, without diacritic marks, designed to convey the approximate pronunciation to an English-speaking reader. The glottal stop is represented by an inverted comma (').

Greetings, etc.

English	Arabic
Greeting:	
Peace be upon you!	es-salamu 'alekum!
Response:	
And peace and God's mercy and blessing be upon you!	we-'alekum es-salam warahmet allah wabarakatuh!

This greeting is only used to Muslims. For Christians the greeting is:

May your day be a happy one!	naharak sa'id!
Response:	
May your day be a happy and blessed one!	naharak sa'id we-mubarak! *or* naharak laban! (*literally, "may your day be as white as milk!"*)
Greeting:	
Good morning!	sabahkum bil-kher! *or* sabah el-kher!
Response:	
May God grant you a good morning!	allah yisabbe'hkum bil-kher!
Greeting:	
Good evening!	mesakum bil-kher! *or* mesikum bil-kher!
Response:	
May God grant you a good evening!	allah yimesikum bil-kher! *or* mesakum allah bil-kher!
On going to bed:	
May your night be happy!	leltak sa'ida!
Response:	
May your night be happy and blessed!	leltak sa'ida we-mubaraka!

English	Arabic
On visiting or meeting someone the first question is:	
How is your health?	izayyak? *or* kef halak (kef kefak)? *or* esh halak?

Response (first merely expressing thanks):

God bless you?	allah yibarik fik!
or God preserve you!	allah yih fazak!
and then:	
Well, thank God!	el-hamdu lillah!

After a member of a group has taken a drink the others' say, raising their hands to their heads:

Enjoy your drink, sir!	hani'an ya sidi!
Response:	
May God grant it pleases you!	allah yehannik!
On handing something to someone:	
Take it!	khud!
On taking something:	
May God increase your good deeds!	kattar allah kherak! *or* kattar kherak!
Response:	
And yours also!	ukherak!
On leaving:	
In God's care!	'alallah!
or In God's protection!	fi amani'llah!
or Let's go!	yalla bina!
To someone setting out on a journey:	
In safety!	ma'as-salama!
Response:	
May God preserve you in safety!	allah yisallimak!
Meeting someone on a journey:	
Welcome!	ahlan wa sahlan! *or* marhaba!
Response:	
Twice welcome!	marhabten!

English	Arabic
To a visitor:	
I beg you (to come in, to take something, to eat something)!	tafaddal (tefaddal, itfaddal)! *fem.* tafaddali (itfaddali)! *plural* tafaddalu (tefaddalu, itfaddalu)!
Will you not join us (in a meal)?	bismillah! (*literally, "in the name of God"*)
Response:	
May you enjoy it!	bil-hana!
Take care! Beware!	u'a!, *fem.* u;i!
I am under your protection: save me!	ana fi'ardak!
My house is your house!	beti betak!
Be so good; do me a favour	i'mil ma'ruf!
Exclamation of surprise:	
What God wills (happens)!	mashallah!
As God wills!	inshallah!
By God!	wallah! *or* wallahi!
By your head!	wahyat rasak!
By the life of the Prophet!	wahyat en-nabi!
By the life of your father!	wahyat abuk!
O heavens!	ya salam!

Months and days of the week

January	yanayir
February	fibrayir
March	maris
April	abril
May	maya
June	yunya
July	yulya
August	aghustus
September	sibtambir
October	uktobar
November	nufimbir
December	disimbir
Sunday	il-hadd
Monday	il-itnen
Tuesday	it-talat
Wednesday	il-arba'
Thursday	il-khamis
Friday	ig-guma'a
Saturday	is-sabt
year	sana
month	shahr
week	usbu', gum'a
day	yom

Useful Words and Phrases

above	fu'u
address	'unwan
after	ba'd
afterwards	ba'den
air	hawa
air mail	al-bardi al-gawi
airport	matar
almond	loz
always	daiman, tamalli
America	amerika
American	amrikani
angry	za'lan
apricot	mishmish
An Arab	ragil 'arabi
Arabia	bilad el-'arab

Arabic Alphabet

Name	Independent	Final	Medial	Initial	Transcription	Pronunciation
alif	ا	ـا	—	—	ʾ ā	glottal stop
ba	ب	ـب	ـبـ	بـ	b	b
ta	ت	ـت	ـتـ	تـ	t	t
tha	ث	ـث	ـثـ	ثـ	ṯ	th (as in 'thing')
gim	ج	ـج	ـجـ	جـ	ǧ	g (hard)
ha	ح	ـح	ـحـ	حـ	ḥ	h (guttural)
kha	خ	ـخ	ـخـ	خـ	ḫ	ch (as in 'loch')
dal	د	ـد	—	—	d	d
dhal	ذ	ـذ	—	—	ḏ	th (as in 'the')
ra	ر	ـر	—	—	r	r (rolled)
za	ز	ـز	—	—	z	z
sin	س	ـس	ـسـ	سـ	s	s
shin	ش	ـش	ـشـ	شـ	š	sh
sad	ص	ـص	ـصـ	صـ	ṣ	s (emphatic)
dad	ض	ـض	ـضـ	ضـ	ḍ	d (emphatic)
ta	ط	ـط	ـطـ	طـ	ṭ	t (emphatic)
za	ظ	ـظ	ـظـ	ظـ	ẓ	z (emphatic)
ʾain	ع	ـع	ـعـ	عـ	ʿ	(a harsh guttural sound)
ghain	غ	ـغ	ـغـ	غـ	ġ	gh (guttural)
fa	ف	ـف	ـفـ	فـ	f	f
kaf	ق	ـق	ـقـ	قـ	q	k, q (velar)
kaf	ك	ـك	ـكـ	كـ	k	k (palatal)
lam	ل	ـل	ـلـ	لـ	l	l
mim	م	ـم	ـمـ	مـ	m	m
nun	ن	ـن	ـنـ	نـ	n	n
ha	ة	ـه	ـهـ	هـ	h	h
waw	و	ـو	—	—	w (ū)	w
ya	ي	ـي	ـيـ	يـ	y (ī, ā)	y

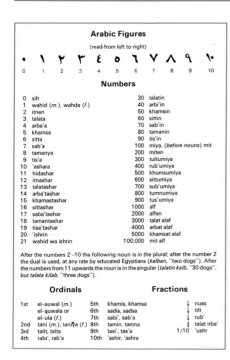

Arabic Figures

(read from left to right)

•	١	٢	٣	٤	٥	٦	٧	٨	٩	١٠
0	1	2	3	4	5	6	7	8	9	10

Numbers

0	sifr	30	talatin
1	wahid (m.), wahda (f.)	40	arbi'in
2	itnen	50	khamsin
3	talata	60	sittin
4	arba'a	70	sab'in
5	khamsa	80	tamanin
6	sitta	90	tis'in
7	sab'a	100	miya, (before nouns) mit
8	tamanya	200	miten
9	tis'a	300	tultumiya
10	'ashara	400	rub'umiya
11	hidashar	500	khumsumiya
12	itnashar	600	sittumiya
13	talatashar	700	sub'umiya
14	arba'tashar	800	tumnumiya
15	khamastashar	900	tus'umiya
16	sittashar	1000	alf
17	saba'tashar	2000	alfen
18	tamantashar	3000	talat alaf
19	tisa'tashar	4000	arbat alaf
20	'ishrin	5000	khamsat alaf
21	wahid wa ishrin	100,000	mit alf

After the numbers 2–10 the following noun is in the plural; after the number 2 the dual is used, at any rate by educated Egyptians (*kalben*, "two dogs"). After the numbers from 11 upwards the noun is in the singular (*talatin kalb*, "30 dogs", but *talata kilab*, "three dogs").

Ordinals

1st	el-auwal (m.)	5th	khamis, khamsa
	el-quwala or	6th	sadis, sadsa
	el-ula (f.)	7th	sabi', sab'a
2nd	tani (m.), taniya (f.)	8th	tamin, tamna
3rd	talit, talta	9th	tasi', tas'a
4th	rabi', rab'a	10th	'ashir, 'ashra

Fractions

½	nuss
⅓	tilt
¼	rub'
¾	talat irba'
1/10	'ushr

English	Arabic
arm	dira'
arrival	wusul
arrive	yusil
ask	is'al
at	'and
automobile	'arabiya, otomibil
autumn (fall)	kharif
back	dahr, wara
bad	battal
baggage	'afsh
baker	khabbaz
banana	moz
barley	shi'ir
basket	guffa
bath-house	hammam
bazaar	suk
beans	fasulya
beautiful	kwaiyis, gamil
bed	serir
bedouin	badawi
bee	nahla
beer	bira
before	kabl
behind	wara
below	taht
bench	mastaba
beside	gamb, 'and
better	ahsan, kher
between	ben
big	kebir
bill	hisab
binoculars	naddara
bird	ter
bite	'add
bitter	murr
black	iswid
blacksmith	haddad
blind	a'ma
blood	damm
blue	azrak
boat	filuka
book	kitab
bookseller	kutbi

English	Arabic
boot	gazma
bottle	kizaza
box	sanduk
boy	walad
brandy	'araki
bread	'esh
break	kasar
breakfast	futur
bridge	kubri, kantara
bring	gab; (imperative) gib!
Britain	ingiltira
British	inglizi
broad	'arid
brother	akh
brown	asmar
brush	fursha
bury	dafan
bus	otobis
butcher	gazzar
butter	zibda
button	zirr
calf	'igl
call	nadah
camel	gamal; hagin (riding camel)
camel-boy	gammal
car	'arabiya, otomibil
carpet	siggada, busat
carriage	'arabiya
castle	kasr
cattle	bakar
cause	sabab
causeway	gisr
cave	maghara
cemetery	karafa, gabbana, madfan, makbara
chair	kursi
change (money)	saraf
cheap	rakhis
cheese	gibna
chemist's	saidaliya, agzakhana
chicken	farkha
Christian	nusrani
church	kinisa
cigar	sigara afrangi
cigarette	sigara
class, first	berimo
class, second	sekondo
clean (adj.)	nadif
clean (verb)	naddaf
clever	shatir
close (verb)	kafal
clothes	hudum, malabis
coat	sitra
coffee	kahwa
cold (noun)	bard
cold (adj.)	barid
color	lon
consul	kunsul
consulate	kunsulato
convent (of dervishes)	tekkiya
cook (noun)	tabbakh
corn	kamh, ghalla
cost: what does this cost?	di bikam?
cotton	kutn
country	watan
cow	bakara
crocodile	timsah
cup	fingan
customs	gumruk
cut	kata'
dark	'itim
dark-colored	ghamik

English	Arabic	English	Arabic
dates	balah	fresh	taza
daughter	bint	friend	habib, sahib, sadik
day	yom, nahar	fruit	fakha, fawakih
dead	mayyit	garden	ginena
deaf	atrash	garlic	tum
dear	ghali	get off (riding animal)	nizil inzil
too dear	di ghali ketir	we want to get off here	ninzil hina
deep	ghamik	gift	bakshish (tip)
desert	gebel, khala, sahra	girl	bint
diarrhoea	ishal	give	ada
died	mat	glass	kubbaya
difficult	sa'b	go	rah ruh
dinner	'asha	gold	dahab
dirt	wasakha	goldsmith	gohargi
dirty	wisikh	good	tayyib kuwayyis
district	balad	goods	buda'a
do	'amal	goose	wizza
doctor	doktor	grapes	'inab
dog	kalb	gratuity	bakshish
donkey	homar	grave	turba
door	bab	green	akhdar
drink (verb)	shirib, ishrab	guide	turguman
dry	nashif	hair	sha'r
duck	batta	hairdresser	hallak
each	kulli wahid	half	nuss
ear	widn	hammer	shakush
earth	ard	hand	id, yadd
east	shark	harbor	mina
eat	akal kul	hat	burneta
I should like to eat	biddi akul	head	ras
egg	beda	healthy	salim
Egypt	masr	hear	simi'
embankment	gisr	heart	alb
embassy	sifara	heavy	tekil
empty	fadi	help	sa'id, yisa'id
England	bilad el-ingliz	here	hina
English	inglizi	high	'ali
enough	kifaya, bass, bizyada	hill	gebel, hadaba, tell
entrance	dukhul	hire	ugra (fare)
envelope	zarf	hold	misik
Europe	orobba, bilad el-afrang	home	bet, watan
European	afrangi	honest	amin
evening	'ashiya	honey	'asal
everything	el-kull	horse	hosan
eye	'en	hospital	mustashfa
face	wishsh	hot	sukhn (*food, drink*), harr
fall (autumn)	kharif		(*weather*)
far	ba'id	hotel	funduk, lokanda
father	ab(u)	hour	sa'a
fear	khaf khof	house	bet
feather	risha	how?	izayy
fee	ugra	how much?	kam
festival	'id	hungry	ga'an
field	ghet	hurry (verb)	ista'gil
fig	tin	hut	isha
find	laka	ice	telg
finger	sub'a	ill	'ayyan, marid
fire	nar	illness	marad
fish	samaka	immediately	halan
flag	bandera	in(side)	guwa
flea	barghut	interpreter	turguman
flower	zahra	intoxicated	sakran
fly (noun)	dubbana	iron	hadid
fog	shabura	island	gezira
food	akl	Jew	yahudi
foot	rigl	judge	kadi
for	'alashan	jug	ibrik
forbidden	mamnu'	keeper	khafir
foreign	gharib	key	muftah
forget	nisi	knife	sikkina
fork	shoka	knock	khabbat
fortress	kal'a	know	'irif
fountain	sebil	lady	sitt
fowl	farkha	lake	birka

English	Arabic	English	Arabic
lame	a'rag	narrow	dayyik
lamp	lamba	near	kurayyib
land	barr	necessary	lazim
lane	hara	neighbor	gar
language	lisan, lugha	neighborhood	bilad
large	kebir, 'azim	never	abadan
late	wakhri	new	gedid
laundry	ghasil	news	khabar
laugh	dihik	newspaper	garida
lavatory	twalett, kabine	night	leil
lay (down)	hatt	nilometer	mikyas
lazy	kaslan	no	la
lead (noun)	rusas	noon	duhr
leave	tarak, yitruk	north	bahari
left	shimal	nose	manakhir
leg	rigl	not	mush
lemon	lamuna	now	dilwakt
letter	gawab	Nubia	nuba, bilad el-barabra
lie (verb)	kidib	number	nimra
light (noun)	nur	oasis	waha
light (verb)	walla'	obelisk	misalla
little (adj.)	sughayyar khafif	often	ketir
little (adv.)	shuwayya	oil	zet
lock (noun)	kalun	old	kadim
locomotive	wabur, atr	olives	zetun
London	londra	onion	basala
long	tawil	only	bass
look for	dauwar	open (verb)	fatah
lose	dayya'	orange	burtukan
low	wati	out(side)	barra
luggage	'afsh	ox	tor
lunch	ghada	pack (verb)	hazam
mad	magnun	pain	waga'
make	'amal	palm	nakhla
man	ragil; (human being)	pants (trousers)	bantalun
	insan	paper	warak
market	suk	parents	waliden
marriage	farah	passport	basabort
mat	hasira	pay (noun)	ugra
match	kabrita	pay (verb)	dafa'
meal	akl	peach	khokha
meat	lahm	pen	risha
medicine	dawa	pepper	filfil
melon	shammam	perhaps	balki, yimkin
merchant	tagir	physician	doktor
midday	duhr	piastre	kirsh
middle	wust	pig	khanzir
midnight	nuss el-leil	pigeon	hamama
milk	laban	pilgrim	hagg
minaret	ma'dna	pistachio	fustuk
mineral water	moyya ma'daniya	plain (noun)	suhul
minute	dakika	plate	sahn
mirror	miraya	please	min fadlak
mist	shabura	plum	barkuka
mistake	ghalat	pocket	qeb
Mohammedan	Muslim	poison	simm
monastery	der	policeman	polis askari
money	fulus	pomegranate	rumman
money-changer	sarraf	pond	birka
month	shahr	poor	fakir, maskin
moon	kamar	port	mina
more	aktar	porter	sheyal
morning	subh, sabah (early); daha	postcard	tazkaret busta
	(forenoon)	post office	busta
mosque	gami'	pot	kidra
mosquito	namusa	poultry	firakh
mother	umm	pound (£)	gineh
mount (riding animal)	rikib	prayer	sala
mountain	gebel	pretty (good)	kwayyis
mouth	fumm	previously	kabl
much	ketir	price	taman
music	musika	prophet	nabi
name	ism	pyramid	haram
napkin	futa	question	su'al

English	Arabic	English	Arabic
quickly	yalla, kawam	sphinx	abul-hol
railway (railroad)	es-sikka el-hadid	spoon	ma'laka
rain	matar	spring (of water)	bir, sebil, 'ain
razor (blade)	mus	spring (season)	rabi'
ready	hadir	square (noun)	midan
receipt	wasl	stamp, postage	busta
red	ahmar	stand up	kam
register	tasgil	star	nigma
reliable	amin	station	mahatta
religion	din	stay	fidil
remain	fidil	steamer	babur el-bahr, markib
rent	ugra, agar	still	lissa
rest (verb)	istirayah	stone	hagar
rice	ruzz	stop!	ukaf, 'andak!
rich	ghani	straight on	dughri
(to) right	yamin	street	tarik, darb, sikka
rise	kam	strike	darab
river	nahr	strong	shadid
road	tarik, darb, sikka	stupid	balid
roast (adj.)	mashwi	sugar	sukkar
roast (noun)	rosto	suitcase	sanduk
roast (verb)	shawa	summer	sef
roof	sath	sun	shams
room	oda	sunrise	tulu' esh-shams
rope	habl	sunset	maghrib
ruin	kharaba, khirba	sunshade	shemsiya
run	gara	sweet	helu
saddle	sarg	Syria	esh-sham
salt	malh	table	sufra, tarabeza
sand	raml	tailor	khayyat
satisfied (had enough food)	shab'an	take	khad
		taxi	tax, taxi
say	kal	tea	shay
school	kuttab, maktab (*elementary*); madrasa (*secondary*)	teacher	mu'allim
		tent	khema
		thank you	kattar kherak
scissors	makass	theater	tiatro
scorpion	'akraba	there	henak
sea	bahr	thing	haga
see	shaf	thirsty	'atshan
servant	khaddam	ticket	tazkara
shave	halak	tie (up)	rabat
sheep	kharuf	time	wakt
shine	nawwar	tip	bakshish
ship	markib	tired	ta'ban
shirt	kamis	tobacco	dukhkhan
shoe	gezma	today	en-nahar-da
shop	dukkan	toilet	twalett, kabine
short	kusayyar	tomb	turba
show (verb)	warra	tomorrow	bukra
shut	kafal	tongue	lisan
sickness	marad	too little	shuwayya
silent, be	sikit	too much	ketir
silk	harir	tooth	sinn
silver	fadda	toothpaste	ma'gun es-sinan
sing	ghanna	towel	futa
sir	afandi; (*to a European*) khawaga	town	madina
		travel	safir
sister	ukht	tree	shagara
sit	ka'ad	trousers (pants)	bantalun
sky	sama	true	sahih
sleep	nam	ugly	wihish
slippers	fantufli, shibshib	understand	fihim
slowly	shwayya shwayya, 'ala mahlak	unnecessary	mush lazim
		valley	wadi
small	sughayyar	vegetables	khudar
small change	fakka	very	ketir, kawi, khalis
soap	sabun	village	beled
son	ibn, walad	vinegar	khall
sort	gins	visit (noun)	ziyara
soup	shurba	wages	ugra, kira
sour	hamid	wait	istanna
south	kibli	waiter	garson
speak up	itkallim	waken	sahha

English	Arabic	English	Arabic
war	harb	mosque	gami
wash	ghasal	hill, mountain	gebel
watch (noun) (hour)	sa'a	island, peninsula	gezira
water	moyya	bath-house	hammam
water-melon	battikh	pyramid	haram
weak	da'if	village	kafr
weather	hawa	ravine, watercourse	khor
week	gum'a	artificial mound	kom
well (adj.)	salim, mabsut	station	mahatta
well (noun)	bir, sebil	mosque	masgid
west	gharb	town	medina
wet	mablul	religious school	medresa
when?	imta	square	midan
where?	fen	river	nahr
where from?	min en	fortress	qala
white	abyad	bridge	qantara
why?	ashshane eh; leh	castle, fortress	qasr
wide	'arid	cape	ras
wind	hawa, rih; khamsin, samum (*desert wind*)	street	sharia
		road, track	sikka
window	shibbak	artificial mound, hill	tell
wine	nabid, nebit	river, valley (usually dry)	wadi
winter	shita	small mosque, chapel	zawiya
wish (verb)	talab		
with	wiya		
without	min gher		
woman	mar'a, hurma		
wood	khashab		
work	shughl		
write	katab		
year	sana		
yellow	asfar		
yes	aiwa, na'am		
yesterday	embarih		
yet	lissa		
young	sughayyar		

Glossary of Topographical Terms

spring	ain
gate, door; defile	bab
lake; river (Nile)	bahr
house	beit
well, cistern	bir
lake, pool	birka
port	bur
road, track, lane	darb
monastery	deir

Accommodation

Hotels

In spite of the considerable efforts that have been made to develop the hotel industry the capacity of Egyptian **hotels** is still insufficient to cope with the growing demands of tourism. In recent years a number of the international chains, among them Sheraton, Hilton and Marriott, have built hotels with pools, shops, entertainment and international menus. Hotels with a high standard of amenity are for practical purposes to be found only in Port Said, Alexandria, Cairo, Luxor and Aswan; and only hotels in the two highest categories (see below) are likely to match

Hotels on the Corniche road, Luxor

Hotel Tariffs

Category		Rate per night in £E	
official	in this guide	1 person	2 persons
*****	L	100–200	120–240
****	I	36–100	50–120
***	II	26–80	40–100
**	III	24–60	36–90
*	IV	10–24	12–36

The higher rates generally apply to hotels in Cairo and other Delta cities, and for rooms facing the Nile (you can expect to pay less in Upper Egypt and for rooms without a Nile view).
Tax and a service charge (12%) are added to the bill.
In 4 and 5 star hotels payment must be made in hard currency.

up to European or North American standards of comfort. Individual travelers will find it practically impossible to get a room unless an advance booking has been made.

Youth Hostels

There is now about a dozen **youth hostels** in Egypt. To obtain admission visitors must produce a membership card issued by their national youth hostels association. The maximum stay in the same hostel is three days, but this may be extended if the accommodation is not required for new arrivals. There is no age limit. Current overnight rates are 80 piastres in Cairo, Alexandria and Luxor, and 60 piastres in other cities.

Information: **Egyptian Youth Hostel Association,**
Sharia Dr Abdel Hamid Sayyid 7,
Maaruf,
Cairo;
tel. 75 80 99.

Bungalow, Jolie ville Hotel, Giza

Camping

This is becoming increasingly popular with now a number of sites, particularly in the Sinai along the Mediterranean and Red Sea coasts. A detailed list of sites can be obtained from tourist offices. "Camping sauvage" (i.e. not on camp sites) should be avoided.

Food and Drink

The restaurants of the large hotels usually offer an international menu. The everyday cuisine of Egypt is very similar to that of other Arab countries: there are practically no characteristically Egyptian dishes.

The Arab dishes which visitors will encounter in Egypt are usually very fatty, and sometimes rather too highly seasoned for Western tastes, while sweet dishes tend to be too sweet. Egyptian cuisine as a whole lacks the refinement of many other Mediterranean cuisines, and visitors will only rarely find a dish which particularly appeals to their taste.

Much use is made of mutton, beef and poultry (but not pork, which is prohibited by the Koran), usually grilled, more rarely stewed in a herb stock. The meat is accompanied by rice, black beans, dark brown bread and a variety of salads, vegetables and sauces, highly seasoned with herbs and spices.

The sweets and pastries, in line with Arab tastes, make abundant use of sugar, honey or syrup, oil, almonds and other nuts to produce a variety of tempting and nutritious confections.

MEAT DISHES

molokhiya	a spicy soup containing meat, rice and garlic
kebab	lamb on the spit
kofta	grilled meat balls
fata	boiled mutton and rice mixed with breadcrumbs
ta'amia	rissoles of minced meat and broad beans
kalawi	kidneys grilled with herbs
hamam mashwi	grilled pigeon
hamam fil tagen	roast pigeon on rice, with cream
gambari	prawns
dolma, wara inab	vine leaves stuffed with minced meat and rice
mosaka	aubergines stuffed with minced meat

VEGETABLES, ETC.

ful medames	black beans in oil, with lemon and salt
kusa	a gherkin-like vegetable, courgette
humus	a thick sauce made with chick peas, lemon, sesame oil
tahina	a sauce made from ground sesame, groundnuts and spices
dima	spiced tomato sauce
salata beladi	green salad
'esh beladi	dark brown or white bread

SWEETS

mahalabiya	rice or cornflour pudding with rose water and nuts
konafa	a cake with a cream or nut filling
ataif	pancakes dipped in syrup
baklawa	a pastry with nuts, honey, syrup and oil

Drinks

The most popular drinks throughout Egypt are tea (black) and coffee, prepared in the Turkish way.

The national beer "Stella", similar to the Belgian variety, is rather light and cold bottled: imported beers are only available in large hotels and better class restaurants.

For wine see next page.

Fruit juices, carbonated drinks and drinking water should be used from sealed bottles. Never drink tap water or have ice cubes.

kahwa	Turkish-style coffee
shay	tea
karkade	iced mellow-blossom tea
bira	beer
nebit	wine (see next page)
erkesus	a brown liquorice drink

arak	date brandy
asir fakh	fruit juice
lamun	lemon
tienshoke	prickly pear
gawafa	guava
roman	pomegranate
'asab	sugar-cane
ma'daniya	mineral, water

Wine (*nebit, nabid*)

In ancient Egypt the vine was cultivated from the earliest times. There were vineyards all the way along the Nile Oasis from Alexandria to Aswan, yielding grapes which were made into wine. Many reliefs and paintings dating from different periods (e.g. the wall-paintings in the Theban necropolis) depict the grape harvest and the making of wine, as well as the various vessels in which wine was stored or drunk. There are also hieroglyphic inscriptions recording the output of wine-producers and the turnover of wine merchants.

The old-established tradition of wine-making was continued by the Greeks and Romans, and Roman poets celebrated the quality of Egyptian wines imported· to Rome. When Islam arrived in Egypt from the Arabian Peninsula, however, wine-making died out, since Mohammed had prohibited the faithful from drinking any alcoholic liquor.

Wine-production did not revive in Egypt until the end of the 19th century, when a Greek named Nestor Gianaclis acquired some land to the SE of Alexandria and planted vines which he brought in from Greece, Italy and France. The area was one in which there had been vineyards in the time of Ramesses II and the Romans had later produced their *vinum mariticum.* After the First World War Gianaclis's son-in-law Nicholas Pierrakos extended the vineyards and improved the quality of the new Egyptian wines to such an extent that they became popular among the upper classes of the population and at the Court.

After Egypt became a republic the Gianclis estate was nationalized under Nasser's land reform program and combined with other wine-making establishments in the Alexandria area to form a single large State enterprise.

The wine-growing estate of Abu Hummus, on the north-western fringe of the

Delta, now covers the considerable area of 17,300 acres and produces some 3,963,012 US gallons/150,000 hectolitres of wine annually. The workers on the estate are mainly bedouin who have taken to a settled life, with the addition of some seasonal workers brought in during the grape harvest (June to September).

Since Islam still prohibits the consumption of alcohol, Egypt cannot export its wine to the neighboring Arab States, and efforts are now being made to find markets in Western countries. Much of the output (mainly white wine) is distilled in Alexandria to produce brandy for export; some is sold within Egypt to the considerable minority of Coptic Christians and to tourists (who will find it available in restaurants and shops); and the rest of the grape crop comes on to the market in the form of table grapes or raisins.

Egyptian Wines

WHITE WINE	Characteristics
Cru des Ptolémées	light-colored, very slightly sweet
Reine Éléopâtre	golden yellow, sweet; a dessert wine
Muscat d'Egypte	heavy, sweet; a dessert wine
Nefertiti	light, sweet, with an aroma of muscatel
Castel Nestor	light-colored, sweet, with a delicate bouquet
Village Gianaclis	greenish, dry
ROSÉ WINE	
Rubis d'Egypte	light-colored, dry
RED WINE	
Omar Khayyam	dark red, dry, heavy, with an aroma of dates
Château Gianaclis	dark red, smooth, dry
Pharaoh's Wine	dark red, light, dry

Manners and Customs

Visitors to Islamic countries who want to understand the behavior and attitudes of the inhabitants and to avoid unnecessary difficulties in dealing with them should take care to regulate their own conduct in such a way as to avoid offending local susceptibilities.

Muslims have a different way of life and different modes of thought from those to which the Western visitor is accustomed. They have different values and different habits, which tourists should avoid disregarding or disparaging. Since to the Muslim religion, law, politics and economic life are all bound up together, criticism in any of these fields may be felt as a slight on his faith.

Unduly light or casual clothing should be avoided, particularly when visiting mosques; shoes must be taken off before entering a mosque, and entry is not permitted during the periodic prayers. Kissing and other displays of affection between the sexes in public are regarded with extreme disapproval. – Female visitors should, for their own protection, avoid unduly revealing dress; women with bare shoulders or wearing shorts are regarded as fair game. In country areas it is advisable to wear a head-scarf. In general women who are "decently" dressed are treated with respect. Women engaged in needlework are regarded as especially virtuous.

Great discretion is necessary in photographing women, children, poor people or beggars, since this is regarded by Muslims as infringing human dignity and may on occasion lead to violent reactions. Much that the tourist regards as picturesque is to the native merely primitive and backward: here too, therefore, great care should be exercised in taking photographs. Features of military importance, including airfields, railway stations, bridges, etc., should not be photographed.

Offence will be caused by visitors who show amusement at the muezzin's call to prayer or at men engaged in the act of prayer. – During the Ramadan fast (see box below) eating, drinking and smoking in public must be avoided during the day. It is regarded as discourteous not to accept an invitation; refusal is possible only with an adequate excuse. In the Islamic social order relations of acquaintanceship and friendship imply obligations: the host's whole household is at the disposal of a guest, and the same hospitality is expected of visitors when they receive guests.

A visitor to a Muslim house must never ask for pork or for alcohol, but he can eat and drink freely whatever he is offered. When the guest takes his leave it is customary for him to make an appropriate gift to his host. When asking for directions

The Faith of Islam

The overwhelming majority of the Egyptian population profess **Islam**, one of the great monotheistic world religions, with a total of some 530 million adherents throughout the world. The word Islam means submission to God. Believers in Islam are known as **Muslims**; they do not like to be called Mohammedans.

The life of Muslims bears the strong impress of their religion. The basic requirement of the Islamic faith, as laid down in the **Koran**, the Muslim sacred book, is unconditional obedience to the will of *Allah*, the only true God. The prescriptions of the Koran are supplemented by laws derived from the traditions recording the deeds and utterances of the founder of Islam, the Prophet *Mohammed* (b. in Mecca *c.* 570, d. in Medina 632).

Every field of Muslim life is regulated by laws, rules and customs which differ from country to country (Sunnites, Shiites; various schools of theology and brotherhoods) but are all based on the *five fundamental duties of Islam*:

1. the **profession of the true faith** (*shahada*): "I testify that there is no God but Allah, and Mohammed is his prophet."

2. **prayer** (*salat*), to be performed five times daily, after ritual ablutions. The words to be recited (in Arabic always) and the actions of prayer are precisely specified. During prayer the believer must face in the direction of Mecca.

3. **almsgiving** (*zakat*). Every Muslim is obliged to give regular alms (between 2½% and 10% of his income) for the poor and needy.

4. **fasting** (*saum*). During the fast of *Ramadan* (the ninth month of the Muslim lunar year) no food or drink may be taken, and smoking and the inhaling of perfume are prohibited, between sunrise and sunset.

5. the **pilgrimage to Mecca** (*hagg*). Every free Muslim of full age is required, if his health and financial situation permit, to make the pilgrimage to the principal shrine of Islam, the Kaaba in Mecca, at least once during his life.

There are also a number of important prescriptions on the believer's food and drink – a ban on pork, blood and alcohol, a requirement to eat only meat that has been ritually slaughtered – and detailed regulations on bodily cleanliness and on the behavior of married people (polygamy being permitted), parents and children.

Within the family the husband enjoys absolute authority. The wife remains in the background, with the house and family as her province. The family is, as a matter of course, the extended family. Thinking, feeling and behavior are conditioned by the needs of the community.

Throughout the Islamic world there is now an increasing consciousness of its own values and possibilities, and increasing stress is being laid on the religious and cultural traditions of Islam.

---

or other information from someone in the street it is advisable to seek confirmation by putting the same question to a second or even a third person.

Tipping

Given the low rates of pay and the high level of unemployment in Egypt, **bakshish** (a tip) plays an important part in the life of the country. Many families depend on the supplementary income they gain from performing small services, selling matches and souvenirs, and so on. Moreover the faithful are required by the Koran to support the needy, and accordingly the Egyptians themselves always give bakshish for any service rendered. The principle is that bakshish must be justified by some help or service rendered, but that in these circumstances it is obligatory. A beggar can be dismissed with the phrase "Allah ya'tik" ("May God give to you"), an importunate youth with "Ma fish bakshish" ("Nothing doing").

Since practically all the Egyptians with whom visitors come in contact will expect a gratuity, it is advisable to keep a good supply of small change. In hotels and restaurants between 10% and 12% is added to the bill, but an extra tip of 5% is normal. Porters should be given 25–50 piastres. Taxi-drivers and bus-drivers also expect bakshish, 25 piastres for a short trip, more for a longer one.

Spas

The dry climate of Aswan is good for rheumatism, colds, etc. The hot sulphur and saline springs of Helwan (a suburb of Cairo), at temperatures of up to 91 °F/ 33 °C, are used in the treatment of rheumatism and skin diseases.

Water Sports

There are attractive bathing beaches on Egypt's Mediterranean and Red Sea coasts, and many hotels have swimming-pools with perfectly safe water. Because of the danger of bilharzia infection, however, bathing in inland waters should be avoided at all costs. Beaches which have been developed for the holiday trade have facilities for a variety of water sports (surfing, sailing, etc.).

Diving

The Red Sea, with its coral reefs and abundance of underwater life, is popular with snorkelers and scuba divers. The principal holiday centers are Ain Sukhna and Hurghada (fully equipped diving center). If you bring your own scuba gear you may need an adaptor for the air cylinders. Divers should note that the coral reefs of the Red Sea are "protected" and persons removing pieces as "souvenirs" can expect heavy fines.

It should be borne in mind that there are more poisonous species of marine creatures in tropical waters than in more temperate latitudes. Fire corals, actinias (sea anemones) and jellyfish (including the Portuguese man-of-war, *Physalia physalis,* and the Mediterranean diced jellyfish, *Charybdea marsupialis*) give severe stings; lance and diadem sea-urchins have poisonous spines which break off easily; the red firefish, scorpionfish and stone-fish have poisonous fin-spines; and moray eels, rays, barracudas and sharks can also be dangerous. It is advisable, therefore, to inquire locally about possible hazards before diving in unfamiliar waters. Attention should also be paid to local regulations on underwater fishing.

Snorkelers in particular can easily forget that salt-water and strong sun can very quickly cause sunburn: it is a good plan, therefore, to wear a light-colored cotton shirt or T-shirt. Caution is advisable in touching unknown marine creatures for fear of stings; stout rubber gloves will give protection. On no account should you feel inside cavities in banks of coral.

Golf

There are golf-courses at Cairo (Gezira Sporting Club, 18 holes; Mena House Hotel, 9 holes) and Alexandria, and visitors are readily admitted to temporary membership.

Entertainment

The programs of entertainments for tourists frequently include *belly dancing* – though the performances arranged for foreigners are sometimes very different from the traditional style.

Looking after your health

As in many other hot countries, the non-acclimatized tourist must take sensible precautions to safeguard his health. Adequate protection against the sun (head-covering, sunglasses, protective cream) is essential; and exposure to the midday heat should be avoided. In order to compensate for the body's loss of water by perspiration it is necessary to drink a lot and to take plenty of salt, either in food or in the form of salt tablets.

It is easy to get a stomach or intestinal infection from eating unpeeled fruit, salad or food bought in the street or from drinking dubious water. Charcoal tablets are usually ineffective; the best plan is to consult your doctor before leaving home and take suitable medicines with you. The water is usually safe to drink in the cities, though heavily chlorinated. Bottled mineral water is obtainable everywhere.

To forestall possible infections it is advisable to use hot tap-water for washing fruit and any dishes or cutlery used, and also, after cooling, for brushing teeth. Water heated to at least 135 °F/57 °C (too hot to bear on the naked hand) is not completely sterilized but is at least pasteurized: i.e. it will kill most of the pathogens liable to cause stomach and intestinal infections.

In spite of the considerable measure of success achieved in controlling it **bilharzia** (schistosomiasis, hookworm disease) is still prevalent in Egypt. The hookworm lives mainly in stagnant or sluggishly flowing fresh water, and its larvae penetrate the skin and establish themselves in the liver, from which they make their way into other parts of the body, particularly the intestines and bladder. So far as possible, therefore, contact with stagnant or sluggish water should be avoided.

Eye infections (trachoma) are not uncommon. They are transmitted by flies or by direct physical contact: it is unwise, therefore, to lend your binoculars or camera to a stranger. – Frequent showering can bring on *"Nile fever"*, an irritation of the sweat glands.

Precautions against *malaria* are necessary during the summer months, particularly in the Delta, the Fayyum and other oases, and parts of Upper Egypt. Since the prophylactic treatment should begin some two weeks before departure, you should consult your doctor in plenty of time.

Calendar

Three different calendar systems are in use in Egypt. The **Muslim calendar** has a purely lunar year of 12 months, alternately with 30 and 29 days; the normal year has 354 days, the leap year 355. The Muslim New Year thus moves right through the *Gregorian calendar,* which is also used in Egypt, in the course of 33 solar years. – The **Coptic calendar** is of importance only in the religious life of the Copts, who for other purposes use the Gregorian calendar. The Coptic year begins on August 29 and is based on the Julian calendar.

Figured carpet from Harrania

The **weekly day of rest** is **Friday**.

Holidays and Festivals

Public Holidays:

February 22 (Union Day)
April 25 (Sinai Liberation Day)
May 1 (Labor Day)
June 18 (Evacuation Day)
July 23 (Revolution Day)
August 2 (Nile Day)
October 6 (Armed Forces Day)
October 24 (National Liberation Day)
December 23 (Victory Day)

The religious festivals are governed by the lunar calendar, the main ones being *Bairam,* a three-day celebration following the month-long fast of Ramadan, the Spring festival *Sham el-Nessim* and *Kurbam-Bairam* celebrating the sacrifice of sheep.
During the fast of Ramadan all daytime activities are reduced to a minimum.

Shopping and Souvenirs

Visitors will find a wide range of wares in the **bazaars**, including in particular leather goods, shoes, carpets, spices, perfumes, galabiyas (jellabas: the long flowing cotton garments which are the everyday wear of the Egyptians), vases, metal plates, mother-of-pearl jewel cases, alabaster figures, papyrus, scarabs, gold and silver jewelery.

Shopping is an affair that requires plenty of time; for bargaining is a form of social communication practiced not only in bazaars but in most ordinary shops, and a customer who pays the price asked without haggling is something of a disappointment to the shopkeeper. As a broad rule of thumb the customer should counter the asking price by offering about half that amount, and after further bargaining might expect to settle for somewhere between two-thirds and three-quarters of the original price. In the main tourist centers it may be possible to bring the price even lower. It should be borne in mind, however, that because of the low

Particularly attractive are the **figured carpets** made in the village of Harrania, SW of Cairo. This craft was established as a social experiment by the art scholar Ramses Wissa Wassef with the object of developing the spontaneous creative urge of fellahin children. The carpets have no standard patterns, and each one is individual and unique. Their decorative themes include the scenery of the Nile Valley, scenes of everyday village life, plants and animals.

Egyptian wage rates most goods are fairly cheap anyway and that it hardly becomes visitors from more prosperous countries to drive too hard a bargain.

Caution is required in buying alleged "antiquities", which almost invariably turn out to be fakes. Genuine antiquities are only occasionally offered for sale, and in any event it is in practice impossible to get an export license. Excellent copies are, however, on sale in the Egyptian Museum in Cairo.

Opening Times

Shops in summer are usually open from 9 a.m. to 12.30 p.m. and from 4 p.m. to 8 p.m. (Mondays and Thursdays until 9 p.m.). Winter hours are from 9 a.m. to 7 p.m. (Mondays and Thursdays until 8 p.m.). Most shops close on Sundays. Bazaar stalls have similar hours.

Banks normally open at 9.30 a.m. and close at 2 p.m., Sunday to Thursday. Most banks close Friday and Saturday.

Offices close on Friday, others on Sunday.

Monuments and historic sites are generally open from 10 a.m. to 4 p.m. daily. Museums, however, do not always comply with these times.

Information

Tourist Information Offices

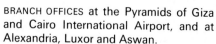

HEAD OFFICE:
Misr Travel Tower,
Cairo – Abbasia;
tel. 82 20 16, 82 54 47
and 82 39 36.

BRANCH OFFICES at the Pyramids of Giza and Cairo International Airport, and at Alexandria, Luxor and Aswan.

Egyptian State Tourist Office,
630 Fifth Avenue,
New York, NY 10020;
tel. (212) 246 6960.
3001 Pacific Avenue,
San Francisco, CA 94415;
tel. (415) 346 9704.
168 Piccadilly,
London W1V 9DE,
tel. (01) 493 5282.

Tourist Police
HEAD OFFICE:
Shari Adly 5,
Cairo;
tel. 91 26 44 and 91 20 98.

BRANCH OFFICES at the Pyramids of Giza, Cairo International Airport (Heliopolis) and Cairo Central Station, and also at Alexandria, Luxor and Aswan.

Misr Travel
HEAD OFFICE:
Shari Talaat Harb 1,
P.O. Box 1000.
Cairo;
tel. 75 00 10 and 75 01 68.

BRANCH OFFICES at Shari Qasr el-Nil 43, Cairo, and at Alexandria, Port Said, Suez, Damietta, Tanta, Luxor and Aswan.

Automobile et Touring Club d'Egypte (*ATCE*)
Shari Qasr el-Nil 10,
Cairo;
tel. 74 33 55, 74 33 48 and 74 31 91.
Shari Salah Salem,
Alexandria;
tel. 96 94 94 – 95.

Embassies and Consulates

Egypt

Embassy,
2310 Decatur Place, NW,
Washington, DC 20008;
tel. (202) 234 3903–4.

Consulate,
1110 Second Avenue,
New York, NY 10022;
tel. (212) 759 7120.

Embassy,
26 South Street,
London W1Y 9DE;
tel. (01) 499 2401.

Consulate,
19 Kensington Palace Garden Mews,
London W8 4QL;
tel. (01) 229 8818–9.

Embassy and Consulate,
454 Laurier Avenue,
East **Ottawa;**
tel. (613) 234 4931 and 234 4741.

United States
EMBASSY:
Shari Latin America 5,
Garden City,
Cairo;
tel. (02) 355 7371.

CONSULATE:
Shari Gamal Abdel Nasser 110,
Alexandria;
tel. 80 19 11.

United Kingdom
EMBASSY:
Shari Ahmed Ragheb,
Garden City,
Cairo;
tel. (02) 354 0850 and (02) 354 0852.

CONSULATE:
Roushdy Pasha,
Alexandria;
tel. 4 71 66.

Canada
EMBASSY:
Shari Mohamed Fahmi el-Sayed,
Garden City,
Cairo;
tel. (02) 354 3110.

Airlines

EgyptAir,
Shari Adly 6,
Cairo;
tel. 92 09 99; reservations 747 4444.

Nifertiti Airlines,
c/o EMCO Travel Tours,
Shari Talaat Harb 2,
Cairo;
tel. 97 04 44.

British Airways,
Shari Abdel Salam Aref 1,
Cairo;
tel. 75 99 77 and 75 99 14.
Midan Saad Zaghlul 15,
Alexandria;
tel. 3 66 68.

Mallawi	Museum
El-Minya	Museum
AUSTRALIA	
Melbourne	National Gallery of Victoria
Sydney	Australian Museum
	Nicholson Museum of
	Antiquities
AUSTRIA	
Vienna	Kunsthistorisches Museum
BELGIUM	
Antwerp	Vleeshuis Museum
Brussels	Musées Royaux d'Art et
	d'Histoire
Liège	Musée Curtius
Mariemont	Musée de Mariemont
BRAZIL	
Rio de Janeiro	National Museum

Breakdown Service

The Automobile et Touring Club
d'Egypte runs a breakdown service on
the main trunk roads in the Delta.

International Telephone Codes

From the United Kingdom to Egypt
010 20

From the United State or Canada to
Egypt   **011 20**

Direct dialing from Egypt to the
United Kingdom, the United States
or Canada is possible but be prepared for some delays.

Museums with Egyptian Material

EGYPT

Alexandria	Graeco-Roman Museum
Aswan	Museum (on Elephantine)
Cairo	Egyptian Museum
Luxor	Museum of Ancient Egyptian
	Art

Obelisk from Luxor in the Place de la Concorde, Paris

CANADA

Montreal	Ethnological Museum
	Museum of Fine Arts
Toronto	Royal Ontario Museum

CUBA

Havana	National Museum

CZECHOSLOVAKIA

Prague	Náprstkovo Muzeum

DENMARK

Copenhagen	National Museum
	Ny Carlsberg Glyptotek
	Thorwaldsen Museum

FRANCE

Avignon	Musée Calvet
Grenoble	Musée de Peinture et de Sculpture
Limoges	Musée Municipal
Lyons	Musée des Beaux-Arts
	Musée Guimet
Marseilles	Musée d'Archéologie Méditerranéenne
Nantes	Musée des Arts Décoratifs
Orléans	Musée Historique et d'Archéologie de l'Orléanais
Paris	Institut d'Egyptologie
	Musée du Louvre
	Musée du Petit Palais
	Musée Rodin
Toulouse	Musée Georges Labit

GERMANY (Democratic Republic)

East Berlin	Bodemuseum
Dresden	Albertinum
Leipzig	Ägyptisches Museum

GERMANY (Federal Republic)

West Berlin	Ägytpisches Museum
Essen	Museum Folkwang
Frankfurt am main	Liebieghaus
Hamburg	Museum für Kunst und Gewerbe
	Museum für Völkerkunde und Vorgeschichte
Hannover	Kestner-Museum
Heidelberg	Ägyptologisches Institut der Universität
Hildesheim	Roemer-Pelizaeus-Museum
Karlsruhe	Badisches Landesmuseum
Munich	Staatliche Sammlung Ägyptischer Kunst
Tübingen	Ägyptologisches Institut der Universität
Würzburg	Martin-von-Wagner-Museum

GREECE

Athens	National Museum

HUNGARY

Budapest	Szépmüvészeti Múzeum

IRELAND

Dublin	National Museum

ITALY

Bologna	Museo Civico
Florence	Museo Archologico
Mantua	Museo del Palazzo Ducale
Milan	Museo Archeologico
Naples	Museo Nazionale
Palermo	Museo Nazionale
Parma	Museo Nazionale di Antichità
Rome	Museo Nazionale
	Museo Barracco
	Museo Gregorio Egiziano (Vatican)
	Museo Nazionale Romano delle Terme Diocleziane
Rovigo	Museo dell-Accademia dei Concordi
Trieste	Museo di Storia e d'Arte
Turin	Museo Egizio
Venice	Museo Archeologico

JAPAN

Kyoto	University Archaeological Museum

MEXICO

Mexico City	Museo Nacional de Antropologia

NETHERLANDS

Amsterdam	Allard Pierson Museum
Leyden	Rijksmuseum van Oudheden
Otterloo	Rijksmuseum Kröller-Müller

POLAND

Cracow	Muzeum Narodowe
Warsaw	Muzeum Narodowe

PORTUGAL

Lisbon	Fundação Calouste Gulbenkian

SPAIN

Madrid	Museo Arqueológico Nacional

SUDAN

Khartoum	Sudan Museum

SWEDEN

Linköping	Östergötland Museum
Lund	Kulturhistoriska Museet
Stockholm	Medelhavsmuseet
Uppsala	Victoria Museum

SWITZERLAND

Basle	Museum für Völkerkunde
Geneva	Musée d'Art et d'Histoire
Lausanne	Musée Cantonal d'Art et d'Histoire
	Musée Cantonal des Beaux-Arts
Neuchâtel	Musée d'Ethnographie
Riggisberg	Abegg-Stiftung

UNITED KINGDOM

Bristol	City Museum
Cambridge	Fitzwilliam Museum
Dundee	Museum and Art Gallery
Durham	Gulbenkian Museum of Oriental Art and Archaeology
Edinburgh	Royal Scottish Museum
Glasgow	Art Gallery and Museum
	Burrell Collection
	Hunterian Museum
Leicester	Museum and Art Gallery
Liverpool	Merseyside County Museum
	School of Archaeology and Oriental Studies

London	British Museum		**Minneapolis (MN)**	Institute of Arts Museum
	Horniman Museum		**New Haven (CT)**	Yale University Art Gallery
	Petrie Collection		**New York (NY)**	Brooklyn Museum
	Victoria and Albert Museum			Metropolitan Museum of Art
Manchester	University Museum		**Palo Alto (CA)**	Stanford University Museum
Norwich	Castle Museum		**Philadelphia (PA)**	Pennsylvania University
Oxford	Ashmolean Museum			Museum
	Pitt Rivers Museum		**Pittsburgh (PA)**	Museum of Art
			Princeton (NJ)	University Art Museum
UNITED STATES			**Providence (RI)**	Rhode Island School of Design
Baltimore (MD)	Walters Art Gallery		**Richmond (VA)**	Museum of Fine Arts
			St Louis (MS)	Art Museum
Berkeley (CA)	Robert H. Lowie Museum of		**San Diego (CA)**	Museum of Man
	Anthropology		**San Francisco (CA)**	De Young Memorial Museum
Boston (MA)	Museum of Fine Arts		**San Jose (CA)**	Rosicrucian Museum
Cambridge (MA)	Fogg Art Museum		**Seattle (WA)**	Art Museum
	Semitic Museum		**Toledo (OH)**	Museum of Art
Chicago (IL)	Field Museum of Natural		**Washington (DC)**	Smithsonian Institution
	History		**Worcester (MA)**	Art Museum
	Oriental Institute Museum			
Cincinnati (OH)	Art Museum		**USSR**	
Cleveland (OH)	Museum of Art		**Leningrad**	Hermitage
Denver (CO)	Art Museum		**Moscow**	Pushkin Museum of Art
Detroit (MI)	Detroit Institute of Arts			
Kansas City (MS)	William Rockhill Nelson Gallery		**YUGOSLAVIA**	
	of Art		**Zagreb**	Arheološki Muzej
Los Angeles (CA)	County Museum of Art			

Source of Illustrations

G. Angelidis (pp. 102, 104; 257, top left)

Anthony-Verlag, Starnberg (pp. 252, 262, 296)

Dr P. Baumgarten, Stuttgart (pp. 7, 14, 56, 57, 60, 67, 72, 74, 83; 84, two; 99, 101, 103, 125; 127, right and below; 128, two; 129; 136, four; 145, 146; 148, foot; 159, 192, 193, top, two; 194, 195; 204, top; 208; 211, two; 214, 215, 218–219; 232, two; 239; 241, two; 244; 257, foot; 258, three; 259; 260, two; 277, 278, three; 311; 314, foot; 325; 362, two; 341, 342, 344, 346, 369, 370)

Bavaria-Verlag, Gauting (pp. 113, 299, 301)

Bildagentur Stuttgart (Eichler: pp. 151, foot; 156, top)

British Museum, London (p. 33)

Dar el-Kitab el-Gedid, Cairo (pp. 156, below; 160, right; 162, 229)

Deutsche Presse-Agentur GmbH (dpa), Frankfurt am Main (pp. 200; 301, top)

Egyptian State Tourist Office, Frankfurt am Main (p. 114)

Dr O. Gärtner, Giessen (pp. 271, 272)

Dr G. Gerster, Zumikon/Zürich (pp. 11, 168, 221; 222, two; 243, 244; 264, two; 265; 352, bottom two)

M. Hecker, Ostfildern (pp. 118, 119; 148, top; 153, 165, 186, 251, 300)

Hetzel-Reisen GmbH, Stuttgart (p. 198, lower left and lower right)

B. Kappelmeyer, Berlin (p. 306)

Koptisch-orthodoxes Zentrum, Waldsolms-Kröffelbach (pp. 76, 77; 78, two; 79, right; 164, two; 270, two; 348, 349)

Lehnert & Landrock Succ., Cairo (pp. 20, 24, 36, 58, 68; 87, top left; 89; 107, top right; 122, 147, 149, 150; 151, top; 154; 160, left; 172, 174, 175; 204, foot; 206; 224; 226, left; 263, 322; 335, right; 337)

Leykam AG, Graz (p. 198, upper right)

J. Liepe, Berlin (pp. 165, right; 375)

Dr G. Ludwig, Mainz (pp. 16, top; 64; 107, top left and foot; 109; 127, left; 130; 132, two; 141, 142; 159, bottom; 178, 179, 101, 182, 183, 187, 188; 193, bottom; 226 right; 235, 236, 249, 250, 254; 257, top right; 269; 286, two; 314, top; 316, 318, 320, 321, 324; 330, two; 332, 335, left; 339; 352, top; 353)

Bildagentur Mauritius, Mittenwald (p. 247)

Prof. Dr H. W. Paschen, Duisburg (pp. 16, 17, 18, 19, 86; 87, right; 93, 120, 133, 185, 253; 342, right)

Bildarchiv Preussischer Kulturbesitz, Berlin (p. 357;

G. R. Reitz, Hannover (p. 98)

Sheraton Hotels, Frankfurt am Main (Zamalek Photo House: p. 198, upper left)

Stern (Ihrt), Hamburg (pp. 134–135)

Studio 7, Cairo (pp. 25; 79, left; 80; 233; 234, two)

Zentrale Farbbild Agentur GmbH (ZEFA), Düsseldorf (title-page; pp. 85, 121, 293, 294, 295)

(In the alphabetical arrangement of names the definite article *el* is disregarded. The names of places beginning with El- should therefore be looked up under the main part of the name.)

AA/Baedeker Travel Guides

The name Baedeker has been famous in guide book publishing for over 150 years, and the latest editions of these books are colourful, detailed and modern. Each book comes with a folded sheet map to make holiday planning simple. The directories have an A–Z arrangement making them easy to use and other sections of the books include practical travel advice, background information and history. Travellers who rely on these books will miss nothing. The titles of books in the series are as follows:

COUNTRY GUIDES

Austria
Caribbean
Denmark
Egypt
France
Germany
Great Britain
Greece
Holland/Belgium/Luxembourg
Ireland

Israel
Italy
Japan
Mediterranean Islands
Mexico
Portugal
Scandinavia
Spain
Switzerland
Yugoslavia

REGIONAL GUIDES

Costa Brava
Gran Canaria
Greek Islands
Ibiza/Formentera
Loire
Mallorca/Menorca

Provence/Côte D'Azur
Rhine
Tenerife
Turkish Coast
Tuscany

CITY GUIDES

Amsterdam
Athens
Bangkok
Berlin
Brussels
Budapest
Cologne
Copenhagen
Florence
Frankfurt
Hamburg
Hong Kong
Istanbul
Jerusalem
Leningrad

London
Madrid
Moscow
Munich
New York
Paris
Prague
Rome
San Francisco
Singapore
Stuttgart
Tokyo
Venice
Vienna